Pulling it All Together

Diary by One of America's First Jewish Women Judges

Anne Freeling Schlezinger Wedding Day, 1939

Anne F. Schlezinger

Pulling it All Together

Diary by One of America's First Jewish Women Judges

Edited by
Ron Duncan Hart

Gaon Books

Gaon Books
PO Box 23924
Santa Fe, NM 87502
www.gaonbooks.com

Copyright © 2011
By Gaon Books

All rights reserved. This publication is in copyright. Subject to statutory exception and to the provisions of relevant collective licensing agreements, no reproduction of any part may be done without the written permission of Gaon Books (editor@gaonbooks.com).

Library of Congress Cataloging-in-Publication Data

Schlezinger, Anne Freeling, 1910-1978
  Pulling it all together: diary by one of America's first Jewish women judges/ Anne Freeling Schlezinger; Ron Duncan Hart [editor].
     p. cm.
  Includes bibliographical references.
  ISBN 978-1-935604-01-3 (Perfect Bound)
  ISBN 978-1-935604-14-3 (e-book)
  1. Schlezinger, Anne Freeling, 1910---Diaries. 2. Judges--United States--Diaries. 3. Jewish women--Legal status, laws, etc.--United States--Diaries. 4. Women--Legal status, laws, etc. (Jewish law) I. Hart, Ron Duncan, 1941- II. Title.
     KF8745.S35A3 2010
     347.73'14092--dc22
                              2010007328

Manufactured in the United States of America.

The paper used in this publication is acid free and meets all ANSI (American National Standards for Information Sciences) standards for archival quality paper.

Cover design by Gloria Abella Ballen

Contents

Foreword	6
Editor's Note	7
Introduction The Integrated Life Of A Modern American Woman: Anne Freeling Schlezinger, 1910-1978 Shulamit Reinharz	9
1931 To 1934: Law School And First Job	65
1935 To 1938: Washington And Professional Beginnings	123
1939 To 1945: Marriage, Mothering, And World War Ii	177
1946 To 1952: Suburban Life In Silver Spring	259
1953 To 1961: Mccarthyism And The Struggle To Survive	319
1962 To 1967: Empty Nest And More NLRB Cases	401
1968 To 1978: Grandmother And Judge	461
Epilogue The Art Of Women's Diary Writing: Anne Schlezinger Orit Rabkin	567
Bibliography	581
Index	585

Foreword

A "Woman of Valor" is the inscription beneath the stain glass memorial window to Anne Freeling Schlezinger at Ohr Kodesh Synagogue in Silver Spring, Maryland. That was my father's idea. It was the way he saw Mom over their nearly forty years together. Only after her death when I read her diaries, legal opinions, and press clippings did I begin to understand what she had achieved in an all too brief a lifetime. How my mother perceived herself, how she was seen by family and friends, and how she was seen in her professional world, suggested very different personas.

When I was growing up, "mom" was what she did. We lived in a world of first generation over achievers from Massachusetts, Pennsylvania, New York, and Ohio. Her first job, after passing the Bar, was as a legal secretary, the only job available to a young Jewish woman lawyer at the time. She subsequently became a staff lawyer, supervisor, and eventually an administrative law judge.

While I was growing up my mother was not different than other working mothers. She left early, got home late, took the bus or drove downtown with dad. Dinner was started by whoever got home first but was always a family affair. Dinner time was for debriefing, starting with me, but equal time for mom and dad. Fairness, balance, and efficiency were part of every aspect of her life, including dinner. Mom had no reservations about her skills (professional and personal) but wasn't quite as sure what this motherhood business was about...But I could make her laugh.

Only as a grown up did I begin to understand the magnitude of what she had accomplished. She went directly from high school to law school. She was admitted to the Bar before she was twenty-one years old. After law school, she moved to Washington, D.C. and went to work for the National Labor Board. She was still on the payroll when she died over forty years later. Her progression from staff lawyer to judge was not an easy one for her. On at least three occasions she used the law to protest inequities. In the early 1950's when her position was held to be patronage and not protected by Civil Service, she lost her job. She sued and was reinstated. Next, she was denied judicial standing because of gender, she again sued and won. Finally to have the same opportunities for case assignment and travel prerogatives as her male counterparts, she once again used the law to support her case and once again prevailed.

Anne Freeling Schlezinger was tough, principled, tenacious, fearless, demanding, fair, and dedicated. In whatever she said or did she stayed the course. She was, and always will be a Woman of Valor.

Ira Schlezinger

Ira H. Schlezinger is a national leader in healthcare planning. He has master's degrees in Public Administration and Organizational Development, and he is the past president of the Amercan Hospital Association's Society for Health Care Planning. He is the recepient of the AHA's Corning Award for Planning Excellence. He is active in community service and in 2008 received the Governor's Award for outstanding service to the arts in Oklahoma.

Editor's Note

Judge Anne Schlezinger was a forerunner of women's rights in the mid-twentieth century. In her chosen profession of law she was in the cohort of early Jewish women lawyers and judges, breaking into the profession in the 1930's. She graduated from Northeastern Law School in 1933 when there were few jobs for attorneys. She worked as a legal secretary until 1937 when she was among the first women hired as a lawyer by the National Labor Relations Board. She worked at the Board the rest of her life.

Judge Schlezinger's diary narrates her personal and professional life for forty-seven years, and it is the story of Jewish professionals, who had more opportunities after the dramatic changes brought about in the World War II years. Anti-Semitism was still a problem in the 1950's, often fused with anti-communism. Misogyny and McCarthyism were other problems that affected her life. Civil Rights legislation in the 1960's under President Johnson led to an expansion of opportunities for women, and Anne was named judge during this period.

Over the last four years I have read and re-read the more than 17,000 entries of Judge Schlezinger's diary, made a selection from each year of a time period that told something in the story of her life, researched the history of the National Labor Relations Board, and interviewed family and friends about her life. This is the result.

I would like to thank Ira and Sandy Schlezinger for their collaboration with this project. They permitted full access to the diaries, family photo archives, and other materials related to Anne Schlezinger's life and work. Through numerous interview sessions and phone calls, Ira clarified information and added details that supplemented information in the diaries.

The excellent essays by Dr. Shulamit Reinharz and Prof. Orit Rabkin bring the life of Anne Schlezinger into a clearer focus, and I thank them for their insightful collaboration. Dr. Reinharz made detailed observations on the entire text, leading to a much improved end result.

I would also like to thank Jamie Nickels for her patient assistance over two years in preparing this manuscript from the hand written originals that are not always easy to read.

Ron Duncan Hart

Ron Duncan Hart is a cultural anthropologist (Ph.D. Indiana University) with postdoctoral work at Oxford University. He is a former Dean of Academic Affairs and worked in Latin America for eighteen years with UNICEF, the Ford Foundation and other international agencies. He has received awards from the National Endowment for the Humanities, the National Science Foundation, Ford Foundation, and Fulbright among others and has published eight books on his research.

Schlezinger Family Tree

Isaac (I.H.) and Pearl (Maiden name Polster)
Six Children and their Families:

Julius	Lena	Louis	Gertrude	Edward	Nathan
Wife Anne	Husband Harry Platzer	Wife Lucille	Husband Alvin Lewin	Wife Madelyn	Wife Bobbie
Son Ira	Daughter Helen Lee	Children: Clifford, Ellen, Marvin	Children: Lois Milton	Children: Anne Howard Joanie	Children: Lynne Nan Joanne

Frihling/Freeliing Family Tree

Abraham and Regina (Maiden name Wagshal)
Four Children and their Families

Louis	Anne	Janet	Clara
Killed in WW II Not married, No Children	Husband Julius Schlezinger Son Ira	Husband Joe Ruscoll Children: Cynthia Richard Jeri	Husband Lou Roland Children: Joyce Steve

Introduction

Shulamit Reinharz

The Integrated Life Of A Modern American Woman: Anne Freeling Schlezinger, 1910-1978

"My Little Page"

Many young people begin a diary with the hope of creating a record of their lives, but most soon give up the practice of regular writing. Anne Freeling Schlezinger was an exception. For forty-seven years starting in 1931 when she was 21, Anne adhered strictly to a daily writing schedule.[1] Her persistence in sustaining her diary was probably facilitated by her decision to write extremely brief entries, almost like those of a farmer's almanac. For this reason, even if she had only a few minutes to spare on a given day, she most likely could manage the 70-100 words of her typical entry right before going to sleep at night.

What is particularly remarkable about Anne's diary, in addition to its longevity and completeness, is its uniformity. For nearly half a century, Anne produced a bare bones daily outline of her experiences, almost always using the same entry topics: the weather, mail and phone calls she received, her meals, her social life, her shopping, her job, her family, her entertainment and her health. She noted the content of her work occasionally and offered only meager comments on world events.[2] Her entries read like telegrams.

---

1   All of my remarks derive from reading the selected diary entries available in this book, which represent only a small fraction of the diary. I assume that the entries not included in this book align with, rather than contradict, my interpretations. Although working with a selection of journal entries makes this project manageable, it also creates large holes in understanding Anne's life. For example, a lot is missing about Ira's military experience.

2   She did mention the "Japs" frequently in her diary entries of 1945: "Announcement first thing this morning that Japan had offered to surrender provided the emperor might be retained on his throne. Want to see the war end as soon as possible, but think we should insist upon *unconditional* surrender." (August 10) "The Allies have replied to Japan that the Emperor *may retain his throne* only subject to the command of the Allied Military Commander. The next move is up to the Japs." (August 11). "Learned in the morning that *the Japs had accepted the Potsdam declaration* last night. Learned later it was again a mistake. But the official announcement finally came in the evening. My celebration consisted of taking Ira and his friends to the corner for ice cream cones, but the city generally went mad with joy." (August 14). "All the government employees," of whom she and Jules were two, "are getting a two-day holiday, but not the poor suckers, the servicemen. We fortunately had an adequate supply of food since all the stores are closed. No mail delivery. I am delighted, of course, that the war has finally ended, but cannot get in a mood for really celebrating until my personal share in it has been completed, namely, until Jules comes home to stay. It is a great relief, though, to know that even if he goes to Japan, it will not be to fight." (August 17). "Hard to realize yet that the war is over. The way the Japs are behaving, I sometimes wonder if it is." (August 20). "Long letter from Sylvia, who tried to call me when the Japs surrendered but could not get the call through. Is depressed by the likelihood that Mort may not be home for quite a while yet. Do not blame her. It just does not seem that the war is really over until the boys are home again, even if we do have unlimited hot water, gasoline, pineapple juice, etc." (August 20). "We have to take off next Thursday or Monday without pay. That is all right with me. But a government that can send millions to arm other countries should be able to pay its servants." (May 22, 1947).

They revolve around these selected themes, hardly varying at all. This manner of writing creates an impression of the writer as a cool, calm, collected personality. But it has a negative consequence as well. All the information appears to have equivalent significance. It is impossible to know what was truly important to her, and what was not. A striking example is the following complete entry:

Thursday, November 13, 1952. Doherty had been reclassified to the same grade as mine, a grade I had when he first came to the Board. The other supervisors are dropping their appeal for reclassification, however, as they are afraid it will make them more vulnerable to discharge when the administration changes. Lunched in the cafeteria with Almira Stevenson. Had coffee in the afternoon with Stasi Dunan. Abe Feller, whom I knew at Justice, committed suicide. Very depressing. Ira missed his Scout meeting – too much homework. Expect he would have brushed it off but for his report card. To the National Theater with Ira and Alice Jaffee to see Phil Silvers in "The Top Banana," a zany thing but I was in just the mood for it, and so was Jules.

In this entry, Anne begins with a statement illustrating employment discrimination against her as a woman. She comments next about the way the change from the Democratic (Truman) to Republican (Eisenhower) administration makes civil service employees vulnerable.[3] She mentions her lunch with her regular companion, Almira Stevenson, and having an afternoon coffee with another friend. The next sentence however, concerns the suicide of a person she knew from work.[4] "Very depressing," is her entire commentary.[5] This brevity is extraordinary because Feller's suicide was related directly to the kinds of interrogation to which she, herself, had been subjected. Perhaps the very appearance of

---

3   Anne was a committed Democrat. In a humorous entry, she noted: "Later listened to Eisenhower deliver a TV political address. It was a good speech, and well delivered, and he even looked well physically. Afraid it might have won him some votes." (October 1, 1956)

4   Her note about "Irv Levy" committing "suicide by jumping off the Calvert Street Bridge" (Friday, February 16, 1951) takes the same form.

5   http://www.spectrezine.org/war/Mendes4.htm: "The purge of American employees holding left-wing views had begun - as reported by Linda Malvern in the Guardian's 'UN Blues' of 1995 (commemorating the 50th anniversary of the UN)...In a matter of years the UN staff was purged in a witch-hunt as systematic & ruthless as the one against Hollywood". This was in reference to the anti-communist campaign of the 50's, masterminded by Senator Patrick McCarran (Senator Joe McCarthy's Svengali), which resulted in the notorious McCarran Act. In 1952 J. Edward Hoover, Director of the FBI, agreed to pass on to Senator McCarran's committee any information they had on the UN's American employees, as a result of which 30 employees were 'interrogated' by the committee - 18 of whom invoked the 5th Amendment. Trygve Lie [secretary general of the U.N. and Norwegian politician] sacked those 18. There was more to come, but this whole dirty episode can best be encapsulated in the following tragic case: Abraham Feller, an American lawyer who had served in FDR's New Deal administration, was the first American to be appointed to the UN - as Trygve Lie's Chief Counsel. In early November 1952, Feller learnt that he faced being subpoenaed by the McCarran committee; on November 10th Trygve Lie announces that he (Lie) is resigning; on November 13th Feller struggles from his wife's grasp and plunges to his death from their Manhattan apartment on the 12th floor."

an extra two-word phrase indicated that this was an important topic. And perhaps she did not write more on this topic lest her diary be confiscated via subpoena. "Ira missed his Scout meeting – too much homework," she continued, as if the nationally reported suicide and her child's homework were equivalent. "Expect he [Ira] would have brushed it off but for his [bad] report card." And then, she's off for entertainment: "To the National Theater with Ira and Alice Jaffee to see Phil Silvers in 'The Top Banana,' a zany thing but I was in just the mood for it, and so was Jules." She was in the mood for zaniness after news of the suicide? Perhaps that's the way her personality worked – always seeking balance.

Even though from an outside perspective the years of Anne's life can be grouped into distinctive time periods (1931-1934: Law School and Graduation; 1935-1938: Washington and Professional Growth; 1939-1945: Marriage, Mothering, and World War II; 1946-1952: Professional Life and Silver Spring; 1953-1961: McCarthyism and the Struggle to Survive; 1962-1967: Mature Years; and 1968-1978: Grandmother and Judge),[6] Anne comments only briefly on these grand topics, perhaps because she did not set out to write her diary with a serious purpose in mind. In fact, she claims (in 1961), to not know at all why she is writing her diary. Her entry about the topic of the diary itself, written 30 years after she began, is one of the longer reflections:

Often wonder why, after all these years, I continue to write these fool things. I almost never look back in them for any purpose, and do not suppose, in view of the great number of these books that I am accumulating, that I ever shall go back over them. By the time I have the time, I shall probably not have the eyesight. But I suppose, if it serves no other purpose, it is a form of self-discipline as I write my little page even when I find it a considerable bore and a great nuisance. Nor do I suppose that all this blithering will be of the slightest interest to Ira or to those who come after him.[7]

The lack of reflective material in the daily entries may also be a structural bi-product of the fact that she wrote monthly and annual reflective summaries to complement the daily notes. In these summaries, she separates the wheat from the chaff. For example, her 1944 summary is as follows:

And so 1944 had dragged to a close. I do not suppose I have ever been so well satisfied to have any other year of my life come to a close. It has been on the whole an unhappy year. It saw Jules go into the army. It saw him seriously ill with spinal meningitis. It saw all his efforts to better his position knocked into the ground, for no apparent reason. <u>*It saw Ira becoming thin and unhappy and resentful. It saw me finally forced to give*</u>

6   Could be labeled otherwise if viewed from the inside, e.g.: A Single Woman Looking for a Man; Finding her Man and her First Job; Becoming a Mother and Consoling her Unhappy Mother; etc.
7   1961 Year End Summary.

up my job, and possibly, as a result, my career. It saw me dragged across the country to visit Jules, and then dragged away from him to be reunited with Ira, whom I had missed far more deeply than I had realized I would. And, seeing how much he had missed me, began to realize how unhappy he must have been when he had to spend so much of his time in Esther's [Anne's maid] exclusive company. I hope and pray that 1945 will be a brighter year primarily that it will see the end of the war, which will not only re-unite our family but will also bring joy to the world. Hope that we shall be able to adopt another child. Hope Jules will find work that will give him joy and satisfaction, and that life will in all ways make up to him for the bitterly unhappy year he had just spent. Have resolved to be more gentle and kindly to Ira. Sometimes speak to him brusquely and peremptorily, and he is sensitive enough to resent it, as well as bright enough to remember about it and make me ashamed of myself. And have resolved to try to make myself worthy generally of the wonderful husband and son I am fortunate enough to have.

But her daily diaries read nothing like this. She even describes "dailies" in terms of what they are *not*:

There is, after all, no vivid description of events of general interest, no profound thoughts, no clever writing, nothing of any interest to anyone who does not care about my routine, humdrum, day-to-day doings. Cannot imagine anyone caring. For one thing, anyone who liked reading could find so many things to read so much more interesting and worthwhile.

I do not think Anne's description represents low self-esteem. Rather it is an avid reader's realistic assessment of the difference between her diary and fine literature.

It might have been vanity and conceit when I began, and when some of the people I met and worked with seemed to my uncritical eyes among the world's greatest, and I a noteworthy person because I had met or worked with them. I am now, however, a little more realistic in my evaluation of people, including myself. I suppose, then, that I continue with this blithering nonsense year after year to be a habit that I am reluctant to bring to an end.

This last reflection is the most telling – Anne used a diary to record the people with whom she was acquainted. One might even label her collection of notebooks, "A Diary of People I've Met." Unfortunately, in most cases, she did not note anything about this myriad of people. This terseness can be expected since the diary was not written to be read by anyone other than its author.

Introduction

Anne seemed determined to provide an accurate and nearly complete record of the people with whom she interacted. For example, she started her diary, as so many people do, on a January 1 (in her case, 1931). "Saw the New Year in with Lloyd Tuinby, Mimmie Begirs and Dick Little." This first sentence provokes the question as to why Anne recorded the names of [nearly] every person she spends time with every day. The reason may be that Anne saw people as unique individuals worthy of respect (i.e. she did not write, "Saw the New Year in with friends."). And second, she cared about details, including the recording of exact names. The latter is a valuable skill for a lawyer or judge.

Anne's first entry recounts Lloyd Tuinby making a fool of himself, and her not accepting his subsequent profuse apology. Although she states that she "expects not to hear from him again," when Lloyd does call two days later, she responds by inviting him to her home. In the next ten days or so, Anne had several more interactions with him until she considered herself "well rid of Lloyd. He had the makings of a fine chap but wrong bringing-up."[8] This short-lived relationship suggests that Anne was somewhat flexible in her relations with others, but that she was also ready to cut people out of her life if they did not measure up.

Anne's *last* entry (in this collection[9]), written on Tuesday, May 9, 1978, had all the usual elements: weather, health, family, friends, food, phone calls. "A cool rainy day. Jules took me to Radiology. Dropped me there. I went from there to the Clinic for, much later, a spinal treatment. Jules stopped at the clinic before leaving for the airport. Stopped, I hope, worrying about me. Helen came to the clinic, brought me some goodies, which, after we got home, the (grand) kids and I had for luncheon. Ruth picked up the kids at Dulles and brought them home. During supper Charlie Smith from Jules' office brought us some fresh-caught frozen trout. Jules called form N.Y to check on whether Charlie, who had trouble calling us about the fish, had made connections."

A New Approach To Reading A Diary

In my recent book, *Observing the Observer: Understanding Our Selves in Field Research*,[10] I offer a simple new approach to the analysis of field notes that applies just as well to the analysis of diary entries. This perspective examines notes in terms of the various selves of the researcher. What emerges from such a reading is an understanding that is different from that which emerges from reading field entries sequentially. For example, here are two randomly selected excerpts of consecutive days of Anne's diary:

---

[8] January 19, 1931.
[9] This collection contains no entries from May 10, 1978 to August 15, 1978, the day of her death.
[10] New York: Oxford University Press, 2010.

Monday, May 6, 1946
Jules and I lunched at S&W. First time in years. The food was good, but the crowds were discouraging. Sent Mother S. some bath salts for Mother's Day. Will send Mother F. her usual check. Henry Lehman came home with us for dinner. We had the roast. Henry ate a fantastic quantity of food, especially meat. Apparently starved for some home cooking. We had coffee after dinner, and I was awake most of the night.

Tuesday, May 7, 1946
Oral argument in Gear Mfg. Houston and Reilly present, and it seemed quite clear they held divergent views. The coal strike is having the disastrous consequences everyone expected. Hope it is settled soon – with the miners getting a decent break. Not so tired during the day as I had expected to be, but I was ready for bed much earlier than usual in the evening. Lillian Freireich Purcell called. She and Sid are visiting Pearl, both recuperating from illnesses.

Read sequentially, these two entries are a hodgepodge of disconnected information. An alternative way to read them, however, is by subject matter, i.e. in the first, lunching, relation with Jules, evaluation of restaurants, celebration of Mother's Day, relations with mother and mother-in-law, a particular person (Henry Lehman), friends, cooking, and obtaining food; and in the second, work, stamina, phone calls, social network, typical week-days. The idea is to read *all* the notes creating an exhaustive list of categories from excerpt number 1, then adding 2, and so forth. Using this inductive approach, I have come up with many categories with which to analyze Anne's diary entries. From these I have selected a few for reasons of space: a) Anne as a reader, b) Anne as a social networker, c) Anne as a drinker, d) Anne as a mentee, e) Anne as her parents' daughter, f) Anne as a Jew, g) Anne as a mother and h) Anne as a professional. Combining these multiple perspectives presents a rather full portrait of Anne the person. But what is most important is that the categories emerge from the data themselves.

Of course, there are many more categories – some of which are quite important - than can be discussed in this chapter. For example, I could have chosen to include a discussion of "Anne the employer," a topic that could make use of numerous entries about her maids. An exploration of employer/maid relations could uncover interesting class dynamics and questions of women's solidarity. Another topic I chose to ignore is the traveling that Anne and Jules did – e.g. their trip to Europe in August 1957 and to Israel in September 1967, among many others. Other topics could be "Anne the daughter-in-law," "Anne the sister," and "Anne the shopper." But every researcher has to prioritize. Each research project is by definition, incomplete. Over and above this technique of deriving analytic categories from Anne's own writing, the reader requires some historical contextualization and some explanatory notes about unfamiliar terms.[11]

Historical Contextualization: The Social Issues Of The Day

Anne Freeling was born in 1910, and sadly, lived for only 68 years. In 1978, her life was cut short by lymphoma.[12] When she was 46 and living in Washington, D.C., she underwent a "cancer test" behind her husband's back: "Took my cancer test at Public Health. Will be notified of the results in 2 or 3 weeks. Got a ride to Silver Spring with Max Rosenberg, and Jules picked me up there. Have not told Jules yet about the cancer test."[13] It would be interesting to know why Anne hid this test from Jules. Was this a common practice among wives at a time when cancer was almost too dreaded to mention? And for which cancer did she undergo a diagnostic test? Seven years later, she had an office physical checkup and wrote elliptically: "Nothing wrong, apparently, as far as the doctor could tell *at this point.*"[14]

These diary entries include many mentions of Anne's not feeling well: "Felt a bit headachy,"[15] "We had scrambled eggs for supper. I fixed some sandwiches for Ira when he came home, and then went to bed fairly early, feeling fine, but woke during the night with a miserable sick headache."[16] "Much too woozy to go to work or to services."[17] "Something did not agree with me, and I went home very sick, and spent another horrible night."[18] The overall impression she gives is of a person with decent health and a lot of energy, and thus her encounter with lymphoma comes as a shock to the reader. Anne's succumbing to lymphoma may also have been characteristic of the period in which she developed the disease. Her chances of going into remission and her survival rate would probably have been much greater now.

---

11 Another technique, which I did not employ in analyzing this diary, is based on a word search. For example, here are some entries that use the word "afraid. "I was afraid I would be too tired with three nights of school in a row." "Tired of the whole racket but cannot quit because afraid of Mrs. Fuller's disappointment." "Afraid I have gotten out of the habit of buying." "Afraid my night work is affecting my real job." "I enjoyed it very much – the swings, too. I used to be afraid of them when I was a youngster, but now I can go way up with nary a tremor." "Afraid my eyes are going on the blink again."
12 I do not know the family's medical history, a topic that is useful to explore when one's subject matter includes illness. See Jennifer Rosner, *If a Tree Falls: A Family's Quest to Hear and Be Heard* (New York: Hadassah-Brandeis Institute and the Feminist Press, 2010). Nowadays, lymphoma is defined as a cancer that begins in the lymphatic cells of the immune system and presents as a solid tumor of lymphoid cells. It is treatable with chemotherapy, and in some cases radiotherapy and/or bone marrow transplantation, and can be curable depending on the histology, type, and stage of the disease.
13 September 7, 1956.
14 September 16, 1963.
15 May 31, 1958.
16 September 7, 1964.
17 September 8, 1964.
18 February 12, 1940.

Anne practiced law most of her adult life at a time when few women had entered the legal field. In terms of the U.S. legal environment for women during her lifetime, she was born *before* the passage of the 19th Amendment giving U.S. women the right to vote, and she died in 1978 three years *before* the first woman - Sandra Day O'Connor - was appointed to the Supreme Court of the United States. Had Anne lived fifteen years longer, she would have witnessed the first Jewish woman to be appointed to the Supreme Court – Ruth Bader Ginsburg – in 1993.

On the other hand, a Jewish *man* had already served the Court while Anne was alive: Louis Dembitz Brandeis served as an Associate Justice for 23 years, from June 1, 1916–February 13, 1939, thereby demonstrating that at the time the prejudice against women was far greater than the prejudice against Jews. [Although Brandeis sat on the court while Anne was in law school, she did not mention him in any of her diary entries in this collection.] For two periods during Anne's lifetime *two* Jewish men [and no women, Jewish or non-Jewish] served simultaneously as Justices of the Supreme Court. Benjamin N. Cardozo served from March 2, 1932–July 9, 1938, and Felix Frankfurter served from January 20, 1939–August 28, 1962, each of whom sharing the bench with Brandeis for part of their tenure.

Although Anne did not live to see women judges on the Supreme Court, she was privileged to see many other "firsts" for American women.[19] In 1914, for example, women were admitted to the American College of Surgeons for the first time (Alice Gertrude Bryant and Florence West Duckering); Ellen Richards becomes the first woman to graduate from MIT; Hattie Plum Williams became the first woman to earn a doctorate in sociology; Jeanette Rankin became the first elected female Congressperson; and the first Jewish sorority was established (SDT, at Cornell). Frances Perkins (1880-1965), U.S. Secretary of Labor from 1933 to 1945, was the first woman appointed to the U.S. Cabinet. In terms of gains in the legal field, in 1918 Kathryn Sellers was appointed the first female judge of a juvenile court (Washington, D.C.); the next year, Mary Florence Lathrop became the first woman admitted to the American Bar Association; and in the following year Florence Ellinwood Allen became the first American woman elected to a judicial post.

The year Anne was born, another New England woman, Marion Talbot, published a landmark research-based book that slowly began to shape a new environment for American women.[20] That book, *The Education of Women*, was based on one of the first social science studies conducted in the United States. Talbot compared fertility patterns of American women who had received a higher education degree with a comparable group that had *not* furthered their education beyond high school. The social background of the

---

19   See Shulamit Reinharz, *A Chronological Chart of Women's Sociological Work*, Working Papers Series, #1, Women's Studies Program, Brandeis University. 3rd edition, August 2001. (available from the author)

20   Rosalind Rosenberg, *Beyond Separate Spheres: Intellectual Roots of Modern Feminism* (New Haven: Yale University Press, 1982).

study was complex. Many educated men in positions of authority (e.g. the President of Harvard University and the Dean of its Medical School) claimed *that higher education damaged women's fertility potential.* They asserted that a human body is a fixed, sealed entity, and if energy flowed to the brain, the uterus did not have access to that energy. The energy-deprived uterus would become desiccated and infertile. (The impact of education on *men's reproductive organs* was not studied). Talbot believed that an empirical study could settle the question once and for all. The conclusion of her research was that the *difference in fertility rates of the two groups of women was negligible,* and therefore, studying for advanced degrees did not make women infertile.

A hidden racist argument underlying this entire controversy was the fear that the greater fertility of American Negroes in comparison with that of white women required intervention measures in order to increase the number and proportion of whites in America. Only by keeping white women at home, it was reasoned, could the fertility gap be reduced. Although Anne's later musings about the work/family conflict she was experiencing sound like those of a contemporary woman, it is important to understand that, like today, *the question of women's employment versus exclusive dedication to mothering was being debated on a national scale.* Taking a radical stance against the very concept of "housewife," national speaker Charlotte Perkins Gilman published "Are Women Human Beings?" and "The Waste of Private Housekeeping." Although Anne's diary does not mention her reading these types of books and pamphlets, it is unlikely that she, as an intelligent woman and reader, was not aware of these arguments swirling throughout society.

During the first decade of Anne's life there were also major changes in women's *volunteer* work. In addition to health related fund-raising groups[21] and the multitude of women's pro- and anti-suffrage organizations among blacks and whites, voluntary societies arose to advocate for ethnic and racial groups. In Chicago in 1912, for example, anti-lynching activist, Ida B. Wells, founded the Alpha Suffrage Club, the first Black women's suffrage organization in the U.S. That same year in Baltimore, Henrietta Szold founded the Hadassah Women's Organization, devoted to providing Jewish education for Jewish women and raising funds for medical services in Palestine. Synagogues were also absorbing a lot of Jewish women's volunteer energy. In 1913, Carrie Simon became the first president of the National Federation of Temple Sisterhood. In 1920 when Anne was 10 years old, Martha Newmark requested ordination from the Reform movement, but was rejected on the basis of gender. And in 1922, Judith Kaplan became the first American girl to have a formal bat mitzvah. If Anne had had a bat mitzvah at age twelve, it would have taken place that same year.

For all the symbolic and actual advancements of women that Anne might have experienced or heard about, it was still very much *a man's world.* Gender bias was

---

21 Fund-raising for these groups was almost defined as a civic duty: February 12, 1955: "While we were out, *someone* left the material I am to use in the Heart Fund collection, so I guess I am stuck with that chore." (emphasis added)

something Anne clearly experienced in part by contrasting her conditions of employment with those of her husband. For example, "Took a notion to ask Tom Emerson for a raise. No soap. Only P.I.'s are getting them, and possibly a few others, not including me. Jules got a reclassification and a raise to $4600."[22] This discrimination is all the more significant in that it occurred a short while *after* Anne had acquitted herself so well at a Congressional investigation of the NLRB (National Labor Relations Board), where she was employed. Seven years later she commented on the same topic in her year end summary: "Jules and I were both reclassified on our jobs, Jules' reclassification carrying with it a substantial increase in salary. And I have virtually been promised another reclassification, one which will also be accompanied by a generous increase in salary." But at the end of the next year, she wrote: "There were other good things that happened this year: my becoming a supervisor and getting a P-6 rating; Jules and I getting clearance from our loyalty review boards." There was no mention of a raise.

One of many examples of discrimination in the diaries is Anne's description of a job interview. Readers of her diaries can benefit from overhearing the conversation and listening in on the prejudicial statements: "I decided to go to the office as I figured I would be interviewed today by Beeson. I was, and it went quite badly. He took me completely aback when he said he would consider the fact that I had a husband to support me. He knew Jules was in private practice."[23] Four days later, Anne wrote: "went in to see Beeson *again* to explain why I thought it unfair to consider as a factor in my case Jules' ability to save me from starving. He did not seem too impressed."[24] (emphasis added) At the time, married women's work was considered superfluous and unjustified based on the unfounded and irrelevant assumption that women took work *away* from men. When a woman married or became pregnant, she was likely to lose her job. Most "selfish" of all was the woman who worked for the government, while her husband did the same, which, of course, was true in Anne's case. On Friday, January 12, 1940 Anne and Jules had dinner with friends "for more discussions of my notoriety. I had made the front page again today in connection with husbands and wives in the Government service."

Nowadays, a comment such as the one Beeson made to Schlezinger is illegal in a job-related interview. The attitude toward working women in the 1950's, when these conversations were taking place, might be compared to today's prejudice against immigrants who are wrongly thought to take jobs away from others rather than properly considered as contributing to the economy. One can also see how threatening it might have been to men unused to being challenged to have to work with intelligent women: "Merv explained to me how the Board was going to speed up cases by, among other things, cutting memos

---

22 January 18, 1940.
23 March 11, 1954.
24 March 15, 1954.

down by discussing vital issues only. I had the satisfaction of reminding him that that was inconsistent with the changes he had suggested *last week* in Gromfine's case."25 (emphasis added) Since men had the power in almost every workplace, they could quite easily put women in their place: "Conference with Merv and Gromfine on one of the latter's cases. Apparently Merv did not like the way I had revised it at all. My work has piled up pretty badly again."26 Although the focus of this essay is on Anne the person, the diaries are also useful to read as a record of the times. Through her diaries, we can see what some people were reading, which movies they went to, how they shopped, what daily life was like during World War II and how women were discriminated against, among many other topics.

Anne As A Mentee

A vast research literature exists on the topic of women needing or at least benefiting from mentoring for personal and career enhancement. Anne graduated from high school in Lawrence, Massachusetts and immediately enrolled in the law school at Northeastern University in Boston, receiving no financial aid from her family. As a new student in a demanding course of study, Anne could have benefited from parental guidance in her new role as a woman in an endeavor dominated by men. But her parents were unable to play that role because, as immigrants, it seems that they had not mastered the environment themselves. In addition, her parents had serious emotional problems of their own.

Fortunately Anne soon found what every ambitious young woman needs, an older woman - Mrs. Fuller - who would become her confidante and mentor, a person who would help her navigate the new demands being made on her. As early as January 5, 1931, four days into writing the diary, Anne describes a longstanding relation with Mrs. Fuller: "Had a real heart-to-heart talk with Mrs. Fuller such as I had not had for some time and which I always find so helpful and constructive. If I ever get through this law course it will be due at least 90% to her encouragement." Anne turned to Mrs. Fuller for advice on whether or not to take particular jobs, and she avoided taking actions (e.g. quitting law school) specifically because she knew that Mrs. Fuller would disapprove. "Tired of the whole racket but cannot quit because afraid of Mrs. Fuller's disappointment."27

In a situation that echoes George Bernard Shaw's "Pygmalion," but is even more charming because Anne's Dr. Higgins is a woman, Mrs. Fuller motivated Anne to dress and behave properly: "Mrs. Fuller thinks I have cultivated a more critical judgment of fashion…'cultivation' instigated and urged on by her in her effort to give me a 'high-grade background.'"28 "Mrs. Fuller suggested that next time I have a date, I go to the Coconut

25 April 19, 1948.
26 April 14, 1948.
27 January 15, 1931.
28 January 15, 1931.

Grove or Lido Venice or someplace formal."[29] Anne was also steered in her reading, although she didn't always concur in her evaluation of these books: "Mrs. Fuller presented me with 'Saplio' and 'Carmille.' Have read 'Saplio.' Too much sensuality."[30]

But Mrs. Fuller did more than help Anne polish her appearance and charm potential suitors. She also helped her deal with her internal conflicts, family problems, and anger: "Wrote home at Mrs. Fuller's behest, suggesting that if the folks sent Jean to day school it would be no more than fair to pay part of my tuition, too. Seems selfish, but never got anything yet by being self-effacing. Jean asks so much more that I do, and gets it, and gets applauded for knowing enough to get it. I try to ask for very little, get less, and am considered a fool."[31] Her sister Jean aggravated Anne quite a bit at this time in their lives: "Promised to meet Jean for luncheon. She took so long to dress we had only a few minutes to get our train, when she announced that she had to go downtown to draw out some money. That was the last straw and I simply refused to go at all."[32] Mrs. Fuller didn't even have to be present for Anne to benefit for her assessments: "The members of the household are friendly and pleasant, but not what Mrs. Fuller would call 'high grade.'"[33]

While at law school, Anne found another woman who served not as a mentor, but as a role model: "Judge Emma Fall Schofield, …the [future] Women's Advisor at Northeastern University. She made a charming address and seems genuinely enthused about the idea, from the standpoint of helping the girls, and not just because it is her job."[34] Emma Fall Schofield, graduated Boston University law school and became *the first woman judge* in Massachusetts. Her mother had been the state's *first woman lawyer in a jury case*. Judge Schofield represented the woman Anne might become.

The third professional influence was her boss, Charles Wyzanski.[35] As she was completing law school, Wyzanski persuaded Anne to leave Boston to work with him in Washington, D.C. as a secretary in the Department of Labor. Anne clearly admired Wyzanski's intelligence and used him as a standard by which to measure other lawyers. Her feelings sometimes left her flustered: "Surprise! Charles Wyzanski dropped in to see me first thing in the morning. We had a delightful chat, but because his visit was so unexpected I did not say, or ask about, many things I should otherwise have mentioned."[36] But Anne's relationship with Wyzanski was problematic on many levels – for one, she was Jewish and he was not.

---

29 January 31, 1931.
30 January 24, 1931.
31 January 19, 1931.
32 August 7, 1933.
33 September 18, 1933. "Letter from Mrs. Fuller suggesting certain people I ought to see in Boston…
34 November 7, 1932.
35 Charles Edward Wyzanski, Jr. (May 27, 1906-September 3, 1986).
36 October 26, 1937.

Although he did not always respect her intelligence, or so she thought, Wyzanski wanted Anne to work for him. In a well-known pattern in mixed-gender workplaces, "The Solicitor,[37] after his usual procedure of *ridiculing any suggestions coming from me, had decided to follow them.*"[38] (emphasis added) Wyzanski also appealed to Anne as a woman, and gave her "a lovely gold pin"[39] and "a beautiful compact he had bought in Vienna [with] a note urging me to make up my vacillating mind and come [i.e. return] to Boston"[40] (and work with him there.) "Had a long talk with the Solicitor about my job. Wavered several times, and then we decided I should go along with him [from Labor to Justice] if the job was available!"[41] "Mr. W. left on the noon train for Boston, leaving me in the midst of indexing…[B]efore he left, [he] had insisted on putting my name on the brief, although I had demurred and questioned the advisability of doing so. He also suggested that I be admitted to the Supreme Court so that there would be no question about my appearing on briefs. His compliments are the more appreciated because of their *rarity.*"[42] (emphasis added) Mr. W., as she called him, was inconsistent. "…I left a little bit early, although Mr. W. hemmed and hawed about it. But *I can forgive him anything for a while* – the Seminole brief came back today, with my name appearing on the signature page. That was somewhat of a thrill."[43] (emphasis added)

On the other hand, the fact that whether or not her name was on a brief was left to the good will of her boss, rather than automatically appearing because it reflected her professional input, meant that her advancement was characterized by ambiguity. These are the conditions under which women frequently worked and still work today.

Anne's final significant mentor was her husband and life partner, Jules Schlezinger, a man with whom she established a strong, mutually satisfying relationship. On November 25, 1938 Jules proposed marriage. At first, Anne was not sure: "I am very fond of him, but somehow I cannot picture him as my husband forever and ever." Gradually her attitude softened. With these mentors and role models available to Anne, she ascended to an unusually high position within the law.

Anne As A Social Networker

Long before the current era when social networking has become organized electronically and virtually, Anne understood its significance both for career development and participation in the larger society. As a law student, she sometimes accepted social engagements over

---

37	i.e. Charles Wyzanski.
38	November 8, 1935.
39	September 19, 1963.
40	September 17, 1937.
41	November 8, 1935.
42	October 24, 1936.
43	October 27, 1936.

studying in order to reap possible future rewards: "Peggy wants me and Jean to go out to the dance tomorrow night with some law students. Pleaded much studying, but she and Jean teased until I finally consented to go. Very much dissatisfied with my refusal powers. Must strengthen them. [I told] myself that I would not have surrendered if they had not been law students. *May mean future business.*"[44] (emphasis added)

During Anne's career, there were several potential time slots for one-on-one, face-to-face networking: breakfast, mid-morning coffee, lunch, afternoon tea/coffee, cocktails, dinner and after dinner on a weeknight, compounded by even more such occasions on the weekend. Anne took advantage of all of these opportunities to socialize and build her relationships. In addition, there were non-face-to-face networking possibilities - letters, postcards, and phone calls - all of which she received in large quantities.

One of Anne's earliest diary entries mentions a fleeting social breakfast: "Monday, January 5, 1931. Very warm. Breakfasted with Peggy." When she moved to Washington, she continued this practice: "Breakfasted in the cafeteria with Miss Thrift, and lunched with Mrs. Jewell and Miss Thrift."[45] Next was morning coffee: "morning coffee with Sid Lindner, Earl Bellman, Tom Wilson, Charlie Schneider, and Bob Piper."[46] She even made business dates with people from across the aisle: "Lunched in the cafeteria with Jo Silver. Had coffee in the afternoon with Jerry Doherty, a Republican, and one of the very few happy people around the Board."[47] "Afternoon tea with Mira Stevenson."[48] The cocktail party could erupt at any time of day: "Was in the office [in the morning] a very short time before Jack took Condon, Swope, Jules and me out for cocktails to celebrate his raise."[49]

While a law student in Boston, Anne started her practice of nearly daily lunches with her fellow students and friends: "Luncheon with Anna Clancy – very pleasant but so inconsequential."[50] Anne is telling us that lunch with someone should be consequential! "Luncheon with Thelma Farrington at Hayler's. Bum lunch. Like Thelma quite a good deal – sensible, sweet, modest."[51] "Luncheon with Anna Clancy. Very pleasant. No depth to Anna. Agreeable, but much of her would be boring."[52] "Lunched with Sylvia and her girl friend."[53] "Lunched with Sylvia."[54] "Lunched with Mrs. Fuller."[55] "Took [Clara] to

---

44 January 5, 1931.
45 November 13, 1935.
46 February 18, 1954.
47 November 6, 1952.
48 March 15, 1954.
49 November 23, 1938.
50 January 6, 1931.
51 January 23, 1931.
52 January 30, 1931.
53 November 5, 1932.
54 November 12, 1932.
55 November 15, 1932. Mrs. Fuller is her unofficial mentor.

luncheon at …a German restaurant on Huntington Avenue."[56] Anne loved to eat good food and to explore new restaurants. She also was willing to do the inviting and foot the bill.

Anne realized that her nearly daily social lunches at neighborhood restaurants in Boston or Washington, D.C. were expensive (frequently overpriced) and conducive to weight gain. But her enjoyment of the company, the place, and the food outweighed those shortcomings. "Lunched with Miss Korte at a cute little back-yard garden place."[57] "Lunched at Allie's Inn with Mary and Jean. I blew them, today being payday - $70.83."[58] Taking her lunch with relatives such as her sister Clara or her uncle Phil was a way to keep in constant touch with family. "Lunched at Tally–Ho with Clara."[59] "Phil took the crowd of us to luncheon and dancing – at the Lotus."[60] "Lunched with Clara at Allie's Inn."[61] "Took Clara to luncheon at Madrillon, and what a licking I took!"[62] "Lunched at the Lotus Lantern with Miss Harrington."[63] "Lunched with Clara at the Lotus Lantern."[64] "Lunched with Clara at the Army Navy Tea room. She gets a big kick out of lunching with me it seems."[65] The big kick goes in both directions, it seems. "Lunched at the Washington Coffee Shop with Mary Lou."[66] "Lunched with Frances."[67]

Starting in 1935, Anne began to have larger business lunches. "Lunched at the Latch String with Frances, Kommy, Edith, and George."[68] "Lunched in the cafeteria with Miss Larimer and Miss Patterson."[69] "Lunched with Lee MacKinnon and Miss Larimer at Brownley's."[70] "Lunched at the Latch String with Frances, Ruth, Gladys, Burch and Kommy."[71] "Frances called and asked me to lunch with her, but I had already made an engagement with Mrs. Jewell."[72] "Lunched with Miss Patterson."[73] "Lunched with

---

56 November 21, 1932.
57 August 25, 1933.
58 August 31, 1933.
59 December 7, 1933.
60 September 2, 1933.
61 September 8, 1933. These are her colleagues at work.
62 September 13, 1933.
63 September 14, 1933.
64 September 15, 1933.
65 September 25, 1933.
66 November 2, 1935.
67 November 5, 1935.
68 November 6, 1935.
69 November 7, 1935.
70 November 8, 1935.
71 November 9, 1935.
72 November 11, 1935.
73 November 12, 1935.

Mrs. Jewell and Miss Thrift."[74] "Mrs. Wintersteen took me to luncheon."[75] "Lunched at the Latch String with Kommy, Ruth and May Sweet. Wore my black velvet, and was profusely complimented on my appearance."[76] "Lunched at the Washington Coffee Shop with Mary Lou and Maxine."[77] "Went to the Labor Dept. to finish my research job. Lunched at the Latch String with Gladys Burch. *Got the low-down on people and events at the Labor Dept.*"[78] (emphasis added) "Lunched at Brownley's with Ruth Jewell and Clara, had a pleasant time gossiping about people we all knew. Met Barney Robbins, who gave me a big hand. Shirley's husband happened along, and I was introduced to him – Dr. Eisenberg – I think."[79] "Lunched with Ralph Winkler, who is very bitter about the lousy deal servicemen have received."[80] "Lunched at Tally-Ho with Irene and Grace. Peg Patterson, formally of the NLRB and now Judge Madden's law clerk, came in alone and joined us."[81]

Some of her companions were her relatives (e.g. sisters Jean and Clara), some were her office mates, and some were her friends. As time passed, her luncheons increasingly became business meetings. "Then lunched with Jules and George Wheeler at the Court cafeteria."[82] "Lunched at the Aviation Club with Mary Clark."[83] "Lunched at the Diplomat with Jonah Silver, recently rehired at the Board on McCulloch's staff."[84] "Lunched at the Black Steer with Vivian Asplund."[85] The list is seemingly endless.

Anne knew a great number of people and enjoyed being with them. "Had a pleasant luncheon at Blackie's with some of the TXes."[86] "Went with Ivan Peterson to the Summer Lawrence funeral at a church in Bethesda. Later to the Democratic Club at the Watergate for luncheon."[87] "Lunched with Fannie Boyls."[88] "Walked to Adam's Rib for luncheon with Mira Stevenson."[89] "A pleasant mild day so Sid Ascher and I walked into Georgetown and had luncheon at Chez Odette."[90] "Lunched at Blackie's with Al Somers."[91]

[74] November 13, 1935.
[75] November 14, 1935.
[76] October 2, 1936.
[77] October 3, 1936.
[78] October 6, 1936.
[79] October 20, 1936.
[80] May 9, 1946. Ralph Winkler is a Judge in the NLRB.
[81] June 6, 1947.
[82] May 4, 1942.
[83] June 2, 1961. Anne and Mary Clark became friends, and Mary predeceased Anne succumbing to cancer in March 1976.
[84] June 22, 1961.
[85] September 21, 1964.
[86] May 8, 1969. Tx or TX is Trial Examiner.
[87] November 6, 1970.
[88] November 10, 1970.
[89] November 25, 1970.
[90] March 1, 1971.
[91] March 11, 1971.

"Lunched at Blackie's with Sid Ascher and Ben Lipton."[92] "Lunched at Blackie's with Maller, Ascher, and Hinkel."[93] "Lunched at the Black Ulysses with Abe Muller and Harry Kuskin."[94] "Lunched at Blackie's with Mira Stevenson and Abe Muller."[95] "I lunched at a cafeteria with the reporter, Mary Bagby."[96] "Lunched with Jo Klein and Milt Janus at the Embers Restaurant, complete with cocktails."[97] And so on for the rest of her life. These lunches were essential to her career. And during those lunches, she seemed to show her companions that she could eat and drink with the best of them. Anne's gusto for lunching with others lasted her whole life. A typical day brought an extraordinary set of people into her life: "I went down [to work] with Jules. After the meeting with Powell, there was a meeting in Leedom's office...Had coffee with Mir, Gearhart and Wilson. Lunched with Charlie Schneider. Had tea with London, Leff and Krasnecki. Got a ride home with Jack Mantell."[98]

In the early 1960's Anne complained about overwork, and thus not being able to carve out time for lunch with friends and colleagues. The lunch dates she did make were with long-term friends such as Fannie Boyls, Mira Stevenson, Sid Ascher and Harry Kuskin. Whereas her 1950s luncheons were almost always with someone else, in the 1960s she frequently grabbed a bite alone and on the run. A common entry reads like this: "The rain stopped for a little while around noon so I walked over to the Hot Shoppe for luncheon."[99] "I was very busy, primarily because of getting ready for some rather difficult cases scheduled for tomorrow's Board agenda, so settled for a quick sandwich at the Hot Shoppe for luncheon."[100]

When she became a judge in the late 1960's, the fellowship frenzy of myriad social appointments slowed down considerably. In 1975, she wrote reflectively: "A showery day, but Mira Stevenson and I walked to Blackie's nevertheless. Told her of my hospital plans. Have told very few at the office. But she will be away next week on a hearing, and she has become pretty much my regular luncheon companion."[101] In her last year she ate nearly every meal with Jules, and then sometimes, lamentably, alone.

Anne As A Reader

In his introduction to this publication of her diaries, Anne's son, Ira, has written that his mother "loved to read." The large majority of her diary entries that mention reading

92   March 14, 1971.
93   September 8, 1972.
94   September 12, 1972.
95   September 15, 1972.
96   October 7, 1974.
97   June 5, 1975.
98   October 1, 1956.
99   September 8, 1964.
100   March 22, 1965.
101   June 27, 1975.

corroborate his comment. *Cyrano de Bergerac* is one of the first works that appears in her diaries, a book she reread: "I still get a lump in my throat when I get to his heroic but tragic death. His pretty cousin did not deserve his love."[102] She mentions only a few books of social commentary ("Trying to read some books on immigration but for the most part they are just words and figures to me.") In general, Anne was a critical reader: "Spent the evening reading the papers, and some of the biographical sketches in *Men of Turmoil*. They are interesting and well worth reading, but too uniformly flattering to be entirely pleasing to me. Each one is treated like the hero of his age."[103] A few days later, she wrote: [In the evening] " I decided to stay home and read. Was gratified when I finally found [that] one of the subjects of *Men of Turmoil* was not treated as a hero of unmixed virtuosity. Incidentally the victim was Henry Ford."[104] A little later on, "Finished reading Morris Cohen's *Philosophy of the Law*. Found it enjoyable and instructive despite its iconoclasm."[105]

"I spent the evening reading Anatole France's *Revolt of the Angels*…. Enjoyed his satirical wit very much."[106] "Read Pat Frank's *Alas, Babylon*. Found it interesting and depressing. Some of the people turned out finer and stronger than ever when faced with such awful problems, but others were so horrible." On August 9, 1945, she wrote: "Finished Richard Wright's *Black Boy*, a devastating description of conditions for negroes in the south. A miracle that one like Wright could rise above them, and so far above them." "Finished Steinbeck's *Cannery Row*." Pretty good, but not at all in the class of some of the other things he has written."[107] "Finished *Cuckoo Time*, a zany but rather entertaining story."[108] "Borrowed a book of Dorothy Parker stories. Found them very entertaining, but finally fell asleep over them."[109]

Not all of Anne's reading was serious: "Finished Jane Allen's *I Love my Girlish Laughter*, a light, frivolous thing, but amusing." "Finished Caroline Miller's *Lamb in His Bosom*. Thought it an excellent portrayal of the class and the times about which it was written." Anne pointed out the magazines, particularly the *New Yorker*, to which she subscribed, and the *Reader's Digest* back issues that she looked at. These were sources of comfort. In one entry she wrote: "The usual evening routine – newspaper, crossword puzzle, whatever

---

102   August 9, 1933.
103   Although this book is a collection of essays, no individual is listed as the editor. The full title is *Men of Turmoil: Biographies by Leading Authorities of the Dominating Personalities of our Day* (New York: Minton, Balch & Company, 1935). The book is aptly titled as there is no woman featured among the 37 portraits.
104   November 13, 1935.
105   November 26, 1935.
106   October 9, 1936.
107   August 21, 1945.
108   August 23, 1945.
109   August 25, 1945.

Introduction

book I am reading at the time, shower, and bed." And again, "It was rather a nasty evening, so I decided I would rather stay home and read – just plain lazy, that's all." Repeatedly, "I stayed home to read – what a stay-at-home I turned out to be!" Her friends must have known that she liked to read, and therefore gave her books as presents.[110] She also frequented libraries for more books: "We got two books at the lending library – Iams' *Girl Meets Body*, and Zweig's *The Axe of Wandsbek* – which should offer contrast if nothing else."[111] Anne also read the *Washington Post* regularly, including the thick Sunday issues. Much of her news came from listening to the radio, especially during the war years.[112] Anne was thus both a regular reader and a regular writer. Her life had a definite rhythm and discipline.

The overview of Anne's readings provides a glimpse into the topics of interest or amusement to a highly educated Jewish American woman of the time. "I read Willa Cather's *Obscure Destinies*, and rather enjoyed them, even the ones I had already read."[113] "…read the papers and some P.G. Woodhouse nonsense." "Read a collection of *Mr. Tutt* stories. Rather tiresome." "Read a detective story while I soaked in the tub. Very relaxing."[114] "Finished reading Catton's *The War Lords of Washington*. The subject matter was interesting enough, but I found the treatment dull." "Read *Candy*, which Stella Zanoff lent us. Thought it putrid. Felt we should apologize to Wachtel, to whom Jules sent the book when Wachtel was ill." "Read the first story in *The Pagan Rabbi*, our book club selection, and waded through a second story. Disliked them very much and do not intend to read any more of the book. Curious to see if anyone else in the book club will have enjoyed the stories."

Over the years, Anne also read law books when they were assigned in her classes; and she examined legal briefs related to her work: [I spent] "part of the evening reading back numbers of the Labor Relations Reports which I had not gotten a chance to read." Reading was always part of her life with her husband, Jules: While on a trip to Israel, Jules "bought a paperback of Malamud's *The Fixer* to read."[115] Finished reading Green's *Nothing* – a silly sort of book in my opinion.[116]

Reading was so important to Anne, her family and friends that they organized a Sunday night book club. "Got started reading *The Agony and the Ecstasy*, our book-club book,

---

110   May 19, 1946: "Acquired a large collection of elective stories from Edith. Don't know when I shall find the time to read them."
111   May 12, 1948.
112   November 8, 1938: "Everyone excited about the elections, which seem to be taking strange turns. Spent the evening reading and listening to the news flashed over the radio."
113   October 15, 1935.
114   April 25, 1948.
115   September 21, 1967.
116   April 26, 1950.

very long but easy to read as far as I have gone."[117] "I finished Tuchman's *Guns of August*, a magnificent book, but one that should be studied, not read as quickly as I did, and as all the book club members will do who read it at all."[118] "In the meantime, I am reading *The Rabbi*, which we got from the duplicate pay collection at the library, during the periods I spend waiting for Jules, and have almost finished it. Just as well, as Jules and the Levy's are counting on reading the same copy before the book club meeting on the 22nd."[119] "A lovely crisp sunny day so we stopped at Katz's and did a few other errands, including buying the paperback *Up the Organization*, our next book club book."[120] "A lively discussion of Mee's *Meeting at Potsdam*."[121]

Nearly every entry of Anne's diaries mentions that she read that day. Reading was a sign of her intelligence and her curiosity about the world. In her last few years, Anne's reading narrowed primarily to the *Post*. She mentioned reading, but did not specify *what* she read. Her love of reading continued until the end of her life: "We read the paper together. I had trouble falling asleep from shortness of breath. Used the oxygen mask almost all night."[122] "I managed to read the paper, not easy with a patch over one eye."[123] Anne died four months later on August 15, 1978.

Anne As A Social Drinker

In the second sentence of her first entry, Anne mentions going to a particular café to enjoy some alcoholic beverages. An offhand reference to social drinking appears nearly daily in her diary until she became quite ill. Clearly, Anne liked to have a drink before dinner, and sometimes after dinner as well. Prohibition had ended (the law was in effect from 1920-1933); women were moving into the public (and not just the private) sphere; and public drinking by women was becoming acceptable. In 1935, while still a law student, Anne wrote: "Mary and I lunched at the Washington Coffee Shop. I blew us to drinks, and they were not particularly good." Having alcoholic drinks with colleagues became part of Anne's daily routine: "Some of us adjourned to the Press Club for more drinks."

Drinking with her boyfriend and then husband, Jules, became a way to relax together: "Spent the evening at his apartment drinking cognac and listening to Toscanini's concert." "Jules, Jack, and I had dinner at the Hour Glass. Had drinks, too, which we liked much better than we did the dinner." "Spent the afternoon listening to the radio and drinking. Dinner with Charlie and Hiram Wooster. After dinner more drinking." "Jules and I had

117 September 13, 1964.
118 July 31, 1962.
119 May 12, 1966.
120 March 21, 1971.
121 March 7, 1976.
122 December 14, 1977.
123 April 16, 1978.

a good stiff drink before dinner." "To George's apartment to pick up George and Helen, and to have a drink." "We had drinks, and later coffee and turkey sandwiches and cake." "The Edes came over for dinner. After dinner we sat around a while and had a few drinks. Then downtown." "Jules bought drinks for everyone, not so much because it was a joyous occasion as because it was one of his last flings as a civilian." "We had cocktails, and then a late, and very delicious dinner. It was a congenial little group, and everyone had just enough to drink to sharpen their wits, so it was a gay, delightful evening, and we stayed quite late."

The lifestyle of social drinking was so ingrained in her group of friends, that it became difficult to imagine an enjoyable party without liquor: "Leedom had the entire staff, their spouses, and a few other people over. He does not drink nor serve liquor, but the party was *easier to take than we expected*." (emphasis added)

Anne and Jules had drinks when they were alone, not only when they were out with friends: "Jules was supposed to go to a B'nai B'rith meeting but was too tired, so we stayed home and had a drink by ourselves."[124] Some of Anne's social drinking did not end well: "The Edises, the Wolfs, and Evans from Jules' office came up later to drink and talk. We had a lot of fun, but by the end of the evening I was a wreck." On another occasion, "Jules had too many drinks, ...got home quite late, and pretty well ruined an otherwise wonderful dinner. I was plenty angry." "Mort plied me with liquor and I am afraid I drank too much and 'shot off my mouth' about my disgust with Truman's speech today re drafting strikers." "We ate very late, I made the mistake of two martinis on an empty stomach, got very sick, and had to come home." "Was miserably sick. Am going to swear off liquor for a while."[125] And sometimes, Anne drank alone: "Spent the afternoon listening to the radio and drinking. Dinner with Charlie and Hiram Wooster. After dinner more drinking."[126]

Because she and Jules tried to keep their weight under control, they sometimes deliberately reduced their drinking, usually to no avail. "We went to a movie, and then to Ted Lewis' for a rather good dinner, assisted by a couple of cocktails. We have not been doing much of any drinking lately, since we have both become concerned about our weight, but do break down once in a while." And sometimes she was put off by other people's drink-related behavior: "Then sat around for the rest of the evening drinking excellent cocktails and listening to a long monologue by Larry Lesser on what a brilliant guy Larry Lesser is. It was quite a price to pay even for a good meal and some good liquor."[127]

124 January 31, 1955.
125 May 26, 1946.
126 November 19, 1938.
127 February 20, 1951.

Anne As Her Parents' Daughter

In the first year of diary writing, Anne mentions her mother (Regina) a few times in ways that seem unremarkable except for two perhaps minor points: first, her mother writes to Anne but refers exclusively to Anne's sister, Jean, and second, Anne's father disagrees with the family about an important matter. "Think he is justified," she adds.[128] These are hints of major problems to come.

Anne's mother lived in Lawrence, Massachusetts, about an hour's ride nowadays from Boston, and frequently visited her daughter, Anne, in Boston. On some occasions they had fun together, visited people, ate out, shopped, and did each other's nails. Most of Anne's early remarks were positive: "Mother left this morning right after breakfast, happy, had a wonderful time… Several of the boys at school commented on how young Mother looks – some refusing to believe she was my Mother. Must tell her that. Mrs. Mann told me a little of yesterday's gossip, the gist of which was that everyone liked Mother."[129] But as time passes, we see continuous evidence that Anne's mother hardly nurtured Anne at all.

> *When I got home Mother and Clara were there. Jean had gone to Lawrence, but got back in time for supper. Clara left my laundry on the train Monday, which, after the umbrella episode, I consider quite inexcusable. I got hell once for losing 95 cents; and never lost much of anything since. But she is sensitive and must not be scolded."[130] Anne believed she was being treated unfairly vis a vis Clara, but more important, her mother did not provide a model for positive ways of resolving these conflicts. "Mother and Clara stayed overnight. We all went out for breakfast together. They left before dinner, thoroughly disgusted, Jean told me, with my harshness towards Clara. Did not come up to say goodbye to me or to get my laundry.[131]*

Then, amidst a description of visiting friends with her mother, Anne writes, "Mother had a weeping spell at the realization of her aloneness, and I spent a sleepless night."[132] And a few weeks later, we see how significant her mother's weeping is and how Anne, rather than Clara, is mobilized to help: "Clara went to work as usual. I went to (my uncle) Phil's (law) office at his special request. Seems John wrote to him re a divorce for the folks. He wanted to talk it over with me. The best bet, I fear."[133] It turns out that by 1933, if not

---

128   January 14, 1931. Anne's diary records her receipt of cards and letters from her mother, which also reflected the mother's refusal to have a telephone installed in her home.
129   November 4, 1932.
130   November 26, 1932.
131   November 27, 1932.
132   September 4, 1933.
133   September 21, 1933. Prior to September 22, 1975 when the Massachusetts Senate initially approved a modified no-fault divorce bill providing for dissolution of marriages within sixteen months after a couple had approved

earlier, Anne's parents' marriage had deteriorated to such an extent that "Phil is planning to take a trip to Lawrence to see if he can help with Mother's divorce. It is really the only way out, and I believe both Mother and Father will be happier for it, although it will no doubt mean Father will be more estranged than ever."[134]

There was no divorce. Instead, Anne's mother seems to have dropped the topic, and in her next communications, focused on her pride in Anne. "Letter from Mother, enclosing a clipping from the Lawrence paper, full of misstatements, and carrying my high school graduation picture…Letter from Mother enclosing clipping about radio commentator who stated that I was 'pretty as well as smart.' Apparently the home town is still talking about me." And likewise, Anne was proud of her mother: "Mother left this morning right after breakfast, happy, had a wonderful time, which gave me that all-tired-out feeling."[135] Her mother also reached out affectionately to Anne's future husband. "Jules called me later. Mother has sent him a box of cookies. He was very surprised and pleased."[136]

But the pleasant period did not last. For the rest of her life, Anne was recruited to participate in the roller coaster of her parents' relationship. "Clara and Lou came over after dinner, with a letter from Mother, still very bitter about Father, but a little calmer about it. Asked us to resume sending her money, which we are, of course, doing. I would so like to see them settle things, but suppose it is hopeless. And yet I can think of no satisfactory alternative. It is certainly a vexing problem."[137] Her parents' yoyo marriage continuously involved Anne: "Letter from Mother thanking me for the check. She seems to be getting along a bit better."[138] "Mother and Father still on the outs but she seems a bit more cheerful."[139] "Letter from Mother – same old problems."[140] "Card from Mother, comparatively gay."[141] "Have not heard from Mother for quite a while. Her letters are never pleasant, but I don't like not hearing from her at all for so long."[142] "A letter from Mother, full of anguish and despair."[143]

This sorrowful saga continued for years and contributed to Anne's anxiety: "Have not heard from either Mother or Clara for some time now, and don't like it."[144] "No word yet

---

dissolution, the grounds for divorce, such as proving that the partner was unfaithful, were contentious and difficult for women to accomplish. Divorce was also an expensive matter, and many women did not have access to funds.

134	September 25, 1933.
135	November 4, 1932.
136	November 12, 1938.
137	December 3, 1941.
138	December 9, 1941.
139	December 15, 1941.
140	December 27, 1941.
141	May 11, 1942.
142	December 1, 1943.
143	December 3, 1943.
144	December 9, 1943.

from Mother or Clara although I have written each of them several times. Wonder what's up."[145] "At long last – mail from Mother and Clara… Mother is unhappy, bitterly lonely."[146] A week later, Anne records that her unhappy mother was hinting that she wanted Anne to take her in. Anne also mentions that her mother had received a court order compelling her father to provide financial support. Apparently, her father had become a dead-beat and had removed himself and any sense of obligation from the family.

But the saddest remark of all in this endless tale of woe is Anne's expression of despair at the very fact of having been born to such a couple: "Two cards from Mother, both utterly miserable, and completely at sea as to any remedy. She is not reconciled to living with Baba (Anne's grandmother) for several reasons, including giving up her few paltry possessions. Also I expect she is waiting and hoping for me to break down and ask her to live with me, but I just cannot see it."[147] "Letter from Mother, full of misery…Mother…has been very much on my mind, although I don't believe my working or not would have any effect on that problem. I have been sending her substantial amounts of money, but of course that is not the remedy for her ailment, although it is something she desperately needs since Father had long since ceased to send her any money despite the court order. I don't suppose now that he ever will. Sometimes I wonder if I shall ever see him again. The whole thing is such a horrid mess. And it is not altogether the fault of either one. They were just too wholly unsuited ever to have been able to get along together. There should be some way to prevent people like that from bringing children into the world. When I think of the anguish they have caused me, it does seem grossly unfair."[148] In 1944, both the outer and inner worlds were at war: "Letter from Mother, seeming to reach the ultimate in the depths of despair."[149]

Uncle Phil tried occasionally to help Anne's mother obtain a divorce. "Mother had a trial scheduled for today. Do hope she made out all right, mainly to save her self-respect."[150] But the problems were never resolved: "Phil gave me a letter he had received from Mother, which pretty completely dampened the evening for me. What a problem!"[151] "Card from Mother. The trial was postponed until next Thursday. Wish I knew what to do for her short of having her come here to live with me. She is stubborn about not coming to live with her mother."[152] "Haven't heard from Mother in a heck of a long time, and it worries me. Have written to her several times. Afraid it means the hearing scheduled for last Thursday went badly for her."[153]

145 December 13, 1943.
146 December 15, 1943.
147 December 20, 1943.
148 December 31, 1943.
149 January 6, 1944.
150 January 12, 1944.
151 January 14, 1944.
152 January 15, 1944.
153 January 25, 1944.

Introduction

Anne's mother's unhappiness spilled over onto her relations with other people: "Phil called to tell me he had received a letter from the son of the woman with whom Mother lives to the effect that Mother had made the arrangement completely intolerable. I can understand that. But good Lord, what shall I do?"[154] Anne and her mother had nearly daily contact: "Card from Mother, which did not cheer me up any."[155] Therefore, while Anne was working to support herself and going to law school as well as developing a social life, she also had to take care of her emotionally unstable mother. "Much to my surprise Mother telephoned from Haverhill. Seemed the hearing had again been postponed, her lawyer had backed out, she could not get another, and she wanted me to come there for a day or two. I explained the various reasons why I could not."[156] The only person to whom she could turn was her uncle Phil, who "arranged to have Sam call his friend Dorgan, a lawyer in Lawrence and ask him to get a lawyer for Mother. I wired Mother about it. Hope it will work out all right. She must be represented by someone."[157] But Dorgan's comment was telling: "Sam and Phil called Dorgan, who said he was taking care of Mother himself, that she had driven her other attorney 'nuts,' that she still has romantic notions about winning Father back, and that she was getting money from him regularly. If all that is true, she has been unbelievably selfish in playing on our sympathies and emotions the way she has. I don't suppose I shall ever know the whole truth of the matter."[158]

More than a year and a half later, the cycle is again in full swing: "Letter from Mother, desperately unhappy."[159] This problem weighed on her. In her summary of 1945, a year when the world war had come to an end, she instead wrote that "Mother had been the source of much unhappiness."[160] The next year's summary, referred to the same "dark cloud" in her life: "Ever present is the problem of Mother, whether due to pity or conscience. I do not feel that I owe her the unhappiness that I know would result if I tried to live with her. Yet I know what horrors of sorrow and loneliness must be her constant companions these days. And there is Father too, who has acted badly, but is not entirely at fault for *the eternal mess that our family life had always been.*"[161] (emphasis added)

In 1947, Anne learns that her mother will "have to retire from her job, and then move out here pronto. That seems the obvious and sensible thing for her to do, but I cannot say that I am looking forward to it particularly. I know she will become my responsibility – entirely." Anne was right: "Card from Mother reminding me that she does not even write to

---

154	January 26, 1944.
155	January 27, 1944.
156	January 28, 1944.
157	January 29, 1944.
158	January 31, 1944.
159	August 4, 1945.
160	August 4, 1945.
161	Year End summary, 1946.

Jean or Clara but depends entirely on me."[162] Sadly, Anne's mother tried to pit her daughters against one another. Two weeks before she was forced to retire, Anne's mother wrote about being heart-broken."[163] At the same time, she attacked Anne for giving away a present she had given her daughter, even though Anne told her *not* to buy it for her in the first place. To make matters worse, Anne's mother ignores the fight they were having: "She did not say a word about the recent explosion" as if it never happened. Anne tries hard to distance herself from her mother's manipulation: "Card from Mother bewailing the loss of her job… I am still fed up with her though, and am not going to let my justifiable annoyance be too readily overcome by sympathy, as is usually the case."[164] Remarkably, about 10 months later, Anne makes the following entry in her diary: "Was in the middle of writing a letter home when Mother and Father knocked at the door. They had come by bus from New York. Father looked very well. They seem to be getting along fine."[165] Three days later, a miraculous change seems to have taken place: "Father is apparently sold on Washington, and he and Mother are pretty definitely planning to move here as soon as all their property has been disposed of. Father seems so changed, in character, not in appearance, that it is hard to believe. Too bad it could not have happened many years ago."[166] Both the 1948 and 1949 "end of year summaries," commented on her parents' reconciliation: "Mother and Father coming to visit us, apparently on good terms with each other…Everything considered, a wonderful year…It was good to see Mother and Father getting along happily."

As could be predicted, their affection for each other did not last. By the time of the 1951 year end summary, Anne wrote that she regretted "dragging Jules and Ira to New England in order to include Mother and Father in our vacation only to incur Mother's deep wrath. I feel that Mother is entirely wrong – it might be a symptom of old age – but that does not make her hostility any more palatable. Apparently Father agrees with her, or just does not care one way or the other. After all, he never did write to us or take any pains to maintain some sort of a family relationship." Whatever occurred during that trip seems to have been serious. By the time she wrote her 1952 end-of-year summary, Anne commented that she "had no direct word from Mother or Father *all year*. I would not have thought it possible, until it happened, that they could or would so *completely sever ties* with me. And for, in my opinion, no reason at all." (emphasis added) Clearly both her parents knew how to hurt Anne with passive aggressive behavior.

Everything about Anne's mother seemed to generate commotion. In February 1954, when her grandson Ira was about to have his bar mitzvah, Regina vacillated daily about

---

162   June 5, 1947.
163   May 25, 1947.
164   June 3, 1947.
165   April 19, 1948.
166   April 22, 1948.

whether or not she was "up to the trip." In one note she wrote that although "her ears are bothering her she is coming, but that Father, who feels fine, cannot get away. [Anne] wrote urging that he come with her as I doubt whether she is fit to travel alone. Also, *it would be nice if Ira could have some grandparents present.*[167] (emphasis added) Finally, Anne's mother did not attend: "Note from Mother that she decided she was not up to making the trip after all. I am very sorry to have her and Father miss it."[168] Three years later, Anne's gracious attitude toward her parents persisted: "It was good…to get to Lawrence for a few days, to see Mother and Dad getting along reasonably well, and to provide them with a trip to Boston, which they clearly enjoyed very much."[169]

A few months later, her father was dead. In her despair, Anne accused her mother of partial responsibility: "Mother was at home, alone, but in better shape than we had expected. Father died of a heart attack. She had not even called a doctor…Her legal affairs are in a muddle but she does not want a local lawyer. A mess!"[170] Even the funeral arrangements were described in terms of parental conflict: "We picked up schnapps and coke, and managed a minyan[171] at the house. That would have pleased Father but merely annoyed Mother. Later had Tom Collins, son of Henry C. who was Father's lawyer for many years, come up to discuss settling the estate. *Mother decided we were trying to rob her when we were actually signing everything over to her.* (emphasis added) It was quite a mess."[172] The next day her mother "was in a slightly calmer mood, but refuse(d) adamantly to budge from her determination to stay [in Lawrence] alone at least for the time being. Collins came over with the forms for release of our interests, which we signed…We all left about 3:00, Mother still refusing to accompany any of us but in despair at the thought of being alone. We all felt sorry for her, although we all felt that her *domination of and cruelty toward Father, and her refusal even at the very end to call a doctor, almost certainly hastened his death.*"[173] (emphasis added)

From June 1958 until her own death twenty years later, Anne seems to have had a dutiful relation with her mother who had moved to Washington but did not live with Anne, Jules and Ira. Anne talked to or visited her mother nearly every day and frequently took her out to dinner, to a play, for a ride, for dessert in a restaurant, or to religious services. There were periods when her mother wrote to relatives "her children were of no

---

167 February 25, 1954. Her mother's on-again off-again approach to the bar mitzvah clearly took the attention off the grandson and put it on her. Anne depicts her mother as quite selfish in not understanding the impact on Ira.
168 February 27, 1954. Anne's comment seems quite gracious.
169 Year End Summary, 1957.
170 June 2, 1958.
171 A quorum of ten Jewish men who constitute the necessary group to say certain prayers, including those mourning the dead.
172 June 3, 1958.
173 June 4, 1958.

help, and appealing…for help, although giving no indication of what she wanted [them] to do."[174] She seems to have had paranoid delusions about her relatives stealing from her. And in the month or so following her husband's death, there were times when her "Mother was desperately unhappy."

Anne used her diary to express anger with her mother for her treatment of Anne's father: "So often, when I look at Mother's cozy apartment, her pleasant way of life, the medical attention she receives, the chauffeuring service, and the service and attention in general from the Rolands and us, I cannot help thinking how much Father would have enjoyed it. He wanted to move here for years, but she kept blocking the sale of the house. And with all Jules' and Collins' efforts, the damned house is not sold yet. How I wish I had insisted, while Father was alive, that they give it away if necessary to get rid of it, so he could have had some time to live here and to enjoy being near us all."[175] She also resented her mother's "laziness,"[176] and her requirement that people wait on her for everything. At times Anne continued her pattern of staying away from her mother, when she seemed too toxic. "Not visiting Mother during this period not only because of the operation, but also because of her inevitably nasty remarks each time I go."[177] In hindsight, one might say that because of her own experience of inadequate mothering, Anne was somewhat concerned about her own mothering abilities. Unlike her mother, however, she seems to have succeeded in forming a loving, supportive marriage with Jules and being a loving, supportive mother to her son, Ira.

Anne As A Jew

Anne expressed her Jewishness in numerous ways beginning with a straightforward membership in the Jewish community. When looking for a place to live as a new student in Boston, for example, she "went to the Jewish Community Center to look up rooms in a private family."[178] When she married, on September 1, 1939, she and her husband chose the home of Rabbi Metz to hold the ceremony.

Although Anne had Jewish and non-Jewish friends and colleagues, she had special problems at work when her non-Jewish boss had to deal with her request for time off in order to attend services on Jewish holidays. While she functioned as a legal secretary, she "presented [her] application for leave to [W] who seemed quite surprised to learn that [she] was Jewish."[179] Attending services seems to have been a *privilege* conveyed by non-Jews to Jew, rather than a *right* of Jews. "Put in my leave slip for Saturday. Was told I would

---

174   June 17, 1958.
175   Year End summary, 1958.
176   June 25, 1961.
177   July 6, 1975.
178   September 11, 1933.
179   September 20, 1933.

have to lose a full day's pay, and not entitled to the three remaining hours. Mr. Watts, Asst. Chief Clerk, heard me talking about it to Miss Coordes, but said that was the rule. However, he spoke to Gompers, Chief Clerk, who told me I could break the rule and take the three hours. He was surprised to find I was Jewish, and we had a long personal chat about the tribulations of a Jewish employee."[180] Despite these inconveniences, for most of her life Anne did go to synagogue on Rosh Hashana and Yom Kippur, and as time passed and more Jews had authority in the workplace, the conflicts abated: "Kessel apparently is not sending out any of the Jewish judges during the holiday period even though the holidays come on the weekends."[181]

Anne's Jewish practices could probably be labeled "reform" combined with largely secular eating patterns. Kashrut[182] was not part of her life in any way. Many times throughout the years she wrote about how she loved shrimp and lobster and even exulted at finding a pork product at times when it was difficult to find meat: "Hit the jackpot – a steak, roast, and bacon – from three different stores."[183] It seems likely that her husband had grown up in a family that adhered more strictly to the rules of kashrut, because Anne mentions that when she met Jules' parents for the first time, they went "to a Jewish restaurant for dinner…."[184] Anne's mother-in-law sent Purim packages, commemorating a holiday not always celebrated.[185] Anne and Jules occasionally ate at kosher restaurants: "Decided on the way that, as it was so late, we would have supper at Irv's Corner. The food, strictly kosher, was only fair, but it made a nice change from cooking anyhow."[186]

Although Anne did not keep kosher, she seems to have observed some of the rules for eating during the Passover holiday: "Lunched with Jules and Arthur Gang at Rubin's so we could have some suitable Passover food. It was fairly good, but I have eaten better Jewish food."[187] Passover was an enjoyable celebration: "To the Gangs' for Seder. The dinner was excellent, the company pleasant, and the whole evening a great success. Ira played his role in the services admirably, and in general, behaved beautifully."[188]

On a subsequent Yom Kippur she made the following comment about the difference between her attitude and that of Jules: "We left our offices about 4:00 so I could prepare a large dinner, eat and clean up afterwards, and get dressed in time for the Kol Nidre services.

---

180 September 29, 1933.
181 September 7, 1972.
182 *Kashrut* is the set of rules concerning which foods Jews may eat and in which combinations.
183 May 4, 1946.
184 November 23, 1938. Jules also participated in Jewish communal activities such as attending the United Jewish Appeal dinner and making pledges as well as selling raffle tickets to raise money for Jewish causes.
185 *Purim* package from Columbus. March 16, 1949.
186 May 3, 1966.
187 April 28, 1948.
188 April 1, 1950.

Managed to do so and get to MCJC in plenty of time.[189] The place was jam-packed. I find it very uncomfortable to sit so long in such crowded conditions, but Jules finds pleasure at the thought of so many Jews turning out for religious observances at least once a year. I suppose his is the proper attitude."[190] The High Holiday seating issue was very important and frustrating to Jules. In 1967, their "high-holiday tickets from MCJC" arrived in the mail. "Pretty bad. Jules was so upset, he went tearing off to MCJC. No one was there so he came home, and later went over again, and again nobody was there."[191]

Anne's Judaism had a strong culinary base. She believed in preparing "Jewish meals" around holidays. In 1963, she wrote about "their big dinner - delicious filet mignons – and then to Kol Nidre services, which we enjoyed." Nine years later she "fixed broiled chicken, etc., for a holiday meal. Then we went to services at Ohr Kodesh."[192] Seven years later, Anne did the same thing: "In the evening, in honor of the holiday, I fixed an especially good dinner. After dinner we went to services, held this year at Leland Junior High. New Year's greetings from Mother S. and from Lucille and Louie."[193] In 1963, she wrote: "We had a very good dinner – challah, broiled chicken, etc. Then dressed and went to Rosh Hashanah services at MCJC." Like many people, Anne had a hard time getting through the entire Yom Kippur observance without eating: "In synagogue all day. Fasted until 1 o'clock, but by then Clara and I craved food, so stopped in for waffles and coffee at the Garden T. Shoppe. By the time we …got home for dinner, Clara and I were so hungry we could not eat much. There was a fairly substantial meal considering Mrs. Levin had not been able to cook. The Levin's had all fasted faithfully."[194] Twenty years later she wrote: "To services in the morning. We all went breakfastless, but Ira and I broke down around 2:00 and went out for a sandwich."[195]

Just as she could not manage to fast for the whole day, Anne did not necessarily devote the whole day to religious observance when it would have been appropriate to do so. Sometimes she plunged into housework instead: "We had breakfast – not brunch – and then went to services. After we came home in the early afternoon, had luncheon, which was more like a dinner. Then to the annual open house on Rosh Hashanah at the Saul Jaffes'. It was pleasant, as we see people there we do not see the rest of the year. We did not stay long. Went home and read the paper. I also did some washing, ironing, and housecleaning. A long time since the house has had a thorough cleaning."[196]

189	Montgomery County Jewish Center.
190	September 15, 1964.
191	September 26, 1967.
192	September 30, 1933.
193	September 9, 1953.
194	September 30, 1933.
195	September 19, 1953.
196	September 9, 1972.

Introduction

Anne expressed her Jewish identity through her concern about other Jews. As early as 1935, she noted: "With Hitler enforcing new cruelties against Jews, fifty nations boycotting Italy, and Japan annexing a goodly portion of China, one wonders what it is all about."[197] And yet, she did not comment in her diary on the day of *Kristallnacht* (November 9, 1938) or other times when news of the Holocaust was reported. She reported with dismay that "Japan went to war against us today, bombing some of our South Pacific islands. It had been imminent for some time but was nevertheless shocking."[198] Anne commented once or twice about the events leading up to the creation of the State of Israel: "The Jews are achieving remarkable military success in Palestine, to the obvious chagrin of the British"[199] but expressed no emotion or enthusiasm: "The Jewish State in Palestine has been proclaimed and has been recognized by the United States."[200] She did not mention this momentous fact in her summary of 1948. Another moment of identification occurred in 1972: "Watched some of the Olympic contests. Proud of the young Jewish American, Spitz, who won seven gold medals in swimming, a real record time."[201] Most exciting of all were the steps toward peace: "We watched the Sadat-Begin ceremonies and listened to the speeches at the Knesset. Thrilling."[202]

Yet another aspect of Anne's Jewish identity was her interest in Jewish culture, of which she was sometimes critical: "After dinner Jules and I went to the final MCJC forum meeting to hear a Les Schwartz talk on 'Jewish Literature.' Found the talk a little bit dull and the speaker more than a little bit conceited and pompous."[203] About two decades later, she wrote: "Lighted a yahrzeit candle for my father last night but decided not to go to services tonight as his name was read at the services last Friday. Then to the Fine Arts Theater to see 'Goodbye Columbus.' I did not care much for the parade of sexual activity nor the vulgarization of Jewish middle-class life."[204] They also attended a talk at synagogue Ohr Kodesh by Leo Rosten, "whom everyone – and there was an enormous crowd – found very entertaining. Stayed for the Oneg Shabbat and to talk to a few people we knew."[205] Jewish culture was a component of their travel itineraries as well. When they went to Amsterdam, for example, they visited "the Rijks Museum to see some magnificent Rembrandts" and then had "the taxi driver take [them] through the Jewish quarter where

---

197	November 18, 1935.
198	November 7, 1941.
199	April 28, 1948.
200	May 14, 1948.
201	September 4, 1972.
202	November 20, 1977.
203	April 26, 1950.
204	May 30, 1969.
205	March 12, 1971.

so many innocent people were killed, and the physical destruction is still evident..."[206] A trip to Israel shortly after the Six-Day War brought the following observations "On a bus tour in the morning. Saw many Jewish graves shockingly desecrated by the Jordanians."[207] Five years later, they vacationed on the Iberian peninsula "We...were picked up...on a Cook's tour to Toledo. Found Toledo interesting; though hours were spent on the glories of the cathedral, moments on the old synagogue converted to a church and then to a museum, reminders again of the virtual extinction of Jews on Spain."[208]

The most significant expression of her Jewish identity, however, was Anne's desire, in partnership with Jules, to inculcate a Jewish identity in their son, Ira, and then to leave it to Ira to make choices on his own as he grew older. A small symbol of her success was Ira's choice of *A Treasury of Jewish Folklore* [as a Father's Day present], which seemed to please Jules very much.[209] Jules and Anne enrolled Ira in Hebrew School, which he attended regularly. Ira certainly had internalized his parents' views: "Went to the theater in the evening to see 'The Diary of Anne Frank.' Ira enjoyed 'The Diary' very much, as, he said, did the non-Jewish friends he was with."[210] Jules took Ira to services regularly especially as his bar mitzvah date was approaching. In March 1954, as a culmination of his education and upbringing, Ira became a bar mitzvah. Anne seems to have poured herself into all aspects of the celebration, from participating in the synagogue rehearsal, to controlling and managing the guest list, to recording all the gifts, telegrams, and calls Ira received. Anne's hard work paid off, as she wrote on Saturday March 6, 1954: "There was a big crowd at his bar mitzvah. He was absolutely perfect, charming, at ease. We were so proud of him, and everyone was so effusively congratulatory. My hostesses did a good job and the Kiddush[211] was excellent."

Like many Jewish mothers before and after her, Anne discussed the bar mitzvah in terms of a competition among families. "Nate, Louie, Lucille, Molly, Milton, Howard, and the 5 Pachels came home for luncheon – roast beef, etc. and everything was delicious. Back to MCJC at 8:00 for the reception. Huffman had done a superb job of decorating, all the food was delicious, there was plenty of good liquor, everyone seemed to be having a wonderful time, and a great many people assured me that the bat mitzvah was the most impressive they had ever attended and the reception the most enjoyable."[212] Anne recorded this type of compliment for days to come: "Jules and I are still being congratulated by people who say they never saw a boy participate so fully in a bar mitzvah or heard any

---

206 August 23, 1957.
207 September 17, 1967.
208 August 31, 1972.
209 June 15, 1958.
210 May 27, 1958.
211 Reception.
212 March 6, 1954.

boy do such a perfect job or attended a more enjoyable reception."²¹³ And sometimes the comparative remarks were not in her favor: "Telephoned Columbus. [Jules' mother] said she had heard that the bar mitzvah went splendidly...In the evening we went to the Marmelstein reception at the Center. Theirs was a much fancier affair than ours. They had a Baltimore caterer, very expensive, and the food was beautiful to look at and delicious to eat. They also had a 5-piece orchestra."²¹⁴

Anne not only recorded who came to the bar mitzvah and who declined her invitation, but also what gift each person gave and how Ira reacted. "The Rolands stopped in – Joyce and Steve wanted to see Ira's loot. Ira was delighted to show it. Later the Bisgyers stopped in to deliver a gift for Ira – a wallet – about the fourth he has received."²¹⁵ The single gift that Ira truly wanted – a baby brother – was not forthcoming.²¹⁶ In at least one instance, Ira passed on a gift he had received to the next bar mitzvah boy: "Later to the Jewish Book Store. Bought …a bar mitzvah card to enclose in our gift to Allen, one of Ira's several very nice sweaters."²¹⁷ Ira's bar mitzvah structured a lot of his and his parents' time beforehand, but when it came time to deciding whether he would continue attending Hebrew School after his bar mitzvah, his parents left it entirely up to him: "Ira went to Hebrew School today. We are leaving it entirely up to him whether or not he will continue."²¹⁸

For all her Jewishness, Anne was also partially assimilated into American culture, particularly with its emphasis on gift giving and parties in the Christmas season, which Anne almost always spelled Xmas. Over the years, she recorded, with pleasure, receiving a "Xmas card from the Tramors,"²¹⁹ "from Henry,"²²⁰ "from the Bob Buckleys,"²²¹ "from John Freed,"²²² and more. In 1941 she went "to the Maddens' with the Duddleys and Judge Smith for Xmas carols." That same year, she sent her "Mother a few dollars extra for her Xmas present." Two years later, she wrote that "One of the men at the office, Joe Stein, gave me a little individual bottle of rye for a Xmas present, so I'll have one gift besides Jules!" In a telling comment that year (1943), she writes that she feels "like such a crumb for not having sent the kids (nephews and nieces) Xmas presents – although I dislike the whole business very much – that I shall have to make up my mind to conform. What a nuisance!"²²³ (emphasis added)

213	March 8, 1954.
214	March 14, 1954.
215	March 14, 1954.
216	February 17, 1954.
217	March 13, 1954.
218	March 11, 1954.
219	December 13, 1941.
220	December 27, 1941.
221	December 19, 1943.
222	December 22, 1943.
223	December 21, 1943.

Anne's participation in Xmas rituals was not entirely passive and begrudging. One year she mentioned meeting Jules downtown, and then going with him to Garfinckel's to select the Xmas cards they would be sending. As if to illustrate that she was both assimilated into the American culture and also an involved Jew, she ended the entry by noting she had received a "letter from Gertrude inviting us to Milton's bar mitzvah."[224] She referred to other Christmas activities: "Ira had a delightful time unwrapping and playing with his new toys. They were all very good choices, and should be of interest to him for some time. Drove to the Lincoln Memorial Reflecting Pool to watch the ice skaters, despite a slight drizzle. Then to Fine's for a lot of good things to eat. Home to fix a very enjoyable supper. Jules gave me a lovely white nightgown and flowers. Had gone all the way to Pasternak's to get it. He seemed pleased with his writing portfolio. It was altogether a very pleasant Christmas Day."[225] In some years, however, Chanukah makes an appearance in Anne's diary, usually in the context of gift giving: "Jules and I went down town at noon and sent stuff to all the kids. Glad that is over with. Chanukah check from Mother S. for $30."[226]

Anne As A Mother

From the diary entries included in this book, it is difficult to know why Anne was unable to bear children except for mention of a cyst on her ovary. Whatever the case, Anne and Jules decided to adopt a child and began to seek help in December 1941: "Lunched with Phil at the Madillon. Discussed adoption with him, since he is one of our references, and also my parent-problem. He was very kind about it all."[227] The adoption regulations at the time, at least in Washington, D.C., required that the mother not work outside the home for one year. "Mrs. Brenner is checking with Washington about the baby that is 'available' but which we cannot have because of my working."[228] Even after the government relented, her mother did not. "Called Mother S. She obviously does not approve of my working. Too bad I cannot be contented staying at home, being a wife and Mother. It would be so much better for both Jules and Ira, and probably for me also."[229]

Anne faced an awful dilemma – "wish I knew what was best to do" and many additional obstacles along the way: "Kept my appointment with a Mr. Dummit at 11:00. It took about 5 minutes – just long enough for him to tell me they had far more applicants than babies, had to satisfy Philadelphia first, but I could file an application. I was sore!"[230]

Through the intercession of their friend "Shad," it turned out, next, that Anne's "working [was] *no obstacle* at all."[231] (emphasis added) As the New Year arrived, so did their baby:

224   November 26, 1952.
225   December 25, 1943.
226   December 22, 1943.
227   December 3, 1941.
228   December 21, 1941.
229   May 5, 1946.
230   December 8, 1941.
231   December 15, 1941.

"He is no beauty, but big and healthy looking, had a charming smile and seems bright. We made friends with far less difficulty than we had been led to expect."[232] For the next few weeks, Anne recorded her delight with her new son, Ira, first by visiting him and then taking him home: "Went out to see the baby again. Wheeled him down in his carriage for a while. Got along even better than yesterday. He is a bit afraid of Jules – apparently thinks he is the doctor."[233] "Did a few errands at noon, including a Hogate rattle for the baby. Went out to see him at about 6:00. Fed him part of his supper and played with him for a while, then put him in his crib, all with hardly a whimper."[234] Anne was already describing her days of combining her legal job and mothering activities. "A miserable rainy day. I did not go down [to the office] until about noon, when the rain stopped, and we took the baby for a little ride. He behaved surprisingly well."[235]

Finally, on Wednesday, March 4, 1942, she "picked up the baby at 2:00. He surprised us all by coming without any fuss. His crib was delivered this morning and the new carpets laid, so we were ready for him. He behaved beautifully the entire time. Fussed a little at night, but finally went to sleep. Slept very soundly – at least he did not disturb us. Glad he is behaving so much better than everyone expected, but I am still a little frightened at the prospect of mothering a baby boy. Jules is so happy about it though, that alone makes it all worth it." Like many new parents, Anne recorded how much her baby slept and by May, when he was 14 months old "and much cuter than he was two months ago," she claimed that "only colored moving pictures could possibly do him justice." As time went on, Anne took Ira to the playground where she "Enjoyed visiting with some of the other mothers for a while, but soon got fed up with the conversation, which covers only pregnancies and babies. Wonder if I shall soon become confined to such subjects," a typical dilemma for educated, working women. Anne discusses Ira's milk intake, his transition from the bottle to a cup, and "hope[s she] is not rushing him too much, taking advantage of his good disposition. But one of the words he says, and often, is 'no,' so he could make his protest vocal if he wished."[236]

In a statement that suggests that Jules was a flexible man, quite ahead of his time, Anne writes "Jules now not only wants to help take care of Ira, but actually does much of the work, so today was comparatively easy for me."[237] A concern that frequently arises among women who employ nannies to take care of their children is the quality of interaction between the nanny and the child. "Esther apparently reads to him a good deal but I doubt whether she plays much with him. *I doubt, in fact, that she knows how.*"[238] (emphasis added)

---

232 February 25, 1942.
233 February 26, 1942.
234 February 27, 1942.
235 March 3, 1942.
236 May 15, 1942.
237 May 17, 1942.
238 December 11, 1943.

At the same time that Anne and Jules were getting used to being parents, the army was calling up Jules for military service. Strangely, the draft office was suspicious that Jules had adopted a baby in order to delay his being called up for service! "Called Rogosa, who will write the board that we applied for a baby well before the fateful December 7. I feel we should be treated as though I had become pregnant in September and had a baby in March. It only puts off the evil day, of course, but Ira and I both need him as long as we can keep him."[239] "We certainly did not adopt Ira to evade the draft, and he has two bona fide dependents as a result of the adoption."[240] Aside from all these strange bureaucratic entanglements, Anne and Jules' adoption of Ira was a complete success and made the child and parents very happy.

Anne wrote frequently about Ira, reporting on his activities, accidents, and triumphs. But a constant refrain is her concern that even though Ira is a contented child, he performs poorly in school. For parents as intelligent and intellectual as Jules and Anne, Ira's lackadaisical attitude toward study was very trying.

> *Ira telephoned – apparently homesick. There was a letter from him – such atrocious spelling! – and a letter for him from OSU [Ohio State University], with a notice also to Jules, that Ira was on probation this quarter because of his poor grades last quarter. Ira is finding his present courses very difficult already. Not at all confident that he will get through college but glad he had some experience with it.*[241]

Aside from his academic difficulties, Ira seems to have had a normal childhood, adolescence and young adulthood. His adolescence was filled with characteristic tension vis a vis his mother. "[Ira] is so upset about the death [of his friend's mother] that *he is even affectionate toward me occasionally, a real change in his attitude*."[242] At the end of that year, when Ira was 19, Anne wrote "Ira is concerned that his poor grades at school will not give him much choice of a college to which to transfer next year, and is inclined *to blame all his troubles on me* rather than on his neglect of his studies. He threatens occasionally to move out and work his way through college for the next couple of years, but, in his calmer moments, realizes he could not possibly manage such a program, financially or academically."[243] (emphasis added) Over time, these maturation issues were resolved. "Ira called in the evening. As seems to be customary these days, he was bursting with good

---
239   May 22, 1942.
240   May 27, 1942.
241   June 22, 1961.
242   November 22, 1960.
243   Year End summary, 1960.

news…"[244] Ira went on to earn a Master's degree in Public Administration and a second masters in psychology and to become a successful professional, a devoted husband to a woman who converted to Judaism, a loving son to his parents, and the father of two sons.

Anne As Consumer Of Culture And A Sports Enthusiast

From reading her diary, I conclude that Anne sought a balanced life that was full of entertainment and just plain fun. When she did *not* go out, she berated herself in the third person: "Anne stayed home and worked – the idiot! This must not become a habit!"[245] Although Anne obviously devoted a lot of energy to her work, she tried hard to separate her work from her personal life, even before she married and had a child: "Have so much work, it's driving me silly. And I am interrupted every time I get going on any one matter. It's a great life if I don't weaken. *I have stopped taking work home from the office*, but do not know whether that means that I am weakening or becoming stronger. Time will tell."[246] (emphasis added) One reason Anne did not want to bring work home was that, when she was single, she hoped to use her evenings to date, and then, when married, for entertainment or simply to be with her husband: "My conscience told me to go back to the office, but Jules begged me to stay and visit with him. He won."[247]

One activity Anne particularly enjoyed was going to the movies. She seems to have seen nearly as many movies as she read books. Unfortunately, in numerous entries throughout the years, she indicated that she went to a movie, but does not state which movie it was. During her law school years, she "Saw Zasu Pitts and Slim Summerville, and found them quite amusing."[248] Later she saw "Lawrence Tibbett in 'Metropolitans.' Enjoyed his singing immensely, although the picture itself was stupid."[249] She and her friend Mary Lou "went to see 'Anthony Adverse.' We enjoyed it very much, although I was disappointed in the way it ended. Frederic March was splendid as Anthony."[250]

Jules, too, was a film enthusiast, even more so than Anne. Jules and Anne "went to the Little [theater] to see the Czechoslovakian picture 'Janisek.' It was rather interesting."[251] "Jules wanted to go to a movie after dinner, but I preferred to stay at home and watch TV on a rainy evening. We had an early supper and he went by himself to an early movie. I felt badly about letting him go alone. On the other had, he likes movies generally far better than I do, and it would be quite all right with me if he went

---

244   March 26, 1965.
245   October 20, 1936.
246   October 29, 1937.
247   November 1, 1938.
248   September 16, 1933.
249   November 10, 1935.
250   October 13, 1936.
251   November 29, 1938.

occasionally without me. Probably should not start such a practice, however, when he is already upset about the prospect of my traveling as a TX."[252] During the war years, it seemed to Anne that "all the movies were silly takes on the army."[253] She labeled "Ball of Fire" delightful;[254] the English movie, "Jeannie," charming;[255] Bea Lillie in "On Approval," very entertaining;[256] "The Spiral Staircase," quite good;[257] and "The Seventh Veil" – quite good.[258] "On the Waterfront" was "a very effective movie, and the acting was unusually good."[259] "The Pirate's Progress," a British film, was "amazing."[260] She liked "Brief Encounter," very much.[261] "It began to rain in the afternoon so we went to the movies. Saw a pretty good Blondie and Dagwood picture. Ira loved it, especially Daisy and her pups."[262] "Later we went downtown to see the movie of "The Egg and I," which we all found quite amusing."[263] "Then to see 'Naked City,' quite a good murder picture."[264] And then, "went to the McArthur to see 'The Little Kidnappers.' We all thoroughly enjoyed the picture."[265] "Saturday Night and Sunday Morning," a very good British movie, was well acted.[266] "The Big Deal on Madonna Street," was "an Italian movie, rather amusing, but would have been more so, I am sure, if one knew the language."[267]

One evening in 1946, she and Jules had to go downtown to a movie, "all the Arlington movies having been ordered closed because of the power shortage resulting from the coal strike. Saw 'The Spiral Staircase,' which was quite good."[268] She mentions a Russian movie, "A Summer to Remember" (1961): "We …found the picture charming, particularly the children in it."[269] In the summer of 1962, Anne saw "The Sky Above, and the Mud Below" a documentary on a New Guinea anthropological exploration. On a Saturday night in September 1963, she, Ira and friends "went to see the Italian picture '8 ½.' Enjoyed it – sort

---

252	May 1, 1966.
253	December 28, 1941.
254	December 31, 1941.
255	December 1, 1943.
256	August 9, 1945.
257	August 9, 1945.
258	May 31, 1946.
259	February 13, 1954.
260	September 30, 1956.
261	May 16, 1947.
262	May 17, 1947.
263	May 26, 1947.
264	April 16, 1948.
265	February 6, 1955.
266	June 3, 1961.
267	June 17, 1961.
268	May 10, 1946.
269	July 17, 1961.

of." She saw "The Great Escape," which she labeled "quite interesting, well acted,"[270] "36 Hours."[271] "The Flight of the Phoenix..."fairly interesting,"[272] "an Italian movie, 'A Case of Jealousy,'.....entertaining,"[273] "'Day of the Jackel,' – not so exciting as the book but a pretty interesting movie as movies these days go,"[274] "a new Peter Sellers movie. I found it too wacky to be really funny,"[275] "'Jaws,' the movie was pretty good, but I found the book far more absorbing,"[276] and "Greenwich Village," which she deemed "fairly entertaining."[277] About "The Prime of Miss Jean Brodie," Anne said, "A more intelligent and less sex-filled picture than I had seen in some time."[278]

Anne enjoyed theater, ballet and all the performing arts. She saw Clifford Odets' "Golden Boy," which she considered "one of the best plays I have seen in a long while. My only criticism is that the ending was weak."[279] They saw "My Fair Lady" "and loved it."[280] On Christmas Day, 1941, she and Jules "went to the National to see 'Pal Joey,' which [she] found rather dull and tiresome." "Afterwards Joe, Libby, Jane and her girl friend, and the three of us went to the Ice Capades,"[281] They saw the play, "The Chalk Garden," which they considered excellent[282] and Neil Simon's "The Odd Couple," which she found amusing. They saw, "'He who gets Slapped,' it was not very good but we did see it through."[283] When they saw the Bolshoi Ballet, their expensive seats were "so far front that we could not see the dancers' feet."[284] "To the Library of Congress with Arnold to hear the Kolisch String Quartet. Rather enjoyed it."[285] "We all drove into Baltimore, in our own car, for dinner and a show. Saw 'See My Lawyer.' It was quite amusing."[286]

Many entries in Anne's diaries mentioned "going riding," acquiring the appropriate gear, and changing plans because of the weather. I believe these comments refer to horseback riding.[287] At other times, she writes about "going for a ride," in which she seems to be referring to a car ride. And still other entries refer to bike riding: "Another grand

270   September 7, 1963.
271   March 20, 1965.
272   May 20, 1966.
273   March 27, 1971.
274   August 11, 1973.
275   June 13, 1975.
276   July 5, 1975.
277   April 2, 1976.
278   May 31, 1969.
279   November 30, 1938.
280   July 19, 1957.
281   February 3, 1951.
282   September 27, 1964.
283   March 24, 1965.
284   May 18, 1968.
285   November 10, 1938.
286   September 23, 1939.
287   November 3, 1938: "Lost a pin-ball game to Lush on which we had bet a horse back ride."

autumn day. Walked down to Mary Lou's after breakfast. Had a cup of coffee with her. Then joined a group from Social Security, and went on a two-hour bicycle ride."[288] She did not play poker but apparently she knew how to play golf. [289] Evelyn Promisel asked us to come over tomorrow night to play bridge."[290] Anne was always ready to play a game in which she could make a bet: "Stopped to play a few games of pin-balls, at which I trounced him (i.e. Jules). It is only when I am playing for money that I get trounced, and have lost a good number of dimes and quarters that way."[291]

Anne As A Professional Woman

As is true for most young lawyers, Anne began her professional life doing research on a variety of cases for her boss, in this case, Charles Wyzanski, a lawyer only four years her senior who was also starting his career and trying to find the right job. Wyzanski had brought Anne to Washington, D.C. where he employed her as a kind of advanced secretary when he started in the Justice Department. "Spent the whole day at the Labor Dept. digging out material on majority rule to be used in connection with the Labor Board cases."[292] "Very busy all day, working on the Seminole case."[293] "Very rushed on the Seminole case. Had to work late."[294] "Very busy at the office, working now on the steamship fine case."[295] Wyzanski vacillates between working at the Departments of Justice or Labor, and moving back to Boston. Anne is interested in the newly formed NLRB and in Wyzanski himself. "Another letter from C.E.W., written from New York. He doubts very much whether I can get a job on the NLRB, and thinks I ought to go to Boston in any event. It is so difficult to know what is my best move."[296] Anne tried to strategize her decision-making without a mentor to help her make the best choice. Finally, in 1937 Wyzanski left for Boston, and Anne received an offer from the National Labor Relations Board to serve as a lawyer, the first major step in her career. In her initial assignment [the Ford Case], Anne worked with Julius Schlezinger, quickly taking up a new romantic interest as well as a new job.

Two years later, the NLRB came under investigation by the congressionally appointed <u>Smith Committee</u>. Established in 1935,[297] the NLRB was the organization in which

288 October 25, 1936.
289 September 16, 1933.
290 February 4, 1955.
291 November 1, 1938.
292 October 5, 1936.
293 October 14, 1936.
294 October 20, 1936.
295 October 30, 1936.
296 September 13, 1937.
297 A predecessor organization, the National Labor Board, was established by the National Industrial Recovery Act in 1933, an act that the Supreme Court subsequently struck down.

Introduction

Anne carried out her entire professional career. According to Wikipedia, the "NLRB is an independent agency of the United States government charged with *conducting elections* for labor union representation and with *investigating and remedying unfair labor practices*," the latter being the area of law with which Anne became most deeply involved.[298] (emphasis added) "Unfair labor practices may involve union-related situations or instances of protected concerted activity." The NLRB's mission fit Anne's interests well, in that she was personally, as well as professionally, concerned with promoting fair labor practices and fighting racial/ethnic prejudice as is evident in these two entries that reveal her attitude toward racism:

> *The entertainment committee is in a stew because we discovered that we cannot hold our banquet at the Lafayette, as planned, since it is on an unfair list, and there was some objection to every other possibility – expense, distance, Negro question, unionization, etc.*[299]

> *Dorothy Grimes called to remind me about the sewing circle, which was meeting at her house, so I broke down and went. The group now includes several new members, and it is too large. The conversation in general bores me, and the frequent cracks at Negroes, etc., cause too much discomfort and annoyance. And I cannot fight them all.*[300]

Although Anne does not discuss why she made her decisions at the NLRB, she frequently demonstrated an interest in protecting workers and the United States: "Oral argument in Gear Mfg. Houston and Reilly present, and it seemed quite clear they held divergent views. The coal strike is having the disastrous consequences everyone expected. Hope it is settled soon – with the miners getting a decent break."[301]

The NLRB is a legal structure, a separate kind of legal system, to deal with labor problems. The process begins when charges are filed by or against unions or employers with the appropriate regional office. That office then investigates the complaint. If a violation of the law is believed to exist, the regional office takes the case before an Administrative Law Judge who conducts a hearing. The five member Board may review the decision of that judge. The process does not end there, however, because United States Courts of Appeals can review the Board decisions. This branch of the judiciary cannot enforce its decisions but rather must seek court enforcement to force a recalcitrant party to comply with its decisions. The governance structure of the NLRB

---

298 The Board's jurisdiction is limited to private sector employers and the United States Postal Service; other than Postal Service employees, it has no authority over labor disputes involving governmental, railroad and airline employees covered by the Adamson Railway Labor Act, or agricultural employees.
299 November 8, 1938.
300 March 10, 1949.
301 May 7, 1946.

itself was significant for Anne's professional advancement because it offered a clear career ladder. "The NLRB is governed by a *five-person board* and a *General Counsel*, all of whom are *appointed by the President with the consent of the Senate*. Board members are appointed to five-year terms and the General Counsel is appointed to a four-year term. *The General Counsel acts as a prosecutor and the Board acts as an appellate judicial body from decisions of administrative law judges*. Currently the Board has more than thirty regional offices. The regional offices conduct elections, investigate unfair labor practice charges, and make the initial determination on those charges (whether to dismiss, settle, or issue complaints).

In 2004, retired NLRB Judge Richard J. Linton wrote a history of the NLRB with an emphasis on its early years. The photograph gracing the book's cover was taken at the May 1942 Trial Examiners' Conference. *Every one of the Trial Examiners in the photograph is a white male*. The NLRB's first Chair was J. Warren Madden. In 1937, Anne had already come to Judge Madden's attention, which in turn, opened doors for her:

Attended a Board meeting. J.S.[302] was reporting on two cases to the Board members, Nat Witt and Alec Hawes. Three other "freshman" and I were invited. It was very interesting. I was singled out since Madden recognized me.

Being a woman hampered Anne's career advancement. She worked at the Board for thirty-one years before being named judge, a rank above Trial Examiner, while men were named judges after fewer years of service.

Because Anne's writing is so concise, it is difficult to follow the unfolding of the investigation of NLRB lawyers. In one of her first entries on the topic, she wrote: "Condon, Koplow, and I were served with subpoenas by the Congressional Committee [i.e. Smith Committee] investigating the Board. It was in connection with the union. We spent a good part of the day rounding up files and records, each of us with a constant escort. I am afraid I embarrassed them when I requested permission to go to the ladies' room unescorted."[303] The fact of being investigated by the Congressional Committee influenced the assignments given lawyers such as Anne in the NLRB.

The Smith Committee was a major force in U.S. domestic issues right before the onset of World War II. The December 25, 1939 issue of *Time* magazine described the committee sarcastically as follows:

---

302 Her future husband, Jules Schlezinger.
303 September 25, 1939.

Introduction

> [I]n the caucus room of the Old House Office Building, there opened a Congressional investigation as suave, sophisticated, polite and cynical as a Somerset Maugham comedy. It was the beginning of the Smith Committee hearings of the Wagner Act—that most crucial piece of New Deal legislation, passed to safeguard labor's historic right to bargain collectively through unions of its own choosing.
>
> Last July Congress authorized the Smith Committee to investigate the Wagner Act, to find out whether the Labor Board had been fair, to see what amendments, if any, were needed, and gave it $50,000 as a starter. To tall, solemn, silent Representative Howard Smith of Broad Run, Va., who has hated the New Deal ever since it tried to purge him last year, it gave the delicate job of chairman. With wealthy Lawyer Edmund Toland and 22 attorneys assisting (called brilliant legal lights by the Right, called tools of reaction by the Left), it checked on the work of the three members of the National Labor Relations Board, the doings of its 22 regional offices, its 109 field examiners, its 10,000 cases a year....
>
> First witness was pipe-smoking Dr. William Leiserson, 56, appointed to the Board eight months ago, with a reputation as a labor mediator. Dr. Leiserson stated the case for the NLRB about as well as it has been stated. He denied that the Act needed amendment. He reminded the Committee of the conditions that brought about the Act—the use of labor spies, the discrimination against good union men, the tragedies of violence in labor disputes, the old hostility against labor legislation.[304]

The NLRB, the Wagner Act, and the Smith Committee were political footballs at the time, and women had a symbolic role to play in the chaos as well. Linton quotes a commentator who wrote that:

> Toland's anti-NLRB animus was flagrantly displayed in his examination of Review Division attorneys...The women Review attorneys were treated rudely and disparagingly. Toland shouted at them and [Congressman Harry N.] Routzohn asked personally insulting questions....When the women Judges of today ascend the bench in order to preside in a case, they will recall that it was Judge Boyls, long before she was able to ascend the bench, who suffered verbal abuse from the Smith Committee.

Congressman Clare Hoffman of Michigan also ridiculed the female Review Section lawyers:

> Those girls who are acting as reviewing attorneys for the Board are fine young ladies...but the chances are 99 out of 100 that none of them ever changed a diaper, hung a washing, or baked a loaf of bread. None of them has had any judicial or industrial experience

---

[304] http://www.time.com/time/magazine/article/0,9171,762099-1,00.html

to qualify her for the job they are trying to do, and yet here they are – after all – good looking, intelligent appearing as they may be, and well groomed all of them, writing the opinions on which the jobs of hundreds of thousands of men depend and upon the success or failure of an industrial enterprise may depend, and we stand for it.[305]

Anne's testimony took place in early 1940:

Meeting at 1:00 with Fahy, Lester Levin, Aaron Lewittes, and Lou Gill. Aaron, Lou and I having been summoned as witnesses for Monday morning. Meeting later with Horshy of those who had been subpoenaed for the Union. Another meeting later with Levin, Emerson, and Witt. By then the afternoon was gone. We just had time to dash home and change before going to the Surreys for dinner. Sat around for a while after dinner, and then off to a party given by the Dave Kroottis for the Les Ashers. It was a lot of fun. All the Board people had some good advice for me, of course.[306]

After giving testimony to Toland, she evaluated her performance positively:

Tuesday, January 9, 1940. On the stand all day again, but I really think Toland had not got a thing out of me. Praised by everyone – Madden, Fahy, Witt, etc., etc. A crowd of us had luncheon at the Ugly Duckling, and it was all very gay, and pleasant. I no longer feel the nervous strain, and could go on and on.
Adjourned about 5:00. Listened in at Jules' hearing until about 7:00. Then had dinner at Schneider's with Lagar Teppe, Dave Cobb, and Jules. Home after dinner. Telephoned Lawrence [her mother and other relatives] *and Columbus* [home of her parents-in-law], *but they knew all about my performance, from the local papers and from the radio. Such fame!* (emphasis added)

The next day, she wrote:

Got comfortably settled in the office with my audience around me when the Clerk of the Committee called and asked me to come up and dictate some longhand notes that were put in as an exhibit. They were perfectly legible, so I sat in at the hearing while a stenographer copied them, and answered the few questions that came up on them. Peggy Bennett and Carol Agger[307] *have testified – and very well – and Fanny Boyls got on for a few minutes this afternoon. Why all the women?*[308] (emphasis added)

---

305   Richard Linton, p. 105.
306   January 6, 1940.
307   November 9, 1938: "Luncheon at the Ambassador with Anne Landy, Mary Schleiffer and Carol Agger. *Decided we would have a dance* at the Press Club Tuesday night." (emphasis added)
308   January 10, 1940,

Introduction

Two days later:

Friday, January 12, 1940. Called to the hearing again as a union witness or I should not have gone to work at all. When I got to the hearing, Toland, as he had Wednesday, gushed all over me in a disgustingly affectionate manner, told me what a splendid witness I was, and assured me he had no intention of calling me again, so I returned to the office.

Four days later:

Tuesday, January 16, 1940. Lunched at Childs with Dave Rein and Jack King. Heard that when the group of girls was called to the hearing, Bea Stern spoke to them, and told them, among other things, "after all, no one can expect to be perfect except Anne Freeling and the Chairman." What a compliment! Sol Barkin, in town for a Wages and Hours hearing, took us to dinner at the Ambassador. He was not feeling well, so went to his room after dinner, and we went home. Letters from Gertrude and from Mrs. S. They are quite "set-up" about the publicity that I, as Mrs. Jules Schlezinger, have received in Columbus by newspaper and radio.

Anne realized that the Committee focused on the "girls,"[309] assuming wrongly that the girls were weak and would buckle under pressure. But that was not the case.

Friday, January 19, 1940 The Trial Examiners are certainly not doing as good a job at the hearing as the dumb little women review attorneys did.

Starting with the first weeks of her job at the NLRB, Anne's diary entries briefly mention the various cases on which she is working. She uses internal jargon and initials, but the overall patterns are clear.

Attended a Board hearing on the Todd Shipbuilding case. Found it very interesting. Nat Witt and Jules have devised a different, and for me, more interesting division of the work on the Ford case.[310]

Without making the point herself, one can see that Anne was a hard and efficient worker:

Have finished the commerce part of the Ford case. Decided I might as well work on another case while waiting for Jules to read his part of the record. Alec Hawes gave me

---

309 Anne used the word "girl" as we might use the word "woman" today. For example, "Wednesday, February 21, 1951. Lunched in the cafeteria with several girls, including a Dr. Platt, an attractive girl who had just come to work for Public Health."
310 October 1, 1937.

the Shell Chemical case, an R case.[311] *My R case is quite complicated. I don't seem to be making much progress with it.*[312] *Reported to Alec on my case. Would like very much to know what he thought of my presentation. Back on the Ford case – on discharges for union activities. Lunched alone, with the intention of doing some errands, but had so much work I dashed back to the office. Levitt's petition was denied because of lack of personal injury.*[313]

Midonish suggested going to the Supreme Court to hear Reed and John Davis on the Dravo case. Spoke to Hawes about it, did a lot of telephoning, and then finally did not go. Had so darned much work – checking signatures on petitions with payrolls, and what not. Received a charming letter of congratulation from John Murphy. Back to the office after dinner to finish checking lists of names – stupid, tedious work. But most of the boys were also at the office, and all of them dropped in to see what I was doing, which kept me entertained. The Board was sitting, and was still hearing cases when I left at about 11.[314]

The Board sat until midnight last night but still has not got around to hearing me. Worked on the Ford case all day.[315]

Lunched alone so I could dash downtown and do a few errands. Worked on the Ford case all day. By the time the Board does calls me I shall be full of information about the Ford case rather than about the Shell Chemical case.[316]

Have finished the "unfair discharges" in the Ford case.[317]

Working on the peskiest, but far from most important, part of the Ford case – ownership of the overpass on which the riot occurred. Finally got called before the Board about 5:00. Presented the case to Witt, Hawes, and the two Smiths, Madden being out of town. They decided the questions involved merited Madden's opinion, so I shall have to present the case again.[318]

Have been given a case on which the Regional Director refused to issue a complaint. I do not agree with the R.D. With the Board more than two hours, along with a couple of other attorneys working on similar cases. Finally decided to follow the Globe case.[319]

Got two new cases today. There is certainly no lack of work.[320]

311	October 7, 1937.
312	October 8, 1937.
313	October 11, 1937.
314	October 12, 1937.
315	October 13, 1937.
316	October 14, 1937.
317	October 18, 1937.
318	October 19, 1937.
319	October 21, 1937.
320	October 26, 1937.

Introduction

Anne kept up this hectic pace because she was still on probation as a member of the NLRB legal staff.

They shared my impression of the regional representatives. Korey, the trial examiner on the Mackey case, when he heard that I had it, suggested that I also handle the Columbia Broadcasting case. Alec Hawes thought it a good idea. I now have enough work for the rest of my probation period.[321]

A year later, "Finally got a new case – Mass Knitting Mills."[322] But Anne wanted greater appreciation and fairness. "Was assigned a new case – a dirty trick, I think."[323] As the years passed, Anne tried not to be jerked around at work: "Found another assignment on my desk – just a 1-day case in Baltimore – but complained and got rid of it."[324] "Oral argument this morning in the Geraldine Novelty case…On the agenda for Geraldine Novelty. Completed my Federal Mogul memo and Geraldine decision. Refused to take a new case until some of the old stuff on my desk is disposed of.[325]

"Frank Bloom called to ask if I wanted to come to a Board conference on New York Merchandise Monday. Glad they finally got around to calling me for something. I don't like the office to get along too well without my assistance on cases I review Wednesday."[326] "To the Board on a motion in the Weissman case."[327] "Got a new case – Reynolds Pen."[328] "Back to work. I had been scheduled for the "little agenda" for 10:00 yesterday morning. Everyone at the Board had been miserable over the latest report that Congress would abolish the Board."[329] It is clear that Anne had garnered a lot of respect from her colleagues: "Lunched at the Ambassador with Kami, who told me confidentially that Nat has recommended, and the Board had approved, my going to Detroit to help Cranefield try the case, but Fahy had voted against it because of the Smith Committee, etc. I am flattered."[330] She knew that her co-workers considered her a "whiz" at writing Board decisions,[331] and she was deservedly proud when she "got an excellent on the annual efficiency rating"[332] in 1947.

---

321 October 27, 1937.
322 November 29, 1938.
323 February 24, 1942.
324 May 16, 1969.
325 June 3, 4 and 9, 1947.
326 May 2, 1942.
327 May 1, 1946.
328 May 27, 1946.
329 May 28, 1947.
330 May 29, 1947.
331 May 10, 1966.
332 June 10, 1947.

Anne acquitted herself well during the investigation by the Smith Committee, but she seems to have won the battle and [temporarily] lost the war. Anne's year end summaries of 1951, 1952 and 1953 either do not mention her work at all or do so in very general terms: "I hope…I shall be able to hold on to my job as we need the money, as I should be lost without a job, and as I cannot see myself going into private practice."[333] In 1954, however, job loss was her *first* topic: "the big event for me of 1954 was my discharge from a job I had every reason to believe I was handling competently." By this time, the 44-year old lawyer knew how to fight back. "The Commission's directive confirms my opinion that my discharge was unlawful." With admirable self-confidence, she continued: "Whether the Board complies or forces me to litigate the matter, I have little doubt I will eventually be ordered reinstated." Not only did Anne plan to fight; she planned to win. "That will be quite a victory, and the back pay we can put to good use."

Regardless, the whole process hurt: "The money will not, however, make whole my wounded self-esteem or my damaged professional reputation." And then, in an ironic twist, Anne mentions she is not sure she *wants* to be quickly reinstated. "Actually the likelihood of my being reinstated soon causes mixed reactions in all of us. Jules and Ira would both prefer that I stay at home, doing volunteer work of some sort to keep myself busy and interested."

This complete change of lifestyle had some appeal to Anne: "And I even must admit that there are many advantages to my staying at home, running the household myself, being relatively independent of domestic help, and having more time and energy to devote to Ira's interests." Her fantasy about staying home was brief: "I like working, however, associating with adults, concerning myself with professional problems, and collecting regular and substantial paychecks."

The dismissal that occurred in 1954 continued into 1955 and was a constant topic of conversation with their friends. "The matter has dragged on so long that I plan to go to the Commission next week, and if I do not get some satisfactory answers, will file suit."[334] On February 5, 1955, Anne went "to see Meloy at the Commission. He told me…that the Commission would …see about getting the Board to comply with the Commission's directives. He was quite encouraging."[335] On Valentine's Day (February 14, 1955), she got "a telegram offering my job back beginning next Monday." Anne's prediction of victory was correct. But her colleagues were not pleased. "I have been treated shabbily since my return, but have learned to live with it, and with the hope that that, too, will change in time."[336] By the end of the following year, she could write, "My job is going along all right, although I do

333	Year End Summary, 1953.
334	February 5, 1955.
335	February 7, 1955.
336	Year End Summary, 1955.

not relish the prospect of four more years of the present Republican leadership."[337] At the end of 1957, she was still not content in her reinstated job: "My job goes along in what has now become a rut. I am still in an undesirable office, do no supervision and have not been restored [to the position I held] before my discharge. The only deference to my ability and experience that the present administration pays is to assign very difficult cases to me, and to compliment my work from time to time."[338] Perhaps because of the numerous deaths in her family in 1958, she did not mention her job at all in that year's summary. When she mentioned work at the end of 1959, she wrote, "My job setup is still quite unsatisfactory, but I can live with it for the time being."[339] She was putting on a brave show in that remark, because, in fact, she was very angry.

1960 brought change. But by November 10, she "spent much of the day packing and getting things ready to be moved to the new office…Shall miss my free parking place. But being downtown will have advantages, and having a bright new office with a window, and alone, will be a big improvement."[340] It is extraordinary to think that for the nearly twenty-five years she had worked at the NLRB, she had never had a private office! As part of her new rank in the NLRB, Anne had the opportunity to supervise, a work duty that had previously been denied her. But along with new responsibilities came an enormous amount of new work: "My work is piling up so that I don't know how I shall ever become current again. Yet, though I supervise about a fourth of the staff and issue about half of its case production, Kuskin does nothing but complain about our not producing enough."[341]

This was not a fleeting complaint. Anne actually thought that "the tension at the office…which lately has been greater than ever" was making her very sick.[342] Kuskin had no compassion when she took the day off. And did not stop piling on the work.[343] Anne believed in hard work and in getting rewarded for that work, but the rewards should fit the effort and the work should be fair. That's why eschewed "get rich quick" schemes, such as Pyramid Clubs: "I cannot see getting rich that way. Too accustomed to working for whatever money I get."[344]

Not being rewarded fairly for her work and not receiving promotions in a timely manner were constant irritants in Anne's work life. On July 23, 1962 she wrote that she had learned about an opportunity for advancement to grade 15. She requested that Harry Kuskin, Chief Counsel to Board member Boyd S. Leedom, recommend her. Harry "did not

---

337   Year End Summary, 1956.
338   Year End Summary, 1957.
339   Year End Summary, 1959.
340   November 10, 1960.
341   June 5, 1961.
342   June 6, 1961.
343   June 16, 1961.
344   March 18, 1949.

commit himself, but [I] gathered he would recommend me." The next day Harry reported back to Anne, that he "had spoken to the Judge about the 15 – made a big pitch in my favor, I gathered – but the Judge maintained that he was not ready to make a decision yet. What a rat!"[345]

Anne then tried another tactic – to move to another division of the NLRB: "Raining so I lunched in the drugstore with Arthur Leff. Talked about a transfer to the Chairman's staff, but he had no '15' available and no prospect of one. Ought to shift at my present grade, but am reluctant to do so. Ought to file for a Trial Examiner's appointment application, but it means a very detailed application, and Jules does not like the idea. The jobs have been classified as '16' but it would require quite a bit of traveling."[346] A few days later, she reiterated "Jules is very unhappy at the mere suggestion that I might get a job that will involve traveling."[347] The reluctance of husbands to have their wives be promoted for whatever reason is yet another factor that impedes women's advancement.

The "detailed application" Anne had to present was daunting and perhaps is more of a burden on women than men, given that women typically have a "second shift" of work at home after the first shift at their place of employment.[348] Anne was vigilant about being treated unfairly – even if unintentionally – by virtue of her gender. For example, at a prestigious conference she attended five years later in her first week as an NLRB judge, she "complained to the conference arranger about paying $21 for [her] room. The men were all sharing $21 rooms. I got moved to a smaller room in a different building for $14 a day."[349] Anne was never a pushover, at least she never admitted to being one. While presiding over a case in Brooklyn, she "took a 20-minute lunch break over the reporter's opposition as he was trying to get in another hearing."[350] She wielded enormous power and yet, did not make much of it: "Got exceptions to my decision in the Tulsa case. Issued an order closing the hearing in the Memphis case. And signed my decision in the Saginaw case."[351] She is completely matter-of-fact.

In September 1963, Anne again approached Kuskin "about the 15 – about a year and a half *since* he recommended me, is *still* recommending me, and Leedom is *still* doing nothing about it." "[I] wonder what satisfaction he derives from giving the 15 to no one for all this time." Anne seems to have been fighting her battle for promotion almost alone. Although she did participate in social gatherings of female lawyers,[352] there did not seem to be an

345 July 24, 1962.
346 September 5, 1963.
347 September 7, 1963.
348 See Arlie Hochschild, *The Second Shift*. New York: Viking, 1989.
349 June 10, 1968.
350 August 21, 1973.
351 August 22, 1973.
352 September 29, 1964.

organized group that could fight with her or on her behalf. Trying to make the best of a lousy situation, she ended 1964 with this biting comment: "Things have gone relatively well for me. I never did the get the '15' but *I did get rid of Leedom* as my boss, and that was almost as gratifying. And, while I am a long way from being appointed a Board member, my activity as an applicant for the appointment seems to have raised me in the esteem I value, and has, as far as I can se, done me no hard. And while my chances are slim, I can go on hoping until someone else is named to fill the Leedom vacancy."[353] (emphasis added)

The decisive person concerning her request for promotion was Secretary of Labor Willard Wirtz. Meeting him at a party, she introduced herself as the "same AFS seeking a Board Member appointment" and that she "would be glad of a chance to talk to him about it. He was polite but completely noncommittal."[354] Jules tried to help Anne as well using his social contacts. A few days after Anne met Wertz, "Jules had luncheon with Mike Feldman, who is *convinced my application will fail for lack of adequate political support* and for that reason alone."[355] Two days later, at a party for Mike Feldman, Anne ran into Secretary Wirtz again. Clearly, the politics of appointment and promotion was carried out in social occasions as well as via work evaluations.

By the following May, Anne describes an exam she could take to qualify for the TX [judge] position, an exam that another woman was taking, suggesting that there was a route to a judgeship based on merit rather than favor.[356] Anne was very nervous about the exam. "[It] began at 9:00 [on a Saturday]. We had an hour for luncheon, which I ate in the cafeteria with Mary Clark. Time was up at 3:30 but I turned my papers in shortly before that."[357] Still on edge a few days later, she wrote: "I will be glad when this whole ordeal is over, one way or the other."[358] The tension persisted: "Mary Clark called me, very elated because she found the case on which the exam question was based, and she had the right answer. So, I learned, did the other two from the Board whom I did not know. We are supposed to be graded on our reasoning, not on getting the right answer, but I was terribly disheartened....If I did flunk, it would be terribly embarrassing. And I won't find out until after our trip to Europe. The strain is going to be very hard on me."[359]

Anne traveled in circles that discussed the exam continuously. She kept hearing details about the TX appointment procedures, "some that perk me up, some that let me down. Will be glad when the matter is finally settled."[360] The topic came up at work all the time as well: "All morning at conference in Zagoria's office. At one point he commented

353   Year End Summary, 1964.
354   March 5, 1965,
355   March 8, 1965.
356   May 3, 1966.
357   May 7, 1955.
358   May 9. 1966.
359   May 10, 1966.
360   May 12, 1966.

about 'when' I become a TX, which I amended to 'when and if.' This is being talked about so much around the Board that it will be terribly embarrassing if I do not get a passing grade."[361] At a conference a few days later she saw people she had mobilized to help her win a judgeship: "Roger Traynor mentioned that he had sent the Commission a very good reference. Paul Herzog *never received the form*."[362] The problem repeated itself: "Learned today that Tom Ricci, one of my TX references *never received a form*. Wonder why, when he is a former chief to a chairman and for many years an outstanding TX."[363] (emphasis added) The frustration of not being promoted began to sour Anne's feelings about her career choices. "The 30th anniversary of my coming to work at the Board [i.e. the NLRB]. I stayed too long at the Board."[364]

Throughout the ordeal of waiting, Anne continued to work very hard: Spent "most of the morning in Zagoria's office and most of the afternoon at the sub-panel agenda with Hoffman and Randazzo."[365] "I had the Brown sub-panel agenda this afternoon, with 5 cases on it."[366] "Had a case on the Board agenda with Eleanor Schwartzbach and was in conference most of the rest of the day – the big end-of-the-fiscal-year rush."[367] *Six months into the next year – 1968 – Anne finally was sworn in as a Trial Examiner with the NLRB.* "Quite late in the evening I got a telephone call from Ogden Fields who said the Board had met late in the afternoon to make its TX selections; that Zagoria had given me a big boost, and that I had been selected and would be told officially tomorrow."[368] In general, Zagoria seems to have appreciated Anne. Later that year when they attended a conference together, Zagoria included "complimentary things" about Anne in his speech.[369] For days people congratulated her. Finally, she received a "letter from the Board confirming [her] appointment subject to security clearance and a medical checkup."[370] After her appointment, she began to receive perks that she appreciated: "After some on-again-off-again talks, I have definitely been invited to attend the Federal Bar Examiners' conference in Williamsburg next week."[371] On June 7, 1968 she was sworn in "as a TX so I can go to the conference as a TX."

The NLRB had a clearly defined system for processing cases by allocating them to appropriate pathways. But backlog was always a problem. To cut down on the number of straightforward cases that were going through the elaborate procedures associated

---

361   May 16, 1966.
362   May 18, 1966.
363   June 2, 1966.
364   September 27, 1968.
365   May 23, 1966.
366   June 1, 1966.
367   June 3, 1966.
368   May 16, 1968.
369   June 13, 1968.
370   May 23, 1968.
371   June 4, 1968.

with the panel, an alternative system of sub-panels was created. Anne dealt with cases on panels and on *sub*-panels. Beginning in 1963, Anne mentions subpanel cases frequently. "Had two cases on the subpanel agenda, one with Chuck Thompson and one with Schneur Genack."[372] Two days later she complained in her diary that "I had so much work on my desk that I hardly knew what to do next. Then got tied up all afternoon on the subpanel which I foolishly agreed to take over while Loeb is away."[373] Her workload was overwhelming: "Scheduled for an agenda of some kind every day this week."[374] "Had various cases with various legal assistants on various agendas, so it was quite a hectic day."[375] "Did enough work today to make up for the holiday [Rosh Hashana] on Monday and the sick leave yesterday."[376] "I was very busy, primarily because of getting ready for some rather difficult cases scheduled for tomorrow's Board agenda."[377] Anne was getting the opportunity to present alone: "I had a couple of cases on the Board agenda with Mira [Almira Stevenson], and the one by myself."[378]

A theme running through Anne's comments on her work concerns the relative benefits of working for the government or opening up a private practice. Jules resigned from his job at the NLRB in 1953 in order to avoid a demeaning investigation of his loyalty. The peace of mind inherent in private practice far outweighed the higher salary of government service. In her 1953 year-end summary, she writes: "The unattractiveness of government service at present is brought home vividly to me practically every day that I am at the office – the prejudice, the suspicion, the insecurity, the hostility toward those who remain from an earlier administration." The work continued unabated: "Had a case on the Board agenda with Leo Weiss."[379] Most of her references to work concern stress: "Have several rush matters at the office , and am really being run ragged – knowing, of course, that no one really appreciates it."[380] Strangely, she concludes that her year at work was "considerably improved." Perhaps she had resigned herself to the fact that she had "not been given the promotion that [she] feels has been unfairly withheld for so long, but Zagoria is a big improvement over Leedom in any event."[381] Internalized and external pressure to work hard followed Anne even after she was promoted: "Attended a staff meeting in the afternoon – [Chief Judge] Bokat's usual pitch for more work, longer hours, and quicker decisions."[382] Strangely, soon after her rise to TX, the amount of work she had to do, di-

---

372   September 11, 1963.
373   September 13, 1963.
374   September 25, 1963.
375   November 20, 1963.
376   September 9, 1964.
377   March 22, 1965.
378   March 23, 1965.
379   July 27, 1962.
380   March 31, 1965.
381   Year End Summary, 1965.
382   May 9, 1969.

minished. "Should hand in my Brooklyn decision for stenciling, but have nothing else on which to work."[383] "Would have had a hearing in Tulsa this week but the case was cancelled. Hope I get an assignment on Thursday. Really finished with my Brooklyn decision but have not turned it in because I have no other case on my desk."[384]

Because her assignments involved travel, Anne found herself juggling appointments at home with work out of town. "Life does get complicated for a TX."[385] Her assignments varied as to destination and the amount of time she would have to spend on location. She tried to manipulate these assignments to meet her needs. For example, in November, 1970 she wrote that she "was given an assignment in Chicago, a short simple case. Would like to get a few such cases to be able to get out some production."[386] "Asked Kessel if I could get a short case next week without prejudicing my getting the Tulsa case. He agreed."[387] She also tried to coordinate her travel with Jules', but it was not easy. The accounts Anne gives of her assignments reveal a chaotic system of travel arrangements made, then cases cancelled, then arrangements cancelled, and yet another change. Repeatedly.

Anne was understandably pleased when her decisions were upheld. "Got a Board decision in my Baton Rouge case – affirmed with a footnote modification."[388] And she seemed proud of her independent thinking: "Got to work on the hot cargo case, a type of problem with which I am quite familiar...Getting straightened out on what is involved in my hot cargo case, it is a novel question so the Board may or may not see it my way."[389] "The Board adopted my decision administratively in Capitol Court (Milwaukee), no exceptions having been filed."[390] "Returned to find the Board decision affirming me in Carbide Tools, a case involving a good many issues, so was very pleased by that."[391] It is charming to read the way Anne was pleased – yet modest – about her rise in the ranks: "The stationery I ordered, imprinted with my title of Judge, arrived today. I was pleased with its appearance. Now have to find some occasion to use it."[392] When Anne became a TX, she was obliged to hear cases in person all over the United States. She never liked this aspect of her work because she did not like to "leave Jules behind." He didn't make it easy for her: "Later called Jules. He was a bit fed up with my absence."[393] "Called Jules, who sounded as lonely as I felt."[394]

---

383   November 2, 1970.
384   November 3, 1970.
385   November 4, 1970.
386   November 21, 1970.
387   March 23, 1971.
388   November 6, 1970.
389   November 23, 1970 and November 24, 1970.
390   March 11, 1971.
391   August 8, 1973.
392   September 27, 1972.
393   May 14, 1969.
394   March 16, 1971.

Concluding Remarks

It is reasonable to ask if Anne was an extraordinary woman whose diary (even in part) warrants publication and analysis. After exploring who Anne was, I would answer "yes". She was extraordinary in several ways. *First*, her intelligence, energy, and professional drive enabled her to break the barriers that stood in her way, particularly barriers based on gender. *Second*, her integrity and strength enabled her to withstand the humiliation of security investigations whereas many others in her position left government service or in some tragic cases, committed suicide. *Third*, Anne is a case study of a person who succeeds despite the impairment of her parents. As mentioned earlier, Anne coped with this problem by forming mentor/mentee relationships as well as a large number of friendships. *Fourth*, Anne illustrates that a woman can live a balanced life, filled with social engagements, athletic activities, and "down time" with family, along with very demanding work. Current studies show that the overwhelming numbers of women who reach the top of their professions, as Anne did, are unmarried and childless.[395] That was not the life Anne wanted. In fact, she and her husband successfully adopted a child and would have liked to adopt a second one. And *finally*, Anne's life illustrates how a Jewish woman of the time integrated the demands of religious affiliation with the other demands in her life. Her court documents will show another researcher how her rulings shaped the nation's labor practices, but her personal diary shows how she lived an integrated life.

Shulamit Reinharz is the Jacob Potofsky Professor of Sociology at Brandeis University. She has her B.A. from Barnard College and her M.A. and Ph.D. from Brandeis. From 1972-1982 she taught at the University of Michigan and then returned to Brandeis where she is on the faculty today. From 1992-2001, Reinharz directed the Brandeis Women's Studies Program where she created a graduate program that included the first Jewish Women's Studies M.A. program in the world. In 1997, she created the HBI (Hadassah-Brandeis Institute) which conducts research on Jews and gender, and in 2001, she founded the Women's Studies Research Center, which welcomes eighty scholars each year. She is the author of eleven books, and is working on *A Memoir in Four Hands: Understanding My Father's Experience Hiding in Holland during the Holocaust*.

---

[395] See David Leonhardt, "A Market Punishing to Mothers," *New York Times*, Wednesday, August 4, 2010, B1, B6

Young Anne Frihling

The Diaries

Part I

1931 To 1934
Law School And First Job

When Anne Freeling began diary writing on January 1, 1931, she could not have realized that she was starting a half century long project of describing her life as a groundbreaking woman professional in the twentieth century. Forty-seven years later she had narrated the five central decades of the century that transformed American life, the decades that saw the country change from struggling in the Great Depression to its role of world dominance and wealth. Anne was near the center of power in Washington, D.C., and major national events appear in her diaries, but in her daily entries she focuses on personal concerns of her life and family. Although she was involved in major cases of labor law and media churning political events, she writes in more detail about her personal life. It was a private area, safe and tranquil. On events that we now see of major historical significance, her comments are frequently cryptic and short. When her emotions creep through, she is usually writing about personal issues with her family or the frustration with the slowness of her job promotions. Only when she fell ill with lymphoma in December, 1977 and had to enter the hospital did she falter in writing daily notes. After a two month lapse her last entries were made in April and early May, 1978, when she rallied briefly before she fell silent.

Anne was born in 1910 of Jewish immigrant parents from the Ukraine. The original spelling of the family name was Frihling, but it was later anglicized to Freeling. Throughout her diaries we read about her sisters Clara and Jean, who later changed her name to Janet, and her Mother (Regina) and father (Abraham). Her brother Louis (sometimes called Louie) died in World War II in action in Europe. Her grandmother, Baba Wagshal, was an important presence in her life, and in her early years in Washington the family of her cousin, Sam Wagshal, was important. Her diaries from 1931 to 1952 tell the story of an intelligent young woman who had little patience for the frivolity of the young people around her. She was focused and determined to be a lawyer, but she worked in a world that favored neither Jews nor women in the profession that she had chosen. After she completed law school and passed the Bar the only job she could get initially was as a legal secretary. Later, she was able to get a job as a lawyer with the federal government.

In Washington D.C. she encountered a larger Jewish community and professional world. Her friends were increasingly Jewish, and she eventually met and married a fellow lawyer from that group, Julius Schlezinger. They worked together, and she respected him intellectually. Anne was unable to have children, so they adopted a son, Ira, who transformed her life. Anne repeatedly expresses her emotional identity with her family, her love of Jules and Ira, the torment with her mother, and the bond with her sister, Clara.

In World War II Julius volunteered for the U.S. Army, which lead to a long, lonely time for Anne filled with anxiety. She narrated her feelings and her growing affection for Julius during that time. After the war the two of them returned to their work and professional lives, and realizing the post-war dream they moved to a house in the suburbs. Then, the election of Eisenhower as president in 1952 led to a turning point in their lives. Anne lost her position with the National Labor Relations Board with the new administration; she challenged through an appeal, which led to her reinstatement. In the 1960's she reached professional success with her appointment as an NLRB judge.

Although Anne writes about her professional life, it is within the context of her personal life. It was an important component of her complex network of friends, colleagues, and relatives, all of whom were woven together in the fabric of life through lunches, dinners, social visits, cultural events, and vacations. Although she was spare in describing the emotional details of her life in her entries, there were times when her emotional concerns slipped through. In the 1940's and 1950's she repeatedly questioned herself as a wife and mother, especially in relation to work. At those moments she would reveal the push and pull between her sense of family obligation and commitment to being a professional woman.

The diary entries are a chronicle of her social life, friends, and meals. Many entries are punctuated with references to breakfast, lunch, and dinner. She loved the social context of lunching and dining and regularly identifies locations, companions, and the food itself. Through this chronicling of a life over five decades we can see many of the social, economic, political, and ethnic changes that occurred in the United States during that time period. We see the changes from radio to television, from public transportation to private cars, from urban living to suburban life, and the economic expansion of life that occurred during those years.

The analysis of her diary shows the evolution of her interests, as she grew from a young law student in a pre-feminist era to a judge in a prominent national agency. Although Anne was deeply involved with worker's rights, she seems not to have been involved in women's rights movements. There is no evidence of her being a member of the National Council of Jewish Women, and she does not mention the work of Hannah Solomon in favor of Jewish women's rights. She makes oblique references to the larger women's rights movement but does not seem to have been actively involved with it.

As early as the 1870's the first women in the United States were becoming lawyers (Leary 2009), and by the beginning of the twentieth century women were making a concerted push to gain entrance to the legal profession. The National Association of Women Lawyers was founded in 1899 before the American Bar Association would accept women. The *Women Lawyer's Journal*, which was started independently in New York in 1912, eventually became the publication of the NAWL. Early issues of the *Women Lawyer's Journal* show that women lawyers were teaching in law schools, and there were women lawyers and judges in the areas of domestic relations, children's, and juvenile law in local, municipal courts. By the 1920's most law schools were admitting women at a time when women had just earned the right to vote.

Although women could study law and pass the Bar, many bar associations would not accept them as members. The Maryland State Bar Association did not admit women until 1946, and the Bar Association of Baltimore did not admit women or African Americans until 1957. Ruth Bader Ginsberg mentions that in the mid to late 1950's she was one of nine women in a law school class of 500 men (1978:1ff). Harvard Law School did not admit women until 1950 (Leary 2009). Many of the barriers against women in law were late in falling.

Anne was one of a group of women lawyers who were edging their way into the legal profession in the early and mid-twentieth century, and she represents the early group of women to obtain positions as lawyers at the Federal level. In the 1930's Anne worked in the Department of Labor under Francis Perkins, the first woman to be named to a cabinet post in the United States government, and she met Secretary Perkins personally. Anne assumed that she could have any job that a man could have, but she was thirty years too early to reach her potential and her expectations.

The National Labor Relations Board was in the lead hiring women lawyers and later in naming women as judges at the Federal level. Anne and Fannie Boyls were hired as lawyers by the NLRB in the 1930's when there were few women in such positions. Eventually they were in the first cohort of women judges along with Rosanna Blake and Josephine Klein in the 1960's. At the time of Anne's death in the late 1970's women judges were being named to the Federal courts. Although President Gerald Ford made some such appointments, between 1976 and 1980 President Jimmy Carter named forty-one women to the Federal Judiciary, which is considered the first major breakthrough for women at the national level.

Anne writes modestly about herself, and with career achievement limited by her sex, she focuses on social contacts, lunches, and dinners in detail, reflecting a complex social circle. In sequences of considerable emotional depth she questions and evaluates her feelings toward her suitors, including her future husband, before getting married. Her writing reflects the delight she took in working and the social life associated with it, but she continually questions how that affected her obligations as wife and mother. Anne suffered from migraine headaches that could be debilitating, and she makes occasional references to lost days because of those headaches.

Anne Schlezinger's diary gives a personal day-by-day narrative of the building of the American Jewish professional class of the Great Generation. Like many others of that time period, she lived through the sacrifices of the Depression and World War II and focused on achievement in her life. Sometimes as a reader, we want more information, and then subtly, almost without knowing it, we realize that she has perhaps given us more in her unassuming way than we were able to realize. It is in the details of lunches and dinners, parties, shopping trips, office meetings, trial hearings, and conversations with friends and

The Diaries

colleagues in almost 20,000 diary entries that we realize the legacy of information about life during her time that she has left for us.

This diary is largely an account of her social networking throughout her lifetime. At times she ignores or gives only passing comments to historically important events, but her daily record of the people with whom she had coffee, lunch, and dinner is meticulous. She was superb at networking before we had a term for it.

As a twenty-year-old student in 1931, Anne was living in a rooming house in Boston with other young women, supporting herself working as a stenographer during the day and studying law at the Northeastern Law School at night. Her family was not wealthy, so even as a young law student she worked and lived on what she earned.

Anne grew up in a family in which English was not the first language, and in her diaries in the early years her spelling is weak, and for much of her life she struggled with the spelling of unfamiliar last names. She had entered law school directly out of high school in the middle of the Great Depression. Although she occasionally mentions people losing jobs or economic difficulties, those references are rare. In her diary entries from the 1930's we see her interests, fun, and endeavors as a student. She completed law school in 1933 and passed the bar exam shortly afterwards.

As a young Jewish woman lawyer, she had no professional opportunities in Boston that matched her ambitions, and she moved to Washington, D.C. Even there she could not get a job as a lawyer, so she begin working as a legal secretary with the expectation of eventually getting a professional position.

The most important person to her in the early years was her sister Jean, whom she mentions once or twice daily. The two sisters had different temperaments, so that Anne was frustrated that Jean was not more like her. She had little patience with the young men and women around her, who were more interested in dancing and drinking than more serious matters.

Then, in 1932 Charles Wyzanski,[1] a lawyer in Boston, begsn to appear frequently in the diary and continues until late in the decade. For Anne, emotional and professional ties were intertwined with Wyzanski although she always refers to him in professional terms in the diary. By 1933 he was in the U.S. Department of Labor in Washington, D.C. and arranged a job for Anne there. It was on her application for that job that he learned that she was Jewish. Anne was twenty-three years old at that point and for years she thought that a relationship might develop between them. It never happened. In this volume some 1,800 entries have been selected from important time periods, representing each year of her life.

-- Ron Duncan Hart

---

1   Charles Edward Wyzanski, a graduate of Harvard Law School, was a Solicitor of Labor, U.S. Department of Labor from 1933 to 1935. He was a Special Assistant to the Attorney General in the Office of the Solicitor General from 1935 to 1937. After a brief period in private practice, Wyzanski was a federal judge in the United States District Court for the District of Massachusetts from 1941 until his retirement in 1971.

Diaries. 1931 Through 1934.

1931

Anne Freeling's first diary entries reflect her interests and concerns as a student. Friends, both girl and boy, occupy an important part of her attention at the time. Money issues and job instability are a concern, after all this was the time of the Great Depression. Although she was a more sophisticated diary writer a few years later, these early entries have a spontaneity that is refreshing. Her monthly memoranda give good summaries for each month, and she freely expresses her feelings more in these end of the month comments than she does in daily entries. -- RDH

Thursday, January 1
Saw the New Year in with Lloyd Tuinby, Mimmie Begirs, and Dick Little. Statler Roman Garden Café for liquor.[2] Lloyd and Mim drank more than they could manage – Dick and I not at all. I wore white chiffon and looked so unlike the rest of the crowd – mostly drunken fools - that I attracted quite a good deal of attention on the dance floor and would not go on to display myself a second time. Lloyd disgusted with my lack of sportive spirit, I with his too abundant holiday spirit. He apologized most profusely on the way home, but I would not grant him my forgiveness, so do not expect to hear from him again, and hope I shall not, lest I be tempted to give him another trial.
Rested all day January 1.

Friday, January 2
Mr. Taylor called to dictate. In commenting on a letter to salesmen he got in the phrase "free from fancy frills," and was so pleased at this alliteration as though he were any ordinary man and not the "super-intellect" man he considers himself.
Went alone to Nate Bidwell's office to do some work for him. Got him talking about his kid, Bob, whom he adores and who, I would be willing to bet money, will some day be a noted surgeon.
Lillian Gates and Eva Hendry, girls from Jean's office, over to the House[3] to bowl. They were very pleasant and agreeable and I was glad to have them, and their conversation was so inane I was more than glad to have them go. Did not do any studying. Consider the evening wasted.

Saturday, January 3
Jean[4] overslept and did not go to work at all. Very much annoyed at her. She has had things come her way too much, needs a few swift kicks to make her snap out of it. Mrs. Fuller[5] had a job at Gum's practically cinched

---
2   Although this was during Prohibition, in the first sentence Anne mentions getting liquor at a Café.
3   Anne refers to the rooming house for young women where she and Jean lived as the "House" but later she also calls it the F.S.H.
4   Anne's younger sisters, Jean and Clara, were a continuing presence in her life.
5   Ms. Carrie C. Fuller was one of the most important people in her early years in Boston and was Anne's first mentor. Anne accepted advice from her on culture and life itself. Ms. Fuller also helped her find jobs.

for her but now considers her too unreliable. Lloyd called several times. Wanted to take me skating, to a dance, or anything I wanted. I finally agreed to let him come over with Dick Little, got Jean, played bridge, went to Old France to eat. Was asked to go on a date with Peggy Hyman and on one with Anita Plamondon, but had already promised Lloyd. Lloyd said he enjoyed it very much.

Sunday, January 4
Dinner with Peggy Hyman. She affects a supercilious air which would irk me if it were not so amusing. Her habit of addressing everyone as "dear" unfortunately brands her as a "shopgirl." Has asked me to move into an apartment with her. Should have known better. Walk in the evening with Jean. Sundaes in a new ice cream parlor on Newton Street. Two men bought liquor. Movie underworld type. Clark talkative but unentertaining.

Monday, January 5
Very warm. Breakfasted with Peggy. She wants me and Jean to move with her. Would not consider it. Had a real heart-to-heart talk with Mrs. Fuller such as I had not had for some time and which I always find so helpful and constructive. If I ever get thru this law course it will be due at least 90% to her encouragement. Agency test. Think I hit it just right. If I did I shall make it a rule not to "grind" during a holiday. Phone while at school. Don't know from whom. Might have been George Benstock.
Peggy in the room after school. Wants me and Jean to go out to the dance tomorrow night with some law students. Pleaded much studying, but she and Jean teased until I finally consented to go. Very much dissatisfied with my refusal powers. Must strengthen them. Flatter myself that I would not have surrendered if they had not been law students. May mean future business.

Tuesday, January 6
Sally Penn in the office. As attractive and as dependable as a bubble. Wants me to go on a "real big date" with her some night. Her idea of a good time – plenty of liquor, laughter, and loving. Not mine except for one ingredient. Luncheon with Anna Clancy – very pleasant but so inconsequential. Peggy's date did not call at all. Just as well. Jean and I expected as much. Peggy down to the room to visit. Brought some sewing as she would not disturb our studying. Nonetheless, talked continuously and left too late for us to do any studying. Revealed in her chatter more of her true character. Liked her much better as a result thereof. Would not want her for a friend – pretty but vain, clever but loquacious, pleasant but patronizing. Calls Jean and me the katzenjammer kids and gets a big kick out of us. So do we out of her. So, everybody's happy!

Wednesday, January 7
Bitter cold. Sidney Lanier up from Florida. Disinclined to venture out. Very charming, but not the *dashing* southern gentleman I hoped he would be.
W.V.T. called and dictated some letters in

his old commandeering manner. Must be feeling better. Left early to get to school at six o'clock. Copious notes on all three lectures. Can hear senior boys commenting on fact that I am only a Soph. taking an elective. Annoying. One of the boys walked home from school with me. Asked to come to one of our house dances. Stalled him off. Not my class.

Disagreed with Jean about her favorite Prof's theories. She has implicit faith in him. He derides everything modern – writers and lecturers. He is encouraging Jean to go to college next year rather than evening school. I believe he will prevail unless she meets someone else with a stronger power of words.

Thursday, January 8
W.V.T. called to dictate. Curt but comparatively pleasant. Over to Nate Bidwell's office to do some work. Offered a job there. Shall take it only as a last resort. Know I should find it pleasant to work for him but the remuneration would be small and not certain. Told Mrs. Fuller about his offer. She advised against it. Told me she was trying to make a job for us at the Tuinly Co. If this office should close, which now seems almost certain. If anyone can do it she can and my best bet for the time being is undoubtedly to stick to her.

Last time Lloyd called I was out. Jean answered. He told her to tell me I should call him. If he is waiting until I do, he has a terribly long wait ahead of him. Bowled, studied, bathed, retired. Not an exciting evening, but refreshing and invigorating.

Friday, January 9
Spoke to Miss Niles about selling coffee to the house, but found she was buying from one of our subsidiaries. Think she could have been sold. A "sellable" type.

Marcia Rulinoff up to the room before school with a box of goodies from home. Therefore, very welcome. A charming, pleasant acquaintance but lacks the depth to make of her a true friend – to a girl anyway. Likes to make fine sounding statements whether or not she believes in them.

Announced at school that we would go 4 nights a week for at least the next 4 weeks. Pretty tough. Very discouraged about it all. Would be strongly tempted to quit but dare not have Mrs. Fuller know. I think maybe if I could quit without anyone ever knowing I had started and failed, I should do so. But hate to have people know; hate to admit to myself that I am a quitter.

Saturday, January 10
Miss Campbell called last night, after I left the office, about a job. Am to call her Monday morning.

Shopped all afternoon for a dress. Did not get one – all too fussy. Tried on one lovely red Sunday night dress in which I did look very stunning but did not feel that I could afford it.

Lloyd called several times. Wanted to take me skating, but was willing to take me to a dance or the movies or anywhere I wanted. I wanted to go to Lawrence. He was not too pleased at the idea of the long drive but said he would take me. Then I decided it was too late to go anyhow and too late to go anywhere. Would not go just riding. Gold digger?

Sunday January 11
Ruth Stockwell over for dinner. Very thin, but sweeter than ever. Told us about her operation. Pluckiest and unluckiest kid I know.
Peggy gone home for a while. Sore feet. At dinner – little Alice Mayo, who is growing from a sweet youngster into a hard-boiled kid. Doris Farley, 11th year at the House and still likes it; Dot Wilson, graduate of art school clerking at Jordan's, tired of her job so ready to marry Al. Blames all on school, not herself.

Monday, January 12
Looked up job. Not worth my while. Wanted someone inexperienced, just out of school. Mrs. Fuller seemed somewhat relieved, but maybe I am just flattering myself.
Walked to school with Esther Bornstein. She asked me to go the House dance tomorrow night after school with some boys from her class but I was afraid I would be too tired with three nights of school in a row. Had no dress, anyway. Got Jean to go instead. Two of the boys started to walk home from school with me but I evaded them by saying I had to meet someone else, I did meet Esther. Do not like any of the boys in my class. The stupid ones I cannot tolerate and the clever ones I resent. A hateful way to be. I realize. Due to my always heretofore having been at the head of my class. Hard to take a back seat now.
Very warm. Rained very hard. Met Esther because she had an umbrella and I had not bothered to bring mine. She is sweet and attractive, a loyal friend, but somewhat inclined to be boring.

Tuesday, January 13
Sally called for luncheon date. Did not go – could not be bothered. Anna Clancy called too – different hours. Went alone, which I preferred. Walked to school with Esther. Told me about those romances of hers, which she somehow omitted in our other talks, and about some she has told me about. In spite of her pleasant but aimless chatter I like her because she really is, to use Peggy's expression, "real." Walked home from school with her and the three boys who were going to the dance. Looked for a taxi – could not get one right away. I suggested walking. Boys very glad to do so. One wanted to come over to bowl some evening. Might have let him if I had plenty of spare evenings but not with quizzes. All expressed regrets that I was not to be at the dance. Meaningless, I realize. Jean and Marcia waiting for the boys in the blue parlor. Both looked very nice but rather self-conscious.

> From these earliest entries we see her impatience with frivolous behavior from those who drink too much to those who have little to say. This was during Prohibition Era, but young people had little difficulty in finding places to drink and socialize. Although she mellowed over the years, throughout her life she had a reputation for being practical and speaking directly, qualitites that later distinguished her as a judge.

Wednesday, January 14
Worked very hard. Time only to run downstairs for a little of luncheon. Did some very long affidavits in re the Tuinly Co. for E.W. Goodale. E.W.G. in spite of his grumpiness and disagreeable-appearing exterior is really a kindly-enough soul. Conflict of Laws lecture easy to understand but very long as usual. Bills and Notes lecture difficult for me to understand, as usual. First lecture in Sales. Mr. Lee, I believe, and so do must of the students, is going to be a success. His lecture was clear and instructive. Jokes terrible. Introductions by Mr. Swaim rather "cute" as Swaim is so inexperienced himself, and both are so young. Offered to do Lee's notes. Expressed appreciation, but did not indicate it by his manner.

Letter from home. First one written by mother. Very sweet. Addressed to me but referred to Jean exclusively. From it I gathered that Jean wanted to quit and go back to day school. Everyone favorable to that but Father. Think he is justified.

Thursday, January 15
Very busy in the office as is to be expected at a time when I am starting a new subject and preparing for my Agency final. Have not even done my lecture notes for this week, much less any cases, very much less any review for the exam. Tired of the whole racket but cannot quit because afraid of Mrs. Fuller's disappointment. Maybe foolish. Hope I shall be thankful in the end. Tried on some dresses. Liked a few but not enough to purchase. Afraid I have gotten out of the habit of buying. Mrs. Fuller thinks I have cultivated a more critical judgment of fashion due to my conscientious perusal of *Vogue*, "cultivation" instigated and urged on by her in her effort to give me a "high-grade background."

Bowled an hour with Jean. Studied a while. Never can accomplish much with Jean hammering at that rickety typewriter. Hoping to accomplish a good deal this week-end as Jean is planning to go home. Hope that every week-end, but that is as far as I can get. Ho! Hum!

Friday, January 16
Very busy in the office again today. Have been, in fact, for at least 4 weeks now. About 2 weeks behind in my studying, which I do not like, especially when I feel that if I do get a spare minute I should review Agency for the final. Up to Esther Bornstein's room after school to help her with a Tort case. Pleased with myself at remembering it. Found her not so unusually clever as I had expected, but more intelligent than average, I believe. Ray Wasserman, her roommate, has become quite unsociable towards me, for which I am thankful as I find her gushiness intolerable.

Downcast. Disappointed in myself – with what I have accomplished. Pretty bum in the job, dumb at school, and making about as distinguished an appearance as a dishrag in my old clothes. Have given up almost all frivolities – for a career? I wonder if it will ever be, and, if it does come to pass, will it be worth while.

Saturday, January 17
Jean home. Folks called. Very enjoyable conversation with them all. Promised Ruth Stockwell to go to the movies with her, against my better judgment, which advised staying

in to study, but Ruth leads such a lonesome life. Waited at the agreed place almost a half an hour but she did not appear. Could not call her because she has no telephone. When I got back to the House I learned some "boy-friend" (presumably Lloyd) had been calling me. Stupid evening with nothing accomplished. Would be heartily annoyed at Ruth if I were not worried as to what might have happened to her.

Sunday, January 18
Jerry Langlois and Louis drove Jean in. Went riding. Took pictures. Lovely weather. Louis and Jerry very pleased with the House. Intend to come in more often for bowling and to learn to dance. Jerry quite good-looking and very agreeable, but too short to be eligible. Discussion at the supper table in re the desirability of love and marriage. I, as usual, the dissenting minority. Alice Mays, Delle Croce, Dorothy Wilson.

Monday, January 19
Snow and rain and warm. Real old-fashioned New England.
Weighted almost 122 today. Have gained considerably, but am told that I look much better so do not care.
Met Ethel Meister this noon. Learned she was engaged. Was wearing beautiful diamond. A sweet girl, deserving of happiness. Cheerfulness her main asset. Optimism is a wonderful gift. Wished I had it more abundantly. An outgrowth of self-confidence, which I also lack. Wrote home at Mrs. Fuller's behest, suggesting that if the folks sent Jean to day school it would be no more than fair to pay part of my tuition, too. Seems selfish, but never got anything yet by being self-effacing. Jean asks so much more that I do, and gets it, and gets applauded for knowing enough to get it. I try to ask for very little, get less, and am considered a fool. Well, now I have asked, we shall see what comes of it. Got call tonight while at school. Cannot imagine from whom. Consider myself well rid of Lloyd. He had the makings of a fine chap but wrong bringing-up.

Tuesday, January 20
Had to go down to see old Mr. Currier at the Parker Coffee Company. Delightfully courteous gentleman of the old, old school. Makes one wonder if the ways of this generation really are the finest.
Jean announced she had given Miss Roth notice today that she was leaving. Very disappointed in her. Shows lack of staying powers I never suspected.
Agency quiz tonight in Bates Hall. Chairs so hard and uncomfortable. Difficult to concentrate because of necessity of almost constantly squirming around. Dr. Rogers looked so particularly small up on the stage – seemed nothing but white hair and voice. I like his lectures immensely – clear and comprehensive. Most of the boys do not – because, I think, he answers them so tartly at times. Dance at the house. Seemed to be very small crowd when I came in. Music did not penetrate my studying so continually and annoyingly as it always did heretofore, wonder if I am learning to concentrate. Mrs. Fuller, when I mentioned

my lack of ability to concentrate, said there was a conformation – that when one could concentrate easily one missed out on something else. Interrupted before I could ask her to explain. Beyond me.

Wednesday, January 21
Hectic day at the office because of new ads with pictures. WIT called several times in regard to same, bawled everybody out good and plenty. When CCF[6] told him everyone looked glum and repentant, he said he felt much better. His streak of cruelty showing through.
Bought two dresses: bright red Sunday night dress, white satin collar, very long, quite décolleté; black trimmed with vari-colored wool embroidery and heavy ear lace. Both quite simple but plenty of style.[7]
Mr. Swaim looked very nice tonight. Hair combed. High-grade looking chap, decidedly clever, but somehow misses fire. Some quality missing. Mr. Lee a good lecturer. Sure of himself. Easy to follow. Inexcusably trite jokes. Students decidedly proposed in his favor. Hostile to Swaim. He must have what Swaim lacks. Maybe because Lee seems more on the students' level. Swaim superior. One of the boys who has walked home from school with me rode me home tonight. Unattractive looking, but his nice car an asset. Asked again if he might come to a Tuesday night dance. So hard up I may let him. Don't even know his name.

---

6   Ms. C.C. Fuller
7   Anne was conscious of fashion and her appearance throughout her life, and shopping for clothes was the punctuation for good days.

Thursday, January 22
Received $2.00 from Mr. Currier as a valentine for work I had done for him. W.V.T. and C.C.F. had a real tiff over the phone. It blew over as their storms always do – much thunder but very little damage.
Bought Sales book from Jeanie Fine. Her offices not grand like mine, but a far more pleasant atmosphere prevailed. Anita called me at his office. Long chat. Insistent I come over.
Found when I got home I had my Sales book instead of my Real Property, which I needed. Did not feel like studying anyhow so went over to Anita's apartment with Jean. Anita very effusive. Probably part of her dramatic rehearsing. Met Miss Boll. Think her clever, mercenary, has personality, but is not too high-grade. Met Bud Thompson, Anita's newest boyfriend. Attractive southerner. Studying architecture at M.I.T. but intends to be a writer. Won a prize for a school theme which went to his head. Had the same theme published, and became convinced he was destined to be an author. He, Jean, and I talked books while Anita made love to him. Crazy scene. His views interacting but trite.

Friday, January 23
Both Mr. Davis and Mr. Poland in the office. Two very clever lawyers – Mr. Davis a business lawyer, Mr. Poland a lawyer because he truly loves the profession. Has made a good deal of money nonetheless. Like a pickled herring – small, dried up, tart, agreeable – likeable and admirable on the whole. Both talked to me, asked about school, were politely flattering, but not too encouraging. So far C.C.F. the

only one who has encouraged me to stick it out. Maybe I shall appreciate that fact ten years from now.

Luncheon with Thelma Farrington at Hayler's. Bum lunch. Like Thelma quite a good deal – sensible, sweet, modest. Last Agency quiz tonight. Final comes Feb. 2. Must buckle down to studying. Still maintain that if I should flunk a subject I would quit immediately. Wrote a nice long letter home. Bowled after school. Tired me out. Have grown stiff from lack of exercise. That will never do.

Saturday, January 24
Extremely cold. Mrs. Fuller presented me with *Saplio* and *Carmille*.[8] Have read "Saplio." Too much sensuality. All through I felt pity for Fanny because Jean was going to leave her. When she turned the tables I immediately felt sorry for Jean. The natural pity for the under-dog. Kay Pitfield asked me to usher at one of the Camel Lab. Theater plays, even offered to lend me an evening gown, but I did not care to and had other plans. Pam agreed to go in my place – all enthusiastic about it – then decided she would not care to after all. Vacillating. Met Delly's Spanish girl-friend from Portland. Unusual-charming-would like to know her.

Sunday, January 25
Very cold. Anita Plumondon over to visit. Loves her work but not her living quarters. Three temperamental people and they clash. Wants to move again, and wants me to go with her. She is torn between her sense of decency and Sunny's depravity. A good friend could help her immeasurably, but I have not the time. Necessity breeds selfishness. If I went with her I know I could help her but I should lose time and ambition myself.

Monday, January 26
Sodas at Bailey's with Thelma Farrington. Window shopping. Fine day. Enjoy Thelma's company. Probably because I can feel just a tiny bit superior to her. Mrs. Lely, Mrs. Fletcher, and Miss Bliss in the office today. None of them young, but all beautifully dressed, well-groomed, all have plenty of money, leisure, travel. Wonder if I shall ever be on their plane. Sincerely hope so. Think B. Bliss one of the cleverest, pluckiest, and luckiest girls I know. The only one of the three who has earned her place, but owes a great deal to luck.

Met Jean after school. Went to Chatham's to eat. Jean and I felt quite distinguished – the only girls in the place not smoking.

Returned to find one of us had received a call. Much conjecture, much annoyance. Might have been a date for the dance tomorrow night. Do not know whether I wait tomorrow or go to the movies as we had planned. I intend to go to the movies.

Tuesday, January 27
Left office early. Went to the State Theater

---

8   Clyde Fitch's *Saplio* (1900) includes the story of a courtesan who begs to be seduced and was considered risque for a young woman of this time. *Carmille* is a story about a young courtesan caught between her love for a young man and the offer of a comfortable life by a Baron.

with Jean before 6. Saw Greta Garbo in "Inspiration."[9] Enjoyed the picture very much because of having just read Saplio. Enjoyed it too because of Greta Garbo's unparalleled exotic beauty and her supreme art of acting. Came home in time to hear the last part of an entertainment at the House. Professional impersonators, but they seemed decidedly amateurish after the Garboian spectacle. Coming out of Haynes Hall, saw the boys waiting for the girls for the dance. They all seemed nice enough boys but young and unpolished. There was not one I should have liked to meet. Wonder if I shall ever find a man who meets all my requirements. Doubt it. And if I do, will he know or care that I even exist. It becomes more and more apparent to me every day that I am destined to be an old maid. Better study hard.

Wednesday, January 28
Learned from Mr. Goodale that he and Mrs. Davis were both graduates of Suffolk evening law school. Quite encouraging.
Violet Wood up for dinner. Read a few of her innumerable poems. Rather good considering her youth and lack of training. Somewhat inclined to suit her thoughts to pretty expressions. Jean mentioned that she might get another job and continue at evening school when Violet, who has just started the course, expressed regret at her leaving. I think the remark was incited to some extent by Jean's realization of my disapproval of her showing herself a quitter. I think she will quit nevertheless. Got a ride home from school with the same chap who taken me before, but whose name I still do not know. Asked again to come to one of our dances. Too homely. Boring. Should much prefer to walk home than to ride with him but do not like to seem rude. Wonder what makes me so "uppity" anyhow.

Thursday, January 29
Quite warm. Walked to work. Trying to lose weight (now 120) but finding it quite difficult to do so.
Some of Jean's girl-friends over to bowl. Jean showed them my two new dresses. Admired them, of course. Wonder when I shall get a chance to wear the red one. First time I have ever bought a fancy dress and waited for an occasion to wear it. Expect this will be a lesson to me. Refused to go down to bowl because I was going to review for the Agency final. Had coffee for dinner so it would keep me awake. Came upstairs after dinner, changed my office clothes for bathrobe and slippers, combed my hair and braided it, brushed my teeth, washed my face, and by the time I was ready to study the girls had finished bowling and came up to the room. When they finally did leave I was so tired I thought I would lie down for a minute, and fell asleep, in spite of the coffee. Jean woke me to take my bathrobe off, but I must go right back to bed. So sleepy! Poor Agency!

---

9   Garbo's *Inspiration* was a recreation of the Sappho story. She does not mention *Lady Chatterly's Lover*, which was published two years earlier but banned in the U.S. It was a time when authors and movies explored forbidden subjects.

Friday, January 30
Luncheon with Anna Clancy. Very pleasant. No depth to Anna. Agreeable, but much of her would be boring. Did quite a lot of work for Mr. Goodale. Find him quite disagreeable. No excuse for his surliness as there is for W.V.T. Walked to work in the morning. Had very little to eat all day. Lost some weight (now 120) but not enough. Dinner with little Alice Mays. Told me of her friends down from south. If all she told me is accurate she has an unusual memory. An unusual child in every way as might be expected from her bringing-up. Will be interesting to see how she develops.

Ruth Stockwell called. Wanted to see me over the week-end. Told her I had to study for the Agency final. Have done no reviewing for it yet and this weekend is my only opportunity. She is a fine, sweet girl, but beneath me intellectually so that it is not worth my while to give her too much of my time. Necessary selfishness.

Rode home with my homely boy-friend again. Still do not know his name. Do not care to, either.

Saturday, January 31
Snowing very hard. Bought a bunch of shoe trees. Have formed a good resolution (at C.C.F's suggestions, as most of mine are) to keep my shoes treed, Wonder how long that will last.

Did not feel top-notch. Could not seem to concentrate on Agency. If I were of that temperament would dread the exam. But have outgrown that. Am learning to drink coffee without sugar, at C.C.F's suggestion[10] – again. Marcia Rubinoff, in the room to break the sad news of her departure from the House to an apartment. She is thrilled – particularly at the chance to meet new men. Glad for her. Could not express regret I did not feel. A sweet child but inane.

Danced with Jean in Grandin Hall – minus hose. Even that seemed exciting in this drab existence. Mother Baldwin could not tell the difference anyhow. Had got a run in my stocking - the cause of my daring. Jean told me she saw Freddy York in a grand new car. Thought it would make me sorry I had broken off our acquaintance. Not so at all. He was too old and sophisticated for me. Fascinating when I first met him last winter, but it wore off.

Sunday, February 1
Drove home with Wallace Marden and Jean. Discussed advantages and hardships incident to working one's way through college, as he is doing. I maintained it was the preferable way because character - building. He agreed, but thought he would nonetheless like to have his way paid for him. Jean, of course, all for going to college leisurely - more time and energy for cultural pursuits.

Father gave Jean $100. for her tuition. I up and asked him for some money. He refused in the way which means "You may get it if you tease," but I had my new black dress and red shoes on and felt too uppity and independent to tease. Mother then offered me $10. which I knew she had taken from Louis. I absolutely refused it - not angry - pleasant but very dignified. She gave it to Jean, and Jean, having sense in place of my pride, took it. But I am not sorry. Mother knew she was being unfair in letting me work so hard and sending Jean

---
[10] Ms. C.C. Fuller was an important influence on Anne at this time.

to college, and thought to appease me <u>entirely</u> with that $10. I know they both felt badly when I left. Afraid I have outgrown them in many ways. They almost irk me when I go home. Hard-working, well-meaning, Mother extremely loving, but both uncultured.

Monthly Memoranda 1931

January
Received marks on three tests - 5, 4, and 3. Far better than my first set of marks. Due to a great extent, I believe, to Anita's absence from the House. She took a great deal of my time while she was here, and kept me up late so many nights I was too tired to think.
Only purchases during the month - 2 dresses. See no immediate prospects of a chance to wear my red dress and new red shoes. Mrs. Fuller suggested that next time I have a date I go to Coconut Grove or Lido Venice or someplace formal. My not going to such places is certainly not because I do not care to. She has the pleasantest notions. I only wish I could carry them all out. Have not been home all month. A shame. Unavoidable. Excusable, I think.
Girls who have left the House - Anita, Sunny, Peggy, Marcia, Ruth Munroe, Ruth McHugh - seems it will be my turn next. Job still as unsettled as ever. May go on indefinitely - may get through any day. Uncertainty almost worse than getting definitely discharged.
Altogether not a successful or eventful month in any way. Starting next month with an agency final. Hope to do well, but not doing much besides hoping. Also hope next month to have more <u>special</u> data.

February
Home one afternoon all month and did not miss it particularly. Because of the folks' unfairness on that occasion probably shall not go home again for some time to come. Have not received one letter from them all month. This breach is going to be, I feel, exceedingly difficult ever to patch up entirely. Have apparently lost Anita's friendship either thru her stupid prejudice or because she is too stubborn to call me because it was left last time that I would call her. Did so and left word with Miss Ball. Shall call her again, and will probably never hear from her again.
Felt so keenly last time I was with Ruth that she was simply not up to my par intellectually that I have not bothered to call her since. Nor has she called me. Would be interested to know why, but not enough to call to find out.
Lost Lloyd, about whom I do not care a hang, to Minnie, whom I had done a kindness by taking her on that date. Did hate to have them think they were putting something over on me, but they no longer do since I have seen them several times. Still greet Min the same friendly way, and she looks quite sheepish every time I do. Feel myself so far above both Min and Lloyd. Thrice-blessed vanity. Without it existence would be unbearable.
Job in a more peculiar position than ever. Do not know whether or not I will really have a job. Feel, however, that I can consider it practically gone. A short time more at best. Decidedly a losing month. Friendships, jobs, and what not. Do hope next month is a finding month. Feel that I somewhat deserve it.

1931

March

Rather a hectic month. Fired the first of the month but still on the job at the end. - Had a chance to say my say to the folks even though I accomplished nothing thereby. - Ruth and Anita back on my list of friends. - Acquired a new roommate. Not an extremely worthwhile acquisition in this case but probably a good experience. - Met some nice boys this month. Did not fall for any one of them, of course. Had some rather nice times too. - School quite hectic all month. Too many tests. Got too far behind. Pretty well caught up now. Do not expect ever to get caught up in conflict of Laws, however. Has been a rather tough year at school. Mrs. Fuller only encouraging person. Fonder of her than ever, but do wish she would not talk to me so much. Has given me some good points in these talks, however, so I ought not to kick. - Easter only a few days away. Have nothing for spring but a hat, and apparently no immediate prospects of anything else. Birthday only a few days away. Wonder if anyone will remember it. - All in all a good enough month. Do wish I were on better terms with the family but afraid I shall never feel the same towards them again. Do wish I had some notion as to what I shall be doing this summer.

April

Job still hanging on - much to my surprise. Only one date in a whole month - Larry - and he is nothing to write home about. How I have slipped.

Two finals off my mind - which is certainly something accomplished. Two nice week-ends, which helped a good deal. Mrs. Holm asked Dot to ask me to write. Ashamed that I had not thought of doing so, but will first chance now. Have called home on the telephone several times but have not seen any of the folks except Jean for quite some time now. Do not miss them so much as a dutiful daughter should. Wonder if I have become really estranged? Hope not, oh so sincerely, but afraid I have. A busy month, certainly, but not a very happy one. Not happy with my roommate. Bored with the girls. Tired of the monotony at the office. Worn out with plugging at my studies. Sulphur and molasses is what I need, I guess. So easily annoyed at everybody, even at myself, and when a person cannot get along even with herself, it is just too bad. Wonder if I feel so disgruntled because of being neglected by boy-friends. Hardly believe that is so, as there is not one I give a hang about. Think maybe some keen new clothes would help a good deal. Have been shopping industriously for some time now, but cannot find anything that suits both my taste and my pocketbook. Plenty of things that suit the former. Result of reading *Vogue* of course. Wonder if it is all for the best, but of course it is.

May

A very dark month just past and a difficult one coming.

Job on same status as it has been for some months. A break for me, I suppose. Only big event - changing my room. A change for the better certainly. Not one keen date the whole month. Thought the first time I met Gordon I was going to like him, but he turned out a worse bore than the rest of the bores. Do not believe he ever went to M.I.T. at all. The few other boys I know are all nice enough but so immature.

As for my numerous girl-friends, they have all either left the House, or are about to leave the House. Suppose I shall go home too. Not particularly looking forward to being in Lawrence, to commuting, to sleeping with Jean, etc. Oh dear! Shall I ever be satisfied with anyone or anything - with my friends or with my circumstances? Hate to be as I am, but cannot change my very nature. Everything I have, everything appertaining to me seems so dull and unattractive - and not even useful. -- Better snap out of that pronto.

June
A busy month but not a particularly happy one. Have seen quite a good deal of Ruth S., who tends to depress me. She is, or thinks she is, more unfortunate than any other girl. Is in some ways, but not in many others. So many unpleasant occurrences - hospital, job, etc.

Not happy at home and cannot be. And nothing particularly pleasant to offset the rest. And no prospect of anything pleasant. Shall probably have no vacation, much as I need one. The beau Alice Mays foretold when she read my palm is too long in presenting himself. Mae is a good pal and I like her better than ever, but she is not particularly interesting or exciting. A few of the girls have kept in touch with me. Many have not. They mean so little to me, and I, apparently, mean far less to most of them. I do so wish I could find something to fill this void which is so inexplicable, but yet which is making me so unhappy. I suppose it is due to the fact that I have become accustomed to being busy every evening - every minute.

July
8 piano lessons [written on top of page]
Quite a hectic month. Started with what seemed a large number of friends. Ended with a number far too small to be very flattering. Most the girls who left with such ardent protestations of everlasting friendship have apparently forgotten that any such place as Lawrence exists.[11] The few boy-friends I have met up with have almost without exception turned out to be awful flops. Most of the boys, of course, are here today and gone tomorrow. Many of the girls, however, I shall meet again in the fall. But it will be with an entirely different attitude on my part, I am sure. I shall regard them - and properly so, as mere acquaintances, and shall no longer break my neck in striving to please them.

This month is memorable also in that it marks the end of my job. The prospects for my immediate future are somewhat disagreeable - no sign of a new job - school coming - seemingly permanently established at Lawrence when I feel that I must be in Boston for the winter - and do not particularly anticipate living at the F.S.H. again. I guess some people never know when they are well off, and I am one of those people - but what can I do?

August
Only Boston friend who seems to stick

---

11   Anne moved home for the summer.

in spite of separation is Esther. Anita and Sunny write to me but not because of any fondness for me.

A busy month as for as dates are concerned - met Jimmy H. and still going with him, which is almost a record for me, though I am getting tired of him. Met quite a few people but no one in whom I am particularly interested. Disappointed to learn how small Mae could be, but I thereby discovered what a good sport Irene is.

No job and no sign of one, which is most discouraging. Getting hard up for clothing too. Went several places where I had never been before and where I could wear my long red dress, which was a help, as I was beginning to think I would never wear it out.

Slipping up on my piano lessons. Losing interest. Anything I do with my hands loses interest far sooner than anything that requires only mental exertion.

Next month is the deciding month as to whether or not I go back to school. It begins to look somewhat unlikely - no watch, no typewriter, and no job. So tired of worrying about money and what-not. Have come to the stage where someone decent with some money could tempt me to get married. Would even prefer that to be begging Father for money. -- but I know I'll change my mind when I get a job.

September
September was an eventful month that just flew by.

Landed what everyone but me considers a wonderful job. Started school again, after it seemed for so long I would not be able to do so. Met both Ernie and Lloyd again. Moved back to the F.S.H., to my same old room, with my same old roommate, and moved right out again into a single room, which sounds like an encore of last spring, except that it is much shorter. Rather a "good time" month, too particularly before I left for Boston. Already a way behind in my studies, which sounds so very familiar.

Broke one boy friend's heart - poor Bill. Renewed several friendships that had begun to lag - particularly Mrs. Fuller and Esther. Still going with Jimmy - almost unbelievable. Would have scoffed if anyone had predicted it. Surely cannot last much longer.

October
A busy month and, on the whole, a pretty good one. Met up with many of my old friends - Lloyd, Harry, Kermit, Anita, Sunny, etc., besides making several agreeable new acquaintances - Maurice, Gordon, Bernadette, Lillian, etc. Had some especially good times, too, due for the most part to Louis.

Job which seemed so terrible, working out fairly well, thanks to Mrs. Fuller. Hope she can stay in the office. She wants to as much as I want to have her.

Breaking away from Jimmy, Irene, and the rest of them for which I am just as glad. Nothing to gain from them except a few silly dates.

Finally got a watch, and a new brown outfit, both things I needed badly.

School worrying along as well as could be expected considering how little time I get to study. Will know better when we get the results of our tests.

November
A crazy sort of a month November was. Practically no "dates" worth talking about. Renewed my friendships with Anita, Kay and Sunny, but they are all such strange unsuited friendships.

A little more established at the office although it is a job of which no one can ever be sure. Did not accomplish nearly so much in the way of studying as I could have and should have and would have except for —. Thanksgiving was simply November 26. Still getting a thrill out of my checkbook when I have enough in the bank to be able to use it. Managed, thanks to Louis, to go a few places I had never been to. Think I should have gone "bugs" if not for him, as I am not and cannot be a grind even for a short period of time.

And I am not nearly convinced yet of my ability to handle a tough job and school too. Will take about a year to convince me.

December
Have made a few New Year's resolutions I hope I can keep.

Must try to plan and reason things out rather than let them slide and depend upon intuition to prompt me correctly.

Most now expect to receive only what I deserve, and not special consideration because of my youth.

Will not go out with boys just for the sake of going places and being able to impress the girls with my popularity. Am going only when I really wish to go, and if it is something or somebody worthwhile.

Am absolutely going to cut out telling little white lies, to which I realize I have a propensity, and exaggeration, not nearly so great a fault in me but still present.

Am going to steel myself to tell the girls they cannot sit and chat with me all evening when I have studying which must be done.

Am going to retire earlier and get up earlier. Getting up late and hurrying to get dressed, gobbling an inadequate breakfast and dashing off to work is not a wise way to start the day. Am going to study more faithfully than I ever have.

Year End Summary 1931

1931 has been a strange and a rather eventful year. Worked so hard until June, played so hard all summer, then in the fall came back to work harder than ever. A stupid year as far as friends go. This year saw a change in jobs, hope next year sees another one at its very beginning.

Have changed more I believe than in any other one year. Grew more sedate, more fastidious, more desirous of nice things, more intolerant of stupidity - not egotistic I hope. Am determined not be just Mr. Somebody's stenographer or Mr. Somebody's wife. Hope my ambitions do not end by making me an object of ridicule - but I must have more faith in myself.

I am thankful I have one real friend, Mrs. Fuller, and she is worth a dozen others.

Have much indeed for which to be grateful - family, home, health, job, etc. Appreciate such things as my raccoon, watch, diamond, typewriter, etc. too.

Have at least managed to keep a diary a whole

year after several unsuccessful attempts. Suppose that is something of which to be proud too.

Anne early 1930's. Above with her father. Below reading.

1932

The second year of her diary, 1932, the United States was in the Great Depression. It was the year that Franklin Roosevelt was elected President for his first term. In spite of these national events, Anne's life was focused on law school, her job, friends, and the on-going conflict between her mother and father. She left her hometown of Lawrence, Massachusetts for the urbanity of Boston. She even makes reference for the first time to the possibilities that Washington offers. November was chosen as the sample month because it was an important time in the year for her. -- RDH

Tuesday, November 1
Took the first day of my vacation today because I just had to do some studying. Decided most convenient way to take my vacation, for both me and the office, was a day at a time. Poured furiously all day, in spite of which I went to the library, and almost got washed away.
Got quite a few old notes typed out much to my relief. Reviewed Constitutional Law a little, but not nearly as much as I should have liked.
Const. Law test surprised me, and all of us, by being comparatively very easy. My worrying had been in vain, as it so often is. Mrs. Niam and I had plenty of time to talk it over before Sidney got out, and it looks like we both hit it right. Hope we get our marks pretty soon – being seniors, we ought to get a little better service than usual.

Wednesday, November 2
Worked for Mr. Walker today. He is not so bad when one gets accustomed to him. Guess he decided the same thing in regard to my stenographic ability as he did over none of my letter today. Flatter myself I could get the job of being his secretary if I were not handicapped with the necessity for dashing off quite promptly to get to school.
Mother arrived soon after we got home from work. Nettie and Gertrude drove her in this morning. Spent the day at Fannie's in Cambridge, and at Harvard with Harold, who is very well. I took her out for supper. She would order coffee which I knew would keep her awake. When we came back, went down to Jean's room and gossiped far, far into the night. Jena [i.e. Anne's sister Jean] manicured Mother's nails. I tried to get a hairdresser but they were to be all out, of course.

Thursday, November 3
Up even earlier than usual even though I was taking a half day off. Had Bertha Bernard shampoo and wave Mother's hair. She had to go to work so I attended to the drying. By the time I got her all slicked up and myself dressed, Mrs. Mann arrived and I went to work. Mother spent the afternoon at the Statter, went to Mrs. Mann's house for supper, then came to school with her. Spalding a good scout and did not call on me.
I decided it was too late after school for Mother to go home, so Mrs. Mann rode us both to the house. Jean was out when we arrived, so we had to wait for her. Both of us frightfully tired. I read a few cases, Mother so tired she fell asleep. When Jean came and carried her off, I was glad enough to leap into bed.

Friday, November 4
Lovely weather, but all the girls are wearing their fur coats, and have been for some time now, so I was persuaded against my better judgment to get mine out.
Short lunch hour because of a rush. It is days like this that convince me that it is going to be necessary to get a leave of absence from the office for the last half of the year.
Mother left this morning right after breakfast, happy, had a wonderful time, which compensated me for that all-tired-out feeling. Several of the boys at school commented on how young Mother looks – some refusing to believe she was my Mother. Must tell her that. Mrs. Mann told me a little of yesterday's gossip, the gist of which was that everyone liked Mother. 2000 at the luncheon.

Saturday, November 5
O'Dunne in a friendly mood again. (I had forgotten to wear my Republican pin) and even went so far as to offer me a ticket to the game, which I of course refused.
Lunched with Sylvia and her girl friend. Shopped most of the afternoon without good results. Lovely warm afternoon, of course, now that I have my fur coat out. Met Mary Krools, who invited me out for a weekend. Looks very well. Laura's sister Jeanne living here, looking for a job.
Studied in the evening. Unusually tired and mopey – blamed it onto the unseasonable warmth, and went to bed.

1932

Sunday, November 6
Weather still mild.
Started out determined to clean up all my old lectures, and my typewriter got finicky. Helen and Louis called to ask me to go to a concert but I refused. Went to the library after supper with Jean, and met them there. When they left, some of the boys came over to talk to us. Did not accomplish much, but had some fun. When we got back, Lillian Wager was playing the piano and we stopped to listen. She plays beautifully.

Monday, November 7
Rain and more of it. Everyone talking politics. Everyone under a little extra nervous tension, and wishing it were all over with.
Party after school for the girls to meet Judge Emma Fall Schofield,[12] who is to be the Women's Advisor at Northeastern. She made a charming address and seems genuinely enthused about the idea, from the standpoint of helping the girls, and not just because it is her job. Played some silly childish games to help some of the newer girls get acquainted. The refreshments tasted good after a very dry elongated speech by Dean Churchill. Mrs. Mann did not come to the party – pleaded a headache – but one of the girls walked part way home with me, and then I met Doris Farley with a couple of friends, so had company the rest of the day. Bed after 12:00.

Tuesday, November 8
Got up especially early. Went to the polls with Dottie Peel right after breakfast. I had the honor of casting the first ballot in that Precinct, and it went in with a big X for Hoover, and another one for Ely. The rest I voted Republican, except for Alonzo Cook. Another miserable drizzly morning. Another day with everyone on tenterhooks, guessing and re-guessing how the election will come out. Everyone more interested in the elections than in Const. Law even Dorman, I bet.
Several of the girls had invited me up to get the returns over the radio but I was too tired to stay awake long enough. Got the latest returns, which were not at all encouraging for poor, unappreciated Hoover. If Roosevelt gets it, it will certainly be because he is a Democrat, and not at all because he is the superior man.[13]

Wednesday, November 9
Election returns mostly disheartening. Not only did Roosevelt get it, but he got in by a tremendous margin. Ely got in for which I am glad. Tech. night.
The girls asked me to go but I could not be bothered. Al and some of the other girls came up in their evening clothes so I could pass judgment. Phone rang about 9:15. Undressed-studying.
Gentlemen caller. Slipped on a dress and shoes. It was Winthrop Conant, the nice boy I met at Anita's last year, who could

12   Judge Emma Fall Schofield was the first woman judge in Massachusetts, and in the Fall semester of 1932 she began as the Women's Advisor in the Northeastern Law School. She had been teaching at Portia Law School in Boston since 1913 where she offered classes in deeds, mortgages and easements, and examination of land titles.

13   Although the 1932 election was intensely fought because of the Depression, Anne paid little attention to it or to politics in general, a situation that changed with professional maturity and life in Washington. Her conservative politic views gradually evolved over the next decade.

not get a word in for that fool Buster. I told him last Spring I would go to the Tech. concert because he plays the cello with them. I forgot all about it but he didn't. Jean came up and helped me dress. Wore the gown Helen lent me – black taffeta with sequins and numerous ruffles, long white ear-rings. Looked pretty nice, for me. The girls all amazed at my 11th hour appearance. Winthrop is good looking, good dancer, and can wear a tux, so all in all I had a very good time even though I was so tired.

Thursday, November 10
Naturally I told the girls at the office about my little social splash of last night.
Charlie Wyzanski[14] back, and it seems nice to have him back even though it will make so little difference to me.
Most everyone in the office still down in the mouth because of the election, although most of the faithful Republicans expected it. The Democrats, of course disgustingly triumphant. Got an awful riding in school tonight for having backed Hoover, but I certainly would not backwater. Expected Mary Waits to be heartbroken but she was not even the least bit depressed. Wonder if Hoover minded it all as much as I did. Do not suppose I could comprehend his feelings at being so hopelessly rejected after faithful service. But people as a mass are such fools, and they are not yet educated to the point of being able competently to navigate a democracy.

---

14   This is the first reference to Wyzanski who will be in her life for much of the decade. In August 1933 he offered her a job in his office and the new Roosevelt administration in Washington.

Friday, November 11
Holiday, so I could have slept late, but was up at my usual time from silly habit. A beautiful day, but I was too lazy to go see the parade, or shopping, or anything but just being around.
Ronnie stopped in to see Jean on his way to N.Y. for his birthday weekend. She had bought tickets for tomorrow night to take him to the theater to hear Grace Moore, so asked me instead.
About 9:30 Jean and I took a walk to the Opera House because she wanted to get tickets for something next week. Ticket box closed. Of course, when we get there. Stopped at Old France for a bite to eat and a smoke. Got in after 11:30, tired but feeling much better for the walk. Look ahead for weeks to a holiday, and then accomplished nothing.

Saturday, November 12
The men getting back to work now after the election excitement. Lunched with Sylvia. Back to the office to study, but could not concentrate worth a cent. Started for home, but could not resist the shops. Clara at home with Jean,[15] when I finally arrived. Knew we could not get one ticket for the theater next to the two we had, so insisted Clara go in my stead, to her great delight. Jean wore my raccoon [i.e. coat], to her great delight. Asked Alberta Thompson to go to the library with me, for the walk and something to do, to her great delight. After which the inevitable Old France, and home, to my great delight.

---

15   Jean and Clara, Anne's two sisters.

Sunday, November 13
Clara much enthused about the show. Had my hair shampooed and waved by Bertha Bernard, who did a real good job. Took most of the morning. Clara left for home after dinner.
Jean going to a concert with Alice Healy so asked to wear the raccoon again as it was growing quite cold.
Could not seem to get down to doing anything at home, so went to the library again, Alberta tagging along. After we returned, she insisted on a session with my whiteheads. To bed late again.

Monday, November 14
Started the week off tired. Getting warm again. A swell break for Jean, but tough on the raccoon. Mrs. Hoole not feeling well. Not at work – staying out with her sister. Sincerely hope it is nothing serious.
Work is decidedly pepping up again.
Received my bill from school for tuition - $40 – which is going to make a considerable hole in my savings.[16]
A rather interesting lecture in Common Law Pleading – as such lectures go. Test in the subject next Monday. Allen told us he would confine it to the subject of Demurrers – something which only Allen would be good scout enough to do. The school certainly got a swell break when they got him. He seems a most genuine man.

Tuesday, November 15
Very busy at the office. Mrs. Robinson had some difficulty getting a stenographer who was also a notary to take some depositions. Decided it was high time I was appointed, and called Jean to ask her to get the blanks for me, which she did. Lunched with Mrs. Fuller. When I got home from school, some of my neighbors were lying in wait in the corridor. A few of them had received prior notice that we all must move. The House is economizing by closing certain floors, ours being one. Some of the girls have been in their rooms for years and have accumulated so many things it is really a task to move. I find it a bother to move my few books and clothes, but they have radios, sewing machines, easy-chairs, etc. I left the gang out there bellyaching and went to bed.

Wednesday, November 16
Very busy at the office. I worked most of the day on a memorandum of Mr. Dunne on the Blue Sky Act, covering decisions in all the States. All the men busy, making up for the little time they lost during the election excitement. Too busy to even ask anyone to sign my petition. Received official notice that I must move. Got a much better room at the same rate – outside room on Newton St. on the 900 floor – certainly an improvement on a court room on the 700 floor.
Danced after supper with Jean and some of the other girls, including Lilian Vager, who danced unexpectedly well considering her lameness. Went up to study, but Alice Mays came to see me – helping me move Sat. Gave her some candy and got rid of her. Would have gone to the library but it was pouring. Alberta called – decided I must have a facial. Jean came down to watch – and this went the rest of the evening.

---
16   The tuition for one semester.

Thursday, November 17

B. Loving Young signed my petition as a Selectman. Mr. Foley and Mr. Wyzanski[17] then signed, completing the required signatures – the other signatures were Albert Boyden, Prof. Dorman and Judge Kaplan, who paid me the compliment of recognizing me. Am going to have Jean take the petition up and save me the trip.

Spalding feeling rather witty, so the Evidence Class was rather amusing, which helped keep me awake.

Mrs. Mann looking very tired – more from her social life than work or study. She certainly has an amazing abundance of pep and energy for a woman of her age.

Mrs. Little is obviously going to have a baby. Do hope that does not mean I will get Foley. Someone has to be the goat.

Friday, November 18

The finger I jammed is finally beginning to look like a finger again. Have the bandage off, but it still looks and feels somewhat sore. Imagine if Nan Hill had not taken care of it, it might have been permanently marked because it was a pretty bad gash.

A dry enough lecture in Conflict of Laws. The old story of sitting in a stuffy room for an hour, the windows thrown wide open for air, and then every one of them closed tightly again for the second hour. Result – a cold. Treated myself to the luxury of going to bed early, but Alberta came up and, even though I was already in bed, would come in and talk to me. She was feeling blue and neglected – no dates and complained away until after twelve.

Saturday, November 19

Went back to the office after luncheon to study, but Mrs. Robinson was hanging around, and rather disconcerted with me. Shopped a while, but it started to rain so I beat it for home. Moved my room after dinner. Alice Mays helped me. Jean and Alberta <u>watched us</u>. Gave Alice some soap and took her out to eat. Jean came along with us.

Went to bed as soon as we got back, hoping against hope the noise of the Els would not bother me.

Sunday, November 20

Horrible cold as a result of Friday night. Head so woozy I could not study worth a cent. Ruth Munns called but I stalled her off. Clara in all afternoon. She went to a lecture in the evening with Jean. Alberta heard I was going to the library and invited herself along. Stalled so much we got there just before closing time. Old France on the way back. Up to Al's room for a manicure. Read the Sunday papers. Ruth and Eloise dropped in, etc., etc.

Monday, November 21

Took the day off from work to study for the test, but my cold was much worse and I simply could not concentrate on C.L.P. Went to the N.U. Library[18] in the morning, but was so uncomfortable I had to leave.

Called Clara[19] at school. Took her to luncheon at the Steuben, a new German restaurant on Huntington Avenue. Enjoyed the luncheon and getting away from the sight of books. Clara came to the library with me, and we gabbed until she had to leave to get her train.

---

17 Probably Charles Wyzanski, Sr, the father of the man with whom she will work later.

18 Northeastern University Library.
19 Anne's sister Clara.

Then I made one more valiant attempt to study, but it was no use.

Test turned out to be quite easy and I think I hit it all right. Involved only memory work, fortunately for me, because I was certainly in no state to figure anything out.

Mrs. Mann most solicitous – gave me plenty of advice.

Tuesday, November 22
Back to work looking like the end of a hard winter. Mrs. Little getting bigger every day. Ought to be leaving soon now. How I hope I do not get Foley wished onto me.

Chap in the office selling coupons for beauty parlor work – a stack of them for 50 cents. I bought some, as most of the girls did. At least if I am getting roped in, they cannot ride me. Had promised Mrs. Mann a copy of the last Conflicts lecture. Decided I ought to do it tonight so she could have it to work on before Friday. My typewriter does not like to make carbons, and kicked up much worse fuss than usual. I was determined to do it and labored over it a good couple of hours, but the typewriter won out, and I went to bed, feeling very much like a worn out, abused and futile person, anyhow.

Wednesday, November 23
If I determine to do a thing a certain way, if I cannot do it that way, I do it another way, but I do it. Got to the office shortly after 8:00, and had the Conflicts lecture all typed before the rest of the office got in and waked up. Used my coupons, and got the best looking wave I have had yet – eyebrows done, too, and a shampoo – all for 50 cents. The best bargain I ever got. Everyone keen about the wave.

Had a splitting headache all day. By the time I hit the Evidence class I was up in the air. Everyone telling me how nice I looked helped considerably. By hint of sheer will power and concentrating on Evidence, I finally managed to forget the headache. Guess the terrific pre-holiday bash in the office was too much for me – I must be slipping.

Thursday, November 24
Thanksgiving. Started out cloudy but turned out a beautiful sunny day. Had a fine turkey dinner at the House – plenty of everything. Danced a while after dinner with some of the girls. Kay Pittfield came over and stayed all afternoon. As dippy as ever. Mary Krook going south for the winter. Her sister appointed to a hospital in N.Y. Those kids certainly do get around places. Went to the Thanksgiving party. The usual type of entertainment – somewhat amusing. Disappointed in Grace Williams but then I realize that she was very tired. Almost no one stayed for the dancing. Needed a more exciting place, I suppose, as an outlet for their holiday spirits. Most of the school girls, of course, are home.

Friday, November 25
November is turning out a beautiful month after all the rain we had.

Everyone in the office talking food until the thought of turkey made me shudder. Just completed a long-drawn-out job for Monty and got another one from Hoag. Do not like them because if I stick to them, everyone else thinks I am not doing any work, and if I intersperse them with shorter jobs, they drag on interminably.

What a grand and glorious feeling – and how unusual to be almost up to date in conflicts for a change. In spite of which, I nearly went to sleep during the lecture, as did a number of other students. The atmosphere was almost unbearably humid and Serthuck was not too wide awake himself.

Saturday, November 26
Finally bought a dress in Jackson – a green one at that. Went back to the office to study. Several girls working, but none too busy to stop and chat with me. When I got home Mother and Clara were there. Jean had gone to Lawrence,[20] but got back in time for supper. Clara left my laundry on the train Monday, which, after the umbrella episode, I consider quite inexcusable. I got hell once for losing 95 cents; and never lost much of anything since. But she is sensitive and must not be scolded.

Sunday, November 27
Very cold indeed.
Mother and Clara stayed overnight. We all went out for breakfast together. They left before dinner, thoroughly disgusted, Jean told me, with my harshness towards Clara. Did not come up to say goodbye to me or to get my laundry.
Took myself to the library after supper. Felt considerably better after the walk in the cold air. Expect I shall soon get over being at all sensitive.

Monday, November 28
Beginning to warm up a little after an extremely cold weekend.
Dashed uptown during my noon hour to get the dress I had left to be taken in at the waist. The seamstress did a most satisfactory job.
Both Mr. Dally and Mr. Coleman have tried their hands at Mr. Miller in regard to Mrs. Mays' brief case. It remained that she could have the case when ever she wanted it, but no other satisfaction. Guess I shall have to go down to see him. Last lecture in Common Law Pleading, which means looking for a final soon. Mary Waite absent, which means making a carbon copy of my notes, which means doing them at the office because my portable does not make good carbon copies. Hope I can get time off to study for finals.

Tuesday, November 29
Went down to see Mr. Miller during my noon hour. After a few minutes of pleasant chatting about the affair, he voluntarily offered to return the bag and refund $2 with it. He was mighty decent about it.
Mrs. Mann told me at school she had heard Lillian Wager was ill. We stopped in to see her after school. Far worse than we dreaded. She was out of her mind as a result of a bad nervous breakdown. Her father here from New York, who insisted on taking her home in spite of her doctor's orders that she be immediately placed in a hospital here in Boston. Two boys from Harvard who had known her at Cornell, Carl Freeman and

---

20   Lawrence, Mass. Anne's hometown.

Jerry Blumberg, were being very kind. Had taken her riding all afternoon, and were trying their level best to make the most comfortable arrangements possible.

Wednesday, November 30
Did not sleep a wink all last night, continuously sifting over in my mind the things I might have done to help Lillian avoid her terrible breakdown.
Lillian Wernick stayed in with Jean last night. Came downtown with us this morning. Typically Lawrencian[21] - nothing much to talk about except who is married and who is not married.
Took myself to the library after super and enjoyed the walk alone, and accomplished far more than I do when accompanied by one of the girls. Fussed around doing odd jobs in my room, trying to tire myself out so I would be able to sleep tonight. I have not had a spell of sleeplessness now for quite a while and can ill afford it at this time.

Monthly Memoranda 1932

January
Not an especially happy month. Sick more than I usually am in several months.
Successful enough as far as marks at school go - but how I dread the finals.
Eventful as far as the job is concerned what with taking over the Bank etc, and meeting so many new worth-while people.
Except for Anita and Davison, a total lack of anything social except what goes on at the House. If I did not lunch with Mrs. Fuller as often as I do I should probably forget how to do anything but work and study. One of the things I least want to be is a grind.
Got more clothes and doo-dads than I ordinarily do in one month, which helped keep me mentally balanced. Refused so many times to go to the theater with Louis he has stopped asking me.
I do so sincerely hope and pray by next month I shall have a new job - one where people treat each other with respect. When my employers will realize I am a human being and not a typewriting machine. After W.V.T.'s meanness and F.C.D.'s bullying, I guess the smallest kindness in an employer would overwhelm me.

February
This has certainly been an eventful month, with a happy ending. I am so happy in my present position as contrasted with my former one I am almost afraid to think of it, afraid I shall waken. Have met a few people I found rather interesting, but could not cultivate their friendship because of lack of time.
Have become far more intimate with Violet than I would have believed possible. Have become far more appearance conscious than I ever was, use more cosmetics - even including rouge - and would have many more dresses if I could find them to suit me at a somewhat reasonable cost.
So enthused about my work, boyfriends and dates have, for the time being at least, lost all interest. Suppose that is a good thing

---

21   Anne's hometown Lawrence, Massachusetts.

while my time is so occupied. School has gone along well enough so far although I do feel they are crowding so far too much for Property - no reviews to speak of, no chance to study up, and beginning Property III two weeks before the final in Property II.

March
A very busy but rather uneventful month. Left F.C.D. partly because there was too much work, and went right in where I do about ten times as much, yet because I like the work and like the people I do not mind it at all.
Jean has moved in but I see so little of her it really makes no difference. Greatly relieved to think of two finals being out of the way, although I am afraid I flubbed the second one. Got rather tough breaks on both in regard to the busy day preceding the exam. But I prefer that to not having this job. The heart-rending tragedy of the month - the loss of the Lindbergh baby, still reasons unsolved. I would give a great deal to get my licks in at the kidnappers if and when apprehended. Have not been home since Christmas - the longest interval as yet, I am afraid. My intentions are good, but I just do not seem able to swing it. And as long as the folks come in to see me, there is no particular incentive for me to go home.

April
Not a particularly happy month even though it was my birthday month. Did have some nice times - more family affairs than usual, for which I am glad.
My experience with Mr. Foley was not very pleasant, although it ended happily enough. More girls out of work lately than ever.
My only week-end at home extremely disagreeable.
Had a nasty cold.
Have a very sore foot.
Worried about my Mortgages final, if I stop to think of it at all. Eyes and ears worse than usual.
No clothes for the summer worth mentioning. Tired of school.
Not especially happy about the prospects at home in the midst of all the wrangling, knowing it is too old a story for me to be able to help it.
Enough of woes - hope they are ended for a while.

May
May has certainly been a busy month - in every respect - especially at the office. My job is so far, so good, but the future does not look too promising. Afraid my handicaps of being a female and lacking ancestors who arrived on the Mayflower will prove insurmountable.[22]
Affairs at home more disagreeable than ever, and it now seems clear enough they will never be remedied. Mother complains incessantly, Father hangs onto every nickel as though it were a year of his life, Louis is a lazy ne'er-do-well, in love with every girl who will look at him, and Clara wants to go to college if someone will "send" her. And yet I feel obliged to go home. "Morning Becomes

---

22 She was well aware of the problems of misogyny and anti-Semitism.

Electra"[23] could not teach me anything - merely proved to me the Freelings [i.e. her family] were not unique. Comparatively speaking, a busy month socially.

Decidedly a busy month at school - ending up with the grand climax of the Trusts final - and a head cold.

June
A "regular" June. The hectic finis of school, the silly relapse, the inevitable "seemingly perpetual" desire to sleep.

Turned out a social flop with the emphasis on the "flop". Not a respectable date for eons and worst of all, not a single eligible boyfriend in town. Strangely enough, down in my heart I do not care. Tired of my old dance-hall shieks [sic]. Think I am old and staid enough to prefer an intellectual chap, but a grind tortures me.

The most encouraging feature of the month is the progress I have made on the job. Several of the men really consider me ahead of the other girls, and even Mrs. Robinson is growing to like me, all of which means so much more than any silly date.

July
I have finally succeeded in getting past Mrs. Robinson's crust a little with the result that I am on the 10th floor for a little while anyhow. Mrs. Fuller and I are drifting ever farther apart. I am sorry, but suppose it is inevitable. She predicted it towards the end of the Taylor régime but I refused then to acknowledge the inevitability of it.

Have been home long enough to be glad the end is approaching but have not had enough vacation to be glad the opening of school is also approaching - and still no marks.

It seems to be true that the year ends, and proceeds, as it began, for I had a dull New Year's.

August
A fairly good month. Coming along well at the office.

Marks from school more than satisfactory.

A little more social life. Did not meet anyone I cared to see again, but had some fun.

Affairs at home rottener than ever but I have long given up any thought of changing the situation and so am resigned to tolerate it until I can get out.

The visits from Washington broke the monotony. Phil's enthusiasm, whether assumed or real, for my legal ability raised my valuation of myself, which I think I can stand. Hope it brings results.

September
September was a good month. Enjoyable Labor Day week-end. Did the right thing for once when I visited Mrs. Robinson as she has been markedly more friendly ever since. Got moved back, from which distance I get along far better with my family.

Cannot tell as yet what this year at school will be like except that it will not be any cinch.

Things at the office looking very auspicious if I can only keep un-assigned.

---
23 Eugene O'Neill's play about a dysfunctional New England family, published 1931.

Met a few boys through Jean - all uninteresting. Realize more than ever what an asset Mrs. Mann[24] is going to be, both socially and in a business way.

Fall is very decidedly here and I have had no vacation yet, but think I am going to be glad in the long run I arranged it as I did.

October
October was rather a smooth uneventful month. Most outstanding affair, of course, the progress of my friendship with Mrs. Mann. Like and admire her far more than any other friend I have, if I have any others. Glad to have three tests out of the way, even though I do not yet know the results.

A number of reunions with former girl-friends, none of them at all interesting to me, except Anita. A few agreeable social affairs, thanks to Mrs. Mann, and once to Sylvia Wilson's persistence.

Job progressing fairly well, although I really am entitled to a raise.

The fact that the office people know I am Jewish is some relief. However I may look, act and think differently from most Jews, in the last analysis I am nothing other than Jewish.

November
November always seems to me rather a dreary month in spite of Thanksgiving.

Started off all wrong with the foolish election.

Ended up all wrong with poor Lillian's breakdown.

Thoroughly disgusted with the House because of the low-down way Miss Jeannette[25] acted toward Lillian and her father - which does not tend to make me at all happier.

Disgusted with school in that, after so many tests, we have not received a single mark yet. Everything at the office about the same as usual, except that I am beginning to feel like one of the older girls now.

A few little social flings, which helped break the stupid old monotony of work and study and study and work.

December
It seems about the most outstanding lesson I have learned this year - and I learned it at the very end of the year - is that it is essential to be selfish to attain any success in the business world. One does not get very far, I am afraid, by plugging conscientiously - by giving extra time and energy, etc. In addition to all that, it is necessary to know how to handle the people who matter, to realize certain things please them, and to do those things even though you would not do them otherwise - so long as they are not wrongful. It is not always merit - or merit alone - that is rewarded on this earth.

Mr. Taylor was professedly displeased at my studying law while working for him. I have lost out on two good jobs since then, which I probably would have retained had it not been for school. I have received absolutely no real encouragement since I began this course. A few people have told me I was doing a splendid and difficult thing, all of which amounts to nothing to my material

---

24   Gertrude C. Mann

25   Anne's sister Jean.

mind. Having given up so much time, money, health, good times, material success (of a kind). - I do so hope I will be glad when it is all done, but I cannot help doubting it.

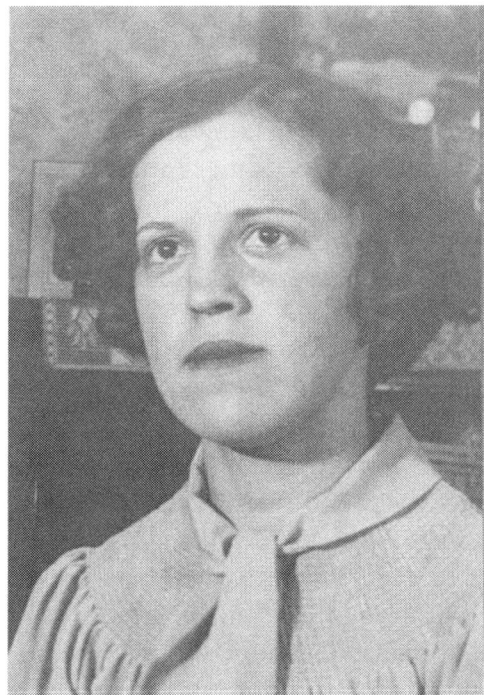

1933

This was an important year for Anne. She graduated from Law School in the spring, and by August she had a regular job as the secretary to Charles E. Wyzanski, Jr., the Solicitor of Labor in Washington. She was unable to obtain a position as a lawyer, and she would be a secretary for the next four years before getting a professional position. Anti-Semitism and misogyny affected not only Anne Freeling, but most of the society during this time period.   -- RDH

Tuesday, August 1

Alice Chakohsky, secretary to Mr. Wyzanski Sr., called in the morning. Charlie had called for her from Washington and told her to get in touch with me in regard to a vacancy in his dept. She told me to call him. He said he would try his best to get me the position, but I would have to help by getting letters from Congressmen, etc. I was almost stunned with surprise, but got into action immediately.[26]

Wrote Mrs. Fuller.

Jerry came with me and introduced me to State Rep. Meeham and State Senator Warren. They were both kind and consented readily to write letters for me. They suggested any number of other prominent local men who would write letters for me, but I do not believe they would count for much in this particular case. Jerry

---

26   After being unemployed for several months and seeing few prospects in Boston, this suggestion of a job in the Department of Labor in Washington was a stunning breakthrough. She would work in the office of the Solicitor of Labor, Charles E. Wyzanski, Jr.

and I caught in the pouring rain coming home, but we were too elated to care.

Wednesday, August, 2
Exceedingly warm. Went downtown with Father about 9:00 am to get letters to U.S. Cong. Connery, but was advised to go to Lynn and see him personally. Got letters from Collins to Connery and, while I was about it, to Sullivan, one of the Bar Examiners. Father took Moe, Clara and me to Lynn. Connery's brother promised he would see that the letter was written. Sullivan said if I were to be called for the orals, he would see I got called in a few days as, if I get the appointment. I must be in Wash., the 10th.

Called on some of Father's relatives. Took them for a ride along the shore. Then drove to Ludwig's Camp at Big Island in Salem, N.H. Ludwig claims to be a friend of the Roosevelts, to have treated them as the family doctor, and that they will do anything for them. He suggested my writing to Louis Howe, the President's secretary, to Wyzanski, and phoning the latter to explain who he was etc., etc. All in his illustrious name. I sized him up as a glorified windbag. We all went for a refreshing swim. Home about 10:30, pretty tired.

Thursday, August, 3
Mrs. Fuller called in the morning. Thought I ought to come to Boston to see some men. Father said he would take me in. Jerry and Clara came along. Saw Mr. Garcelon, who was kind but ineffectual; had big chat with Alice Chakofsky, and was much surprised to learn that I was a constant subject of discussion in the Wyzanski tribe, saw Fred Davis, who was very cordial, turned me over to Mr. MacCormack, who gave me a letter to Mr. O'Connell, Sen. Coolidge's secretary, who lives in Fitchburg. My time too limited to do much with it, but I'll send it along with my own letter anyhow. Called on a number of the other people, but everyone was away on vacation. Called on Dermaine last. He agreed to write a letter for me, and his cordiality towards me, as well as the show of friendliness of everyone else in the office, was the crowning surprise of this whole series of surprises. Now if I can only get this appointment, and if, please God, I can pass the bar, I think I would be sitting pretty pretty.

Friday, August, 4
It certainly felt good just to loll around all day. Note from Wyzanski reminding me that without a letter from Connery he could not present my name. Letter from Mrs. Fuller suggesting certain people I ought to see in Boston, apparently written and mailed just before she phoned me to come in. Had the time, so helped Mother with dinner, whereupon it turned out to be quite a grand repast. Jerry was over for dinner, which made quite a crowd- quite a dinner party. We even borrowed Lynch's freezer and made ice cream. Esther Pinsky called and invited herself and her sister Bessie over. There ensued the usual gab fest. Moe, of course, got considerable attention from the man-hungry Pinsky's. I certainly

have very few friends round abouts whom I would miss or who would miss me were I to leave.

Saturday, August, 5
Called Connery yesterday. Spoke to Cong. Himself, who knew nothing about the matter. Jean called today, and spoke to the wife, who knew nothing about the matter. No word at all from the Bar Examiners, which is highly annoying. Anna Goldblatt over in the evening. She was, as she can sometimes be, most amusing. Would like to spend her vacation in Washington if I am to be there, but we necessarily had to leave plans dangling since my plans are so maddeningly uncertain.

Sunday, August 6
Moe left about 2:30. Taking the 5:00 boat to N.Y. Seemed sorry to leave but felt he ought to get back to work with so much doing on account of the N.R.A. Jerry came over in the afternoon and I wrote some letters for him. He had bought land in No. Andover and is going to start building tomorrow. We all just laid around all evening, rather missing Moe. He was a delightful, easy-to-entertain guest.

Monday, August 7
No mail for me, to my intense disappointment. Mother and I had planned to go to Boston to shop. Promised to meet Jean for luncheon. She took so long to dress we had only a few minutes to get our train, when she announced that she had to go downtown to draw out some money. That was the last straw and I simply refused to go at all. I had asked Mr. Lynch to contact Connery for me. Was thinking of phoning Connery when Lynch came in with a letter from him acknowledging Lynch's request and stating that he had already written to Wyzanski on my behalf. At least that much is off my mind. Everyone in the house seems somewhat depressed and tense, waiting for me to hear from Wyzanski. They consider this job far more worthwhile than passing the bar. I am somewhat inclined to favor the latter. Wish Sullivan would get in touch with me and at least end my anxiety. Suppose I am wanting too much in hoping for both the job and passing the bar.

Tuesday, August 8
Dollar day. Went shopping in the morning. I got two dresses and Clara got one, besides a few other little things. When we got home there was a message for me to get in touch with Wyzanski. Seems Connery does not fit with the Administration, so I must get Farley's ok through Connery. The latter was out of town until Thursday afternoon but his secretary assured me the letter would be sent promptly upon his return. Mrs. Mann and Charlotte meanwhile had dropped in quite unexpectedly and visited all afternoon. They both looked charming, and we enjoyed their visit. They made me promise to come down Saturday for at least the day.
Letter from Sen. Coolidge's secretary trying to be helpful but not at all what I want.
Billy has apparently for some reason decided to stop writing. Maybe he did not like my last letter. Whatever the reason, it is no great loss for either one of us.

Anne Schlezinger

Wednesday, August 9
Went downtown with Mother. Got one of my new dresses which I had left for alterations. Mother got a snappy little brown hat.
Re-read *Cyrano de Bergerac*. I still get a lump in my throat when I get to his heroic but tragic death. His pretty cousin did not deserve his love. Our back yard view is lovelier than ever these days – the river and the valley bathed in sunshine while the hill tops are bathed in a delicate autumnal mist. No mail deliveries Wednesday afternoons, not Tuesday and Saturday afternoons – in order to balance the budget. That eliminates a considerable portion of my favorite occupation – waiting for the mail.
Mr. Sullivan apparently does not intend to keep his promise. I cannot conceive of any other reason than that it is intentional. I hope I am wrong and that he will surprise me any day now – with favorable news. I hope, I hope.

Thursday, August 10
Downtown to get me more clothes. I got nothing but Mother got a good-looking brown dress touched up with orange – most becoming to her. Called Collins to ask his advice about calling Sullivan. He told me the Bloom boy had already been called, but advised strongly against bothering Sullivan again. Called Father and asked him to ask Collins, as though at Father's own suggestion, to call Sullivan. Collins refused and insisted if Sullivan did not communicate with me it was because I had flunked out. But Sullivan promised to let me know either way. I disregarded Collins' advice and wrote to Sullivan, very courteously reminding him of his promise. The least he can do now is answer me. And if, as I myself believe, I have flunked it, I have nothing to lose and will at least gain the ease of certainty. Jerry over all day.

Friday, August 11
Blew myself to a shampoo and fingerwand at the Pink Powder Puff. The girl is a fool but knows her work. Mother and Clara met me there and we went for Mother's dress, which had been left for alterations. Got a ride home with Anna Goldblath, whose vacations had been postponed a few weeks so she still has hopes of visiting me in Washington.
Met Jerry's two sisters. Mother introduced me to them. Typical French mill workers. Have not Jerry's personality and intelligence. Told me of some of their employers' abuses, which I am to right as soon as I get to work in the Labor Dept. Jerry called. His car is still under repairs and will not be available tomorrow. We were planning to go to Marblehead as Mrs. Mann had insisted I come down for at least the day. I am quite disappointed, of course, and Jerry seemed disappointed for me.

Saturday, August 12
Called to Manns to tell them I could not come. They were in town but I left word with Bridget. Down town after luncheon. Clara got a job for Saturdays in the Renee Dress Shop. Jean bought a stunning brown dress in Sutherland's. Ate at the Puritan. Shopped for shoes, tried on dozens of pairs, but could not get suited.
Jerry called. Meehan had brought over the

letter of acknowledgement he received from Wyzanski. Jerry read it to me over the phone. Jerry thought it was splendid – only the usual thing.

Sunday, August 13
Jerry over all day. Exceedingly warm. Repairs on Jerry's car not yet completed. It is now quite unlikely that I shall be able to go on even a short mountain trip.
Jerry brought over the note Wyzanski had written to Meehan – a very nice little note. Wish I knew definitely whether I was going or coming.

Monday, August 14
Mother and I went into Boston in the morning. We both bought shoes, she bought some tableware, and I bought two dresses – considerable difficulty finding what I wanted. Did not have time to call Jean. Made a later train. Arrived home to learn Wyzanski had been calling me all day. Had even called Jean in Boston. Wyzanski tired of waiting – wanted me to come out as a temporary appointee, to be made permanent when I obtained certain other letters. Phoned Sen. Coolidge but he said he had supported Al Smith during the last campaign, and therefore could not write a letter for me. Up very late packing and completing the many things which must be done before such a trip.
Arranged to have Jean try to make an appointment with James Roosevelt through E. Field. My good byes certainly will not occupy much of my time. Hope I have better luck in Washington making friends.

Tuesday, August 15
Bought two hats in Lawrence. Father and Clara came to Boston with me. Bought another pair of shoes, got my money out of the bank, called Jean - Field had been very nice, but J.R. was in N.Y., so Field said he would try again tomorrow. Got the 11:00 train. Parlor car seats quite comfortable and the novelty of the trip kept me interested. Wired Phil from the station what time to meet me. Had the wrong time, so wired again from N.Y., wired the folks on my arrival.
Phil had gone to some stag affair so Mark met me with Gertrude, Mae and young Jerry.[27] No room in Mark's small car for all of us and my suitcases, so we did not get the bags. Rode over to Sam's store, where I saw Sam, Nettie, Lester, and Baba. Then to Mae's house, where I am to stay for the time being. A very attractive home, but not enough room for me to stay indefinitely. Jerry is amazing, clever for such a youngster.

Wednesday, August 16
Reported for work promptly at 9:00. Phil took me. Forbore his morning golf, which is a history making event. Wyzanski was very nice, introduced me around, explained to me that the job would amount to whatever I could make of it and that the former solicitor's secretary would show me the tricks. He had tried to get rid of her, but she was rather old, could not get another job, so

---

27 Anne's arrival to Washington. Her cousin, Sam Wagshal had a deli, and his son Mark picked her up at the train station along with Phil's wife Mae and their child Jerry. Gertrude, Anne's cousin from Lawrence, was also there Waiting for her at Sam's deli was her grandmother Baba and other family members.

he took her back. Imagine how pleasantly that makes her feel towards me.

In the evening we rode over to Sam's store. Saw Ben for the first time since he left Lawrence. An attractive pleasant boy, a bit too serious for his age. Took a ride around the Speedway. Met Lester and took him along. A very pleasant ride. Gertrude is going to try to get a job here and live with me in an apartment.

Thursday, August 17
Mae and I took a cab in this morning.[28] She goes to work – dental hygienist – in the morning the last part of the week, and in the afternoon during the first part. Getting the hang of the work. Mr. Wyzanski is certainly being exceptionally nice. Plenty of places right near the office where I can eat, which is a help. Several pleasant little parks right near the White House, which makes me, feel pretty grand. Imagine the shock I received when the mailman brought me a summons to appear for the oral bar examination.
Phil and Mae were all for going out or having company over, but I was too thoroughly tired to be able to look pleasant. They think I ought to call upon Mrs. Levy, whom they met through me. I knew her at law school, but was never particularly friendly.

Friday, August 18
Mae and I go in by cab, taking turns paying, which makes it cost little more than a trolley. Wyzanski is going to Boston over the week-

[28] When she first arrived to Washington, Anne stayed with her uncle, Phil, who was a lawyer, his wife Mae (or Mary), and their son, Jerry.

end. Called to make plane reservations for him, and was quite surprised to learn that the rates were little more than train fares. Would like to try flying next time I go home. My oral exam scheduled for Tuesday, Aug. 22. Wyzanski suggested if it were on a Saturday or a Monday, I could have Sunday at home, so I wrote requesting a postponement.
A very pleasant young couple with their little boy came over. The man was a lawyer, and he, Phil and I went over my case for the oral exam. They were rather helpful. Clever enough to sell Phil some tickets for a lawn party.

Saturday, August 19
The office seemed stupid without Wyzanski around. Had a long chat with Reitzel, Assistant Solicitor, about the Washington sights.
Went to Sam's store. The whole crowd there. Met Selma, who is quite snappy, with a tendency to be silly.
Mark took some of us to the movies. We all had dinner out.
Mae and I walked home from the store for the exercise. She was in a confiding mood which lasted until about 1:30.

Sunday, August 20
A pleasantly cool day. Went to the office with Phil, and discussed some of his cases all afternoon. It required concentration and I was tired to begin with. Went to the store later. Met the rest of the family. We all went to the lawn party. The usual type of crowd, and the usual supper. Up very late again.

Monday, August, 21
Rained miserably all day. Tired, but glad to

get back to work. The job has not begun to pall upon me yet. Supposed to play tennis with Mark, Lester, and Gertrude,[29] but the weather queered that.

Bertha Levy, formerly of Boston, phoned. She is quite friendly with Mae. We had a nice long chat. She was very surprised, as everyone in Washington seems to be, at the idea of anyone being called and asked to accept a position.

Phil did not come home for dinner, or for the best part of the evening. He spends considerable time and, I suppose, money away from home. Mae is mighty sweet about it, but is reaching the end of her patience. Think I can work Clara into the job in Phil's office, and believe it will be a good thing all around.

Tuesday, August 22
Not raining, but wanting too. Wore my black satin beret, new black dress, black sandals, white gloves, etc., and looked pretty spiffy – for me. Had dinner at Mary Coordes apartment on N.Y. avenue. She works in the Chief Clerk's office. Her roommate, Jeannette, works in the Agriculture Dept., and is a Morman – different enough to be interesting. After dinner Mary and I went riding in her car. We went all through the Congressional Library which, of course, impresses me mightily. The Lincoln Memorial was breathtaking lovely in the evening. His statue is a masterpiece; he looks so kind and fatherly.

Phil was out again. I stayed up and talked with Mae quite a while. Seems I can never get away from the discord of an unhappy marriage.

Wednesday, August 23
Supposed to lunch with Miss Coordes but could not make it. Ate with Miss Kuste because she had an umbrella and I did not, and it was pouring. Terrific storm, which did much damage, but was far worse in Virginia and other places around Washington. In the evening we went to see Mae West in "She Done Him Wrong." One of the most popular pictures of the season, much talked about, but it seemed to me just simply vulgar. And yet nice people have talked about seeing it over again, especially the men folks. Guess I still have a few old fashioned traits. Went to the store afterwards to eat. Stayed and gossiped until I almost fell asleep on the table.

Thursday, August 24
Bumped into Lillian Finkelstein during my noon hour. Chatted with her for a while, and then immediately afterwards met Mae with Jerry.

Must get some more summer clothes. Mine are a wreck and my fall clothes are too warm. Wyzanski must notice clothes because when referring to Miss Robinson, he described what she was wearing pretty accurately. After dinner went to the office with Phil to talk over his cases. I was desperately tired but he was quite insistent.

Almost went to sleep on the job. Phil seems to think I can help him although seems to me, I know very little law, especially D.C. law.

---
29   Anne's cousins Mark and Gertrude. Lester is always with the family.

Friday, August 25
Had a little spat with Wyzanski, but we both got over it. He was particularly nice after it. Lunched with Miss Korte at a cute little backyard garden place. Miss Korte is at the stage of old-maidhood where she appreciates any companionship. Seems to be a good sport, although she dresses like a farmer.

My work is accumulating very rapidly. Have not worked up my pace yet. Supposed to start on the new filing system, but cannot seem to find time. Considerable agitation because I have not been keeping a time sheet, but Wyzanski put his foot down, and I am not to keep one. Went to the offices after dinner with Phil to do some work with him. He seems to think he can accomplish more when he talks over his cases with me.

Saturday, August 26
Insufferably hot. Went down early to buy an excursion ticket for Clara and mailed it to her Special Delivery.

Went shopping. Bought a beige dress and a number of small things. Went to the beauty parlor with Mae and got slicked up. Gert and Nettie came over, and after dinner we all took a ride to the store.

Letter from Clara. Billy Kugell had phoned. Was called for the oral. He wrote, but never received the letter.

Sunday, August 27
Very hot. Mary Coordes, her friend Okie, and I went swimming to Capel Point Beach. Then drove to Annapolis. Arrived 7:05 – Academy gates closed at 7:00. Dinner at the Blue Place – a pleasant little southern place, but the food certainly was not worth what they charged. Delightful ride. Home quite late and tired.

Monday, August 28
Wire from Clara. R.R.[30] ticket sent her, due to some error, dated for next week end. Regrettable, of course. Looks like I shall have to do Phil's work evenings as Graham is not much help as a stenographer. Went to Phil's office in the afternoon prepared to do some work. A friend of his called and suggested a poker game, and Phil succumbed to the temptation. The game was at his house. There were several rather interesting looking men, but, being a poker party, I might just as well have been a thousand miles away.

The men – most of them – were leaving in the morning when I was thinking of getting up and dressing. Phil had left them playing to go to bed.

Tuesday, August 29
Went shopping after work with Mary Lou. A new lawyer in the office – Edward Williams – very young and very pleasant.

Lester is helping Phil with the office work. I went to the office with Phil after dinner to finish up what Lester left uncompleted. Big U.R.A. parade. I saw part of it-and heard the fireworks while in the office.

Considerable difficultly in parking the car, which meant a long walk, home late, and very tired. It really seems too bad to let myself get so run down on a new job, but, under the circumstances, I cannot very well refuse to help Phil with his office work.

---
30   Railroad

1933

Wednesday, August 30
To Sen. Walsh's office for letter of endorsement. He had already left Washington but his secretary gave me a letter. Met Mr. and Mrs. Pogue then and had a nice chat with them.
Mae and Jerry came down and we all had dinner in town. Then Mae and Jerry went to the movies while Phil and I went back to the office for more work. Letter from Jean that she would be in Washington Thursday, but no indication of the time. Met Gertrude.
Letters from Clara and Bee Pounch. Clara apparently quite keen to get out here. I have quite a stack of mail on hand now to answer, but it will have to wait until such time as I am not working both day and night. Afraid my night work is affecting my real job.

Thursday, August 31
Rained all morning.
Jean [Anne's sister] arrived about 10:00. Had seen Kusganoff. He was requested by the Dept. of Labor to leave sooner than he planned, and thinks it must be due to me. Lunched at Allie's Inn with Mary and Jean. I blew them, today being payday - $70.83
Mary gave me and Phil a ride home.
After dinner, Nettie, Gertrude, Mark[31] and his roommate, Chris, dropped in. Mark and Chris left early. The rest of us went to Sam's store to show Jean off. Then we went sightseeing, a nice long ride, and then stopped for something to eat. Did not get home until about 1:30, by which time I had to prop my chin up with my hand to keep my head from drooping.

31   Anne's cousins Gertrude and Mark and their friends.

Friday, September 1
Phoned as usual for my cab. It did not show up so I phoned again, etc., etc., until I finally walked to 14th Street., where there are always many cabs. Not a one today that was not occupied. At 8:55, in desperation, I picked up a ride. The chap was nice and hurried. Arrived at 9:10, had a phone call at 9:05 which CEW [i.e. Charles Wyzanski] answered, looked for me, etc. Do not know who called, but would like to blast whoever it was. Called in on the way home to see Barb Levy and her new baby.
Mae, Phil, and Jean wanted to go places and do things after dinner, but I was much too tired even to go riding. They sat around so long debating where they should go, it was finally too late to go anywhere, so they went out for a ride, and I, blessed sensation, went to bed early.

Saturday, September 2
Phil took the crowd of us to luncheon and dancing – at the Lotus. Then we went to Mount Vernon, and spend most of the afternoon wandering about the house and grounds. Enjoyed it very much. Got home later than we planned, and I had to rush considerably to change my clothes, throw a few things into a bag, grab something to eat and dash for the train. My first experience on an excursion train. The seats were like rocks. The girls were silly and the boys cheap flirts. The colored people all had smelly luncheons, and seemed to eat continuously.

Sunday, September 3
Home about 10.[32] Clara left early in the evening for Washington – much excited. The only Lawrencians who greeted me were the Lynches and Anna Goldblatt. Anna invited me to go to a dance with her and her brother, but that did not appeal to me.
Would have gone out with Mother, but it poured all evening. Very disappointing holiday weather. Is not going to make Clara's trip any more pleasant.

Monday, September 4
Poured all day, but cleared up beautifully in the evening. Just laid around all day. Realized I ought to study my case for the oral exam, but was mentally asleep.
In the evening Jerry sent his brother for us, and Mother and I went over to his place in N. Andover. It is small but attractive, the food is unusually good for that type of place, and I really expect he is going to make good.
He told me he had a good contact with Walsh through his lawyer, Gus Donovan, who is quite pally with Walsh. Mrs. Fuller, also, has written me to the effect that she has an excellent contact with Walsh through a friend of ours. To be sure, it never rains but it pours. Mother had a weeping spell at the realization of her aloneness, and I spent a sleepless night.

Tuesday, September 5
Took the train from Lawrence to Boston. Learned at the Court House that the Board of Bar Examiners was not sitting this week.

[32] On the same day Anne traveled home to take the Bar Exam, Clara traveled to Washington to take the job Anne had arranged for her in Uncle Phil's law office.

Called Hitchcock. They had written to me to come next week, but I did not receive it. Later learned it arrived in Washington today. I went to his office, and he asked me a few questions – mostly personal. Said I got a good mark on the written exam, to my surprise. I then was interviewed by Mr. Powers, who quizzed me on the case I was to have prepared. Both were impressed with my references. Now if they can convince the other members of the Board that ought to be sufficient for my oral, I will be all set, but I have my doubts.
Train 35 minutes late.
The crowd met me. Went to the Congressional Library in time to see it closed. Went to the store for sandwiches and to visit. Bet Clara is the most important feeling person in Washington.

Wednesday, September 6
Had the feeling I had returned home rather than that I had returned to a comparatively strange city.
The men thought the Bar Examiners had been mighty unfair.
The material for my new filing system is beginning to come in. I'll be ruined if my system does not work.
We all had dinner down town. Phil and I did some work while the others visited the Congressional Library. We met them later at the Library, and Phil took us all home. Then Phil, Mae and Jean and I decided to stay at home and retire comparatively early – especially since there is to be a party tomorrow night. Sent Alice Chakofsky a lovely velvet bag from Garfinckels.

1933

Thursday, September 7

Disagreeably warm.

Lunched at Tally – Ho with Clara. Wyzanski there with some other chaps I did not know. He was in back of me. Clara said he stared at me, which promptly made me most uncomfortable. He mentioned seeing me afterwards. Mae had a party at the house. The Winklers came, Ben and a friend of his, and three doctors. No one of them was particularly interesting. We played bridge a while, but there was a good orchestra on the radio, so we soon decided we preferred dancing. Two of the doctors were fairly good dancers. Ben finally admitted he would like to learn how to dance. His friend invited me to one of their club dances, but they are all youngsters. Party broke up about 1:00.

Friday, September 8

Warmer still.

Lunched with Clara at Allie's Inn. Mr. and Mrs. Williams were there. Suppose I may as well get used to bumping into them.

Wyzanski gave me an errand to do at the Dept. of Commerce first thing tomorrow morning. I like doing things like that.

Phil went to bed early, and I felt very much like following suit, but refrained for Jean's sake. Called Mary Coordes. She said she would be glad to take us riding. Stopped at Sam's for sandwiches, cookies, etc., went for a nice long ride, and then stopped to eat on one of the benches beside the river on Mount Vernon Highway. A lovely evening – moonlight on the water, boats with bright colored lights, balmy breezes, and delicious rye-bread sandwiches. Oh, lovely nature!

Saturday, September 9

Terribly warm.

The gang of us lunched together, visited Sam's wife, Annie, then went to Arlington Cemetery, Lillian Finkelstein tagging along all day. The Lee house, the amphitheater, the tombs, and all were most interesting and impressive.

Took Jean around to make her farewells, and then saw her off on the 10:30 bus, which turned into quite a ceremony. We saw to it she got the best seat, a pillow, plenty of food, more than enough kisses, etc.

Sunday, September 10

Considerably cooler today.

We all went to Bay Ridge. Lillian F. tagging along again. Although the water was rather cold, Mae, Nettie, Jerry and I went in. I enjoyed it very much – the swings, too. I used to be afraid of them when I was a youngster, but now I can go way up with nary a tremor. I bought a coat, so enjoyed the drive even though it was quite cool.

Monday, September 11

Still cool. Jean would have relished this weather for tramping around.

Madam Secretary back from her vacation today. A stack of work to be done, and I guess I was the victim.

Clara went back to the office after dinner to do some work. Mae and I went to the Jewish Community Center to look up rooms in a private family. They had a far longer list than I expected. I will certainly be glad to get out and get settled in my own place. Just about fed up with Mary [i.e. Mae] and her eternal complaining. Seems to think because I am

Phil's niece and a law student, it is up to me to find a cure-all, and her complaints lately tend to take on a tone of bawling me out. Got caught in the rain and soaked before we got a cab.

Tuesday, September 12
These days I can wear my long sleeved dresses comfortably, which is something to be thankful for. Letters from Jean, written on the boat, to Mary [i.e. Mae], Phil and me. Mine also contained the N.E.U.[33] Bulletin – the last time my name will appear on the Dean's List. Planned to look at rooms, but spent so long at the Levy's home and at the store that we had no time for anything else. Mrs. Levy's mother, Mrs. Becher, recognized me immediately. The youngest daughter, Edith, who is also here with her mother, is just as pretty as ever, and that is very pretty. The Levy's have a pretty home, the Mr. seems to be a grand sport and the baby is doing fine. Les had made tennis reservations last night but it rained. Supposed to go to Ben's Club meeting tonight, but decided we ought to look for rooms. Nothing but frustrating.

Wednesday, September 13
Wore my old green dress with the plaid trimmings, and everyone liked it very much. Took Clara to luncheon at Madrillon, and what a licking I took! In addition to that blow, I was informed that Mae's sister Lill and her husband were coming out on the 15th for their vacation, which means moving pronto. Supposed to go to a bridge party with Mae tonight, but got excused to go looking for rooms. Mae decided she would rather come along than play bridge. It started to pour, of course, which meant I got a sticking for cab fares. And then we did not find anything satisfactory. Either the room or the furniture or the people were impossible.

Thursday, September 14
Perfectly miserable weather. Lunched at the Lotus Lantern with Miss Harrington.
Trying to read some books on immigration but for the most part they are just words and figures to me.
Some of the people whose rooms we looked at called today to quote more reasonable figures. We looked at a compile of places tonight, and finally decided on Mrs. Levin at 1337 Perry Place.[34] After that we went to the office to do some work. I finished the little there was for me to do, and then left, because it was plain Clara and Phil would have to stay quite late. When I got home, Mae's cousin Sonia was there – a charming Russian Jewess. I stayed talking with them so late, I might as well have stayed at the office.

Friday, September 15
Clara left early this morning with Phil to finish up what they had been working on. And yet Phil is dissatisfied, as he told me in strict confidence, because he complains that her inexperience holds him up. Mae's guests have not arrived yet.
Called Mrs. Levin to announce we had decided to take her room. She seemed quite pleased. Lunched with Clara at the Lotus

---

33   Northeastern University

34   After Jean returned to Boston, Clara and Anne took a room with Mrs. Levin.

Lantern. Trying to put her wise to herself – and her job.

Played ping-pong after dinner with the set Jean sent Jerry. She also sent Phil some ties. Mae asked me to go to the movies. Phil asked me to take a ride down to the store. I was tired and then weather was nasty, so I declined both invitations and went to bed early.

Saturday, September 16
So cold I just shivered and chattered all morning. Phil asked me to play golf with him after luncheon, but I did not feel that any of my clothes were warm enough.
Went to the movies in the evening. Saw Zasu Pitts and Slim Summerville, and found them quite amusing. Saw Nettie and Gertrude off for home [i.e. Lawrence, MA]. They are going all the way by bus. Took Mrs. Wolf and Baba to church – some midnight observance. Got to bed late – and tired.

Sunday, September 17
Bright sunny day – too warm for comfort. Slept a good part of the day while the older folks went to the cemetery. Got our duds moved in to our new home, much to everyone's relief, I'll bet.
Dinner in town. Did some work for Phil. He thought we ought to visit at the house a while, but Clara and I decided to go to bed early. Not so early by the time we unpacked.

Monday, September 18
Lovely warm day – a little too warm, but grateful after that disagreeable cold spell.
Our first meals at Mrs. Levin's did not make too good an impression. The food is good and substantial, and more than enough of it, but it is served most inartistically. The members of the household are friendly and pleasant, but not what Mrs. Fuller would call "high grade."
Clara bought a good-looking and much needed brown silk dress. Mary's sister arrived on Sunday night with her husband and daughter. We got out just in time. Phil and Arthur Segal, Lil's husband, came over in the evening, and we all went to the office. Phil wanted my O.K. on an important letter he was sending to the judge. After much fuss and hullaballoo, he sent it out special delivery but without very essential enclosure.

Tuesday, September 19
Wyzanski warned me today not to be too chagrined if my appointment was not made permanent. He said it seems I was to be the innocent victim of a political quarrel between Farley and the Mass. Senators. These autocrats – so jealous of their momentary power.
Jean writes that most of last year's crowd is back at school, and that some of the law-school boys are rather envious of the heights to which I have attained – a precarious temporary position, and not yet a member of any bar.
Lou Goldstein, the other boarder here, is a queer sort of duck, as annoying at times as he is amusing. Pat and Al are agreeable but quite ordinary. Al is a member of the bar, but he took it three times.

Wednesday, September 20
Presented my application for leave to Wyzanski, who seemed quite surprised

to learn that I was Jewish.[35] Phil is quite chagrined because I do not stop in at the office everyday like I used to, but that was too much of a good thing.

Clara and I are tired of Mrs. Levin's cooking and her stupidity, of Pat's coarseness, of Lou's proud reticence. Al is a pretty good sort, but very much wrapped up in his pretty little Naomi, who was over for dinner and spent the evening here.

It is going to be too bad for me if I have arrived at the point where I gauge all men by Wyzanski's standard. Yet, how can I help it? Went to Temple with Pat.

Thursday, September 21
Clara went to work as usual. I went to Phil's office at his special request. Seems John wrote to him re a divorce for the folks. He wanted to talk it over with me. The best bet, I fear. I maneuvered and got Clara off for the afternoon. Pat, Lillian F., Clara, and I went shopping and then to the movies. We went over to Phil's house for dinner and the evening. Met Max's sister – Lil a nice sort – and her pretty little daughter, Jean Francis. We debated how to spend the evening until it was too late to go anywhere. But for a ride, which we did. Jerry was most delighted to see me, and showed me off to Jean in the most amusing fashion. It is really quite extraordinary what an attachment he has for me.

Friday, September 22
Concocted a nasty head cold somehow or other. A letter from home every day lately.

Apparently things are going from bad to worse. Phil plans to go out there and help. Attended services with Pat and the Wagshal tribe at three different "Shuls." Was introduced to Mike Jolson and several other people. After luncheon Mae induced me to the movies. It was a very long picture and we spent the entire afternoon there, although it was a lovely day to be out. It was all Jerry's doing, and there was no Mickey Mouse picture after all.

Mae, with her continuously nagging and bellyaching is making herself mightily unpopular with me.

Saturday, September 23
Back to one terrific pile of work. Wyzanski's leaving for a two week vacation – a well deserved one. Met Mae and Lil and Frances and Jay and all the rest of them at the hairdressers! Clara came up later. Phil told her she was not satisfactory, and she was furious. Mae and Phil had quite a spat about it because Mae is afraid he wants to take back his ex vamp steno.

Went to a farewell party in the evening. Met a lot of people and a few interesting persons.

Sunday, September 24
Cold getting worse in spite of everything I do. Not enough sleep, of course. Mike Jolson called. Professes to a bad case of love at first sight. Nuts! Lillian I. called to invite me to dinner for about the dozenth time. Some people do not know when to quit. Went riding, and to visit some of Mae's relatives in Ft. Mayer, Va. Nice ride, nice people, good time.

---

35   Anne's first High Holidays in Washington, and Wyzanski learns that she is Jewish.

Monday, September 25
Sam gave me some capsules last night for my cold, and I have noticed some improvement already, although I took only one.
After dinner, I ironed the undies I had washed yesterday morning. Very warm, they had to be done. Lou tried to entertain me while I did the ironing.
Lunched with Clara at the Army Navy Tea room. She gets a big kick out of lunching with me it seems. Phil is planning to take a trip to Lawrence to see if he can help with Mother's divorce. It is really the only way out, and I believe both Mother and Father will be happier for it, although it will no doubt mean Father will be more estranged than ever.

Tuesday, September 26
Pouring in the morning. Umbrella in the office, but had my raincoat. Nothing mattered, however, when I learned I had passed the Bar. The letter went to Phil's house, Mae brought it in to Clara during the forenoon, and Clara phoned me. Met her for luncheon to get the precious letter.
Having a tough tussle with a furniture inventory, specifying what is fit for use in the building. Dinner with Lillian F. Has her little face fixed up quite attractively, and served a pleasant and tasty meal. She suggested our going to see a bowling match – friend of hers. But I was tired so we spent an enjoyable lazy evening listening to the radio, reading the Lawrence Tribune, etc. Mike [i.e. Yoelson/Jolson, brother of Al] called several times.

Wednesday, September 27
Wore a warm dress, because it was cool in the morning, and almost suffocated. First letter of congratulations from Wm. Garbelon.
Lunched with Clara, who is noticeably happier than she has been, since Phil told her yesterday to forget what he had said Sat. – about giving her notice.
Phil left for Lawrence this morning. Wish I were going with him, even though the task awaiting him is rather distasteful.
Mike called a couple of times, but I was too tired to be pleasant. A friend of his from Baltimore was up yesterday. He called so many times because he wanted to take us to a dance at the Shoreham – just my luck to miss out on that. But anyhow, I do not believe we could get along.

Thursday, September 28
Letters of congratulations from home, Mrs. Fuller, etc. Billy passed. Muriel Hunt did not, to my amazement. Seems I was the only N.C. [i.e. Night Class] girl. Do not seem to be many boys from my class either. Of course, Stein, Epstein and Berenson passed. My good luck certainly stood by me that time, considering how thoroughly licked I was before I started the exam.
The stacks of mail I open during CEW's [i.e. Wyzanski] absence give me some inkling how busy he is when here. Mike called and asked me to come over to hear his brother's program. I had already promised to go bowling with Pat and her girl-friend. He called several times, until I finally consented to come. His brother's program was quite

amusing and entertaining. The father and mother were agreeable and friendly. The home was pretty and well decorated. But Mike is not my idea of a boyfriend at all.

Friday, September 29
Put in my leave slip for Sat. Was told I would have to lose a full day's pay, and not entitled to the three remaining hours. Mr. Watts, Asst. Chief Clerk, heard me talking about it to Miss Coordes, but said that was the rule. However, he spoke to Gompers, Chief Clerk, who told me I could break the rule and take the three hours. He was surprised to find I was Jewish, and we had a long personal chat about the tribulations of a Jewish employee.

Went to Synagogue with Clara in the evening.[36] Mike [i.e. Yoelson] was there but I was decidedly cool to him – no use letting him convince himself further than he has that I am in love with him. Later walked home with Baba [i.e. Anne's grandmother]. Then to Mae's house to get some letters which had been sent there. Mae [i.e. cousin Phil's wife] growing distasteful to me, with her continuous complaining.

Saturday, September 30
In synagogue all day. Fasted until 1 o'clock, but by then Clara and I craved food, so stopped in for waffles and coffee at the Garden T. Shoppe. Have another head cold, to my thorough disgust, but the capsules Sam gave me helped considerably. By the time we escorted Baba and her grand bouquet to the store, which by then was opened, and got home for dinner, Clara and I were so hungry we could not eat much. There was a fairly substantial meal considering Mrs. Levin had not been able to cook. The Levin's had all fasted faithfully. In the evening Clara and I went to the movies for something to do. Would have preferred something more exciting.

Monthly Memoranda 1933

January
Have gone in for athletics to the extent of getting my name in the Transcript under Old Man Winter as the only co-ed in the N.U.[37] Ski Club. January marks another turning point in my life. Hope losing this last job means the end of my career as a stenographer.
Realized once more what it was to be ill.
Glad this is the last lap at school, and will be gladder still when it is all over.
Renewed a pleasant friendship. Bee. The girls have all been pretty decent about my bumming breakfasts, etc.
Still seems strange not to be dashing off to work every morning. Makes me wonder if I ever will again.
Hope next month is a happier month, although January was not too tough.

February
A short month but chock full. Made a splendid move when I left the House.

---

36   In Washington Anne gradually became more active in Jewish life than she had been in Boston.

37   Northeastern University

Made a number of new acquaintances, some of whom may develop into worthwhile friends in the course of time. Did more social entertaining than I ordinarily do in about a year. Not doing such keen work at school as I should like. Maybe I'll do better when I get settled down to the routine of the apartment. Maybe I am getting stale. Maybe when I get through and have to struggle for a job again, I will realize how well off I am at this time. Capped the month by getting elected Class Secretary. No great honor, to be sure, but quite a compliment.

Passed up a grand automobile trip, a chance to get in on the Inauguration, because of the Con. Law final - what a tough racket this is.

March
Feb. was certainly an important month - marked a change of residence and, to a great extent, of my whole mode of life. Met the Suffolk gang, who may be valuable acquaintances in the course of time.

Contact with the Mann family developing into a very real and valuable friendship.

Friendship with Mrs. Fuller revivified. Have reached the stage where I sometimes wonder whether I shall ever work on a regular job again.

Met Marvin Webber, who may prove to be worth knowing.

Getting mighty doggone tired of school -- too much of a good thing. Jerry's plans for the Alpine Unit materializing in great shape - which pleases me mightily for his sake and because it may prove to be a good thing for me. Mrs. Fuller, like everyone who knows about it, very much enthused.

April
Rather a pleasant month, although not particularly exciting. Busted up what looked for a while as though it might develop into quite a fine friendship - Billy Kugell.

And now I am 23 - high time I was accomplishing things. This month should have contained a celebration - the end of my final exams. Have passed everything so far, for which I am duly grateful, but somewhat afraid of Evidence.

Must take my graduation pictures soon - cannot realize I am really approaching the end of this long grind - although I may have to begin all over in Sept. for a bar review. But at least that will not be a matter of four long years, not if it means I never pass it. Gosh, what I would give to be over that hurdle - the bar exam.

May
May was rather a delightful month but I shudder to think of the studying I should have done and did not do.

Went home once which is, these days, rather an event.

Clara's school days seem to be over, rather prematurely - tough for the kid. Wish she had a little more nerve and initiative. Billy and I still scrapping at the same old rate. He is rather getting on my nerves, but then I shall not see him for some time after next month, if ever again. Pleased to have made the Dean's List, of course, but I certainly should have done better than I did. Nice to have a few old friends, like Mrs. Fuller and Anita hanging on in spite of my giving them so little attention.

Wonder if any of my new friends will hang on at all. Will probably never see most of the kids from school after next month, after seeing them so often for four years.

June
An extra-special month, since there occurred in it two Big Events - graduation and the bar exam. The former was heaps of fun but the latter was Hell. It was not the fault of the exam, however, since it struck me as being comparatively easy for anyone who had studied conscientiously and was feeling up to scratch. Very much afraid that I flubbed it, neither of the above qualifications applying to me.

There is no sense in looking for a job until I know whether or not I have flubbed the bar exam - until I know definitely, that is. Not keen on losing an entire summer, but cannot very well do anything else. Nothing to contemplate now but a most uneventful summer, and, as for the fall - *quaere*.[38]

Sometimes I am very lucky - wonder if my luck is going to help me through this tough spell.

July
A stupid month, despite my having looked forward to it for so long. Nothing has worked out as I planned it. Those friends I have not neglected have deserted me anyhow.

The only exciting thing I do is wait for the mail, and even then I seldom receive anything worth waiting for. My favorite past-time seems to be playing with the numerous youngsters who infest the neighborhood. A phone call is an event, even though they are almost never for me. My only chums are the Pinskys, who do not know any better than to use double negatives, and whose idea of a keen time is a family outing to Winthrop. What could be a more stupid existence. Another month of this will slay me. Guess I can prepare to be slain.

August
A most eventful month, beginning with the very first day. Marks one of the important changes in my life - a step ahead, I believe. If I should succeed now in passing the Bar and in obtaining a permanent appointment, I should consider myself exceptionally fortunate indeed. Another stroke of luck was having agreeable relatives with whom to live, and an opportunity to make friends.[39]

C.E.W. has disappointed me slightly. I suppose it is inevitable that, being aware, as he must be, of his exceptional ability and good qualities, he should grow a little puffed up with his own importance. There are few chaps so young who could fill his position, but I do regret having him take the attitude that he is what keeps the U.S. government functioning.

September
September was certainly crowded with action for the most part, and marks several steps of progress for me, probably the most outstanding being the fact I have passed the Bar.

Changed my Washington residence, went home to Lawrence, met a number of Washingtonians, received one marriage

---

38 Latin for inquire, in other words, we will find out.

39 This summary overlooks the important details. She was given a job in the Department of Labor in Washington and moved there.

proposal, brought Clara out here, and kept her here, brought Jean out and superintended her vacation, saw Nettie and Gert off for Lawrence, and later Phil, got considerable religion, got a few head colds and a few samples of temperamental Washington weather - and, I passed the Bar.

October
Accomplished a few worthwhile things. Got my new filing system going in pretty good form. Changed my living quarters for the better. Broke Phil of his habit of having me drop in several times a week to do a little extra work. Bought my fur jacket. Got the walk-to-work-in-the-morning habit. Received my permanent appointment. Won a bridge prize. Sat in on a trial at a genuine southern small-town courthouse, such as I thought existed only in American historical novels. Got a noiseless typewriter, and made the Solicitor admit it was a sensible purchase. And, last but not least, I am finally getting the hang of the work, of government red tape.

November
This month had a most auspicious beginning, marking my real entrance into the legal realm.
Not so auspicious in so far as mother is concerned, but she insists on procrastinating, upon giving father a chance to reform, and there is nothing I can do to help her.
Got better acquainted with the Levitans, Mr. Gompers, and the few other friends I have made in Washington.
Wyzanski giving me a little more work to do, in spite of which fact I am convinced he has little faith in my ability. I have doubts myself. Have started to do some reading again - high time. Really ought to buckle down and take a few useful courses before I stagnate completely.

December
Had an unexpectedly delightful Christmas. A few - a very few - social events. Must be something wrong with me.
Don't seem to be getting very far on my job. Have the routine pretty well in hand but, as far as I can see, there is to be nothing but that routine.
Spent quite a bit of money for Christmas gifts - comparatively speaking - but suppose it was worth it in that I get it back in good will. One of the most outstanding facts of the past month is the improvement in mother's status - if it will only last a while!

Anne on left with friends

Anne Freeling completed Northeastern Law School in the Spring of 1933. She continued working as a typist/stenographer in the same day job she had while in law school with the law firm of the elder Charles Wyzanski. While working at the firm, she had gotten to know the son, Charles Wyzanki, Jr. When he took a job in Washington D.C. with the new Roosevelt administration, he found a job for Anne in his office in the Department of Labor. As a young woman and Jewish lawyer, she had little professional future in conservative Boston law circles. Even in the Federal government she was able to obtain a job only as a legal secretary. It took four years for her to get a professional position as an attorney.

1934

No selection was made for 1934. Anne continued her adjustment to work and life in Washington. The highlight of the year was a trip by ship up the East Coast and down the St. Lawrence to Quebec. She made the trip with Frances and Miss J.

On board ship 1934 trip to Quebec

Monthly Memoranda 1934

January
Have progressed quite a good deal in the office. The Solicitor occasionally treats me as though he considered me slightly intelligent.
Had a few social "blow outs" for which I am duly grateful. I am not yet quite old enough to be satisfied to sit around the house every evening with the radio or a book for entertainment.
Got results from my complaints about Miss Harrington, which I think worked out very well all around. And finally kept my much postponed dinner date with her. Rather enjoyed it, contrary to my expectations, but an glad it is over with.

February
One of the most enjoyable months in a long while. The unusual amount of snow was heaps of fun even if it did, and does, make me late for work every morning.
I made some new friends - the chief one being Miss J.
Joined the Center, went swimming, went sledding, bought a riding habit, arranged for Russian lessons, and "stepped out" more than I have in a long while. Went to two formals, which is a record for me.
Saw the beginning of what may prove to be a pleasant romance. Had it "out" with Mrs. Levitan about her charges.
And, what means most of all, seem finally to have my job, such as it is, pretty well in hand. I guess no amount of partying can detract from my paramount interest in my work.
Thoroughly enjoyed the opportunities I had to visit the Supreme Court and Congress, and think the Solicitor was fine to grant me the opportunity.

March
March was an active and interesting month, and, for me, very lively socially. Have at least two boyfriends in Washington - Sol and Irving - on whom I can count for dates. And one in New York - Al. Shirley and Russian keep the rest of my time pretty well filled up.

Have cultivated my friendship with Shirley, Miss J, and some of the girls in the office - all quite worthwhile, I am convinced.
Scheduled to get more money.
Know what Department dance is like.
Know what it is to "take a conference", how the men can dilly-dally, knowing a professor is doing the work, and what flat jokes they can tell, and how the men will laugh and laugh if an assistant attorney general is telling the stupid joke.
Have drifted away from the Jewish Community Center, but if I can manage to get some exercise in some other way, I shall not miss it. They have a very stupid crowd there.

April
Another birthday in the past, a year older - I wonder, a year wiser?
Renewed the slight but pleasant acquaintance with Mr. Wyzanski, Sr. Hope it may continue.
Had some rather interesting dates.
Finally went horseback riding - at least once.
Had my hair cut - far more exciting event, it seemed, for my friends than it was for me.
Clara beginning to step out - to the extent that she is stealing my boyfriends - for which I am very glad. She is quite welcome to Irving Gottlieb's attentions, and it is all eminently flattering to her.
Got short of the Levitans and, even though we are not at present living in a very desirable place, I am just as glad that we are away from there. They were beginning to think they owned us.

May
Certainly the outstanding thing about May was the enjoyable week-end and holiday. And I learned that charming love letters are not certain proof of a true lover - Al taught me that.
Irving Gottlieb calling me again - but it would make no difference to me if he refrained.
Sol still hanging on, but his dates are so few and far between that I can completely forget him between calls.
Here are my old boyfriends all doing complete flops, and no new ones on the horizon - I'll soon be back on the same shelf on which I was parked during my first months in Washington. Guess I'll have to get myself another Shirley - but one less shallow and fickle. Thanks be I still have a job - of a sort - to keep me occupied.

June
Took up golf - and dropped it again.
One new date - Joe Viner - but he apparently is quite uninterested. No very exciting dates. Attending the code hearing probably the most interesting.
Have learned to enjoy swimming in an indoors pool in the summer time - did not suppose I ever would. Learned what it was to work - and work hard- during Washington's hot weather. Beginning to wonder how long I shall be able to stick it out here.
Saw a great deal of the Wagshals and the Winklers. Just as well most of them are out of town - we all need a rest from each other.
Had an extravagant spell - gifts to May, Jerry, Mary, Molly and San, in addition to mother and father - not to forget Sol's penknife. Just as well there is only one June per year.

1934

July

Another trip to Englewood. Becoming quite an experienced traveler - via excursion trains. Arrangements all made for my vacation. Hope it is as enjoyable as I expect.

Had a real quarrel with Sol. Made up, but something was lost in the process.

Irving is hanging on, but I am not making any new friends, and that is bad.

Ran around with May and Phil quite a bit - enough to get fed up with them, especially with Jerry.

And so Jean is now all enrapt with an Afghanistani. She certainly is international in her choice of boyfriends. He sounds interesting enough to make her forget Runganoff. Some of the people in the office still kid me about my trip to Russia. Wonder if I shall ever get there or anywhere further than a couple of weeks trip. Ready to be prejudiced against Reilly for the insane reason that he got the job I wanted, but find myself liking him.

August

Rather a hectic month. Scurried about just before leaving on my vacation, trying to complete my shopping and wangle a new job for myself, all in one breath. Far more successful at the former than at the latter. Wonder if the Solicitor, when he learns of my activity, as he inevitably will, will be displeased. Do not care much.

Hutchie came to Washington.

Considerably fed up with Sol - and with Irving too, for that matter. And the boyfriends I acquired on the boat were all very well - for two weeks. Being fed up with one's job sours one's taste for a number of things.

Well, anyhow, my vacation was a delightful one, despite Frances's illness and Pearl's complaints and Bee's man-madness. People like Sam and Molly, Frances, her brother George and his wife Edith, sort of renew one's faith in human nature, make one wonder if, after all, it may be possible for two people to marry, spend the rest of their lives together, and continue to love each other through the various trials and tribulations of married life. The government should pay people like that.

September

This month has been a worth-while one if for only one reason - my growing friendship with Frances. I value it for a number of reasons, the least of which is the luncheons and dinners I get from or because of her. I value it because she has refreshed my waning ego, made me feel that possibly I am not the ugliest and stupidest person on earth. One's family one takes for granted. One's boy-friends seek one out only because, and only when, it serves their purposes and desires to be in the presence of a female of the species. One's fellow-employees have their own axes to grind.

But Frances thinks I am pretty - and I primp in an effort to please her. She thinks I am intelligent - and I converse with her about things I merely "kid" about with other people. She enjoys doing things for me - and I make a special effort to be generous with her.

She is patient and tolerant, and I am pleasant to her relatives.

October

Have met Mrs. Wyzanski Sr. and liked her far better than I expected. Wonder how I shall like Mrs. Wyzanski Jr. Quarreled with Sol even more this month than usual. Considering that he never argues back and never loses his temper, he is a surprisingly easy individual with whom to disagree.

Have renewed my horseback riding - and enjoy it very much.

Hutchie and Tommy Riddell still write to me, but Dave has decided apparently to put me among his past vacation memories. Still I suppose that is a fairly good average under the circumstances.

Frances is still rushing me. One of these days something will happen, she will ditch me, and I will be very much stranded. Have come to depend upon her to an unwise extent for my recreation. But I shall not spend any time worrying about the aftermath. Cannot help wondering, however, how Kommy feels about taking me to luncheon every day. Bet he thinks Frances is just ramming me down his throat.

November

Well, I have succeeded in proving to myself and to anyone else who might have been interested that I can have a most enjoyable time without a male escort in tow, paying my way and expecting me to be forever beholden to him. I probably could not have done it without Frances, but I have nonetheless done it.

Met Mrs. Wyzanski and found her charming, through not so lovable as her husband had been.

Saw more plays this month than I would ordinarily see in a year. But I have considerable ground to cover to make up for the past years devoted to school or saving money.

Finally succeeded in getting mother to Washington. I know she enjoys it, but would prefer it if Jean were here, if Louie had a job, if she had more clothes and money, if, if and if.

December

So Jean is married - and I do not know when and have never seen her husband.

I suppose that definitely relegates me to the old-maid class. I do not regret that. But it makes me stop and realize that a phase of my life is definitely of the past. I cannot dismiss the thought of marrying with a wave of my hand and a nonchalant remark about "plenty of time" when my younger sister is married. But I am just as far away as I ever was from wanting to marry.

What could have prompted Jean to go about getting married in so informal a manner? Certainly no one would have stood in her way had she gone about it in the conventional way. But I suppose any strange procedure can be explained by the mere fact that one is in love.

But Jean knows she is mother's most dearly prized jewel. And yet, for the sake of a man she has known a comparatively short time, she could proceed to hurt mother so intensely.

Well, who am I to expect any human being to be consistently rational?

Quebec Trip 1934

Anne is the center figure.

Anne with Scotsman

Anne is on the left.

Anne is sitting in the carriage on the left.

On board ship during Quebec trip.
Anne is on the far right.

The Diaries

Part II

1935 to 1938
Washington and Professional Beginnings

Anne Freeling was one of the first women lawyers hired by the National Labor Relations Board (NLRB). Her forty-one-year tenure began 1937 two years after the Board was founded and lasted until her death in 1978. Her diary entries that cover this entire period provide a uniquely intimate insight of the experience by a Jewish professional woman, who had a role in shaping labor law in this country. She came under severe criticisms in Congressional hearings and other forums for her youth and gender. While Wyzanski was Solicitor General he presented Anne at the Supreme Court to be accepted as an attorney to argue cases. Before she had her first job as a lawyer, she was already approved by the Supeme Court to argue cases. She followed the Supreme Court closely and was admitted to argue cases herself. She makes no mention of Justices Louis Brandeis or Benjamin Cardozo, the first Jewish Justices, but it might have because both left the Court in a matter of months after she joined the NLRB and began having more direct contact with the Court. Years later, (see page 434) she makes reference to Justices Goldberg and Douglas when they enter her social network.

Wyzanski resigned his position in the Department of Labor and moved to the Department of Justice, and she moved with him, literally helping him move his office files. In her entries in November, 1935 she refers to him as the "Solicitor" rather than by name in keeping with the professional distance with which she refers to him in the diary. Then, in 1937 Wyzanski resigned his position in Washington and returned to Boston to enter private practice, urging Anne to go with him. Increasingly she refers to him as C.E.W., and she vacillated months over what to do. During this process the opportunity of joining the National Labor Relations Board as a lawyer came up, realizing her goal of working professionally as an attorney. Anne decided to stay in Washington and join the NLRB. She was immediately assigned to work on a case with Julius Schlezinger, which started the relationship that lasted the rest of her life.

Over the next two years she struggled through the process of understanding love and life partnership. For a year she was reluctant to accept Julius' proposal of marriage, but a touching story of dedication on his part led to their eventual marriage in 1939. She wrestled with her feelings and confided those feelings to her diary.

Judaism became more of a part of her life. She mentions going to synagogue with her sister Clara and the observance of fasting on Yom Kippur. Although her social group in Boston was not particularly Jewish, in Washington her circle of friends became increasingly Jewish.

Her sister Clara continued to be an important person in her life, and some people begin to appear who will be present for years, such as her friend Joe Kaminstein, sometimes written as

Anne Schlezinger

"Kami" or "Kommy". Her cousin Sam Wagshal owned a deli in D.C., and the two sisters ate there frequently and had continuous contacts with Sam and his family. Their grandmother "Baba" lived with him, and they visited her.

In 1937 she obtained a position as an attorney with the newly emerging agency to oversee labor law in the United States, the National Labor Relations Board. Anne gained a reputation for strong analysis of cases, and an excellent writer of reviews. She regularly mentions in the diary that her cases were sustained by the full Board with few if any modifications.

Her job was in the Review Division which was the focal point for a number of strongly pro-worker sympathizers who were considered to be leftist and called Communists by conservative groups. Some of them were Jewish, and Anne regularly lunched with them. This group gravitated to the NLRB with the idea that they could help the conditions of workers in the United States. Anne was sympathetic to the cause of workers, but she gives no indication of having been politically involved with the group. In occasional comments she hints at the conversations, saying things like "today the boys got carried away". So, she might have heard comments that went beyond what she was willing to accept, but there is no indication that she was involved in any formally organized group. She did join the Lawyers' Guild, which admitted Jewish and African-American members in contrast to the American Bar Association at the time. The Lawyers' Guild tended to take more leftist positions on social and legal issues. Later, at the time of the McCarthy scare and the security hearings, both she and Jules were confronted with loyalty investigations, a situation complicated by these associations.

Members of the worker-oriented group (later alleged to be Communists) within the NLRB with whom Anne had regular contact in the late 1930's included Allen Rosenberg, Martin Kurasch, Joseph Robinson, David Rein, and Nathan Witt[1]. Of this group David Rein continued being a friend with Anne, and later Julius, for the rest of their lives. There was an important Jewish presence in this group shaping labor law in the United States in the late 1930's, and Anne was in close personal contact with most of the Jewish members of the group.

The initial head of the group was allegedly Herbert Fuchs, the supervisor of the Review Division within the NLRB. In hearings with the HUAC (House Un-American Activities Committee), Fuchs identified seventeen NLRB staffers as members of the group. They were Lester Asher, David Rein, Woodrow Sandler, Jacob Krug, Harry Cooper, Edward Schwunenmann, all attorneys in the Review Division. He also identified Mortimer Riemer,

---

1   Nathan Witt was a labor lawyer who graduated from Harvard Law School. In 1936 he joined the National Labor Relations Board as assistant general counsel and became its secretary in 1937. After he resigned from the board in 1941, he became a partner in the New York law firm of Witt & Cammer. Later he was the full-time counsel to the International Union of Mine, Mill and Smelter Workers. Before the House Un-American Activities Committee in 1948, Whittaker Chambers accused Witt and other New Dealers of having been part of a Communist underground organization within the NLRB.

The Diaries

a trial examiner, John and Margaret Bennett Porter (the husband a Litigation attorney and the wife a Review attorney) and a group of Litigation attorneys Allen Heald, Frank Donner, Bert Diamond, and Ruth Weyand. Most of these people left government service and were professionally active later in their careers supporting workers' rights and/or civil rights.

Allen Rosenberg was from Boston and a frequent lunch partner with Anne. He graduated from the Harvard Law School in 1936 and immediately took a job in Washington. In 1937 he was appointed to the National Labor Relations Board (NLRB) as a legal assistant to Secretary of the Board, Nathan Witt. Rosenberg was in charge of the attorneys representing the NLRB during the Congressional investigations (including the Smith Committee) into activities of the Board from 1938 to 1941 when he moved to the Board of Economic Warfare.

In 1935 the Wagner Act (later revised as the Wagner-Taft-Hartley Act of 1947) was passed, intending to democratize the American workplace. With this law the federal government encouraged worker organization and collective bargaining as a means of guaranteeing workers' rights. The National Labor Relations Board was established shortly afterwards to provide a judicial system dedicated to hearing disputes between employees and employers. The NLRB started prosecuting anti-union employers, and in its first year won all sixteen cases that it argued before the Supreme Court.

Businesses continued to fight unions, even using violence, and in so doing violated the Wagner Act, opening themselves to worker accusations and prosecution. Business oriented politicians argued that the unions and workers had gained too much power and in a conservative backlash in 1938 won control of Congress.

The two major labor unions at the time were split between themselves over how to enforce the Wagner Act. The Congress of Industrial Organizations (C.I.O.) was involved in organizing industrial employees and was considered the more militant or "leftist" organization. The American Federation of Labor (A.F. of L.) was involved in traditional "craft" type industries and was more oriented toward negotiating mutually acceptable agreements with business. The A.F. of L. supported the conservative attempt to limit the scope of the NLRB because it argued that the Board tended to support the CIO.

In late 1941, many of these people shifted to other jobs in the government and war effort, and they continued with productive professional lives in future decades. A few stayed with the NLRB, including David Rein and Ruth Weyand. It is clear that by the late 1930's and 1940, the NLRB was under attack by conservatives for what they considered to be harsh judgments against corporations. Pro-business conservatives used arguments about youth, inexperience, and leftist tendencies with the intention of inhibiting the work of the NLRB.

At a meeting of the NLRB in November, 1938 a photograph was taken of the judges and lawyers attending. Of the 159 people in the photo, there was a small group of women, including Anne Freeling and Fannie Boyls and fifteen others. Approximately ten percent of the early NLRB staff were women, an unusually high number of women attorneys for a Federal agency in the 1930s.

--Ron Duncan Hart

Anne Schlezinger

Diaries. 1935 Through 1938.

1935

By 1935 Anne had been in Washington for two years working as the secretary for Charles Wyzanski, the Solicitor General in the Department of Labor. She was frustrated that she had not been able to get a professional position as a lawyer. Her fortunes were tied to Wyzanski. When he took a new job in the Department of Justice in November, she went with him. Her social life was closely tied to her family, especially Clara, Frances, cousin Sam Wagshal, and her grandmother Baba. She ranks this as one of the most boring years of her life up to that point. She was twenty-five years old. --RDH

Friday, November 1

Amazing how much there is for me to do in spite of all the new assistants.

The Solicitor is not coming in tomorrow – going places with his mother. Seems like he might have suggested my taking the morning off, but he merely reminded me that I could complete some indexing I was doing. Shopped a bit at noon but did not find anything I craved to own. Not a word from Frances. Her love for me had certainly cooled considerably, and I am just as glad it has.

Spent most of the evening drilling Clara in shorthand for the test she is taking tomorrow. Dorothy came up and drilled and was drilled for awhile. Between breaking in new stenographers and drilling Clara, I shall soon be considerably fed up with shorthand, typing, filing, etc.,etc.

Saturday, November 2

The announcement of Mr. Wyzanski's resignation was made today, so I no longer have to keep the news secret.[2]

Lunched at the Washington Coffee Shop with Mary Lou. Went riding with Lee and Helen Koonty. Saw some people take a nasty tumble, which served to cool temporarily everyone's ardor.

Miss Griebel came back from the hospital today. Clara fears she did not do very well on her examination. She is handicapped by her extreme nervousness. Dinner at Fireside with Clara. Stopped by for Dorothy and the three of us went room hunting, but did not find anything we liked in our price range.

Sunday, November 3

Went to the Tavern for breakfast, just for the sake of variety. Went for a long walk with Mary Lou. Stopped in her apartment a while to visit Gladys,[3] who was still in pajamas. Then stopped by for Clara, who also was undressed. Went riding. Stopped to look at a few places that had been advertised – but not what we wanted. Mary had some trouble with the car, so we spent a goodly part of the evening at a repair station. Home early, where I finished reading a few old magazines, bathed, and went to bed real early.

Bought myself a new green bag just to make myself feel better. Mr. Reilly gave me a lovely copy of *Men of Turmoil*[4] as a going away

2   Wyzanski moved from the Justice Department to Labor.
3   Gladys Birch was a frequent lunch companion with Anne and Kommy.
4   *Men of Turmoil* (1935) was about the dominate personalities of the day, including Roosevelt,

present, and I do not even know yet that I am going. He certainly is a thoughtful individual. Could not tell anyone in the office about it because it might sound like asking for more gifts. Picture postcard from Frances. Clara and I had dinner at Sam's and planned to visit Baba, but she was attending a meeting of one of her societies. Therefore, we got home early and, besides the newspapers, there was nothing to read, since I had not brought home my new book, so I reread some of the "Reader's Digest."

Tuesday, November 5
Lunched with Frances, who returned because the Civil Service people tried to get in touch with her, but she did not seem at all anxious for a new job. Our new file clerk, so called, it seems not only cannot file, but also cannot type, and does not know the fundamental rules of spelling. She exhausted my patience, and I finally asked the Solicitor for another girl. I warned the Solicitor when Miss Esper first came down that I did not believe her experience was adequate. Rode home with Mary Lou. Dinner at Fireside with Clara. She went to the Bible Class at the Center with Dorothy, but I stayed home and read a few chapters in my new book. Did not feel particularly well, so went to bed early.

Wednesday, November 6
Lunched at the Latch String with Frances, Kommy, Edith, and George. Supposed to go to a Community Chest meeting, but could not get away from the office. Rather disappointed, because Josephine Roche and John Dickinson

Mussolini, Hitler, and Stalin.

were among the scheduled speakers.
The girl from the Endion Club called in regard to a vacant double room at $47.50 each. Too expensive. And only a few days ago she impressed us with her long waiting list. Mary drove Anne Lawrence around to interview some of the people who had answered Anne's ad for a room. I went along. The places were all impossible.
Dinner at Fireside – Mary, Clara and I. Read some of the biographical sketches in my new book.

Thursday, November 7
Began to pour when I was half way to the office, and I got soaked. Did not get thoroughly dry all day, my head ached miserably, and I felt all dragged out. But could not go home – too much work to do. Lunched in the cafeteria with Miss Larimer and Miss Patterson. The Solicitor knew I did not feel well, but suggested I wait until Monday to take sick leave – the brute!
Mary came by to give me a ride home, but decided to stop on the way to have her hair cut. I was feeling by then like the end of a long, hard winter, but she wanted me to sit and keep her company while she had her hair cut. Fortunately it did not take long. When I finally did get home, I fell out of my clothes and into bed – dinnerless and ambitionless.

Friday, November 8
Felt wobbly in the morning, but went to work anyhow, and gradually began to feel better. Lunched with Lee MacKinnon and Miss Larimer at Brownley's.
The Solicitor, after his usual procedure of

ridiculing any suggestions coming from me, had decided to follow them. Miss Saulsbury, Mrs. Schultz, and Miss Chaffef are being assigned to this office; Miss Esper is being sent back to the Textile Board. Had a long talk with the Solicitor about my job. Wavered several times, and then we decided I should go along with him if the job was available! Saw Sol on the way home, and waved at him, which was all the incentive he needed to call me. But I turned him down – again.

Saturday, November 9
Did not feel quite myself yet, so decided I would not ride.
Lunched at the Latch String with Frances, Ruth[5], Gladys Birch and Kommy. Francis and I went shopping after luncheon, but neither of us bought much of anything. Then home. Francis asked me to go home with her, but I was desperately tired and wanted to lie down. Dinner at Sam's. Visited Baba all evening. She talked enough to make up for all the times we had not called on her. Phil came up to invite her to go to the movies, but she turned him down. After all, a movie is a movie, but a chance to talk is a chance to talk.

Sunday, November 10
A pretty day, and I should have been out and doing, but I felt disgustingly lazy, and completely surrendered to the feeling.
Got up late, went out for breakfast, and spent most of the afternoon reading the papers.
Dinner at Sam's. Invited Baba to go to the movies with us, but this time she turned us down to go riding with Phil. Saw Lawrence Tibbett in "Metropolitans."[6] Enjoyed his singing immensely, although the picture itself was stupid. It started to rain on the way home, but we were too carried away with 'Pazliacci" to mind that.

Monday, November 11
The Solicitor is away for a couple of weeks, but I have a plenty to keep me busy and contented. Frances called and asked me to lunch with her, but I had already made an engagement with Mrs. Jewell. She is a nice sort, and I enjoy her company very much indeed.
Mr. Rowe began work today; as did also Miss Chaffety, the new file clerk. And still we do not seem to have enough people. Clara got home so late, I ate alone at Fireside.
Spent the evening reading the papers, and some of the biographical sketches in "Men of Turmoil." They are interesting and well worth reading, but too uniformly flattering to be entirely pleasing to me. Each one is treated like the hero of his age.

Tuesday, November 12
Got a new typist in today – Miss Thrift.
Missed out on another Community Chest meeting. But, I suppose, as long as I contribute and collect, missing a meeting does not matter.
Lunched with Miss. Patterson. Got caught in the rain, but it was not wet enough to matter particularly. Both our "bosses" be-

---

5   Ruth is not identified by last name, but she was an important companion during this time. The only Ruth at the NLRB at this time was Ruth Weyand.

6   Lawrence Tibbett, the leading operatic baritone of the day gave a magnificent performance in this story of backstage life.

ing out of town, we took a little time to go shopping, although we nonetheless got back within an hour.

Clara and I had dinner at Fireside.

Clara went to Bible class with Dorothy. Mary Lou and I went roller skating, and had a lot of fun. And I did not fall even once.

Wednesday, November 13
With the able stenographic assistance now at my command, and with a minimum of interruptions, I am sailing through the I.L.O.[7] indexing with gratifying ease and rapidity. Stanley Reed called everything is OK. Rained all day. Breakfasted in the cafeteria with Miss Thrift, and lunched with Mrs. Jewell and Miss Thrift. Left my cigarettes in the cafeteria, but fortunately they were not in my cigarette case.[8]

Rode home with Mary Lou. Clara and I had dinner at Fireside. After dinner Clara and Dorothy went to a lecture at the Community Center. The subject did not appeal to me, so I decided to stay home and read. Was gratified when I finally found one of the subjects of "Men of Turmoil" was not treated as a hero of unmixed virtuosity. Incidentally the victim was Henry Ford.

Thursday, November 14
Mrs. Wintersteen took me to luncheon.

I took a little extra time to go to the bank, where upon I bought a new green dress and got a manicure, and was broke again.

Planned to leave early and get my hair fixed, but Mrs. Jewell did not feel well and went off to see the doctor. The Solicitor maneuvered a raise for Collins, so that he is now getting $1500 – little enough for a family-man, but good pay for a messenger. Clara and I had dinner at Sam's. The usual evening routine – newspaper, crossword puzzle, whatever book I am reading at the time, shower, and bed. I will not die of too much excitement, at any rate.

Friday, November 15
Breakfasted at S&W with Clara. And, this being pay day, I was feeling magnanimous, and blew her to luncheon at Cornwell's. Met May there – enough to spoil any luncheon. Went shopping with Clara and helped her pick out a hat. Mrs. Lubin died in childbirth. I tried to help Mr. Lubin the only way I could – by trying to take care of the ILO work that had been turned over to him, and that had been merely accumulating on his desk. Governor Winant was splendid about helping me, and thereby helping Mr. Lubin.

Dinner at Fireside with Clara and Miss Witherow. Clara went to a Bible class or something with Dorothy, but it was rather a nasty evening, so I decided I would rather stay home and read – just plain lazy, that's all.

Saturday, November 16
Planned to take the morning off, but came down to get some ILO material out for Mr. Lubin. Left about 10:30. Lee picked me up at 11 to riding. Enjoyed the ride although it was rather cold. Glad we did not wait until afternoon to go, since it started to rain.

Went to the Hot Shoppe for luncheon. Their barbecue certainly hit the spot. Let-

---

7   International Labor Organization.
8   Her son Ira was unaware that she had ever smoked, and it seems to have been for a brief period.

ter from Mrs. Fuller, who is now working at Tyler, Emes, Wright and Hooper's office, and finds the job to be not quite all she had expected. Dinner at Fireside with Clara and Miss Witherow. Clara went to Dorothy's after dinner, but it was a wet disagreeable night, and I was glad to stay in, and read, go to bed early.

Sunday, November 17
Clara went to Francis's. She had made a date yesterday, including me, but I cannot see anyone making dates for me.
Mary, Anne Lawrence and I went looking for rooms, in spite of a miserable cold downpour. Anne went for dinner, and I went to Mary's. Had a lot of fun, making fudge, preparing dinner, etc. Spattered hot grease all over my dress while frying chicken. I never put on an apron until it is too late. Some chap from Mary's dancing class was coming up in the evening to practice dancing. Mary wanted me to stay, and I should have liked to, but my dress looked so messy, I went home. Clara got home just a few minutes before I did.

Monday, November 18
With Hitler enforcing new cruelties against Jews, fifty nations boycotting Italy, and Japan annexing a goodly portion of China, one wonders what it is all about.
Lunched in the Latch String with Frances, Ruth and Kommy. Left the office early, had my hair done, washed and waved.
Dinner at Sam's. Clara went right home, but I visited Baba for a while. Sam's business is about ready to fold up, and it may mean Baba's going to Lawrence to live, an eventuality about which she talks as though she were going to the North Pole regions. She would be better off, but I suppose one is not better off unless one thinks one is.

Tuesday, November 19
Lunched at the Latch String with Frances, Gladys Birch and Kommy.
Such a pretty afternoon, I decided I ought to play hooky – with Mr. Reilly's permission. Bumped into Mr. McGrady, who took Frances and me to the Willard Corner for cocktails. Did a few errands.
Dinner at the Tally – with Frances, Kommy, and Florence – the latter's treat. They went to the National, but I was not interested. Started to rain, but stopped by the time I got home. Clara was out. I got completely settled with a book when Irving called and invited me to a party. I was surprised into accepting, and regretted it all the while I was dressing. I noticed it had started to rain again, however, which was all the excuse I needed to call Irving back and call off the date. Stopped raining by the time I got upstairs – but, anyhow with a sigh of relief, I got comfortably settled with a book.

Wednesday, November 20
Lunched at the Ugly Duckling with Frances and Kommy. Enjoyed it, although I ate too much.
Long letter from Hutchie, who is readily exerting himself to see if he can help me to get a legal job in Boston. I am surprised, and very grateful indeed.
Invitation to attend a farewell dinner to the

Solicitor next Monday, given by the Secretary. I will be, if I go, the only young and non-official guest there.

Went shopping with Mary Lou. Dinner at the A&W. Mary went home, Clara went to a lecture at the Y, and I stayed home to read – what a stay-at-home I turned out to be!

Thursday, November 21
Lunched at the Latch String with Francis,[9] Ruth and Kommy. Shopped around for the Solicitor's farewell gift. After work I stopped around for a dress to wear Monday night. Did not find one, but did get a perky little black velvet hat. Dinner at Sholl's with Clara. Phil propositioned me – he to go in business, I to run his law office.

Went to Francis's. After turning her apartment inside out, she found an old black lace evening dress. After cutting it down to fit me, we had enough for puff sleeves and a collar. I shall wear it with a crimson girdle and carry a matching chiffon kerchief. I am also borrowing Francis's black satin slippers. In return, she wanted me to stay all night, but I begged out of it.

Friday, November 22
Lunched at the Latch String with Francis, Kommy and Mrs. Behneke.

After much discussion, shopping and re-shopping, we bought the Solicitor a green onyx penholder, with two life-time pens, appropriately inscribed. Mary and I had dinner at the S&W. Then we went to her apartment. I completed my borrowing splurge with her black evening bag and gloves. She and Gladys, who were going out to play bridge, stopped in to look at my outfit for Monday, Francis having brought the dress down at noon. I staged a dress rehearsal, black lace, green silk, and India print. Clara, who had dined at Phil's, came home during the proceedings. They approved of the black lace outfit.

Saturday, November 23
Distributed my vases, plants etc. Willed my desk to Mrs. Jewell, Mrs. Schwartz to sit in the same room. Mary and I lunched at the Washington Coffee Shop. I blew us to drinks, and they were not particularly good.

Shopped a while. Much too cold to go riding. Did not buy anything but the groceries for tonight's supper. I splurged on some cakes from Napoleon's for dessert. Clara and Gladys managed to arrive when Mary and I had finished preparing supper. We had welsh rarebit and I thought it was excellent.

Sat around a while and talked. I read almost through the latest Reader's Digest. Mary was going out to play bridge, and Gladys, per usual, was sleepy, so Clara and I went home early.

Letter from Louis, and one from Sam, Mollie[10], Elias and Dorothy coming.

Sunday, November 24
Sunday morning breakfast – at about 11:00 – at Mrs. Uhler's house – Mary Lou, Clara, Sadie, her charming young son, Marcus, and I. Brought our roller skates, but decided it was a bit too chilly, so stayed indoors. Went home to get into respectable clothes, picked

---

9 Frances is sometimes spelled Francis.

10 Anne's brother Louis, and her cousin Sam Wagshal and his wife Mollie. Dorothy was a regular companion for Anne and Clara during this period.

up Dorothy – she and Clara riding in the rumble seat – and went to the Corcoran Art Gallery.[11] I thoroughly enjoyed poking around at my leisure. To Allie's Inn for dinner. Then Mary Lou went home. Dorothy came up to our house. Spent a good part of the evening trying to give me a manicure that would match the crimson accessories I planned to wear with my dinner dress. Dorothy also insisted on swapping watches with me, hers being a yellow gold baguette.

Monday, November 25
Lunched at the Latch String with Frances and Kommy.
After luncheon the Solicitor and I moved over to Justice, both of us well loaded down with his personal belongings. The offices are not nearly as sumptuous as the ones we left. Miss Connors, who shares my office, seems both agreeable and competent.
Had my hair done. Did not leave me much time to dress. Ruth and Frances came up to pass judgment, and to give me a ride down. Everyone told me I looked very well, which was encouraging. Glad to see none of the women were escorted – not the Secretary nor Miss Anderson nor Miss Jay. Rather a nice dinner. Everyone vied to say the most flattering things to the Solicitor. The Secretary won – she was permitted to talk the longest. Some of us adjourned to the Press Club for more drinks. Reilly took me and Chapelle home.

Tuesday, November 26
Wyzanski (no longer the "Solicitor") came in at about 9:30, looking quite pale. He took a $2000 cut for this job. Lunched at the Latch String with Frances, Kommy, Gladys Burch and Lee MacKinnon. Practically nothing to do so far but fuss around about supplies, etc. Mary and I went to the Fox after work to see the Marx Brothers in "A Night at the Opera." It was amusing in a silly, slapstick way. The stag show was of the same order. We got some good laughs out of it though. Dinner at Ceres. Went for a short ride. Then home. Finished reading Lorris Cohen's *Philosophy of the Law*. Found it enjoyable and instructive despite its iconoclasm.

Wednesday, November 27
Since it was a half-holiday, and I did not have much of anything else, I wore my new green dress and black and green hat.
Justice was about the only Department that got off for the half-day.
Lunched at the Latch String with Frances and Kommy. Went shopping. Bought a few little things, including a girdle. Every one of my girl friends will be convinced it was her influence that reformed me.
To Frances's apartment, where she straightened out the hem of my new dress. She is also going to wash and block my bouclé suit. Clara was not coming home for dinner, so I ate alone at Fireside. Spent a very quiet evening, with my newspaper and crossword puzzle.

Thursday November 28
Poured torrentially all day, and spoiled a good many people's Thanksgiving sentiments.
Dinner at Tally–Ho with Dorothy, her sister Harriet and her young Aunt Rae. It was a good dinner, even though most of the con-

---

11   Corcoran School of Art near the White House.

versation turned on what we could have done if it had not rained.

Adjourned to Bancroft Place after dinner, where we ate candy, and continued to regret the weather.

The girls left in the evening to go over to Dorothy's before leaving for New York. They were disappointed, and I was disappointed for them. It was their first trip to Washington, and they may not be able to come again for some time.

Friday, November 29

Pleasant, clean, cold day.

Miss Connors took the day off, but I still was not overburdened with work. Mr. Wyzanski said if I continued to have so little to do, he would keep me busy looking up law, but that, apparently, would be a desperate last resort. Lunched at Reeves' with Ruth Jewell.

Went over to the Dept. of Labor to get a binder, and came back, in the middle of the afternoon, apparently without being missed at all. Dinner at Fireside with Clara and Miss Cochran. Clara went to Dorothy's, and Miss Cochran and I, for something to do, went to Mary's. She and Gladys had some girls up for dinner. We arrived in time for cake and ice cream and tea. Miss Cochran can be, and was, quite entertaining. We stayed until about 12:00.

Saturday, November 30

Discovered that my appointment had not been formally approved and I may not be paid until January 1. Mr. Wyzanski was quite distressed about it, and wanted to lend me a "couple of hundred dollars." Labor was much quicker to accept my resignation than Justice was to appoint me.

Lunched at Loft's with Mary Lou and Miss Connors. Shopped with Mary Lou. Met Dr. Flory, who took us to call on Dr. Rosenberg. Had cocktails in The Latter's ultra-modern bar. They wanted us to stay for dinner, but we declined. Dashed home to see if the people had come from Englewood. No one was at home, so I took myself to Fireside for dinner. When Clara got home, she told me she had not heard from them. The drinks had made me groggy, so I went to bed early.

Monthly Memoranda 1935

January

So far the prophecy that the year will be spent as New Year's was spent has held true. Mine has developed into a stupid humdrum existence. To work 5 1/2 days a week, and the same things happen day after day even if we have moved into a new building. And weekends I spend with Frances, and invariably do the same things every week-end. And occasionally I have a dinner engagement - when Kommy happens to take us to dinner. And if I desire to go to the theater or otherwise find amusement, I can jolly well take myself.

And yet I realize fully that if I had someone to beau me around, the poor chap would develop to have so many insurmountable faults that I should become intensely annoyed with him.

It certainly is a most uncomfortable way to

be, anyone would agree, but that is how I am, and I cannot change - even if I really did wish to change.

February
February was rather a routine sort of month, with few occasions to break the monotony. Most of whatever excitement I experienced was derived from newspapers and accounts of Supreme Court doings.

The dedication of the building furnished a bit of variety. The Solicitor was away from the office for more than two weeks - longer than he has previously been away at any one period. I have been rather pleased with myself at discovering how well I could struggle along without his guidance. Not that I presume for one moment to think I can do his work, but I have taken care of a number of lesser tasks which he would ordinarily handle if he were here. And such matters as I could handle, I turned over to the proper people, and it is an important part of any executive's tasks to know the proper authorities to whom to refer matters.

My friendship with Frances is still flourishing, except that I am getting a bit fed up with it. In return for Kommy's treats and Frances' hospitality I am obliged to spend the major portion of my leisure time with them. I have not been overwhelmed with other invitations, but nonetheless there are occasions when I should prefer not to feel obliged to be with them and to entertain them. What price popularity?

March
The end of March finds me a discontented person indeed. I am fed up with Clara, with Frances, with Kommy, with my job and with Washington. Not working hard, not studying, not accomplishing anything or in any way advancing myself, yet I seem to be more run down and ailing than when I was working my fool head off and going to law school nights. I need a change badly, and simply buying new clothes is not satisfying the urge. And all the time I rail and rant, I know well enough that I am going to slide along with the tide and do nothing about effecting a change, just wait until someone, somehow, someday offers me a change.

April
I know now how beautiful Spring in Washington can be. Do not believe I ever saw such lovely profusions of lilosa, wisteria, phlox, iris, violets - and such heavenly fragrance. And I am sure the cherry blossoms were lovelier this year than other years - and I am not in love either.

Renewed my acquaintances with Anita, who said she was surprised to find me so unchanged, and I felt decidedly the same about Anita. I suppose if she has not sobered up by now, she will go through life regarding the whole affair as one huge joke, enjoying herself and making friends everywhere she goes! The contrast in our dispositions is sharply drawn. We are as different as the poles, and I often wonder whether Anita is not by far the cleverer of the two, with all her flip gaiety and thorough enjoyment of life.

Contemplating again going to Geneva to work for the I.L.O.[12] If I could get a

---
12   International Labor Organization

reasonably good salary, and could go with the understanding that I should not be obliged to remain longer than a year, I think I would be a fool to pass up the opportunity. Do not know when I could get to Europe otherwise. And as for giving up my job, that would certainly be a small loss, since it amounts to nothing at all now and shows no signs of leading to anything. My complete flop as a legal light is most discouraging, and it may be that a trip to Geneva, a complete change in atmosphere and surroundings, would be good for my sadly deflated ego. And it would be an interesting experience, to say the least.

May
Thoroughly fed up with my job, with Washington, with my so-called boy-friends, and with my status in general. Too stupid to get a legal job. Too stupid to go to Geneva as secretary to the delegation or in any other capacity. Too lazy to study further in an effort to get somewhere. Too diffident to accomplish anything through such contacts as I have made, such as they are.
In other words, I am fed up with everything and everybody, and most particularly with myself. What a state of affairs!

June
No sign of a new job. I have grown to dislike my work intensely, and yet cannot seem to effect a change. Am I overly ambitious, or just stupid? And I convinced myself all through law school that, unlike so many other girl graduates, I would do something with my law education. It would be amusing if it were no so pitiful.
Irving, apparently, has thrown me over, and I, apparently, have thrown Sol over, which leaves me high and dry as far as boyfriends go. I might just as well go to Geneva, or anywhere else I can, as far as anyone missing me is concerned.
Some people, like the Solicitor, for example, have so much, and it is my lot to be thrown always into contact with such people closely enough to know how much I lack.
Mrs. Winterstein heard that they were taking people on at Justice, including some women lawyers. I promptly began to agitate for such a job for myself, with the same results as I got from my previous periodic attempts to get a different job. I fail in some respect, it seems, and cannot overcome the obstacle because I cannot ascertain with any certainty exactly what it is.
Well, the Solicitor will be back from Geneva in a few days, whereupon I shall not have time to think about a new job, unless he gives me a chance to go to Geneva, which, from his silence on the subject, seems rather impossible.

July
July was not a happy month for some members of the family, having lost Aunt Fanny and Molley's baby.
It contained additional disappointments for me. The Solicitor practically destroyed all my hopes of going to Geneva. My ambition to tour the West on my vacation is apparently an impossibility due to the lack of a car. What

looked like a chance to get a legal position was entirely based on a vain hope.

And as for boyfriends, there simply are not any, despite Mr. Reilly's frequent references to my dissipation hangovers, etc., which he believes to be either true or funny.

Well (sigh) I seem to be getting nowhere rapidly, to be going constantly around in silly little circles.

August
August may or may not be a turning point in my career. If my run-ins with the Solicitor eventually result in my getting a job on the Social Security Board, I will finally be on the way to a legal career. If I remain as the Solicitor's secretary, I shall probably die a stenographer.

Well, I did one outstandingly good deed this month anyhow - taking Mother with us to the Cape. She is an extremely trying person at times - trying to both Frances and myself - and her expenses are entirely on me. But my conscience will be salved for some months to come, as far as being a dutiful daughter is concerned. I am glad that my vacation took in the Cape instead, as I originally planned only Lawrence.

September
I accomplished one thing in September that should, I suppose, satisfy my ego more than it does - got a raise in salary without asking for it. The idea of it means far more than the actual money, however much or little it may be.

But what I really want - a legal job - is just as far away, it seems, as ever, and that is very far away.

And it is so difficult to know whether to remain with the Solicitor, and take my chances of advancing with him, or to take my courage in my hands and try my fortunes on an entirely new ship.

I was glad of the opportunity I had to get better acquainted with my father. Because of the unhappy state of affairs at home, we had drifted farther apart than I had supposed or realized. Everyone to whom I introduced him seemed to like him. And his intelligence and knowledge of affairs in general were most satisfying. Louis could take many cues from him. But Louis lives in a mist of poetry and imagination that prevents his seeing clearly on mundane problems.

Neither Father nor Louis liked Jean's husband. Father gave Jean a beautiful diamond ring set in platinum. It should seem out of harmony with her communistic beliefs.

October
October has been an eventful month. My work has grown far more interesting and more exciting, savoring somewhat of the executive. And, because, or in spite of, all that, there is a possibility that I shall soon be on a new job. The regrets at leaving the old job (if I do) will be stifled by my gratification to think that the Solicitor preferred me as his secretary, and by the excitement and novelty always attendant upon a new enterprise.

Socially speaking, the month of October was a complete flop, with very few occasions to break the monotony.

November
November was an outstanding month in at least one respect - my transfer from Labor

to Justice. The results thereof remain, as yet, to be divulged.

Socially, there was only one event that meant anything at all, and that of course, was the farewell dinner to Mr. Wyzanski. Gave me an interesting opportunity to observe under an unfamiliar guise some of the people I had known only as more - or - less dignified officials. Most of them acted and re-acted pretty much as one should have expected. The Secretary[13] was a charming hostess, except that I thought she talked too much. Miss Jay was her usual disagreeable self, under a very thin veneer.

Have made what may prove to be an interesting friendship - Mary Cochran, who lives at the house. She is a beautiful blonde, whom I like to have around if only because I enjoy looking at her. She was at one time extremely wealthy, has traveled extensively, but has nothing left now except a quantity of exquisite clothes, an intense desire for more travel, and her memories, which are her greatest possession.

This phase of her life she tries to consider as just another experience, but I know it must be very difficult for her at times. She seems pitifully grateful for a little attention - she, who is obviously accustomed to having the world at her feet.

December

This year ended as quietly as it began. I was, and am, pretty much dependent upon myself for entertainment. How fortunate that I can enjoy reading as much as I do, and gain my thrills and experience vicariously. The outstanding event of 1935, as far as I am concerned, is my transfer to the Department of Justice. Since I am destined to be a "career woman", my job, such as it may be, has to constitute the most important thing on my horizon. It is just as well, my friends being as few as they are, and as tedious as some of them are. I could wish, however, that my work might be a bit more exciting and absorbing.

Anne at desk in Solicitor's office, Department of Labor

Anne with Charles Wyzanski

---

13   Frances Perkins, Secretary of Labor

1936

In 1936 Anne's fortunes began to turn. She enjoyed her work and being in Washington. She was frustrated by not being able to get a position with the United States' delegation to the International Labor Organization (ILO) in Geneva. She was restless and ready for a change. It would not come until 1937 and then in an unexpected way. Frustrated with her professional life, her emphasis is on her social life.   --RDH

Thursday, October 1

Went to the doctor at noon. The father was out of town, so the son took care of me. He seems to know what it is all about, but I prefer one doctor to treat me.

Mr. Peak took me home from class, but had to leave immediately as he was due somewhere to listen to the President's speech. I listened to it, and to Al Smith's speech also. It seemed to me that Al had it all over the President on this particular occasion. Mr. Roosevelt is at times just a bit to unctuous for me to swallow. But everyone was surprised when Al came out expressly for Landon.

Friday, October 2

A bit busy for a change. Even had to work a few minutes overtime.

Lunched at the Latch String with Kommy, Ruth and May Sweet. Wore my black velvet, and was profusely complimented on my appearance.

After dinner Clara, Dorothy, and I decided to go to Schule,[14] but when we arrived the place was closed. They had apparently had sunset services. However, we did the next best thing and took a long walk; window shopped on F Street, had some ice cream, and went home pleasantly fatigued.

Saturday, October 3

A lovely autumn day. Lunched at the Washington Coffee Shop with Mary Lou and Maxine. After luncheon Mary Lou and I went shopping. Jack picked us up about 4:30 and took us home. After dinner Dorothy, Clara and I went to a dressmaker recommended by Rose Hornstein, a Mrs. Basch. I left my green dress and my brown shirt to be taken in and shortened. Between my clothes stretching and the styles calling for shorter skirts, all my left-over things will have to be altered. Such a nuisance!

Sunday, October 4

Another beautiful sunny day. Went bicycling with Mary Lou in the morning. Went for a ride, returning home just in time for dinner. Glad I bestirred myself in the morning, as I could not budge any of my roommates for the rest of the day or evening.

Read the papers, listened to the radio, washed gloves, ate, mended, did some "homework" for my taxation course, ate, listened to the radio, talked, ate and went to bed.

Monday, October 5

The Supreme Court opened today. Now the fun will begin.

---

14   Synagogue, also spelled Shul

Spent the whole day at the Labor Dept. digging out material on majority rule to be used in connection with the Labor Board cases. Lunched with Clara. Said hello to a number of my old cronies. Went to the doctor. After dinner Mary Lou and I went roller skating. Ran into a lot of hills, mostly down-grade, which resulted in traveling far more speedily than I might otherwise have chosen to do. But it was a lot of fun.

Tuesday, October 6
Went to the Labor Dept. to finish my research job. Lunched at the Latch String with Gladys Burch[15]. Got the low-down on people and events at the Labor Dept. Went to class — my last one, since I have decided not to take the course. It involves more accounting than I seem able to comprehend. Larry Peak took me home, but first we went for a long ride out Mt. Vernon way, and then to the Hot Shoppe for something to eat. He has traveled extensively and is an interesting conversationalist. He tried to persuade me to continue with the class, and asked if he could see me anyhow.

Wednesday, October 7
Stella Margold called to tell me she had taken a very large apartment and had an extra bedroom — and she wanted to know how I like our apartment. I assured her I was very happy with it.
Lunched at the Latch String with Kommy. Mr. W. went to New York to attend the Frances Perkins Dinner.[16] I went to the Labor Dept. to look up one or two more references, visited in the Solicitor's Office, and then "skipped." Did a few errands. Went to the doctors. After dinner Dorothy, Clara and I went to the dressmaker's. Brought along some more things for her to do, but then decided not to leave them as her house was so very dirty.

Thursday, October 8
Mr. W. returned during the middle of the afternoon sometime. It must have been quite a party.
Lunched at Epstein's with Rose Furr. Went shopping with her.
Went shopping after work. Bumped into Mary Lou, so we shopped together. I finally bought a green sport coat after all my shopping for a copper-colored coat. After dinner Mary Lou and I went to call on Mildred and Paul Jones. They have an attractive home and are pleasant folks, but a bit dull. I was rather glad when we finally got away.

Friday, October 9
Lunched at the Latch String with Kommy. It had rained all morning and was pouring at noon, but he came anyhow. It was a warm gentle rain which I did not mind in the least, but he probably could not see a thing.
I had made an error in something I looked up, and was told about it, of course. Went to the doctors.
Clara and I had been invited to Marty's for dinner tonight. Clara went.
I spent the evening reading Anatole Francis's *Revolt of the Angels*.[17] We have had a phone <u>installed at last.</u>

---

15   Birch is sometimes spelled Burch by Anne.
16   Frances Perkins was the first woman to serve in a cabinet position in the U.S. She had a major role in establishing Social Security and supported other labor reforms.
17   Anatole France's *Revolt of the Angels* has overtones of the religious conflict in *Paradise Lost* and is a protest against tyranny and violence.

Saturday, October 10
Letter from the Democratic National Committee offering me the privilege of becoming a member of the National Pro-Roosevelt Association of Women Lawyers. Mr. W. left early to go to a rehearsal for Mr. Eliot's wedding, so I left early also, did a few errands and then met Kommy at the Tally-Ho for luncheon. We went to my apartment after luncheon, walking part of the way because it was so pleasant after the rain. I walked home with him later also, but rode back.

Mary Lou and Mrs. O'Brien came up to tell us about Tom Eliot's wedding which, as members of his office staff, they had attended. They stayed very late, discussing all sorts of things.

Sunday, October 11
Mary[18] was spending the day in the country with Jack, which left me to my own devices for any active exercise, so I took myself a walking in the morning. Dorothy's aunt Ray and Saul came in for the day. They had dinner with us and then went sightseeing. They returned later in the evening, and we had a most amusing game of Monopoly, all except Hazel, who can enjoy only poker and that only when she is playing for money.

Their train did not leave until 1:45, so they stayed quite late, but no one minded except Hazel.

Monday, October 12
A delightful autumn day – an additional reason why it should have been a holiday.

Kommy called me in great glee because he had received a letter from Frances. I lunched with him at the Latch String. The letter was very long and more fascinating than many travel stories I have read. I am happy for her, but I confess, I am a bit envious.

Big-heartedly helped Mr. Rosenwald on a rush case, and found myself working until 6:30. Kommy was coming up at 7:30 to have me type some letters for him, so I had time for only a glass of milk. By the time we finished and I accompanied him home, I was more sleepy than hungry so went right to bed.

Tuesday, October 13
Sent Louie[19] a check for his birthday. That usually proves to be the most acceptable gift I can send.

Went to the doctors in the morning before going to work. Went to the beauty parlor after work.

I am getting quantities of mail these days – mostly from the Democratic National Committee. After dinner Mary Lou and I went to see "Anthony Adverse."[20] We enjoyed it very much, although I was disappointed in the way it ended. Frederic March was splendid as Anthony. We went to the Hot Shoppe after the movie and then home.

---

18   Mae or Mary was married to her uncle Phil, the lawyer.
19   Anne's brother Louie.
20   "Anthony Adverse" is an adventure epic adapted from a best-selling novel. The story follows the globe circling tale of Anthony Adverse, the illegitimate heir to the fortune of a cruel stepfather, Don Luis, who had left the boy in the hands of the church after killing his real father. Later, Anthony gets revenge.

1936

Wednesday, October 14
Very busy all day, working on the Seminole case. I had made a luncheon date with Kommy and managed, but with considerable difficulty, to keep it. Loren had been ill, so that I imagine it is even more unpleasant for Kommy to stay at home than it would otherwise be. Mr. Wyzanski gave me so many things he thought I ought to read, and so little time in which to read them, that I took them home. I conscientiously looked through them after dinner, but with the radio blaring forth and my three roommates talking above the noise of the radio, I doubt whether any of what I was reading made an impression on my tired mind.

Thursday, October 15
Wore my black velvet. I was not feeling particularly well, so the compliments that outfit inevitably invokes were very gratifying.
Lunched at the S & W with Mary Lou, pay day meaning a trip to the Riggs Bank. Spent the entire afternoon in the library, with very little to show for my efforts.
Clara and Dorothy went to the movies. Their absence mean a comparatively peaceful evening, which I was in a mood to appreciate. I read Willa Cather's *Obscure Destinies*, and rather enjoyed them, even the ones I had already read.

Friday, October 16
Lunched at the Latch String with Kommy. Met Gladys Burch there. She seems to resent Kommy's obvious preference of me as a luncheon companion. Wore my new pink collar with my black dress, pink gloves and was generally admired. Had quantities of work, which, as a conscientious secretary, I should have stayed after 4:30 to do, but it was pouring rain and for a variety of reasons, I decided I would take myself home on time. As it was, there was a bad traffic jam, and I got home just in time for dinner.

Saturday, October 17
A lovely autumn day. Lunched with Mary Lou at the Candlestick. Walked up Connecticut Avenue to her apartment, stopping en route to do a few errands. Visited with her until I had to go home for dinner. It was such a pretty evening that I was tempted to go out, but, being unaccustomed to so much walking, I was tuckered out from my excursions in the afternoon. However, since it was Saturday night, we all sat up very late just clowning and fooling around.

Sunday, October 18
Another grand revivifying day. Went walking in the park in the morning. Mary Lou came up for dinner. After, all five of us went to the zoo. Visited the hybrid bears, among others. Ate popcorn and peanuts just to get into the proper frame of mind. And fed the animals, despite the signs. On the way back we stopped in for milk shakes. And we were not home long before we began on supper. It is well for our figures that there is only one Sunday per week.

Monday, October 19
Letter from Sam. A marriage announcement

and a letter from Frances. That, of course, necessitated lunching with Kommy, even though I was terrifically busy. Had to work late as a result.

Kommy came up after dinner with a box of candy. I read the letters he had received from Frances and Nick – all of them most interesting and unusually well written. I had typed a letter to Frances for him. He sat around and visited a while, being a little bit used to the girls by now. I went home with him and enjoyed the little jaunt very much.

Tuesday, October 20
Lunched at Brownley's with Ruth Jewell and Clara, had a pleasant time gossiping about people we all knew. Met Barney Robbins, who gave me a big hand. Shirley's husband happened along, and I was introduced to him – Dr. Eisenberg – I think.

Very rushed on the Seminole Case. Had to work late and go to the doctors, but got home in time for dinner. Was cordially invited to attend a National Luncheon of the country's leading women lawyers in New York, sponsored by the National Pro Roosevelt Association of Women Lawyers, a non- partisan organization. It is to laugh. Wonder how they define "non-partisan." Went to a lecture at the Center, to find it had been postponed.

Wednesday, October 21
Mr. Rosenwald gave me an extra application for an absentee ballot. Lunched at the Palais Royal with Rose Furr.

Worked late again, but finally got the Seminole brief off to the printer. Mr. W. confessed that he had rushed on it because he expected to be called to Boston "any day now" to present at the birth of his sister's baby.

Hazel went to Mary's to play bridge. Mary had asked me to come too, to play or not as I preferred. But I preferred to stay at home. I was tired enough to be able to enjoy an evening of just lazying around the apartment.

Thursday, October 22
Kommy called to invite me to lunch at the Latch String with Ruth, Mae Sweet and himself. Not so terribly busy today, so that I was able to leave at 4:30. Met Mary Lou and went shopping with her. Got home just in time for dinner.

Spent the evening reading, finished Anatole Francis, "Revolt of the Angels." Enjoyed his satirical wit very much. Finished a Wodehouse story in the Saturday Evening Post. Did not consider it nearly as funny as some of his that I have read. And then went to bed.

Friday, October 23
Letter from Ann Clancy, who is trying to arrange a get-together in New York for February 22.

Lunched at the Latch String with Kommy and Ruth. Met Galdys Burch there. She was "burnt up."

Worked hard, and late, on the Seminole brief. Mr. W. was peeved because Messsrs. Soremon and Hearn insisted that their names be put on the brief. He said it would be more to the point if my name were put on the brief, that my assistance had been far more valuable. Was I flustered! Irving Gottlieb called. Do not know how he got the number. Chatted quite a while and then suggested that he drop around to see me, but the suggestion was vetoed.

Saturday, October 24
A beautiful day, although I did not get much chance to enjoy it.
Mr. W. left on the noon train for Boston, leaving me in the midst of indexing. I did not get away from the office until about 3:00. Everyone else had left early on account of the horse show, etc. But maybe it was worth it, since Mr. W., before he left, had insisted on putting my name on the brief, although I had demurred and questioned the advisability of doing so. He also suggested that I be admitted to the Supreme Court so that there would be no question about my appearing on briefs. His compliments are the more appreciated because of the rarity.

Sunday, October 25
Another grand autumn day. Walked down to Mary Lou's after breakfast. Had a cup of coffee with her. Then joined a group from Social Security, and went on a two-hour bicycle ride. It was great fun. Met Sol sitting in a bench and reading. Mary came home with me for dinner. After a little rest she took us for a long ride. The park was beautiful indeed, although the foliage here is not so brilliantly colored as that at home. We all went to the Hot Shoppe for supper. Then home, to read the Sunday papers, listen to the radio, and rest.
Finished Caroline Miller's "Lamb in His Bosom."[21] Thought it an excellent portrayal of the class and the times about which it was written.

---

[21] A Pulitzer Prize winning novel about the Old South, specifically the poor people of the south Georgia backwoods, who never owned a slave or wanted to fight a war. It is a story of social customs of nineteenth century rural Georgia.

Monday, October 26
Miss Bartz's mother is sick, so she asked me to take charge of the front office in her absence, much to the resentment of the other girls.
Had to take a matter up with Mr. Rosenwald. The official discussion being completed, he turned it to a personal one, in the course of which he told me a great deal about himself, and asked a number of questions about me. He then proceeded to ask me what a lonesome chap could do for amusement in this town. I withheld my advice.
Lunched with Kommy, who had received two letters from Frances. He came up in the evening (with another box of candy). I typed a letter to Francis and one to Sam asking him to take care of various subscriptions for Francis. Clara and I saw Kommy home. (Went to the doctors after work.)

Tuesday, October 27
Mrs. Bartz passed away this morning. She had been an invalid for years, so it may all be for the best, but it is hard to lose a mother in any event.
Stayed in the front office most of the day, so did not get a change to confer with Mr. Rosenwald about his pressing personal problems. Mr. W. came back this morning, not yet an uncle.
Lunched with Miss Quinn, one of my favorites in the office. Since Mr. Reed was not in, I left a little bit early, although Mr. W. hemmed and hawed about it. But I can forgive him anything for a while – the Seminole brief came back today, with my name appearing on the signature page. That was somewhat of a thrill. Had my hair done.

Wednesday, October 28
Dashing back and forth between – Mr. Reed's office and my own just about wore me out. After much beating around the bush, Mr. Rosenwald made a date with me for Saturday night. As I had suspected, he was hesitant because he feared he might be stepping on Mr. W's toes.
Several of the men seemed quite enthused about my name appearing on the brief, and insisted I must become a member of the Supreme Court so that my name might appear in the Reports, so I set the wheels in motion.
By the time I got home, I had a sick headache and a sick stomach. Threw up my breakfast and luncheon, had a cup of tea for dinner and went to bed.
(Miss Wheaton and I were delighted to buy the flowers for Miss Bartz's mother.)

Thursday, October 29
Took time off in the morning to go to the doctor. Since his violet ray lamp got broken, I do not seem to progress so rapidly.
Kommy called to tell me he had mail from Shanghai, where Frances had been visiting, and so, of course, I had to lunch with him.
Several of the girls went to Mrs. Bartz's funeral. I didn't go because I had too much work, because I did not know Mrs. Bartz and because it is bad enough to go to a funeral when one had to go. Went shopping with Mary Lou. Bought a flowered blouse with a metallic thread running through it.
Mary dropped in after dinner and wanted me to go for a ride, but I was in lounging pajamas, and dog-tired. So she visited for a while. Got a long letter from Louis and one from Sam, so I am "up" on all the family gossip.

Friday, October 30
Lunched with Kommy and Ruth at the Latch String. Bought a pair of black suede shoes and some new pink satin underwear after work. Very busy at the office, working now on the steamship fine case. Dorothy wanted to go to schule after dinner, but I was too tired and Clara did not feel like going. Also, I had to do some pressing with which I could not entrust the heavy-handed Daisy. So everyone stayed home except Hazel, who went to visit her poker-playing cronies. Heard an excellent speech by ex-President Herbert Hoover.

Saturday, October 31
A lovely day. Lunched at Cornwell's with Mary Lou and Miss Connors. Meandering up Connecticut Avenue, Mary and I met Kommy, had a soda at Munnally's and then walked Mary to the hairdresser's. Kommy came home with me and I read to him. Clara, Dorothy and Hazel went out after dinner, so when Harold Rosenwald finally arrived I was alone. We sat around a while, and then started to go out, but heard some neighbor's radio blaring forth the President's speech, so came back to hear it. When we did finally leave, he did not want to go to any place where there could be a mob dancing and cutting up. So we went to two or three cocktail rooms, could not get in for the crowds, and finally wound up at the Carleton. Discussed Mr. W. most of the evening. Decided that R. [i.e. Rosenwald] is rather a bore.

Monthly Memoranda 1936

January

I hope it is not true that the beginning of the year is a clue to the end of it, and all the interim, since I started it by moving and by meeting a new boyfriend who is a complete mope. And, mope or no, even he has stopped calling me. And Frances and I are on the outs, seriously it seems this time.

And although Shirley has started calling me again, she irks me more than she pleases me. And we are all ready to move again, but cannot find a suitable place. And I want and need some new clothes, but am reluctant to burden myself with additional things to move. It looks like I had better not only stick to French, but start at least one other class.

February

I have lived through another February 29th and am still single and completely lacking in "prospects". Dearie me!

Had a very satisfactory trip home, insofar as everyone was well and seemed quite contented with his or her respective lot, an unusual state of affairs for my tribe. Had an opportunity to wear my ski-suit, which, in Washington, is indeed an occasion.

Maneuvered a new job for Clara, so that she is now "off my mind". The new job is an improvement in every respect, and she is far happier than she was working for Phil. Relatives are all right - in their place.

March

The crowning event of the past month was our decision to take an apartment instead of a room. I think, and sincerely hope, it will work out satisfactorily.

Saw Mother, Jean, Sam and Molly, and was happy to see them all looking particularly well and happy. My "friendship" with Frances has apparently come to an end, and my "friendship" with Stella Margold has apparently been renewed. But the latter certainly does not compensate for the former.

Mary Lou has turned out to be my "old faithful". I should be thoroughly ashamed when I think how I neglected her for Frances.

April

Had a birthday.

Lost a case in the Supreme Court.

Took sick leave.[22]

Became finally convinced that Frances and I are entirely "through" with each other.

Heard about a possible three months job in Geneva, and agitated to try to get it.

Saw Walter Hampden in "Cyrano de Bergerac" - a real treat.

Ended, for the time being, my French studies because of an argument about religion. And had a most delightful visit with the Fullers, becoming more than ever fond of and attached to Carrie Fuller.

And the apartment project is quite a success, despite Minna's unpopularity. I hope she keeps her promise to move because of the <u>excessive expenses</u>.

---

22   Anne suffered from severe migraine headaches for much of her life, but she does not specify the nature of her sickness at this time.

April was, indeed, a very full month, with enough activity and events to keep me happy, - well, most of the time.

Now I should like to start May off by hearing that I am going to Geneva. Although I am not optimistic enough to proceed with the preparations for the trip, I shall continue to expect that I am going until I am informed to the contrary. Miss Patterson has proved to be a good sport and a real friend in connection with maneuvering to get me the Geneva job. Mrs. Wyzanski, apparently, will be delighted to get rid of me for a least a few months. And I have always been anxious to go abroad. So everybody will be happy. Having had my first airplane ride, a trip to Europe automatically becomes the next thing on the schedule.

May

May has been rather an interesting month. The first accomplishment was getting rid of Minna.
The White House garden party.
My Geneva bubble exploded.
Have gone in for bicycling in a big way, and like it. Got some new clothes, which everyone, including myself, liked very much.
Drove to Winchester with Mary and Jack, a most enjoyable trip. Have more - or - less renewed acquaintance with Frances. Whether more or less remains to be seen. I have a tentative engagement to lunch with her on Tuesday. Hope it is not too awkward.

June

What a month!
Started out by acquiring a new roommate, a splendid acquisition in every respect. And Frances and I are friendly again - something, I believe, that only her imminent departure for China could have accomplished.

She is a grand person in so many ways, if only she would not overdo the grand traits. My athletic activities increased during the month of June, something which pleases me exceedingly. I have completed a course of tennis lessons, which gives me great satisfaction. Of course I almost never get chance to play, but, nonetheless, I have completed a course of tennis lessons.

And what an unconstitutional month it has been! Federal legislation, state legislation, the Supreme Court, the various lower courts - a heterogeneity of bungling legislation and contradictory court of opinions. Beginning with the New York Minimum Wage Law, on down through R.R. Retirement and the Fruehauf case - bang, slash, snip!

Getting a taste of a lazy job such as I have not had since I worked for Warner V. Taylor. And I do not like it any better than I did then. And I was studying law at least part of that time, which helped considerably to prevent me from getting bored. The solution seems to be to take a course of study.

July

Frances has left for China, and I am delighted that we parted good friends.
Made my debut in the movies. Am not taking the next train for Hollywood.
Had the usual discussion and debate about vacations. Mr. Wyzanski won this time, but not entirely by fair means, since he had to use the

threat that he may leave the Department in the fall. Mr. Hiss[23] has left on vacation, after which he is not returning here, but is taking a position with the State Department. Wonder what effect, if any, that will have upon Mr. Wyzanski's plans - and, consequently, upon mine.

August
Have spent more time at home this vacation than I have since I went to Washington. Just as well, I suppose. I am getting a good rest. Mother is very happy, and the money I should otherwise have spent on my vacation I can give to her. But, as far as excitement is concerned, this vacation is a complete flop. I have spent some pleasant days, however, thanks mostly to my friends in Boston.
Relations between Mother and Father are, if possible, more hateful than ever, which does not tend to make visiting at home more pleasant, but does put us under a greater obligation to come home.

September
Wonder if I shall ever again spend as much time loafing in Lawrence as I did on my last vacation. In a way I am glad I did it, since I made somebody happy. But then again, hearing George Gray tell of his adventures in South America, and Miss Quinn tell of what she saw in Europe, etc., I wonder if I was wrong not to try to go someplace new to me also. But where I should have gone, or with whom, is more than I can figure out even now when it is too late to do anything about it.

October
Got a little male attention, for a change, and, as usual, decided it was not so enchanting as it seems to be when it has been lacking for some time. But I think I should like, one of these days before I get too old, to go on some rip-roaring dates with a dancing fool who cannot carry on an intelligent conversation, but can keep me amused and gay all evening. The people I meet nowadays seem so staid and sober.
Well, I got my name on a brief, and that should keep me happy for a while.

November
Finally got admitted to the Bar of the Supreme Court of the United States - for what it may be worth.[24] Had a very enjoyable visit with Father, Louie and Ben Franks. Father can be so agreeable when he wishes. And Mother can be so generous according to her lights. It is nothing short of tragic that their lives, and their children's lives, have been so full of unhappiness and misunderstanding. But I am afraid that their hatred of each other can never be altered now. The example is enough to turn anyone against marriage.[25]
I have become quite pally with Kommy. He is a good scout, and for more entertaining than many much younger folks I know.
Things at the office are running along much the same smooth lines. I have been rather

---

23 This is a reference to Alger Hiss who appears a couple of times in her diary.

24 At 26 years old she was admitted to the Bar of the Supreme Court, which allowed her name to be on cases appealed to that Court.

25 The example of her parents not only made her hesitant toward marriage, but once she was married she was committed to having a good relationship.

busy, which is gratifying. Hazel turned out to be a blackguard and an ungrateful wretch. It seems to me that I expect very little of people, and yet always get much less. And here we are with the necessity of moving again. We are one of the wondering Tribes, all right.

December
The superstition that one does all year what one did the first day of the year seemed to come true. We spent a goodly part of the year agitating about a place in which to live. How can I worry about the Spanish Civil War when civil war is raging in my own home, as it has for years, and as it will continue to do as long as the combatants live! I cannot be hardhearted enough not to come home, because of Mother's loneliness. But I certainly do not enjoy my visits. And as for making Mother happy, whatever I give her she gives Jean, and whenever anyone says anything to me in the least complimentary, she say, "But you should see my daughter Jean."

1937

By 1937 Anne was twenty-seven years old. She had worked four years as a secretary to Charles Wyzanski with no possibility of a position as a lawyer. She was beginning to think that she might not be able to get a professional job and maybe she was too old to get married. Wyzanski does not seem to have used his influence and position to help her professionally, probably because she was such an excellent assistant, and he did not want to lose her. Although Anne still wondered about the emotional possibilities with Wyzanski, for all practical purposes there was no future in that relationship. It was Wyzanski's decision to resign and leave Washington that broke the logjam emotionally and professionally for her. After he left, her life began to change. In September she was offered a position with the National Labor Relations Board as a lawyer.   -- RDH

1937

Monday, September 13
Another letter from C.E.W., written from New York. He doubts very much whether I can get a job on the NLRB, and thinks I ought to go to Boston in any event. It is so difficult to know what is my best move. Lunched at Cerews with Clara. Went shopping and finally bought a hat – small, black, with a veil.
Sadie Wine came up for dinner. Clara went bicycling in the evening with Ernie Goodrich. Ruth, Sadie, and I walked up to Fourteen Street to shop. It was a cool, brisk evening, and the walk was most enjoyable. Stopped for some Weyman ice cream. Then to Sadie's apartment for a very short visit. I enjoy Sadie's company, but Ruth's "New York-ishness" annoys me.

Tuesday, September 14
Lunched at Tally–Ho with Frances, Nick, Edythe, Bob, Jack, and Kommy.
Had dinner rather early. Went to Kol Nidre services with Ruth, Sadie, Cecile, and Clara.[26] Saw Baba and several other members of the family there, also a few friends. Mike Yoelson[27] told me he had wanted to take me to a party at the Shoreham a few days ago, but Lester had told him I left town. Les confirmed the story. Just as well, no doubt, as Mike's only asset is his half-brother, Al Jolson, while his liabilities are many.
It was a delightful evening, and I enjoyed the walk to schule and back home more than anything else. The schule was too crowded and stuffy for comfort.

Wednesday, September 15
A beautiful balmy autumn day. Clara, Ruth and I walked down to the 8th Street Temple. Met Cecile there. The place was almost deserted, and the English services seemed dull in comparison to the unintelligible but stirring Hebrew ritual so we went back to schule. We fasted until about 5 o'clock, when my head began to ache pretty badly. Cecile, Clara, and I had a bite to eat, but it was too late by then, and the headache persisted. Phil gave us a ride home. Cecile came home with us for dinner. I hardly ate a mouthful, but it was enough to make me violently sick to my stomach. Sadie called, and Mike, but I would not speak with either of them. Ruth went to the theater, Clara and Cecile to the movies, and I to bed. And that's Yom Kippur.

Thursday, September 16
Had a rush job to do for Mr. Reed. He came out just as George and I finished checking it, and hearing George say there were no errors, commented that not many people rated 100% in their work.
Lunched at L.S.[28] with Kommy. Frances and Nick have gone to New York again.
Long letter from Louie,[29] who wants a new job, for which I do not blame him, and seems to think all I have to do is ask Nick or Mr. Wyzanski, and he will have a job. I should so like to help him, but he has so few practical business assets.

26 Anne's sister Clara, Cecile Neuhauser, Sadie Wine, and Ruth Weyand (?).
27 Al Jolson's half brother Mike was interested in Anne for some time, but she rejected his attentions.
28 Latch String.
29 Anne's brother Louie.

Clara and I went to the theater to see "Brother Rat."[30] It was a lively comedy, very well played, and we both enjoyed it immensely. And tomorrow I see Nat Witt.[31]

Friday, September 17
Went over to see Nat Witt, but he was called into a board meeting. While waiting for him, I chatted with Hi Shulson[32], Howard Lichtenstein[33], John Porter, and Allen Greenberg. Hi invited me to luncheon. I enjoyed turning him down. Got tired of waiting, so made an appointment for tomorrow.
Received from C.E.W. a beautiful compact he had bought in Vienna, and a note urging me to make up my vacillating mind and come to Boston.
Lunched at L.S. with Kommy. Had the afternoon off in honor of Constitution Day, so had my hair permanented.
Dinner with Kommy at the Silver Bowl. Then to the apartment. Had tickets to hear the President speak at the Sylvan Theater, but it was cold and disagreeable, and had rained all morning, so no one else wanted to go. We stayed home and talked all evening.

Saturday, September 18
Had a very pleasant chat with Witt[34] and, later, with Fahy. I will know my fate within a week. Lunched with Mary Lou and Clara. It was a pretty afternoon, so we went walking in Rock Creek Park.
Ruth had Norman up for dinner. Went to a dance at the Bell Haven Country Club with George Gray and two other couples. The boys were all good dancers and loads of fun. I liked the girls too, but they were very young. George is a sweet old thing.

Sunday, September 19
Slept late. Lazied around most of the day. Finally got disgusted, dressed, and dropped in on Mary. They were about to drive up to Martha's for sodas so I went along. Then we went for a ride. When I got home, I was told that Hi[35] and a friend of his had wanted a date with Ruth and me, but made a date with Clara in my absence. In order not to be home when the boys came, I went to the movies with Mary Smida.

---

30   "Brother Rat" is a comedy about cadets at VMI. Ronald Reagan and Jane Wyman met while working on the film. They later married.
31   First NLRB contact for a position.
32   Hyman Schulson was an attorney at the NLRB in 1937-38. For most of the rest of his life he worked in Zionist affairs and had a role in negotiations leading to the establishment of Israel.
33   Howard Lichtenstein had a distinguished career in labor law. The Howard Lichtenstein Distinguished Professorship was established in his name at Hofstra. As a senior partner in the law firm of Proskauer Rose Goetz & Mendelsohn, he was considered an authority on administrative law. In addition, Mr. Lichtenstein was a strong advocate for the teaching of legal ethics.

---

34   These "chats" must have been the interviews for the position with the NLRB. Witt was shortly named the Executive Secretary of the NLRB, and Charles Fahy was General Counsel. In 1940 Fahy was named Solicitor General of the U.S. Later, he was appointed to the U.S. Court of Appeal, D.C. Circuit where he served the rest of his life.
35   Hyman Schulson. See footnote 29.

Monday, September 20
Charming letter from Carrie Fuller demanding to know what's what. Answer: nothing. Quite busy at the office. Miss Bartz is still on vacation, and George starts school again Wednesday. He wants me to substitute in the front office for him. He gets in at 3:00. I am not particularly enthused about the idea, but should like to accommodate George. Frances and Nick were due back today. I suppose I ought to call on them, but they are so busy with their own affairs that I feel simply in the way when I am with them. Spent a quiet evening at home listening to the radio and reading *Time*. Heard Maxwell Anderson's first radio play, done for the fist time – very interesting.

Tuesday, September 21
Lee MacKinnon called to break our riding date because of unexpected out-of-town guests.
Miss Connors returned to the office today. We lunched together at Palais Royal. Sadie called – wants me to go to Boston with her this weekend. But I am making no plans until I hear from the Board.
After dinner Mary Lou and I went for a very long walk. It was a beautiful evening – full moon, except for a few minutes, when it rained a little – and we both enjoyed the walk very much. I enjoyed the feeling – rather rare these days – of being physically tired.

Wednesday, September 22
Working for Mr. Reed. Had a rather interesting morning. Paul Freund – surprise of surprises – commented on my new hair-do. Lunched in the cafeteria with George. The food was pretty bad but George is good company.
Supposed to visit Frances and Nick in the evening, but I was tired and did not feel well, so called it off.
Sadie Wine came up to visit in the evening. She is such a cheerful, exuberant person that her visit perked me up a good deal. She has job worries too, and said the visit did her a lot of good. So everyone was happy.

Thursday, September 23
Worked for Mr. Reed again. Lunched in the cafeteria with George, Steve Farrand and Paul Freund.
Nat Witt called and asked me to come over to see him, which I did. He told me that the Board would give me a 3 months appointment at my same salary, and suggested I get a leave of absence for 3 months. He said he and Fahy had recommended a permanent appt. at more money, but the Board demurred because of my lack of legal experience.
Sadie Wine came up for dinner. She, Clara and I went to the theater to see Gertrude Lawrence in "Susan and God."[36] It was very well done. I enjoyed it. The story contained much food for thought.

Friday, September 24
Mr. Reed said he would grant me the leave of absence. But I learned that would mean losing all my accumulated leave, so decided to resign. He assured me he would take me back anyhow, if possible but hoped it would not be necessary.

---

36 A play about a women whose religious devotion causes strain within her family. Later, it was made into a movie with Joan Crawford as the lead.

Lunched at L.S. with Kommy and Clara. She came back with me to see Mr. Smith about getting my job, but there are Civil Service complications that may prevent it.

George Gray came up for dinner. A friend of his was to pick us up after dinner to help us move my accumulated junk from the office. Something happened, however, and the boyfriend did not show up. However, we enjoyed having George for dinner anyhow – even in spite of Grace having found it necessary to take the afternoon off.

Saturday, September 25
George's friend had gone to Apt. 216. Nat Witt called. Looks like I may lose my leave anyhow. Made my farewells. Luncheon party at the Madrillon – Misses Connors, Furr, Drenstl, Quinn, Wheaton, Ruth and Clara. Back to the office to show Ruth around the building. Paul Freund moved my stuff, Ruth, Clara and me home. Stopped in for just a minute, but soon found an excuse to leave.
Clara and I went to call on Sadie and Eve. Amy Orent also dropped in. Spent a pleasant evening.

Sunday, September 26
A dull dark day. Did not get dressed until after dinner, when Clara and I dropped in on Mary Sinda, Mary Lou being out with Jack. She had two guests for dinner. We had dessert and coffee with them; sat around and chatted for a while, escorted the guests part way home, and then ambled up to Martha's for sodas.

Monday, September 27
Raining, but my spirits could not be dampened.
Nat Witt chatted with me for a few minutes about the Board's procedure, then assigned me to an office with Joseph Robinson[37], a very pleasant person. Introduced to so many people I shall probably not remember half of them. Given a great quantity of material to read, but had too many visitors to get much done. Lunched at Tally-Ho with Kommy.
Telegram from C.E.S. – "Am betting on your happiness and success in new job."
Long letter from Dorothy. Letters from Anne Clancey and Pauline Colahan.
Clara and I went to Mary Lou's birthday party. Had rather an enjoyable time, although I should have liked to get home and to bed earlier than I did. Should have done some more reading too. However…

Tuesday, September 28
Mail from home – happy about my job. Letter from Sam, who does not know about it yet.
Lunched at the Bavarian Inn with Charlie Horshy. He is a good scout and always cheers me considerably. Read a lot more stuff, and received a great deal more advice – for what it was worth. But everyone was very agreeable.
Received so many invitations that I felt constrained to attend the Lawyers Guild[38] meet-

---

37 Witt, reputedly head of a secret leftist group within the NLRB, assigned Anne to an office with Joe Robinson, also alleged to be a member of the group.

38 The National Lawyer's Guild was founded in 1937 as an alternative to the American Bar Associa-

ing this evening. Tom Emerson was Chairman. Some of the discussion was interesting, much of it stupid. Most of it centered around the Spanish situation.[39] I got fed up and left about 10:30, but they were still going strong.

Wednesday, September 29
Assigned to work on the Ford Case with Julius Schlezinger.[40] I like J.S., and the case seems very interesting.
Lunched at the Press Cafeteria with Schulson, Selley, and Lippman[41]. Chester Ward[42] dropped in to see me, and to present me with a complimentary subscription to *Labor Relations Reports.*
Attended a Board meeting. J.S. was reporting on two cases to the Board members, Nat Witt and Alec Hawes. Three other "freshman" and I were invited. It was very interesting. I was singled out since Madden recognized me.
Wonderful letter from Carrie Fuller, who is as thrilled and excited about my new job as I – or even more so.

The dressmaker came to the apartment to give us some fittings. Took most of the evening, but I managed to find a little time to do some reading.

Thursday, September 30
Perfect autumn weather. Walked both to work and home from work.
Lunched at S&W with Miss Connors and Miss [Fannie] Boyls, the latter a female lawyer also with the Board. Miss Connors had some mail for me, but no check.
By the end of the day it was quite apparent to me that the arrangement for the division of work between me and Julius Schlezinger was not possible. It looks like I might have to drop it. I was disappointed, and he seemed even more so.
Letter from Jean[43] asking me to pull political strings to help Joe get a job, and making numerous protestations of sisterly affection despite my determined estrangement. Such hypocrisy!

Friday, October 1
Attended a Board hearing on the Todd Shipbuilding case. Found it very interesting. Nat Witt and Jules have devised a different, and for me, more interesting division of the work on the Ford case. Lunched alone at Cornwell's because I had several errands I wanted to do. Worked until almost 6:00, and then walked home. Ruth and I went to the Mormon concert – a delightful half-hour. Spent most of the evening reading. Wonder how long my eyes will hold out under this strict regime. However, in the office, when I get tired of reading, I

---

tion in protest of the ABA policy of excluding African-Americans and Jews from membership.
39   Spanish Civil War, Fascists against Republicans.
40   On Anne's second day at the NLRB she was assigned to work on a case with Julius who would become her husband two years later.
41   Hyman Schulson, Solaman Lippman, Selley unidentified. Lippman started with the NLRB but later had a long private practice career in labor law. For 25 years he was the general counsel of the old Retail Clerks International Union. In 1972 he founded Lippman, Semsker and Salb of Bethesda. He was also attorney for the National Organization for Women, the House Education and Labor Committee.
42   An attorney and recognized scholar on labor law.

---

43   Joe Ruscoll, Jean's husband.

can look at the pictorial exhibits, most of them gory and brutal things. I also wonder whether this job and these associates will make me a little liberal instead of a little conservative.[44]

Saturday, October 2
A beautiful day. Ruth, Clara and I had luncheon in the Tally-Ho garden. Went shopping. I bought a sport dress, black and white plaid with blue trimming.
After dinner Clara and I visited with Sadie and Eve. Eve talks so much about "Raum" that it is, at moments, rather awkward. Maybe she suspects that I know him other than Mr. Wyzanski's associate.

Sunday, October 3
Rained all day. We did not even bother to get dressed. May Lou and Mary C. dropped in for a short visit during the afternoon. Ruth and I got fed up by evening, so, although it was still raining, we took ourselves for a walk. Stopped at the delicatessen for some stuff and brought it home for supper.

Monday, October 4
Justice Black[45] took his seat on the bench today, amid a storm of acrid criticism. Lunched with Sellery and Burstein at the Open Door Cafeteria. They were both with the Puerto Rico Construction Administration, and I enjoyed lunching with them very much.

They don't take their mission to emancipate the working classes quite so seriously as do some of the other boys.[46]
Rained all day, but let up in the evening for a while. Clara and I went for a walk, ended up at the drugstore for sundaes. Met Ruth and Esther there- also supposed to be out walking.
Arnold was supposed to be back today, but nary a word did I hear from him.
Worked at home for a while.

Tuesday, October 5
Lunched at the Roumaxian Inn with Joe Robinson, Millard Midonick, a chap by the name of Wolf and another by the name of Rosen. Wore my new dress. Sellery exclaimed that I looked very pretty.
Ruth came to the office again for an interview, but it looks pretty definitely now like she will not get the job. I am sorry because she is so disappointed.
The dressmaker brought our things up, including my pink evening dress. Now I shall take the things to the cleaners, I have clothes to wear. But shall I have places to wear them – at least, to wear my evening clothes? I needn't worry about the others.

Wednesday, October 6
Lunched at the Tally-Ho with Kommy. Felt rather guilty about having neglected him so, but when I can lunch with such entertaining young men, he suffers by contrast. But I still enjoy his company very much anyhow.
Hy Schulson wanted to pay his bet tonight. I was glad I had a good excuse not to go with him.

---

44   One of the few oblique references to the political climate of the NLRB at that point.
45   Justice Hugo Black went on to be the fourth longest serving judge in the history of the Supreme Court and one of the most influential judges of the twentieth century. He defended civil rights.

46   Another reference to the political climate.

Cecile Neuhauser came up for dinner. She, Ruth, Clara and I went to the National to see Constance Cummings in "Madame Bovary."[47] The whole thing was interesting and excellently played. Constance Cummings was superb – and beautiful.

Thursday, October 7
Lunched at Childs' with Joe and Jules.
Have finished the commerce part of the Ford case. Decided I might as well work on another case while waiting for Jules to read his part of the record. Alec Hawes gave me the Shell Chemical case, an R case. Arnold called me at the office and asked if he could see me tonight. I told him to come up fairly late, so I could have time to get my hair washed and waved. About nine when he arrived, and he talked so long about his trip that it was too late to go to the movies. We did finally go for a long ride, however. He had an interesting, but tiring trip. Was pleased about my new job. Invited me to the Harvard Navy game a week from Saturday. But made no other date, although he told me how much he had missed me, how glad he was to see me again, how nice I looked in my new dress, how pretty I looked to him – with or without lipstick.

Friday, October 8
Lunched at the Embassy Grill with Marty Kurash and Warren Sharfman.[48] They were both rather foolish, and I had a lot of fun.
My R case is quite complicated. I don't seem to be making much progress with it. Ruth left this afternoon for New York. Heard Marty and Joe[49] making a date to have dinner down town, so invited them to our house. Clara dropped in at the office and visited with some of her old friends.
Joe and Marty left fairly early, which suited me as I was tired. Marty, who is lame, I know, enjoyed it all very much.
Shirley Colby called and invited us in for bridge. Carla went, but I begged off. Sadie called and asked me over, but I turned her down too. Went to bed early instead.

Saturday, October 9
Lunched at Cornwell's with Mary Lou, Miss Franklin, Sadie, and Clara. Shopped all afternoon with Sadie and Clara – and did not buy a thing.
It was pouring in the evening, but quite undaunted, Clara, Sadie and I went shopping on 14th Street. Clara bought come shoes, and we got some delicatessen at Sam's new store. But about all I accomplished by my exertions was plenty of exercise and wet feet. However, it was all rather fun – even the walking in the rain – and at least I know now what I am going to buy.

Sunday, October 10
Cloudy, disagreeable weather. Mary Lou and I went walking in the morning. Too threat-

---

47   Flaubert's masterpiece about a provincial doctor's wife who has multiple affairs and lives extravagantly to escape the banality of small town life. Anne regularly attended theater during this period.
48   Sharfman was at the NLRB in the late 1930's but continued to be active in Washington legal circles for several decades, including the Civil Aeronautics Board.
49   Martin Kurash and Joe Robinson, both identified as active in the clandestine Communist group.

ening to do any of the several other things we had tentatively planned.

Mary Smida came up for supper and the evening. Ruth home with a lot of new clothes and talk.

Monday, October 11
Reported to Alec on my case. Would like very much to know what he thought of my presentation.

Back on the Ford case – on discharges for union activities. Lunched alone, with the intention of doing some errands, but had so much work I dashed back to the office. Levitt's petition was denied because of lack of personal injury. A meeting at 4:30 of the so – called lawyers' union. We had a lot of fun, but I shall be surprised if their program reached fruition.

Supposed to go shopping on 14th Street with Mary Lou, but decided I had better stay at home and work. Ruth's friends Ester and Clara dropped in, and Shirley Colby – so I gave up any idea of working.

Tuesday, October 12
Lunched with Midonish, Joe Friedman and Joe Robinson. Midonish suggested going to the Supreme Court to hear Reed and John Davis on the Dravo case. Spoke to Hawes about it, did a lot of telephoning, and then finally did not go. Had so darned much work – checking signatures on petitions with payrolls, and what-not.

Received a charming letter of congratulation from John Murphy. Back to the office after dinner to finish checking lists of names – stupid, tedious work. But most of the boys were also at the office, and all of them dropped in to see what I was doing, which kept me entertained. The Board was sitting, and was still hearing cases when I left at about 11. Howard[50] took Allan Rosenberg, Marty Kurash and me to the Hot Shoppe for a bite. Sat around talking all hours. I was completely exhausted – but glad Columbus discovered America.

Wednesday, October 13
A cold rainy day. The Board sat until midnight last night but still has not got around to hearing me. Worked on the Ford case all day. Because of the weather, lunched at the drugstore across the street with Joe Robinson and Allan Rosenberg. Brought some stuff home from the office to read. I have a tremendous accumulation of miscellaneous Board material to read. Wonder if I shall stay on the Board long enough to get it all read. The only exciting event of the evening was a visit from the dressmaker. I know how busy Arnold is, but he might find time to call once in a while to say hello, so I'll know he has not forgotten me.

Thursday, October 14
Lunched alone so I could dash downtown and do a few errands. Worked on the Ford case all day. By the time the Board does call me I shall be full of information about the Ford case rather than about the Shell Chemical case.

Has become so cold that I ordered my raccoon [i.e. coat] out of storage for game Sat-

---

50   Probably referring to Howard Friedman, an attorney at the Board.

urday. Clara stopped at the office for me, and we went shopping together – for groceries. I took some work home, looked it over after dinner, but was tired and did not try to do much. After all, it is also important to know when to stop.

Wrote a few letters, but still have many more to write. I just do not seem able to catch up with myself these days.

Card from Jean thanking me for the information I procured for Joe.

Friday, October 15
Lunched at the Hotel Washington with Charlie Horsley. We had a grand luncheon, starting off with bluepoints, and I always enjoy his conversation.

Arnold called me at the office and again at home to make definite arrangements for going to the Harvard-Navy football game tomorrow. Alec Hanes said I could get off early – as long as I was rooting for Harvard. Tried to arrange to report to the Board this afternoon – but no soap. Two new lawyers came in today and another one is coming in tomorrow. Wonder if I shall ever get to know them all. Got my raccoon out of storage for the game, my pink evening dress from the cleaners for the celebration after the game, and hope I'm all set.

Saturday, October 16
A glorious sunny day. Eve Braverman and Dave Hether were in our car. Joined in Baltimore by Lenny Raum, Marvin Braveman and their girl friends. Met Alec and Mrs. Hawes, Allan Rosenberg, Mark Winkler, and a number of others I knew. Had a grand time. The game was 0-0.

Everyone was so tired after the game that what was going to be a large party dwindled down to Arnold, Marvin and myself. We went to the Shoreham for dinner and dancing. Saw Jules there. Had a nice time, but we were all too tired to be very jolly.

Sunday, October 17
Went to the cocktail party at 1718 Q. Street. A big crowd, most of them from Justice or the Labor Board (including the Witts, Sellery and Burnstine) so I had a grand time. Went with Eve and Marvin Braverman. Got a little better acquainted with Lenny Raum, who seems to be a very agreeable sort. "Fixed" Clara up with Moe. Harold Leventhal took me home.

Monday, October 18
The combination of being unwell, too much excitement, and irregular meals all weekend was too much for me, and I was frightfully sick all night.[51] But got up and went to work nonetheless. Lunched at the Roumanian Inn with Joe, Warren, Howard, Midonick, Kamination, Allan and Jules.

Have finished the "unfair discharges" in the Ford case. Staff meeting from 4:00 to 5:00. Clara stopped by for me, and we went to the grocery store.

I worked for a little while after dinner, wrote some letters, and went to bed, not too late, and not too early or I should not have been able to fall asleep.

---

51   Anne suffered with migraine headaches and sometimes does not clearly state if it is a migraine or other ailment.

Tuesday, October 19
Pouring rain. I nonetheless went out at noon because I had to do some errands. Most of the boys "ate in."

Working on the peskiest, but far from most important, part of the Ford case – ownership of the overpass on which the riot occurred. Finally got called before the Board about 5:00. Presented the case to Witt, Hawes, and the two Smiths, Madden being out of town. They decided the questions involved merited Madden's opinion, so I shall have to present the case again.

It had stopped raining when I left the office, so I stopped for groceries. Pouring worse than ever when I left the store.

Brought home some work. Shall not make a habit of it, but just until I get going.

Wednesday, October 20
To [Supreme] Court at noon with Asher. Lunched at the Cafeteria. Met many of my old friends. Heard part of Paul's argument in the jigsaw puzzle case. He did well enough, but is not another Wyzanski by any means.

As for Judge Black – I may be prejudiced, but he does not look particularly "judicious" to me. Got Arnold two symphony tickets for his birthday – for next Tuesday, although his birthday is Wednesday. But I thought he would rather hear a good concert Tuesday than a mediocre play Wednesday.

Moe called Clara and took her to the opera. Ruth went to a lecture at the Center. Anne stayed home and worked – the idiot! This must not become a habit!

Thursday, October 21
Paul[52] got quite a bit of publicity because at one time he said something about changing the rules, just as the Court sometimes does. Hughes[53] commented that the Court was not a game. "No," shot back Paul, "but it is a puzzle." Was told to wait around in the morning, and again in the afternoon, for the Board, but through someone's error was not called.

Have been given a case on which the Regional Director refused to issue a complaint. I do not agree with the R.D.

To the theater to see the Lunts in "Amphitryon 38." It was clever and amusing, and very well acted. But it was more than risqué, it was positively smutty. The Lunts, it seems to me, are able enough actors to warrant a better vehicle. Met Hy Schulson, Mark Johnson, and their friend Al Siegal at the theater.

Friday, October 22
Arnold called to thank me for the tickets and to ask for a date for tomorrow night. With the Board more than two hours, along with a couple of other attorneys working on similar cases. Finally decided to follow the Globe case.

Dick Wolf[54] is leaving the Board. Nat Witt is getting his job, and Tom Emerson will be the new chief.[55] I am selfishly sorry to see Nat leave Review, but glad it did not happen a few weeks ago. Tom and I lose no love for each other.

Have lost my fountain pen and miss it very

---

52   Perhaps Paul Nachtman, an attorney with the Board at the time.
53   Chief Justice Charles Hughes of the Supreme Court (1930-41).
54   Secretary General of the NLRB
55   Of the Review Division of the NLRB

much. Received a perfectly wonderful letter from Carrie Fuller. She has certainly stood by me and provided me with irresistible inspiration. There were times, when I was going to law school, when I did try to resist it.

Saturday, October 23
Lunched at Cornwell's with Mary Lou, Clara and Anne Lawrence. Went shopping. I bought an evening wrap in Garfinchel's – black, velvet, long, lined in white, with a white fur hood. Also bought a pair of black, toeless, dressy, sandals. To the beauty parlor.
Arnold [Raum] suggested we go to the movies as he was tired, had a cold, etc., etc. He stalled around so much I suspect he was not keen even about going to the movies, but I did not want to sit around all evening, so we went to the movies.

Sunday, October 24
Cecile Neuhauser came up to cook Hungarian Chicken Goulash for us. Preparing dinner, and eating it, took the best part of the day. It was a lot of trouble, but a grand dinner. Sat around for a while digesting it. Cecile had to leave about six, so Clara and I walked her home, for the company and exercise.

Monday, October 25
Took most of the day to get my decision written, but I finally did, and got a stenographer to type it. Hope it suits, but don't suppose it will. Also, finally got to see Alex Hawes about the compliant Mrs. Rosoeter had dismissed, and won him to my way of thinking, that the compliant should have been issued.

Did a day's work at the office, but did not stay late and did not take any work home. I do not want it to become a habit. And yet I have so much to do – so much to learn. Compromised by spending part of the evening reading back numbers of the Labor Relations Reports which I had not gotten a change to read. Did go to bed early, however, because I have a very heavy schedule ahead of me.

Tuesday, October 26
Surprise! Charles Wyzanski dropped in to see me first thing in the morning. We had a delightful chat, but because his visit was so unexpected I did not say, or ask about, many things I should otherwise have mentioned. Bought a black felt riding hat. Maybe I'll go riding one of these days soon.
Got two new cases today. There is certainly no lack of work. Wore my brocade gown and new wrap to the concert. Was much complimented. Arnold told me I looked "regal" – and he is not much of a one for compliments. Met a number of people we knew at the concert. The concert was delightful. Fritz Kreisler was the soloist, Eugene Ormandy conducting the Philadelphia Symphony. Arnold being a musician could find things to criticize, but not I. Clara and Ruth were both out, so we stopped at the apartment. After 12 Arnold got his birthday kiss.

Wednesday, October 27
Our regional conference began this morning. Some of the speakers from the regions were interesting. Others were obviously

talking just for the sake of talking. The A.F. of L. – C.I.O.[56] Peace Conference had come to naught, as I expected. Lunched at the Chamberlin with Joe, Henry Lehman and Monty Wolf. They shared my impression of the regional representatives.

Korey, the trial examiner on the Mackey case, when he heard that I had it, suggested that I also handle the Columbia Broadcasting case. Alec Hawes thought it a good idea. I now have enough work for the rest of my probation period.

Supposed to go to the Guild[57] meeting tonight, but it was pouring rain, I was tired, and phooey to the Guild anyhow.

Thursday, October 28
Regional Conferences again today. My eyes were badly inflamed from sitting all day yesterday, in a smoking atmosphere, so I took care to sit near a window today. Brought my riding clothes to the office yesterday but it poured almost all day yesterday and was very cloudy today. Lunched at the Chamberlin with Howard Lichtenstein and Joe Kaminstein.

Several of the boys urged me to go to the Regional Banquet tonight. But I decided not to go. Certain of the regional representatives were being too attentive to be altogether to my liking, and I did not care to encourage by being around them while everyone was in a party mood. Went to the National with Clara instead. Saw Charlotte Greenwood in "Leaning on Letty." Found it, and her, rather amusing.

---

56   American Federation of Labor, the conservative union and the Congress of Industrial Organizations, which was more militant. They competed.
57   National Lawyers' Guild

Friday, October 29
Eve Braveman called me for luncheon, but I had already promised to go with some of the boys. She was very cordial, and urged me to call her or to spend an evening with her.

Everyone in the office and from the field made a point of coming in to inquire where I had been last night. I suppose I should have gone, but what the heck?

Have so much work, it's driving me silly. And I am interrupted every time I get going on any one matter. It's a great life if I don't weaken. I have stopped taking work home from the office, but do not know whether that means that I am weakening or becoming stronger. Time will tell.

Saturday, October 30
Lunched and shopped with Clara and Mary Lou. Bought a number of things for the apartment. Arnold had called just before I got home, and said he would call again, but did not. George Gray did call, however, to ask me to go to a Halloween party with him. We went to the River Bend. There were eight couples, all nice kids. George knew a lot of other fellows there, all of whom asked me to dance. Home about three – very weary – but it was a lot of fun.

Sunday, October 31
A beautiful autumn day. To Mary's in the morning – not too early. Walking all afternoon with Sadie and Clara. Home just long enough to change, and them to Sadie's for supper. Stayed there all evening. Heard several wonderful radio programs, including Erma Sach on the General Motors program – her voice seems too beautiful to be human.

Monthly Memoranda 1937

January
January first, and all the rest of the month have been decidedly quiet and uneventful. If the superstition is true, I shall spend many boring hours in the course of the coming year. However, things could be much worse. I am far happier in our present living conditions than under any of the previous arrangements we have tried. Our apartment is certainly the most attractive place we have lived in Washington, and I find it no hardship to dispense with a fourth roommate. As for my "career" - I have what I suppose I should consider quite a good job.

February
Such a dearth of dates and things to do I never did see. Sam's visit fortunately broke the monotony, but even then I could find nothing more exciting for his entertainment than the movies and dinner at May's. I certainly am slipping - or have slipped. He insisted that he had a very enjoyable visit, but of course he would.
Well, the argument of the Labor Board cases was exciting. Looks like I shall have to get my thrills that way.
And Howard Lichtenstein, who bet me a kiss, and won is not even interested in collecting his winnings. I have lost what sex appeal I might once have had!

March
I wonder if all this hectic excitement about the Social Security case does not mark the beginning of the end, since my boss has been sticking around largely in order to try the labor Board and Social Security cases. And when he leaves, then what? I should not care to stay in the Department of Justice as just another stenographer - even if I could. And I should not care to go to the Department of Labor with Horshy as Secretary to the Solicitor - even if I did get the chance. But I am not gong to worry about such matters. Uncertainty in regard to my various jobs has always been more or less a matter of course, and seems quite natural now.

April
Went through a spell of a depression around the time of my birthday such as I have seldom, if ever, experienced. And do not know exactly what caused it. Wonder if it was the realization that I was becoming an <u>old</u> old maid. Wonder if it was because my boss had rooting for him in Court such a very pretty girl. I really do not believe that I am in love with him, but so many people seem to think I am that I sometimes suppose I may be wrong. Is it possible to be in love with a man and not be aware of it?

May
Such a great deal has happened this past month - the arguments in the Social Security old age pension case, winning both Social Security cases, being told I should soon have to hunt another job (unless I wished to remain after Wyzanski left, which I don't), Van Devanter's resignation, presentation of the Connery-Black wages and hours bill, etc., etc. It seems rather too bad to have to leave Washington when we are so comfortably

settled. But there is the consolation that I my get a much better job out of it. However, I shall miss my boss of the past four years. I have found considerable fault with him upon occasion, and believe I was at times justified, but on the whole he has been a pretty decent boss as bosses go in this workaday world.

June
There have been so many changes this past month - losing one roommate and acquiring another, losing one boss and not acquiring another, at least, not a boss in whom I am at all interested. There have been some compensations for my losses, however. Looking for a new job soon acquaints one with those who are real friends. Among such I know I can count Eugene O'Dunne and John Murphy. Whatever Charles Wyzanski has done or may do, I consider that he more or less owes to me. And the men in the office have been most kind about urging me to stay. Arnold Raum has turned out to be rather an agreeable acquisition as a boyfriend. My dates are so rare these days that almost anything is a treat.

July
The past month certainly ended up in a blaze of glory, socially speaking. And the whole month was a very full one, between working for Mr. Reed, entertaining Miss Calahan, getting acquainted with Sadie Wine and her friends, finding a new maid, going home, to the seashore, to New York, and to Boston, looking for a job, handling C.E.W's personal business, and welcoming Frances and Nick[58] back to Washington. I am glad that I have been fairly well occupied, and so pleasantly, since I thus had no opportunity to miss Charles Wyzanski, whose absence I had expected would leave a great gap.

August
My social life is much improved, thanks to Arnold. But the job situation looks pretty dark. If I only knew definitely what I wanted to do, and where, I might concentrate on it, and then I <u>might</u> get somewhere. But with C.E.W. in Europe, and my lack of actual legal experience, and my indecision as to whether I want to work in Washington or Boston, I am rapidly getting nowhere. Well, if nothing else turns up, maybe I'll go to Manila with Frances and Nick. The thought of a complete change of scenery is quite intriguing. And the distance from home would not worry me at all.

September
At long last I have achieved my ambition to be a lawyer, in deed and in name. And I am thrilled and happy as a result of the achievement. Another happy result is the respect and admiration of my friends. It would have been so easy to go on being a secretary, to C.E.W. or to someone else, with the assurance that I excelled in my job. But to start at the bottom as a lawyer required some sacrifice and difficulty. However, I am sure I shall be happy in my choice - if only I can make the grade. If I fail, it will not be for lack of trying.

October
Well, I have been a lawyer for a whole

---

58   Frances returned after a year in China, and she and Nick were married in the meantime.

month now, and like it more each day. The greater responsibility, the opportunity to use some initiative, are positively inspiring. Although I was so downcast about it at the time, it was a lucky day for me when Charles Wyzanski decided to leave Washington. From his attitude when I saw him last, I have a suspicion that he is not altogether happy in his choice. He will, of course, do any job exceedingly well, but Ropes, Gray lacks the color and excitement with which his work here abounded. And my social life is on the up - and - up. In short, everybody is happy.

November
Had such a lovely Thanksgiving. Arnold was particularly sweet. And Lenny and Clara seemed to get along so well. And the dinner went off even better than I had expected.
I really have much for which to be thankful - a pleasant apartment, an interesting job (drat Tom Emerson!), pleasant friends, some new clothes, and lastly, and chiefly, Arnold.[59] He is so sweet tempered and kind and charming that it is good for my soul, for my crabbed disposition, to be able to spend some time with him occasionally. And I do think he likes me. I certainly hope so. But I wish he might be just a mite less preoccupied with his work.

December
This year ended very pleasantly for me. My job has been made permanent, I am working on C cases,[60] and I think I am going to get a raise. And I am glad that Arnold called me and that I spent New Year's eve with him. And although I am sorry he has been ill, I am glad that was the reason, and not indifference, for his not calling me. I really do not believe that I am in love with him, but I do miss him when he does not call. And Mother was anxious to meet him.
If 1938 continues to give me, as 1937 has, a moderate measure of success in my work, continued friendship with Arnold, Frances, some of the boys at the office, and a few others, I shall be kept reasonably content - I believe. And my newest girl friend, Eve Braverman, I think I am going to like more and more as time goes on. And Mary Lou continues to be my old faithful.

---

59   Arnold Raum
60   C Cases refer to unfair labor practices, and R Cases refer to representation (i.e. union) hearings.

Anne with Julius Schlezinger

1938

By 1938 Anne's life is becoming what she had dreamed. She has an interesting and exciting professional life with challenging cases in labor law, and she is surrounded by dozens of young men lawyers who are intelligent. Gone are the frustrations and doldrums of 1935, replaced by a happy social life and professional future. She is confronted by Jules' proposal of marriage and her own doubtfulness. Altogether 1938 was a very good year.

Tuesday, November 1
Shopped assiduously at noon, but no luck. Meeting of the Entertainment Committee at 4:30.
Meeting of the boycott Committee at 5:00. Jules,[61] who has been working at home, called and asked me to have dinner with him. Insisted he would be glad to wait no matter how long the meeting took. We were joined at dinner by Stanley, Dorothy having gone to the races. Stanley left shortly after dinner. My conscience told me go back to the office, but Jules begged me to stay and visit with him. He won. He was very sweet, made a point of telling me why he did not like Edna. It was very late by the time he got talked out and consented to take me home. He said I have done him a lot of good – by being such a patient listener, I suppose. Lillian is working days beginning today.

Wednesday, November 2
Cut a luncheon meeting of the Boycott Committee to go shopping. Found a hat and gloves that I liked. All set now for a while.
Such a pretty afternoon that I decided to go riding. Edna and Lish went with me. Had a perfectly glorious ride. Rather late to go home for dinner, so I stayed down town and had dinner with Edna at Child's. Went back to the office after dinner, but it was quite late by then, and Jules, who was also back, insisted on my going along home with him. Stopped to play a few games of pin-balls, at which I trounced him. It is only when I am playing for money that I get trounced, and have lost a good number of dimes and quarters that way.

Thursday, November 3
Lost a pin-ball game to Lush on which we had bet a horse back ride. Entertainment Committee after work. Lillian and Clara both went out after dinner. I had a grand time all by myself – a lazy, luxurious tub bath, manicure, a thorough brushing of my much neglected hair, etc.,etc. Finished Jane Allen's *I Love my Girlish Laughter*, a light, frivolous thing, but amusing, which Lillian had recommended to me. Listened to the radio, to program that would ordinarily bore me silly. And felt more thoroughly relaxed than I have in a long while.
My suit arrived and is very nifty.

Friday, November 4
Lunched with Henry Lehman and Dave Rein.[62]

---

61   By the Fall of 1938 Anne's relationship with Jules had become closer. She was 28 but unsure of him.

62   Rein was promoted to Judge in 1946, Anne would be promoted twenty-two years later. After the Alger Hiss trial in 1948, he was accused of being a member of the leftist group within the NLRB.

Kommy asked me to go walking with him this evening, but despite an almost full moon, I chose to go back to the office instead.

We got a maid through Jules asking the Surreys' maid. She started Monday, and seemed to be working out all right, but announced tonight that her husband got a job in Philadelphia and she must leave tonight. What a nuisance!

Jules was at the office, but did not take me home because he was staying much longer than I was. However, he did take enough time off for a few games of pinball and a coke – which, as loser, I had to buy him.

Saturday, November 5
Joe Friedman called to tell me about the long quotation from American Radiator that would appear in the Annual Report.[63] Left about 11:30 for Baltimore – Jules, Stanley, Jack and I. Dorothy had packed a luncheon for us, which we ate on the way. The game was fairly interesting except that it poured all through the second half, and we got soaked through. I was wearing my new tweed outfit. I know the rain will not hurt it, but I should have preferred not to christen it that way.

Dinner at Mrs. K's Toll House Tavern – wine and everything. Spent the rest of the evening at Stanley's, Dorothy looking very fragile and lovely in scarlet-and-cream satin lounging pajamas. Home not too late, but very tired.

Sunday, November 6
Supposed to go riding with Stanley but we decided it would be two muddy underfoot.

Dinner at Greenway Inn - not nearly so good as our own café, we all agreed.

Ineg sent a friend of hers – Ruth Eason – whom we hired. She is a little older than most of the maids we have had, which may be an advantage. Went to the office about 8:00. George Koplow was there. He told me that several of the other boys, including Jules, had been down, but apparently had not returned after supper. I called Jules when I got home – shortly after 10:00. He had worked all day, was very tired, and was just about to go to bed. We chatted for a few minutes, however, long enough for him to invite me to the Board banquet and dance.

Monday, November 7
A warm sticky day – very unseemly.

To the beauty parlor at noon. Met Lillian after work to go shopping for a dinner dress. Did not find anything I liked well enough to purchase.

Ruth prepared a good enough dinner but seems not to have done anything else all day.[64] She does not serve very well, but I suppose she will learn. She seems to be quite intelligent.

Jules and Kommy had dinner at Wally Cohen's. Stopped in to see us on their way home about 10:00, quite unexpectedly. It was a beautiful evening, full moon, but Lillian and I were wearing house coats, and were too lazy to change, so just fooled around in the apartment.

Tuesday, November 8
The entertainment committee is in a stew because we discovered that we cannot hold our

---

63 Anne's work on the case with American Radiator was to be quoted in the Annual Report, giving more visibility to her opinions.

64 Anne and her apartment mates, Clara and Lillian, hired a maid. Ruth.

banquet at the Lafayette, as planned, since it is on an unfair list, and there was some objection to every other possibility – expense, distance, Negro question, unionization, etc. Everyone excited about the elections, which seem to be taking strange turns. Spent the evening reading and listening to the news flashed over the radio. Jules is all tied up in knots over the annual report, and will not have much for me until some time next week. And I am doing practically no work. Yet I do not feel that I ought to go home just for a few days or longer and miss the Regional Conference.

Wednesday, November 9
Luncheon at the Ambassador with Anne Landy, Mary Schleiffer and Carol Agger. Decided we would have a dance at the Press Club Tuesday night.
The Republicans are making great inroads into the Democratic holding.
Arnold Cutler[65] invited me to a concert tomorrow night. I had to buy a ticket for a rally – also tomorrow night. But anyhow, I have at least one holiday date, although I should much have preferred that it be with Jules. He is having company for the holiday – a girl friend, I suppose – so I shall probably not see him at all. Well, maybe it is just as well if we do have a respite for each other.

Thursday, November 10
Bought a white sweater at noon to wear with my new suit. Koplow, Mapes and I bought Condon a book credit,[66] today being his birthday. I think he was very surprised – and touched. Union meeting at 4:30. When I left at about 6:00, they were still counting ballots. Jules called me later to tell me that not only had I won, but every "administration" candidate had won, most of them with sizable majorities. Although I don't care a hang about being Chairman of the Labor Board Problems Committee, I was gratified of what amounted to an overwhelming expression of confidence in Jules. Jules also told me he had to work tonight and all day tomorrow. To the Library of Congress with Arnold to hear the Kolisch String Quartet. Rather enjoyed it. Then to the Hot Shoppe and home.

Friday, November 11
Apparently the boys had a celebration at Jules' apartment last night. Kommy called just after I left to ask me to come over. Lillian said he sounded decidedly tight, and the place sounded like a night club. A gorgeous day. Lillian and I took a long walk in the morning, and were abut to leave on another walk in the afternoon when Jules, Marty and Jack dropped in. I was so angry with Jules, who had told me so repeatedly the last few days about the necessity for his working nights and holidays, and who, nonetheless, was always available when the boys wanted him, that I refused to go for a ride or a walk or even to be civil to them. They did not stay long. Jules told Lillian in an aside that he had been working all day, and had just come out for a breath of air, and that the celebration last night had not lasted long. Maybe I was too hasty. Stanley Surrey called to ask me to go riding on Sunday.

---

65   Cutler was an attorney at the NLRB.
66   Gift certificate

Saturday, November 12
Wyzanski called. He is in town here for about a month to argue a case for the Government. Wants me to notify him when U.S. Smelting is decided by the Board.
Lunched at Child's with Jules and Kommy. Then did some errands – a couple for Jules. Came back to the office, and typed a couple of pages for Jules, who really is in a stew over the Annual Report. He gave me a ride home since he had to take some stuff out to Faley's house. Kommy took me to dinner at 2929 – lost a bet. Jules called me later. Mother has sent him a box of cookies. He was very surprised and pleased. Spent the evening at his apartment drinking cognac and listening to Toscanini's' concert. Made up all our differences. I am glad that Jules has apparently learned to tolerate my ridiculous moods. The boys had stopped in for just a few minutes Thursday night, and he just took about an hour off from the office Friday.

Sunday, November 13
Went riding with Stanley Surrey in the morning. It was a warm, sticky day, I did not enjoy the ride so much as I usually do. During the afternoon took a nap, read the papers and some P.G. Woodhouse nonsense, and in general, completely relaxed. Dinner with Jules at the Olmsted's. Then to see a silly movie. Got home rather early. He did not stop in at all since he wanted to get to bed fairly early for the first time in a long while. His report is nearing completion, enough so that he has his head about water, and he was more nearly his old kidding self than I have seem him for weeks. It did my heart good, because the kid has been working terribly hard.

Monday, November 14
The Regional Conference started today, but the sessions were not open to the Washington people. Got in touch last week with a new maid through the Surrey's girl, who sounded much better than Ruth. Clara and Lillian interviewed and hired her one evening when I was not at home. We let Ruth go Saturday. The new maid did not show up today, leaving us holding the bag. Dinner downstairs at 2929.[67] Spent most of the evening trying on evening gowns and trying to decide what to wear to the dance tomorrow. Everyone seemed to have a different idea on the subject. Finally went to bed without having decided the momentous question.

Tuesday, November 15
Called Nick Dallant to wish him a happy birthday. Must get up to see them soon.
Spent most of the day at the Regional Conference. Quite interesting. Left a bit early to go to the beauty parlor. Then home, where there was a great flurry of pressing, fixing, supper, and just general fussing. Jules got Dorothy Surrey to call me about what I was wearing. He sent me – to my surprise – a perfectly exquisite orchid. I wore my pink chiffon, the orchid in my hair, and for once in my life, really created a sensation, both at the cocktail party Jules had in his apartment, and at the dance. I was rushed, cut in on, promised boys' halves

---
67   The Parkwest apartments at 2929 Connecticut, NW where Anne and Clara were living.

of dances, and had a perfectly marvelous time. I was really the belle of the ball for once. Even Horshy, who was there, was astonished. And Jules was so proud!

Wednesday, November 16
Wore my orchid to the office on my suit. It was still beautiful, and showed off wonderfully well on the black jacket. Lunched at Child's with Dave Rein. The Conference today centered around the legal discussion, and was very interesting. Everyone was still raving about how gorgeous I looked yesterday and thought I looked pretty well today too. Gosh, what an orchid will do for a girl! To the Trans-Lux with Jules, Condon and Al Bernstein. Dinner at the Ambassador with Jules and Dave Rein – Dutch treat.
Jules took Dave and me home. Dave asked me to come up and visit with him for a while, but I went home instead, looked at the newspaper, and went to bed fairly early.

Thursday, November 17
Lunched at the Old Vienna with Tom Ray, a friend of Condon's who is just back from Spain with a wounded leg.[68]
Meeting after work of committee chairmen to pick committees. I think I drew a very good group. Jules was driving Ray and Condon to McLean to pick up Ray's bags. They asked me to go along, but it would have meant crowding them, so I did not go. Had dinner at the Burlington with Marty, Dave, Harry Sellery, George Koplow. Met Jules's party going to dinner as we came out. Again they asked me to join them, but I wanted to go back to the office for a while. Jules called me at home. He had gone to the office just after I left. Wanted to know if I would excuse him from our date to go to Bowie Saturday since he wanted to go to Philadelphia for the weekend, inasmuch as I would be busy Sunday. I excused him. Made a date for tomorrow and for December 6. Dorothy and Stanley [Surrey][69] had dropped in to see me before I got home.

Friday, November 18
People are still talking about my orchidaceous appearance last Tuesday. It is most gratifying to Jules as well as to me.
Bought several things at noon, including a white angora sweater. Jules, Jack, and I had dinner at the Hour Glass. Had drinks, too, which we liked much better than we did the dinner. Jack had to go to a meeting right after dinner. Jules and I took a walk, looked over the movies but did not find anything we wanted to see, so went up to his apartment, read the paper, listened to the radio, and fooled around until all hours. He is going to Philadelphia for the weekend. I think it is rather a good idea not see each other for a couple of days.

Saturday, November 19
Don't know whether it was because Jules

---

68   This refers to the Lincoln and Washington Battalions within the International Brigade that fought against the Fascist forces in the Spanish Civil War. Some 500 Americans fought, many of whom were later alleged to have socialist or communist associations.

69   The Surreys were frequent dinner companions over the next several years.

went out of town, or what, but I had fully a dozen requests for dates. Finally wound up by going to Charlie Horshy's. Stopped at Justice first to visit with Wyzanski for a while. Spent the afternoon listening to the radio and drinking. Dinner with Charlie and Hiram Wooster. After dinner more drinking. Did some "double-crostics" which were a lot of fun. Charlie had to go to the office for a while, but by then Wooster and I were getting along like a couple of old friends. When Charlie took me home, we went into the park for a driving lesion, but were advised by an officer to leave because of the sniper, which we did. But all in all, I had a swell time.

Sunday, November 20
Did not feel very peppy in the morning but Stanley insisted on my going riding with him, so I did. Got home just in time to change to go to the concert with Marty. Arnold Raum called just before I left to ask me to go for a drive.
We heard Lawrence Tibbett. I enjoyed it very much. Then to Peters for dinner. Met Dave Rein there. I had had a slight headache all day, and the Russian food was the last straw. I was quite sick by the time we got home. Marty left after a few minutes. He was awfully sweet about the whole thing. Jules had called to ask me to dinner. I called him back. He asked me to go to Philadelphia with him for the holiday. Most of his family will be there, and the plans sound quite exciting.

Monday, November 21
Had fully a half dozen meetings scheduled in the course of the day, but attended only one - that of my own committee at 4:30. Shopped at noon. Got a number of things, including a gorgeous black housecoat, pajamas, stockings (lisle), underwear, etc.
Jules had a dinner engagement so I ate at the S&W with Koplow and Rein. After dinner, to the Guild to hear Berle, who was introduced by Judge Stephens. I found Berle very interesting, and not too far beyond my comprehension, as I had been warned he would be. Jules took me home. He is very excited about our trip to Philadelphia – most delightfully so.

Tuesday, November 22
Shopped again at noon today, but not with so much success as yesterday.
Got a $200 raise,[70] which pleased me greatly. Spent a few minutes on the anxious seat when Condon got his notice before I got mine. Dinner at 2929 Connecticut[71] with Jules, Clara and Lillian. Then Jules and I had to go to a Union meeting, his first as ex-president. I made my first report as a committee chairman – very badly, I am sure. Jules was very hurt because there had been much talk of buying him a present in appreciation of his services to the Union, and all he got was a superficial sort of speech by Harry Sellery, followed by some half-hearted applause. After all the sacrifices he has made for the Union. I comforted and soothed him as best I could.

Wednesday, November 23
To the beauty parlor in the morning. Was in

70   $200 raise in the yearly salary.
71   The Parkwest apartments where Anne, Clara and Lillian shared an apartment.

the office a very short time before Jack took Condon, Swope, Jules and me out for cocktails to celebrate his raise. It was very early, but we had out luncheon anyhow – at the Hour Glass. Then to do an errand with Jules. I got some lovely black satin mules. We got our things and left around 3:00. Traveled most of the way at a rather sickening rate of speed. Got to Philadelphia about 7:00. Freshened up a bit at his brother Nate's[72] apartment. Then to a Jewish [i.e. kosher] restaurant for dinner with Mr. and Mrs. Schlezinger, who seem to be good, plain, simple folks. We got along fairly well. Nate had an engagement after dinner. The old folks wanted to go to bed early. Jules and I went up to my very nice apartment. He was all for going places, but I was tired, a bit sick, and it was late, so we didn't.

Thursday, November 24
Jules came over to take me to breakfast. Met the rest of the crowd at his folks' place. Went to see the Penn-Cornell game – three couples, including the Pachels.[73] It was very cold, and started to sleet right at the beginning of the game. I was not well, into the bargain, and all in all, was pretty miserable. Picked up the folks, and went to Walters for Thanksgiving dinner, which was just so-so. Planned to go dancing, but Freda Bull, Nate's girlfriend from Indianapolis, was too tired, and Nate had a bad rash on the back of his neck, and the Pachels decided they ought

72   Nathan S. Schlezinger, M.D. taught at the Jefferson Medical College in Philadelphia and later became a widely published scholar on neurology.
73   The Iz and Rebecca Pachel appear for the first time in the diary, and they continue to be friends for the next three decades before contact is lost.

to go home and see to their baby. I was not in the dancing mood, and the weather was terrible, and there were no good movies, so Jules went out and bought some magazines and we spent a quiet, cozy evening in my little apartment.

Friday, November 25
Breakfast with Freda at Schraffts. She knew Jules before she knew Nate, and seems to prefer him. She is most disturbingly pretty and vivacious. There was so much snow and slush that we bought galoshes. We all had luncheon together, after which I went shopping with Mrs. S. for gifts for her five grandchildren. She bought me a hanky for being such a good child.
Dinner at the Jewish restaurant. Home to change. Then the four of us went to the Walton roof. Had a lot of fun, but there was a long, dull floor show, during which we left, despite the $2.50 minimum.
Jules asked me tonight not whether I would marry him, but when I would marry him. He really took me unawares. I am very fond of him, but somehow I cannot picture him as my husband forever and ever.

Saturday, November 26
Breakfast at Huyler's with Freda, whom I know quite well by now, and am inclined to like very much despite her prettiness. The Pachels joined us for luncheon at Tendfers. Then to a matinee to see Frank Craven in Thornton Wilder's "Our Town." It was excellently done, and, in spots, quite stirring, but on the whole, rather depressing.
Very cold and more snow, so we were not too

sorry we had not gone to the Army-Navy game. Dinner in the restaurant at the railroad station where we saw Mr. and Mrs. S. off for Wilkes-Barre to visit his sister. Home to change, and then to a party given for us by some friends of Nate's. It was very jolly. Jules is being so sweet, so solicitous, so sort of husbandly.

Sunday, November 27
Jules paid for my room before I could prevent it. I finally persuaded him to toss for the money, but I won. To the Parcels' for breakfast about noon. Fooled around there until about 2:00, and then left for home. It was a pleasant day, but the roads were pretty bad. We did not stop for dinner until we got to Baltimore. Ate at Millers. Home about 9:00. Jules stayed a few minutes to look at the papers and then went home. I then had to tell Clara all about the weekend. Apparently she and Lillian had decided that Jules was going to propose. I seem to be the only one who was surprised. Clara and Lillian are all for it, and have most of my plans already made for me. Edna Loeb called me Thursday afternoon to make a date with me for the Altschulaer chap I met with her at a Guild meeting.

Monday, November 28
Supposed to go to a Boycott Committee meeting at noon, but had too many errands to do. Got my raccoon [coat] out of storage. Bought two orchestra seats for "Golden Boy" at $2.75. I am taking Jules.
Dinner with Jules, and his folks at Gendleman's, a kosher restaurant. After dinner we went to Jules' apartment. The Surreys and Kommy came up to meet Mr. and Mrs. S. I planned to take Jules to dinner also Wednesday before the theater, but the Surreys, who have tickets for the same evening, invited us for dinner. Dorothy was unusually cordial, surprisingly so until I gathered that Jules had told them he hoped to marry me. I wish Jules would not take the matter so much for granted, and indicated my wishes to him. Up until all hours telling Lillian, who was out last night, about the weekend.

Tuesday, November 29
Shopped with Mrs. S in the forenoon. It was a lovely day, and I rather enjoyed hanging around with her. Met Mr. S. and Jules for luncheon at Child's. Finally got a new case – Mass Knitting Mills.
Dinner with the Schlezingers at Gendleman's. Saw Mr. and Mrs. S. off on the 8:30 train. Then Jules and I went to the Little to see the Czechoslovakian picture "Janisek." It was rather interesting. Got home fairly late, despite which Jules insisted on stopping in for a while. Despite anything I can do or say, he proceeds on the assumption that I am going to marry him, and what is more, that I am going to marry him in the very near future. I do not like his assuming so much, because I am not at all sure that I am going to marry him at all.

Thursday, November 30
Luncheon at the Lafayette Hotel with Kommy. Jules happened to lunch there with some of the boys and did not seem a bit pleased to see us.
Wyzanski called to inquire whether his case had been decided yet. Jules and I had dinner at the Surreys'. Then to the theater to see Clifford Odets', "Golden Boy," one of the best plays I have seen in a long while. My

only criticism is that the ending was weak. After the theater, we all went to the Willard for cocktails. Had a lot of fun. So late by the time we got home that Jules did not come in at all. However, Lillian and Clara were still awake, so I had to stay up long enough to tell them everything – about the play, about the cocktails, but especially about Jules.

Monthly Memoranda 1938

January
1938 has started quite auspiciously, I think. All goes well with the job. My chief complaint, in fact, is as to Arnold, who cannot be so very fond of me if he can be satisfied with seeing me so infrequently. Mother had a pleasant visit with us, which makes me happy.
Have made a number of new friends, most of them at the office, several of them interesting and worth-while.
Jules is being attentive, but I shall not let myself get too interested in him. He is too likeable - too fickle - and too young.
If only Arnold were a bit more attentive, everything would be lovely.

February
February has been most exciting socially. Having Arnold call again, at long last. Making some rather interesting new friends, like Arnold Cutler. And of course the Guild convention was just one party after the other. And the Union cocktail party was heaps of fun.
I wonder if I shall ever see any of the people I met during the Guild weekend. I should rather like to get better acquainted with Joe Winer. But he has probably forgotten by now that I even exist. Well, such is life in Washington.
As for the job, changing rooms - and roommates - has been rather exciting. I have a much brighter office now, but far too much sociability. It makes things very pleasant, I must admit, but does not tend to increase production.
But I must not get too discouraged. My zeal and circumstances combined to pile up several cases on me at once, something I may be wise enough to avoid in the future. I am more - or - less satisfied with what I have accomplished to date. However, a raise would be most reassuring.

March
March has been rather a hectic month, what with dates and union activities, and my various athletic endeavors, and my raise, and shopping for new evening clothes, and the Modern Forum, and the cherry blossoms, and the early spring weather, and Clara's birthday, and solving roommate and apartment problems for various of my friends, and getting some decisions out, and wondering if I would ever be able to straighten out the American Radiator muddle, etc., etc. Life, on the whole, is very gay and exciting and full. I like being 27 and an attorney on the National Labor Relations Board.

April
Am now 28 years old, and, with my hair turning gray so rapidly, am really beginning to feel rather antiquated. Have not seen Arnold since the first part of the month. There have been plenty of others around to

keep me busy, but no one I like as well as I do Arnold. And although my social life has been so full, and rather exciting, for the most part it has consisted of just one drinking brawl after the other.

I continue to be "a great big outdoors girl" - more so than ever, in fact, having substituted tennis and golf for bowling and roller skating. It's all a lot of fun, and it does keep me fit.

My work continues to interest me a good deal. However, I shall be happy when American Radiator has gone out, and when Cating and Sommers have gone through the courts O.K. Ruth's change in plans settles our housing problem for the time being - settles it insofar as we probably will make no change until she does leave. A problem deferred is not a problem settled, I know, but I refuse to worry about the future. I can always find enough present worries to keep be occupied.

May
Despite a rather dull May 30th weekend, it has been quite a gay month socially - lots of doing, even if it was not all exciting.

And, in view of Gertrude's visit, I have done my duty by my Washington relatives for another year or so.

May 27th was C.E.W's[74] birthday. I thought of sending him a card, but then decided I would not. I have an idea he prefers to be considered by me as just another former boss, and if that is what he wants, that is what he will get.

As for the job - I can tell better when some of my cases have been ruled upon by the C.C.A.

---
74   Charles Wyzanski, Anne's former boss.

June
This has been an exciting month in Washington, what with Congress adjourning, after passing the Wages and Hours Bill, and what with the President issuing an Executive Order providing for the blanketing in the thousands of people under Civil Service. This has been an exciting month on my job too, what with American Radiator finally going out, and Columbia Broadcasting coming back. It has been fairly interesting socially also, what with a number of old friends - beaus and otherwise - remembering my existence, even to the extent of taking the time to come and see me. Such friends include Sol, whom I found as unattractive as ever; Arnold Raum, whom I found most disappointingly dull; Sam, who came because he preferred to ask me to do him a favor in person rather than by mail; Marjorie Frank, who bores me to tears; Charles Wyzanski, who would not take more than a minute of his time to talk to me; Charlie Horshy, who is being particularly attentive because I can be useful to him in connection with his Labor Law course; and George Gray, who, I think, really likes me, since he spends his hard-earned money so freely on me, and does not even ask to kiss me good-night.

July
July started out disappointingly inasmuch as I was deprived of the exciting Fourth I might have enjoyed had I not been unwell at the time. However, there have been compensations. We showed Jean and Joe a fine time, and I had rather an interesting weekend, everything considered.

And Arnold Raum called at least to say goodbye, which shows that he has not entirely dropped me.
And Albert Stern may prove to be an interesting addition to the list of boyfriends.
And Lenny Ackerman is proving to be a very handy person to have around upon occasion, but not too long at a time.

August
This has been a pleasant month socially, despite the many people out of town. Of course, things did lag pretty badly while Jules was away, but they picked up considerably ass soon as he returned. And then there were Arnold Cutler and Al Stern and Lillian's young friends and Arnold Raum, and, possibly, a few others. But lately they have all become just fill-ins for Jules - yes, even Arnold Raum, who was the favorite for so long, but appears to be willing to relinquish his position. I really think I prefer Jules anyhow.

September
September has been a merry month. If I could have squeezed in a bit of a vacation, it would have been well nigh perfect. Well, I did get out of town.

October
Month after month slips by, and still I do not get home or away on vacation. I seem to have acquired a ridiculous phobia that I must not go until the Stihli decision has been issued. And that case seems to be a jinx for getting held up for one reason or another. Although Lenny seems to have permanently deserted me - a loss which I can tolerate with very little suffering, Arnold Raum has come back into the fold - more or less. I am rather pleased that he has, although Jules is very definitely number one man these days, and has been for a surprisingly long time, everything considered. I am becoming very accustomed to having him around - unwisely so, I sometimes think.

November
November 1938 marks a turning point in my life, maybe more important than I now realize. To think that Jules - the good - looking boy in the next office, whose dates I enjoyed so much - should propose to me! And to think that I may, in time, accept. The likelihood becomes stronger, the prospect more pleasant, the longer I contemplate it. However, I still am a long way from having definitely made up my mind. He is younger than I am; he has no money at all and probably never will have much; he is not a good lawyer generally speaking; he is somewhat lacking in culture and refinement; he is not literary or intellectual; and not interested in becoming such. But he is sweet and kind and considerate and generous - to a fault. He appears to be very much in love with me, but will, I expect, always have an eye for a pretty girl.
I wonder if I have been foolish in slighting Arnold Raum the way I have. I wonder if I am being too encouraging to Jules when I am so far from making a decision.
I wonder…
I am very gratified about my raise - very much encouraged. Some of my fellow workers who have graduated from "the better law schools" and who are so much superior to me in many ways - masculine, etc. - did not get raises. I was

a bit surprised, since I have not turned out any great quantity of work the past few months. Maybe the Board would just as soon have fewer decisions, if the few result in settlement and consent decrees rather than litigation.

December
December has been such a gay month, thanks to Jules. He becomes dearer to me every moment, Arnold more and more just a part of my past. Arnold Cutler and Jackie and all those others have never counted for much anyhow, just means of passing the time pleasantly. And I grow more and more accustomed to the idea of being Jules's wife. He and his friends have done a thorough job of minimizing those objections I have seen fit to discuss with them. At first it all seemed quite incredible, but it is beginning to appear very likely. Am I giving in to the pressure that is being exerted upon me from all sides, or am I really falling in love with this boy?

Anne in center back with group 1936

1935-38 Summary

The period of 1935-38 was a pivotal one for Anne Freeling. Four years out of law school she was still working as a secretary and stenographer, but in the middle of the depression, fortunate to have a comfortable job. Although she escaped the worst impact of the Great Depression, she was held in place, at least in part by misogyny. In the 1930's women, and Jewish women, had few opportunities to advance professionally. In her diary she wonders what this invisible force is that is causing her to lose opportunity after opportunity for a professional position.

She started from a conservative place in politics, and in 1932 she voted for Hoover, thinking that Roosevelt would be a disaster. Even in 1936 she was still intrigued by Alf Landon and thought he was a better candidate than Roosevelt, even though the latter won the most lopsided presidential election in the history of the U.S. Coming from that conservative political background, she was given a job in the National Labor Relations Board, which in 1937 had attracted a significant number of attorneys with pro-labor political positions. Many of those people became her friends within the NLRB.

Anne's working on labor cases with a group of worker oriented lawyers correlated with her shifting toward liberal social and political positions. Her association with this group of lawyers, some of whom were denounced during the McCarthy period, probably affected her professional career later.   --RDH

Anne and Julius Schlezinger on their Wedding Day 1939

The Diaries

Part III

1939 to 1945
Marriage, Mothering And World War II

From the time of Anne's marriage to Julius (Jules) Schlezinger in 1939 through the next decade, which included World War II, she shows particular concern for her husband. Although she had met Julius' parents in November, 1938, she was still not sure about marrying him. In 1939 she discovered that she had a cyst on her ovaries and that she would not be able to have children. Julius had proposed marriage to Anne within months of their having met. During that time Julius was hospitalized briefly, and Anne visited him daily. The loyalty of each through these health crises seems to have forged a special bond between them. Shortly afterwards Anne accepted his proposal of marriage, and they quickly arranged the wedding. Her grandmother, Baba, and sister, Clara, were present along with Julius' brother, Nate, and friends. In 1941 Clara met Lou Rolands (spelled Rowlands initially in the diary) who became her husband.

Anne's decision to marry Jules at this point seems to have been less about love than a decision about him being a good life partner. Knowing that Anne could not have children, they began exploring the possibility of adopting a child, and in early 1942 they were able to adopt their son, Ira. In her diary entries during Jules' absence in World War II we can see her emotional attachment for him growing. She desperately wanted him to return and be with her and Ira, and in her entries from 1944 and 1945 we see her open up emotionally. She worried over Julius' professional opportunities much more than she did about her own.

Just as Anne was finding a tranquility and happiness in her personal life, things were heating up in her professional life. The NLRB came under congressional investigation, and Anne was highlighted as being representative of the problem. As a part of this move to the right on issues of labor, Congress set up the Smith Committee to investigate the NLRB. In Roosevelt's attempt to stop the investigation, he revamped the leadership of the NLRB, eliminating employees suspected of pro-CIO sympathies, especially in the Review Division. Anne was working in that Division and was in close contact with many of the suspected lawyers.

When the Smith Committee hearings started, Anne was the first witness called for the Review Division. The Committee had friendly media coverage, and its accusations of leftist tendencies in the work of the NLRB were widely believed. The House approved the Smith Committee's business-friendly revisions of the Wagner Act, but they stalled in the Senate without being passed. After World War II, many of the same recommendations were re-introduced and passed as the Taft-Hartley Act. The NLRB had other problems at the time and was denounced by the Supreme Court for ordering the re-instatement of strikers who lost their jobs as a result of breaking the law during strikes. Because of these problems, the NLRB lost momentum and became more conservative in the prosecution of cases.

Anne makes reference to the "red scare" in February of 1939, and the anti-communist and anti-worker movements continued into the 1940's and 1950's. As a lawyer with the National Labor Relations Board, Anne was continually affected by these political threats. She was investigated more than once by the FBI, and she was dismissed from the NLRB for a period in the early 1950's during the McCarthy Era.

Anne's happiness after her marriage and adoption of Ira opened a new world for her. She worried about her mothering skills and was delighted with Ira's achievements and distraught about his lack of eating and development at times. Anne and Jules lived in the Buckingham Apartments in Arlington, and the Goor family became their best friends. Anne and Jeanette Goor shared baby sitting, errands, and long talking sessions, while their sons, Ronnie and Ira, played. Ron Goor,[1] remembering the apartments, said that it was a two-story brick complex that occupied a city block. The apartments were built along the streets lining the four sides of the block with the interior space left as a park/playground. Children could play in the interior space while mothers' supervised them through the apartment windows, or mothers would meet and talk while their children played.

The difficulties and loneliness of World War II were devastating to Anne, as her husband and brother went off to war in Europe. Julius was in combat in the final drive into Germany, and he won a bronze star for his actions. Her brother, Louis, was missing in action and his body never found. The certainty/uncertainty of his fate left her with an emotional pain that was never resolved. Julius did return uninjured much to her happiness.

As Anne matured, her friendships became more stable. As a student, her sisters, Jean and Clara, were her constant companions. For the first few years in Washington before she met Julius, she began to form friendships from work. In addition to her sister Clara, who was her roommate and constant companion, her regular friends were Kommy, Frances, and later Arnold Raum. During the early and mid-1940's she was a very close friend with Jeanette Goor, and they raised their sons together. After moving to Silver Spring in 1948 her life, work, and friendships stabilized into long term patterns, but there are interesting cases of people who appear in her diaries for a period of time then disappear. Anne mentions Grace McEldowney a dozen times or so from 1949 to 1956, then Grace vanishes without further reference. Evelyn Promisel was a frequent lunch companion from 1952 to 1965 and then she also disappears. Evelyn and her husband Nate met socially with Anne and Jules in the late 1950's, but the last the last few entries are about not accepting invitations to go out with them. The last reference to them as a couple is in 1962. Anne gave no comment or explanation, but the social relationship with the Promisels obviously ended.

-- Ron Duncan Hart

---
1   Ronald S. Goor became a scientist (Ph.D. in biochemistry, Harvard and M.P.H. from Harvard School of Public Health). He and his wife Nancy are the authors of best selling books on health, including *Eater's Choice: A Food Lover's Guide to Lower Cholesterol*, *Choose to Lose: A Food Lover's Guide to Permanent Weight Loss*, *Eater's Choice Low-Fat Cookbook*, and *Choose to Lose Weight-Loss Plan for Men*. They have also collaborated on nine non-fiction award-winning children's books. Dr. Goor worked for most of his career with the National Institutes of Health.

Diaries. 1939 Through 1945.

1939

During 1939 Anne's work continued even as clouds of opposition gathered around the NLRB. The major focus in her life was the relationship with Jules. Although they had been seeing each other regularly since they met in 1937 and Jules asked her to marry him in November, 1938, Anne is conflicted about getting married. Her parents' difficult marriage was one factor that made her reluctant. Both Jules and Anne had health problems during the year and were in the hospital. Anne learned that cysts on her ovaries meant that she would never be able to have children. The fact that Jules wanted to marry her as she was, a working woman unable to have children, seemed a turning point for her. She decided to marry. The fact that her roommate Lillian got engaged in June was another factor that might have contributed to her decision in August to put aside her fears about being married.   -- RDH

Monday, February 27
Lunched at the Guaranty Grill with Andy Toth. His work is not going very well, and he is consequently discouraged and down-in-the-mouth.
Stehli is being typed in final form - glory be! But we lost three cases in the Supreme Court today. It makes me shudder to think what they would do with Stehli after what they did with Fansteel, Columbian and Sands. To a Guild[2] meeting, at which Gutknecht and Quilici were present. The red scare is probably going to bust the Guild considerably because so many of the big shots are afraid of the publicity. The meeting was long, but rather interesting, and, in spots, highly amusing.

Friday, September 1
The war started, and Jules and I got married, all on the same day.[3]
I did some errands with him in the morning. We were married at one o'clock at Rabbi Metz's home. Those present[4] were Baba, Mae, Phil, Jerry, Clara, Edward, Nate S. and Nate G., Marty and Kami, Stanley, Dorothy and Do. It was a lovely ceremony, but a bit too long. We then had to go to Jules' apartment, while he packed.
Received a great many telegrams. Finally "got going" about 4:30. Drove along Skyline at sunset-beautiful. Had a fairly good dinner at Skyland. Then went on to Charlottesville. Stopped at the Queen Charlotte Hotel. It was small and inelegant, but clean and rather pleasant. And we had a private bathroom, which are not so prevalent around here as in the North.

Saturday, September 2
Took a short walk in the morning. Had a fine breakfast at the Hotel. Drove around the University grounds, then to Monticello. Went through with a guide. It was most interesting and impressive.

---

[2] National Lawyer's Guild which was formed in 1937 to admit Jewish, African-American and other minority group lawyers, not admitted by the American Bar Association. A number of NLRB lawyers were members.

[3] Germany invaded Poland on this day, the opening attack starting World War II. This sentence is haunting in that Anne had a fear of marriage because of the fighting she had seen between her parents. She was twenty-nine years old.

[4] Anne's grandmother, Baba, her uncle Phil and his wife May, her sister Clara, Nate Schlezinger, Anne's friends Kami and Dorothy, and other friends.

Did not take off again until about 12:30. We had another beautiful day. Everything had certainly been lovely so far. Good roads and very fine scenery.

Stopped overnight at the Wythe Hotel in Wytheville. Had dinner at the Hotel. Then went for a walk along Main Street. It was after nine o'clock by then, but all the stores were open, all the farmers being in for their Saturday shopping and jamboree. It was an interesting thing to watch. Everyone seemed very gay and cheerful and unbathed.

Sunday, September 3
Another beautiful day. Left in the morning, after a very pleasant walk and a very poor breakfast at the Greyhound Bus depot.

The scenery was beautiful almost the whole way. It was quite warm, even when we got into the mountains, so must have been a scorcher in the lowlands.

Took a room at the Riverside Hotel in Gatlinburg. Had a wonderful dinner at the hotel – fried chicken, hot biscuits, jams, stewed apples, and several other delectable dishes. We both stuffed ourselves, and did away with only half the food served to us. Walked about after dinner, sat on the porch listening to the news flashed about the war, which England and France have now entered, as Poland's allies, and went to bed, not too late. Met Miss Jay, vacationing with Judge Fay Bentley.[5]

---

5   Fay L. Bentley was a judge on the D.C. juvenile court from 1934 until she retired in 1958. She was the only judge at that time who was trained in both social work and law.

Monday, September 4
Another idyllic day except for one brief rainstorm in the afternoon, following which the air was sweeter and the scenery lovelier than before.

Breakfasted at the hotel, lunched at The Fox, and dined at the hotel. We have, with few exceptions, been getting scrumptious food, and such quantities of it!

Did a great deal of tramping and climbing, more than we should have, I am afraid, because Jules, who has not yet completely recovered from his operation, was completely fatigued.

The hotel moved us into a far more attractive and desirable room.

Went for a delightful ride in the evening, and to bed about eleven o'clock.

Tuesday, September 5
A lovely day, almost too warm. Breakfast at the Fox. Jules and I had a fuss about his reading the newspaper at the breakfast table.

Lunched at the Norris Restaurant. We were both fairly impressed with Norris, its comfortable little homes and plentiful room around them. Then on to the Dam. Went through the power house with a guide, then for a boat ride on the lake.

Back to Gatlinburg in time for a shower and rest before dinner. Ate at the French Tavern, and decided we liked it the least of all the places where we had eaten. That was probably partly due to a box of spiced pecans which accompanied us this afternoon. To the movies after dinner, and then home and to bed.

Wednesday, September 6
Another gorgeous day. The weather had certainly been kind to us.

Breakfasted at the Hotel. Had a fried-chicken luncheon packed for us, and went off into the hills. Climbed to the top of Clingman's Dome, a short but very strenuous climb. Did a great deal of walking, clambering over rocks, and so forth. Ate our luncheon sitting on some rocks out in the middle of a mountain rivulet. Everything tasted wonderfully good.

Back in the evening to bathe and dress. Had dinner at the Hotel. Went out to watch the square dancing for a while. Then home and to bed.

Jules was especially sweet all day after our fuss yesterday. And he did not read the paper at breakfast.

Thursday, September 7
And still another lovely day. Breakfasted at the Fox. Bought some souvenirs, and checked out. Was sorry to leave a place we had enjoyed so much.

Drove through beautiful country. Made very fortunate selections of places where to stop and eat. Climbed Chimney Rock at $1.10 per person for the privilege. It was really too strenuous for either one of us, and we had seen as lovely spots in the Smokies free of charge. Would probably have stopped overnight at the Cliff Dwellers Inn, but the old geezer who sold us the tickets to Chimney Rock oversold the place so much that Jules and I were prejudiced against it. Drove and drove until we finally found a tourist home we liked outside of Charlotte, North Carolina.

Friday, September 8
A very warm day and it got warmer and warmer as we approached Myrtle Beach. The swanky hotel where we had planned to stop had closed for the season, but we finally found accommodations we liked at the Driftwood. But between the heat and the ferocious, man-eating flies, I almost went daffy. Fortunately, it got much cooler in the evening, but even then there were more and bigger insects around then I have ever seen. Had a pretty fair dinner, went into town to a movie, just because the theater was about the coolest place in town, then home and bed, already thoroughly fed up with the place.

Saturday, September 9
Went swimming in the morning. The water was warm, smooth, and very pleasant. But the heat, and more particularly the flies, spoiled everything. We finally got so disgruntled about the whole thing that we packed up and left right after luncheon, and started back for the Smokies. It was very warm driving, but the thought of getting back to the Smokies made us happy. And along toward nightfall it got much cooler, almost cold, in fact, deliciously cold. Stayed overnight at the Franklin Hotel in Brevard, North Carolina. It was only a fairish sort of place, but all the more desirable places were already occupied and it was then around eleven o'clock. Maybe this is a silly kind of a honeymoon to take, but most of it had been lovely.

Sunday, September 10
A beautiful day. Slept too late to get breakfast at the hotel, so walked into town and breakfasted at a nice little café. Pulled out

right after breakfast. Took one of the most beautiful drives of the whole trip. Stopped a few times to walk, to look and to admire. Stopped also to look at a few hotels, but did not like the accommodations for one reason or another. But we finally came upon Onitaluga Inn, which was the place we had been looking for this entire trip. It was perfectly situated, beautiful views and trails all around it, a little artificial lake, boats, a rustic building which looked like it had grown there, and modern plumbing, tub and a shower.

Monday, September 11
A lovely day. Took a long walk after breakfast. The Inn is located in a perfectly beautiful spot. Went into Bryson City after luncheon to do a few errands. Then came back and went rowing on the lake. Lufty, the splendid German Shepherd who belongs to the inn-owners, has adopted Jules and me, and accompanies us everywhere, even in the boat.
After dinner sat around for a while visiting with the folks. Then drove into town and fooled around for a while just to be doing something. Did not care about the only movie that was available, so went home, to bed, early again. Our room is delightfully cool. Everything about the place is grand except the food, and that leaves much to be desired.

Tuesday, September 12
Another glorious day. Had a luncheon packed, and left shortly after breakfast to go up to Wayak Bald. It was beautiful trip, although the gravel road was terribly dusty. Found a pleasant spot to have luncheon, but the basket, when we unpacked it, was very disappointing. We decided that although Onitaluga was in such a beautiful spot, we would leave because of the lack of good food.
Back in time for dinner, which was the best meal we have had there yet, but we are leaving despite it.
Drove into Sylva. Thought we might go to a movie, but I had seen the only picture that was playing. Besides I was very tired. Got some of our snapshots, a few of which were pretty bad.

Wednesday, September 13
Took a walk down along the river after breakfast. Pulled out about eleven. Went to Gatlinburg. Had a marvelous fried chicken luncheon at the Fox. Discussed the various places where we might go, and wound up by heading for Columbus. A large part of the drive was very beautiful, but we had to go too far before we found a good stopping place. Saw North Carolina, Tennessee, Virginia, West Virginia, and Kentucky. Some of the scenery in Kentucky was as grand as anything we had seen in the Smokies, but the miserable hotels in which the coal mine employees had to live were a depressing sight.
Had an excellent steak dinner at a roadside restaurant near Pikeville, Kentucky.
Finally stopped for the night at the Governor Covell Hotel, after midnight, thoroughly worn out.

Thursday, September 14
Slept late, and had a leisurely breakfast in the Grill Room. Then off again. It was very

warm in Huntington, and got warmer as we went on. Discovered, after we started, that we were only a few minutes from Ohio.

Got to Bexley around 2:30. Mr. and Mrs. S were at the hotel next to the Temple, this being Rosh Hashanah.[6] We took cold showers, rested a bit, then went over to see them. The gang of us, except Mama and Papa, who eat at the Temple, went to Gertrude's for supper. After supper we went over to the hotel again to visit for a while. Talked about going to a movie or something, but wound up by going home and to bed. Today was the hottest September day on record here.

Friday, September 15
Had a grand sleep, and got up feeling very rested and refreshed. Put on a girdle when I got dressed for Temple, for the first time since the day of my wedding. Another scorching hot day.

Had a grand cold chicken luncheon after the services, and after much handshaking and greeting and introductions. Stayed at home for the rest of the afternoon.

After supper, to the Mendlowitz' apartment, where we had some champagne, with Louie and Lucille, and Merman and Myrtle Katz. Then the whole gang of us went to a movie. Then to Mills for something to eat. Got into an argument about the Wagner Act,[7] and were there all hours. Herman was the only one who could see beyond his nose on the subject.

6　　So they could walk to services.
7　　Compliance with the Wagner Act, officially the National Labor Relations Act, was the judicial responsibility of the NLRB. Anne was passionate in defending it. Since Jules' family was in business, some of them would have questioned it.

Saturday, September 16
Slept rather late. Another very warm day. In addition to Mr. S's $1000,[8] and Ed's $75, we are getting $25 from Nate and $25 from Louie, and a Toastmaster from Gertrude.

Left after luncheon, after many fond farewells and much kissing.

Stopped at a couple of pottery places, and got a few vases, pitchers, etc.

Had a very pleasant trip. Stopped for the night at the Summit Hotel. Showered and changed, had an excellent dinner, then dropped into the Baron Munchausen Room for a champagne cocktail and to see the floor show. Then to bed.

Sunday, September 17
Had an excellent breakfast at the Hotel. Walked around a bit, and looked at the papers and sent a few last minute postcards before leaving. Had a perfectly delightful trip, although rather sad, since it was the end of our honeymoon.

Got to Jules apartment about 4:30. Picked up his mail. Then took a lot of stuff out to our new apartment, which is completed, and looks lovely, even without any furniture. Back to Jules' apartment to bathe and change. Then out to 2929[9] to get my mail and to see Clara. I had received a few more felicitations, a large quantity of bills, some exquisite gold-and-white pajamas from Carrie Fuller, a very lovely blue leather monogrammed desk clock from Dumaine. Dinner at Arignoe's. Slept at Jules' apartment.

8　　Jules' father.
9　　2929 Connecticut Ave., N.W. The Parkwest Apartments where Anne and Clara had lived.

Monday, September 18
Spent the entire day shopping and running errands. Lunched with Jules, and we went to the bank to open joint checking and saving accounts.

By the time I met Jules again at 4:30, I was completely fatigued. But we went to Baylors' nonetheless to order a few more things, and then out to the Surreys' for dinner.

Sat around for a while after dinner, and then went out to Buckingham[10] to unwrap the box spring and mattress, the only things delivered so far. Jules was all for getting some linen and sleeping out there, but it was too much like camping out to suit me. Although I am sure it would have made more comfortable sleeping than his studio couch.

Tuesday, September 19
Downtown in the morning to shop all day again, although it almost killed me. Bought a number of little things, which take such an amazing long time to select.

Letter from Mother, enclosing a clipping from the Lawrence paper, full of misstatements, and carrying my high school graduation picture. Jules and I had supper at the Hot Shoppe.

Went to see Elise Goodman, and to pick up the thing she got for me at her mother's shop – table linen, bedspread, lace runners, etc. Left early enough to take a load of stuff out to the new apartment. Again Jules wanted to stay overnight, but I demurred, so we came back to Adams Mill Road. I have barely enough energy left to undress myself and get into bed.

Wednesday, September 20
Spent most of the morning on the telephone, arranging for a maid, etc.

Received a very good looking hammered aluminum tray from Lillian and Ben.

Lunched with Jules. Did a few errands. Then to the beauty parlor. Met Jules again later to do some errands together. Then out to Buckingham to take the things we had bought. Back to Adams Mill Road to move some more things.

Had dinner at a very pleasant little Italian place in Arlington.

Spent the night in Buckingham. I became unwell, about a week later than I was due. I was a bit worried because, although I do want to have children, becoming pregnant on my honeymoon was too much of a good thing.

Thursday, September 21
The employment agency had sent a maid out, but she did not show up.

I felt pretty miserable, but I got up and fixed Jules' breakfast anyhow. Planned to go back to bed, but the telephone man came to install the phone, and the laundry man and milk-man etc., came, one after the other, in a steady stream. Finally dragged some clothes on and went downtown about one o'clock, and Jules and I drove into Baltimore to a furniture wholesale house. Selected a chair in a few minutes. Tried then to leave, but we had an extremely persistent salesman, who succeeded in keeping us there

---

10   Anne and Jules moved into the apartment in Buckingham as soon as they returned from their honeymoon in 1939. They lived there until moving to their Silver Spring house in 1948.

three hours, so that it was then too late to go anywhere else.

Had a nice dinner at the Mayflower. The place was full of Congressmen returned for the special session, which opened today.

Friday, September 22

I finally succeeded in getting a maid at about 11:00, and together we got the apartment pretty well cleaned up.

She left about 4:00. And I left shortly after. Picked up Clara and Jules at the Labor Department and we went to Rabbi Metz's shule for the Kol Nidre.[11] We left about 7:00, and went to the States Hotel for dinner. Then to Jules' apartment, where we had a glass of cognac. Packed a few things, took Clara home, and went home ourselves. It was very late by then, and I was terribly tired.

Saturday, September 23

Jules stayed home, but we did not sleep late. Went into town to look at furniture. Selected several things we liked at Style, but they are so very expensive. Stopped at the Euclid Street shule to see Baba.

Stopped at the Surreys'. We all drove into Baltimore in our own car for dinner and a show. Saw "See My Lawyer." It was quite amusing. The whole evening, in fact, was very pleasant except the long, tiring drive back to Washington late at night. I could hardly hold my head up, and I know Jules was very tired too.

Sunday, September 24

A beautiful day, and my last day of freedom from the office, yet we spent most of it at Adams Mill Road packing Jules' trunk.

Jules telephoned home to find out how they all felt after their Yom Kipper fast. Despite all my good resolutions, by the time we got home, bathed, and got to bed, it was late again, and we were both thoroughly exhausted again. This must cease.

Monday, September 25

Got a very warm reception at the office. Was back only about an hour or so, however, when Condon, Koplow, and I were served with subpoenas by the Congressional Committee investigating the Board.[12] It was in connection with the union. We spent a good part of the day rounding up files and records, each of us with a constant escort. I am afraid I embarrassed them when I requested permission to go to the ladies' room unescorted.

Jules and I had dinner at the Neptune Room. Spent the evening looking at new cars. Got home about 11:00. Card from Louie asking for his birthday money in advance. Telephone call from Nate wanting to know how we were getting along.

Tuesday, September 26

Majestic went out last week but, I learned, the plant burned down a couple of months ago. There is some suspicion of arson. The Board had decided to dismiss the appeal in Joe Lowe, so I wrote a Third Amendment to Direction of Election.

---

11 Rabbi Solomon Metz, Adas Israel Congregation, located at 6th and I Streets, NW at the time.

12 Subpoenas from the Smith Committee. Anne would be called to testify in January, 1940.

Went to Style with Cokin to look at the pieces we had selected. He told me they were very expensive but good, so I ordered them. Dinner with Jules at the Arlington Grill. And again we spent the evening looking at new cars. Our car is in excellent condition, but Jules had a notion he would like a sedan. We can afford it, so he shall have it.

Wednesday, September 27
Received a silver cake knife from Charles Wyzanski,[13] and a red blanket from Mother. Lunched at the Madrillon with Charlie Horshy. Enjoyed it very much.
Reported Mass. Knitting to Leiseron once more. He decided to dismiss the 8(3). Smith is dissenting. I am to draft both opinions. Pep talk at 4:30 from Madden, Smith, Fahy and Emerson to the entire Review staff – must turn out more decisions.
Jules and I had dinner at the Arlington Grill. Looked at cars some more. Then home so he could bathe and pack. He left about 11:30 to take the sleeper to New York on business. Wish I could have gone, but did not dare ask for more leave.

Thursday, September 28
I was picked up at the bus stop by a Mrs. Fenner, who gave me a ride into town. Executive Committee meeting at noon. A whole gang of us had luncheon at a little delicatessen on K Street. To Claire's[14] for dinner.
Jules telephoned me from New York – from the British Pavilion at the World Fair. He expects to return late tomorrow night.
Clara had nothing to do, so she came with me to the union meeting. It was a rather interesting meeting, but the usual forensic battles made it last too long. Went to Adams Mill Road to spend the night, although the place was rather a mess.

Friday, September 29
Dorothy called. Stanley is going to the hospital tonight for an appendectomy. She wants me to dispose of their football and theater tickets.
Downtown at noon to buy a number of things in the way of house furnishings. Turned down a dinner invitation at the Wagshals.[15] Kami broke a dinner date with me because he had a chance to get a free meal at the Levy's which I thought was pretty low-down. Ate alone at the Arlington Grill.
Jules arrived about 11:30 with a box of candy, and very glad to be home again – I certainly was glad to have him home again.

Saturday, September 30
A lovely day, but a bit too warm. Lunched with Jules and Jashie. Then Jules and I chased around and did a number of errands, including picking up and disposing of Dorothy's tickets. Home about five to do some shopping in the neighborhood. Then out to a dinky little neighborhood restaurant, where we had excellent steaks. Then to a local movie, where we saw a silly but amusing picture. Then home, quite late, very tired, but happy. Got a package from Nyach, a clock from Clara and a set of Community Plate[16] from Sam and Molly.

13   Anne's former employer.
14   Claire Rosen, a regular lunch and dinner companion.
15   Anne's cousin Sam Wagshal who was a focal point of her family activities in Washington.
16   Silver plate flatware from Oneida.

Monthly Memoranda 1939

January
Wish I could make up my mind definitely about whether or not I am going to marry Jules. It would be fairer to him and much easier on me. I am very fond of him, certainly, but not madly in love with him. However, I doubt very much whether I shall ever be madly in love with anyone. I would not mind being a couple of years older than he is, but sometimes I seem a thousand years more mature than he is. He is sometimes so sweet and lovable, and at other times so damned inconsiderate. I just don't know my own mind - and sometimes I wonder if he really knows his.

February
February started out with Jules' birthday, and it has been pretty much Jules, Jules, Jules all the way through. Several exciting things happened this month, notably Jules' new job and our trip to Florida. Jules seems to be very happy in his new work - so far, and the trip was one of the most delightful vacation I have ever enjoyed.

And, after so many months, Stehli is almost ready to be issued, which will be a load off my mind until the respondent brings it to court. After the debacle in the Supreme Court last Monday, and with public opinion what it is, anything is likely to happen. And the case is not too strong at best.

Poor Jules, who asked me last November to marry him, is still waiting, and very impatiently, for his answer. But I cannot bring myself to rush into marriage, which I am still old-fashioned enough to consider a life-long proposition, until I am reasonably sure that Jules is the One meant for me.

March
A good deal of celebrating during the month of March, what with Clara's birthday, Kami's divorce, my raise, and Do's pregnancy.

The most radical thing I have done, of course, is go out with Arnold.[17] But if I am not going to marry Jules - for a while yet anyhow - I think it is fairer to both of us if we stopped going out with one another exclusively. We are getting very much talked about already, and it is not all entirely savory to me. And the fact remains that I still like Arnold a good deal. Does that mean I do not love Jules? How I wish I had someone with whom I could talk about all this, or a mind that knew what my heart was saying in its hesitant, stammering way.

April
I am beginning to feel more and more like a cad for the way in which I keep Jules dangling in mid-air. We have such good times together, but I know that he is unhappy, and that makes me unhappy. But he will not take no for an answer, and I still cannot bring myself to say yes. If something does not "break" soon, I shall find myself doing something drastic, like writing to Dorothy Dix. If only Jules were not unhappy, I could go on like this indefinitely. But I suppose that does not make good sense.

---

17   Arnold Raum

Other than my "Jules problem", everything seems to be hunky-dory, particularly now since I got another raise, indicating that someone considers my work to be still satisfactory. Everything considered, $3000 is a pretty good salary for me to be earning. With Jules making $3800,[18] we would be sitting pretty. But that, of course, is not the only consideration. Jules is so sweet and so generous and so much in love with me - but I don't want to get married!

May
May has certainly been a busy month - what with Jules, Arnold, the dentist, reporting and re-reporting to the Board, getting elected recording secretary of the Union and performing my duties as such, the White House, and the trip to Lawrence.
My work has not been going so well as I should like. I seem to get stymied on everything, and I do not want to accumulate too many cases, particularly during the summer time. And I seem no nearer making up my mind about Jules.

June
What a month June has been! Many events have occurred which must needs have a lasting effect.
There is Lillian's engagement, which means finding a new roommate. And, if I do get married anytime soon, it will make Clara's living arrangements a real problem. And of course there is the necessity for my operation, with the possibility of the many serious consequences which may ensue from it. But come what may, it certainly made me realize how much, and how truly, Jules loves me - so much more than I deserve. Then, there is the problem of my work, which seems to me to remain pretty much at a standstill, despite my great desire to get things cleaned up before I go to the hospital - and, possibly, before I get married. I am getting badly fed up with my work anyhow, but cannot decide whether it is due to the heat, to thinking so much of Jules and marriage, or to having been so long on the same job.
I have about decided to marry Jules - maybe this summer yet - although I am still not altogether sure that I am marrying him because I am in love with him or simply because of the force of circumstances. I do wish things could be as clear in my mind as they are in Lillian's for example.

July
What a life - being engaged, Jules having an operation, going to Philadelphia twice to see him, and finally getting to Columbus - and the family. The die is cast now. It is still difficult for me to picture clearly in my mind Jules and me as a domesticated married couple. Can I possibly measure up to his expectations of me? Can I ever possibly become a domesticated, wifely sort of being. I somehow cannot picture myself as a mother, although I do want to have children. It is all very puzzling. Shall I feel like this right up to the day I am married? Will I feel like this after I am married? I doubt it. I hope not.

---

18 Both were lawyers in the same agency with approximately the same experience, but the difference in salary for the woman is notable.

1939

August

August 1939 marks a definite turning point in my life, since I have finally decided to get married, and to marry Jules. It seemed for so long that I should probably never marry, and then again it seemed for quite a while that Jules and I were not meant for each other. But here we are, on the verge of getting married, and we are both very happy. I know that I am, and I am sure that he is.

September

I have been married a whole month now. It still does not seem possible, after so many years when I was definitely not the marrying type. Jules is a dear, really too good to me. He is a bit on the lazy side, and somewhat untidy - but then so am I. But he is so kind and generous and good natured that I fully expect he will spoil me badly after we have been married for a while.

There is one fly in our very lovely ointment, and that is the way all our friends, except the Surreys, have neglected us. We expected, and had practically been promised by a number of people, parties and dinner invitations galore. But to date, there have been no parties, and no dinner invitations except from the Surreys and Clara. Yet we were both rather popular before we married. I should like very much to know what the reason can be for people shunning us since we got married. But we have each other, and our work, so what the heck?

October

I am now an old married woman. Life seems little different than it was before I got married, but with more problems and responsibilities. Jules has a great many little faults that irk me a good deal, particularly since they are so unnecessary and so constant. He seems to be - and I believe he is - very much in love with me, but he nonetheless manages to say and do the wrong thing about nine times out of 10. I often wonder if I did the right thing in letting him shake my determination never to marry.

November

Except for maid trouble and the Smith Committee, everything appears to be progressing very smoothly and happily. The trip to Lawrence proved to be, on the whole, a rather pleasant affair. I had been afraid that the situation at home might prove a terrible shock to Jules. He was aware of unfriendly relations, of course, but the situation, on the surface, was not nearly so bad as it might have been.

I have been rather toying with the idea recently of getting a part-time job of some kind that would give me more leisure time. But I do not know what job that would be. I am not working too hard on my present job, but my conscience bothers me because I do not give my work more of my time and energy. I wonder how other married women with jobs and with children, can ever get caught up with themselves. It seems that they must neglect some phase of their lives, or maybe it is only a case of having a competent maid.

December
The most memorable date of 1939 is, of course, September 1, the date on which I got married and on which World War II broke out. It took me a long time to make up my mind about marrying Jules, but it has all worked out beautifully. He is a very sweet person, patient with and considerate of all my silly moods, to a far greater extent than I deserve. Life seems very pleasant these days. I only hope that they will continue so.

Editor's Note:
This year, 1939, is the last time Anne wrote monthly summaries. From 1931 to 1939 she had written in diaries given by the Fidelity and Deposit Company of Maryland (later United States Fidelity and Guaranty Company), and those diaries provided space for the monthly summaries. Starting in 1940 she wrote in commercially produced diaries, and they did not provide space for monthly summaries.   -- RDH

Year End Summary 1939

By the end of 1939 Anne had accumulated a prodigious resume of work with the NLRB. She had worked on eighteen cases that included some of the largest corporations in the United States, such as the Columbia Broadcasting Company, Shell Chemical Company, and Ford Motor Company. She had worked on some cases that seem to have been particularly complicated according to her diary comments, such as American Radiator Company and Stehli and Company.

As a lawyer in the Review Division of the Board, her job consisted in reviewing the case documentation of each case assigned to her. She then presented an oral summation of the case to the Board itself based on the evidence, which included transcripts of testimony, exhibits, the findings of the Trial Examiner of the Board, pleadings, and any other relevant material. She had to review decisions made at the field level and present the case to the Board to be upheld or overturned.   -- RDH

Anne and Julius on honeymoon

Anne, Julius, Mother Schlezinger
in Columbus, Ohio

1940

This was Anne and Jules first full year of marriage, and she writes about it in the Year End Summary in glowing terms. She had a promotion at the NLRB, and she received considerable attention in the national press about her work and her appearance before the Smith Committee, which was named for the conservative congressman from Virginia, Howard Smith.

Conservatives in the House of Representatives were opposed to the work of the National Labor Relations Board. They created a special House committee to investigate the workings of the NLRB and named Smith as the committee chair.

In turn Smith made an alliance with William Green, the president of the AFL (American Federation of Labor) who also opposed the NLRB on the grounds that he considered it to be controlled by leftists who supported the CIO (Congress of Industrial Organizations), led by John L. Lewis. The hearings by the Smith Committee tended to be sensationalist and created major news stories. The legislation proposed by the Committee passed the House but was eventually defeated by Roosevelt's supporters. As a compromise, Roosevelt began replacing the more left-leaning lawyers in the NLRB, many of whom had been Anne's friends.

Her appearance before the Committee was covered in the *Saturday Evening Post*.[19]

---

19   Vol. 213, No. 8, August 24, 1940, "Juvenile Jurists", Willard Edwards, pp. 29 to 44.

The article begins,

"The young woman in the witness chair surveyed the investigating committee with calm assurance. Members of the committee stared back curiously. Photographers crouched around the witness. The crowd in the hearing room leaned forward eagerly.

"The echoing caucus chamber of the Old House Office Building in Washington, D.C., furnished the setting...The witness said her name was Mrs. Julius Schlezinger, but that she was better known in the offices of the Labor Board as Miss Anne Freeling. She was a review attorney with the board...Her age? Twenty-nine..."

Anne was the first witness, and she was on the stand for two complete days, far longer than other witnesses. Congressmen focused on her youth and her lack of experience with litigation before taking a position with the Board. The fact that she was selected as the first witness indicates how much was focused on her.

The long article describes her work with the Board and that of the other witnesses called. The purpose of the hearings seems to have been establishing the youth of many of the lawyers and their lack of experience to act on cases with some of the largest corporations in the United States.

In her diary (January 10) Anne questions why so many women were called to testify. Since almost 90 percent of the lawyers with the Board were men, the focus of the Committee on women, who tended to be younger and less experienced, did not represent a balanced view.

In discussing the treatment of the women lawyers who were cross-examined by the Smith Committee, labor historian James Gross says, "The women Review attorneys were treated rudely and disparagingly. Toland shouted at them and [Congressman Harry N.] Routzohn asked personally insulting questions."[20] -- RDH

Monday, January 1
Went for a ride to the fruit stand. When we got back, Ben and Lillian had arrived. We had breakfast, then sat around and talked, had some cognac, and talked some more.
After they left, Jules and I went for a long ride in the country. It was a cold but bright day, and the drive was very pleasant.
To a movie in Bethesda, and then to the Bethesda Grill for a steak dinner. Home, to read for a while, bathe, and hop into bed – the end of a very delightful, and all too short, holiday season.

Tuesday, January 2
Postcard from Howard Friedman,[21] from Miami Beach. According to him, Clara is having a marvelous time. Lunched at S&W with Peggy, Mrs. Spalding, and Miss MacAldowney, two new Review attorneys.
Worked most of the day with Kami on General Motors, and went in with him to report to Nat Witt, who kidded me a good deal about Jules, as he usually does.
Edna did not come in – "too much fun" – so Jules and I ate at the Hot Shoppe on the way home, and spent a quiet evening at home.

Wednesday, January 3
Reported to the Board this morning on General Motors. In the course of the discussion it was decided that I should go to Detroit to assist the Trial Examiner during the hearing. The Board and Nat kidded me a good deal about getting my husband's permission.[22]
Spoke to Clara on the phone, but could not get together. Edna fixed a very good dinner. She certainly has her good points – and her bad ones. Fooled around all evening, reading and what-not. I just seem to get so tired these days I have no desire to go gallivanting around in the evening.

Thursday, January 4
Lunched at S&W with Clara. She looks very well and apparently had a marvelous time. Something in my luncheon – I suspect the salad dressing – did not agree with me, by the end of the day I felt very woozy. The crowning point was getting home to find that Edna had failed to show up. Jules had a night session, so he went downtown to eat. I curled up on the sofa and went to sleep. Got up later to drag off my clothes and get into bed. Got up once more when Jules came home to wash my face and brush my teeth. Felt terribly weak, as though, I had been sick for a long time.

Friday, January 5
Felt a little better, so went to work. Lunched at the Ambassador with Marcia and Miss Anschoss, a new review attorney. Jules and

---

20   1981. *The Reshaping of the National Labor Relations Board.* Albany: State University of New York Press. Page 183.
21   Anne's NLRB colleague Howard Friedman, apparently on a trip to Miami with Clara.
22   Occasionally Anne refers to misogynistic statements.

I left a little early and went out to Best's, but could not find anything I liked well enough to buy. Then I went to the beauty parlor and Jules went to Al's Motors.

Fixed supper ourselves, Edna having failed to show up again, although her clothes are still at the apartment. I suppose she is on a drunk. Edetha is going to work for Clara, and I don't know where to turn now for a maid. Andetha is coming in tomorrow to clean, at least.

Saturday, January 6
Meeting at 1:00 with Fahy, Lester Levin, Aaron Lewittes, and Lew Gill, [with] Aaron, Lew and I having been summoned as witnesses for Monday morning. Meeting later with Horshy of those who had been subpoenaed for the Union. Another meeting later with Levin, Emerson, and Witt. By then the afternoon was gone. We just had time to dash home and change before going to the Surreys' for dinner. Sat around for a while after dinner and then off to a party given by the Dave Kroottis for the Les Ashers. It was a lot of fun. All the Board people had some good advice for me, of course.

Sunday, January 7
Stopped in to see Frances for a few minutes during our usual Sunday drive.

Clara dropped in with Harold. Brought us some jellies form Florida. Also received a twin waffle iron from Jules' Aunt Henrietta. In the afternoon to the National Symphony Concert with Dorothy. Met our husbands at Awignine's, where we had dinner. By the time we finished dinner it was snowing very hard, but Jules had promised we would stop in at the Bergs', so stop in at the Bergs' we did. I should have liked to get to bed early, but we didn't. Got my name in the papers in connection with the hearing.

Monday, January 8
I was called to the stand first, and grilled on review work in general and American Radiator in particular. At noon we dashed back to the office to talk to Tom. Had a sandwich, on the run. I was on the stand all day; have to go back tomorrow. Everyone had been very kind about telling me what a good job I am doing, but it is an ordeal nevertheless.

Jules and I had a good stiff drink before dinner. Ate at the Hot Shoppe. Then went to the movies, in an attempt to relax. But everything reminded me of the hearing.

Much publicity!

Tuesday, January 9
On the stand all day again, but I really think Toland[23] had not got a thing out of me. Praised by everyone – Madden, Fahy, Witt,[24] etc., etc. A crowd of us had luncheon at the Ugly Duckling, and it was all very gay and pleasant. I no longer feel the nervous strain, and could go on- and on. Adjourned about 5:00. Listened in at Jules' hearing until about 7:00. Then had dinner at Schneider's with Lagar Teppe, Dave Cobb, and Jules. Home after dinner.

Telephoned Lawrence and Columbus,[25] but they knew all about my performance, from the local papers and from the radio. Such fame!

23   Edmund M. Toland was the General Counsel of the Smith Committee and led the questioning of witnesses.
24   Nathan Witt, head of the NLRB; Warren Madden, and Charles Fahy, division heads.
25   Anne's hometown of Lawrence, MA and Jules' hometown of Columbus, OH.

Wednesday, January 10
Got comfortably settled in the office with my audience around me when the Clerk of the Committee called and asked me to come up and dictate some longhand notes that were put in as an exhibit. They were perfectly legible, so I sat in at the hearing while a stenographer copied them, and answered the few questions that came up on them. Peggy Bennett and Carol Agger have testified – and very well – and Fanny Boyls got on for a few minutes this afternoon. Why all the women?[26]
Dinner at the Silver Bowl with Bill Rice, Kami and Babs. Then to the Brown apartment, where Bill is staying, for a drink. Then home and to bed, so tired. Letter from Lawrence, with clippings.

Thursday, January 11
Lunched in the drug store with Jack Krug and Dave Rein.[27] I am still being showered with compliments to an amazing extent. It is all very flattering, but, it appears to me, considerably exaggerated. Left the office a little early and went shopping with Jules. We were joined later by Clara. Jules bought a suit, a sport jacket, and some underwear, and I bought two new dresses. By that time I was thoroughly fatigued, so we took a cab to the parking lot, but the cab driver had a slight accident, so we were further detained. Went to Howard Johnson's for dinner, then home to read for a while, and then to bed, to stay awake most of the night with cramps.

26 To Anne that the disproportion number of women suggested that they were being targeted.
27 Jack Krug and David Rein were lawyers at the NLRB.

Friday, January 12
Called to the hearing again as a union witness or I should not have gone to work at all. When I got to the hearing, Toland, as he had Wednesday, gushed all over me in a disgustingly affectionate manner, told me what a splendid witness I was and assured me he had no intention of calling me again, so I retuned to the office.
Jules had a yen for some delicatessen, so we went to Sam's for dinner – and for more discussions of my notoriety. I had made the front page again today in connection with husbands and wives in the Government service. Something did not agree with me, and I went home very sick, and spent another horrible night.

Saturday, January 13
Was awakened in the morning by Jules, dressed and ready to leave, coming in to kiss me goodbye, so I stayed home. He came home at noon, and I fixed luncheon. Then he went to the Guild's Administrative Law Conference. I should have liked to go, but still felt weakish.
Drove over to the Hot Shoppe for dinner, although, it was so terribly foggy out that it took the best part of the evening to drive there and back. When we got home we stayed there, wrote letters, read, and went to bed. Jules would have liked to go out, despite the fog, but I just did not feel equal to it.

Sunday, January 14
A miserable, rainy day, so spent most of it indoors, and a considerable part of it ini-

tiating our waffle iron. It was a lot of fun, and we finally produced some very fine waffles. Late in the afternoon we went for a long ride, despite the weather. Stopped at the Howard Johnson's in Falls Church for supper. Then to a movie at the Buckingham Theater. Jules packed his overnight bag, and left about 10:00 to take the sleeper to New York. I hated to see him go, even for one day. We both would have gone for the weekend if I had not been ill.

Monday, January 15
Lunched with Clara. Turned in the credit slip at Foster's for a bread tray, a set of coasters, and a tie rack. Letter from a poor chap in Los Angeles who heard over the radio about my "labor relations" and thought I might be able to help him.
Jules got back about 4:30, so I got a ride home. I went down on the bus this morning.
We walked over to the Buckingham Grill for dinner. Then home, to read for a while, and to bed. Card from Sam Wagshal, who is vacationing in Florida. Letter from Ruth Samson commenting on my recent notoriety. My fame was fleeting, but rather pleasant while it lasted.

Tuesday, January 16
Lunched at Childs with Dave Rein and Jack King.
Heard that when the group of girls were called to the hearing, Bea Stern spoke to them, and told them, among other things, "after all, no one can expect to be perfect except Anne Freeling and the Chairman." What a compliment! Sol Barkin, in town for a Wages and Hours hearing, took us to dinner at the Ambassador. He was not feeling well, so went to his room after dinner, and we went home. Letters from Gertrude and from Mrs. S.[28] They are quite "set-up" about the publicity that I, as Mrs. Jules Schlezinger, have received in Columbus by newspaper and radio.

Wednesday, January 17
Lunched at the Ambassador with Kami, who told me confidentially that Nat has recommended, and the Board had approved, my going to Detroit to help Cranefield try the case, but Fahy had voted against it because of the Smith Committee, etc. I am flattered. Dinner at Clara's. On the way, saw a beautiful white jersey dinner dress in the Embassy Shop window, stopped in, and bought it. Had an excellent dinner. Sat around for a while, and then went home, taking the few books and things I still had at 2929.
Letter from George Gray, from the Philippines. Very happy to hear from him. Letter from Aunt Henrietta. The family is really "taking me up."

Thursday, January 18
Took a notion to ask Tom Emerson for a raise. No soap. Only P.I.'s are getting them, and possibly a few others, not including me. Jules got a reclassification and a raise to $4600.
Shopping at noon. Bought some evening and other underwear. Fixed supper at home – and a very good one.
Letter from Mother enclosing clipping about radio commentator who stated that I

---

28   Jules' mother.

was "pretty as well as smart." Apparently the home town is still talking about me. Interviewed several maids and hired the one who was available to start tomorrow. Hope and pray she works out all right.

Friday, January 19
Shopping at noon with Clara, even thought it was a nice cold day to stay indoors. The Trial Examiners are certainly not doing as good a job at the hearing as the dumb little women review attorneys did. The maid who came in today arrived late, worked slowly, and bungled things so badly that she made me nervous. I finally paid her off and fixed supper myself. It was a very good supper, and of course put Jules onto one of his favorite subjects again – why I don't quit my job and become a housewife, even if I kept a cook and merely supervised –which just doesn't appeal to me as the way to spend my life.

Saturday, January 20
Lunched at the Ambassador with Jules and Gene Levenson. Then Jules and I went shopping. I finally wound up in a beauty shop in Clarendon, where, through sheer accident, I found an operator who could really "do things" with my hair.
Home to dress. To George's apartment to pick up George and Helen, and to have a drink. Then on to the Troisha, where we were joined after dinner by Gene and his date. Everyone admired my dress and complimented me highly. Jules was pleased and proud. It was very late by the time we took everyone home and got home ourselves – but it was a grand evening.

Sunday, January 21
Slept late. Took a walk, had a scrumptious breakfast, read the papers, then dressed and went out. Stopped at the home of our latest prospective maid to leave a key. Then on to visit the Reins, Selma being ill. There were several other people there, and we had a very pleasant visit. Then on to Mrs. Delin's for the grandest smorgasbord supper I have ever eaten. It was proceeded by gliing, a Swedish drink, which was delicious, quite potent, and fascinating to watch in the process of making. We all stuffed ourselves, drank and drank, gabbed, took pictures and had heaps of fun. Home not too late.

Monday, January 22
Although I have been to Jules' hearings a few times, I have never heard him put on a witness, so I dashed up there at about 11:30, only to have him complete his presentation a few minutes after I arrived. Hattie came in the morning and worked all day. She cleaned fairly well and did a tremendous amount of laundry. Dinner was fairly good. I think she would work out all right with a little training, but don't know that I shall be able to train her since Jules and I may both be going out of town in a week or so, I for about two weeks and Jules for about a month. Letter from his folks in Florida.

Tuesday, January 23
Lunched alone in order to do a little shopping. The Solway draft is in the pool, and my departure for Detroit is still very much up in the air. What to do in the meantime?

Hattie fixed a splendid dinner – a delicious roast and all the trimmings. To the theater to see Ethel Waters in "Mamba's Daughters."[29] The acting was excellent, and the whole thing very well done, but it was all rather depressing. On the whole, however, I am glad we went to see it. Came out of the theater into a white world and a driving snow storm.

Wednesday, January 24
We were pretty well snowed in, but Jules insisted on taking the car downtown, as we did, after much time and trouble. Everyone else seemed to have a least as much time and trouble as we did getting to work. Had a very good dinner. Let Hattie go early without doing the dishes lest she have trouble.
Took a warm bath, then sat around reading with a nightie and bathrobe on, and, of course, was sniffling by bed time. I should have known better, but I felt so darned warm.
Card from Mother telling me she is sending more clippings.

Thursday, January 25
Wore my new black and white dress, and was much complimented. Supposed to go to a meeting of the in-service training committee at 4:30, but my cold was so miserable that I skipped it. Had too much to do anyhow – buying candy, nuts, etc., at the last minute.
Bill Rice and Clara came up for dinner. The meal left much to be desired. The Edises, the Wolfs, and Evans from Jules' office came up later to drink and talk. We had a lot of fun, but by the end of the evening I was a wreck. Evans very kindly offered to take Clara and Bill home, which relieved Jules of the task.

Friday, January 26
Stayed home from the office. Jules fixed some orange juice and tea for me before he left. Pele came over at noon and fixed luncheon for me. She stayed until Hattie came. Jules came home early, bringing me some things to read.
Hattie served my supper to me in bed, and Jules ate his off a tray to keep me company. Poor Hattie! She is really trying very hard, but just cannot make the grade.
My cold was much better by evening, but Jules absolutely forbids my going back to work tomorrow.

Saturday, January 27
Jules fixed breakfast for me again, but I was well enough to fix my own luncheon. Finished *The Country Lawyer*,[30] then new issue of *Fortune* and the new issue of *Life*. Jules had to spend most of the afternoon downtown.
Got up for dinner, which was pretty bad. Paid Hattie off, and then let her go.
Some of the gang were giving Henry Lehmann[31] a farewell party tonight, but Jules put his foot down on that. So, we just stayed home and read and fooled around and went to bed early. I feel like I have been laid up for months.

---

29   A play based on a novel by the same name published by DuBose Heyward in 1929 about racial boundaries and tensions in Charleston, South Carolina.
30   1938 book by Francis Lyman Windolph describing the work of small town lawyers.
31   Usually written Henry Lehman. He was a regular NLRB lunch companion for Anne from 1937-39.

Sunday, January 28
Henry came over for breakfast, which Jules still insists is the best meal of the week when I fix it. Then, since it was a little warmer out than it had been, the three of us went for a long ride. Met the Surreys at the Neptune Room for dinner. Ran into Arnold Raum[32] and the rest of the Q Street gang and gobs of other people we knew. It was a regular Old Home Night. Stopped in to visit Clara for a bit. Then home to pack on the chance that I shall be leaving for Detroit tomorrow.

Monday, January 29
Back to the office. In a complete flurry all day getting ready to go to Detroit. Lunched with Jules. Bought a new black bag and shoes – very stunning. Jules took me to the train later. I certainly hated to say goodbye to him. But he is going to the Philadelphia regional office tomorrow for a month, so it would have been goodbye anyhow. Took the B&O 5:30 train. Jules bought me a drink and a big box of candy and some magazines. I read, had dinner, read some more, and retired. It was a ramshackle old rattly train, and darned drafty.

Tuesday, January 30
Checked in at the Statler, where Pratt[33] had arranged to have me meet Rickel, the Trial Examiner, and get acquainted.
Then to the hearing. I sat on the bench with Rickel, who announced on the record that I was the review attorney and "technical assistant." I don't believe he liked the idea, but he had no choice.
The hearing adjourned within about an hour. To the Regional Office for a conference. Luncheon with Boweu, Burno, Diammock, Cranefield and his wife. Dinner with Rickel, and cocktails later at the Statler bar. To bed very late.

Wednesday, January 31
Slept fairly late. After breakfast, went to the office. Read transcript, wrote letters and talked. Long letter from Jules.
Had a fairly good picture of me in the *Detroit Free Press*. Moved to the Wolverine. The boys are staying there, and it is much cheaper than the Statler and will serve my purpose just as well. Ben Fitzgerald moved my things. Dinner at Stouffer's with Rickel and Bohat. I like the latter very much, and we had a very pleasant dinner.
Had a nightcap in Burns' room with Burns and Fitzgerald. Sat around talking all hours of the night. Fitz is a very nice boy just out of school.

---
32 Anne's boyfriend before Jules.
33 George Pratt, Chief Trial Examiner until July, 1942.

Year End Summary 1940

Anne on the beach

It has been a wonderfully pleasant and exciting year - testifying before the Smith Committee and becoming something of a national figure; going to Detroit for the General Motors hearing, for all the world like a "big shot", and making a number of new friends there; getting transferred to Briefing and later to the Trial Examiners' Section, both steps upward; having such a wonderful birthday celebration, with roses, orchids, champagnes, and beautiful gifts; having mother in for such a pleasant visit; having hired a maid whom Jules and I both rate as pretty near "tops"; going on such a perfectly marvelous trip to the West; attending two delightful weddings; taking so many short trips, for both business and pleasure; helping Lou[34] and Kami get new jobs; having the Detroit office try to "draft" me; experiencing so many little triumphs on my new job; attending the thrilling farewell banquet for Foley; getting such a lovely fur coat and so many other pretty clothes; going to so many delightful parties and on so many thrilling "dates"; and, last but by far the best of all, having such a generous, patient, understanding, loving, adorable husband. It was truly a perfectly wonderful year.

---

34 Lou Roland, sister Clara's husband took a job in St. Louis.

1941

As war clouds gathered over the nation and the world, Anne and Jules continued their professional lives, and they explored the possibility of adopting a baby. Anne continues to wonder whether she should work as a wife and prospective mother. After the Japanese attack on Pearl Harbor and the entry of the United States into war against both Japan and Germany, it was clear that their lives were about the change dramatically. -- RDH

Monday, December 1
Lunched at The Candlestick with Claire. Getting along with the Curtiss-Wright record, which is ridiculously long.
Odessa is finally getting the curtains up, and the apartment is beginning to look like something. Maybe soon I can begin entertaining again.
Jules wanted to go the movies after dinner, but I was rather tired, so reneged. He went for a walk while I rested. When he came back, we played cards again. It is certainly getting to be a habit.
Then took a nice leisurely bath, read the *New Yorker*, listened to the news flashes, and then to bed.

Tuesday, December 2
Shirley Berg stopped in the office on her way from the dentist and we lunched together. Getting really fed up with Curtiss-Wright. No mail from home for a couple of days. Hope that's good news.
After dinner went to a Lawyers Guild meeting. It was very sparsely attended and delightfully brief. Elected a new slate of officers, including Tom Emerson as president. Joe Eggert, one of the Buckingham evictees, reported on the District Rent Control Bill that was passed today. And Guild meetings are good places to meet old friends.

Wednesday, December 3
Lunched with Phil[35] at the Madillon. Discussed adoption with him, since he is one of our references, and also my parent-problem. He was very kind about it all.
Jules had to work late so I rode home with the Edes. Jules got home in time for dinner. Clara and Lou came over after dinner, with a letter from Mother, still very bitter about Father, but a little calmer about it. Asked us to resume sending her money, which we are, of course, doing. I would so like to see them settle things, but suppose it is hopeless. And yet I can think of no satisfactory alternative. It is certainly a vexing problem.

Thursday, December 4
To the beauty parlor at noon. Almost finished with the Curtiss-Wright record.
The Edes came over for dinner. Odessa fixed an excellent turkey dinner. Later the Treusches and the Reiters came over. We had drinks, and later coffee and turkey sandwiches and cake. Everyone seemed congenial and to be having a good time. Jules and I enjoyed it very much. It was quite late by the time everyone left and we got things put away. And when we finally got to bed, it was to sleep only fitfully since we had both too much coffee.

---

35   Anne's cousin Phil, the lawyer and son of Sam Wagshal.

1941

Friday, December 5
Finished the record and conferred most of the day with Howard.
After we got home, Nate telephoned about an appointment on Monday.[36] Jules told him he was going out of town, and then they proceeded to make the appointment for me.
A few minutes later Edward telephoned, having talked to Nate meanwhile and heard that Jules was stopping in Columbus. Card from Eve - very busy and very happy.
Clara and Lou stopped in for a while to wish Jules a pleasant trip, etc. Stayed long enough to furnish Jules with a good excuse for not packing, since I insisted on his getting to bed at a reasonable hour.

Saturday, December 6
Our closets were painted this morning so we lunched at Howard Johnson's on the way home. Jules showered and changed, and just threw his things into a suitcase. The Edes[37] picked us up and took us to the airport. Jules left on the 4:35 plane for Columbus, then tomorrow evening to Minneapolis to try some cases.
I went to the Edes' for dinner. Later we all went to a movie. Stopped afterwards at Howard Johnson's. Then they took me home. Urged me to stay overnight, but I was leaving for Philadelphia in the morning, so decided to sleep at home, although the place was a terrible mess, with everything out of the closets.

Sunday, December 7
Took a cab to the station, and got the 10:00 train, breakfasted on the train. Nate met me. They had breakfast when we got back, so I had to eat again.
Japan went to war against us today, bombing some of our South Pacific islands.[38] It had been imminent for some time but was nevertheless shocking. Tore ourselves away from the radio and went for a long delightful ride to Valley Forge, the radio on the entire way.
To the Russian Inn for dinner. Then home again, to read some of the "Extras." It's time all right. I was very tired, but we were all too excited to go to bed for hours.

Monday, December 8
Kept my appointment with a Mr. Dummit at 11:00. it took about 5 minutes – just long enough for him to tell me they had far more applicants than babies, had to satisfy Philadelphia first, but I could file an application. I was sore! Took the 12:12 train back, and got to the office at 2:45, much to everyone's surprise. Worked on Curtiss-Wright for a while. Then a long weary trip home on the bus. Odessa had straightened the place out, but had gone home, as I told her to do. I fixed some supper, read the papers, worked for a while, and finally to bed. A discouraging day. And, worst of all, no letter from Jules.

Tuesday, December 9
The bus service is atrocious. Mrs. Langbein telephoned and asked me to come to her office to clear up a few details. Told me I would be required to give up working for a year.[39] We

---

36 Jules' brother Nate making an appointment with an adoption agency in Philadelphia.
37 Claire Rosen Edes and husband.
38 Refers to the bombing of Pearl Harbor, which led to the U.S. entering World War II. War was declared on Japan, Monday, December 8.
39 This is the adoption agency in Washington

have passed our tests so far, and they have a baby in mind – but I made no definite answer. Wrote Shad[40] about this matter. No mail from Jules, which was a great disappointment.

Letter from Mother thanking me for the check. She seems to be getting along a bit better. Dined in solitary splendor. Clara telephoned and asked me to come over but I was not in the mood. Did some work. Listened to the President's war speech. We make speeches while Japan drops bombs.

Wednesday, December 10
The CCA sustained Norristown Box in one short paragraph, which was something of a triumph for me.

Howard's indecisiveness got on my nerves pretty badly today, and we had quite a little spat. We got over it, however, before quitting time, fortunately, since I had a dinner engagement with him.

The Ringer[41] family joined us and we all went to Wearley's for dinner. Then to the Little to see Chaliapin[42] in "Don Quixote," an old film showing signs of wear. They drove me home. Card from Jules which he wrote from Chicago but forgot to mail and a letter from Minneapolis. He is full of nothing but war talk again.

Thursday, December 11
Howard[43] and I are just about finished, thank heavens. Caught a terrible cold somehow and was pretty miserable.

Rode home with Claire, who came for dinner. Letter from Jules, who is working very hard, being entertained a good deal, and having a wonderful time, but – the war.

After dinner Claire and I went to the Volunteer Civilian Defense Bureau and signed up for a whole bunch of things. Don't know how we shall find time but are going to try anyhow. Back to the apartment for some hot tea and more news flashes. Then Claire went home and I wrote Jules and went to bed.

Friday, December 12
McNally[44] is still seriously ill so I am revising Gates Rubber in accordance with the memo I wrote months ago. No mail from Jules.

Gave Odessa her Xmas gift so she would have time to change it if necessary before going on her vacation.

To a Civic Association meeting on Defense with Clara and Lou. The management had a representative present; and all is now peace and harmony between us as we prepare to fight the common enemy. There were several good short talks by representatives of the Army, Red Cross, Civilian Defense, U.S.O. etc., and much enthusiasm by the audience – altogether a splendid meeting.

Saturday, December 13
Began with a sleet storm in the morning,

---

where they were able to eventually adopt their son.
40   Someone helping with the adoption.
41   William Ringer, who would serve as Chief Judge of the NLRB from 1947 to 1961.
42   Feodor Chaliapin, Russian opera singer and considered one of the best bass soloists of the time. The only sound movie he made was "Adventures of Don Quixote" in 1933.
43   This is apparently Anne's colleague Howard Friedman working on the Curtiss-Wright case.
44   NLRB Judge Patrick H. McNally.

which had started last night, and a deluge of rain all day. Lunched downstairs in the drug store, and worked most of the afternoon, even skipping a union cocktail party.

The DeKovens picked me up and we all went to Claire's for dinner.[45] She had a cousin there from Chicago, and of course Bernice, so it was a nice little party. Claire asked me to stay over, but the DeKovens offered to take me home and I accepted their offer. Found a card and a letter from Jules, a Xmas card from the Traynors, and an enthusiastic note from Odessa who is delighted with the new uniform. It was certainly worth while coming home.

Sunday, December 14
After breakfast I tidied up the apartment, got dressed and walked to the corner to mail a letter to Jules and to get the paper. Jules telephoned, and was very pleased to hear how industrious I had been. Is enjoying his work very much, but is terribly worried about the damned war.

The Surreys[46] surprised me by dropping in during the afternoon for a fairly long visit. Clara telephoned and asked me to go to the movies with them, but I was tired, and wanted to do a little work, so I stayed at home. Worked for a little while, AND THEN relaxed with the *New Yorker*, and then to bed.

Monday, December 15
Lunched at the Tally-Ho with Claire. To the Board on Webb's Bonafide Mills. Got slapped down. The Board is really getting conservative when it dismisses a case Webb sustained.[47] Home with Claire for dinner. Later we went to the Arlington Recreation Room and played some ping pong. Enjoyed it very much. Same old argument about staying over, but I finally persuaded her to take me home. Had a letter from Jules and one from Mother. Jules keeps complaining about not getting enough mail from me although I write every day. Hope I am not mis-addressing them. Mother and Father still on the outs but she seems a bit more cheerful. Letter from Shad - my working no obstacle at all [for adoption of baby].

Tuesday, December 16
Had a bad headache all day. Could not get out of a luncheon date on Guild business at the Tally-Ho, so went, and ate a much bigger luncheon than I would have alone.

Pratt[48] made a speech exhorting us to work nights and Sundays to get our important defense work out. Sounded silly to me.

Got a ride home with Dan Byrd.[49] Went to bed immediately, and got sicker and sicker. Odessa was very kind, but there was nothing she could do to help. I had to insist on her going home because she was so afraid to leave me alone. Postcard from Jules, still complaining about not getting enough mail from me.

Wednesday, December 17
Went to the office, but felt a bit sickish all

---

45   Claire Rosen Edes and her cousin Bernice. The DeKovens are not identified and do not appear again.
46   Friends Stanley and Dorothy Surrey.
47   After the 1940 hearings by the Smith Committee FDR replaced some of the more liberal lawyes on the NLRB, and it did become more conservative in prosecuting corporations.
48   Chief Judge George Pratt.
49   Not identified and does not appear again.

day. Odessa bawled me out when I got home for going to the office. Told me Ann Reiter had called when I was in bed last night. Called her back, and was asked to dinner Friday evening.

Claire asked me to dinner tonight but I decided I had better go home and mollycoddle myself a little. Odessa fixed some very good broiled chicken for me.

Letter from Jules, who seems to have perked up a little. Xmas cards from the Carl Bullocks and the Joe Friedmans.[50]

Wrote Jules a good long letter, wrote a few other letters, read for while, and went to bed good and early.

Thursday, December 18
Mort Riemer and I went for the oral argument in Feinberg but no one showed up for it. That won't help the respondent any.

Claire asked me to dinner again but I wanted to say goodbye to Odessa, who is leaving tomorrow for Ohio for the holidays.

Duffy[51], who got in last night, called after dinner, and took Claire, Bernice and me downtown to see the world premiere of "The Corsican Brothers,"[52] a rather lukewarm affair. Then to the Hot Shoppe for a drink and much talk. Home very late, but wrote a few more paragraphs on Jules' letter before retiring. Received a card and a letter from him.

Friday, December 19
To the beauty parlor at noon. After work out to the Reiters' on the bus. Ann had a few other people, but Fred got tied up at the office and could not get home for dinner. Had a delicious dinner which Ann had cooked. Attended a first-aid lecture in the lobby of their apartment house. Then back to the apartment for much talk, principally about the war. The Hechingers, who were there, have a son at camp for whom they want Fred to arrange a transfer. Apparently he gets many such requests, and was very sweet about it. They took me home, very late. Special delivery from Jules – he may be home this Sunday night. I certainly hope so.

Saturday, December 20
On top of everything else, Jules' office is being moved to Pittsburg, Lou[53] to St. Louis, etc., to make room for defense workers.

Lunched with Bob Koretz.

To the Maddens' with the Duddleys and Judge Smith for Xmas carols. There was a large crowd and a very pleasant one. Then home. Did not bother to go to Edna's party. Clara and Lou stopped in. Cards from Mother and Jules. Then a wire from Jules that he was coming home tonight. To the airport to meet him, but his plane had come in early and he went directly home. We finally got together. It certainly was good to see him again. And there was so much to talk about!

Sunday, December 21
Jules called Columbus when he got in last night so we did not call today. Served as an air raid warden in a test raid this morning

---

50   NLRB colleagues.
51   Duffy Edes, Claire Rosen's husband.
52   A 1941 swashbuckling movie starring Douglas Fairbanks, based on the original story by Alexandre Dumas.
53   Lou Rolands, sister Clara's husband.

with a very charming neighbor, Mrs. Earl, as my assistant.

To the Edes' in the late afternoon. Then to dinner at L'Escargot with the Edes, her cousin Ralph, Bernice and Lou, and the Treuschers. After a very good dinner we all went to see the new Disney picture "Dumbo" which we all found perfectly charming and very relaxing.

Letter from Shad. Mrs. Brenner is checking with Washington about the baby that is "available" but which we cannot have because of my working.[54]

Monday, December 22
Jules probably will not be moved to Pittsburgh. Irv told him about the baby available here, apparently very desirable. Wish I knew what was best to do.

Lunched with Mary Persinger. Xmas cards from Phil Wolfe, the Ringers[55] and the Herrups.[56] Sicolia is cleaning for us in Odessa's absence.

Fixed a delicatessen supper. To an air raid wardens meeting with Mrs. Earl. Then home to wash dishes and tidy up. Nate telephoned to tell us they might not be able to come down until New Year's Day. He expects to be called up for service in three months in spite of Bobby's pregnancy. Pretty tough luck!

Tuesday, December 23
Mailed to Mother S. the hanky Jules bought her in Minnesota for $2.50 – a gyp! Sent Mother a few dollars extra for her Xmas present.

Picked up another terrible cold, I think at the meeting last night. Pretty miserable all day. And a rainy day into the bargain!

Home to clean up and rest for a while. Then to Howard Johnson's for dinner, which was rather good. Then home to read for a while, play some cards, take a hot bath, and go to bed reasonably early.

Winston Churchill is at the White House mapping out a war plan for the Allies with the President while the Russians really fight this war.

Wednesday, December 24
Supposed to have 2 hours off for shopping, so left at noon for the day. Jules took me to luncheon at the Madrillon. Then he bought me a luscious white nightgown and I bought him the *Holmes Pollock Letters* and *The Black Lamb and the Grey Falcon*, 4 volumes, and $15 worth of books, which should keep him occupied for a while. Bought a number of other little things.

Cards from the Teples, the Lesters, the Ruchels, and Romeo Cammisa, our former messenger now at Fort Devens, and the Crocketts. Had a delicious dinner at a Chicken In the Rough place. Then to the Reiters' for a very pleasant evening.

Thursday, December 25
A pleasant, rather warm day. Went for a long walk after brunch. Jules went for another walk later, and came back with some lovely flowers.

---

54   This refers to Ira, the son they will be allowed to adopt in another couple of months.
55   William Ringer, who served as Chief Judge from 1947 to 1961.
56   Al and Eve Herrup.

To the Surreys' for eggnog. She had just a small congenial group, and it was quite enjoyable. Then downtown to meet the Edes, and to O'Donnell's for dinner, although I had completely ruined my appetite at Dorothy's. She gave each of her guests a small gift – gave me some very nice candy.

After dinner we went to the National to see "Pal Joey,"[57] which I found rather dull and tiresome. Then home – on the whole a lovely day!

Friday, December 26
Japan had bombed Manila mercilessly although it had been declared an open city. What could one expect? Jules received cards from Lazer Tepes and Elias Lieberman.[58]
Got ambitious and cooked dinner tonight. The steak was not so good, but dear, sweet Jules insisted it was the fairest of the meat, and that the rest of the dinner was excellent. But I knew he was just being kind.
I was very tired, so got into lounging clothes. Jules tired to read aloud to me but I kept falling asleep, so we finally gave up and I went to bed.

Saturday, December 27
Lunched at Childs over near Union Station. Then to a church nearby for Charlotte Lyerly's wedding. It was a simple lovely ceremony. We got a chance to kiss the bride after the ceremony so skipped the reception, and went shopping instead.
Fixed dinner again to retrieve my reputation. Made fried chicken – my first attempt – and it was really good. So was the rest of the dinner. I felt much better. Xmas card and postcard from Henry Lehman, whom Jules had seen much of in Minneapolis. Letter from Mother – same old problems. Read for a while, until I got very sleepy, and then went to bed.

Sunday, December 28
A dull cloudy day.
Jules took a walk before brunch, and we both took a short walk after brunch. I felt lazy and spent most of the day in a negligee reading the paper and just sitting around.
Had some "Ma Froman" chicken sent over for supper. It was good, but we both decided that the chicken I fixed last night was better.
After supper we walked over to the Buckingham movie to see a silly, but somewhat funny movie about the army, as all, the movies lately seem to be. Home early enough to read for a while, listen to the news flashes, and have a snack before retiring.

Monday, December 29
Downtown at noon to do some errands. The stores are still crowded – with people exchanging gifts.
Finished the N.Y. Merchandise record today. And Marty will be away for a week yet. Odessa got back today, and we certainly were glad to see her. She pitched right in and did a tremendous amount of laundry and cleaning. After dinner we stopped in to see Clara and

---

57   "Pal Joey" is a musical based on a book by John O'Hara with music and lyrics by Richard Rodgers and Lorenz Hart. The story is about an unsuccessful singer who is cynical but then discovers love. The 1957 film starred Frank Sinatra and Rita Hayworth.

58   Elias Lieberman, a poet and educator, best known for his poem, "I Am An American," was associate superintendent with the New York Board of Education at this point.

Lou.[59] They are having a hard time deciding whether to move to St. Louis or have Lou get another job. Lou likes his work very much but Clara doesn't want to move from Washington – so far from everyone.

Tuesday, December 30
Lunched at the Claridge with Joe Robinson. Helen's agency is moving to Chicago and he has other problems, but mainly he is filled with pride for his son. Long letter from Madelyn about the furniture she and her decorator have selected – sound sumptuous. Card from Bobbie – they won't get in until Thursday.
Test black-out tonight. With Jules' assistance, I put out the lights in the hallways and patrolled my block. It was highly successful. Saw Mrs. Earl for a few minutes. They are moving tomorrow – had to or give up their dog. Rather sorry to see her go because she was a pleasant neighbor and co-air raid warden.

Wednesday, December 31
Lunched with Mary Persinger, Ann Wolf, and Molly Perkins, who were over to see Pratt [i.e. Chief Judge George Pratt] as a union committee. He is taking on several new trial examiners although there seems no need for them.
The Edes came over for dinner. After dinner we sat around a while and had a few drinks. Then downtown. Saw a very delightful movie, "Ball of Fire." Walked around downtown for a bit. Then home for more drinks and a lot of fooling around. I fixed some scrambled eggs and stuff to sober everyone up as well as to feed them. It was about 3:00 or 4:00 before the Edes finally left and we tumbled into bed.

59   Lou Roland, Clara's husband.

Year End Summary 1941

Cannot say that I am sorry to see 1941 come to an end - the year of my operation and this country's entry into the War, both extremely distressing occurrences. I realize of course, that 1942 may be far worse, since this is such a horribly devastating war, but at least I won't again have to go through the horror of realizing that I can never bear a child. But the horror of having Jules drafted into the Army, which seems so imminent, may be even worse. I suppose I really ought not to complain about anything in my present lot.

Hope I am not doing Jules, as well as myself and some poor baby, a grave injustice by not having given up my job and adopting the baby. If only New York would give me a definite answer, I should know how to proceed - either to wait for a baby from New York, or to accept the one here and resign from my job. I really believe I should do the latter, but it is an extremely difficult thing for me to persuade myself to do. So many of my girl - friends with young babies found it too boring to stay home with them. And I should find it even more so, I am afraid, as undomestically inclined as I am. And I do not feel that the welfare of the baby requires it. If I did, that would make all the difference in the world. A few months I should gladly give up to it, but a year can seem a frightfully long time. Or if I could foresee Jules' future as far as the draft is concerned, that would greatly facilitate my arriving at a decision. Would hate to try to bring up a baby on $21.00 a month, or to use up all our savings in the process. Well, time, and time alone, will tell.

1942

The turning event in 1942 was the adoption of their son Ira. With motherhood Anne discovers something within herself that she did not expect. At the end of the year she says that because of Ira and her happiness, the year has passed incredibly fast. On the other hand, the fear of Jules being drafted into the Army pervades her vision of the future. She longs for the war to end. Life and work continue even with all of the changes. 　　　　　　　　　-- RDH

Monday, February 23
To the Board on Bradford Machine. A very short and unexciting discussion. We got off a bit early because of the holiday, so I went home with Dan. Stopped in to see his young son, who is an adorable child.
To Marvin's for dinner. Finally met Al Herrup, a pleasant person, apparently very wealthy. Eve looked splendid and seems to be very much in love.
After dinner we had some drinks, listened to the President's speech, got into a very heated argument about it, and got home very late. Herb Marx was there – no other guests.
Letter from Madelyn describing her new house furnishings. Yum!!

Tuesday, February 24
Was assigned a new case–a dirty trick, I think. On top of that, Ragosa is ill and the baby has a cold, so we could not see him.
Eve stopped in to visit. We had a nice long chat. It is refreshing to see someone so much in love.

We both brought work home, but just as we were about to start the Rolands,[60] Sylvia and Mother came in, a day ahead of time, but no one bothered to let us know. They had not had dinner yet, so they all went out to eat except Mother, and I scraped together something for her to eat. Then I had to fix the guest bed, got her things unpacked, and by then it was time for bed.

Wednesday, February 25
Finally got Langbein to take us out to see the baby. He is no beauty, but big and healthy looking, had a charming smile and seems bright. We made friends with far less difficultly than we had been led to expect. Jules got back to the office to learn that Gardner had been trying to get him for hours. Turned out he wanted to offer him the job as head of the Children's Bureau at $5600. So this was quite a day!
Pitiful letter from Spier thanking us for what we had done. To the theater with Mother to see "Louisiana Purchase," which we found very entertaining. Jules went to the office, waited for us and took us home.

Thursday, February 26
Went out to see the baby again. Wheeled him down in his carriage for a while. Got along even better than yesterday. He is a bit afraid of Jules – apparently thinks he is the doctor. Finished my record today. The report is pretty bad but I am not going to undertake to rewrite it. Jules went back to the office to work after dinner. Claire stopped out for a

---
60　　Sister Clara and husband Lou.

while to visit with Mother and me. Jules got home while she was still here, and we all sat around gabbing for later than we should have – particularly Jules, who is working under great pressure.

Do Levy called to talk about the baby. She is quite excited and pleased about it.

Friday, February 27
Finished conferring with Gus and revising the report – after a fashion!

Did a few errands at noon, including a Hogate rattle for the baby. Went out to see him at about 6:00. Fed him part of his supper and played with him for a while, then put him in his crib, all with hardly a whimper.

Had a delicatessen supper at Bassin's. Then home. Mother got home shortly after we did, and had to be told all about the visit. She is very anxious to see him, of course, but I think he has enough strangers to worry about for the time being, and we should be bringing him home in a few days.

Saturday, February 28
To the Board on Curtiss-Wright. They are sustaining it.

Mother came downtown at noon. Jules took us to Olmsted's for luncheon. Then he went back to the office, and Mother and I went on a shopping spree, for the most part things for the baby. Wonder if he will ever use all of them. Buying them was a lot of fun.

Letter from Bobbie,[61] telling us among other things what time Nate's train would get in tomorrow. Mother went to Clara's after dinner. I curled up on the sofa with one of my baby books, and poor Jules did some more work. I shall certainly be glad when that brief is finally completed.

Sunday, March 1
Nate came in at about noon. We met him, took him to luncheon, for a ride, then out to see the baby. He was quite delighted with him. Made no examination since he seemed as obviously healthy and "at least normal." He played with us in very friendly fashion for quite a while.

Home to rest for a while. Then to the States Restaurant for a very good dinner. Nate left about 8:00 and we went home, Jules to work a bit and I to read. Supposed to go to Clara's since she was entertaining some of the relatives, but I just was not equal to it.

Telephoned Columbus. They were all pleased and very excited.

Monday, March 2
Spent most of the morning with Rogosa discussing preparations for the baby. Spent most of the afternoon buying some of the things she told me to get.

Did a little work in between on my review report.

Nate telephoned to give us some information about pediatricians. A really beautiful letter from Edward with a $100 check from Mother Schlezinger. The baby will now have a nice bank account. Wonder how I will do as a mother. Expect I am going to find it far harder work than being an attorney in the T.E. Division.[62] I am worn out just getting ready for the job.

---

61 Jules' brother Nate and wife Bobbie.

62 Trial Examiners' Division or Judges Division.

Tuesday, March 3
A miserable rainy day. I did not go down until about noon, when the rain stopped, and we took the baby for a little ride. He behaved surprisingly well. Lunched at Tally-Ho with Babs and Kami.[63] They are leaving tonight for St. Louis. Then to the office to do a little work and straighten up a few matters.
Some of the baby's things were delivered today, and are almost cute enough to eat. Letter from Bobbie, thrilled at Nate's glowing account of the baby, telling us a highchair was on the way. Sleeping very badly these days – nervousness I suppose, and I need a lot of rest, with the baby on a 5:30 schedule.

Wednesday, March 4
To the office late for about an hour to finish up. Said my goodbyes.[64]
Picked up the baby at 2:00. He surprised us all by coming without any fuss. His crib was delivered this morning and the new carpets laid, so we were ready for him. He behaved beautifully the entire time. Fussed a little at night, but finally went to sleep. Slept very soundly – at least he did not disturb us. Glad he is behaving so much better than everyone expected, but I am still a little frightened at the prospect of mothering a baby boy. Jules is so happy about it though, that alone makes it all worth it.

Thursday, March 5
Up much earlier than we are accustomed to. The baby behaved beautifully all day, except that he demands too much attention, and I hate to add to the ordeal of his change by just letting him fuss.
Mrs. Hathorn gave me a lovely warm snowsuit that Tucker had outgrown.
Bobbie and Nate[65] sent us the loveliest high chair I have ever seen, blonde wood and leather, and in one simple motion it breaks down into a low chair and table. Mother and the Rolands[66] came over in the evening. Although I was obviously so sleepy I could hardly hold my head up, they stayed quite late, hoping the baby would waken so Lou could seem him.

Friday, March 6
The baby slept a bit later today, for which I was grateful.
Mother and Clara came over early and we played with him so much that he fussed terribly when left alone in his crib for a nap. And I am trying to break him in to the "toidy seat," which he hates.
Rogosa called. I called Schwartz to ask him a few questions. Several friends and people from the office called. Mother Schlezinger called from Columbus – could not wait until Sunday to see how we were getting along. Long letter from Gertrude. Mother, Clara and I went to the store in the afternoon, and we all bought things for the baby. Took him for a long walk.
Jules and I went to bed early, and were asleep in about two shakes. He was thoroughly exhausted also.

---

63   Joe Kaminstein had been Anne's most frequent lunch partner and friend from 1934 to 1940. Their lunches began to be less frequent after she was married in 1939.
64   Anne took leave for a period from the NLRB as a part of the adoption agreement.
65   Jules' brother and his wife in Philadelphia.
66   Anne's sister Clara and her husband Lou.

1942

Friday, May 1
Dietz[67] came over about 11:00. Jules came home for luncheon so we could get both interviews over with. She is a pleasant, young, enthusiastic thing.
Long letter from Madelyn. They will move into their new home any day now.
Card from Lou from Dallas. Apparently enjoying his trip very much.
Mary Miller came over after dinner to stay with Ira while we went to the Buckingham movie. Saw a fairly good picture. Particularly enjoyed the air-cooling after a record breaking warm day. And enjoyed being out in the evening, even if only for a neighborhood movie and an ice cream cone.

Saturday, May 2
Ira was 14 months old today, and much cuter than he was 2 months ago. Took some snapshots of him, but only colored moving pictures could possibly do him justice.
Frank Bloom[68] called to ask if I wanted to come to a Board conference on New York Merchandise Monday. Glad they finally got around to calling me for something. I don't like the office to get along too well without my assistance on cases I review Wednesday.
Fleet Hathorn[69] spent the evening with us, his family being out of town. Since he could sleep late tomorrow, he stayed and stayed.

Sunday, May 3
A pleasant day, not quite so warm as yesterday. Mother Schlezinger telephoned. I have not been writing as frequently as I should.
Claire and her mother, and Gene Leverson[70] came over to visit, Gene very hot in his uniform, but also very handsome. We all lounged around in the back yard, drinking lemonade and playing with Ira.
Gene stayed for supper and for a little while afterwards, but left fairly early since he had to go back on the bus and since he has to get to work quite early. I had washed and wiped all the dishes, so was glad to flop on the sofa in "undress" with a book.

Monday, May 4
To the Supreme Court to see Jules sworn in as a member. Saw several old friends there, including Fahy, who moved Jules' admission.[71] Then lunched with Jules and George Wheeler at the Court cafeteria.
To the office after luncheon. Got a warm reception from everyone, including Denhan, who is no doubt very pleased to have me no longer there.
The Board conference took only a few minutes since everyone was in agreement.
Two cards from Mother, both written before she received my letter acknowledging receipt of the suit for Ira. She was afraid it had gone astray.
Ira was, as usual, delighted when I got home.

---

67 Only reference. Not identified.
68 Frank Bloom, the Chief Trial Examiner, the term used for judges.
69 Fleet Cooper Hathorn was from Augusta, GA. and a neighbor of Anne and Jules. He was known for his conservative views.
70 Anne's firend Claire Rosen. Gene Leverson has not been identified.
71 Charles Fahy, who had formerly been at the NLRB, was Solicitor General at this point. As S.G. he argued more than 70 cases before the Supreme Court.

Tuesday, May 5
Letter from Mother, relieved that we received the suit, thanking me for the check, and promising to get herself something pretty with it. She and Nettie are becoming friendly again, which is a very good thing.

A pleasant day so I kept Ira out even more than usual to make up for yesterday, since Odessa does not keep him out as long as I usually do. Did a good deal of walking and running after Ira, and was thoroughly tuckered out by evening.

The war news is very bad these days, as Japan conquers more and more territory. If only the Russians can keep up their splendid fight against the Germans, I believe everything will come out right in the end.

Wednesday, May 6
Ira received from the Pachels a beautiful set of military brushes and comb, all silver-backed and monogrammed. Since he had the set I bought for him, I shall put this one away for a while until he may be able to appreciate it more. He has certainly been fortunate in the number and the appropriateness of the gifts he has received.

Rogosa is long overdue for her visit. I certainly do not miss her, but hope she has not become ill. Don't know what would keep her away so long except illness. Jules is going to Columbus this weekend for the laying of his father's gravestone, and may go to California next month on official business. Looks like I am stuck at home though with Ira.

Thursday, May 7
Downtown in the afternoon. Bought three dresses and some things for Ira. Met Ruth Weyand,[72] relaxing between arguments, so invited her home for dinner. We went home with Jules. Fleet Hathorn also came for dinner.

After dinner Hathorn, Ruth and I went to register for ration books. Then back to the apartment. Sat around chatting, but almost every topic hit upon wound up in an argument, Hathorn being a southerner and Ruth a very outspoken liberal. A very pleasant cool evening so we took Ruth all the way home. A ride seems a luxury now, with all the talk of rationing gas. Joe Friedman[73] called – Edna had a son Tuesday night, a bit ahead of schedule, but all doing fine.

Friday, May 8
A bit cooler today, and it had a marked effect on Ira's appetite. Eating everything we gave him like his old self again. Jules got home a bit early to pack a few things. Finally, with much difficulty, got a reservation on the train. Could not get one on a plane although he had been trying for a week. Left about 7:45 to get the 8:30 train.

I got into pajamas, and made myself comfortable in bed with some magazines.[74] Hathorn

---

72   Ruth was a lunch companion with Anne and a litigation attorney at the NLRB. Anne was on leave at this point, and she was probably happy to visit with a colleague. Ruth was active in feminist causes (Hartmann 1998:227-229) and African American issues (Smith 1999:589-591) as well as workers' rights.

73   Friend of Anne and Jules, an NLRB lawyer, who later became Jules' law partner. Sometimes called Jo-Jo.

74   Anne was a frequent reader of the *New Yorker*, and entertainment at home in the evening included Anne and Jules reading aloud to each other from the magazine.

knocked at the door, but by the time I got a dressing gown on, he shouted that he was sorry he got me up and beat it, and I let him go, with a big sigh of relief, although it was still quite early.

Saturday, May 9
A pleasant day. Met Claire and her mother downtown in the afternoon, and we all shopped together. They came home with me and stayed for dinner. Claire called home around 8:00 and learned Duffy had come in unexpectedly about 6:45, so they beat it home. Duffy had gone out in the meantime, but they finally got together.
Heard Johnnie downstairs crying very hard. His folks were out, and the woman staying with him apparently could not quiet him, so I went down. I got him quiet quickly enough, but then he would not let me leave until his folks got home. That kept me up much later than I should have been up, but the Wuestefeldts seemed duly appreciative.

Sunday, May 10
Mrs. Wuestefeldt came up to thank me again, which seemed like much ado about nothing.
Received some lovely carnations from Jules, who had the card signed with Ira's name.
Jules telephoned. Will be back tomorrow morning. Marcia and Sid Hertzmark came over. Ira put on a great performance. Marcia just about ate him up. The poor thing wants a husband and children so badly herself. She brought Ira a very attractive toy animal. He is certainly the greatest one for receiving gifts in this family.
Put Ira to bed, had a lonely supper, then read until time to put myself to bed. This, my first Mother's Day.

Monday, May 11
Card from Mother, comparatively gay; a Mother's Day card from Gertrude and Al, and a long and very interesting letter from Henry Lehman, who is in the Signal Corps at Geiger Field, Spokane. Jules came home for breakfast and to freshen up before going to the office. Overnight trips on a Pullman wear him out, but he will have to get used to them. The war news seems a little brighter. Hope it is not just propaganda.
Claire called to ask if we would like to drive to Philadelphia with them for the weekend. We want to see the new baby, but it does not seem feasible to drive for the whole weekend with Ira. Would like to get away for a bit, though.

Tuesday, May 12
Letter from Sam, thanking us for the sweater, and exulting over his new son.
Letter from the Board that I was off the payroll, and could be paid for the day I worked or save it as annual leave when I returned. I chose the latter as it was much less trouble for the accounting division.
Took Ira to the playground. He had a great time on the swings. Fell off once, but got up and on again without a whimper. He is certainly a brave lad. Enjoyed visiting with some of the other mothers for a while, but soon got fed up with the conversation, which covers only pregnancies and babies. Wonder if I shall soon become confined to such subjects.

Wednesday, May 13
Long letter from Clara,[75] who seems to be getting quite fond of St. Louis. Card from Mother, suggesting we take her along on our vacation to help take care of Ira.
Mouritsen called for some information on Curtiss-Wright which I could give him only after consulting my notes, so went to the office for a while in the afternoon. Enjoyed getting back, if only, to break the monotony. Jules likes the three dresses I bought last week, so I think I shall keep all three of them, which gives me more clothes all at once than I have had in a long time. He still wants me to get some dress-up clothes, although there seems to me to be remarkably little need of them.

Thursday, May 14
Card from Mother. She is certainly becoming a faithful correspondent. Jules signed up today for a gasoline rationing card. What tremendous clerical jobs these registrations must entail. Finished putting on my slipcovers. Will finish our spring-cleaning sometime before summer, I hope.
Collecting our snapshots to put into albums. We have quite a collection of them even though we are not particularly camera enthusiasts. Stayed up ridiculously late listening to some of the comedy radio programs and reading. Jules was air-raid wardening.

Friday, May 15
Long letter form Madelyn, exulting in her beautiful new home. A warm pleasant day. One of the good things Ira does is keep me outdoors more than anything else could.
I am trying to break him from the bottle. He is not fussing about it at all, but is drinking far less milk. Hope I am not rushing him too much, taking advantage of his good disposition. But one of the words he says, and often, is "no," so he could make his protest vocal if he wished. The office is in a quandary as to how they can give me per diem for the Annapolis conference when I am off the payroll. I would just as soon skip it, and will certainly not go at my own expense.

Saturday, May 16
Letter from the Board notifying me officially that I was on leave of absence.
Stanley called. Roger Trayner was in town for the day only. Asked us over but it was pouring rain and we were busy with the baby. The Surreys[76] are in their new home and are encountering many problems, not the least of which is gas rationing.
Went to one of the neighborhood movies in the evening. The picture we saw was definitely second rate, but the ride over and back seemed something of a treat with the non-use of cars seeming so imminent. I drove for a while this afternoon, and despite the rain and Ira, did quite well.

Sunday, May 17
A rather cool day but had Ira out a good deal to make up for yesterday.

---

75   Lou Roland, sister Clara's husband, had accepted a job in St. Louis, and they moved there in March, 1942. Clara was pregnant at the time and had a miscarriage on the trip to St. Louis.

76   Stanley and Dorothy Surrey were frequent dinner companions.

It was pleasant not to have to sterilize bottles, but I wish Ira were drinking more milk. He does not fuss for his bottle, but neither does he drink his milk from his cup as he should. Jules now not only wants to help take care of Ira, but actually does much of the work, so today was comparatively easy for me. I reciprocated by fixing a steak and other things Jules likes for supper. Spent a lazy evening reading the *New Yorker* and the paper and listening to the news commentators until time for bed.

Monday, May 18
Letter from Mother. Price ceilings went into effect today. Our grocery bill as a result was considerably smaller than it would have been last week. Letter from Bobby enclosing snapshots of Lynn, who looks very sweet and lovely. Bobby is happy that the Army turned Nate[77] down, although he is keenly disappointed.
Ira was in a bad temper most of the day. He apparently realizes we have taken away his beloved bottle, and he greatly resents it. He is drinking some milk, but far too little for his own good and my peace of mind. Had an appointment last Saturday with Dr. Schwartz but he called it off because of the rain.

Tuesday, May 19
Received an announcement of the birth of Frederick Ethan Friedman, and a long letter from Carrie Fuller giving me the history of our co-workers at Amosheag,[78] most of whom seem to have done quite well.
Since this was one of Odessa's early days, I planned to go downtown to shop and for a change, but the weather looked threatening, and, far more important, Ira was getting over his fussing about the milk, and drinking very well out of a glass, and I did not want to break the charm.
Mildred Wainwright keeps calling to urge me to go to the staff conference in Annapolis, but it all seems a silly jaunt, and I do not believe I shall go.

Wednesday, May 20
Had the showers today that were threatening yesterday, but we got outdoors quite a bit anyhow. Ira is almost always delighted just to be outside. And he seems particularly happy these days, getting over his little bad spell.
The war news seems a bit better these days. I do hope it ends soon, and ends right. Walked to the corner after dinner, had ice cream cones, quite a spree. But it was a delightful evening and the walk was refreshing. Jules was very tired and went to bed a bit early. I was tired too, but not sleepy, so stayed up and played solitaire until I became sleepy.

Thursday, May 21
Card from Mother. Ira's bonds arrive today. Our hot water is being rationed to conserve fuel. That will be a nuisance, particularly with a youngster. But it appears to be necessary. Downtown at noon. Lunched with Jules at the Madrillon. Sent Madelyn and Edward a tray with an English hunting picture painted on it. Bought some things for Ira and for the house. Had arranged yesterday to have Mary Miller come in this evening so we could go out, but it was raining so hard and I was so

---

77   Jules' brother Nate.
78   This might refer to the history of the Amosheag Manufacturing Co. case from the late 1800's. Her use of "our co-workers" is interesting.

tired we called it off. She seemed just as well pleased. Spent the evening arranging snapshots in our and Ira's albums.

Friday, May 22
A card from the draft board instructing Jules to report for a physical examination. He had been placed in Class I without any notice. I was greatly perturbed but he was quite calm about it. He came home at noon, as much to soothe me as for any other reason.
A charming letter from Reba Pachel urging us to visit them. Rained most of the day but we got out a few times between showers. Called Rogosa, who will write the board that we applied for a baby well before the fateful December 7. I feel we should be treated as though I had become pregnant in September and had a baby in March. It only puts off the evil day, of course, but Ira and I both need him as long as we can keep him.

Saturday, May 23
A pleasant coolish day. Jules came home for luncheon. We took the 3:00 train. Ira behaved beautifully, far better than we had expected. He fussed hardly at all, and was practically no bother. Nate met us. Got to the apartment in time to bathe and feed Ira, and let him play a bit before going to bed. He made himself completely at home.
Lynn seemed a tiny thing since we're used to Ira, but she is sweet, and I think will look just like Bobby. She gave up her crib for Ira, and slept in her basket. Nate and Jules slept in another apartment so Bobby and I could be with the babies, an excellent arrangement, everything considered. Mother Schlezinger called.

Sunday, May 24
Another very pleasant day. The Pachels came over in the afternoon *en masse* although it was a long trip and they have only an A gas card. Ira found it all very exciting, especially Johnny.
We left on the 3:12 train. Ira again behaved admirably, and was the pet of everyone in our car. He seemed to enjoy the whole trip very much, but was evidently delighted to get home again to his own play pen and toys and crib and whatnot. I was rather glad to be home again myself as we had crowded Nate and Bobby's small apartment pretty badly.

Monday, May 25
To Rogosa's and Crowley's for letter to the draft board stating that we had sought to adopt a baby before December 7. Lunched with Jules at Olmsted's. Home on the bus about 4:00. Reunions with Ira when I have been out are always delightful.
Charming letter from Helen Lee, who is being very brave about her pending tonsillectomy. Mary Miller came over; we went to the National to see "Arsenic and Old Lace," which we both found very entertaining. If only everything were not clouded over by the threat of Jules being drafted soon. I can hardly bear to think of it.

Tuesday, May 26
Spent most of the day in the back yard with Ruth Wuestefeldt while Ira and Johnny more or less played together. Ira is fussing about drinking his milk. Afraid I have made too great an issue of it, and his objections are entirely psychological. It wound up by his going to bed supperless, but just as cheerful as ever.

Jules walked to the corner for something after dinner, but I was to tired even for that much exertion. Made myself comfortable on the sofa with a *New Yorker* for a while, and we both went to bed good and early.

Wednesday, May 27
Card from Mother, and letters from Clara, Bobby and John Fried. John wants to come down for the weekend. Expects to be drafted shortly unless his commission comes through in time.
Jules went to take his physical exam at 7:30. He was gone for hours, although the exam consisted only of taking a blood count, because there were so many ahead of him. He seems to feel there is a strong likelihood that he will be drafted – and soon. And it just isn't fair. We certainly did not adopt Ira to evade the draft, and he has two bona fide dependents as a result of the adoption.

Thursday, May 28
Letter from Madelyn, reveling in the new house she had and in the new baby she is soon to have. Broke my glasses while roughhousing with Ira. Should have known better than to be wearing them. Left them to be repaired when I took Ira to Dr. Schwartz. Did some more errands afterwards, and then stopped at Jules' office and came home with him. Ira behaved admirably despite unusually warm weather, much exertion, excitement and being fussed over. The doctor seemed well satisfied with Ira's progress, which was comforting in view of the change from the bottle, the hot-weather and what-not.

Friday, May 29
No word yet from the draft board. Jules had expected to be notified immediately that he was in I-A. Downtown in the afternoon to get my glasses. Would have taken Ira but it was too doggoned hot. Stopped in at the office for just a few minutes, then home with Jules.
Some years this would have been a lovely holiday weekend, but this year Memorial Day is just another working day for Jules. I do hope that next Memorial Day we are celebrating the end of this war.
Cleaning closets, throwing away mementoes of all sorts in tremendous quantity. No room for sentimentality in our apartment now that we have Ira.

Saturday, May 30
Jules got home with John Fried at about 2:00. We had luncheon, then went down in the back yard to lounge and play with Ira. Claire asked me to get her some cokes at Dubarry's for tonight, so we took them over and brought Ira to visit them.
Later we left Odessa with Ira and went to Claire's for buffet supper. She had about 20 other people, but it was all handled smoothly and expeditiously. Played games afterwards. Felt quite young and gay and giddy again. It was all fun. John enjoyed it too. Home much later than we had intended.

Sunday, May 31
An extremely warm day. What with Ira's breakfast, our brunch, and Ira's lunch, I had quite a busy morning. Jules took John down in time to get the 2:00 train. Only Jules uses tires and gas that way nowadays.

Later we went to the Surrey's. Their place is going to be lovely, but is still in quite a rough state. We stayed for supper, having brought some canned food for Ira. He had a grand time with the dog, the woods, and a whole house in which to roam.

Telephoned Columbus. Mother is excited about the possibility of our coming there on Jules' next trip west.

Year End Summary 1942

This has been a good year in that we acquired a son who has developed beyond our fondest expectations. He is bright, lovable, affectionate, good-looking, and has practically all the good traits any mother could wish for in her son. If he continues as he has been going, he will make us very proud of and happy with him.

He has brought so much sunshine into our lives that he helped us immeasurably to lean up against a brutally prejudiced draft board and its attempts to shanghai Jules into the army. He will also no doubt help us to bear it when Jules is called up, which is almost inevitable in the next few months.

On top of everything else, he has been interesting enough to make almost an entire year at home fly for me so swiftly that I can hardly believe it has passed. I, the determined careerist, who struggled so hard and sacrificed so much to achieve my status as an attorney, content to keep house and cook and tend a baby - how I have changed. It is largely because Ira is such a wonderful baby, but just as much because Jules has been such a kind, considerate, generous, loving husband. It still astonishes me at times that he chose me for his wife when I hear other girls commenting on how handsome he is and or what a splendid husband he makes.

The great regret of my life will always be my foolishness in putting him off for a year when he was begging me to marry him. It is certainly the most foolish thing I have ever done. I have paid dearly for that foolishness and will never finish paying for it.[79]

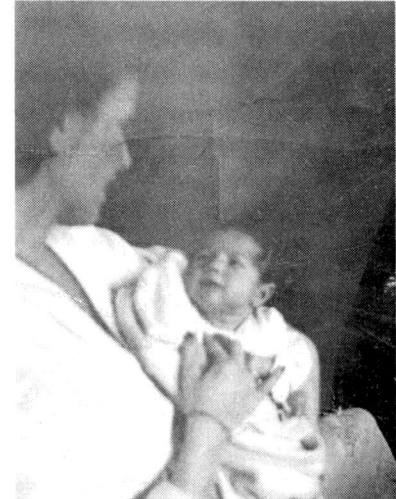

Anne with baby Ira

---

79 Her accusing herself of foolishness in not immediately accepting Jules' proposal of marriage is very different from the premarital Anne. Saying that she "will never finish paying for it" suggests a tragically deep sadness. What produced such a dramatic feeling on her part? It is unclear whether she is referring to the delay in the marriage as perhaps suggesting her lack of confidence in the marriage and Jules (for which she is sorry) or whether she had thoughts that an earlier marriage date might have meant that she could have given birth to a child.

1943

Anne had taken leave from the NLRB when she and Jules adopted their son, Ira, in March 1942, and she stayed home taking care of him until May 1, 1943. At that point she was re-instated and went back to work, but she had trouble finding a maid who would also take care of Ira. By May 10 she wrote this in her diary, "If I do not get a satisfactory maid soon, afraid I shall have to give up the idea of working for a while. Jules is betting that I will give it up." She did find a maid, but having someone who would be there consistently was a problem for years. Jules was classified as 3-A by the draft board because of vision problems. He tried to join the Air Corps but failed the physical. In the meantime many of their friends were being drafted. All year Anne worried that Jules would be drafted, and by year's end he was entering the Army. -- RDH

Friday, January 15

A fairly warm day, so Ira got out morning and afternoon, much to his delight. Ira is badly in need of rubber pants, but the local shop could let me have only one pair. Even babies' things are getting scarce.

Jules took the car to work in order to keep the battery alive and to bring the Reins[80] home to dinner. Beulah fixed quite a good roast chicken, and the dinner generally went very well. Sat around drinking and talking until a very late hour, surprisingly so since the Reins had to go home by bus. But enjoyed seeing them again.

---

80   David Rein, a colleague from the NLRB, and his wife. He was a frequent lunch companion.

Saturday, January 16

A very warm pleasant day. Too bad Jules could not have the afternoon outdoors with Ira. Ira and I spent most of the afternoon with Irene and Marilyn at one of the playgrounds. Rather to my surprise, Ira remembered all about playgrounds, and had a wonderful time on the various contraptions.

Walked to the corner after dinner to get some books, and missed a call from Mother Schlezinger. Called her back. She had merely become lonesome. Mrs. Braverman called. She and Marvin have both been quite ill. I must try to call on her.

Sunday, January 17

A very warm day. Jules and Ira went to the corner in the morning, and we all went out in the afternoon.

The Russian counter-offensive continues to meet with astonishing successes. It is most gratifying. It seems to me Germany cannot last much longer. But it is little enough I know about it. Jules gave Ira his bath, and both of them had a delightful time. Too bad they cannot have a little more time together, but I am grateful for each Sunday that Jules can spend with us. Who knows how many more of them they will be together?

Monday, January 18

Letter from mother. Poor Jean lost her baby. This family certainly has bad luck in recreating itself.[81] Letter from John Fried, who may be here this weekend.

---

81   Anne could not have children, and her sister Clara had a miscarriage a few months earlier.

Ed telephoned from Philadelphia. Has been attending a convention in New York. Stopping here tomorrow.

Went to see Dr. Cox in the morning although it was raining very hard. He dismissed me as cured but recommended I continue my home treatments for a few days more. That was most encouraging.

Finished Elliot Paul's *The Governor of Massachusetts*, which I found only slightly interesting.

Tuesday, January 19
Card from mother. Card from Kami,[82] who is stationed in Aberdeen, Md. Ed got in, in the afternoon. Jules left the office early and came home with Ed. Jules had a grand time playing with Ira, and Ed had a grand time talking about Ed.

Beulah fixed a very good dinner. She can usually be counted on to do all right if we stick to chicken for company dinners. Stayed up quite late, Jules and Ed having their inevitable argument over almost any subject raised.

Ed brought us a delightful picture of Howard. We should have some photos taken of Ira - best of all, some moving pictures.

Wednesday, January 20
Very cold. Jules planned to take the car to work, and we were all to go along but he could not start the car.

Jeannette Goor stopped in with Ronnie,[83] and a few minutes later Irene with Marilyn. The three youngsters had a grand time. Ira was a splendid host, gave crackers to each mother before taking one for himself, while the other two kids just gobbled - and all of his own accord.

Ed was having difficulty getting a train out, but at Jules' suggestion and much to Ed's surprise, got a reservation on the noon plane. The Russians have lifted the siege on Leningrad.

Thursday, January 21
Had planned to step out tonight with the Silvians. They could not go because his father was coming in, but we decided to go anyhow. I went downtown in the afternoon to do some errands. Got a wonderful ABC picture book for Ira, among other things. Stopped by for Jules at his office. Went to the movies first, and then to O'Donnell's for dinner. Had planked steak, but it was not so good as the last one we had there. The place was very crowded and the service as a result very unsatisfactory. I realize it cannot be helped, but it nevertheless tends to spoil a meal. Home not too late.

Friday, January 22
Letter from Clara, who seems to be getting along very well. I hope everything goes well with her. I should like to see at least one little Freeling born into this world.[84] Card from mother, who is just living for her next visit here and to St. Louis.[85] Took Ira downtown in

---

82   Joe Kaminstein, her friend and most frequent lunch partner during the 1930's.

83   The Goor family, their neighbors in Buckingham Apartments and their best friends for many years. Jeanette was Anne closest friend in this stage of her life.

The husband, Charlie Goor, worked at the Pentagon.

84   Her sister, Clara, was pregnant again at this point,

85   St. Louis, where Clara lives.

the afternoon and got him some new shoes. Ordered some galoshes for him but I shall be lucky if I get them. Bought some really warm bedroom slippers for myself. Then to Jules' office since he had the car downtown. Ira took the entire staff by storm.

Beulah fixed a real Friday night dinner - and a very good one.

Saturday, January 23
No mail at all, which suits me well.
Told Beulah not to come in today at all since she is coming in tomorrow. But dinner was no problem since we had chicken soup and chicken left over. Just as well since it was a pleasant afternoon, and Ira and I stayed out quite late. Too bad Jules could not be with us.
Ira not only picks up and puts away his things, helps to dust and make the bed, but has also begun to help with the dishes, wiping the silverware more or less dry and putting it in the drawer. He is getting to be a real help.

Sunday, January 24
Another pleasant day, and we all spent much of it outdoors. Beulah stayed out with Ira after we left for the Rein party. Enjoyed the party very much. Saw a number of old friends and a few new ones. Ate and drank so much neither of us wanted any dinner, so let Beulah go when we got home. Ira was still awake, so we had a chance to kiss him good night. Finished reading Smith's *Last Train from Berlin*,[86] Seemed like an honest factual account of what occurred in Germany before and during the war. Smith seems to have some good ideas.

Monday, January 25
Letter from Madalyn, who finds time to write even though she has no maid, a big house and a small baby. Letter from Wells that the appeal on my efficiency rating had been turned down. No reasons were given and I had never been given the hearing to which I am entitled.
A very warm day, and we spent much of it outdoors. Ira enjoyed it very much, except that he missed the other children, none of whom was out when he was.
Finished Ellery Queen's *Calamity Town*, a very interesting mystery story. Jules had guessed at the solution but I did not until too close to the end to count.

Tuesday, January 26
Called Bloom[87] to gripe about the appeal committee's decision and, with his encouragement, protested it and am to get a hearing.[88] Rained all day. Took Ira to the Goor's in the afternoon. He and Ronnie played together very amicably.
Beulah was to stay while we went to a movie,

---

86   Howard K. Smith's memoirs of his experience as a reporter in Berlin during Hitler's rise to power and for the first years of World War II. After he was allowed to leave Berlin in December, 1941 he wrote about things that censors had forbidden, such as the psychological manipulation of the German people by Hitler and the group around him and brutal physical treatment. He told of people forced to join the war effort, obligatory Nazi Youth groups, and other organizations. This was a clear denunciation of Nazi Germany.

87   Frank Bloom, Chief Trial Examiner.
88   Although Anne was not actively working with the NLRB, she maintained her connections there, maintained her status, and visited the office.

but got an urgent phone call and had to go home. Jules went to the corner for a walk, and came home with ice cream and chocolates, which helped to pass the evening.

The Roosevelt-Churchill meeting in Casablanca was thrilling, but the announcement of the results did not justify the build-up it got.

Wednesday, January 27
Beulah's apartment had been broken into, but the boys were caught and everything recovered.

Jeannette and Ronnie came over to spend the morning, since it was snowing, and stayed for lunch. Finished Silone's *Fontamara*, a very moving tale of the horrible effects of Fascism in Italy from its very beginning.

Had Fine's deliver some groceries, including a splendid looking roast, but when Beulah got through with it, it was rather tough. Think I shall handle the roasts in the future, not having produced a tough one yet. Beulah is probably not yet sufficiently familiar with an electric stove.

Thursday, January 28
A terrible day of sleet, snow and ice. Jules was late, so took the car, and regretted it very much, especially on the way home, which took hours and a precious lot of gas. Beulah could not get in at all, but telephoned to say she had tried.

Jeannette called and asked Ira and me to come over, but I was sensible and stayed in to mollycoddle my cold. Could not go to bed for keeping an eye on Ira.

Fixed dinner of a sort.

Jules walked to the corner later for some groceries we needed and got a book for me. I stayed up, foolishly, instead of staying in bed.

Friday, January 29
Card from mother.

Stayed in bed most of the day with a steaming kettle beside the bed. Beulah managed to get in, although late. Jules also had a pretty bad time with transportation, and got home quite late for dinner. Had promised to dine with the Silvians, but canceled it because of my condition.

Feel badly about not being able to get downtown to buy Jules a birthday present, but maybe I can get one yet. At least I took a subscription to the morning *Post*, which he has been wanting, but that is hardly a birthday present.

Saturday, January 30
Transportation was so bad that many people were dismissed early, including Jules. He stopped to pick up some galoshes for Ira and a box of candy, and still managed to get home a little earlier than usual.

Dressed first thing in the morning, determined not to lie a-bed any more, but could not go out because it snowed some more, nd my cold seemed to get worse from my sitting around in the apartment.

Finished a lending library book Jules got for me, a silly sort of English mystery called, I think, *Death in a Small Town*.[89]

[89] Anne read 4 books during this week. 3 novels and Smith's description of Nazi Germany. She was always an avid reader, but during this time when she was staying home with Ira, she read extensively.

1943

Sunday, January 31
Jules got up with a cold - now that mine is getting better. Nevertheless we all went out to play in the snow and had a grand time. Had to be wary of the enormous quantities of snow falling off the roofs. The sidewalks had not been cleared at all, making it almost impossible for Ira to walk, but he managed to scoot around pretty well.

After supper we got into bed with books, papers, candy, Kleenex, the radio, a bottle of rye and two glasses, a steaming kettle, and a few other things handy. It was very lazy and luxurious and pleasant.

Wednesday, December 1, 1943
Have not heard from Mother for quite a while. Her letters are never pleasant, but I don't like not hearing from her at all for so long.

Lunched with Jules today at the 400 Club, and did some errands. Shopping is pretty discouraging this Xmas.

Working full time these days, what with the long luncheon hours, and work-a-plenty to be done. Stayed downtown his evening. Saw a charming English movie, "Jeannie," and then to Harvey's, where we had a very good dinner even though it was meatless day. Altogether a delightful evening.

Thursday, December 2
A pleasant very warm day. Esther brought Ira downtown. I was not able to get him any shoes or a haircut, both of which he needs badly, but we all had a wonderful time in Woody's Toy Department. Had dinner in the Tea Room. Ira ate about $1.50 worth of food, every crumb and drop of it. I was mighty pleased with him. Bought a cuddly doll for Lynn and a box of various preserves for Bobby. When we got home it was high time to put Ira to bed, and by the time I had bathed and looked at the paper, it was my bed-time as well.

Friday, December 3
A pleasant warmish day. Aaron Warner stopped in at the office, looking very well and seeming very happy.

A letter from Mother, full of anguish and despair. A letter from Claire about her wonderful son. Duffy[90] expects to be inducted shortly.

We had a number of meat points that were to expire tomorrow, so Esther "went to town," and we had a truly delicious steak and all the trimmings.

Should have done our packing, as little of it as there was, tonight, but became engrossed in a detective story, and finished it too late to do anything but go to bed.

Saturday, December 4
A very pleasant day. We made the 9:55 train with no undue rushing. The chair cars were surprisingly uncrowded, and so was the diner, where we had brunch.

Arrived at the apartment to find only Lynn and the maid there. Bobby and Nate[91] got their signals mixed but we finally all got together. Had a dull but useful afternoon. The Pachels came over in the evening, and

---

90   Duffy Edes, husband of Claire, Anne's close friend.

91   Jules' brother Nate and his wife Bobbie in Philadelphia. The Pachels were long time friends.

several other people. Reba was the life of the party with her tales of her three sons. Everyone stayed very late, and then Bobbie and I did the dishes.

Sunday, December 5
Could have slept all morning, but not with the two kids around. Left about 3:30. Nate and Lynn took us to the station. Ira had not taken a nap, and proceeded to fall asleep in the diner, so we cancelled our orders and returned to our seats. Ira spent the rest of the trip napping or howling. By the time we arrived, however, he was rested and wide awake, so we stopped at the Dodge Hotel for dinner – hit another meatless menu – and then went home. A fairly enjoyable weekend but probably not worth a precious day's annual leave when mine are so scarce.

Monday, December 6
Ira seemed happy to be at home again, but was sad to see both of us leave.
Lunched with Rosalie Seveig. Like all the other single girls in town, she gets pretty lonesome for male company, for which I know no cure. Had a lot of work, but managed anyhow to leave at my regular early hour. Ira had gone on a rampage in the kitchen, and ruined several things, some of them rationed. I made him stay in his room for awhile, which was very severe punishment for him. After he had gone to bed, I read for a while, worked for a while, and went to bed fairly early.

Tuesday, December 7
Two years ago today I was in Philly. How different things were then.

To the beauty parlor at noon. Home early again.
Phil called. Had tried to get us over the weekend. The Winklers were in town en route to Florida and wanted to see us. Phil urged that we have Mother come here to live with Baba.[92]
Received two beautiful wine decanters from the Silvians. Garfinckel's forgot the "Do not open before Xmas" stickers.
Took Ira to the barber for a haircut. Got him some gloves and a new suit.
Worked, read, listened to the radio, and went to bed.

Wednesday, December 8
Downtown at noon. Sent Mother S. a wool shoulderette, and Ira a "bouncee-babe." Hope that will keep Ira occupied and out of mischief. Today he broke Esther's glasses, on which she is very dependent.
It is something everyday, more or less serious. Tried to get him some other toys as well but it is almost impossible to find anything worth buying.
Esther has apparently been reading to Ira a great deal because he can now recite several nursery rhymes from memory, which we think quite a good stunt.

Thursday, December 9
Note from Helen Lee thanking us for the pen and stationery. Got my pen back today. Will see if I can keep it out of Ira's reach for awhile. Have not heard from either Mother or Clara for some time now, and don't like it. Came home from the office, and then I drove to the

---

92   Anne's cousin Phil and her grandmother Baba.

Hot Shoppe for dinner. Tried to get Ira some new shoes but was not successful.

Got some work done to make up for having left early. Ira had contacted quite a bad cough, as a result of which all three of us spent a bad night. The flu epidemic has me worried.

Friday, December 10
Ira's cough seemed much better, but it was a damp day so we kept him indoors. His "bouncee-baby" was delivered, which solaced him a great deal for being kept indoors. But he by no means confines himself to bouncing up and down on it. He bounces with such momentum that he causes it to slide, and thereby travel all over the house on it.

The farmer had no chickens today, which complicated matters, but we managed out of what few stores we still maintain. They are quite adequate, as a matter of fact.

Saturday, December 11
Kept Ira in again today just to be on the safe side. Stopped at Fine's on the way home and picked up a fairly good supply of food stuff. Went to Safeway after dinner to get a few more things we needed over the weekend – if I can still call Sunday a weekend.

Ira is being even naughtier than usual, but of course allowances have to be made when he is kept indoors for a few days. Esther apparently reads to him a good deal but I doubt whether she plays much with him. I doubt in fact that she knows how.

Sunday, December 12
A delightful sunny mild day. We celebrated it by taking Ira out morning and afternoon, and he loved it. He behaved beautifully and was in excellent spirits all day, as a result of which we all had a lovely Sunday. Mrs. Braverman called. Marvin is a Navy Lieutenant stationed here. Called Ann Reiter. Fred is in Italy.

We found ourselves with three Sunday papers today, so part of the day and much of the evening were spent in wading though them.

Monday, December 13
Quite a cold day, but Ira seemed entirely rid of his cold so Esther took him outdoors.

Terribly busy at the offices, and still the assignments continue to come.

No word yet from Mother or Clara although I have written each of them several times. Wonder what's up.

A gift for Ira from the Wagshals[93] which we did not open.

Worked late at the office and worked at home, but still did not make a dent in it. Just carrying too great a load and the OPA clearance system slows everything down.

Tuesday, December 14
My secretary, along with about half the staff, out sick. Quite a nuisance. Had to call off one conference because all the appropriate Rationing people were out sick.

Ira had already received two gifts from Columbus, and I have not sent anything yet.

---

93 Anne's cousin Sam Wagshal.

Don't know what to do about it. Have not even been able yet to get anything for Jules – let alone for 8 nieces and nephews – and with 2 more on the way!

Wednesday, December 15
At long last – mail from Mother and Clara. Lou has not been inducted yet – is awaiting another physical. Mother is unhappy, bitterly lonely, but says nothing about living with Baba. I expected she would not care for the idea much, but it has many advantages.
Very cold. Esther and Ira went to the store nevertheless, and seemed none the worse for it. Esther's clothes seem so pitifully inadequate – my old spring coat – that I do not see how she stands it, although she seems to mind the cold less than I do.
Stayed up quite late finishing a mystery story.

Thursday, December 16
Another cold and windy day. Esther and Ira stayed in, which was probably just as well.
Some of the sick folks are beginning to drag back to the office, which is a good sign. Was particularly glad to see Mrs. Fisher back. Her substitute was even a worse steno that Mrs. Fisher.
Finally managed to get Ira some shoes in Clarendon, cheap ones that I did not like, but the only thing in his size I have been able to locate anywhere. Did a few more errands, and then home, very happy to have some new shoes for Ira.

Friday, December 17
Another very cold day. The flu epidemic is about over. We were lucky indeed to escape unscathed. I was particularly concerned about Ira since he seems so susceptible to colds.
Long letter from Lucille, very happy in her new home.
Jules' transfer, and his being prepared to go overseas, are apparently being rushed frantically.
Stayed downtown for dinner at the Madrillon with the Reins. Will probably not see Dave again until after the war. They went home after dinner, and we went to the movies. All in all, a very satisfactory evening.

Saturday, December 18
A lovely mild day. Downtown at noon. Got leather writing portfolio for Jules.
Extremely busy at the office. Home to find the draft board had sent Jules another IA card, which was just about the limit. Apparently they are still not reconciled to relinquishing him. He is going to volunteer for induction Monday morning.
Spent the evening working and reading. We were both pretty tired after our evening of dissipation, comparatively speaking, so went to bed at a reasonable hour even though it was a Saturday night.

Sunday, December 19
Another lovely mild day. Telephoned Columbus. Mother had a cold, but otherwise everyone and everything was fine.
In the afternoon we drove over to visit the Bergs. Ira and Susan had a lovely time playing together. Wish we knew some children as nice as Susan in our neighborhood.
Xmas card from the Bob Buckleys.

Had supper of a sort at home. Ira had had a full day and seemed glad to get to bed. He behaves so well when we are at home as compared with what goes on in our absence that I am convinced he is not altogether to blame.

Monday, December 20
Jules volunteered for immediate induction, but cannot be inducted before January 5. Seems a study of his x-rays indicated he may be suitable for military service.
Meanwhile the board notified FEA he cannot leave the country. He is pretty unhappy about it all, I am afraid.
Two cards from Mother, both utterly miserable, and completely at sea as to any remedy. She is not reconciled to living with Baba for several reasons, including giving up her few paltry possessions. Also I expect she is waiting and hoping for me to break down and ask her to live with me, but I just cannot see it.

Tuesday, December 21
Lunched at Olmsted's with Jules and Westley. Had cocktails and an excellent luncheon.
What with being kept indoors more than he likes, and what with one thing or another, Ira is just almost impossibly naughty these days. He had destroyed a great many things, and has Esther just about at her wit's end.
A book of 25 war stamps for Ira from Lucille. I am feeling like such a crumb for not having sent the kids Xmas presents – although I dislike the whole business very much – that I shall have to make up my mind to conform. What a nuisance!

Wednesday, December 22
Jules and I went downtown at noon and sent stuff to all the kids. Glad that is over with. Chanukah check from Mother S. for $30.
V- Mail[94] Xmas card from John Freed.
Ira has now learned to recite a number of nursery rhymes quite well. We are quite pleased with him on that score. If only he were not so mischievous and destructive.
Would have liked to go to a movie tonight but could not get anyone to stay with Ira. Too many Xmas parties I guess.

Thursday, December 23
Jules and I both left a little early today.
Esther wants to go home for a few days, but instead of going while we are at home, plans to go on Monday because of the transportation problem. It is a nuisance but there is not much I can do.
Did a lot of marketing since the stores will be closed on Saturday. Then to the Hot Shoppe for dinner. Ira had had no nap, but surprised us by behaving perfectly.
One of the men at the office, Joe Stein, gave me a little individual bottle of rye for a Xmas present, so I'll have one gift besides Jules!

Friday, December 24
Ira prepared for Santa Claus by breaking my glasses, mussing all Jules' ties and breaking the tie rack, and a few other misdeeds.
Jules and I home about 3:30 after our respective office parties. First thing we had to do was discipline Ira. When that was out of the

---

94   "Victory Mail" was the system used in World War II to expedite one page letters to and from people in the military overseas.

way, we all went outdoors for a little while. Esther seemed pleased with her gifts. She wanted to be off until Thursday but I told her I preferred she get back by Wednesday. It remains to be seen whether or not she will comply with my request.

Saturday, December 25
Ira had a delightful time unwrapping and playing with his new toys. They were all very good choices, and should be of interest to him for some time.
Drove to the Lincoln Memorial Reflecting Pool to watch the ice skaters, despite a slight drizzle. Then to Fine's for a lot of good things to eat. Home to fix a very enjoyable supper.
Jules gave me a lovely white nightgown and flowers. Had gone all the way to Pasternab's to get it. He seemed pleased with his writing portfolio. It was altogether a very pleasant Christmas Day.

Sunday, December 26
Two-and-a half days really seems like a long vacation these days.
Poured all day, which was too bad, since it meant keeping Ira indoors. Jules went out a couple of times despite the rain, and despite Ira's protests at not being allowed to join him. Nevertheless we all had a pleasantly lazy day playing with Ira's toys, eating, napping, listening to the radio, reading etc.
The war news is quite good. Jules is being inducted again tomorrow, so the war may be really going to hit home now. The President had ordered essential government workers deferred, but Jules had volunteered nevertheless.

Monday, December 27
Marilyn Schultz came to stay with Ira. I spent most of the morning at Justice in conference with Andrews et al. Had a terrific schedule for the afternoon, but had to come home to let Marilyn go.
Jules telephoned to tell me he was in the Army. He would have to volunteer!
It could have been put off a few weeks at least, and maybe indefinitely under the President's new order. He had gone to Richmond on the train, at his own expense, instead of on the special bus.
The trains were running very late, so it was quite late when he got home. He seemed glad it was over with, although rather surprised since Nate[95] told him on the phone last night there was no chance he would be inducted.

Tuesday, December 28
Jules stayed home with Ira and I went to the office. Had a very hectic day, and was hardly able to break away by 5:30.
Jules telephoned Nate but Bobby said he was still at the office. He telephoned back a few minutes later. Was very surprised to hear Jules had been accepted. We later telephoned Mother Schlezinger, who was not happy about the news, but took it pretty well.
Ira behaved so much better, and is obviously so much happier, when Jules or I or both of us are at home than when he is left with Esther that it bothers my conscience terribly. Toy for Ira from Clara.

Wednesday, December 29
Left Ira with Jeanette Goor for the morning.

---

95 Jules' brother Nate in Philadelphia.

Jules came home at noon and spent the afternoon with Ira.

I had another hectic day and was again late in getting home. We went to the Hot Shoppe for dinner.

Esther telephoned in the afternoon – will be back on the job tomorrow morning. It is about time.

Edward telephones from Columbus to get things straight. Mother apparently got things pretty confused. Edward was rather chagrined about it all. He had enjoyed the prestige of having a brother going to Chungking to do intelligence work, and will now have to eat his words.

Thursday, December 30
Letter from Clara. Lou is to be inducted January 5. Meanwhile they are happy to be together for a while.
Lunched with Jules at Olmsted's. FEA wanted to request him from the reception center, but found it had no authority to do so, which was a great disappointment to Jules and consequently to me. Esther was back at work this morning. We had a long talk about Ira's behavior, which was so much better in her absence. Hope she got some ideas out of it as to how to best handle Ira. Of course his new toys are a big help in keeping him contented.

Friday, December 31
Letter from Mother, full of misery.
Lunched at the Willard Coffee Shop with Marie Berger, very enthusiastic about her work with United Nations Relief. Bought her a cocktail to celebrate the New Year.
Nate telephones in the evening. Another daughter, Jo Ann, was born this morning, very small, but both mother and child doing fine.
And here almost a whole week of Jules' furlough gone. The time seems so short. Spent a quiet New Year's Eve by ourselves, without even a drink – in fact we did not even stay up to see the New Year in.

Year End Summary 1943

Seems that most of the year was occupied with waiting for Jules' induction notice. The year ended – appropriately I suppose – with Jules on the verge of leaving to become a soldier. I have grown accustomed to the idea in all the time it had been pending, but am still far from happy about his departure.

Although I returned to work principally because of the probability of Jules' leaving for the Army, now that he is in the Army I am filled with doubts as to whether I should continue too work or stay at home with Ira. It has been bad enough to leave Ira as much as I have, but to continue leaving him so much when his Daddy has left him for an indefinite period seems a much tougher break than he deserves.

Also I seem to find less and less gratification in my work. I much preferred Aaron to Bryon as my boss. And I dislike my present co-worker, Reg Watt, for no particular reason except that he is just generally not my type.

There is, of course, some satisfaction to being a professional career woman at a fairly substantial salary, but the satisfaction is much diminished by the amount of thought I have to devote to maids, marketing, housework, and first and foremost, Ira's care and welfare.

Mother, too, has been very much on my mind, although I don't believe my working or not would have any effect on that problem. I have been sending her substantial amounts of money, but of course that is not the remedy for her ailment, although it is something she desperately needs since Father had long since ceased to send her any money despite the court order. I don't suppose now that he ever will. Sometimes I wonder if I shall ever see him again. The whole thing is such a horrid mess. And it is not altogether the fault of either one. They were just too wholly unsuited ever to have been able to get along together. There should be some way to prevent people like that from bringing children into the world. When I think of the anguish they have caused me, it does seem grossly unfair.

So many things in my life seemed grossly unfair, until Jules came along, and made up for all the rest. And now he must leave me – for months and maybe for years.

I should, of course, miss Jules very much under any circumstances, but I shall miss him more than ever now that we have so few close friends left in town. And the few we have we seldom see, what with gasoline rationing, our respective small children, the difficulty of finding sitters, the complications of trying to entertain with Esther running the house, etc., etc. If I had any kind of a home to go to, I would think I would pack up and go home with Ira, for a while at least. But I have no such haven. I don't believe I would be comfortable living in Columbus with the various Schlezingers, and [not comfortable] on the various Schlezingers. So it appears that I must of necessity stay put. To work or not to work, though, is the question that is seriously disturbing me and which only I can decide. Jules' family would send me some money, so, with our savings, we could get along all right. But much as I love Ira, to spend all my time with him, without even the excitement of having Jules come home in the evening, would I am afraid, not make me happy. And if I am not happy it would certainly reflect on Ira. But that is no argument; because he would unquestionably be better off with me than with Esther under any circumstances. I just do not know what to do.

One thing for which I am very grateful in all this mess is that we have all so far maintained good health despite some pretty bad epidemics. To have one of us, particularly Ira, become ill would be just about the last straw. I suppose some of the credit for his continued good health must be due to Esther, and I appreciate that.

Well, I cannot say that I am sorry to see 1943 come to an end. I am trying very staunchly to hope for and expect better thing from 1944. If only the war would end, all these other problems would settle themselves.

1944

This year saw Jules inducted into the Army and leaving for basic training. They sold the car, which they had decided Anne would not need. As Jules left, Anne quit her job to spend more time with Ira because she felt that her daily absence combined with the long term absence of Jules would not be good for the child. The Schlezinger family helped her with expenses while Jules was away in the Army.

This was a long, slow year for Anne. Jules was in training, and there was uncertainty if he would be shipped to Europe or the Pacific Theater. She visited him whenever possible, once on a long trip to California. These visits became so important to her to maintain contact with Jules.   -- RDH

Ira and Jules

Saturday, January 1
A regular working day as far as we were concerned. Our holidays began and ended with Christmas for the "duration."
Jules and I did manage to come home a little bit early, after all we shall have so little time together. And I do make up for it by working at home.
Jules broke a lamp while romping with Ira. Between the two of them they have managed to put most of our lamps out of commission. Shall try to have some of them repaired before trying to buy new ones.
Went to a movie after supper, and enjoyed it very much. Disappointed to learn, when we came home, that Carl Auerback had called, apparently with some information Jules wanted about OSS. Too late to call back when we got home so will have to try tomorrow.

Sunday, January 2
Unable to get Carl, who had apparently gone off for the day. Jules was quite disappointed. Other than that we had a rather pleasant lazy sort of day.
Ira and I drove to the airport with Jules, who took the 4:45 plane to Columbus. Ira and I came home in a luxurious airport limousine. But it was darned lonesome without Jules already.
After I got Ira settled in bed, and a few things straightened out, I went to bed myself with a book, and a very poor light, but somehow it seemed less lonesome.
And then Jules was always so good about taking care of the windows and two radiators at night and on these cold mornings.

Monday, January 3

Poured all day. Someone called about 9:00 to tell me Esther was waiting for the rain to slack because she had a cold. She finally arrived at almost 10:00. She sounded husky, but seemed all right other than that. Of course she had no umbrella or galoshes, despite her cold and the torrents of rain.

Spent the afternoon visiting banks re-ration banking with Duncan of the district office. Found it rather interesting.

Obtained from Carl the information he had and wired it to Jules. Jules telephoned me to discuss it a little more fully and to tell me what further to do.

Letter from Madalyn, note from Nate giving us Pachel's address in the Navy (how can I complain in view of that!), and notice that our last stock had been sold.

Tuesday, January 4

Esther got in very late again this morning. This will have to be halted.

In conference all day with representatives from some of the field offices on ration banking problems. Made me pretty late in getting home.

Letter from Clara. Lou is being inducted tomorrow. She sounds quite brave and philosophical about it all.

Called Jules to report, but he had gone out for a walk. He called back a little later. Ira was not yet in bed so he had a chance to talk to his daddy. Bob Matthew's wife called to ask us to dinner Saturday. Worked for a little while, and then relaxed with a magazine until time for bed. Still raining.

Wednesday, January 5

Long letter from Helen Lee. Esther arrived on time for a charge. Wire from Jules that his flight was cancelled, so he will arrive by train tomorrow morning. In the course of all this nasty rainy weather I have picked up a pretty bad head cold. Esther also has a cold, but, thank heavens, Ira has not caught it from either of us.

Seemed particularly lonesome without Jules tonight because I had been expecting him back. But I shall have to become accustomed to missing him.

Ira is being particularly sweet and affectionate toward me these days, almost as though he is trying to comfort me for Jules' absence. He apparently misses Jules keenly also, and asks for him continually.

Thursday, January 6

Jules got home just as I was leaving. He went to the office later. We lunched together at Schneiders with Westley and Lou Wierner. It looks like OSS is off. Jules is certainly not getting a decent break from anyone these days. He deserves so much better of fate.

To the Hot Shoppe for dinner. Did some marketing on the way home. Pretty well out of everything since Esther has not done any marketing at all this week.

Letter from Mother, seeming to reach the ultimate in the depths of despair.

Did quite a bit of work in the evening. Sold our play pen and pad for three dollars. Must replace it with a toy chest. Afraid my eyes are going on the blink again.

1944

Friday, January 7
Byron is quite unenthusiastic about my taking next week off, but cannot very well object. He could be a little more gracious about it however. Jules stayed downtown after work to have a cocktail with Mrs. Coleman. I dashed around and managed to get a scrumptious steak and all the trimmings. Jules had too many drinks, however, got home quite late, and pretty well ruined an otherwise wonderful dinner. I was plenty angry.
Lou telephoned from New York to inquire about AMG, etc., as he has also been inducted into the Army.
Letter from Lou about the same matter. Letter from Al Levin reminding me about the invitation to make my home with them should I find things too difficult without Jules.

Saturday, January 8
Aaron Warner visiting at the office. Looked very well, but did not seem so thrilled with it all as he had at first.
Very busy at the office, but managed to get everything pressing pretty well cleaned up. This was Jules' last day at the office, so he had a number of things to finish up before he left. It seemed good today to drive to work and home since it is probably the last time for a long while.
To the Bob Matthews' for a delicious dinner and very pleasant evening. They both seem to be grand people. He apparently thinks very highly of Jules. Too bad he did not have more influence on his friend Maggs.

Sunday, January 9
Quite cold. I was completely lazy and stayed in all day, to Jules' great disgust. He advertised the car for sale in today's *Star*. We got surprisingly few calls, and no one interested enough to come to see the car.
Helen Griendstein stopped out to visit during the afternoon. She seems a lonely unhappy little soul.
Ira at least is very happy, particularly at the idea that both his mommy and daddy are going to be home with him for a whole week. I can see already what a bad time I shall have of it when the furlough ends. Esther had not the facility for keeping him entertained, and never will have. And nursery schools will certainly mean illness.

Monday, January 10
Letter from Lou, who has decided to take his chances on going into the army as an ordinary private. Jules is inclined to do likewise. OSS[96] seems to be out, and AMG had many disadvantages, including no chance at all of OCS.[97]
More ads about the car, more phone calls, but still no sale. Jules is quite chagrined about it all.
The war news sounds quite good these days. The Russians particularly are "going to town" in fine style.
Talked to Phil[98] on the phone. He has written Mother, and feels confident his letter will

---
96 OSS - Office of Strategic Services, the intelligence organization prior to the CIA.
97 OCS - Officers' Candidate School through which Jules could have become an officer in the Army.
98 Anne's cousin Phil, a lawyer.

be very effective. I hope he's right.
Talked to Ann Reiter on the phone. Fred is on the march, but still in Italy.

Tuesday, January 11
Jules turned down an offer of $800 for the car – by far the best offer so far – because it meant surrendering the car today.
We all went downtown in the afternoon, I to get a permanent, Jules to demonstrate the car, and Ira for the ride. I got what looked like a very nice permanent. Certainly glad it was over with for a few months.
Called Helen Koplow, but she has joined George at Battle Creek, Michigan, and subleased her apartment here. Called Selma Rein,[99] but she has gone to the West Coast to see Dave off for overseas duty, and subleased her apartment here. I believe I would do likewise if I had only myself to consider, but it gets rather complicated to try to move Ira around from one camp town to another.

Wednesday, January 12
Sold the car to a dealer for $725, delivery to be made on Sunday.
Downtown in the afternoon. Rented a safe-deposit box in which Jules stored our bonds and a few other valuables. Bought Jules a "Dopp-kit." Got a few other errands done.
Had asked the Silorains to dinner this week, but they had to go out of town. No one else we especially cared to have over.
Phil called. They are taking us to the theater Friday night. As painless a way to spend an evening with May as I can imagine, if I have to spend an evening with her at all.

Mother had a trial scheduled for today. Do hope she made out all right, mainly to save her self-respect.

Thursday, January 13
Received a very attractive suit for Ira from Philadelphia. Talked to Nate later, who said he had sent it just because he was Ira's godfather. Downtown in the afternoon. Got several errands done, including gifts for the Herrup and Edes babies. Ira, of course, had a wonderful time.
Later to the Little Tea House for dinner, since that seems to be Ira's favorite restaurant. He enjoyed it very much again, and was particularly intrigued with the open fire.
Would have liked to go to a movie this evening, but Jules had received the statements of our earnings, so began to work on our income tax returns. Just as well since it will save me a few headaches, and he does not seem to mind too much wrestling with the pesky forms.

Friday, January 14
Tom Emerson telephoned. Wanted some information about ordinances for a speech to be made by Bohles. Using the car a great deal since it is our last chance.
Took Ira to the Zoo in the afternoon. He had a wonderful time. We did too.
To the theater as guests of May and Phil to see "Marianne." The play was pretty bad. Later ran into Mark,[100] his wife and mother-in-law, and Gertrude, whose husband had just gone overseas. Jules bought drinks for everyone, not so much because it was a joyous occasion as because it was one of his

---

99   NLRB colleague David Rein's wife.

100   Mark Wagshal, Phil's brother, and Gertrude, cousin from Massachusetts.

last flings as a civilian. Phil gave me a letter he had received from Mother, which pretty completely dampened the evening for me. What a problem!

Saturday, January 15
Downtown in the morning. Got several errands done when it began to hailstorm and we had to go home. Got Ira a toy chest, which should be a big help, and several toys intended to keep him happy when Jules and I have to leave him.
Sleeted, rained, and snowed all day, but we went out in the afternoon anyhow to do some errands in the neighborhood shops.
Jules spent most of the evening finishing up the income tax returns. Too bad he had to spend his time that way, but I suppose it is all for the best.
Card from Mother. The trial was postponed until next Thursday. Wish I knew what to do for her short of having her come here to live with me. She is stubborn about not coming to live with her Mother.

Sunday, January 16
Awoke to a beautiful white snow covered world. Spent much of the day outdoors playing in the snow. Ira loved it.
Jules delivered the car this afternoon. He felt quite sorrowful about the parting.
Mother S. telephoned just before he got back, so he called her so she could bid him farewell. Charlie Joseph came over to deliver some papers to Jules and to visit a while. He is an agreeable person and we enjoyed his visit very much.

It had been such a delightful week but it had gone by so quickly I can hardly believe it has gone, and that tomorrow is the day Jules leaves, for heavens only knows how long. It is going to be awfully hard on both Ira and me, but I am afraid harder on Ira.

Monday, January 17
Spent our last few hours together quite uneventfully. Jules left by cab at 3:30.
Letter from Claire Edes just after Jules left saying Duffy had been given another 6 months' deferment, and congratulations. Did not make me feel any better.
Bill Wise telephoned. Was sorry to have missed Jules as he wanted some advice on how to get into the army at a higher salary. He has refused a deferment, wants to get in, but has a wife and three daughters who must be supported.
Bought a bond with the proceeds from the car. Sent Joyce some galoshes, rubbers, etc., that Ira had outgrown. Have a lot of Jules' things to give away.
Jules telephoned. Took an hour to put the call through. He was terribly tired and had to get up at 5:00 am tomorrow.

Tuesday, January 18
Ira did not like the idea of my leaving him this morning, but fussed much less than I feared he would.
Many of the people at the office made kind remarks about Jules and very flattering remarks about my new hair-do.
Esther fixed a fairly good supper. Shall have to watch out that she does not slacken up too

much in Jules' absence, as she has a tendency to do.

Jules telephones again, much earlier than last night. He is tired and sleepy, and is not enjoying the food but otherwise is getting along well enough. He now has his uniform so he feels a little like a soldier. Ira had a chance to speak to him, which made both of them happy. Ira seems remarkably understanding about the situation.

Wednesday, January 19
Esther got in quite late this morning, but insisted she could not help it, had left in time, but could not get the jam-packed buses to stop for her. Apparently to make up for it she fixed a particularly good dinner this evening, including steak and apple pie. But I could have enjoyed it so much more if Jules had been enjoying it with me. The darndest part of it all is that it may be such a long time before we shall be able to have our meals together again.

He telephoned rather late this evening so he could report if his name was on the shipping list. It was not – yet. He was told that he had done exceptionally well on his tests, but all avenues of advancement seem closed nevertheless.

I am apparently just being investigated for my war agency job.

Thursday, January 20
I miss Jules so much more when I am at home with Ira. Much less fun to fix supper at home with Jules not around. Sunday, of course, will be the worst of all.

He called in the evening. Very weary from scrubbing and polishing floors, but not complaining. Still not on the shipping list, but does not know what that indicates. He told me the boys were permitted to have visitors, which I had not known. Will try to arrange to go up with Ira on Sunday if the train schedule is at all decent. He just started to give me his mailing address when the operator told us our time was up, although it seemed to me we had just started to talk. And he was sounding so lonesome.

Friday, January 21
Thank you letter from Eve and Peter Herrup.[101] Notice from the dentist that I am due for a prophylaxis. Lunched at Scheider's with Wes. Told me of some chap who had been at the office that had seen Jules last night, weary from his floor scrubbing.

The train schedules are terrible for Ira. Don't know what to do about visiting Jules. Will probably go on Sunday and just try to manage somehow.

Jules did not call tonight, which means he is again not on the shipping list. It would be wonderful if he could be stationed near here but I suppose that is expecting too much.

Bill Wise called. He passed his pre-induction exam and expects to be called about March 1. And Sally with her three daughters in St. Louis!

Saturday, January 22
Just comfortably busy at the office. Letter from Clara, who also found the three weeks'

---
101   Called Al Herrup in an earlier reference.

furlough far too short. My first check from the Army – for $80. Letter from Jules. Jules also telephoned, so thrilled about my coming tomorrow that we should have to go regardless of inconvenient train schedules. Not that I would give them a second thought for myself, but it is going to be hard on Ira dragging around at all hours of the night.

Did some work in the evening, knowing I should have no chance tomorrow.

Sorry I had told Ira about our proposed trip as he stayed awake very late talking to himself about it. He probably misses Jules more than he indicates.

Sunday, January 23

Ira was up before the crack of dawn ready for his trip. I managed to restrain him sufficiently to wait until after his nap.

We took the 4:30 train. Jules met us at camp at the bus stop. He looked very well, and felt well except for a head cold he got as a result of K.P. in the freezer room. We had supper at a cafeteria at one of the recreation rooms, a very ordinary meal, but Jules said it was the best he had had all week. We spent the evening walking and sitting and talking. Shortly before we left he checked the shipping list for tomorrow, and found his name on it, which made me doubly thankful we had come. As a matter of fact Ira withstood the trip far better than I did, and when we reached home at almost midnight was far more chipper than I, and called for something to eat.

Monday, January 24

Ira amazed me by getting up at his usual hour. Got piled up again today with a lot of work. Nate telephoned from Philadelphia. Was very sweet, urged me to come any time I could or cared to, to telephone and reverse the charges whenever I had the urge to talk to someone, and to call on him for any help I might ever need. Telephoned Mother S to tell her about seeing Jules. She was very happy to hear about him, but distressed to think of him at a camp, having supposed he would be immediately placed in an office. She thinks Joe has been sent overseas.

Worked for quite a while in the evening, and then dragged off to bed, physically and emotionally exhausted.

Tuesday, January 25

The civilian clothes Jules had worn to camp came back today. Made me a bit sad.

Lunched with Marie Berger, who was in the building for a conference.

Haven't heard from Mother in a heck of a long time, and it worries me. Have written to her several times. Afraid it means the hearing scheduled for last Thursday went badly for her. A lovely warm afternoon. I got home early, and Ira and I stayed outdoors until supper-time. Ira broke the glass top on the coffee table today, and unscrewed the switch of the desk lamp, which I was able to fix. His explanations and apologies were so profuse I could hardly punish him.[102]

No word yet from Jules, which must mean he is in the course of a long trip.

---

102 Both Ira and Ronald Goor remember this event. They were playing inside with a metal toy gun, and in the play the gun fell and broke the table top.

Wednesday, January 26
It seems Ira is on one of his destructive rampages again. Today he broke one of my really choice dishes. I hate to see so many things destroyed, and I hate the necessity for disciplining him.
Phil called to tell me he had received a letter from the son of the woman with whom Mother lives to the effect that Mother had made the arrangement completely intolerable. I can understand that. But good Lord, what shall I do?
And still no word from Jules, who must be going all the way across the country. I hate to think of his being so far away, and distance will greatly complicate plans I might have made to try to join him. I suppose I should just about get settled somewhere when he would be shipped overseas.

Thursday, January 27
A very sweet letter of thanks and sympathy from Claire Rosen Edes. Ira really went to town today – more dishes broken, a drape pulled down, his room pulled to pieces – all while he is supposed to be taking a nap. It is no doubt partly Esther's fault, but how can I train both Ira and Esther the few minutes I have morning and evening?
Claire telephoned. In town for a couple of days for a conference. She had certainly worked things out better than I have. Card from Mother, which did not cheer me up any.
And so many girls have their husbands, their children, and folks with but one thought – to help then in every way possible. If I had time to think about it, I would be feeling very sorry for myself.

Friday, January 28
Still usually managing to leave early, but very busy all the time. I am at the office and doing some work every evening. Between that and Ira and my household responsibilities, I don't get too much time to worry about Jules and to feel sorry for myself.
Much to my surprise Mother telephoned form Havenhill. Seemed the hearing had again been postponed, her lawyer had backed out, she could not get another, and she wanted me to come there for a day or two. I explained the various reasons why I could not.
Took Ira to the barber shop for a haircut. He behaved admirably and I was very proud of him. If only he would behave a little better at home.

Saturday, January 29
Lunched in the cafeteria with Claire.[103] She looked well, and things seemed to be going splendid with her.
She telephoned in the evening just as we were finishing dinner, but I told her to come out anyway, and I fixed something for her to eat. She fussed over Ira, which he liked very much. And, after he went to bed, it was pleasant to sit around and talk with her, even though I get a chance for so little words. She would have spent the night, but when she called her brother's house she was told there were other friends of hers there so she went home.
Phil[104] arranged to have Sam call his friend Dorgan, a lawyer in Lawrence, and ask him to get a lawyer for Mother. I wired Mother

---
103   Her friend Claire Rosen Edes.
104   Phil Wagshal, Anne's cousin, and his father Sam Wagshal.

about it. Hope it will work out all right. She must be represented by someone.

Sunday, January 30
Mother S. telephoned, but I had no news for her. If Jules had been in the army little longer I should begin to think he was being shipped overseas. It is a week-and seems years-since I have heard from him. And Tuesday will be his birthday!

Not cold, but quite windy, so we went outdoors for a walk, but did not linger long. Ira had apparently assumed that Jules would come home or that we would go to camp on Sunday. He was keenly disappointed. He talks quite knowingly about his soldier-daddy, but cannot understand much of it-except that it had taken his daddy away for quite a long time. Worked for a while, read for while, finally realized I was getting no call tonight, and went to bed.

Monday, January 31
Spent most of the day at Justice on the municipal legislation program but managed to get away long enough to go the beauty parlor.

Five letters from Jules, who is at Camp Blanding, Florida. His first two had been misrouted by the post office. He was not able to telephone, and a corporal who had promised to wire me had not done so. That was a tremendous relief. I was really getting worried. Sam and Phil called Dorgan, who said he was taking care of Mother himself, that she had driven her other attorney "nuts," that she still has romantic notions about winning Father back, and that she was getting money from him regularly. If all that is true, she has been unbelievably selfish in playing on our sympathies and emotions the way she has. I don't suppose I shall ever know the whole truth of the matter.

Year End Summary 1944

And so 1944 had dragged to a close. I do not suppose I have ever been so well satisfied to have any other year of my life come to a close. It has been on the whole an unhappy year.

It saw Jules go into the army.

It saw him seriously ill with spinal meningitis.

It saw all his efforts to better his position knocked into the ground, for no apparent reason.

It saw Ira becoming thin and unhappy and resentful.

It saw me finally forced to give up my job, and possibly, as a result, my career.

It saw me dragged across the country to visit Jules, and then dragged away from him to be re-untied with Ira, whom I had missed far more deeply than I had realized I would. And, seeing how much he had missed me, began to realize how unhappy he must have been when he had to spend so much of his time in Esther's exclusive company. I hope and pray that 1945 will be a brighter year primarily that it will see the end of the war, which will not only re-unite our family but will also bring joy to the world.

Hope that we shall be able to adopt another child.

Hope Jules will find work that will give him joy and satisfaction, and that life will in all ways make-up to him for the bitterly unhappy year he had just spent.

Have resolved to be more gentle and kindly to Ira. Sometimes speak to him brusquely and peremptorily, and he is sensitive enough to resent it, as well as bright enough to remember about it and make me ashamed of myself. And have resolved to try to make myself worthy generally of the wonderful husband and son I am fortunate enough to have.

Julius Schlezinger 1944
Camp Blanding, Florida

1945

The year began with war in Europe and in the Pacific. Jules was shipped to Europe to fight on the German front. Mail arrived sporadically and often after long delays. Anne agonized over his well-being and used contacts to try to obtain a good posting that would use his education and skills. Nothing worked; he fought as an infantryman. The surrender of Germany brought her great happiness, but then it began to appear that he might be sent to the Pacific front after the war ended in Europe. In the end he was not, and in August he was discharged to go back to his position in the Department of Labor.

While Jules was away, Anne felt that she should stay home with Ira and not work. She resigned her position to be with him. The Goor family lived near them, and Anne became a good friend with Jeannette, the mother, and Ira with the son about his age, Ronnie.

President Roosevelt died without seeing the war victories against Germany and Japan. -- RDH

Monday, April 9
Two letters from Jules, both written earlier than the one I received on Saturday. A pleasant day and Ira and I spent much of it outdoors. The Liftins and Goors suggested we join them at the Hot Shoppe for dinner, but I did not think Ira was sufficiently recovered for that [i.e. from chicken pox].
A big bunch of lovely spring flowers arrived in the evening, from Jules, a delightful surprise, and about the only bright spot in an

otherwise drab, dull birthday. So I am now 35. I sometimes feel twice that, and, with my hair graying so fast, no doubt I sometimes look twice 35.

Tuesday, April 10
Long letter from Jules written before the Saturday letter. Birthday card from Madalyn. Still not permitting Ira to play with other children since he has a few spots that linger on and…we manage to spend a good deal of time outdoors by ourselves.
Hannah and Sylvia came over to visit in the evening. We went to the drugstore for sodas. Then came back to the apartment, and sat around gabbing all hours for the most part about Hannah's marital troubles, of which she seems to have a plenty.
Joe Friedman called. Is certainly doing everything he can to put the Bernstein proposition through. Should certainly like to know what developed from Bernie's call.

Wednesday, April 11
No mail from Jules. Wonder if he is on his way to join Bernie..
Ira's hearing seems to be normal again, which is a great relief to me, and must also be to him. I am nevertheless still anxious to have him examined by Davis, but he still has a couple of spots to get rid of before I can take him downtown.
Washed my hair for the first time in a good many years. It came out looking pretty weird, but at least it was much cleaner than it had been.
Ronnie has chicken pox. He apparently got it from Joe Dale as there would not have been time for him to have developed it from Ira.

Thursday, April 12
Shocked and saddened by the news of President Roosevelt's death. It is a great calamity, for the Jews, for the country, and for the world. I am sorry, for him, that he could not live to see the culmination of the war and the fulfillment of his ideals for the post-war world.
Planned to go to the movies with Sylvia but I could not get a sitter, and neither of us felt much like it when we heard the news. Instead she came over so we could condole with each other.
Received a pink blouse from Clara for a birthday gift, not the sort of thing I should select for myself, but I think I shall be able to use it.
Card from Mother.
Nothing from Jules.

Friday, April 13
Mary back at work, and gave the place a good cleaning with Ira's "help."
The rug was picked up today for cleaning and storage. Glad to get rid of it.
Did some errands for Jeanette since Ronnie now has chicken pox.
President Roosevelt is being mourned not only by this country but also by many foreign countries. I find it deeply depressing to contemplate the changes in world events that will result from his untimely death.
Still no word from Jules. I have a hunch he is on his way to join Bernie. Will be glad when I hear what it is all about.

Saturday, April 14
Spent most of the morning at the grocery store, and was rewarded by getting a comparatively abundant supply of meat.
Received from Bobby and Nate three very well chosen toys for Ira and a box of salt water taffy for me.
Card from Clara. Nothing from Jules.
All the stores, movies, etc., were closed this afternoon and evening in memory of Roosevelt. Even the government offices were closed this afternoon.
Felt that Ira had finally reached the stage where he could play with other children with no danger of their catching chicken pox from him, so let him play outdoors for a while without my standing guard, a relief for both of us.

Sunday, April 15
A rainy morning.
Wes stopped in for a few minutes. He and Ira had a wonderful romp together. Too bad it had to be right at noon, but Ira managed his luncheon pretty well anyhow.
Nate telephoned to ask how Ira was and what we heard from Jules.
Took Ira to the movies after his nap to see "The Three Caballeros." He enjoyed it very much, although I found it difficult to explain to him some of the Walt Disney fantasy. It was quite a treat for him after such a long period of confinement and restriction.
Sylvia had suggested coming over with Johnny, but I figured Ira would enjoy the movie even more.

Monday, April 16
Another drizzly day, but we got out in the morning and afternoon. Letter from Jules. He and Bernie finally got in touch with each other, but there appear to be serious obstacles in the way of Jules getting on Bernie's staff. Afraid it will be a bad blow for Jules to lose this last chance to do something for which he is really qualified in this war.
Mary did not come in but at least she called.
Sent Jules another package although he has not yet received any of the others I have sent him.
Truman seems determined to carry out Roosevelt's plans as far as possible, which is a good sign. The war in Europe, always about to end, goes merrily on.

Tuesday, April 17
Rained all day. Ira and I are getting on each other's nerves terribly from being cooped in together too much, with the result that we squabble a good deal, poor Ira usually getting the worst of it. Will have to get hold of myself.
Jose Dale came up for a while, and we visited Ronnie for a while, but it was not enough of a change to break the evil spell.
No mail from Jules, which did not help mend matters.
Letter from Madalyn, apparently, written at Mother's request, asking for some of the package requests I have received from Jules. I had written Mother I could spare some.

1945

Wednesday, April 18
Still no word from Jules.
No Mary, and no word from her yesterday or today, so I suppose she has retired again. Will probably not take her back again.
In the evening to the movie at Ft. Myers with Sylvia and Hannah. Saw "The Enchanted Cottage," which I found rather depressing. Hannah had the car, Wes being out of town, but she had a lot of difficulty with it on the way home. It was a cold windy night, and we were glad to get home finally. And we had not gone anywhere to eat because Hannah had to be home to release her sitter at 10:00. She was at least an hour late.

Thursday, April 19
Picture postcard from Jules for Ira mentioning that he is now in Germany. He is apparently in a combat unit, and not even Bernie, with all his prestige and influence, could get him transferred.
Sent Lynn two birthday gifts selected by Ira, and bought him a sweatshirt selected by him. He has very definite ideas not only as to what he likes, but also as to what Lynn would enjoy.
Finally got my hair done. Left Ira with Ronnie, for which both Ronnie and Jeanette were very grateful.
Got some housework done in the evening since Mary has apparently really retired this time.

Friday, April 20
Four letters from Jules, now "deep into Germany," feeling fine and finding it all rather interesting. No word as to whether or not he is in combat himself. No word about Bernie, but I am afraid that was a great disappointment to Jules, one of a long series of disappointments. Joe Friedman pointed out to me that something might still come of it when it would mean staying in Europe rather than being transferred to the Pacific, which was a rather comforting thought. Joe has certainly been splendid about this whole matter. It is reassuring to run across someone occasionally who seems like a real friend.
Hannah got a chicken for me from her farmer, the first we have had since we returned from Philadelphia.

Saturday, April 21
Card from Mother. No word yet from or about Louie. The reports of conditions found in German prison camps almost make one lose all faith in human decency.
Sylvia came over in the afternoon with Bonnie and Johnnie. We had sodas at the drugstore, went for a walk, and then spent the rest of the afternoon in the back yard. Many of the girls have already made arrangements for their summer vacations. Some of them sound very attractive. I suppose Butch and I will stay put. Too bad the family has made New England so unattractive.
Ira's improved eating habits are beginning to show results. He looks and feels much better.

Sunday, April 22
A cool day but sunny and pleasant. Wes took Ira and Jr. for a little ride in the morning. Sylvia and her charges came over in the af-

ternoon. We took the kids to a playground. They had a wonderful time. Bonnie, as usual, created a great sensation among the dog-hungry children of Buckingham.

I roasted the chicken Hannah got for us. It was delicious, the sort of thing Jules would enjoy very much.

Finished Godden's "Take Three Tenses." Pretty good. Wish I could write. Would be one thing I could do and still stay at home. But I can't, and I am too lazy even to try.

Monday, April 23

Would have gone downtown but the weather report kept promising rain. It did not rain all day.

Ira developed a red eyelid. Could not get hold of Stein, but boric acid and a rest soon made it look much better.

Ira has a passion for climbing fences. He did so at Hannah's this afternoon, and ripped both his jacket and overalls very badly.

Guess Mary is really gone this time.

There should be some word from or about Louie soon. Hope he is all right. Those damned Nazi fanatics -- I don't know what would be an appropriate punishment for them.

Tuesday, April 24

Rained all day.

Marketing with Jeanette and Ronnie in the car. Got sandwiches and stuff at the drug-store and had a picnic luncheon at Jeanette's in celebration of Ronnie's being able to go outdoors again.

Card from Mother. I am her only hope for remedying her impossible situation. Letter from Clara - she will accept my invitation for a visit if there is no chance of Joyce catching chicken pox from Ira. As through I should suggest it otherwise!

Mother S. telephoned. I have been lax about keeping in touch with her and shall try to do better. When I don't hear from Jules, though, I hesitate about calling or writing to her.

Wednesday, April 25

Three letters from Jules, badly battered, containing German money and stamps. He is in combat, his baptism of fire having occurred on my birthday. But his wonderful spirit is quite undaunted. I can "take it" too if only it does not go on too long.

Rained all day. Jeanette and Ronnie came up and spent the afternoon with us. Sylvia called to chat on the phone as she does almost every evening now.

Jeanette has a new maid whom I shall engage also. Pretty sore at Mary, but would like to have someone in case Clara comes. Don't want her to feel she has to clean house when she is here as a guest on her first visit in years.

Thursday, April 26

Two letters from Jules. Has received no packages yet but requests more. The food and living conditions generally are very bad apparently, as is to be expected, I suppose, on a battleground.

Louise Wells decided to drive out to the Ruchel party. Ira enjoyed the ride with Slug and Sally about as much as he did the party. It was, as always, a very pleasant party, even though, as happens to me so often, I was the only woman there whose husband was in the service.

Lucky that we had a ride since it was pouring by the time we came home.

Poor Ira was very conscious at the party of Slug and Anthony and some of the others having younger brothers and sisters along to look after.

Friday, April 27

Jeanette's new 'jewel' of a maid was supposed to come in today but did not show up.

Cool and very windy but I took Ira downtown anyhow. Got him some new shoes and did a few other errands.

Note from Bobby thanking us for Lynn's birthday gifts.

Nate also telephoned to inquire about Jules, and said Lynn had been delighted with the gifts Ira selected.

No mail from Jules, but I no longer expect to hear from him every day. I just hope the intervals between letters will not be too long.

Fear I am ruining my eyes by too much reading, but what else can I do with so much free time?

Saturday, April 28

To the dentist in the morning where we both had our teeth cleaned. From there to see Dr. Davis, who arranged to remove Ira's tonsils on Monday. I liked Davis very much and was glad I had decided on him.

Then to the Tally-Ho for luncheon. Met some old Labor Board friends there. Could not help resenting their not being in the army.

Sylvia came over in the afternoon with Bonnie and Johnny. We sat in the back yard while the children played in the sandbox.

Great excitement in the evening over a report that Germany had finally capitulated, but it proved to be a false report. Germany's collapse is expected momentarily, but I have heard that so many times over such a long period of time.

Sunday, April 29

Many people expected word of German's surrender to come through today officially, but it did not.

In the afternoon we met the Liftins at the corner for ice cream. Then we all went to Lubber Run Park. It was very pleasant there, and the two youngsters and Bonnie seemed to be having a wonderful time. Should have brought some eats along and made it a picnic as so many others were doing, but we had been afraid it would be too cool and damp.

Jules would have enjoyed an afternoon like this so much - tramping around in the woods with his son, his wife, his friends, and a dog.

Monday, April 30

Arrived at Doctor's Hospital about 11:00. Liked it so much better than Columbia - newer, cleaner, better service, and altogether more pleasant. Ira enjoyed every moment of the preparations, even having his finger pricked and being wheeled away. The next few hours were not so pleasant, but they were not too bad. By evening he was feeling rather perky again and begging for something to eat. He managed to get down a whole glass of crushed ice and a little bit of milk. I did not have the heart to eat, so went out for a bite of luncheon while he was in the operating room, and just skipped dinner. We had a somewhat restless night, but not too bad.

Tuesday, May 1
Home by cab about 10:30. No mail from Jules. It appears from the newspapers that his outfit has been designated as an army of occupation. And they would not release him to work with Bernie.
Letter from Clara with some snapshots of her cute chubby daughter.
Official notice from OPA of acceptance of my resignation.
Jeanette and Ronnie brought Ira some blocks. Sylvia and Johnny brought him three toys, some bananas, and, for me, some home made cinnamon buns. Ira stayed in bed, but had a wonderful time with his guests and all his new toys.
Seemed good to be home again. Even a good hospital can be unpleasant.

Wednesday, May 2
Ira was up and around the house all day, without even taking a nap, apparently without ill effect.
Long letter from Jules, who has been vacationing at a resort. The only way he could rate a vacation is by being injured, but he offered no explanation. The letter was dated April 20.
Jeanette did my marketing, and brought us some ice cream. She and Sylvia have certainly been splendid about all this.

Mussolini is definitely dead, and there is a report, not yet confirmed, that Hitler is also dead. I hope Hitler's death was as degrading as Mussolini's apparently was, although they really deserved a long, lingering, horrible punishment.

Thursday, May 3
Two letters from Jules, dated April 17 and 18, the earlier one describing intensive fighting, the later one the vacation resort. Despite his reiterated statements about feeling well except for his loneliness, I am still afraid that he rated a vacation only because he had been injured on the 17th.
Card from Mother, very smug because none of her four children had had a tonsillectomy.
Wes called. Just back from New York. Hannah staying there a while longer.
Rained all day. Ronnie spent the morning and afternoon with Ira, and Jeanette did the marketing again.
Ira still eating very poorly.

Friday, May 4
Note from Bobby enclosing a long letter from Jules to Nate which they considered particularly fine and worth preserving. I am becoming convinced that Jules for some strange reason rated a vacation, and that he was not injured.
Wish I shared Jules' noble sentiments about his participation in this fight for freedom, but I do not, not with so many of his contemporaries participating so much more comfortably at home. And Ira needs him so much, for many reasons, to counteract the effects of my nasty disposition, among others.

1945

We took a walk in the afternoon when the rain let up. Bought some ice cream for the Goors and ourselves.

Saturday, May 5
Card from Clara. Has to postpone her trip because Joyce is having her tonsils removed this morning. Too bad that little thing has to go through it. Note from Hannah.
Ira and I were out most of the morning, fortunately, since it rained in the afternoon. It had stopped, however, by the time we finished dinner, and since Ira had eaten a fairly good meal, we celebrated and went to the corner for ice cream. First time we had been out after dinner for a long while.
Mrs. Ritchie, a neighbor, gave us a great quantity of stuff from her garden, a great help since our larder is quite low.

Sunday, May 6
In the morning we drove over to Clarendon with the Liftins to feed some ducks and chickens in someone's backyard. The children enjoyed it. Walked around and window-shopped until it was time to come home for luncheon.
Ira's appetite is very erratic, but generally poor. I still hope it will improve shortly as a result of the tonsillectomy. He is so thin!
With V-E day so imminent, there is already talk of who will be discharged from the army, but, with Jules in the army of occupation, I am afraid it is going to be a long time yet before we get together. And it has been so long already, such a big part of Ira's life.

Monday, May 7
Germany has surrendered!
Took Ira to see Davis about his ear complaints and his lack of appetite. Got some ear drops and some advice.
A lovely warm day. The Liftins came over and we spent the whole afternoon outdoors.
Letter from Madalyn. Get-well cards for Ira from Mother S. and Helen Lee and from the Lewises.
Nothing from Jules. Wonder what chance there is of his coming home. Very little, I am afraid.
I am glad that most folks seem to be taking V-E day pretty soberly. After all, there is a lot of war to be fought yet.

Tuesday, May 22
Mail from Jules finally. Four letters dated April 26 and 27 and May 2 and 3. One of them was meant for his mother. He has been in the Sudetenland in the alpine region, with heavy snow in May, and is now with the First Army, which almost surely means a transfer to the Pacific. If he does go to the Pacific with the First Army, he will probably get a 30-day furlough at home, which would be a big help. Note from Gertrude accompanying the "requests" from Jules which I had sent Mother and which she was returning. My box of goodies was no doubt part of what Mother had prepared for Jules.
Spent the evening listening to the radio while I did the ironing.

Wednesday, May 30
Memorial Day! To remind us that this insanity called "war" has gone on and on, down

through the ages. What chance is there of stopping it now?

Used the washing machine in Hannah's building to wash the small rug in Ira's room. Wish Buckingham supplied laundry facilities and outdoor clothes lines.

No mail was delivered today. For some, at least, it was a holiday. Had dinner with the Goors. As always it was a good dinner and very pleasant, particularly since she fed the children first so we could eat in comparative peace. Charlie [i.e Goor] is quite excited about his new job. Wish Jules were around, thinking about jobs, new or old.

Thursday, May 31
Two letters from Jules dated May 14 and 23, the letters setting a record for speedy delivery. Now that he is no longer fighting, he has more time to be lonely and homesick. His remarks about how much he loved me only saddened me. I was not cheered up by hearing that Hannah and Wes were driving to New York; nor by a letter from Claire about how busy she and Duffy were both on their jobs and socially, even though she did very kindly urge us to come for a visit.

It will be a good thing when Ira gets back to school and I have less opportunity to vent my foul temper on him. I am brutal to him at times, at far too many times. And he is so sweet and so deserving of better treatment.

Sunday, July 1
Extremely warm.
Jules called in the morning. Thought he would be home very late tonight or some time tomorrow.

Mrs. Coston gave us some sweet peas in honor of Jules' homecoming. He arrived at about 1:00 a.m. very happy to be at home again. He talked practically the whole night. Had had a lot of tough battle experiences but came through with flying colors. He had a number of battle trophies although most of them had been stolen by the rear echelons, a mighty low-down trick. He brought me some lovely lingerie, but too small, and some exquisite perfume. He brought Ira some toys and a number of books in French. He looks very thin but brown and healthy.

Wednesday, August 1
To Clarendon by bus in the afternoon. Took Ronnie along. Did some shopping. Jules bought Ira several toys as farewell gifts, and little planes for both Ira and Ronnie.[105]

Borrowed the Borkin car in the evening. Took Ira for a ride to the airport. Then home to put Ira to bed. Had Mrs. Costin listen for him again while we went to the Mayflower to dance, to drink, and to remember the many other occasions when we had been there without the shadow of war and prolonged partings hanging over us.

Nate telephoned from Philadelphia to say goodbye to Jules.

Thursday, August 2
Letter from Helen Lee thanking Jules for the souvenir gifts he had sent her.

---

105   Ron Goor remembers this day and seeing Jules with a duffle bag and helmet in his hand. Jules gave Ronnie a leather pistol holster as a souvenir.

Have had no luck at the store the last few days, so Jules' farewell meals today were all very simple, but he seemed to enjoy them nevertheless. He also particularly enjoyed his shower, his easy chair, and the other few little luxuries we have at home.

Jules left by cab at 10:45. The parting was very hard on all of us, but hardest of all, I am sure, on Jules. If only it would all end soon.

Jules called Columbus before he left. His mother too hated the thought of our little home being broken up again.

Friday, August 3
A warm, humid day. It seemed strange and lonely without Jules around.

He telephoned at noon. Expected to leave for Bragg in the afternoon.

Had a headache most of the day which by evening had developed into a sick stomach. Sent Ira down to have dinner with the Goors. Jeanette brought him home later and put him to bed.

Jules telephoned again about 11:00 from Union Station. Said he would have come home had he known he would be at Meade all day. Is already horribly lonely and homesick.

Felt a bit better so got up, had some tea, read the paper, heard the midnight news, and then went back to bed.

Saturday, August 4
Took Ira to Dr. Stein in the morning for a Schick and TB test. He had gained another _ inch but only _ pound, and is still quite small for his age.

Letter from Hannah, who is in Utah with her brother, who is at a military hospital and apparently in bad shape. Letter from the Pa. R.R.[106] admitting the error but requesting the ticket stubs before making a refund – and Jules long since gave them to Ira to play "train" with. Letter from Mother, desperately unhappy.

Had dinner at the Evens Coffee Shop with Jean Cohen, Bob having gone fishing.

Felt quite peaked [i.e. piqued] all day, but managed somehow. Hadn't the strength, though, to tackle the horrible accumulation of housework.

Sunday, August 5
Got started on the housework bright and early this morning and made a noticeable dent in it.

Jules called from Fayetteville, where he was staying on a weekend pass. Found the town terribly crowded and seemed quite discouraged about our coming there. Will try to come home this coming weekend. Called Mother S. since Jules said he was unable to get a call through to Columbus without waiting several hours. A week seems a long time now to wait to see Jules, and it is very doubtful at that.

Ira already misses Jules greatly, but takes his absence, as he does practically all situations, in his stride.

Monday, August 6
Our scientists have devised a new "atomic" bomb, and have used it on Japan with apparently devastating results. I hope it will result in hastening the end of the war. Its potentiali-

---
106   Pennsylvania Railroad

ties are wonderful, but also frightening.

Card from Mother. A red-letter day at the store. Succeeded in getting both bananas and soap flakes.

Nate telephoned. He had been in touch with the Penn R.R., which is no doubt one of the reasons for the polite letter we received. The refund is, however, still forthcoming.

Getting caught up a bit on my letter writing, which I have greatly neglected while Jules was here. Read a collection of "Mr. Tutt" stories. Rather tiresome.

Tuesday, August 7

To the beauty parlor in the morning leaving Ira in Jeanette's care.

Jeanette received a letter from Sylvia in which Sylvia said she thinks she would prefer to wait for Mort to come home until he came to stay. Her remarks were apropos of Jules' furlough having ended. I can see her point, but am grateful for the 30 days despite the painful parting which was the inevitable end.

Letter from Sam, who was vacationing with Bobby. Clara and Joyce had spent a few days with them, so they knew of Jules' homecoming and departure. Wonderful cool nights for sleeping and Ira and I make the most of them.

Wednesday, August 8

Letter from Jules written Sunday. Six pages of loneliness. Ira and I went downtown in the morning just for a change. Returned just in time to get a call from Jules. The Treasury request is being acted on, but he may be moved before final action can be taken. The weekend at home now looks very doubtful. Another letter from him in the afternoon mail.

I was quite downcast by his news, but was considerably cheered when the news came out that Russia had declared war on Japan. That news plus the atomic bomb should certainly expedite considerably the end of the war. Hope Jules is still in this country when it ends. Poor Louie. No word. Looks pretty hopeless.

Thursday, August 9

Jeanette took Ira over while Jean Cohen went downtown. We lunched at the Tally-Ho, then went to the Little to see Bea Lillie in "On Approval," a very entertaining English movie. Altogether a pleasant outing.

Letter from Jules written prior to our telephone conversation. He was still expecting to be at Bragg a couple of months for training.

Finished Richard Wright's *Black Boy*,[107] a devastating description of conditions for Negroes in the south. A miracle that one like Wright could rise above them, and so far above them.

Listened to the President's radio speech. Fell asleep.[108]

---

107   After joining the NLRB Anne became more conscious of social justice issues, and it shows in her reading and opinions over the next decades.

108   President Harry Truman spoke to the nation, 10 p.m. Washington time about Germany and Japan. A second atomic bomb had been dropped on Nagasaki that day, and the next day, August 10, the Japanese offered to surrender.

On the use of the atomic bomb, he said, "The world will note that the first atomic bomb was dropped on Hiroshima, a military base. That was because we

Friday, August 10

Announcement first thing this morning that Japan had offered to surrender provided the emperor might be retained on his throne. Want to see the war end as soon as possible, but think we should insist upon unconditional surrender.

Letter from Jules stating, among other things, that he doubts that the war will end soon. Form card from the Penn. R.R. Our claim for a refund will be handled in due course.

The results of Ira's TB and Schick tests appear to be neutral, for which I am duly grateful. He seems to be getting safely past the whooping cough season, although the Barnett twins still have it, and infantile[109] seems to be on the wane.

Saturday, August 11

The Allies have replied to Japan that the Emperor may retain his throne only subject to the command of the Allied Military Commander. The next move is up to the Japs.

wished in this first attack to avoid, insofar as possible, the killing of civilians. But that attack is only a warning of things to come. If Japan does not surrender, bombs will have to be dropped on her war industries and, unfortunately, thousands of civilian lives will be lost. I urge Japanese civilians to leave industrial cities immediately, and save themselves from destruction."

Source: Public Papers of the Presidents of the United States: Harry S. Truman, Containing the Public Messages, Speeches and Statements of the President April 12 to December 31, 1945 (Washington D.C.: United States Government Printing Office, 1961) page 212.

109   Anne lists the worst childhood diseases of the time. Infantile paralysis which was a crippling disease with no vaccination or cure. The Schick test was for diphtheria. TB and Whooping Cough were the other concerns.

Card from Mother.

Jules was supposed to arrive, if he came in, about 9:00. I had just about given him up when he arrived at almost 11:00. He was so glad to be at home again it was almost pitiful.

The last request for his release has been disapproved. What fantastically bad luck he seems to have! Present plans are for his division to leave for a West Coast P.O.E. on Friday. At least, I hope, he will miss the fighting in the Pacific.

Sunday, August 12

The President and Byrnes were at their respective desks at 8:00 am, and everyone else was glued to the radio, but there was no response from the damned Japs.

Combined supplies again with the Goors, and we had a delicious picnic luncheon at Lubber Run.

Jules called Columbus and Philadelphia. Jules had to leave at 6:00, so terribly early. Charlie drove us to the station.

Jules hated to leave. He is again bitterly unhappy. He found combat, with all its dangers and hardships, far more pleasant than garrison life in this country.

Monday, August 13

Back to the old routine without Jules.

Letter from Clara. Lou[110] is supposed to be working with Fahy but, as an enlisted man, cannot be permitted to do legal work. What a nonsensical rule!

Jules telephoned in the afternoon. The disapproval of his request has been overruled, and

110   Sister Clara's husband, Lou Rolands.

is being acted upon. We talked for a long time because Jules obviously hated to say goodbye. If he gets a discharge, it will mean a year in Europe. Hope he is doing the right thing.

I succeeded this morning in getting bananas both for Jeanette and myself. She more than reciprocated by getting two chickens this afternoon and letting me have one. Have somehow caught a nasty cold.

Tuesday, August 14

Learned in the morning that the Japs had accepted the Potsdam declaration last night. Learned later it was again a mistake. But the official announcement finally came in the evening. My celebration consisted of taking Ira and his friends to the corner for ice cream cones, but the city generally went mad with joy.

A call came through from Jules about 9:00, but he had left the booth by then. Thought he might be on his way home, but he did not show up. No definite announcement yet on discharges except that a great many men will be discharged as soon as possible. Hope Jules and Lou get out soon. Let the new fellows replace them. Poor Louie!

Wednesday, August 15

All the government employees are getting a two-day holiday, but not the poor suckers, the servicemen. We fortunately had an adequate supply of food since all the stores are closed. No mail delivery.

I am delighted, of course, that the war has finally ended, but cannot get in a mood for really celebrating until my personal share in it has been completed, namely, until Jules comes home to stay. It is a great relief, though, to know that even if he goes to Japan, it will not be to fight.

To Jeanette's in the evening with several other people for a V-J[111] drink.

Jules woke me about 12:30 am on the phone. Still thinks he will be going to Japan.

Thursday, August 16

Jules arrived about 3:00 p.m., a complete surprise. Got a 3-day pass to clean up some questions regarding his possible discharge. Managed to get a ride on an army plane.

The grocery store was closed again today, but between what we could get at the delicatessen and what we had, we managed pretty well. Gasoline and fuel oil rationing have been ended, and other restrictions will soon be raised. It still seems strange to think of the war being over, to listen to the news broadcasts without hearing about battles and casualties, and to realize that soon all the things that have been so scare will become available. We need a great many things, and can soon, I hope, begin to plan to get them. Called Columbus.

Friday, August 17

A mad dash at the store for pineapple juice, reduced from 60 points to none. Got a rib roast of beef, my first in years.[112] It was Grade B, but looked good, so I took a chance on it. Downtown in the afternoon. Jules called on Joe and some other Treasury people while Ira and I did some errands. We met later at the Trans-Lux. Then to Olmsted's for dinner. Had

---

111 Victory Japan.
112 Meat was difficult for civilians to get throughout the war years.

some really superb roast beef. Then home on the bus, a very pleasant outing for all of us.

We have one very difficult jig saw puzzle with which Jules has become very intrigued. He spent the remainder of the evening working on it. Hard to realize yet that the war is over. The way the Japs are behaving, I sometimes wonder if it is.

Saturday, August 18

Having wonderful weather, mild days and cool nights.

Fixed my roast for dinner, keeping my fingers crossed, and it was superb, tender and delicious. We all enjoyed it very much, and I was delighted.

Jules had to go to Joe's house for a few minutes in the evening, so he borrowed Charlie's[113] car and took Ira and Ronnie along to play on Jane's new jungle gym. After Ira was in bed and asleep, Jules and I went to the Buckingham movie. Mrs. Coston listened for Ira.

Jules' car picked him up at 2:00 am. The next time I hear from him, he should either be discharged or en route to Japan. I hope it is the former. It is high time he get a decent break in the army – by getting out.

Sunday, August 19

Jules called in the evening, sounding very happy as he told me he was about to be discharged. His company leaves for the west coast tomorrow morning, thence for Japan. I called Joe Friedman.[114] Mother S. and Nate[115] to convey the glad tidings. Gertrude[116] called later to get Mother's version of what had happened straightened out. They are, of course, pretty excited about the news.

Now to see how this new turn of events develops. Jules will have to go to Germany, but at least it will be as a man doing a job, and not as a private on police duty. It should help him to regain some of the self-esteem he has lost.

Monday, August 20

Card from Mother. Long letter from Sylvia, who tried to call me when the Japs surrendered but could not get the call through. Is depressed by the likelihood that Mort may not be home for quite a while yet. Do not blame her. It just does not seem that the war is really over until the boys are home again, even if we do have unlimited hot water, gasoline, pineapple juice, etc.

Ira persists in trying to climb trees despite my having forbidden it and today, as was inevitable, he fell from a fairly considerable height. He was more frightened than hurt. Nevertheless he received only censure, not sympathy, from me.

Finished *Everything Rustlers*, a silly story about ridiculous people.

Tuesday, August 21

Ronnie had a cold. It will be nothing short of a miracle if Ira does not catch it.

Rather warm and humid, but this had been on the whole, as far and weather is concerned, a wonderful summer.

---

113   Charles Goor, Jeannette's husband.
114   Jules' best friend and later law partner.
115   Jules' brother Nate.
116   Anne's cousin Gertrude from Lawrence.

No word from Jules since Sunday. Hope there has not been a hitch in his getting discharged.

Finished Steinbeck's *Cannery Row*.[117] Pretty good, but not at all in the class of some of the other things he has written.

Spent the evening doing my ironing, a helluva way to spend a beautiful moonlit evening. Wonder how many more I shall be spending alone.

Wednesday, August 22

Letter from Jules written on Monday. He is still cheerful about getting discharged, and is doing everything he can to expedite it. His gang left on Monday morning for the west coast P.O.E.

To the beauty parlor in the morning. Since Ronnie still had a cold, I took Ira along to the beauty parlor with me. He enjoyed it, but got bored before I could get from under the dryer.

On the way home Ira bought a writing tablet and a box of Mickey Mouse cookies for Ronnie as well as for himself. Ronnie was grateful, and promised to buy the identical things for Ira when Ira caught a cold.

Thursday, August 23

Official change of address card advising me to address Jules c/o the postmaster at San Francisco. Think it must be a mistake. It just must be a mistake.

Poured all day. Let up for a while in the afternoon, but resumed as soon as Ira and I started to go out. That was better, anyhow, than having it resume a little while after we had left.

Finished *Cuchoo Time*, a zany but rather entertaining story.

Government employees are going back on a 40-hour week, and holidays are to be resumed. A job is becoming more and more attractive, and I am afraid, harder and harder to get.

Friday, August 24

Again it poured all day. Went to the store in the afternoon just to get out for a few minutes. Ira was sweet about staying at home by himself. In fact he has been remarkably sweet about being cooped up for two days with only me for company.

Jules called in the evening, and I was particularly glad to hear from him. He hopes to be home by Sunday night. It still seems too good to be true. Wish he were coming home to stay. It is going to be hard for all of us, and so difficult to explain to poor Ira.

Nate called. Helen Lee might stop off here for a couple of days. Hope she does although I don't know where we would all sleep.

Saturday, August 25

Took Ira to the doctor in the morning. He was ok. Had gained since March 10 three pounds and 1 1/2 inches, which Stein thought quite good. He should be heavier, though, I think.

The weather cleared up nicely in the afternoon. Took a chance and let Ira play with Ronnie outdoors although Ronnie was still

---

117 Anne's continuing awareness of social justice issues in her reading.

sniffling a little. Did not permit them to play together indoors.

Got a good looking steak today, but shall save it until Monday, when Jules should be here for dinner.

Claire's cousin Bernice called. Is now living here with her husband and promised to bring him out for a visit. I have owed Claire a letter for months.

Sunday, August 26
Very cool in the morning, but warmed up nicely in the course of the day.

Spent most of the morning cleaning house, in honor of Jules' homecoming.

In the afternoon we drove out to Great Falls with the Goors. Had a pleasant outing. Ronnie came over to luncheon. Ira sometimes, embarrasses me, by inviting Ronnie over when I have very little food available.[118] Borrowed a book of Dorothy Parker stories. Found them very entertaining, but finally fell asleep over them. Just as well since Jules did not get home until 4:00 in the morning. I awoke when he came in. It was worth it. His joy at being a civilian once again was very contagious.

Monday, August 27
Ira's joy at finding his daddy at home this morning was a great joy to Jules and to me. He assumes now that Jules is home to stay, and is going to find it difficult to see him depart again for Germany.

Jules takes great delight in wearing civilian clothes, and in the realization that he does not have to return to the army. The life of a G.I. is apparently a pretty miserable affair. Glad it is all over with for him.

Had saved the steak I bought on Saturday so we had a wonderful dinner tonight.

Jules called Columbus and Philadelphia. Nate was out, and called back after Jules and I were asleep. Helen Lee is there, and is coming here for a few days.

Tuesday, August 28
Downtown in the morning. Jules made some calls at the Treasury and Labor while Ira and I took care of some bank business. We met later at the Tally-Ho for luncheon, where Ira and I both behaved quite badly.

Had a light supper, consisting mainly of shrimp, of which both Jules and Ira are extremely fond.

Nate called to tell us Helen Lee was coming from Thursday to Saturday instead of Wednesday to Friday as originally planned. Complicates our plans to celebrate our anniversary Saturday night, but we can work it all out somehow. Still don't know where we are all going to sleep.

Wednesday, August 29
Jules went to Clarendon to call on the draft board and the OPA board. I cleaned house, thoroughly and strenuously, since we were having our first dinner guests in a long time.

The Goors came for dinner. I had a rib roast of beef, which turned out to be perfectly delicious. Everything else turned out very good, and we all ate a great deal. I was very

---

[118] Notice the number of references to food scarcity in recent pages.

happy that it had turned out so particularly good since I owe the Goors so many dinner invitations. The service went very smoothly too. I was, on the whole, quite proud of the entire affair. And so were Jules and Ira.

Thursday, August 30
Ira was invited to lunch at Ronnie's house with a couple of other guests, so it became a "party." Jules went downtown. Had a very successful trip. Is going back on the Labor payroll, to be borrowed by the Treasury. He will go to Germany as a lawyer, rather than in a CAF classification, and for 6 to 9 months rather than a year.

Jules came home about 5:00 with Helen Lee. We had very good broiled chicken for dinner. Nate called to make sure Helen Lee arrived all right. Took Helen Lee to the Buckingham movie. Jules stayed with Ira. Jules slept on the sofa so Helen Lee could sleep with me.

Friday, August 31
The Goors lent us their car, and we took Helen Lee, Ira and Ronnie sightseeing.[119] It was very hot, Helen Lee was much more interested in stopping as often as possible for ice cream than the sights, we had to wait to pick Charlie up at 5:30 although we were ready to come home much earlier – all in all, it was quite a bust. Anniversary gift from Mother S., $25, a very nice note from Ed. Card from Mother. Letter from Clara.

Hannah called. Got home today. Her brother is still quite ill, but is improving. Jules took Helen Lee to the Greystone for dinner. It was too late for Ira to go out to dinner, so we dined at home.

Year End Summary 1945

It is with no regret that I see this year end. I am grateful that Jules came through the war alive and well, but we have been separated so much.

Losing Louie was a bitter blow. And Mother had been the source of much unhappiness.

My career is shot to pieces, and I have not, by sacrificing it, accomplished nearly so much good for Ira as I had hoped for. He is still a poor eater; he is still too nervous and high-strung. I am sure all these faults are attributable to my attitude and actions toward him, but cannot seem to control myself. And I do try. I had no idea before all this how cruel and sadistic I can be.

But he is a happy, sunny child, and I hope that when Jules comes home to stay, and we resume a more normal family relationship and way of life, Ira will be even happier. He certainly deserves it.

It will be a happy day too when Lou gets back and Clara can resume life on an even keel.

And may our children never know what it is to go through a war either as a fighter or as a waiter for a fighter.

---

119   Ron Goor remembers that they had a 1940 Chevrolet. Car production ended in the United States in 1942 as all the factories were converted to the war effort. Car production resumed in 1946.

1945

Buckingham Apartments, 1940's

Jules and Anne

The Diaries

Part IV

1946 to 1952
Suburban Life In Silver Spring

In the late 1940's and early 1950's Anne Schlezinger and her family found stability. Anne's return to work was a psychological boost for her, and Ira was old enough to begin school. Anne and Jules were both successful professionally, and in 1948 they bought a house in Silver Spring and move into a neighborhood with a good school district. Since Anne worked full-time, she hired maids to help take care of the house, prepare food, and help with Ira. Finding reliable maids was a continuing problem. The family bought a dog, Pal, for Ira, a car for themselves, and a television set. Anne's sister Clara, and her husband Lou Roland [sometimes spelled Rowland], moved close to them. The two sisters had been roommates for years, and they visited each other frequently.

Anne and Julius' house in Silver Spring was in a quiet cul-de-sac. Their neighborhood, including the immediate neighbors, the Harlows and Grimes, was not Jewish. The Grimes' son, Tommy, became one of Ira's good friends, and they carpooled to school. There were a few Jewish families in the general area, especially the Levys, and they became close friends for the Schlezingers. Ira remembers that the neighbors were cordial, but there was not much social life between Jewish and non-Jewish families.

The Silver Spring house was a center of social life for the family for the next twenty-five years. It had two floors and a basement, where the living quarters for the maid were located. The maid had the privacy of her own entrance. (Kommy) Kaminstein and Joe Friedman (to be Julius' first law partner) continued being important friends. They continued visiting with the Goor, Pachel, and Purcell families.

As 1952 ended Eisenhower won the presidential election, bringing the first change in government in twenty years. Since Anne and Jules both worked for the federal government, that left uncertainty in their lives for several months, as the new administration took office. Given the communist scares of that time period, both Jules and Anne were required to pass loyalty reviews, and Jules eventually quit government service over this issue.

Starting in 1946 they took their first summer vacation. Later, the summer trip quickly became a highlight of the year, and initially, these vacations were driving trips, usually to one of the family hometowns. Later, they began to vacation at the beach. First, they went to the Delaware beaches, but in the 1950's and 60's they almost always went to Cape Cod and Hyannisport, which permitted Anne to also visit her family in Massachusetts.

-- Ron Duncan Hart

Diaries. 1946 Through 1952.

1946

In 1946 Jules was back with the family, which made life easier in many ways. The loneliness that Anne had felt for the past two years was over. She returned to her job with the NLRB, and once again found satisfaction in her work. Her sister Clara and husband Lou moved back to Washington from St. Louis, and the two sisters were able to renew their frequent visits.

In late August they took a vacation trip to the beach in Delaware where five year old Ira discovered the ocean and apparently enjoyed himself thoroughly with Jules. They visited Jules' brother Nate and his family in Philadelphia and saw some of the important sites in that city. -- RDH

Wednesday, May 1
Lunched at the Dragon with Jules and Kaminstein, who seemed much the same as ever. Enjoyed seeing him again after so long. To the Board on a notion in the Weissman case. Ira seems very happy to be back at school. Brought home his May Day "creations" today. Hope he is going to stay well now for a long, long time.
Owe a number of letters but never seem to be in the mood for letter writing these days.

Thursday, May 2
Lunched at the Madrillon with Mary Lou. Seemed pleasant to see her again, but we had remarkably little to talk about. Finally remembered to call Garfinckel's about having my coats picked up for storage. Have neglected it far too long this year. Hope the moths have not ruined my gray coat. The raccoon by now does not owe me a thing. John Freed called. Working in Baltimore. Coming home tomorrow with a girl friend.

Friday, May 3
Stayed downtown after work. Went to the Statler for cocktails. Later met John and his friend Sylvia and we went to the Balalaika. Had quite a good dinner, several drinks, a few dances, and a lot of fun. Home at a reasonable hour. Jules took Vera home, but not before she had expressed great displeasure at the idea of coming in on Saturdays. Then why did she agree to it when I hired her? Will my maid problems never cease?

Saturday, May 4
Rained all day. Vera and I compromised. She will not come in any more on Saturdays and I will pay her a dollar less.
Hit the jackpot – a steak, roast, and bacon – from three different stores.
Took Ira to see Pinochio. For the first time he got upset at the "sad" parts of a movie.
Jules sold some of his army clothes to a fellow going to Germany. Much rather have the $55 than the clothes.

Sunday, May 5
A pleasant day, but Ira was laid up. Coughing and sneezing again. Weekends are apparently just too much for him.

Then Silvians[1] came over for a while. Beginning to happen every Sunday. And they insist on our spending our Friday evenings together.
Called Mother S. she obviously does not approve of my working. Too bad I cannot be contented staying at home, being a wife and Mother. It would be so much better for both Jules and Ira, and probably for me also.

Monday, May 6
Jules and I lunched at S&W. First time in years. The food was good, but the crowds were discouraging.
Sent Mother S. some bath salts for Mother's Day. Will send Mother F. her usual check.[2]
Henry Lehman came home with us for dinner. We had the roast. Henry ate a fantastic quantity of food, especially meat. Apparently starved for some home cooking. We had coffee after dinner, and I was awake most of the night.

Tuesday, May 7
Oral argument in Gear Mfg. Houston and Reilly present, and it seemed quite clear they held divergent views. The coal strike is having the disastrous consequences everyone expected. Hope it is settled soon – with the miners getting a decent break.
Not so tired during the day as I had expected to be, but I was ready for bed much earlier than usual on the evening. Lillian Freireich Purcell called. She and Sid are visiting Pearl, both recuperating from illnesses.

1 Wes and Hannah Silvian with whom Anne and Jules visited frequently.
2 Anne's mother, Regina Freeling. She calls Jules' mother, Mother S.

Wednesday, May 8
Jules decided the car was using too much oil so brought it in this morning to be fixed. Had to leave it for a few days.
Lunched at the Madrillon with Jules.
Ken Robertson, who always rides with us, took his car today so we got a ride home. Fred, Bob, and Sid Reiter came over this evening. Anne was not in town. Fred was still in uniform – a colonel – although on his way out of the army. Sid is interested in working in the labor field.

Thursday, May 9
Lunched with Ralph Winkler, who is very bitter about the lousy deal servicemen have received.
Card from Mother. Card for Ira from Levins.
Jim Mann came to dinner, and it turned out to be one of the best meals any of us had ever eaten – fresh shrimp, the wonderful steak we got last Friday, done just right, and lemon meringue pie. The Rains came over later for drinks, and we all had a very pleasant visit. Jim could not get over raving over the dinner.

Friday, May 10
Had my hair done at noon at Gabriel's. Got a good shampoo and quite an attractive set, although, Jules' only comment was that I had combed my hair nicely.
Had to come to Arlington after work to pick up the car so had dinner at home. Then downtown to a movie, all the Arlington movies having been ordered closed because

of the power shortage resulting from the coal strike. Saw "The Spiral Staircase," which was quite good. Then to the Hot Shoppe. Then home.

Saturday, May 11
Ira's report cards for the last several weeks have been excellent. Hope he keeps it up. Marketed all morning but got no meat at all. Downtown in the afternoon. Got Ira some white shoes, got another small white table top radio, and got a number of needed household items. Card from Clara. She expects Lou in 2 or 3 weeks.
It is a great relief to have the coal strike settled, even temporarily. Pearl Purcell called. We are to try to go over on Tuesday.

Sunday, May 12
Called Columbus but only to talk to Joe. Jules and Ira came back from their usual walk to the corner with a lovely gardenia corsage for me. Jules also prepared and served breakfast.
Went for a ride in the afternoon and stopped to look at some houses which were for sale. Saw one we liked, but it was far too expensive for us.
Had dinner at the Hot Shoppe.
Started out a warm sunny day, but wound up pouring. The lights went out for a while. Ira bathed by candlelight to his great delight.

Monday, May 13
To the Board again on American Gear, but were merely told again it was being put off for another oral argument. What a waste of time, particularly when the chances are about 1000 to 1 that the Board will merely sustain the Trial Examiner, I go to the contrary notwithstanding.[3]
The truce on the coal strike is encouraging. Hope it gets settled, with the miners getting a decent break in the settlement. Just about that time, I suppose, the railroads will be on strike.

Tuesday, May 14
Neglected to take an umbrella to work today. Got caught in the rain on the way back from luncheon. After work Jules and I got our signals mixed, and I had to come home on the bus. Jules admitted later it was all his fault, but that did not keep me dry.
In the evening to visit the Purcells – Pearl, Morris, Lillian and Sid. Had a pleasant-enough visit although I still find Lillian a terrible bore. Pearl is entirely out of her class. Morris seemed nice too.

Wednesday, May 15
Have been waiting a week now to report Weissman to Gene. We were to get at it today but he was out all day. Heard he had lost his father, and would be out for a couple of days.
Managed to get a few bananas and some pineapple juice at noon today. And Vera got a chuck toast. Have used no bread for two days, our little contribution to the wheat famine. But we live so well compared to so many people that whatever we can contribute is too little.

3   As a lawyer in the Review Division, Anne's job was to review and comment on the decisions of the Trial Examiners (i.e. Judges) who heard the cases.

1946

Thursday, May 16
Card form Mother thanking me for the Mother's Day gift. She sounded almost cheerful. Letter from Sam Wagshal inviting us to Bobby's bar mitzvah in July.

Jules and I stayed downtown. Had an excellent dinner at Hogate's. Then to the AVC forum, when Benton, Shirer, Warburg and someone from Poland presented a very interesting discussion about State Dept. short-wave news broadcasts. Afterwards for a coke with Bill Wise.

Ira had Ronnie to dinner. Gather they had a fine time.

Friday, May 17
Card from Clara. She expects Lou Monday or Tuesday. Called Arnold again, but he says he is doing all he can.

Jules' papers are being processed at APC for a P-7 job. He is very happy at the prospect of getting a P-7 and of leaving Labor. We celebrated with a very good luncheon at Olmstead's.

Vera is going to Lynchburg for the weekend to see her Mother. With the threatened railroad strike and what-not, I wonder if she will get back in time for work on Monday.

Saturday, May 18
Marketed all morning but go no meat or anything else to justify our time and trouble.

Ira was very mischievous and I was very cranky so we both had a very disagreeable time. In the evening the Morris Purcells, the Sid Purcells and Papa Purcell came over. Lillian and Sid [Purcell] are going back to Cleveland tomorrow and Papa Purcell to Allentown. The railroad strike had been postponed for a few days.

Sunday, May 19
A lovely day. We went for a walk in the morning, Ronnie coming along with us. We went for a ride, plus Ronnie again, in the afternoon. For a swan-boat ride around the basin. The children were thrilled with it. Saw part of the jet plane demonstration, another thrill for the two boys.

Spent the rest of the afternoon resting in the backyard. Acquired a large collection of detective stories from Edith. Don't know when I shall find the time to read them. Mother S. called, pleased with her gift.

Monday, May 20
Learned in the course of the afternoon that Vera had not shown up. Ira was with the Goors, and not at all disturbed, but it was extremely annoying.

Planned to eat out, but when we got home Ira was so completely dirty that we had to eat at home. Managed to scare together enough food for a rather good dinner.

Ran into Ed Teple on the street, and Claire Edes called; both are here for a Federal Security conference.

Tuesday, May 21
Vera called this morning. Not able to get back yesterday because the buses had been too crowded. Maybe. But what can I do? Quit my job I suppose.

Lucky enough to get a chuck roast at noon. Meat is very hard to get. So is bread, and several other important items.

Libbin decided I would skip reporting the Weissman case; let him look over the memo. And then shoot the case along to the Board. That suits me fine.

Wednesday, May 22
Lunched with Jules at the Dragon. Not busy so took the time to do a few errands. Finished my memo in Weissman, Libbin read and approved it in a few minutes, and it is being prepared for circulation to the Board. With Thorrens it would have taken several days and much haggling over minutiae. Thorrens got back today but I did not submit the memo to him.

The Edes, The Teples, and Carl Bullock came over. We had a very enjoyable visit except that everyone stayed far too late.

Thursday, May 23
Lunched at the Candlestick with Henry Lehman. Arnold told me Clara's application had been put on top. Wrote her about it but doubt if she will get the letter since the railroads have gone on strike. That is going to be calamitous if it lasts any time at all. Have no work to do. Just reading cases.

The Purcells stopped over in the evening with some steak and Crisco [that] Pearl had bought for me. A mighty nice thing for her to do. They stayed for refreshments but left at a reasonable hour.

Friday, May 24
Jules had rather a bad cold but does not like to stay at home with Vera only to keep him company.

Lunched at the Tally-Ho Garden with Grace MacEldowney and Irene Shriber. Downtown to pick up a few things for Ira. Jules and I went to the Trans-Lux after work. Then met the Reins at Treasure Island for dinner and dancing. We all enjoyed it, but left rather early since Jules was obviously not feeling well. Vera offered to go home by bus but Jules insisted on taking her.

Saturday, May 25
A very warm day. We went marketing with fairly good results. Spent much of the day in the backyard so Jules could sun-bathe.

Supposed to go to the Liftins' in the evening. Jules did not feel like going but agreed I should anyhow, so I went with the Goors. She had several couples, and plenty to eat and drink. Mort plied me with liquor and I am afraid I drank too much and "shot off my mouth" about my disgust with Truman's speech today re drafting strikers.

Sunday, May 26
Was miserably sick. Am going to swear off liquor for a while. And poor Jules with his cold. Rained most of the day. Ira visited with Ronnie for quite a while, which was a big help.

Telephoned Philadelphia. Nate was out but talked to Bobby. Nate is feeling much better.

Perked up a little in the evening. At least I was able to sit up and take some nourishment. Ira broke one of my necklaces while I was a-bed.

1946

Monday, May 27
Jules stayed home today to nurse his cold. To the beauty parlor at noon. Ira went to Ronnie's birthday party. Jeanette picked Ira up at school so he could attend. Gather that Ronnie was very pleased with the camera we gave him.
Letter from Clara. Lou is back. They are very happy to be together again, and hoping to have an apartment down here soon.
Got a new case – Reynolds Pen.
Came home early since I knew Jules would be bored. Worked in the evening for a while.

Tuesday, May 28
Jules stayed at home again today. Turned out to be a cold rainy day, and I was dressed most inadequately for it. It finally stopped raining in the late afternoon, so Jules and Ira came down and took me home.
Ira looks particularly well these days, and feels so wonderfully that he just effervesces all the time. It makes one feel good just to look at him, although he can be very wearing when taken in large doses. Poor Jules would so like another child, but I cannot see it.

Wednesday, May 29
A pleasantly cool sunny day. Jules went to work – too bored to stay home any longer. Bet Vera was glad to have him out from under foot. His cold has not been cured yet, however, although he is doctoring it very conscientiously with a variety of remedies.
Vera had expected to work tomorrow, and was very pleasantly surprised when I told her she could have the holiday off.
I find the thought of the holiday depressing. Reminds me too much of poor Louie.

Thursday, May 30
A warm sunny day. Spent much of the day sunning ourselves in the backyard, which should help Jules greatly in getting rid of his cold.
In the late afternoon we drove to the airport. Would have had dinner there but were excluded from the dining room because Jules was not wearing a coat. Had dinner instead at Howard Johnson's in Alexandria. It was not very good. Louie used to like to eat at Howard Johnson's in Lawrence.[4]

Friday, May 31
My office roommate, Paul Bisgyer, left this morning for a 60 day assignment in Philadelphia. A great many people were on holiday. The office seemed deserted.
Lunched with Jules at Allies' Inn. Got circus tickets for Saturday afternoon. After work to the movies to see "The Seventh Veil" – quite good. Then to Mrs. K's for an excellent dinner, although we arrived just too late for the wonderful steaks everyone else seemed to be eating. Ira went to Lou's birthday party this afternoon – apparently had a wonderful time.

Jules, Ira, and Mother Schlezinger

---
4   Anne's brother Louie who died in WW II.

Year End Summary 1946

This was a good year since it brought Jules home again and restored our family life to something like normalcy. It also brought Clara and her family back where we can see them occasionally. But there have to be a few dark clouds. They are Louie's failure to come home from the war, and Mother's constant misery. Even though Louie and I drifted so far apart, we were for many years very close to each other. The though of what might have happened to him is a constant dull ache of the heart.

And ever present is the problem of Mother, whether due to pity or conscience. I do not feel that I owe her the unhappiness that I know would result if I tried to live with her. Yet I know what horrors of sorrow and loneliness must be her constant companions these days. And there is Father too, who has acted badly, but is not entirely at fault for the eternal mess that our family life had always been.

I am glad to be back at work since I am more contented while working than when staying at home. Maybe Jules and Ira would be happier if I stayed home, but I doubt whether it would make much difference to either one of them.

Ira seems a normal, healthy, happy, affectionate child, for which I am deeply grateful.

1947

Anne was still hoping for another child, but she was busy with work, marriage, mothering, and running the household. She received a promotion on her job, which was encouraging. They began looking at houses in Silver Spring with plans to move from the Buckingham Apartments where they had lived since they were married. On September 1, the day of their eighth anniversary they signed a contract to buy a wooden lot and began construction on a house that included "the works", extra bathroom, den, and maid's room. Anne's entries comment on life at the office and the cases on which she was working. --RDH

Friday, May 16
Jules has been given the title of Acting Assistant General Counsel, which makes up, but only partly, for the shabby way the office has treated him recently.
Lunched with Fanny at the Candlestick.
To the movies after work. Saw "Brief Encounter," which we liked very much. Then to Hogate's, where we had a very good dinner. Took a walk after dinner along the waterfront.
Ira had dinner this evening with the Goors. Charlie was working late so Jeanette could handle both Ronnie and Ira. Ira apparently ate more, and better, than Ronnie did. He is eating well these days. Hope he continues.

Saturday, May 17
Jules went to the office in the morning. Ira

enjoyed having the whole morning to play outdoors with Ronnie, and I had a lazy pleasant morning devoted largely to the newspaper and a bath. After Jules came home we went to do our marketing.

It began to rain in the afternoon so we went to the movies. Saw a pretty good Blondie and Dagwood picture. Ira loved it, especially Daisy and her pups.

Got some delicatessen for supper. At this rate I shall soon forget whatever I have learned of cooking. Even if I were willing, Jules does not want me spending weekends in the kitchen.

Sunday, May 18

Ira's Sunday School term ended today. Jules was the carpool driver.

In the afternoon we went for a ride along the Mt. Vernon Highway. Parked along the highway and went for a walk in the woods. It was pleasant, but too damp to spend much time there. Discovered a new place where we can get prepared chicken boxes, closer than any of the others, and the chicken seemed much better. We were delighted with our discovery.

Telephoned Columbus. Helen Lee is being confirmed and Joe is getting married on Sunday, June 1. We shall have to miss those occasions, but hope to attend Ellen's wedding on June 15th.

Monday, May 19

Lunched with Margaret Farmer at the Candlestick. She is a nice enough person, and obviously wants to be friends, but I find her so dull.

Letter from Sam[5] urging us to come over May 30th, as I had indicated we might. We probably shall go although it will mean Ira would miss Ronnie's birthday party and his Sunday School picnic. There will be many compensations, though.

Letter from Mother. She is sending some things I am to give Baba, and including some things for me. I have asked her so many times not to do so as she should not waste her money and I never like the things she sends.

Tuesday, May 20

Lunched with Irene at Tally-Ho. Then scooted downtown and bought a pair of white shoes. They were $18.75, not worth it, but there is a limit to the extent to which I can fight inflation by not buying.

Ira had been falling asleep later since the nights became warm. He does not seem sleepy during the day, but it just does not seem that he can not be getting enough sleep at this rate.

Theodosia got our slip covers on today. They looked cool and fresh, although they are somewhat the worse for wear. Ira was very pleased with them. He enjoys a change very much, and is very home-conscious.

Wednesday, May 21

Now that I have some white shoes I can begin wearing my cotton dresses, although they are all a wee bit tight, and quite a bit short by present standards. I have lost a little

---

5   Sam Wagshal, Anne's cousin, inviting them for Memorial Day.

weight since the weather got warmer, but am still much too heavy. Wish I could really diet, but I have such a big appetite.

Card from Mother. It seems pretty definite that she will have to retire from her job, and then move out here pronto. That seems the obvious and sensible thing for her to do, but I cannot say that I am looking forward to it particularly. I know she will become my responsibility – entirely.

Thursday, May 22
We have to take off next Thursday or Monday without pay. That is all right with me. But a government that can send millions to arm other countries should be able to pay its servants.

Lunched with Irene Shriber at the Chicken Hut. She seems to be getting more and more sour on life.

Long letter from Helen Lee. She is leaving in a few days for Columbus, and can hardly wait to get there. She is to be a bridesmaid at Ellen May's wedding.

The package from Mother arrived. Doubt whether I shall be able to use many of the things she sent me. Will keep a few and send back the rest.

Friday, May 23
Lunched in the Tally-Ho garden with Marcia Hertgmach. She "let her hair down" a little, and is apparently not nearly so contented with her lot in life as appears in a casual meeting.

We went to a movie after work. Then had a wonderful steak dinner at Fan and Bill's. Had to go for a walk after dinner, we both had eaten so much.

Ira had Ronnie come to dinner. Gathered from Theodosia they had a fine time. Ira hardly seems to miss us on Fridays. He is a pretty self-sufficient little guy. And that, I think, is going to stand him in good stead.

Saturday, May 24
Downtown in the morning. Jules went to the office while Ira and I went shopping – after we all had an excellent breakfast at Ceres.

Went marketing in the afternoon at Shirlington. Stopped in to see Clara. Her baby may arrive almost any day now, probably in about a week.

It was very warm, so in the late afternoon we went to a movie. The picture we saw was dull, but at least we were all cool. Then home for a very good delicatessen supper. Ira got to bed quite late, but he had enjoyed his day, and his evening, so much it was with the loss of a little sleep for him.

Sunday, May 25
Rained quite hard in the morning. When it cleared up Ira went outdoors in the wet grass until his shoes got soaking wet even though he was wearing rubbers.

He refused to go anywhere in the afternoon. Did not want to wear his old shoes or to break away from his erector-set project. We finally left him at home and drove to Baba's to give her the things Mother had sent for her. She was delighted to see Jules and me again, although she cannot remember altogether who we are, and was thrilled with her gifts. Telephoned Philadelphia to let them know we might be along next week.

1947

Monday, May 26
Downtown at noon. Did several errands. So much to do to get ready for our trip. So many gifts to buy I don't know where to begin.
Card from Mother. She has only two more weeks on her job, and is heart-broken to lose it. Paul Bisgyer had a baby son yesterday.
Marcia came home with me for dinner. She brought Ira some candy. Theodosia fixed roast chicken and a very good dinner. Later we went downtown to see the movie of "The Egg and I," which we all found quite amusing. Theodosia stayed with Ira as she is getting some time off at the end of the week. She takes plenty of time off anyhow, one way or another.

Tuesday, May 27
Had quite a bad headache in the morning, so decided to stay home. Spent most of the morning in bed. Got up about noon, showered and dressed, and drank some tea. Then out in the backyard for the afternoon, largely in order not to be under-foot for Theodosia. After an afternoon devoted to the neighbors and their babies, I realize anew how much more fun working is.
Jules had to work tonight so he stayed downtown for dinner. Ira sat at Jules' place, and had a wonderful time being "Mr. Schlezinger." Theodosia and I played along with him. He was most amusing.

Wednesday, May 28
Back to work. I had been scheduled for the "little agenda" for 10 yesterday morning. Jules phoned at 11:30. Meanwhile the building had been torn apart searching for me by Norman.
To the beauty parlor at noon. Jules had to stay downtown for a farewell party for Cook, the departing director. I had a miserable, hot, jam-packed ride on the bus. Everyone at the Board had been miserable over the latest report that Congress would abolish the Board. Then I got a card from Mother, giving me hell for giving Baba the purse she had intended for me, and being generally nasty. That was too much, after I had told her so many times not to send me anything, and I wrote and told her so. I am fed up with her.

Thursday, May 29
Everyone at the Board had to take a payless day to make up for a budget deficit so I took mine today. Card from Mother to the same effect as the one yesterday. Nuts!
Met Jules at the Hot Shoppe for luncheon. Picked up Ira at school and drove to Philadelphia. Had a flat tire on the way, in an out-of-the way spot, and had no tools, but finally got it changed. Then ran into a cloudburst, so did not arrive at Bobby's until about 8:00. Had a very good warmed-over dinner. The kids had a very exciting time with each other and with the things we brought them. Jules, who had been very tense from the strain of his job, was, by evening, completely relaxed. That alone makes the trip worthwhile.

Friday, May 30
A lovely day, sunny but with a pleasant cool breeze.
We had a delicious breakfast, and left almost immediately afterwards. Had a delightful

trip. Lunched at a Howard Johnson place. Ira saw the Pulaski Subway, the Holland Tunnel, the big ships at the wharves including the Mauretania, the big buildings including the Empire State, the George Washington bridge, and finally, Nyach and the Wagshals. He and Bobby hit it off beautifully. Bobby took him in tow, and we hardly saw either of them for the rest of the afternoon.

Had an excellent dinner at a rustic restaurant called Jerry's place. We occupied Bobby's room. Bobby and Ira, to the latter's great delight, shared the guest room. The Wagshals were all delighted with Ira.

Saturday, May 31
Another perfectly lovely day. Ira went off with Bobby and his gang for the entire morning. We bought some gifts at the store and Sam gave us some things for Ira and Joyce.
We left about noon, by the "back road." Made good time, and had a beautiful trip.
Bobby's maid fixed a super chicken dinner. Everyone was astonished at the quantity of food Jules ate.
We started out for a movie after the children were in bed, but missed the train, could not make other satisfactory connections, and finally wound up at a local ice-cream parlor. But we were all feeling rather giddy and a lot a fun anyhow, and got to bed at a decent hour.

Sunday, June 1
Another lovely day, although a bit warmer. Went out the golf course with Nate in the morning. He lost several balls, so our birthday gift of 6 balls came in handy. Left about noon. Stopped to see the Pachels. Had a pleasant trip, although we ran into quite a bit of traffic, and Ira was becoming rather travel-weary.
Picked up some delicatessen and had supper at home.
Think Ira enjoyed the trip tremendously, but also that he was rather glad to get home. So was I.
Another card from Mother. Printed card from May and Jerry thanking us for our expressions of sympathy. Bill from Gude's. Jules paid $7.50 for my Mother's Day plant, my idea of real extravagance.

Monday, June 2
Today was the alternate payless day. The office was pretty well deserted. Suspect a good many took both days off.
Sent Bobby Wagshal a woolen shirt in a handsome plaid. Hope it fits and that he likes it.
Jules came home for dinner, but went back to the office right after dinner.
The Purcells dropped in for the first time in a long while. Brought us some bananas, which we were very glad to have although they were rather expensive. Jules got home just as they were leaving. According to Ira's weekly report from 1-C, he still eats too slowly, but reads well, and needs practice in his number work. I think he is doing very well despite the school.

Tuesday, June 3
Oral argument this morning in the Geraldine Novelty case. Lunched at the Dragon with Frances Steyer.

Sent Helen Lee an overnight bag for a confirmation gift. Still have several gifts to buy. Jules came home for dinner, but quite late, after Theodosia left. He worked at home most of the evening. I used to think he lacked ambition but now he seems to have almost too much of it.

Card from Mother bewailing the loss of her job, promising all sorts of presents for Baba, and not saying a word about the recent explosion. I am still fed up with her though, and am not going to let my justifiable annoyance be too readily overcome by sympathy, as is usually the case.

Wednesday, June 4

Lunched at S&W with Frances Steyer and Eleanor Schwartzbach.

On the agenda for Geraldine Novelty. Had a little run-in with Reynolds, which had become the usual procedure when we get together.

Stayed downtown this evening as we have to go to Ira's operetta on Friday. I had come to work without a coat and it was quite cool, so Eleanor insisted I borrow hers as she was going directly home, which was generous of her.

We saw "The Well-Digger's Daughter," an amazing French picture at the Little. Then had a very good dinner at the Neptune Room.

Thursday, June 5

Lunched at the Candlestick with Irene. I find her pretty dull company but cannot always turn her down.

Theodosia fixed a very elaborate "company" dinner because we thought Pachel, who was in town for the Law Institute meeting, was coming here, but at the last minute he decided to go to his sister-in-law's instead. Jules went back to the office after dinner. Nice break for Theodosia as it means a ride home for her instead of two or three bus transfers.

Card from Mother reminding me that she does not even write to Jean or Clara but depends entirely on me; an honor I should like to forego after all these years.

Friday, June 6

Lunched at Tally-Ho with Irene and Grace. Peg Patterson, formally of the NLRB and now Judge Madden's law clerk, came in alone and joined us.

Hurried through dinner. Left Ira at the school at 7:00. We went to the Sylvan Theater at 8:30. But at 8:30 there was a terrific rain and hail storm. After it stopped there was considerable uncertainty about whether or not to proceed with the show. It was finally decided to go. It went off quite well in spite of the wet stage and the wet seats and the muddy ground. The children all seemed amazingly bright and wide-awake considering the lateness of the hour. Ira did not get to bed until about midnight.

Saturday, June 7

Jules went to the office in the morning. Ira slept until about noon, but then got up feeling wonderful. Lunched at the Hot Shoppe. Spent most of the afternoon shopping for a pair of sandals for Ira. Finally found them at our old stand-by Turner's. Sent Howard a pair of white pants for his birthday.

Picked up some delicatessen for supper. Shall certainly forget what little I knew about cooking at this rate. Poured most of the evening. Just as well they got the operetta over with last night.

Clara telephoned. She is going to the hospital on Monday according to her doctor's latest prediction.[6]

Sunday, June 8

Went to the Carleton for a delicious breakfast, plenty to eat, excellent service – "the works." Ira ate a wonderful meal.

In the afternoon Ira and I went to a movie while Jules worked at home. Visited the Rains for a while until we got tired of exclaiming over their wonderful baby.

Picked up some chicken and shrimp for a very good dinner.

Jules worked some more in the evening. I lengthened one of my dresses. They all need it, what with the style for longer dresses and my increased size. I really should start some serious dieting. Am ashamed of my figure.

Monday, June 9

Farewell luncheon for Marcia at the Carleton by Melvern Krelow, Eleanor Schwatzbach and myself.

Completed my Federal Mogul memo and Geraldine decision. Refused to take a new case until some of the old stuff on my desk is disposed of.

---

6   Anne's sister Clara who was pregnant.

Jules went back to the office after dinner. Lou called me to let me know that Clara had a son at about 9:00 this evening, a big boy, Stephen Phillip, and both were getting along fine. Glad for them the suspense is over. Nice too that it is a boy since they already have a girl. The news, of course, has caused Jules to renew his plea for another child, but it does not seem to best to me.

Tuesday, June 10

Catching up with my reading of *Labor Relations Reporters*,[7] etc., until Bob finishes going over the work I have turned in to him. Got an excellent on the annual efficiency rating.

Lunched with Fannie at the S & W. Thought I had been dieting, but nevertheless had gained a little. I should diet more strictly because I am too heavy for comfort or good looks. Sent Clara a baby blanket. Card from Mother, all set to move to Washington.

Jerry Wagshal called. Mother had written to ask if she could stay there while she looked for a place but they have no room for her. She will, of course, wind up here.

Wednesday, June 11

Terribly warm, somewhere in the 90's. Lunched with Irene. Should have done some shopping, but it was too warm.

Got into a heated argument with Newman and Fuchs about writing the Reynolds decision. I lost.

Jules may not be able to get away next week.

7   *Labor Relations Reporter* is a publication that summarizes decisions on labor law at the Federal and State levels. Currently produced by the Bureau of National Affairs.

What with one thing and another, we went to the Willard after work and got delightfully tight. Then to see a movie. Had dinner at the Occidental. Got home quite late but Theodosia did not seem to mind too much. She will not stay Friday and may get all next week off.

A very warm night but I was still slightly tight and had no difficultly in falling asleep.

Thursday, June 12
Augusta, Irene, Grace and I took Eleanor to the Carleton Grill for luncheon in honor of her birthday. Really meant to do a lot of work on Reynolds today, but as occasionally happens, I had almost a steady stream of visitors all day. Ira received his final report card today, marked down from "outstanding" to "average" in the major subjects, and promoted to 2A upon condition that he does supplemental work in reading and arithmetic. Convinced it is a low-down trick to assure his going back to Congressional [i.e. school], but it certainly will not work.

A very hot night. Between that and my anger at Congressional, I did not get much sleep.

Friday, June 13
Downtown at noon. Got Jules a cotton bathrobe for Father's Day. Cooler, thank heavens, but pouring by 5:00. Got a ride home with Dan Sachs, who even waited while I picked up a dress at the cleaner's, and then took me right to my door. Ira and I had dinner, then Theodosia and her husband, and then Jules, who got home quite late, very tired – but we are going.

He had gone to see Miss Meehl at the school and told her a thing or two. She is supposed to mail us a proper report card. Remains to be seen. They are completely untrustworthy. Announcement from Clara and Lou. Ed Rains came over to visit.

Got pretty completely packed tonight so we can leave fairly early tomorrow morning.

Saturday, June 14
Breakfasted at home and left about 8:00.
Rained practically all the way, but it was nevertheless a pleasant trip, and in many spots, a beautiful one. Ira traveled like an old hand at the game.

Lunched at The Chimney Corner, Red House, Maryland.

Made the trip in 11 hours, quite a stunt for our little old Ford. Dinner at Mother's.

After Ira was asleep we went to a party at Gertrude's given for the bridal party. It was a large, elaborate, and lovely party. Met the prospective bridegroom and some of his family, all very attractive people. Met Miriam, Joe's war bride from Czecho-Slovkia. She is a plump, pleasant, attractive girl despite her horrible concentration camp experiences.

Sunday, June 15
Ellen Day was married at the Temple at 4:30. It was the most beautiful wedding I have ever attended. The Temple was jammed. After the ceremony there was a sumptuous chicken dinner for about 300 guests at the Temple. Home then to put the children to bed.

Later to a reception at the Seneca Hotel. Well over a thousand people there, a dance band, and plenty of refreshments. When the

Schlezinger's throw a wedding, they really do things up brown. It was the first wedding Ira had attended. I think he enjoyed it very much.

He has lost an upper front tooth, and looks very cute and funny whenever he smiles, which is most of the time.

Ira and Baba

Anne's mother, Regina, on left, Grandmother Baba in center, Anne on right, and Ira in front.

Year End Summary 1947

Well, 1947 has been a pretty good year, everything considered. We have had good health, for which I am always grateful. We got started on what I hope will eventually be our lovely new home. And Ira, so far, has "made the grade" in grade school. Jules and I were both reclassified on our jobs, Jules' reclassification carrying with it a substantial increase in salary. And I have virtually been promised another reclassification, one which will also be accompanied by a generous increase in salary.

One big disappointment had been our inability to get another child, or even any slight encouragement as to our prospects.

But maybe 1948 will be an even better year, will bring us another child, will see us settled in our new home, will permit Ira to attend a fine school, will continue Jules' success in his work, and will raise me to a P-6 classification at the office.

Another of Ira's accomplishments had been his good work at Sunday School, including making a start at learning Hebrew.

Best of all is his increase in height, weight, and robustness. He is huskier, and healthier looking now than he has been for several years.

1948

In 1948 Anne, Jules, and Ira moved from the Buckingham Apartments in Arlington where they had lived since they were married nine years earlier. They moved to a house in Silver Spring, which was to be their house for the next twenty-five years. The Goors had been their close friends during the time. Ronnie Goor had been Ira's primary playmate since they were old enough to play. They were seven years old at this point and would continue to see each other on occasion. Anne was promoted to supervisory status at the NLRB, something for which she had been waiting. -- RDH

Thursday, April 15
Lunched at the Maxwell House with Frances Steyer. Did a couple of errands. Got Jules a new billfold he needed badly. Frances is working for Lou Roland now – says she likes him very much.
Conference with Merv and Gromfine on one of the latter's cases. Apparently Merv did not like the way I had revised it at all.
My work has piled up pretty badly again. Should probably have worked this evening, but by the time Ira had gone to bed I was tired and not in the mood for work.
Maybe we should fix up the extra room in the house as a den for me.

Friday, April 16
On the Board agenda with Gromfine.
To the dentists' at noon to have my new fillings polished. Took only a few minutes,

Anne was happy. Jules was back from the Army; Ira was healthy and growing; and, she was back at the NLRB.

but Bogdonoff was running behind schedule so I had to wait for about a half-hour before he got to me.

Decided to have dinner before going to a movie, but several places we stopped at were already crowded and had long waiting lines, so we finally wound up at a little Chinese restaurant. Then to see "Naked City," quite a good murder picture. Had ice cream sodas after the movie. And with all that, we were home by about 10:00. We are spoiling Irene for staying late should the occasion ever arise. Wonder if we shall have a live-in when we move.

Saturday, April 17
Managed to get to Silver Spring before 9:00. The painting is just about completed, and looks very attractive. The light fixtures look well too, although a couple of them were put in the wrong places and a couple were the wrong ones.

Did some shopping – got some clothes for Ira – and our marketing.

In the evening we got a sitter from Arlington Hall, and went to the Herb Davids'. The Vernons, the Gangs,[8] and the Fishers – all new people to me – were also there, an interesting group and we had a very pleasant evening. Message from the painter to come out to see the final results.

Sunday, April 18
To Sunday School for the model Seder.
Telephoned Columbus. Broke the sad news that we were not coming to Columbus for the Seder weekend.

[8] Arthur and Florence Gang were Silver Spring neighbors, friends, and members of the close-knit Sunday Night Book Club.

To the Home for the Aged to give Baba[9] the $10 Mother sent. Her mind is failing badly. She does not recognize people, and lives in the remote past.

Out to Silver Spring, where we met the Rolands.[10] They liked the house. Some of the paint colors are not exactly what we had in mind, but are quite close. Probably should have stayed around yesterday.

Ira got his Sunday School report card – a very good one. Wonder how he will do on his grade school report card from his new teacher.

Monday, April 19
Downtown at noon to get another slip in exchange for the one Clara sent me.

Lunched at the Candlestick with Grace MacEldowney.

Merv explained to me how the Board was going to speed up cases by, among other things, cutting memos down by discussing vital issues only. I had the satisfaction of reminding him that that was inconsistent with the changes he had suggested last week in Gromfine's case.

Stopped at Fine's on the way home to get some Passover foods. Was in the middle of writing a letter home when Mother and Father knocked at the door. They had come by bus from New York. Father looked very well. They seem to be getting along fine.

Tuesday, April 20
Mother and Father got up and had breakfast with us. They went over to Clara's later to spend the day.

[9] Anne's maternal grandmother.
[10] Anne's sister Clara and her husband Lou.

On the panel agenda with Gene Threadgill. One of the things we bought at Fine's yesterday was a roast, which we had for dinner tonight. It was delicious. We all ate a great deal. The folks seemed to enjoy everything very much.

Letter from Helen Lee. Note from Sam enclosing the snapshots Bobby took. They were too dark to be any good.

Jules' turn to have the poker game here tomorrow, but he called it off because of the folks being here.

Did not do anything this evening but sit around and visit.

Wednesday, April 21
Mother and Father came downtown about noon, and we went to the Madrillon for luncheon. They seemed to enjoy it. Father insisted on paying the check. Later they cabbed out to Sam's, then to see Baba, and then back to Sam's. They had dinner at Sam's. We drove over after dinner to get them. Sam was still gloating over his Supreme Court victory against the Bakery Drivers Union. The folks bought Ira a very handsome white palm beach suit at Garfinckel's.

We drove home, put Ira to bed, and, after he was asleep, took the folks to Clara's. She has better sleeping facilities for the two folks; so they will stay there for a while.

Income tax refund for me of $38.

Thursday, April 22
Lunched at the Dragon with Irene Shriber. Took the time to do a couple of errands although I was extremely busy at the office. Talked to Mother on the telephone in the evening. She and Father had been downtown today, but did not call me because they did not want to bother me at the office. Too bad, as I could have suggested some points of interest for them to see. As it was, they merely walked around downtown. In any event, Father is apparently sold on Washington, and he and Mother are pretty definitely planning to move here as soon as all their property has been disposed of. Father seems so changed, in character, not in appearance, that it is hard to believe. Too bad it could not have happened many years ago.

Friday, April 23
To the beauty parlor in the morning. Mother and Father spent the day at Sam's and visiting Baba. They came to the office about 5:00, and we took a cab to Jules' office. When Jules was able to get away, we went for a ride. Wound up near Silver Spring so stopped at the house although it was beginning to grow dark. They liked it very much. Father was favorably impressed by some of the structural details, about which his experience makes him far more expert than we are.

Then to Balalaika. Had a fairly good dinner, a fairly good time. Had a few drinks, which ran our bill up outrageously. The folks stayed with us tonight, Jules sleeping on the floor so as not to disturb Ira.

Saturday, April 24
Mother and Father decided to forego going out to the house again, but to go instead to May's for luncheon with the Rolands. We

dropped them at Clara's after breakfast, and made our farewells.

Looks like we shall move into the house on about June 15.

Lunched at Hecht's.

Then downtown to see the movie "Sitting Pretty," which we all found very entertaining.

Went through some of the motions of a Seder dinner for Ira's benefit. It meant enough to him that he even gave up his Saturday night radio programs without a protest.

Did not hear from Mother and Father, so assume they left tonight as planned. Wonder if they will move here.

Sunday, April 25

No Sunday School today because of the holiday. A pleasant warm day.

We sat in the backyard in the morning reading the newspaper.

In the afternoon we went for a ride. Stopped near the canal. Went for a walk along the towpath. Sat there for a while, just being lazy. Ira finally got bored, so we went home. Took a tub bath in the evening. Read a detective story while I soaked in the tub. Very relaxing. Could not do that while Ira was awake as he would inevitably want to do likewise, which would be the end, no doubt, of many of his books.

Monday, April 26

Downtown at noon to return the white suit Ira received from Mother. Garfinckel's will call when the colored ones come in. Ira and white Palm Beach just are not a good combination. Bought myself a seersucker suit. Jules did not like it, so I shall have that to return tomorrow.

Ira received his report card, exactly the same as his last one. Suspect Mrs. Stoner merely copied his last grades. We are handicapped in helping him at home since he no longer brings home graded papers. In any event, it is clear that he will be promoted in June to the third grade. After that, it is up to the Parkside School. I hope it does more for him than the Kate Weller Barrett School has.

Tuesday, April 27

To Garfinckels' to return the seersucker suit. Met Irene Shriber there, so we lunched and shopped together, but I did not find anything in my size that I liked well enough to buy.

An invitation to a White House garden party on May 4th. Rate it now that I am a P-6. Used to go from P-1 on up, but the requirements were changed last year.

Claire Edes, in town for her annual regional conference, came over to spend the evening. She looks very well, and is her usual energetic self. Duffy is apparently doing very well in private practice. It was good to see her again, and to talk about our mutual friends.

Wednesday, April 28

A rainy day. On the Board agenda on a petition to rehear Pullman-Standard. Denied.

Lunched with Jules and Arthur Gang at Rubin's so we could have some suitable Passover food. It was fairly good, but I have eaten better Jewish food. It was a change from the usual routine, however.

Irene has lost her purse. She did not mind too much about the money, what little there was in it, but was anxious to get back the other things, particularly her social security card.

The Jews are achieving remarkable military success in Palestine, to the obvious chagrin of the British.

Thursday, April 29
Lunched at the Trans-Lux Restaurant with Irene Shriber. Then downtown for a little while, but did not buy anything.

Duffy Edes came to town today, and stopped in at the office to see me. He is still very enthusiastic about the advantages of private practice over government employment.

Drove over to Shirlington in the evening to pick up some clothes at the cleaners, and for the ride.

A set of sketches of scenes in the Philippines from Ira Rubin, rather interesting and attractive – a very thoughtful thing for him to do. Wonder how the Silvians are getting along there.

Friday, April 30
To Ogilire's in the morning for a scalp treatment.

Lunched at the Candlestick with Grace MacEldowney. Bought a birthday gift for Anthony Ruche at the Play Center.

Very busy in the afternoon. Glad of the extra time when Jules was late in picking me up.

We went to a movie, and then to Ted Lewis' for a rather good dinner, assisted by a couple of cocktails. We have not been doing much of any drinking lately, since we have both become concerned about our weight, but do break down once in a while.

Wonder if we shall continue our Friday night outings after we move, or if we shall be too "broke" for such splurges.

Saturday, May 1
Stopped at the Buckingham office to give tentative notice that we might move June 15th. Then picked up the Edes and took them out to see the house. Took them downtown, had a quick luncheon at a Howard Johnson, and then to Anthony Ruche's birthday party. They took the whole crowd – 20 children and a number of adults – to Glen Echo [Park]. It was a drizzly sort of day, but the children had a good time anyhow. Back to the house for ice cream and cake. I had gone for a ride in the "tub" in the fun house, and had to skip the refreshments. Did our marketing on the way home.

We were all pretty tired by evening.

Sunday, May 2
Not Jules' turn to drive, so we had a pleasant, leisurely brunch, and read the paper in peace until Ira got home.

After Ira's luncheon we went for a ride. Rented a boy's bike at Hains Point and Jules tried to teach Ira to ride a two-wheeler. Ira, I must admit, was not a very apt pupil.

Later we went to a movie, since it was beginning to rain again. Went to the Virginia, near Alexandria. Afterwards we went to the Red Lobster near there for dinner. The food was perfectly delicious, and Ira ate a tremendous meal. We got more satisfaction out of seeing that than out of our own dinners, good as they were. Ira is doing very well, but I should like him to be a bit heavier.

Monday, May 3
Ran into Ann David at Garfinckel's, so we shopped together for a while, and then we lunched together at the Maxwell House.
Irene fixed the roast for dinner that we bought Saturday, and fancy fixings to go with it. Everything was delicious, especially the roast, which was "out of this world." We all ate a great deal, especially Jules, who stuffed himself so that he could hardly stir from the table.
Telephoned Nate. When he comes here to deliver his lectures, Bobbie is coming in to join him for the weekend. Too bad we cannot put them up in our new home. But it won't be long now!

Tuesday, May 4
Panel agenda on one of Gromfine's cases. Otherwise not especially busy these days, for a change.
To the White House party in the afternoon. There was a mob there, and it meant standing in line for hours. That was more – far more – than the hand shaking ceremony and glass of punch were worth.
Quite late in getting home for dinner. Told Irene to leave but she stayed and served my dinner anyhow. Jules was attending the United Jewish Appeal dinner. He pledged $100.
After putting Ira to bed, I spent a pleasant, restful evening sprawled on the sofa with a detective story Gromfine had brought me.

Wednesday, May 5
Full Board agenda on one of Wenzel's cases. Gray had raised the question, but he was voted down 4-1. A victory for our side.
A cool day. I was wearing a wool suit and a silk blouse, and was nevertheless uncomfortably cool at noon.
Letter from Bobbie thanking us for the birthday gift we had sent Lynn. We sent her a set of the building bricks that Ira – and especially Jules – have enjoyed so much.
Irene was complaining that she had a cold and her chest hurt. Reassuring that her chest x-ray was all right – or so she said, and I have no reason to disbelieve her.

Thursday, May 6
Irene telephoned early this morning that she was not well enough to come in. Ira went to the office with me. Jules picked us up at about 11:30 and took us to the Hot Shoppe for luncheon. Then we left Ira at school and went back to work. Jeanette took care of Ira after school until I got home.
Jules stayed downtown to have dinner and go to a rally on Palestine with some people from his office. I did not want to go enough to arrange for a sitter, etc. Jules, however, came home greatly inspired by the entire evening, but particularly by Moshe Shertok of Palestine, the principal speaker, and, I gathered, a real orator.

Friday, May 7
Raining quite hard in the morning. Irene called that she was not coming in again. Took Ira to the office. Jules took us back to Arlington at noon. Lunched at a Hot Shoppe. I came home again in time to meet Ira after school, and stayed at home.
When Jules got home, we went to the Hot Shoppe in Shirlington for dinner. Afterwards

satisfied one of Ira's great ambitions – to go to a movie in the evening. And we got out in time to hear the "Ozzie and Harriet" program, a fitting climax to Ira's night of thrills. He got a 100 on an arithmetic paper today, and felt that he had been fully rewarded for his success.

Saturday, May 8
To Silver Spring in the morning. Were told that we can move in on June 1 or any time thereafter. Our larder was so depleted that we breakfasted at the Hot Shoppe and lunched at Manny's delicatessen.
Bought a gift for Bruce Goldstein and sent one to Joan. Did our marketing. Then home just in time to make Ira presentable for Bruce's birthday party – late this year due to the birth of Esther's third son.
Card from Mother. Had a fine trip. Will come back for our housewarming with Father as well as Jean, Joe, and Cynthia. How jolly!
Sent her and Mother S. telegrams for Mother's Day. Just had not had time to get gifts for them.

Sunday, May 9
Jules took the children to Sunday School. Brought me a lovely bunch of flowers on his return.
Rented a bike for Ira again this afternoon. He finally got the hang of it and did quite well.
Drove out to Silver Spring. Ran into the Efron's, who went through our house. Sam was most enthusiastic about it.
To the Chicken-in-the-Rough restaurant on Connecticut Avenue, where we had a delicious dinner. The rest of the evening was spent in bathing Ira, shampooing his hair, cutting his toenails and fingernails, and preparing some clean clothes for him for tomorrow. I trust Irene will be in tomorrow.

Monday, May 10
Very busy all day, with work a plenty left over for tomorrow. Luncheon at the Tally-Ho for all the Board's women lawyers – about 20 of them. I shared a table with ,[11] Norma Hatfield, and Stasi Thannhausen. Ruth seems to be pregnant although she is still, as far as I know, unmarried.
Very warm day.
Too warm after dinner to stay indoors so we went for a walk around Buckingham. My flowers have lasted remarkably well. Hope Irene enjoys then during the day. I see so little of them myself. But I cannot discourage Jules altogether from buying me flowers as I probably have already from buying me gifts.

Tuesday, May 11
Irene "overslept", so Ira went to the office with me, and she picked him up there. I am getting more than fed up with her frequent tardiness.
Downtown at noon to look for cotton dresses, but did not find any.
In the evening I unpacked the few summer

---

11   In September, 1949 Ruth married Leslie S. Perry a leader in the African American community in Washington, D.C. He was an attorney with the N.A.A.C.P. and activist for African American rights (See Perry 1947:283). They were married in Canada, and the marriage created some controversy. Ruth was an Assistant General Counsel at the NLRB at the time.

things that I had thought worth putting away at the end of last season. They are nothing to brag about, and quite unstylishly short. I need so many things, but have so little time in which to shop for them. They are so expensive, too, a thought which must be borne in mind with a house to be paid for starting next month.

Wednesday, May 12
Lunched and shopped with Irene Shriber, but neither of us found anything we wanted to buy.
Took a walk in the evening. We got two books at the lending library – Iams' *Girl Meets Boy*, and Zweig's *The Axe of Waudsbek* – which should offer contrast if nothing else.
Wonder if we shall spent most of our evening reading when we are living in the house, or if we shall find ourselves occupied with household duties. Hope we shall be able to find a good maid – a real housekeeper with a sense of responsibility, which Irene is not and has not. Nor does she have enough interest to develop.

Thursday, May 13
Raining at noon. Lunched at the Women's University Club with Grace MacEldowney and Fannie Boyls.
Nate was in town, but was tied up all day and all evening. Iz Pachel was also in town, and came to dinner.
Irene cannot stay tomorrow evening, so agreed to stay tonight. We took Pach to the station after dinner. Then to the movie to see "Gentlemen's Agreement," which we thought was quite good.

Wonder how it will seem – when and if we get a maid to live in - not always to have to watch the clock when we go out.

Friday, May 14
Had my hair cut and permanented. Got many compliments.
Irene brought Ira downtown at 5:00. We met Jules and Nate at the Statler. Bobby could not get anyone to stay with the children, so could not join us.
We had dinner at the Statler Colony Room. Because it was late or because the food was so good, we all ate a great deal, Ira surprising all of us by the quantity he ate and the gusto with which he ate it. Nate insisted upon taking the check, which was outrageously high. We visited with Nate for a while, and then had to go home to get Ira to bed.
The Jewish State in Palestine has been proclaimed and has been recognized by the United States.[12]

---

12   Although Anne commented only occasionally on international events, the creation of the modern state of Israel was one of importance for her.

Year End Summary 1948

It has been a most satisfactory year, notable especially for the completion of, and our moving into, our new home, with all the changes in our way of life brought about thereby. Although we have made so little progress about getting the house furnished, it is a lovely house, and I know we are going to be happy in it. Our delight with Parkside School would warrant our having moved in any event.

The only fly in the ointment is the difficulty we are having in finding a really satisfactory maid, but I hope we shall succeed in doing so soon. There were other good things that happened this year: my becoming a supervisor and getting a P-6 rating; Jules and I getting clearance from our loyalty review boards, Mother and Father coming to visit us, apparently on good terms with each other; and Sam and Bobby coming to see us, the last time I was to see Sam alive. It is still hard to believe that Sam is gone, and Phil and Louie. Whenever I hear of someone appearing after a long absence, I wonder if Louie will appear again some day. They were all three so young to die, especially poor Louie, just married, and just ready to embark on a really adult way of living.

1949

This was a good year. Anne and Jules were busy furnishing their new house. Her sister Clara and husband Lou moved into a house in the same area, and they were delighted to have them so close. They went to Columbus, Ohio for vacation in August and visited with Jules extended family. From there they went to Niagara Falls and on to Quebec, one of Anne's favorite places.

Then they went to Massachusetts and visited Anne's family and spent some time at Cape Cod, which would become their favorite family vacation place for the next few years. They celebrated their tenth wedding anniversary on the Cape, and over the next few days drove back through New York with a stop in Philadelphia to visit Jules' brother Nate and his wife Bobbie.

In her daily entries Anne writes about office life, cases, social life around lunches and dinners, and family news.   -- RDH

Tuesday, March 1
A very cold, windy day. I still have several errands to run for Ira's party, but put them off because of the weather.
Ira has received in the mail two packages form Columbus and one from Philadelphia, and a $25 bond from Mother S. He is accumulating a fine nest egg of bonds.
To a PTA meeting in the evening. Ira had claimed that he is doing much better work lately, but there was nothing in his room to indicate any improvement. Miss Moore did not seem to be present.

Jules is sticking to his diet, and even passed up the delicious PTA refreshments after the meeting.

Wednesday, March 2
Ira wore his new cowboy outfit in honor of his birthday. He looked handsome, and was thrilled with it.

Jules went to the dentist about noon, so we lunched together at the Hot Shoppe.

Waited in the evening a half-hour past the usual time, then went home by bus and cab. Jules got to the office shortly after I left, stopped at Crisfield's for the fried shrimp platters we had ordered at Ira's request, and still got home before me. I was in a pretty foul mood, but we had a lovely dinner anyhow, and a pleasant evening with Ira – what there was left of it. We had planned to attend a lecture this evening by Dr. Arnold Gesell, but I refused to go or even to listen to Jules' explanations.

Thursday, March 3
Lunched with Irene Shriber at the Crescent. Did several more errands for Ira's party. We have received acceptances so far from everyone we invited except the Ruchels.

Ira received birthday greetings from Milton and Lois Ann, Dr. Zeller, the rabbi in Arlington, and Turner's Shoe Store.

Spent much of the evening wrapping favors for the "fish pond" for Ira's party. Have one gift per child plus a couple of extra ones.

Jules and Sam have to go to Baltimore to get their new license plates. We planned to make an outing of it, with dinner and a show, but called it all off when we learned that Ford's Theater in Baltimore is being picketed because of race discrimination.

Friday, March 4
Called the Ruchels. Both children are coming. They had delayed RSVP-ing until they saw whether or not Martha would be rid of her cold in time. That should make a pretty good sized party.

Had finished all my shopping for the party at noon today, but we went marketing after dinner so we would not have it to bother with tomorrow.

Evelyn made some lovely cookies for the party. She is going to stay and help us tomorrow, and seems almost as excited about the whole affair as Ira is. Hope it is a good party. I want his first party in his new home to be a memorable one.

Saturday, March 5
Got Ira's "Mickey Mouse" cake at the Hot Shoppe, and two bricks of ice cream at Gifford's, one with pink hearts, the other with green shamrocks. Got some jonquils to add still another gay note.

We had the Rolands, the Goors, the Ruchels, Sylvia and Johnny Liftin, and Tommy Grimes. Everyone seemed to enjoy the games, the refreshments, and the favors very much. Ira got a fine selection of gifts, including both toys and wearing apparel.

Evelyn helped with the refreshments, straightened out after the party, and served supper, for which I was very grateful. I will make it up to her.

1949

Sunday, March 6

Efron's turn to take the children to Sunday School, so Jules and I were able to eat a pleasant, leisurely breakfast.

Telephoned Columbus. We have been extremely dilatory about sending Irwin Howard a baby present. Hope we can do so soon.

Ira's teacher had instructed the class some time ago to make clothing scrap-books and to sketch their front doors. Ira had neglected to carry out either assignment. He really buckled down to work today, however, and had completed both tasks before he went to bed. He seemed to enjoy doing them, and had a great sense of accomplishment when he finished.

Monday, March 7

Grace McEldowney called me for luncheon, but I already had a date with Barbara Kaiser, and Grace refused to join us. I spent so many lunch hours recently preparing for Ira's birthday party that I owe several calls. Barbara and I lunched at the Candlestick. She is an intelligent girl, although extremely loquacious, and I enjoy her.

Miss Moore, according to Ira, was pleased with the work he had done over the weekend, and commented that she liked the clothing book because it did not look like his father's work. Hope she meant that, because it was Ira's work. We helped him only with the spelling of a few words.

Tuesday, March 8

Lunched with Irene Shriber at Fan and Bill's. We are now scheduled to move at the end of the week, so thought we might as well eat decent food while we could.

The Harlow dog, Stumpy, was run over and killed today. It was an unusually cute, friendly dog, and everyone in the neighborhood was saddened by his untimely death.

After dinner we picked up Hope Efron and went to a Sunday School PTA meeting and MCJC[13] meeting combined. Ira's teacher was not there, so when Hope had finished her conference, we left, and went to the movie in the neighborhood to see "The Snake Pit," an unusually adult, intelligent, well-acted picture.

Wednesday, March 9

Had a luncheon date with Grace McEldowney, but got tied up so late with a Board agenda that she had left before I was free.

Jules and Sam went to Baltimore in the morning for their new plates, etc. Wes Silvina picked me up in the morning, and Jules was back in ample time to take me home in the evening. Jules had put me to shame on this diet business. He had stuck to it with remarkable faithfulness, and has already lost several pounds. I have followed it only occasionally, and have lost no weight at all. I should exercise more will power, but I get so doggone hungry.

Thursday, March 10

To the beauty parlor at noon. Told them we were moving, and got an embarrassingly effusive farewell.

---

13 Jewish Sunday School PTA and Montgomery County Jewish Center combined meeting.

Got a ride home with Paul. Ira had taken a notion to burn up newspapers in an old stove the builders had left in the basement, and got the whole house full of smoke. The ideas that kid dreams up!

Dorothy Grimes called to remind me about the sewing circle, which was meeting at her house, so I broke down and went. The group now includes several new members and it is too large. The conversation in general bores me, and the frequent cracks at Negroes, etc., cause too much discomfort and annoyance. And I cannot fight them all.

Friday, March 11
Our moving has been postponed again for at least a week. A number of Trial Examiners, some of whom have always been considered "tops," have received notices that they failed to meet the standards set up under the Administrative Procedures Act. It is an outrage. I hope their appeal is successful.

Postcard from Stasi Thannhauser, who had gone to Mont Tremblant in Canada for the skiing.

To see the Silvians in the evening. Had a dull time looking at all their souvenirs of Manila. Don't know how I managed, at one time, to see so much of Hannah.

Saturday, March 12
To Dr. Stein's for Ira's check-up. He weighed 58 1/4 and measured 49 3/8, a gain of 7 1/4 pounds and 2 1/8 inches – very gratifying. Then to the dentist, where Ira got more fillings.

Lunched at the Habbord House. To Peerless. Ordered yellow summer drapes for all the first-floor rooms, and a mirror over the fireplace mantel.

Took Ira to the children's barber shop at Hecht's for a haircut. Sent a toy to Ellen's baby. Finished our marketing, having done part of it yesterday evening.

To the Efron's in the evening. Kim sitting with Ira. The Bob Bursteins, the Ira Roths, and the Bill Lundeens were there, all highly intelligent people. A pleasant evening.

Sunday, March 13
No Sunday School today, but a Purim party at the armory in the afternoon. The Silvians came over and went to the party with us. Jo seems a nice kid, but Hannah is impossible. Clara telephoned. They were going to look at houses, and would have stopped in to see us, but I explained that we would be out most of the afternoon.

After the party, which was noisy and hectic, we went for a pleasant, relaxing ride.

I fixed a yummy eye-of-the-round roast for dinner. Heard Evelyn come in about 10:30. How wonderful not to have to worry about her showing up on time!

Monday, March 14
Finally got together with Grace McEldowney for luncheon. We ate at the Good Earth.

No indication now of when we shall move to the new building. This whole affair has been handled with amazing inefficiency.

Jules walked over to the Kramers after dinner to turn in the proceeds of our sales of chances in the Montgomery Jewish Community

Center television raffle. Reported that they seem to be very agreeable neighbors. We should get better acquainted.

Sylvia Liftin telephoned to invite us to dinner Friday evening. Glad to get an invitation that is not for a Saturday evening.

Tuesday, March 15
Evelyn rode down with us in the morning to pay an overdue insurance bill, and then went home on the bus. She did not disappear for a week, as Mable did when she had an insurance matter to take care of.

By noon we were getting a nasty combination of rain, snow, and cold, so Irene Shriber and I lunched across the street at Trois Mousquetaires. Neither of us had a hat or an umbrella, but we managed all right with the aid of our morning papers and fleet footedness.

Jules built a roaring fire in the evening. It was most enjoyable.

Jules had now lost 6 ½ pounds.

Wednesday, March 16
Wes surprised us all by stopping by in the morning and offering to drive today. We accepted the offer. It was Sam's turn to drive, so he and Hope were delighted.

It appears now that we are definitely scheduled to move our new offices this weekend.

Note from Molly Wagshal. She is planning to spend a few days with us at Easter-time, but does not mention whether or not Bobby will accompany her.

Purim package from Columbus. Jules promptly went off his diet, although he had not done so for Evelyn's lemon cream pie yesterday or her banana cream pie today, both of which were delicious. Sylvia called to change the date to tomorrow.

Thursday, March 17
Did not wear green, although a good many others at the office – men and women – did. Getting ready to move is quite a chore with all the books and stuff I have accumulated in the comparatively short time I have been back at the Board. We went to the Liftin's for dinner. The Norman Altmans were also there. We had cocktails, and then a late, and very delicious dinner. It was a congenial little group, and everyone had just enough to drink to sharpen their wits, so it was a gay, delightful evening, and we stayed quite late.

Ira invited Tommy Grimes to have dinner with him. Evelyn fixed them a lovely dinner, with lots of "green."

Friday, March 18
A rainy, snowy day. Lunched at Aux Trois Mousquetaires with Grace McEldowney and Meg Flexner – in the nature of a farewell party as they are remaining at the Rochambean for a few weeks. I am being moved this weekend.

Have been asked by a number of people at the office and also by some of the neighbors to join Pyramid Clubs. Have refused them all. Do not want to take the time that is necessary. And cannot see getting rich that way. Too accustomed to working for whatever money I get.

Ordered some food from Capon Springs which arrived today. Hope it is good.

Saturday, March 19
To Stein's in the morning. All three of us getting tick shots. We got the second in the series of three today. It did not bother Jules or Ira, but it left my arm very sore.
A new clothing store opened in Silver Spring today, and gave away various things as an advertising stunt. We got there too late for most of the gifts, but I did get a lovely gardenia.
Evelyn has been suffering a good deal with sinus trouble, so we urged her to go to a doctor, and encouraged her by driving her downtown to her doctor's office. She is such a top-notch maid; we do not want her getting sick.

Sunday, March 20
Wes came over in the morning with Jo to return our folding bed. He helped Jules take Ira's train table from the spare room to the basement.
A cool but sunny day. Took Ira to Rock Creek Park for a while as he had a notion he wanted to do some leaping from rock to rock in the Creek.
Telephoned Columbus. Got bawled out for not acknowledging Ira's gifts. Put it off for Ira to do himself, as he did at Christmas.
Had a very good dinner at Crisfield's, followed by dessert at Gifford's. Jules observed his diet at dinner, and had only sherbet at Gifford's.

Monday, March 21
Evelyn rode down with us so she could stop at her doctor's for a sinus shot.
Started in at the new building. Spent much of the day getting our offices inhabitable.
Lunched in the cafeteria with Iz Gromfine.
Ira came home from school early with an upset stomach. Evelyn fixed him up in short order, with a lot of fuss and attention that he loved.
Thank you letter from Ellen, with pictures of her baby, who looks and sounds adorable. Card from Mother.
Ira had bought four glasses with his allowance Saturday for my birthday gift, but he could not wait, so we began using them. He wrote several charming thank-you letters for his birthday gifts.

Tuesday, March 22
To Lansburgh's at noon to do some household errands. Lunched there.
Another pleasant, mild day, but a rainy evening. Spring, so far, has given us delightful weather.
The mirror over our mantel was installed today. It looks tremendous, and I think will be very effective when it is supplemented with other decorative touches. It is not installed entirely to our satisfaction, but maybe that can be remedied.
Ira was fine fettle today. His illness was apparently only momentary. Thank heaven for his wonderful good health and good spirits. We are indeed fortunate.

Wednesday, March 23
Lunched in the cafeteria with Iz Gromfine and Elenor Schwartzbach. That place is going to become a bad habit, but there is no better place in the vicinity.
Evelyn entertained her girlfriend and two boyfriends this evening. She requested permission in advance, and offered to pay for their refreshments. I assured her she was free to entertain, and to help herself to refreshments. Apparently her party went off very well, and all her guests complimented her on her room and on the refreshments.
Finished reading Catton's *The War Lords of Washington*. The subject matter was interesting enough, but I found the treatment dull.

Thursday, March 24
Lunched in the cafeteria with Barbara Kaiser, Ruth Smalley, and Elsie Austin.
Got a ride home with Paul Bisgyer.
Note from Molly Wagshal confirming the fact that she is coming for Easter and clarifying the fact that Bobby is coming with her. Invitation to Joyce's sixth birthday party.
Decided to skip the sewing circle tonight. Instead went with Jules to a movie in Hyattsville to see "Chicken Every Sunday." Enjoyed the movie, and also the ride there and back. Wonder if the sewing circle missed me at all.

Friday, March 25
Jules picked me up at noon, and we went to Herzog's at the waterfront for luncheon. Then to Lansburgh's, where we bought a green bathroom scale. Would have done some other errands but it was raining quite hard.
Clara telephoned to tell me how much she liked the pink nylon sweater I sent her for her birthday. Also told me Jean had a son on the 18th.
Note from Mother, who is with Jean, written on one of Jean's baby announcements, with a PS by Jean.[14]
We all went to Hecht's in the evening. Bought Evelyn a 3-way mirror, with which she was delighted, and a pink nylon sweater for Joyce.

Saturday, March 26
To DuStein's for the last of our tick shots. Back to Silver Spring to do our marketing. Then home for luncheon, to find a man from Peerless putting up our drapes, which look very well. That looked like an all day job, so we finally left him to finish his work, while we went shopping. Got Ira some new shoes. While we were marketing, Ira stopped in at a new pet shop, and was given two goldfish as a souvenir of the opening. Then we had to get a bowl, food, and instructions for them.
It was quite late when we finished our errands, so went to the Steak House for a very good dinner.

Sunday, March 27
A very warm day, hitting 83 in the afternoon.
We planted the rose bush I bought yesterday. Hope it will grow.
I went with Jules to pick up the children after Sunday School. Had dinner at noon – a steak that was one of the best we had ever eaten.

---
14   Anne's sister Jean.

Went to Joyce's party via the 14th Street Bridge and the Tidal Basin to see the cherry blossoms. They were out enough to have attracted hordes of sightseers. Ira insisted upon stopping at the Goors' after the party, but they were not at home. Probably out house hunting, as they and the Rolands and so many others spend most of their Sundays that way.

Monday, March 28
Evelyn had spent the day in the country yesterday, and returned very late, but she was nevertheless up early and had a good breakfast for us. Bless her!
Lunched in the cafeteria with Herb Shenhin.
Jules had received an invitation for us to attend a reception this Saturday afternoon at the Italian Embassy for Count Sforza. That created a clothes problem.
Westley stopped in after dinner to return a book he had borrowed, and stayed a while to visit with us. Although he and Hannah seem to be getting along fairly harmoniously now, I doubt whether there is much real affection between them.

Tuesday, March 29
Jules offered to go shopping with me, but indicated there was an argument this noon at the Supreme Court he would like to hear. Barbara Kaiser also offered to go, and I accepted her invitation. We lunched at the cafeteria in the other building, then shopped at Garfinckel's and Schwab's, but did not find any dresses worth buying. I need a lot of new clothes, quite aside from the Italian embassy party. Gave some of my old dresses, which were too small for me, to Evelyn. They are too large for her, but she can probably adjust them, and she seemed delighted to get them.
The Gangs telephoned. They would like to have us run a Seder.

Wednesday, March 30
Downtown at noon by myself. Did a couple of errands, but bought no new clothes. Jules seems particularly anxious that I look well for the Italian Embassy shindig on Saturday, and I am trying hard, for his sake. One problem is the weather. It was extremely warm today, about 80 during the afternoon, but by Saturday, of course, it is liable to turn cold again.
Under Evelyn's care, Ira's goldfish, my rosebush, and the Valentine's Day plants are all flourishing. Evelyn seems to enjoy taking care of them, and has expressed a wish for more flowers and a dog. We should oblige.

Thursday, March 31
The weather turned cloudy and much cooler, and by noon it was pouring. Jules picked me up anyhow, and we went to Garfinckel's, but, even with his inspiration, I still did not find anything. We lunched at the 400 Club.
Jules built a roaring fire in the fireplace after dinner. It really felt good, as the wind blew and the rain poured down outdoors.
The tile-man and the painter were both around today filling in cracks caused by the house settling. Wonder when we shall be through with all that.
Suffered with acute indigestion during the night although we had had a very simple, wholesale meal.

Year End Summary 1949

Everything considered, a wonderful year. A wonderful vacation. It was good to see Mother and Father getting along happily.

Getting our wonderful home furnished at last. At least we have the carpeting installed. Our maid situation got messed up again with Evelyn's leaving, but I hope, and think, that is just a temporary problem.

Having the Rolands move into the same locality has been pleasant. Ira likes having relatives around, to visit and to be visited. He and Joyce are becoming close friends as they see more of each other. And Stevie is a delight to all of us.

Ira had only one bad accident, cutting his leg, and that seems finally to have healed up all right. Other than that, we have all enjoyed good health.

Our social life has maintained a pleasant, enjoyable pace.

And, last but not least, Jules and I have both made satisfactory progress in our respective jobs, financially and otherwise. I am well satisfied with the status quo in all important respects and in most of the unimportant ones.

1950

By 1950 Anne and her family were well established in their Silver Spring home. They bought a Buick and the same year made a long driving trip through the West where they visited the major sites. In North Dakota they went to Mt. Rushmore, in Wyoming they visited the Big Horn Mountains National Park and saw a rodeo, then to Yellowstone. From there they went to Montana and visited the Glacier National Park and saw a powwow and stayed some days on a horse ranch. On the way home they stopped in Columbus to visit with Jules' family.

In an interesting side note Anne's cousin Sam Wagshal wrote an article in the January issue of *Reader's Digest* in which he described his relationship with Supreme Court Justice Wiley Rutledge who frequented Sam's delicatessen where they talked about politics and other things. Justice Rutledge invited him as a guest to the inauguration of President Truman and sat in the section with family members (Wagshal, 1950).   -- RDH

Saturday, April 1
Ira got off some "April Fool" jokes before the rest of us were fully awake. He had apparently been looking forward to it for some time.
The three of us went to the library and did errands in the morning. After luncheon we took Ira to Clara's then Jules' and I kept an appointment he had made with a Buick agent. Had a demonstration ride, and got a very fair offer, but Jules was not quite ready to close the deal. The Buick is more expensive

than the line he originally contemplated purchasing.

To the Gangs' for Seder.[15] The dinner was excellent, the company pleasant, and the whole evening a great success. Ira played his role in the services admirably, and in general, behaved beautifully. I helped Florence clean up afterwards, which made us quite late in getting home, but Ira took it all like a trooper.

Sunday, April 2
A beautiful warm, sunny day. We did quite a lot of work in the yard, and enjoyed it very much. Jules rather enjoys outdoor work, and if he can get both Ira and me to work along with him, is especially delighted.
Telephoned Mother Schlezinger. She seems to be getting along all right, but Gertrude, who is still in Florida, is still ill.
Drove into Silver Spring in the afternoon to buy some flowers for the table. Other than that, we stayed at home all day, and we had no visitors. That gave me ample time to prepare a Passover dinner, and I needed the time. Cooking dinner and participating in the Seder service was a hectic combination, but it was fun, and the dinner was quite good, and we all enjoyed the dinner and the ceremony thoroughly.

Monday, April 3
Called Miss Morrow and cancelled our drapery order until fall. Seems foolish to hang them when the open-window season is just about to arrive. They will make them at their leisure during the summer.
With three legal assistants away, I am busier then ever. For one thing, I am handling many details which, if they were here, they would handle themselves.
David Whitten stopped in after dinner to play with Ira, and they soon became engrossed in a Parcheesi game.
Jules and I went shopping. Thelma broke the refrigerator butter-dish, and we are having considerable difficulty in finding a replacement. When we completed our shopping, we went to the Silver to see "When Willie Comes Marching Home," an entertaining movie, which Jules found especially funny.

Tuesday, April 4
Lunched in the dining room with Bob Freehling and Dick Brownstone.
Had three cases on the sub-panel agenda, one with Weuzel, one with Balice, and one of Clem Miller's which is now in my lap, Clem having returned to the San Francisco Regional Office. It was a hectic afternoon.
In the evening Jules and I went to a P.T.A. meeting. Mrs. Zeller, as usual, outlined the business part of the meeting, the two speakers were both interesting and informative, and the coffee-and-cookies were refreshing, so it all added up to a successful meeting.
Apparently a great many visitors come to the school from a great many places to study its programs and activities. It is a wonderful school. Jules and I are completely sold on it. Only wish Ira could have started there earlier than he did.

---

15   Arthur and Florence Gang lived in the neighborhood and were close friends for the rest of their lives.

Wednesday, April 5
A hectic day. Got a number of draft decisions back with inconsistent changes made by different Board members, and had to do a great deal of running around trying to get such changes reconciled.
Lunched in the dining room with Bob Freehling.
Had an enforcement conference in the afternoon on Doherty's Dixie Mercerizing case. The enforcement attorneys found all our findings amply supported by the record.
Ira's Easter vacation began today. Too bad it was a rainy disagreeable day, when yesterday was sunny and very warm.
In the evening we drove Thelma and Ira to Silver Spring so Thelma could pick up some things she wanted at the drug store. Took them both home, and then Jules and I went to the movie to see "The Man on the Eiffel Tower," an interesting picture with beautiful photography.

Thursday, April 6
Still extremely busy at the office. It should begin tapering off soon when I get issued the several decisions left behind in various stages of progress by legal assistants going on field details.
Announcement from Barbara Kaiser of the birth of her daughter Margaret.
Hope Efron telephoned and invited Ira to spend the day with Mark tomorrow. Ira accepted with alacrity and was surprisingly pleased and excited at the prospect. Apparently he has been squabbling quite a good deal with his playmates in the neighborhood, and I am afraid he is not wholly without blame for it.
A chilly evening, so we had a fire, the first in some time. It was very pleasant.
Thelma went out for the evening.

Friday, April 7
Lunched in the dining room with Peg Patterson, Kay Loomis, Elsie Austin, and Mag Flexner. Brought Peg up-to-date on *l'affaire* Threadgill.
Ira spent the day with the Efrons, and apparently enjoyed it very much; especially the double-feature cowboy movies Hope took them to see in the afternoon.
Jules and I went marketing in the evening.
Birthday cards from Madelyn and Mother Schlezinger, the second with a twenty dollar check enclosed. Have not heard anything from the folks in a long while although I have written them a few times. Do not expect to hear from them particularly on my birthday, but am surprised to hear nothing from them for so long. Clara has apparently not heard anything either for some time.

Saturday, April 8
Did a number of errands in the morning.
Thelma's girl friend stopped by for her at noon. We took both of them to the terminal. Then to the Buick agency, and drove a car over to see how it would fit into our garage. It just gets in. We placed an order for one – a green super 4-door sedan.
Then to Franklin Simon's, where Ira, as secretly as possible, bought some hose for my birthday gift. It was quite an occasion

as he was paying for the gift out of his own money, which he finds it difficult to accumulate on 25 cents a week, and with his naturally generous traits.
We went home for dinner.
The weather is cold and windy and cloudy. Too bad for all those to whom the Easter parade is important.

Sunday, April 9
Ira gave me the hose, and Jules gave me a lovely white topper. Ira delivered the eggs he and Thelma had colored to his friends, but received eggs only from Tommy and Dicky Grimes.
The Gangs stopped in to visit. We always enjoy them. Wish they would move out our way as they talk of doing.
Clara telephoned to say they could not call on us as Stevie had a temperature, but would like to have us visit them. We did. She gave me a very attractive pink linen jacket.
After we left there we went for a long ride in the country. Then, at Ira's suggestion, we went to Brook Farm, where we had a very good dinner. It was quite late when we got home – in fact Ira fell asleep on the back seat of the car, something he had not done in a long time – but it was a lovely birthday, and we all three thoroughly enjoyed it.

Monday, April 10
To Garfinckel's at noon. Exchanged the white topper, which was too large, for a yellow one, which was somewhat cheaper but nevertheless more becoming. Bought myself some gold earrings.

Had Thelma put Ira and David Whitten on the shuttle bus, and I left the office early and met them at the terminal and took them to Walter Reed for their first swimming lesson. Jules picked us up afterwards and took us home. I was pretty tired, having had to wait for the boys almost two hours on my feet, but we went shopping after dinner anyhow. For one thing, I wanted to exchange the pink jacket, which was too small. Hecht's did not have it in my size, but expected more of them, so I had to get a credit slip.
Then to the Silver to see Oliva DeHavilland in "The Heiress," an excellent movie in which she did a superb acting job.

Tuesday, April 11
Pouring at noon, but I had a hairdresser appointment and kept it in spite of the weather. A couple of my "permanent" curls did not "take" properly, and I had to get them done again.
Had two cases on the sub-panel agenda, one of Doherty's, who was on field detail, and one of Wenzel's, who was available.
Received a picture postcard from Jerry from Jerome, Idaho.
Brenda Whitten took the boys for their swimming lesson this afternoon, and picked them up afterwards. Ira, for reasons I could not follow entirely, had not enjoyed the swimming lesson yesterday at all, but enjoyed it today very much. Hope he really learns to swim this time. He had no fear of the water at all, so should do quite well once he gets the hang of a few strokes.
A cold evening. I was glad we had no

occasions to go out and could spend the evening reading in front of the fire.

Wednesday, April 12
Ira returned to school today, his Easter vacation over. He said he enjoyed his vacation, but no doubt he would have enjoyed it far more had the weather been more pleasant, and had his 5-6 o'clock swimming schedule not disrupted any possible afternoon or evening excursion.

Had two cases on the full Board agenda today, one Doherty's and one of Clem Miller's, both of which I had to handle alone. Both of them required revisions in the draft decisions, but I managed all right.

Brenda Whitten again took care of the swimming pool transportation, and will do so until Saturday unless she calls on us before that.

We stayed in again this evening. Thelma went out. She does not go out, it seems to me, so often as she used to. As long as she shows up in good time in the morning, she is welcome to her occasional night out.

Thursday, April 13
Had made a luncheon date with Katie Goldman, when Vivian McConnell called and asked me to lunch with her and Peg at the waterfront. Katie did not want to take the time for that, but excused me. I invited Grace McEldourney to join us. Vivian and Peg picked us up, and we went to Hogate's, and had a delicious luncheon. Then for a ride to see the cherry blossoms. It was an unpleasantly cold day, but, from the inside of a closed car, the cherry blossoms, which were in full bloom, looked lovely.

Ira passed a swimming test, and was given a button inscribed "I was taught to swim by the Y.M.C.A." We were all very happy that he succeeded in obtaining the button, particularly after David Whitten had received one yesterday.

A cold night and we all stayed at home. The mild winter was very pleasant, but we seem to be paying for it now with a cold, nasty spring season.

Friday, April 14
Postcard from Gertrude Lewin, still in Florida. She must be really ill to stay away from home so long.

Still hectically busy at the offices but things may quiet down next week.

Got a ride home with Paul Bisgyer,[16] so got home shortly before Ira returned from swimming. He was bursting with news that he and David were doing so well that they had been told not to return tomorrow so the instructors could concentrate on the boys who had not yet passed the test. Glad Ira made the grade, and that he was able to hold his own along with David.

Jules and I went marketing after dinner just to get it done and over with and not have to bother about it on Saturday. Frank Bloom died. And he was only in his 40's.

Saturday, April 15
To Hahn's in the morning to buy Ira some

---

16 Bisgyer was an NLRB colleague with whom Anne occasionally had lunch and rode home.

sneakers and Jules some sport shoes. Then to Hecht's to get Ira some more blue jeans. The Buick agency had telephoned while we were out and left the message that our car was in route and should be available in a few days. Now that we have decided on a car, Jules is very impatient to get possession of it.

In the afternoon, Sam Efron and Mark picked up Jules and Ira, and they went to the Lone Ranger Rodeo. I stayed at home and read. Just as well because the rodeo turned out to be mainly a souvenir selling affair, and for the most part a sadly phony affair. Ira and Mark enjoyed seeing the Lone Ranger and Silver, but even they found most of the performances dull.

Drove over to the delicatessen to get some stuff for supper.

Sunday, April 16
Fixed a steak and all the trimmings for dinner. Jules and Ira went for a little walk while I was preparing dinner, and lost track of the time so completely that they did not get back until long after everything, including the steak, was ready. That ruined my disposition for the rest of the day.

Joe Friedman stopped in. Is house-hunting, and would like to live in our area, but cannot find anything suitable.

The Rolands stopped in to visit.

Ira played most of the afternoon in the piles of dirt near the new houses being constructed in our area. By the time he came in to get cleaned up for supper, he was about the dirtiest human being I have ever seen.

Monday, April 17
Thelma did not show up and did not call. A hectic morning, but we managed. Ira carried his luncheon. I lunched in the dining room with Irene Shriber.

Left the office early, and got home before Ira returned from school. Did some cleaning. Ira was, as always under such circumstances, very sweet and helpful.

Thelma's girlfriend called. When she heard Thelma was not in she called Thelma at home and then called me again. Seems Thelma went for a long drive in the country, the car broke down, she did not get back until this afternoon and went right to bed and was still asleep.

Called Mable, but she was not available for the next few days.

Went to Crisfield's for dinner, to Gifford's for dessert, and to the library to return some books. Jules was in a gay mood, having had a highly satisfactory conference with the Attorney General.

Tuesday, April 18
Lunched in the dining room with Katherine Goldman.

As busy as I am, I consented to take on another field person here on detail, a Harry Cranford. Probably should have refused, with my maid complications on top of everything else. Still no word from Thelma, who may be too ashamed of herself to call me – or who may just not care one way or the other about her job.

Had two cases on the sub-panel agenda this afternoon. Jules volunteered to go home early in order to be there when Ira got home. I left when I finished my work, about 4:00, and Jules and Ira met me at the terminal. We went home and I fixed dinner.

Do not know what to do about a maid. Can hardly take Thelma back now, but hate to go through the calls and interviews and breaking-in if I advertise.

Wednesday, April 19
A lovely warm day. I could really enjoy this weather if my maid problem were not so pressing. I do treat maids well, but have been unlucky at keeping a good one.
Lunched in the cafeteria with Helen Hoffman and Iz Gromfine.
I left early to get home before Ira did, but can hardly continue to do that much longer. Jules went to a Civic Association Meeting in the evening. I should have liked to go, because it promised to be and was an interesting meeting, but I had to stay at home to "sit" with Ira. Made some calls re maids, but none of them brought results. Mabel called me about 9:45 to let me know she could come out tomorrow and stay for a few days. She is only a temporary solution, but if she gets the laundry done and Ira looked after for a few days, that will be a tremendous help, and will give me a chance to look around for someone more "permanent."

Thursday, April 20
Mable did not show up and of course did not call.
Telephoned Brentano's and had a book sent to Lynn as a birthday gift. Shopping is out of the questions these maid-less days.
Letter from Jerry Doherty, who is enjoying his Seattle detail, and enjoyed the trip out there, very much.
Lunched in the dining room with Harry Barnford, Pat Kalders, Dave Findling, and Ida Klaus.
Home early again.
Called a couple of girls who had applied last time I advertised, and whose numbers I still had. They had jobs though, and did not think it right to quit. Why can't I find someone like that – other than Evelyn? Called Evelyn also, but she still did not know of anyone who wanted a live-in job. Will advertise over the weekend, and pray that we get someone reliable this time. Too bad I wasted Evelyn's training-time on Thelma.

Friday, April 21
Called Thelma, who answered the phone, told her I was advertising, and suggested she pick up her things. She said she would tomorrow at 10:00. No further comment. The Employment Service called me about an applicant, and gave me her reference the check.
Lunched in the cafeteria with Grace McEldowney, Mag Flexner, and Gladys Bestor.
Jules picked Ira up after school and took him to his office.
Letter from Jonah Silver, on detail in New York.
After work we went for a little ride. Then to Hendrix, where we had a cocktail and Ira had tomato juice, and then all three of us had really superb steak dinners.
Then home, to get Ira cleaned up and in bed, to straighten out the house a bit, and to pray that we shall soon have a maid again. Belated

birthday card from Gertrude Lewin, back in Columbus [Ohio].

Saturday, April 22
Thelma arrived shortly before 10:00, packed her things, left the sweater and flashlight I had given her, said she was sorry and would be glad to come back any time I needed her. Got in touch with the reference for Carrie Gray, the Employment Service applicant, and it was highly satisfactory, so made an appointment for 11:00 this morning. She was prompt, the interview was satisfactory, I hired her, and advanced her $5 to buy a uniform. We took her back to the terminal, and then to Caithness Buick to pick up our new car, a very handsome green sedan. When the paperwork was completed, we went to the Hot Shoppe for luncheon. Did some errands, and then home.
Cancelled my ad. for tomorrow and Monday when I hired Carrie, but I had to leave it in for today. Got a few calls during the little time I spent at home, but Carrie it is.
Took Tommy Grimes and Ira to see the movie "Cinderella."

Sunday, April 23
Telephoned Columbus, only to learn that Mother S. had fallen getting out of the bathtub and is now confined to bed.
Rained all day. Jules had to drive the Sunday School carpool. After luncheon we picked up Carrie and moved her possessions (pitifully few). Left her to straighten out her room and to fix dinner, while we went for a ride. Stopped to show the Rolands our new car.

Carrie fixed an excellent dinner and served it very well. There are a few things we like done differently, but by and large she is far more experienced and competent than Thelma was, or than Evelyn was when she first came. She is 38, separated from her husband after 14 years of marriage, had no children, and is completely "broke." I think she can use some good meals too – and she will get them.

Monday, April 24
Lunched in the dinning room with Harry Kuskin and Merv Bachman. We have been invited to the Bachman's Saturday evening. Carrie said she would "sit."
She managed very well with breakfast, and apparently, with Ira's luncheon. We went home to change our clothes, and saw that she had prepared a fine dinner for Ira and herself, which they were eating together in the breakfast nook. Both Evelyn and Thelma would have served Ira alone and then eaten alone. Ira seemed much happier this way.
We went to the Federal Bar Association dinner at the Statler, Jules looking very handsome in a new tuxedo he bought last week. The President was there and made the principal talk. There were many other notables, cabinet officers, Supreme Court justices, etc. Afterwards we went to the cocktail room for drinks with the Creightons. A very enjoyable evening.

Tuesday, April 25
Jules drove the new car to work for the first time. It presents a real parking problem because of its width.

At noon Jules and I went to Mayer's to look at some new dining room furniture. Selected another living-room lamp. Have one more to select.

Had two cases on the sub-panel agenda, one with Hank Wenzel and one with Harry Barnford.

Got a ride home with Paul. He suggested we stop this evening to see his new television set, but neither Jules nor I was in the mood. Went to the library and did some marketing.

Read Owen Lattimore's *The Situation in Asia* inasmuch as Jules had the book and the author was receiving so much publicity because of Senator McCarthy's Communist accusations. Found the book dull as it dealt with a subject so unfamiliar to me. Doubt that there is any truth to McCarthy's charges.

Wednesday, April 26
A mild sunny day.

Downtown at noon with Irene Shriber and Dick Brownstone to look for bargains in Garfinckel's clearance sale. Only Dick bought anything. We lunched at the Dragon.

Carrie seems to be working out very well. Best of all, she and Ira hit it off beautifully.

After dinner Jules and I went to the final MCJC forum meeting to hear a Les Schwartz talk on "Jewish Literature." Found the talk a little bit dull and the speaker more that a little bit conceited and pompous. Stopped to chat with several people on the way out, which made us rather late in getting home. Have sold $11 worth of 25 cent chances for MCJC. Think I have had enough of MCJC for a while.

Finished reading Green's *Nothing* – a silly sort of book in my opinion.

Thursday, April 27
Another warm sunny day. Maybe spring is really here at last.

Downtown again at noon, this time with Helen Hoffman and Iz Gromfine. We did some errands, then lunched in a Sholl Cafeteria in deference to the serious diet Helen and Iz are observing, in contrast to my half-hearted, on-and-off diet.

Nate called from Philadelphia to discuss arrangements for our joint excursion to New York.

Max and Kate Goldman, and Bernie Balicer and his girl friend stopped in this evening. We had some drinks. Carrie came up later and served scrambled eggs, toast and coffee. They stayed quite late, but it was a fairly pleasant evening. They all admired the house and the new furniture quite extravagantly.

Long letter from Thelma's sister pleading with me to take her back.

Hank Wenzel has announced his engagement.

Friday, April 28
Lunched in the cafeteria with Carol Pollack. It was a pretty day, so we went for a walk after luncheon.

Jules has adopted the practice, when Sam drives the carpool, of riding in front with Sam, leaving me to ride alone in back. He argues that is proper as a driver should not be required to sit alone like a chauffeur, while I argue that it is improper for Jules to sit in front while I sit alone in the back. We are both stubborn, so it looks like a knock-down-and-drag-out argument.

In the evening we went to the Al Sommers', who were entertaining in their new home. That had quite a large group, Board and non-Board couples, and we had quite a pleasant time. I rather like Laura Sommers, yet years go by without my seeing her. It is no doubt as much my fault as hers.

Saturday, April 29
Let Carrie go early as she was coming in to "sit" in the evening.

Did our marketing, got Ira's haircut, stopped at the Buick place for some adjustments to the car, home to change Ira's clothes and give him a quick luncheon, and then deposited him at the Ruchels' for Anthony's birthday party. Jules and I then stopped at the Hot Shoppe for luncheon. I did some shopping while Jules worked on the lawn. When Ira came home – the party had gone to a roller-skating rink, which he enjoyed - we had dinner.

Carrie arrived in a cab promptly at 8:00 as arranged, but it seemed to me she was tipsy. I accused her of it but she denied it, urged us to go ahead, assured us everything was all right, etc., etc. We finally went, with some misgivings, to the Bachmans'. The Gromfines and the Art Leffs were also there. I called home, and everything seemed to be under control, but I was a bit heart-sick all evening, although I tried not to show it. Otherwise, a pleasant evening.

Sunday, April 30
A rainy day.

Carrie came up all dressed; with her hat on, to ask if she was supposed to fix breakfast. I told her she was not, so she left for the day. She was sober enough this morning. I do not know what to do about her. She bought two new uniforms yesterday although she is apparently very hard up financially. But I cannot trust Ira with her if she is a drinker.

Ira went to Sunday School in the morning. Other than that, we all stayed home all day. Telephoned Columbus. Mother S. is still laid up pretty much, but had improved sufficiently to be able to come to the telephone.

In the evening Jules went to a meeting at the Trittons' of the householders in our block to try collectively to prevent new houses in our block from going up much closer to the street line than our houses, which are set back 40-45 feet.

Year End Summary 1950

This was on the whole a very good year. The sad spot, of course, was poor Louie's funeral. And his death seems so terribly a waste as the wars go on and on.

Although Ira had mumps, and had to miss school because of illness for the first time since kindergarten, we all for the most part enjoyed very good health. Jules got mumps also, but he was over it by the time he realized he had it. And the effect of mumps which most men dread so held no threat for Jules.

We acquired a luxurious new car, which we have enjoyed a great deal, and in which we have had many wonderful trips, long and short. And I finally broke down, learned to drive, and got a license. It proved so easy when I finally got around to it that I can see although I would not admit it to Jules - how ridiculous it was for me not to have done so years and years ago.

We are gradually getting the house furnished and decorated. Jules is impatient to go ahead with it much faster than I am doing, and I have had to keep a tight rein on him in order not to wind up with a great deal of expensive furniture we should not enjoy living with after a while. When we have finished, however - if we ever do - I shall probably have to admit again to myself that it was something that should have been done years sooner. One of the chief difficulties has not been attributable to me, and that is the fact that so many things have been, still are, and will continue to be difficult to obtain because of war shortages.

Our jobs have been going along well enough, nothing startlingly new, good or bad.

Ira's school work has improved a little, but we have finally resigned ourselves to the realization that he is not a scholar. When I think of the trouble that I used to go to to get books, and he had so many which he can hardly be bothered to read. And a set of encyclopedias - what a treasure I should have thought them. To him they constitute a chore. But he is a sweet, healthy, lovable, intelligent, good-looking child, and one cannot have everything. I appreciate him, and am not complaining. It is just that I want to do so much for him, and want him to be able to absorb and enjoy and appreciate it all.

1951

In August they went for vacation to the beach in Delaware, staying near Rehoboth. Anne caught a serious cold during the trip and spent much of the time indoors, but Jules and Ira enjoyed the beach. They went on to Massachusetts and picked up Anne's parents for a trip through the Berkshires. They came back through New York City and met Jules' brother Nate, his wife Bobbie, and their children for an anniversary week-end in the City. This was their twelfth anniversary, and Ira was ten years old. The conflict between Anne's parents continued to be a problem, but they had stability in their work situations, with their group of friends, and with Ira's growth. -- RDH

Thursday, February 1
A nasty day, but, having waited until the last minute to get Jules' birthday gift, I had to go downtown. I got him a green sleeveless sweater from me and a desk blotter from Ira.
Ira has no school today because of the weather. Carrie fixed a festive dinner, including a birthday cake with candles.
Jules got a birthday card and check from Mother S, a telegram from Lucille, and cards from the Levins and from Agnes and Marion.
Not much of a birthday celebration, but the best I could mange in this weather, etc.

Friday, February 2
The Montgomery County schools reopened today although the roads were still icy and traveling even on foot very hazardous.
Farewell party this afternoon for Sam. Jules invited me, but as he generally does not ask me to his office parties I got uppity and refused to go to this one. I drove the car home and took Paul home. Jules telephoned about 7:00 to ask if I wanted to come downtown for a movie, but I did not. He ate supper by himself at Union Station and came home via streetcar and cab. I suppose I was mean not to have gone to the party with him, but I just did not like the way the invitation was extended.

Saturday, February 3
Discovered at noon that our tickets for the Ice Capades matinee were actually for the evening performance, and no matinee tickets were available. We went to the Friedmans'[17] about 5:00, had a drink while the kids played, and then had supper. Afterwards Joe, Libby, Jane and her girl friend, and the three of us went to the Ice Capades, leaving Robert Friedman and Pal in the care of a sitter. We all went in our car. We all enjoyed the show very much, and the three kids had no difficulty whatsoever in the remaining wide awake. By the time we took the Friedmans home and picked up Pal, Ira did not get to bed until well after midnight.

Sunday, February 4
Nate[18] telephoned from Philadelphia. They expect to get in tomorrow evening in time for

---
17   Joe Friedman, Jules' law partner. They left the son Robert and the Schlezingers' dog, Pal, with a sitter.
18   Jules' brother Nate.

dinner. We telephoned Columbus. Mother S. is still very concerned about Helen Lee taking her current leave too seriously.

The Rolands came over in the afternoon. Clara and the kids rode over with me to pick Ira up. Despite going to bed so late last night, Ira went to Sunday School and to his youth group. We wanted him to go to bed early tonight though so we turned down the Rolands' invitation to eat out with them. I got a bit fed up with them anyhow. They permit Stevie to run wild in our house in a way I consider inexcusable. Ira would not be permitted to do so in their house.

Monday, February 5

Carrie arrived by cab quite late claiming she had been ill.

Mrs. Grimes took Ira along with their two boys to the barber shop for all three to get haircuts.

Got a ride home with Paul. Letter from Gertrude. Our share for Mother's birthday party is $97 which, with our traveling expenses, made it a really expensive occasion.

Bobby and Nate arrived late, but we held dinner for them, and Carrie turned out a really fine dinner despite the delay. They brought us a lovely box of chocolates.

Duffy Edes telephoned. He is in town in connection with the Wage Stabilization set-up, and does not know whether he can find time to come out to see us.

Tuesday, February 6

Had four cases in the subpanel agenda with Stasi and Hank.

Jules' new secretary, Elise Havenner, rode home with us, and will apparently be a regular rider. Sam, of course, no longer rides with us since he is at the Pentagon. He was much better company than the Havenner gal.

To a PTA meeting in the evening. A psychiatrist showed a movie on child-raising and then conducted a discussion about it. He was pleasant but unimpressive, and the program was not so interesting as it might have been.

Nate and Bobby left this morning after breakfast. Ira gave them a bunch of books he felt he had outgrown.

Wednesday, February 7

Lunched in the dining room with Irene Shriber. The weather was terrible – rain, snow, and ice in various combinations. We took Paul Bisgyer and Mrs. Havenner home. The driving was so slow and so skiddy that it seemed to take forever. Carrie had been promised the evening off to see her doctor about a breaking-out on her face, and decided to go despite the weather. Jules took her to the bus terminal, an extremely generous gesture in view of the driving hazards. Ira and I fixed supper while Jules was gone. Ira can be very helpful when he takes a notion to try, as he did this evening.

Thursday, February 8

Could not get the car out of the garage because of the ice. Mr. Harlowe saw us struggling and offered to take us to work. We accepted gratefully. His car had been out overnight, and anyhow his driveway does not have a sharp incline like ours. Home with Herb David. We had invited several people from Jules' office to come over this evening, but suggested a postponement in view of the driving difficulties, and they agreed with alacrity.

It had been below freezing all day and was very cold at night. Jules and Ira nevertheless got out and worked on the ice in the driveway.

Luckily Carrie managed to get in this morning in plenty of time.

Friday, February 9
Had a date with the Zarkys for this evening, but Norma cancelled it because of the driving difficulties.

A letter from Agnes Smith, and a map from Norma Zarky showing how to get out to her place.

Duffy Edes called just as I was preparing to leave the office at about 5:20, and offered to come out to dinner. We were glad to have him but had planned a very un-company dinner and it was too late to change anything. We picked him up, and he kept us waiting 30 minutes past the appointed time, which was annoying and seemed quite unnecessary. Nevertheless we enjoyed his company. Took him back to the Willard about midnight.

Saturday, February 10
To Hecht's in the morning to get a birthday gift for Dick Burns. Took so long getting it and some Valentines that we had no time to market before luncheon. We did that after luncheon while Ira was at Dick's party. Needed a lot of groceries, and everything was so outrageously expensive that we spent $38 – and on stuff that will for the most part be used up in a week.

It seemed quite a warm day, but the temperature did not get any higher than 34. Just much warmer than it had been.

We ate the first part of our supper in the breakfast nook, and the second part in the den watching television. Nice occasionally to not have a maid around.

Sunday, February 11
A pleasant mild day. Ira, as usual, was away most of the day, between Sunday School and his youth group. The Rolands, as usual, were around most of the day. I should think they could find something more exciting for their kids to do, especially with Ira away during most of their visit, and with me leaving to pick him up while they are there. They used to ride over with me, but decided today they would not ride with Pal, who was already in the car, so they stayed at home and Pal went with me.

I fixed a porterhouse steak dinner that was one of the best yet.

Monday, February 12
Carrie did not show up and did not call. Had Ira carry his luncheon and, as he had a Valentine Party after school, he would be busy all day. Quite warm so we let Pal run loose, and moved his bed and water to the garage. I went to the beauty parlor at noon. Went home early. Ira and I fixed supper. Jules came on the train, and Ira and I picked him up at the station.

Called the woman with whom Carrie stays weekends. Gathered she did not stay there last night, but the woman had seen her with her eye blacked and her face badly cut. She must have been in a drunken brawl. Called Thelma, but she had a Government job. Don't know what to do now.

Tuesday, February 13
A man called me at the office to tell me Carrie was ill, and that her nephew was supposed to have called me yesterday. I indicated to him what I thought of her.
Felt lousy – probably aggravation about Carrie – but stayed until after the Subpanel agenda and then drove home. Managed to get the house cleaned up a little, fix supper of a sort, go out to buy refreshments for tonight, and get them ready to serve.
Our party, postponed from last Thursday included the Tony Burches, the Sid Grosses, the Lou Allmans, and the DuBois. They were a very congenial group, and the entire party, including the refreshments, went off very well. Jules and I cleaned up afterwards.

Wednesday, February 14
Stayed at home, really ill. Stasi called to ask how I was. Ira was glad of the chance to come home for luncheon. Jules sent me for a Valentine a tremendous bunch of gladiolas with the longest stems I eve saw.
Marion came home with Jules for dinner. I had fixed a roast, which was good, but the rest of the dinner was pretty mediocre. Marion then sat with Ira while we went to the theater to see "Death of a Salesman," with which we were very much impressed. The Efrons drove down and home with us. Marion had refused to stay overnight, so we went directly home so Jules could take her home. The Efrons had the same situation.

Thursday, February 15
Felt better but stayed at home again anyhow. Jules waited until about 10:00 for a woman the U.S. Employment Service said would be out at 9:30 but never showed up.
Stasi called again.
Someone called and asked for Carrie. Suspect she was calling for Carrie to see if she still had a job. I indicated clearly she did not.
Letter from Bobbie, from Florida, enclosing a dollar she had borrowed to tip Carrie. What a waste!
Ira came home for luncheon.
Mayer's delivered our sofa pillows, made over, and in our opinion much better looking.
I did a little cleaning and a little laundry and fixed dinner. We played cards in the evening, and watched television after Ira went to bed.

Friday, February 16
To the office. Everyone sympathetic.
Jules called and invited me to drive out somewhere for luncheon, but I was not in the mood and did not want to take the time. Went to the cafeteria alone and joined Herman Marx.
Put an ad in the *Star* for Saturday and Sunday. Could not get away from the office until about 5:00. Jules left then also. Ira had managed very well except that when an applicant from an agency called, he merely said I was not in and did not have her call

me at the office. He had heard me instruct Carrie not to refer all calls to the office but to take messages.

Went marketing after dinner.

Irv Levy committed suicide by jumping off the Calvert Street Bridge.[19] How terrible!!!

Saturday, February 17
Received a good many responses to the ad, but only one I considered seriously enough to interview, and she showed up smelling of liquor. That left me completely discouraged on the subject of housekeepers. Still no word from that tramp of a Carrie although she has clothing, money etc., still in her room.

I am also getting completely fed up with preparing meals, washing dishes, etc., and am likely to go on a binge of dining out weekends – even if we have a housekeeper by next weekend.

Clara telephoned. She is shopping for some furniture and wants to use Mayer's decorating service but without any extra cost.

Sunday, February 18
Pal was one year old today, but we were too concerned with maids to do much about celebrating his birthday.

Telephoned Mother S. The Rolands came over as usual. I was in no mood for a visit but tried not to show it.

Interviewed three applicants. The one we liked best, Margaret Powe, was pretty and well recommended, liked the job and we settled on her. She agreed to come in this evening at 8:00. She telephoned at 8:00 that she would be a little late and did arrive soon afterwards. I appreciated her calling. A boyfriend brought her in a car both times. I hope she will be ok, and will stay a reasonable time before she gets married again.

Monday, February 19
Margaret seemed to take hold of everything so readily that I felt perfectly free to leave with Jules for the office. I do not feel altogether relaxed about her only because it is hard to believe that so young, attractive and intelligent a girl will stay on a job where she is so much of the time alone.

Lunched in the cafeteria with Mag Flexner, Irene Shriber, and Milt Janns.

I had sent Mother one of the clippings about Jules. She got the *Lawrence Tribune* to print an article with picture about me, somewhat inaccurate and greatly exaggerating my importance. But it probably made her happy and did no real harm.

Tuesday, February 20
Downtown at noon and bought some black shoes.

Had cases on the subpanel agenda with Stasi and Jerry.

After work to a cocktail party given by the Schweitzers, who are attached to the French Embassy. It was a lovely party, not a mob scene, with an apparently endless supply of delicious champagne. After the party, the Boyntons, the Myrons, and we went to the Larry Lessers'

---

19   Irving Levy was a labor lawyer defending workers' rights. He had previously worked in the Department of Labor. His law partner was Joseph Ruah co-founder of Americans for Democratic Action and active in civil rights issues.

for a delicious steak dinner. Then sat around for the rest of the evening drinking excellent cocktails and listening to a long monologue by Larry Lesser on what a brilliant guy Larry Lesser is. It was quite a price to pay even for a good meal and some good liquor.

Wednesday, February 21
Lunched in the cafeteria with several girls, including a Dr. Platt, an attractive girl who had just come to work for Public Health.
Edith Bisgyer invited us over Saturday evening but we already had an engagement.[20] Margaret served a really magnificent dinner this evening, including broiled chicken and a lemon meringue pie as good as any I have ever eaten. She asked if she could get off to go to a movie this evening. I agreed, but she did not go anyhow when she saw what a cold, rainy evening, it was. We like her so far very much, and hope she will work out all right for a long time. Still no word from Carrie.

Thursday, February 22
Ira had school today. We let Margaret off when she finished breakfast and straightening out. Took her to the terminal to show her the bus stop, etc. Ira came home for luncheon. We had cold broiled chicken. It was still wonderful.
After Ira came home from school, we went to a movie. Home to give Pal his supper, intending to go out for dinner ourselves, but Pal was not around. Got fried shrimp platter at Crisfield's to bring home – a good idea as they were delicious, and by the time we got home with them Pal was there.
Played cards. Ira beat Jules and me – watched television, and finally to bed.

Friday, February 23
Margaret showed up in plenty of time to fix breakfast. A windy but rather pleasant day. Walked to the Hickory House for luncheon with Dick Brownstone. Stopped at the Gayety to get tickets for the Lunts' coming show but the line was so long I could not wait.
Margaret fixed a wonderful turkey dinner and served it beautifully. After dinner we had a fire in the fireplace – the first in quite a while. It was very cozy, playing games with Ira, and reading after he went to bed, before the fire – so much as that we did not go out even to do our marketing. Must begin to plan for Ira's birthday party.

Saturday, February 24
Did our marketing in the morning. Margaret fixed a very elaborate luncheon as she was staying on today.
Did some shopping in the afternoon. Dressed in the late afternoon and went to the Frank Browns' cocktail party in honor of the Boyntons. It turned out to be a much larger and more elaborate affair than we had expected – even included – special traffic policemen.
I filled up, as usual, on hors d'oeuvres, but Jules did not and was hungry, so we went to the Silver Fox, where we had very good lobster dinners. Then to the movies to see "Harvey," which we enjoyed so much we saw it through completely after seeing the second half.

---

20   Wife of Paul Bisgyer, Anne's longtime office mate at the NLRB with whom she occasionally rode home.

Sunday, February 25
A pleasant mild day.
I took Ira over for his youth group when he telephoned to ask if we could drive a group of children to the zoo. Jules went. He was gone so long that I was sorry afterwards that I had not gone too. It seemed a long, lonely afternoon. The Rolands did not show up – the first Sunday they have missed in a long while.
Margaret left this morning at practically the crack of dawn. Was picked up by her boy-friend – that is real devotion. I do hope she will stick around for a while – I so hate changing maids.

Monday, February 26
Margaret showed up in good time.
Walked downtown at noon, did some errands, and walked back to the office.
Ira brought two boys home from school to play. Margaret gave them cake and lemonade.
Carrie stopped by this afternoon to get her things. Margaret told me Carrie still showed the effects of a severe beating. The fool, when she could have had comfort and security with us. I cannot feel sorry for her.
Mrs. Wilkinson called to tell me there was a vacancy now for Ira in the tumbling class. I postponed his participation a week in view of his birthday party excitement this coming weekend.

Tuesday, February 27
Left the car for a checkup and rode to work with Wes Silvian.
To the Supreme Court for a while to hear Dave Findling argue a case. He did very well. Lunched there with Stasi Dunas. Back to the office just in time for the subpanel agenda, on which I had cases with Jerry Doherty and Bernie Balicer.
Clara telephoned to let me know she had passed her driving test this morning – her second try.
I rode home with Paul Bisgyer. Hank Wenzel had announced that he is leaving the Board to go into private practice in New York.

Wednesday, February 28
Irene Shriber announced that she is marrying Dave Polier. Very nice for both of them.
Lunched in the cafeteria with Herb Shenkin.
Herb and Duffy Edes came out to dinner. Margaret served a delicious dinner and they both ate as though they had not eaten a decent meal in weeks. We had a cocktail before dinner and highballs afterwards.
They left at a reasonable hour, and as Herb had his car we did not have to take Duffy downtown. Duffy is staying with Herb – very nice, when he is getting $50 a day plus $15 per diem and traveling expenses while serving as a Wage Stabilization consultant.

Year End Summary 1951

One of the most pleasant things that had happened to us this past year was acquiring Margaret as our housekeeper, and having her stay with us so long. I sometimes am ashamed of the importance I place upon having and keeping a good housekeeper because I recognize that it results largely from my laziness, as a good housekeeper saves me so much trouble and inconvenience. That is not the whole or even the main reason, however, for my appreciation of Margaret. She and Ira have become so close because of her patience with and understanding of him that in many respects he prefers to share his interests with her rather than Jules or me or anyone else. Jules too is fond of her and enjoys having her around. She has never objected to the extra work Pal causes, and has cheerfully undertaken little serving jobs and other duties which I would not ordinarily ask a housekeeper to do. And on top of all that, she keeps the house clean and fixes excellent meals. Of course she does run around a good deal in the evening, but that is her business entirely.

One of the things I regret about the past year is the way I botched things up on our summer vacation, first by catching that miserable cold in such a stupid way, and then by dragging Jules and Ira to New England in order to include Mother and Father in our vacation only to incur Mother's deep wrath. I feel that Mother is entirely wrong – it might be a symptom of old age – but that does not make her hostility any more palatable.

Apparently Father agrees with her, or just does not care one way or the other. After all, he never did write to us or take any pains to maintain some sort of a family relationship.

Anne in Office at NLRB

1952

The election of Dwight Eisenhower as president in November signaled a coming change in their lives. Anne and Jules had supported Adlai Stevenson and were disappointed when he lost. In other aspects this was a year of stability. The maid, Margaret, brought continuity to the household; Ira was doing reasonably well in school; and, their group of friends was good. The problem of her parents continued to brother Anne; they did not communicate with her the entire year much to her chagrin.   -- RDH

Saturday, November 1
Very warm but overcast, apparently as a result of the many forest fires in the area. Ira went with me to finish up our marketing in the morning. Margaret was picked up after luncheon. Ira went to the Blair football game. I stayed at home, watched the Ohio State-Northwestern football game, and felt rather lonesome. Later Ira and I had supper in the den while watching television. He enjoyed that very much even if there was nothing particularly interesting to watch.

Sunday, November 2
Jules telephoned in the morning. Got me up, in fact, and none too soon as I had to get the boys to MCJC by 10:30. Developed a bad headache in the afternoon. Went to bed, and evidently slept very soundly as the Koplous stopped by once and the Rolands twice, and rang the doorbell until Ira, who was playing outdoors, noticed them and made my excuses for me. Hannah Sullivan telephoned after I woke up, and I am afraid I was rather short with her. Jules had arranged to have Sid drive tomorrow, but he called and asked me to drive as his car was in the repair shop. Fortunately by the time he called I was feeling a little better.

Monday, November 3
Rain was threatened, so Ira went with me. When we got to Sid's, Irv was there and ready to drive although he is changing jobs and dropping out of the carpool. After much discussion, I wound up driving. Went downtown at noon. Finally found a watchband that would fit my watch.
Pouring in the afternoon. Ira got a ride home with Mrs. Harlowe. I drove home – good practice at least.
Jules got home around 11:00, while I was watching Stevenson deliver his last pre-election speech. Most of the remainder of the radio and television time this evening had been bought by Republicans. Margaret, Ira and I did get to watch "I Love Lucy" though – Ira having no school tomorrow.

Tuesday, November 4
Ira was home from school but had to go to Hebrew school.
Jules picked me up at noon and we went to Hogate's for a very fancy luncheon with cocktails.
Many people pessimistic about the election, but when Pete Ward offered us a share in the large bets he has made, we splurged for $50. Had cases on the subpanel agenda with Marion Ladwig and Max Rosenberg.

Margaret had an especially elaborate meal in honor of Jules' homecoming. I was not hungry but had to do it justice. The election returns started out definitely pro-Eisenhower and continued that way to an amazing landslide victory. We went to the Gangs for an election party and midnight supper – it was more like a wake.

Wednesday, November 5
Max Rosenberg asked me to drive somewhere with him for luncheon, but I was not in the mood for anything gala. Lunched in the cafeteria instead with Stasi. A pretty day, so we went for a little walk afterwards.
Rode home with Dick Brownstone, very depressed about the possibility of losing his job.
Margaret's sister Helen was moving into a small apartment, so Margaret went off this evening after dinner to make arrangements for Geneva to live elsewhere. Geneva is Helen's nurse as much as she is Margaret's, but Margaret evidently had a far stronger feeling of family responsibility.
But the election results outshadow everything else.

Thursday, November 6
Margaret telephoned in the morning and asked me to fix breakfast so she could get Geneva settled and come in later.
Lunched in the cafeteria with Jo Silver. Had coffee in the afternoon with Jerry Doherty, a Republican, and one of the very few happy people around the Board.
Ira's scout carpool miscued again so we had to take him to the meeting. Waited around MCJC then until it was time for our Hebrew School PTA meeting to begin. Ira's teacher, Mrs. Mir, was not there so we could not get a report regarding his progress. Otherwise it was a satisfactory meeting, people seem generally more pleased with the operation of the school this year, and the new rabbi is an improvement.

Friday, November 7
Ralph Winkler and Irv Jaffe rode down with us this morning. Irv works at Alien Property on Fridays.
Lunched in the cafeteria with Max Rosenberg, Jo Silver, Helen Rosen and Almira Stevenson, all still bemoaning the election and what it is likely to mean. Home with Jules, who also took Dave Cohen and Irv Jaffe home.
Jules and I did the marketing after dinner while Margaret and Ira watched television. Margaret put away the groceries and then went out.
We are signing Ira up for group dancing lessons. Should fix up the basement, but everything seems so temporary nowadays.

Saturday, November 8
Marvin telephones from Nate's house to let us know that he and Lois would be here tomorrow morning. Margaret volunteered to come in if we needed her.
Downtown in the forenoon. Took Ira to the dentist to get a filling polished, bought an iron at L&F, and looked at wedding gifts at Garfinckel's and Bertram Shrier's but did not make a final selection. Lunched at the Ambassador Grill.

Home in the late afternoon. Jules had to go to the tailor, so picked up some delicatessen for supper on the same trip. We ate on paper plates in the den while watching television – good food, fun, and an absolute minimum of work. Thus life goes on in spite of the election results.

Sunday, November 9
Margaret called in the morning to ask if we wanted her to come in. Said if we didn't need her before that, she would drive to Baltimore with some friends, but would return by 5:30.
Marvin and Lois called from Aberdeen in the morning to say they would be later than they first said. They arrived about 3:00. Bought us a box of candy. Rested from their trip. Telephoned his folks in Columbus and her mother in Cleveland.
To Mrs. K's Toll House, where we all had especially delicious dinners. Then home, to sip cocktails until Margaret arrived. Drove downtown to the Dupont to see "The Lady Vanishes," still an excellent movie although quite old. Jules and I had seen it many years ago.

Monday, November 10
A rainy day. Marvin and Lois were in bed when we left. We took Ira to school. Paul Bisgyer rode down with us.
Lunched with Jo Silver, Max Rosenberg, and Arthur Leff. Rode home with Ralph Winkler. Marvin and Lois, who did not get up until 11:00, were home from their sightseeing about 5:30. After dinner we sat around and made conversation. They showed no interest in going out. Their idea of the way to spend a honeymoon seemed very peculiar to both Jules and me. They have a car, and I am sure they can afford to do a little stepping out. They are not at all romantic toward each other and act like a couple married many years. Jules and I went out to do some marketing.

Tuesday, November 11
Ira had to go to school, but Jules and I had a holiday. When Marvin and Lois finally got up, we breakfasted and went sightseeing. Stopped at Shrier's and got them an electrically-heated glass tray for their wedding gift. They seemed thrilled with it. After covering a number of places in town, we drove out to Mt. Vernon, stopping at the Seaport Inn in Alexandria for luncheon. Then home. Ira, who also had to go to Hebrew School, got home later than we did. After dinner sat around all evening trying to make conversation. Except when we drag them around, they don't stir.

Wednesday, November 12
Marvin and Lois left when we did, with profuse expressions of gratitude for hospitality and gift.
To Lansburgh's at noon, where I had my hair done and bought two flannel nightgowns for Margaret's birthday present.
Home with Bob Freehling, now part of Paul Bisgyer's carpool. Jules stayed downtown as Kirks had invited all the branch chiefs to cocktails and dinner at the University Club.

Ira brought his report card home today – two D's and two C's – much worse than any of us had expected. He seems shocked by it himself – enough, I hope, to inspire him to work a little harder. One trouble is not taking things seriously enough.

Margaret went out after dinner.

Thursday, November 13

Doherty had been reclassified to the same grade as mine, a grade I had when he first came to the Board. The other supervisors are dropping their appeal for reclassification, however, as they are afraid it will make them more vulnerable to discharge when the administration changes.

Lunched in the cafeteria with Almira Stevenson. Had coffee in the afternoon with Stasi Dunan. Abe Feller, whom I knew at Justice, committed suicide. Very depressing. Ira missed his Scout meeting – too much homework. Expect he would have brushed it off but for his report card. To the National Theater with Ira and Alice Jaffe to see Phil Silvers in "The Top Banana," a zany thing but I was in just the mood for it, and so was Jules.

Friday, November 14

Woke up with a slight headache. Considered staying at home, but then went to the office. Lunched in the cafeteria with Robbie Robinson. Had afternoon coffee with Stasi Dunan, Helen Rosen, and Max Goldberg.

Ira brought home an A on a spelling test, with a note on it commending him for doing better work.

Margaret seemed very pleased with the two nightgowns I gave her for her birthday. She rushed off right after dinner, evidently all set for a big weekend. She asked to be off tomorrow as she was getting a ride to Harrisburg to see her father. Nate and Bobbie telephoned from Philadelphia to invite us to visit for the Thanksgiving weekend. We shall probably go.

Saturday, November 15

The President signed an order making Alien Property income-tax returns available to Congressional probers. Jules' will show his $500 payment to Warner Gardner for defending him in the loyalty attack.

Notice from the school that Ira should have his eyes tested.

The Gangs came over to visit most of the afternoon – evidently their children's favorite form of entertainment. By the time they left and we had dinner, it was time for Ira to go swimming with a Boy Scout group. All of which meant he had no opportunity to do the homework he should have done. He enjoyed the swimming very much, but got home quite late, so will be tired tomorrow.

Sunday, November 16

Jules stopped at Hofbergs on the way back from MCJC, and we had a scrumptious breakfast. I went with him to pick up the boys.

Telephoned Columbus. Mother urged me to come soon for a visit even though Jules was there so recently. The Rolands visited all afternoon. I made an excuse not to have dinner with them as I had to give Ira some time this evening for study. We went to Crisfield's for dinner. When we got home, Jules and Ira went to work on Math. It was a hectic and prolonged session as Ira had apparently made a great many errors, some of them through sheer carelessness, which made Jules quite short-tempered with him.

Monday, November 17
Margaret did not show up. She called in the afternoon to say she got back late from her trip and was going right out to the house – and then did not show up again. When I called, Geneva said she was ill. Fishy!
Lunched in the cafeteria with Stasi Dunan and Grace McEldowney.
Had dinner at Louie's Steak House. Then Jules and Ira had another heated session on Math. Ira had brought home another A in spelling. Glad of it, but that, after all, is memory-work. It is Ira's reasoning powers that worry us.
Jules went to a B'nai B'nith stag party with Bill Levy. He got home about 12:30. Heard Margaret come in a little later.

Tuesday, November 18
Government employees were given an extra hour off today to greet Eisenhower on his way to the White House for a conference with Truman. Stasi Dunan and I used the time to go shopping. Had coffee in the afternoon with Jim Shaw.
Went home with Ralph Winkler and his carpool.
To a membership meeting at MCJC in the evening. Took Evelyn Promisel as Nate could not go. Most of the candidates we supported won – for a pleasant change. The meeting was well attended, so we had the pleasure of seeing a number of old acquaintances and meeting many new ones. The meeting lasted until after midnight but it was never boring.

Wednesday, November 19
Lunched in the cafeteria with Helen Rosen and Myra [also written Mira] Stevenson. To the Supreme Court in the afternoon to hear Bernie Dunare's first argument there. He was excellent. Got a ride up with Lou Becker and a ride back with Sam Ross.
Pouring rain in the late afternoon. Ira got out of school a bit late, missed the carpools and the bus, and walked home in the rain. Poor kid! Margaret saw to it that he took a warm bath and put on dry clothes. Spent a pleasant lazy evening at home. Florence Gang called about theater tickets, Mickey Rosenfeld called about a children's dance group, and Hannah Silvian called to weep on my shoulder about Wes.

Thursday, November 20
Rained all day.
Lunched in the cafeteria with Dick Brownstone.
Had coffee in the afternoon with Joe Silver and Max Rosenberg. Ira brought home no homework – insisted he had none – and went to his Boy Scout meeting.
Mrs. Nir called to say that Ira had caught up with the rest of the Hebrew class and was capable of keeping up except that he was evidently lazy about studying. She said that

he should spend at least a few minutes each day studying Hebrew. But most of the time he maintains that he has no assignment and therefore spends no time studying. I watched some television programs with Jules and some others with Margaret.

Friday, November 21
Poured all day.
Jules and I stopped at the school for a conference with one of Ira's teachers and the guidance counselor. Ira's work is not up to par, and they evidently felt he was capable of doing better.
My feet felt wet when I got to the office so I went down for coffee with Dick Brownstone and Ralph Winkler. Lunched in the cafeteria with Stasi Dunan. Had afternoon coffee with Paul Bisgyer, Bob Freehling, Herb Lipsitz and Sid Ascher.
Poor Ira had to walk home again in a downpour. He bathed and dressed, and we took him to the Rosenfeld's for his first ballroom dancing lesson right after dinner. He enjoyed it very much. We marketed while he was taking his lesson.

Saturday, November 22
Herb Brownell has been named the new Attorney General,[21] which Jules does not consider good news from his standpoint.
In the morning we bought Ira new shoes. Had to stay at home in the afternoon as the Ohio State – Michigan game was being broadcast only on FM. Ohio State won for the first time

---

21 Attorney General of the United States and head of the Department of Justice named by the new Eisenhower administration. Jules worked in Justice.

in several years, and had been the underdog, so Jules was very happy. Joe Friedman called, and they exchanged congratulations.
We went to Kushner's for a fairly good seafood dinner.
Jules went to a special Civic Association meeting about the new tax rates. I stayed at home with Ira. After he went to bed, I watched television until Jules came home and we went to bed.

Sunday, November 23
Ira was given some candy as an award for an extra assignment he had done for Hebrew school. Clara telephoned to suggest, if we were eating out, that we have dinner together. We had had a large breakfast as Ira is back on his 11:00 Hebrew School schedule, so skipped luncheon and went to Brook Farm in the late afternoon for dinner. The meal was rather second-rate, but fortunately the children's dinners were better than ours. We all went in our car, including Pal. It meant quite a bit of crowing and confusion, but the kids and Pal loved every moment of it. Glad Ira has some local cousins, and that they are so fond of one another.

Monday, November 24
Ira won two pencils at school as an award for being runner-up in a spelling match. Hope these awards will inspire him to do his work more conscientiously than he had been doing it.
Drove down to Herzog's with Stasi Dunan for luncheon. The food was not good, but it was a change from the cafeteria's poor food at least.

Had coffee in the afternoon with Ralph Winkler, Horace Rucker, and Charlie Schneider. Went home with Ralph and his carpool. After dinner Jules and I went to the National to see "The Shrike," with Van Heflin in the lead. The play was unusual and interesting, Van Heflin did a splendid acting job, and we had excellent orchestra seats.

Tuesday, November 25
Lunched in the cafeteria with Max and Catherine Goldman. Then dashed to Garfinckel's to look at their sale shoes but did not buy any.
Had cases on the subpanel agenda with Max Rosenberg and Stasi Dunan. Afterwards went down for coffee with Stasi, Adelaide Kelly and Augusta Spaulding joined us.
A very attractive bowl from Marvin and Lois as a thank-you gift – most unexpected.
Jules and I did a few errands in the evening. Got a box of candy at Gifford's to take to Philadelphia with us.
Ira seems quite excited about his trip, his first with us in quite some time.
Tom Polster called from N.Y. re wife's immigration problems.

Wednesday, November 26
I went down with Sid in the morning. Jules took the day off as he had several days annual leave he had to use before December 20, and as he wanted to have a plumber in to do several jobs that needed doing.
I went to Lansburgh's at noon to get my hair done.
Left the office early and took the street car to the terminal. Jules met me there and we went to Garfinckel's and selected our Xmas cards.
Margaret evidently had one of her cab-driving friends visiting her most of the day. She dashed off after dinner to have her hair done. Her mother had wired her some money and she is going home for the weekend.
Letter from Gertrude inviting us to Milton's bar mitzvah.

Thursday, November 27
Margaret decided not to go to Columbus for so little time and was left with no plans. I called Bobbie, who would have liked to have her but no room. Too bad we did not call earlier. We left Pal at the Aspin Hill kennels again. Lunched at a Howard Johnson en route. Arrived in the early afternoon, which gave the children time to play and get reacquainted before dinner, which was at about 6:00. Nate took some flashlight photos, and showed some movies we had taken at different times and at different places, in a few of which we appeared.
Telephoned Columbus.
Sat around and chatted a while after the kids got to sleep, and then we all went to bed fairly early.

Friday, November 28
Quite cold but clear and fairly sunny.
After luncheon the children went to a local movie, and Bobbie, Jules and I went downtown. Bobbie and I shopped while Jules called on Pachel and got a haircut. We all met at 6:00 at Nate's office. We were to go out to dinner by ourselves and the maid was to feed the children. I had had a very slight headache earlier in the day, which by 6:00 was a full-

fledged migraine. Nate gave me some pills which only made matters worse. They finally took me home, I went to bed, and they went out the Blue Bell Inn for what they told me later was a terrific dinner. Too bad I missed it and, worse, messed up part of their evening.

Saturday, November 29
I felt quite all right again. In the afternoon the three of us took Lynn downtown to the dentist. Nate met us there and took us to the Colonnade for a delicious luncheon. Shopped for just a little while, during which I bought shoes and a hat at Bonwit Teller's. The children began to grow impatient then, so we took them home.
Jules took Ira and the three girls to Williamson's for dinner to clear the way for Bobbie's big dinner party. Nate got home too late to take them. I greeted the first guests as neither Bobbie nor Nate was dressed when they arrived. It was a very fancy party, 18 guests, lots of delicious food and all kinds of liquor, three people to serve, etc., etc.

Sunday, November 30
It snowed during the night. Ira was out playing in it long before we were out of bed. We went to the Pachels' for brunch. Ira had a wonderful time in the snow with the Pachel boys.
The roads were clear, the day was sunny, and we had a very pleasant trip except that some detours confused Jules and we went considerably out of the way. By the time we picked up Pal, it was time for dinner, which we ate at The Town and Country Inn. The mail included a note from Marion and Lois thanking us most effusively for our hospitality.

The Kaplans telephoned and asked if they could drop in. We told them we had just returned from a trip but to come ahead. Had drinks by the fire, so cozy.

Year End Summary 1952

The event of 1952 most likely to affect our lives was the change in administration, the first in our many years of government service. How much we shall be affected remains to be seen. It is too indefinite for us to make any plans about it, so we shall just coast along in the status quo as long as it lasts.

I have had no direct word from Mother or Father all year. I would not have thought it possible, until it happened, that they could or would so completely sever ties with me. And for, in my opinion, no reason at all.

Ira is well and happy, and is, I believe, doing better work in school since we cracked down on him following our conference with his teacher and counselor. He is blossoming out a bit socially also since he began taking dancing lessons.

Margaret is still with us – something of a record for keeping a live-in maid. She has annoyed me a good deal with her frequent days off, but on the whole she has been a wonderful housekeeper for us.

Pal is still with us also – and that is something of a record for keeping a dog, in our neighborhood at least. As a matter of fact, if we do not lose our jobs, I should be content to go on in the coming year just about as we have in the past year.

The Diaries

Part V

1953 to 1961
McCarthyism and the Struggle to Survive

In 1953 Anne and Julius celebrated their fourteenth wedding anniversary. Anne was forty-three years old. She had been a lawyer with the National Labor Relations Board for sixteen years, giving her some seniority. The election of Eisenhower had brought in a new Republican administration for the first time in twenty years, and both Anne and Julius faced uncertainty in their jobs. Anne was terminated by the NLRB. The new administration made a broad argument that government positions were political patronage, including hers with the NLRB. However, not everyone at the Board was terminated, suggesting the real cause for her loss of position might have been her association with the group of alleged Communists in the NLRB in the late 1930's. Although she never seems to have been a member of the group, she did associate with them socially quite frequently. Later, she sued the government for reinstatement and won, and she went back to work with the Board.

This was the time of McCarthyism. When Julius was threatened with a "loyalty investigation," which he found outrageous, he decided that private practice would be better than government work under those circumstances. He joined two friends, Joe Friedman and Mel Locker, to set up their own law firm. A few years later they expanded by adding Naiden.

During this time they were active in the Sunday Night Book Club that remained a focal point of their social lives for decades. Other families in the Club were Bill and Ruth Levy, Irv and Alice Jaffe, Arthur and Florence Gang, and the Middletons. Ruth Levy became Anne's best friend. Anne mentioned her for the first time on Februry 16, 1954 when Ruth called to say that she and Bill would sponsor the Oneg for Ira's bar mitzvah. From then on, she appears every few days in the diary until the last entry in 1978.

As a working professional, Anne felt that she needed help with household chores, and she wanted someone to be there when Ira arrived home from school. Finding a maid who could work consistently was a continuing problem.

The family members who continued to be important were Anne's sister, Clara, her husband Lou Roland, and the Wagshal family, as well as her mother and father. Anne's other sister Jean (who changed her name to Janet) and her husband Joe Russcol appear occasionally. Anne refers to Janet as Jan normally in the diary. The death of their father and the increasing dementia of their mother made this a disturbing time for the three sisters.

The Schlezinger family played the most important role, including Mother S., Jules' brothers Nate, Lou, and Edward and his sister Gertrude Lewin among others. Nate and his wife Bobbie continued to live in Philadelphia, which permitted them to visit with some frequency. Lou and his wife, Lucille, lived in Schlezinger hometown, Columbus, Ohio, as did Gertrude and her husband, and Edward and Madelyn. -- Ron Duncan Hart

Diaries. 1953 Through 1961.

1953

By 1953 they were in their fifth year of living in Silver Spring and adapted to suburban living. Anne was satisfied with her work situation. When the new Republican administration under Eisenhower began making significant personnel changes in the government, and McCarthyism was reaching a peak at this time. Jules went into private practice, and Anne had to fight to keep her position.

Anne's colleagues in the NLRB represent a new generation of lawyers. None of the names from the activist period pre-World War II period were left. Anne had worked with the Board for sixteen years, and she would work there another twenty-five years.

For vacation they went to Cape Cod, visiting Anne's family in Lawrence, and having a relaxing time at Provincetown and Hyannisport. Jules and Ira went for regular swims at the beach, but Anne only occasionally mentions being at the beach. Her comments are more oriented to the meals and the evening entertainment. -- RDH

Tuesday, September 1
Ira gave us a very attractive tray and glasses set and Jules gave me a beautiful stole in honor of our anniversary. And Merv told me Rodgers was keeping none of the supervisors! Lunched with Jules at Hogate's. Home with Herb. Had misplaced my key and Ira was at Ronnie's again. I had brought some work home so sat on the front steps and sweated it out.

In the evening to Mrs. K's Tea Room for a lovely dinner. Met the Raums[1] there.
Elsie telephoned from Ocean City. Her cottage was not available but at Jules' request she had reserved a place for us for the weekend. Anniversary card from Marion, thank-you note from Darlien and Jerry, and a very amusing letter from Eve Herrup.

Wednesday, September 2
Elouise called and came in. Ira went swimming and to a movie with Tommy Grimes.
Had cases on the Board agenda with Brownstone, Rosenberg, and Krasnecki. Rodgers was there.[2] The boys[3] all did a magnificent job but so far none of them has been "chosen." McCarty and several other drones have been. So far he has taken people from the Board, which is good, but all at lower classifications than mine, which is bad.
Lunched with Krasnecki, Al Somers, and Earl Bellman.[4]

---

1   Anne's former boyfriend Arnold Raum and his wife.
2   William P. Rodgers. In 1953 he was the Deputy Attorney General of the U.S. for the new Eisenhower administration, and he was apparently attending NLRB reviews to chose people for Department of Justice positions. He had previously been involved in both the Alger Hiss case and the Julius and Ethel Rosenberg cases. He was later named Attorney General and then served as Secretary of State under President Nixon.
3   Anne's assumption is that only men were being considered for jobs in Justice. She was a joint presenter on the three cases mentioned, but she had no expectation of being a candidate.
4   Somers and Bellman were NLRB judges. Anne and Krasnecki were lawyers.

Home with Jules. It was so late, and so hot, that we went to the Hot Shoppe for supper. Afterwards, bought Ira some shoes at Halin's. Anniversary cards from the Levins and the Ed Schlezingers.

Thursday, September 3
Bernie Balicer was in the building around noon so I lunched with him and several of the other boys.
Attended an organizing meeting of GS13's and above. Decided we should organize, as we are otherwise unrepresented for collective bargaining purposes. And we are going to have to do some negotiating with the Board.
Ira[5] went swimming and to a movie with Ronnie, then came home with him, but so late we were all a bit alarmed by the time they showed up. Fixed a very good dinner with the help of some Chicken Delight boxes. We ate in the backyard. Ira and Ronnie went to bed about 10:00, giggling over their plans to stay awake for hours and were asleep almost immediately.

Friday, September 4
Hot, but not quite as hot as it had been.
Had a case on the Board agenda with Ben Gueshin, a highly disillusioning experience for both of us. Lunched with Stasi Dunan, Dick Brownstone, Mel Welles, and Art Christopher.[6]

Another meeting of the supervisors' organization.
Jules and I came home a bit early. Elouise had already left. Ronnie left about noon.
Fixed a very good dinner, which we ate on the porch. Had fixed a rather fancy breakfast, which we also ate on the porch. Might really become a cook when I lose my job.
Packed our bags. Late in the evening went for a quart of milk, a little ride, and frozen custard cones – all four of us.

Saturday, September 5
Had planned to get an early start, but it was 8:00 before we got away. A cloudy morning, making the driving pleasant, but warm and sunny when we got to the beach about 11:00.[7] Our housekeeping cottage was quite nice, but not too clean and lacking a number of things. We went to the boardwalk for luncheon and to do some shopping. Then to the beach. The water was rough but not too cold, and we all – including Pal – had a wonderful time.
The Grosses visited us in the afternoon. Later we went to the Ship Café for dinner. The food was good but the service was terrible.
Then to the boardwalk. Ran into the Bisgyers, the Flaxes, and the Bellmans.[8] Played some of the games; Ira went on some of the rides; and then home and to bed.

Sunday, September 6
A beautiful day. The water was rougher than

---

5   Ira and Ronnie were twelve years old at this point.
6   Many people appear briefly in Anne's diary but seem to have been at the NLRB for a limited time, such as Gueshin. Others, such as Welles and Christopher are there for long periods and become judges. Many women, such as Stasi Dunan, appear for long periods in her diary but never become judges.
7   Delaware shore. A number of their Washington friends were there.
8   NLRB colleagues.

ever, but exciting and enjoyable. We fixed both breakfast and luncheon at the cottage. Spent practically all day on the beach, but were "at home" long enough for the Grosses to visit at one time, and the Bisgyers and Flaxes at another time, to admire our place which is evidently far more livable than where they are all staying.

Had dinner at the Sandpiper. Then to the boardwalk. Met the Flaxes and Bisgyers again. Ira went on some of the rides with Bonnie and Freddie Flax, and with Naomi Neiman who is here with the Flaxes. It made the same rides he went on last night far more enjoyable to him when he was with friends about his age.

Monday, September 7

Pouring in the morning. Fixed breakfast and luncheon. The Grosses visited us. Telephoned Columbus. In the afternoon stopped to say goodbye to the Bisgyers, Flaxes, and Grosses, and then visited Gladys Boestor in her new and ultra modern cottage. Met her husband for the first time.

The sun came out in the late afternoon, so we went to the beach. The water was rough but we have become accustomed to it. Later the Bellmans stopped by, and we all drove to the Dinner Bell in Rehoboth for dinner. Afterwards to the boardwalk. We played a number of games, much to Ira's delight. Enjoyed the company of Earl and Helen Bellman[9] far more than we had expected we would.

Tuesday, September 8

We were quite cold last night – except Ira, who was permitted for the first time to have Pal sleep with him. Bright and sunny day, but the breeze was a bit crisp. Ira went crabbing and for a little ride on a horse that belongs to the motel owner, and we played Scrabble. To the boardwalk for luncheon. Then on to the beach. The water was delightful but the air a bit cool for me, so I left before Jules and Ira did. We had planned to stay until tomorrow, but Jules and Ira found the beach house lonesome and we decided to leave today. Had a pleasant trip home. Got there about 6:30. Fed Pal. We went to the Silver, where we had a very good dinner. Did some marketing. Then home to unpack.

New Year greetings[10] from the Bill Levys and Marion Mynot. Ira had a postcard from Evelyn Gunter and a ticket to a ballgame with the Knothole gang.

Wednesday, September 9

Joe Friedmen[11] telephoned before we were up to discuss with Jules forming a law partnership with Mel Locker. Later in the day Paul Myron called and said he had to see Jules. Jules was convinced it was about his loyalty file. What a bitter farce that is!

We did more marketing. Bought a tie for Jules. Lunched at Hofberg's. In the evening, in honor of the holiday, I fixed an especially good dinner. After dinner we went to services, held this year at Leland Junior High. New Year's greetings from Mother S. and from Lucille and Louie.

Discussed at some length the pros and cons of Joe's offer. Jules will almost certainly accept it. There is so little choice, for one thing.

---

9   Earl Bellman was a judge with the NLRB.
10   Rosh Hashanah, Jewish New Year.
11   This partnership was established, and later Naiden joined them.

Thursday, September 10

Elouise came in, as arranged, a little later than usual. Gave her directions, then left for services. Afterwards we had an elaborate holiday meal in the dining room, best linens, silver, etc. Elouise had everything just about ready when we got home, and was very helpful. Shortly after we finished, Joe, Libby and Robert Friedman arrived. Joe and Jules discussed the proposed law partnership at length. It sounds attractive, and Jules may have little choice but to accept it. The Friedmans had just about left when the Rolands[12] arrived, and Jules discussed at length with Lou the pros and cons at this time of private law practice. The New Year is starting with a promise of many changes.

Friday, September 11

Jules went to the office to see Myron. Senator McCarthy[13] had asked for Jules' personnel file, everyone got scared – Townsend being in Europe – and Jules set their minds at ease by announcing his resignation to the effect in two weeks. And so a loyal, hardworking, patriotic government employee gets booted out. But it is probably all for the best that he is getting out. And what a happy coincidence to have the offer from Joe at this time.

Ira and I went to services in the morning, did some errands in the afternoon, and spent the rest of the day at home. In the evening Jules and I went marketing. Lou Roland telephoned to ask what Jules had decided.

Saturday, September 12

New Year's greetings from the Levins and from Helen Lee, Jerry and Eric.

In the afternoon we all went to the baseball game, Ira as one of the Knothole Gang, and Jules and I separately. It was a fairly interesting game and the day was quite pleasant except for one brief shower.

We had all eaten so much junk at the game that we were not hungry, so had a late light supper in the den while watching television. Fixing three meals – of any kind – at home in any one day makes me feel quite virtuous and domestic. Actually, in fairness to Jules and Ira, I should devote myself far more than I do to the domestic and culinary "art."

Sunday, September 13

Drove over to MCJC[14] in the morning to work out Ira's transportation schedule. They were supposed to have worked out a cab-ride arrangement, but it is not yet ready to function, so he will ride over, temporarily, with the mother of one of his classmates and come home with Evelyn Promisel.

We ate all our meals at home again today. I did not mind except that by the end of the day I felt that I had spent practically the whole day in the kitchen.

---

12   Jules' law partner, Joe Friedman and his family, and Anne's sister Clara Roland and her husband Lou.

13   Senator Joseph McCarthy and the investigations of people considered to be Communists or sympathizers. Jules had been president of the Washington chapter of the National Lawyers Guild, considered leftist by some, and he knew many of the early NLRB lawyers accused of being Communists. To avoid the potentially devastating problems from a McCarthy investigation, he resigned his position in the Department of Justice and opened a private law practice with Joe Friedman and Mel Locker.

14   Montgomery County Jewish Center.

Dropped in on the Rolands for a few minutes to see their recreation room, now practically completed, and most attractive and livable. We probably should do likewise but our house seems so much too big already.

Monday, September 14
Mrs. Grimes took Ira and Tommy to school. I went back to the office, to the gossip, rumors, back-biting, and bitterness now prevalent there – to such an extent that although everyone was friendly and cordial to me, I came home with a headache. Ira had tried to make some popcorn, had burned it, the whole house smelled and the kitchen was a mess. That was almost the last straw. I managed to fix supper of a sort, and went to bed shortly after supper.
Jules had met at noon today with Joe and Mel and worked out some of the details of their proposed association, but much remains yet to be resolved – the firm name, for one thing. I hope it all works out all right, for the sake of all of us who are involved.

Tuesday, September 15
We took Ira and Tommy to school this morning.
Lunched with Helen Rosen, who is appealing her RIF notice.[15] Her husband was RIF'd some time ago and had not yet found another job. A New Year's greeting card from some people named Kossow whom neither Jules nor I could recall ever having met. In any event, with Jules going into practice, we shall have to be far more diligent than we have been in such matters as sending New Year's greetings and socializing with the right people. Joe and Mel have some pretty extravagant ideas. It will take plenty of substantial fees to meet their expenses and leave anything over.

Wednesday, September 16
Bernice Balicer was visiting at the office. A pretty day so we walked to the Hickory House for luncheon and walked back to the office.
Home with Ralph Winkler.[16] Am going to have to find a ride down when Jules leaves his government job.
Ira rode his bike to school today, but was home later than usual as he always has errands to do when he rides his bike. He did some homework after dinner while Jules and I went marketing. Note from Hannah Silvian. Wes had been RIF'd but is appealing. She wants me to let her know whether or not his appeal is sustained. He has not sent her any alimony as yet.

Thursday, September 17
Sid Gross was back from his job-hunting trip to New York – a few leads, nothing definite. Morning coffee with Joe Silver, Sid Lindner and Helen Rosen. Attended a combined union – supervisors meeting at noon to hear a report on the Board's latest "bargaining" session with the Union. Lunched afterwards with a big group.
Home with Ralph Winkler.
Called some maids who had advertised for jobs. One was to come out this evening for an interview but did not show up.

---

15   Reduction in Force notice of being terminated from a job.

16   Ralph Winkler, friend, Chief Counsel to Board member Gerald Brown and later NLRB judge.

The partners tossed a coin to see whether Jules or Mel would be second in the firm name. Jules lost. He has also been outvoted as to the expensive quarters Joe and Mel prefer.

Friday, September 18
Had a case on the Board agenda – a motion in an old case of Balicer's so I went in alone. The atmosphere, which used to be so chummy, was frigid. During the day Rodgers' lieutenants interviewed many of us, and asked the most insulting stupid questions.[17] Lunched with Harry Kuskin and Ralph Winkler.[18]
Home with Herb Silberman as he had waited for me to finish my interview although I could have come home a little earlier with Jules.
Changed my clothes in a hurry, and we went to the Dinner Bell for dinner. Then to Yom Kippur services at Leland Junior High. All the Board people who were there were still buzzing about the Rodgers interviews. He must be a complete heel.

Saturday, September 19
To services[19] in the morning. We all went breakfastless, but Ira and I broke down around 2:00 and went out for a sandwich. There was a break of 1 1/2 hours in the afternoon, during which we went home.
I had left a roast in the oven on the automatic controls, so we had a very good dinner with relatively little work or delay.

A warm pleasant day. We did some marketing, but other than that it seemed pleasant just to stay at home for the rest of the day and evening.
Jules telephoned Columbus to check on how Mother felt after the holidays. Announced that he was going into private practice and would be in Columbus to try to drum up some business.

Sunday, September 20
Ira was picked up for Hebrew School and for breakfast at MCJC with the boys who have been bar mitzvah and those about to be. In the afternoon we barbecued hamburgers in the backyard. They were very good. The weather remained fair but it threatened to rain from time to time so we could not relax entirely.
Jules and I did a little work on the mailing list for his announcements, but much remains yet to be done.
Max Rosenberg telephoned to let me know that his second son was born yesterday. He was quite excited. Called principally in order to let me know he would not be at work on time tomorrow morning.
Ate supper in the den while watching television.

Monday, September 21
Ira and Tommy went to school on their bicycles.
Had morning coffee with Sid Lindner, Ralph Winkler and Stasi Dunan. Attended a union meeting at noon. Afterwards a large group of us lunched together – to discuss the favorite subject nowadays, the crummy way

---

17 Again, William Rodgers, deputy Attorney General, relates to September 2 entry.
18 Both Chief Counsels to Board members.
19 Yom Kippur services.

the Board is treating legal assistants.
Home with Jules.
We had roast beef for dinner, cooked with the help of the automatic controls.
Evelyn Gunter telephoned, thinks the people for whom she has been working are about to leave town, and proposed that we try a full-time but live-out arrangement. That might be a happy solution.

Tuesday, September 22
Elouise was on the job bright and early. She has been a real help. Had morning coffee with Max Rosenberg, Joe Silver and Tom Wilson.
Met Jules at Garfinckel's at noon. Shopped for a dress for me, but did not find anything. Wound up at Lansburgh's, and lunched on the balcony.
Jules, Joe and Mel signed a 5-year lease today for a very expensive space in a new building to be completed November 1st at 17th and K Streets.
Home with Herb Silbermen.
Fixed broiled chicken for dinner. Later we went to Gifford's for dessert.
Talked to Evelyn again on the telephone. She does not want to work part time. I have liked cooking part time.

Wednesday, September 23
Had morning coffee with Joe Silver and Tom Wilson. Lunched with Stasi Dunan. Had afternoon coffee with Dick Brownstone. Came home with Sam Ross. We had cold broiled chicken for dinner. It was delicious. Cannot decide what we should do about Evelyn. Her reliability and other good qualities seem very attractive after Margaret. On the other hand, she will have a long trip. Also, I will be paying her about as much as I would a live-in maid while getting considerably less service. Elouise has been able in the two days she works to keep the entire house clean and to do the laundry. I have managed the meals surprisingly well, and Ira had enjoyed his "independence."

Thursday, September 24
Had morning coffee with Joe Silver, Helen Rosen and Max Rosenberg. A lovely day so I walked to Hecht's and walked back without having bought a thing.
Evelyn called. Definitely wants the job. Guess I will try it although we are all a bit regretful at letting Elouise go as she has done a splendid job. She cleans and launders expertly, and Ira likes her very much. We went to the Villa Rosa for a very enjoyable dinner. Then went shopping, but were unsuccessful again. Did really want a new dress for the party tomorrow.
Came home from the office today with Ralph Winkler.[20] Am going to have a problem after tomorrow getting to work. May try public transportation.

Friday, September 25
Had morning coffee with Max Rosenberg, Joe Silver, Tom Wilson and Art Christopher.[21]
Downtown at noon. Lunched, bought a

20   Winkler was one of Anne's oldest friends at the Board.
21   These were NLRB regulars. Rosenberg and Anne frequently lunched during this time. Later, he was promoted to NLRB administrative judge (1964) and continued until his retirement in 1980.

dress, and had my hair done – all in record-quick time.

Jules and I left a little early, went home to get Ira, then to the party in Jules' honor at the Carlyle Hotel.[22] There was a large crowd, plenty of liquor and food, and everyone being so complimentary and gracious. Then speeches were made by Tom Creighton, Colonel Townsend, Roland Kirks, Hal Baynton, and Judge Bazelon, all lauding Jules so brightly that Ira and I were mighty proud. I had not appreciated how highly he was regarded. Afterwards a group of us had dinner at Longchamps. Jules was presented with a handsome brief case.

Saturday, September 26
We all slept rather late. Jules and I went marketing after breakfast while Ira did some work around the yard.
In the afternoon visited the new Garden Shop opened by the Herb Davids yesterday. Met a number of acquaintances there.
Later to the Joe Friedmens' to decide together some questions about furniture for the offices. Mel was there for a little while. We had a few drinks, and then a very informal but very enjoyable supper. Ira and Jane hit it off beautifully. We should try to have them see more of each other as long as they seem to enjoy each other's company so much.
Did not stay too late as Ira had been up so late last night. Joe is contagiously optimistic about the new firm.

---

22   This was the going way party for Jules, who left the Department of Justice to enter the private partnership with Joe Friedman and Mel Locker.

Sunday, September 27
We evidently have a carpool on Sundays with the Mattells and the Marmelsteins. The boys go in a cabpool during the week. The entire arrangement seems to be quite satisfactory.
At the Rolands' request we went with them to look at one of the furnished Post Homes of '53. They went on to look at others and then to eat out. We went home and fixed a delicious barbecue mid-day meal. They stopped in again afterwards to visit and talk some more about Jules' partnership arrangements. There seems to be a note of longing in Lou's voice whenever he discusses it. Everyone wants out of government service these days. Ira had picked up a head cold, probably from playing so hard and getting overheated yesterday at the Friedmans.

Monday, September 28
Ira's cold seemed better so we took him to school. I worked at home until I went to pick up Evelyn about 11:30. Showed her around, and then Jules and I had luncheon. Afterwards he took me to the office and went to keep an appointment with Joe and Mel.
Had afternoon coffee with Art Leff,[23] Charlie Schneider, Horace Ruchel and Lou Libbin.
A staff meeting at which the Board announced its latest personal action in lieu of the revoked RIF[24] – the discharge of several people, including Stasi and Joe,[25] and the transfer of others, including me, to the "ghost staff."

23   Chief Counsel to the Board Chairman Frank McCulloch and later NLRB judge.
24   Reduction in Force, being terminated from a position.
25   Stasi Dunan and Joe Silver (?)

Home with Sam Ross.
Evelyn fixed and served a very good dinner.
Got Elouise a job with the Ralph Winklers.

Tuesday, September 29
Jules took me to the terminal, where I got a streetcar and then he went on to school with Ira and Tommy. Had morning coffee with Max Rosenberg and Sid Lindner.[26]
Libbin called a meeting of the "ghost staff." As it is top-heavy with supervisors, Bob Freehling and I will work as independent operators.[27] Lunched with Sid Lindner, Dave London and Charlie Schneider.[28] In the afternoon got a C Case to review – the first in a long while.[29] Home with Ralph Winkler. Find coming home to Evelyn's housekeeping very pleasant. Gave her a blouse, not too good, but she seemed pleased with it.
By evening, much to my chagrin, I seemed to be sniffling pretty badly. Nate telephoned from Philadelphia.

Wednesday, September 30
A very warm day – in the 90's. Ira went on his bike, Jules took me to the terminal, and I went downtown on the trolley.
A meeting of the supervisors' organization. Stasi Dunan, Dick Brownstone and I walked to the Art Gallery for luncheon. Had coffee with Max Rosenberg and Joe Silver.
My cold got worse and worse. Home with Sam Ross. Joe Friedman came over after dinner to discuss a few matters with Jules, who had worked at home all day – except when he was watching the opening World Series game on TV. Sid Gross stopped by to leave some things Jules had forgotten at the office. It would not hurt him to offer me a ride down occasionally, after all the rides home I saved him.

Year End Summary 1953

As the year drew to a close, we seemed to be getting along splendidly except for two problems that have been with us on and off for a number of years – Ira's poor grades at school and the lack of a real housekeeper. The first is, of course, the more serious as Ira is reaching the point where his poor school work will affect his eligibility for college and thus his whole way of life. The second is important because we are all so much happier and more contented when we have someone who can keep house and cook, particularly if it is someone reliable as well as competent.

Jules seems to be doing well in his new endeavor, and that is very gratifying to all of us. It may be a long time before he can equal the income he had in the government, but the peace of mind and satisfaction he feels at being out of the government at present are worth thousands of dollars. It might have been different if Stevenson had been elected, but he was not. By the time a change in administration does occur, I

---

26   Both NLRB judges.
27   Independent operators were paid on a per diem basis and were not listed as permanent employees. Although she did not totally lose her job, she was moved to a more vulnerable position.
28   All NLRB judges.
29   The NLRB has two types of cases. C cases refer to charges of unfair labor practices; and R cases are petitions for representation filed by individuals, employers, or unions.

hope he will be so well established in private practice that he would not consider going back into government work even if he could. The unattractiveness of government service at present is brought home vividly to me practically every day that I am at the office - the prejudice, the suspicion, the insecurity, the hostility toward those who remain from an earlier administration. I hope, nevertheless, that I shall be able to hold on to my job as we need the money, as I should be lost without a job, and as I cannot see myself going into private practice.

1954

In 1954 Anne was 44 years old and in mid-career, but her loyalty was under question, which cast a shadow over her. The Eisenhower administration decided that her job was a patronage position and not a regular civil service position, and she was dismissed from the NLRB, which was a big blow to Anne. She appealed and threatened litigation. Eventually her case was reviewed and reversed. The fact that the FBI had been investigating her on grounds of loyalty (i.e. Communist sympathies) immediately before her dismissal leaves in question the true reason for her being terminated.

The bright point in the year was Ira's bar mitzvah. It was a special event for family and friends. In August they took a family vacation to the New York lake country and then on to Quebec. Anne's first long vacation had been to Quebec twenty years earlier as a young single woman working in Washington. That trip had been by ship. They returned to Quebec for other vacations, and it was a place that she liked. They visited Anne's parents on the way back.   -- RDH

Monday, February 15
Ralph and Herb being out of town, Jules took me to the terminal and I went downtown on the trolley while he took the car to a repair shop. Had morning coffee with Mira Stevenson. A lovely warm day so I walked downtown and back at noon.
The FBI is conducting <u>another</u> investigation

of me.[30] They have inquired of Paul Bisgyer[31] and Sam Efron.

Came home with Mira Stevenson. Joe Friedman brought Jules home. Our car will be ready tomorrow evening. Sam Edes[32] stopped in to see Jules today – <u>may</u> come to dinner tomorrow. A note from Mother that she does not feel up to the trip here for the bar mitzvah and enclosing a check for $25. Helen Lee and her husband are the only other ones who have declined so far. Acceptance from Carroll Cahan, the Gangs, and Allan Marmelstein, and a postcard from Bobby and Nate. Ira got an invitation from Allan Marmelstein.

Tuesday, February 16
Very warm-record-breaking, in fact. Ira had a head cold though and stayed home this morning but went to school in the afternoon.

I went down with Mira Stevenson. Had morning coffee with Tom Wilson, Winn Newman, Eleonor Schwartzbach, Dave Davidson, and Noah Minkin.

Went to Jelleff's at noon. Finally bought a dress in the French Room – navy blue silk with a small red print.

Afternoon coffee with Charlie Schneider, Bob Piper, Sid Lindner, and Art Leff.

Duffy Edes stopped at the office about 4:00, sat around until 5:00, and then we both rode home with the Brownstones. Jules picked up our car on his way home. Dezorah served her first company dinner, not bad thanks to a luscious steak. I have hired Agnes and given Dezorah notice. Hope I am doing the right thing.

Ruth Levy called to say they were coming but lost the card. They are sponsoring an Oneg Shabbat as their gift to Ira – a most generous gift.

Jules took Duffy to the Willard about midnight.

Wednesday, February 17
Ira insisted upon going to school on his bike although the weather looked threatening, and it was pouring before he got half way to school. I went down with Jules.

Had morning coffee with Sid Lindner, Bob Piper, Charlie Schneider, and Tom Wilson. Had no luncheon.

Had afternoon tea with Dick Brownstone, Helen Rosen, and Ogden Fields. Came home with Jules.

Acceptances from the Mark Winklers and the Joe Friedmans.[33] Evelyn Promisel telephoned – the FBI had been inquiring there.

Ralph Winkler[34] telephoned – is back and will pick me up in the morning.

Ira's suit and my dress were delivered today. Jules and Ira liked my dress very much. Jules' only criticism was that I should have bought more than one dress.

Ira said the bar mitzvah gift he would like best is a brother. Poor kid.

Thursday, February 18
Pal was four years old today. Ralph picked

---

30 These are the problems that haunted Anne during this time because of her associations with leftists in the NLRB in the late 1930's.
31 Long time NLRB colleague and friend.
32 Samuel Edes, NLRB colleague and friends
33 Joe Friedman, law partner with Jules.
34 NLRB judge and close friend with the Schlezingers.

me up in the morning. Had morning coffee with Sid Lindner, Earl Bellman, Tom Wilson, Charlie Schneider, and Bob Piper.[35]

To Lansburgh's at noon to have my hair done. Walked over and rode back.

Had afternoon tea with Dick Brownstone, George Hadjinoff, and Herb Lipsitz.

Came home with Ralph.

Beeson was confirmed, after a long and heated debate, by the close vote of 45-42. I won $1 from Piper. Should have gone shopping this evening, but Ira got home so late from Hebrew School that, by the time we finished dinner, there seemed to be little point in going. Beeson's[36] confirmation, although expected, makes me hesitate to buy too many clothes. Staying home would make a difference in what I should need.

Friday, February 19

Ralph was not going in today so I went down with Jules. Had a case on the agenda. The Board members seemed unusually congenial and decided the case with the utmost liberalness.

Rode downtown at noon with Mira. Walked back. Had afternoon coffee with Max Goldman, Bernard Greenfield, and Elilu Platt. Came home with Paul Bisgyer.

Ira was knocked down on his bike on the way home from school – late because he had stopped to watch a basketball game. Told the driver he and his bike were all right, but he was shaken up and his bike was damaged. Neither the driver nor any of the onlookers offered him any assistance. He went to bed early. Later Jules and I went to the Ira Jeffes'. The Leon Ulmans, Sid Grosses and Saul Elsons were also there. It was a congenial group and a very pleasant evening. Acceptance from the Sharfmans, Rosses, McConnell, Johnson, and Steve Seligson.

Saturday, February 20

Acceptance from the [Sid] Lindners, offering to help, the [Mel] Lockers, the Benensons, the Sam Wagshals, and the Leonard Saxes, and from Sara Shostech. The Paul Brands sent regrets, and Marvin and Lois wrote a letter.

Ira went to services in the morning. We went shopping. Later picked him up, took Dezorah downtown and said goodbye to her, went to Duke Zeibut's for luncheon, and then did some shopping. Like most of our expeditions lately, we look at clothes for me and wind up buying only things for Ira.

Stopped at Schusters, a new kosher caterer that opened today, and got some things for supper. Had it opened a little earlier, we probably would have selected it for the bar mitzvah reception. I hope Hoffman will do all right but he impresses me as operating on a shoestring.

Jules went to MCJC[37] again this evening. We were planning to go but the Marmelsteins offered to take Ira so we stopped at home and played Scrabble.

---

35 Lindner, Bellman, Schneider, and Piper were frequent lunch and coffee companions with Anne.

36 Albert C. Beeson was an industrial executive named to the governing Board of the NLRB. His nomination was sharply protested by Democrats and organized labor because the NLRB had been constituted as a neutral judicial body without representatives from either industry or labor. Anne interpreted Beeson's confirmation as swing to the right and a threat to her job.

37 Montgomery County Jewish Center.

Sunday, February 21
Jules drove the Sunday School carpool. A rainy day so I got up to make sure Ira had a good warm breakfast before he left for Sunday School.

Pal was gone again all last night and a good part of the day. He must be courting more ardently than ever. Jules and Ira went to MCJC again in the afternoon to do some research preparatory to writing a bar mitzvah speech for Ira.

After they came home we went out for dinner, first to Schusters, which was too crowded, and then to Louie's Steak House, where we had a very good dinner.

Called Agnes, who was supposed to come in tonight so I could show her around tomorrow, but she was "out." I took it that she had changed her mind without bothering to tell me, although she had originally been most anxious to get the job. Would have thought she would consider Dezorah if not me.

Monday, February 22
No word from Agnes – my guess was right. A lovely day and I was not going to let her unreliability spoil it. Ira had to go to school. Jules and I lazied around for a while, then went shopping. Bought a large supply of liquor for the bar mitzvah and for ourselves. Lunched at the Chuck Wagon.

I had left a veal roast in the oven and set the clock. Got home in time to fix the potatoes, etc., and we had a delicious dinner.

Called the Pollacks about Elouise, but she has been "indisposed" for about a week. They offered me the use of a room for my bar mitzvah guests. The Stevensons and Friedmans have offered to put up people.

Very generous.

Helen Bellman telephoned to sympathize about the accident.

Ralph Winkler telephoned to say he would pick me up in the morning.

Barbara Weinstein, a new neighbor and a friend of Ira's, delivered her response – will "gladly" attend the reception.

Tuesday, February 23
I went down with Ralph. Had morning coffee with Mira Stevenson.

Met Jules at noon. We shopped for furniture for Ira's room. Lunched on Lansburgh's balcony. Had afternoon tea with Winn Newman. Home with Ralph.

Acceptance from the Bellmans, Baums, Davids, Lindenbaums, Liftins, Bayntons, Bazelons[38] (if they can leave another affair early enough), Ulmans, Jay Wolf, Bob Levin, and Richard Mattel. A note from May Wagshal[39] accepting – she had sent the invitation along to Jerry and Darlien. Regrets from the Raums and from Bell Herskowitz. A postcard from Molly vacationing in Florida with Bobby.

Nate telephoned from Philadelphia. Expects to get in late Friday evening and will stay at a patient's suite at the Shoreham.[40] They are giving Ira luggage.

Wednesday, February 24
Ira's bike had been repaired so he rode it to school today. I went down with Jules. Ralph was going in too late for me.

38   Judge Bazelon.
39   Phil Wagshal's wife. Jerry is their son. The Raums refer to her once boyfriend Arnold and his wife. They were social friends in the 1940's.
40   Jules' brother Nate stayed in the suite of one of his patients in the Shoreham.

Had morning coffee with Sid Lindner, Bob Piper, Charlie Schneider, and Tom Wilson.
Had a case on the Board agenda with Mira Stevenson, my first appearance at an agenda as a supervisor in quite a long time.
Came home with Ralph and Sam Ross. Ira had forgotten his key and was waiting for us on the doorstep. Also waiting was a handsome box of fruit which Mel Locker's parents had sent from Florida. Acceptances from Zola La Follette and George Middleton, the Findlings, Jaffes, Minskoffs, and Rubins. The Bachman's declined because Merv was out of town. Jules' medical check-up revealed enlarged glands of some sort, which will probably mean an exploratory operation. I pray that it is a very minor matter. We have been so lucky as to our health and I hope it will continue.

Thursday, February 25
Jules took Ralph and me down this morning. Had morning coffee with Art Leff, Sid Lindner, Bob Piper, and Charlie Schneider.[41] Lunched with Helen Rosen.
Ralph and I came home with Sam Ross. Acceptances from Madelyn Kramer, Mrs. Coleman and Mrs. Stanley. Apparently the FBI had been inquiring about me form Abe Harris – they are really going back a long way.
Note from Mother that although her ears are bothering her she is coming, but that Father, who feels fine, cannot get away. I wrote urging that he come with her as I doubt whether she is fit to travel alone.

---

41 Sid Lindner, Arthur Leff, and Charles Schneider were judges and friends of Anne, and the latter two served later as Chief Judge of the NLRB.

Also, it would be nice if Ira could have some grandparents present. Ira opened some of his gifts – a globe from Marvin and Lois, broken; two ties from the Bazelons that can be worn only with Windsor knots, and he has none of the right type of shirt for them; and a chain from the Bogdonoffs – none of us knew what it was for.

Friday, February 26
I went down with Ralph. Ira went on his bike and Jules went by himself. Had morning coffee with Winn Newman and Jim Shaw.
Met Jules downtown at noon. Bought a red hat, lunched at Reeves, and then he went to pick up a new steam iron while I got a girdle. Afternoon tea with Sid Lindner, Max Rosenberg, Helen Rosen, and Charlie Schneider.
Came home with Ralph and Sam Ross.
Ira received a very handsome portfolio from the Sid Grosses.
I fixed a broiled chicken for dinner – and very good it was.
Later to services at MCJC, mainly so that Ira could see what the Friday night services were like as he may participate in them next Friday night. Stayed for the refreshments afterwards so he got to bed rather late, and he gets up rather early on Saturdays.

Saturday, February 27
Elouise had promised to come in today but did not show up and did not call. That really left me in a jam.
Jules took Ira to services early, and we went over later as there was a bar mitzvah and we wanted to observe. Downtown afterwards to

do some errands. Then home to clean house, do some laundry, hang the new curtains we had bought etc. So tired by dinner time that we went out to Villa Rosa and then, for an additional treat, went to Gifford's for dessert. Note from Mother that she decided she was not up to making the trip after all. I am very sorry to have her and Father miss it. Acceptances from the Pachels – all 5 of them, the Dunans, from Nina Hoffman. Ira received a brush-and-comb set from the Sam Rosses, which was very kind of them as Sam has had to go out of town and does not expect to be back by Saturday.

Sunday, February 28
A lovely warm day. I did a great deal of telephoning trying to line up a maid, but had no luck.
Telephoned Mother Schlezinger.
Nate telephoned to ask if he could bring Nan. We assured him we would have a maid to look after her – but it is dubious. Gertrude telephoned to let us know Al could not come because his foreman is ill, but she is flying in on Friday with Milton and Howard. She and Al and Milton all talked to Ira, which pleased Ira a great deal.
We went to the Center to talk to Sol Silverman, to Hoffman's house to see him, for a ride as it was such a pretty day, and then home.
I fixed a roast for dinner – and very good one it was. Did some ironing in the evening. But I cannot mange the work with all these guests coming. Shall have to ask Dezorah to come in, as unsatisfactory as her work was. And she may be tied up with school or another job.

Monday, March 1, 1954
Called Dezorah, who said she could come in beginning Wednesday.
Went down with Herb and Ralph. A very rainy day.
Lunched with Mira Stevenson, Helen Rosen, and Will Newman.
Afternoon tea with Charlie Schneider. Beeson was in all day but will be sworn in tomorrow.
Jules saw the surgeon today and does have to undergo exploratory surgery. Came home with Herb, Ralph, and Herb's brother-in-law. Herb had to do some errands so we were rather late getting home, but I managed quite a good dinner nevertheless.
An acceptance from Teddy Adelman, a check for $5 from Bell Herskowitz, a belt from the Ed Rains, and an invitation to Jules and me for the Jaffe bar mitzvah – a luncheon at the Hotel 2400.
Would give a great deal now for a maid who could fix a birthday cake and company dinners, etc.

Tuesday, March 2
Dezorah telephoned to say the doctor wanted her mother to stay in bed another week, and Dezorah had to nurse her, so could not come in to work.
Went down with Herb, Ralph, and Herb's brother-in-law, whom we dropped at the station. Attended Beeson's swearing in.[42] He made a calm, reasonable, and rather encouraging speech. Had coffee afterwards with Charlie Schneider and Earl Bellman.
Lunched with Kate Goldman, Rosanna Hulse, and Gladys Boester.

---

42   See February 18, 1954 entry.

Had afternoon tea with Bob Piper, Charlie Schneider and Henry Sahm.
Home with Herb and Ralph.
Jules and Ira got home from MCJC about 7:30. We went to Stone House Grill for dinner. Ira had a complimentary birthday dinner. He received a Dopp kit from Carroll Cahan, an album from Mrs. Coleman and Mrs. Stanley, a jacket from Ellen May, and a sweater from the Maybrooks – very handsome of them as we had not even sent them an announcement.

Wednesday, March 3
Such a frustrating day. Went down with Ralph and Herb. Pouring rain. Would have cancelled my appointment for a permanent but staff meeting was scheduled, and I did not want to meet Beeson looking like a witch. Then could not get a permanent because of a scalp irritation so got a set, which in this weather was a complete and expensive waste. Then the staff meeting was postponed. And the maid who was supposed to come in did not. Then Ira called after school, had found the front door unlocked and was afraid prowlers were in the house, so he waited for us at the Benensons. I cam home with Ralph and Herb, fixed dinner, cleaned up, and then Jules and I went to MCJC to straighten out a few details. Ira was reassured enough to left alone by then.
Nate from Mother – they are sorry but cannot come. Note from Dezorah telling me how much she enjoyed and appreciated working for me. Note from the Bogdonoffs – cannot come Saturday.

A desk set from the Pollacks, a muffler from the Lindenbaums, and pajamas from Madalyn's sister, Gloria Wells.

Thursday, March 4
Went down with Ralph and Herb. Lunched with Dave Davidson and Noah Minkin.
Had our staff meeting this afternoon. Beeson sounds like a very fair and reasonably individual.
Jules picked me up, then we picked up the tape recorder we are giving Ira, then to MCJC to watch Ira's rehearsal, then to Schuster's for supper, then home. Later Jules went to the terminal to pick up a maid who was supposed to work through the weekend but she did not show up. Mrs. Benenson's maid had been in today, which was a big help.
Ira received cuff links from the Liftins and from Joe and Miriam Schlezinger, and records from Earl Bellman. He received a $10 check from Uncle Morris and Aunt Lena. Many of these gifts are from people to whom we had not sent invitations and from whom we did not expect gifts. Molly called from New York. Coming in tomorrow. Will stay with the Rolands.

Friday, March 5
Jules and I took leave today. Called Dezorah, who agreed to come in for the weekend. Nate called to say Nan was sick and he was coming alone. Called Louie in New York to find out when they would arrive. Marketed. Got corsages at Gudes, a white orchid for me, purple ones for Clara, Mollie, Gertrude, Ruth Levy, and Lucille, gardenias for Ben Lindner, Evelyn Promisel, Alice Jaffe, and

Sylvia Benenson. Picked up Gertrude, Milton, Howard, Louie, and Lucille at the airport, took them to luncheon, then to the Woodner. Met them later at Mrs. K's, where we had a delicious dinner. Then to MCJC, Ira participated in the service and did quite well. Afterwards there was the Oneg Shabbat given by the Levy's in Ira's honor.[43]

Louie gave Ira a gold watch. Ed and Al gave him $25 each. Mother S. gave him a $25 bond and a $50 check, Millie $20, the Rolands $20, and Allan Marmelstein $5. He also got a belt from Helen Lee, splendid books from the Bayntons, Days, Baums, and Nina Hoffman, a bar mitzvah album from Evelyn Polster, two shirts from the Promisels, a chess set from the Benensons, a globe from Barbara Weinstein, and Nate arrived tonight with two handsome suitcases.

Saturday, March 6
Ira received a number of wires, including some from the Katzes, Meltons, Oppenheimers, and Schattensteins. There was a big crowd at his bar mitzvah. He was absolutely perfect, charming, at ease. We were so proud of him, and everyone was so effusively congratulatory. My hostesses did a good job and the kiddush was excellent. Nate, Louie, Lucille, Molly, Milton, Howard, and the 5 Pachels came home for luncheon – roast beef, etc. and everything was delicious.

Back to MCJC at 8:00 for the reception. Hoffman had done a superb job of decorating, all the food was delicious, there was plenty of good liquor, everyone seemed to be having a wonderful time, and a great many people assured me that the bat mitzvah was the most impressive they had ever attended and the reception the most enjoyable.

Ira received atlases from the Jaffes and the Levins, a shirt and vest from the Lindners, a multicolor pencil from McConnell and Johnson, $25 from the Pachels, a $25 bond from Sam Wagshal, a handsome desk lamp from the Friedmans and Lockers,[44] and so many things from the kids at the reception that I could not possibly keep track of them.

Sunday, March 7
Ira was up early and full of pep. A lovely day. The boys played and we talked after breakfast. Then had a snack, left the boys at a movie, took Nate to the station, met the Rolands and Molly at Jules' office – which they admired greatly – then they took Molly to the station and we picked up Gertrude, Louie and Lucille at the Wooden and took them to the house. Served them some of the food we brought home from the reception. Later managed to squeeze the bags and all 8 of us into the car, took them to see Jules' office, did a little sightseeing, then to the airport. They all left on the 7:15 plane for Columbus. They all assured us they had a wonderful time, had never attended a more impressive bar mitzvah or a more enjoyable reception.

Then home, all of us very tired. Had some supper and, later, fell into bed. Dezorah was a big help. Have to start looking for a maid again – if I have a job.[45]

---

43 Bill and Ruth Levy were neighbors, and Ruth was Anne's best friend from the 1950's to the 1970's.

44 Jules' two law partners.

45 Anne's uncertainty about her professional

Monday, March 8

I came down with Jules, Ralph and Herb having gone out of town.

Jules and I are still being congratulated by people who say they never saw a boy participate so fully in a bar mitzvah or heard any boy do such a perfect job or attended a more enjoyable reception. "Stood by" all morning for my interview with Beeson[46] but was not reached,

Got a ride home with Frank Kleiler. I had lunched rather late with Max Rosenberg. Was not very hungry for dinner, but nevertheless fixed quite an elaborate meal with broiled chicken as the main feature. After dinner made up packages of hors d'oeuvres and sweets from the enormous supply we brought home from the reception, and Jules and Ira delivered them to the Promisels, Benensons, Harlowes, Grimes, and Levys.

Ira received bar mitzvah cards from Bobby Wagshal and the Shostecks, a handsome pair of bookends from May Wagshal, a shirt from the Rubins, and a manicure kit from the Dunans.

Tuesday, March 9

Jules took me to work and Ira to school – had to give a ride as he was so laden down with bar mitzvah cake for his school friends.

Had morning coffee with Sid Lindner, Dave London, Bob Piper, and Tom Wilson. Lunched with Ruth Smalley.

Had afternoon tea with Sid Lindner.

Got a ride home with Sid. Ira received a telegram from the Rabbi, delivered by phone to him at the Center on Saturday night, congratulating him on his bar mitzvah performance and again expressing regret that he was unable to attend the reception because of a prior engagement.

Fixed dinner at home. Am becoming quite adept at hurried but adequate meals. Need someone, though, to do the cleaning and laundry, and should have someone to cook at least when we are entertaining guests.

Wednesday, March 10

Again Jules took me to the office and Ira to school – Ira laden down again with bar mitzvah cake.

Ralph and Herb got back today, and both stopped in first thing to tell me how impressed they were with Ira's bar mitzvah and how much they enjoyed the reception.

Had a case on the Board agenda with Mira Stevenson. Beeson was present. It went pretty well.

Had morning coffee afterwards with Mira, Dave London and Bob Piper. Lunched with Mira and Helen Rosen.

Ralph and Herb went home earlier than I wanted to leave, so I waited and went home with Mira and her husband.

Have been quite tired lately – I suppose the strain of preparing for the bar mitzvah and the concern about whether or not Beeson would retain me on his staff. Have been going to bed much earlier than usual. Will have to snap out of it as it must be quite tiresome for Jules.

---

future was with her even during the happy week-end of Ira's bar mitzvah.

46   The new member of the governing Board of NLRB whose nomination was opposed. See February 18 entry.

Thursday, March 11
I awoke with a headache, and it was a snowy-rainy day, but very foolishly, no doubt, I decided to go to the office as I figured I would be interviewed today by Beeson. I was, and it went quite badly. He took me completely aback when he said he would consider the fact that I had a husband to support me. He knew Jules was in private practice.[47]

Skipped luncheon. Had afternoon tea with Max Goldman, Sid Ascher, and Henry Sahm.

Ira went to Hebrew School today. We are leaving it entirely up to him whether or not he will continue.

Felt much better. Went down with Jules in the morning – in such a hurry to get there – but came home with Herb and Ralph.

Fixed dinner at home. Edward called. Said Howard enjoyed his visit tremendously. Nate called. Said he did not think an operation was necessary from his study of the x-rays and knowledge of Jules' history.

Friday, March 12
Went down with Herb and Ralph. Had morning coffee with Sid Lindner, Dave London, and Bob Piper. Lunched with Carol Pollack, Mira Stevenson, and Charlotte Hankin. Had afternoon tea with Art Leff and Earl Bellman.[48]

Came home with Herb and Ralph.

I had left a roast in the oven on the automatic timer so dinner was soon prepared.

After dinner we all went to Hecht's to exchange some of Ira's gifts which he needed in larger sizes.

Thank-you notes from Gertrude and Milton, Millie Wagshal, and the Cantor, the first three for the good time they had, the Cantor for the reception and the $25 check Jules gave him for doing such a fine job of preparing Ira. A card and note from the Ruscolls.[49] Ira was in a real fight at school today. I am afraid he got the worst of it, and to make it worse for his spirit, the fight was with a seventh grader – a "rookie" at Eastern.

Saturday, March 13
Helen Gibson came in to do housework, a big help.

We went to Allan Marmelstein's bar mitzvah. A rainy day and the crowd was less than half as big as the one last week. Allan was excellent but lacked Ira's poise. Ira went off afterwards for luncheon and a movie with Richard Mattell. Jules and I did some errands. Lunched at the Wagshal's. Sam is supposed to be getting me some big-wig Republican support but I have not much faith in help from that source. Meanwhile our lunch plus a few things we bought came to nearly seven dollars.

Ira received a handsome leather portfolio from the Saul Elsons. We had dinner quite late as Ira sat through a double feature. Later to the Jewish Book Sore. Bought some records for Ira to present to the Cantor, and a bar mitzvah card to enclose in our gift to Allen, one of Ira's several very nice sweaters.

---

47   Misogynistic references seem to have been made with some frequenty to women in the NLRB.
48   Leff and Bellman were both judges, and Leff was Chief Judge for one year.
49   Anne's sister Jean (Jan) and her family.

Sunday, March 14
Ira slept rather late. He could have made it to Sunday School by rushing but we decided that he might as well skip it.
Telephoned Columbus. Mother S. said she had heard that the bar mitzvah went splendidly.
The Rolands stopped in – Joyce and Steve wanted to see Ira's loot. Ira was delighted to show it. Later the Bisgyers stopped in to deliver a gift for Ira – a wallet – about the fourth he has received.
Ira got started on his thank-you notes. In the evening we went to the Marmelstein reception at the Center. Theirs was a much fancier affair than ours. They had a Baltimore caterer, very expensive, and the food was beautiful to look at and delicious to eat. They also had a 5-piece orchestra. The Cantor was there, and thanked us profusely for some records we got for him at the Jewish Book Store.

Monday, March 15
Went down with Herb – Ralph was on sick leave. Went in to see Beeson again to explain why I thought it unfair to consider as a factor in my case Jules' ability to save me from starving. He did not seem too impressed.
Lunched with Frank Kleiler, Ogdon Fields, and Henry Sahm.
Had afternoon tea with Mira Stevenson. Herb wanted to leave early, but when I refused to go he insisted upon waiting until quitting time for me. Ira's friend Celica Brill gave him another wallet today.
Fixed hamburger for dinner tonight. We all agreed it was about the best hamburger we had ever eaten.

Ira worked some more on his thank-you notes. Jules or I dictate them and have to spell almost everything for Ira. Sometimes I despair of Ira ever becoming an educated man, despite the Cantor's faith in his intellect and diligence.

1954 Continued

Friday, August 20
We had breakfast...Then we picked up the folks...Later went for a very pleasant ride around Cape Ann. Had dinner in Gloucester at the Studio Restaurant. The dinner was good but we particularly enjoyed the location. We ate on the verandah overlooking the water, and the boats and seagulls and fishermen, etc., kept us constantly entertained...It was a lovely evening, complete with a magnificent sunset...

Anne with parents

Year End Summary 1954

The big event for me of 1954 was my discharge from a job I had every reason to believe I was handling competently. Glad that the year ended on an encouraging note. The Commission's directive confirms my opinion that my discharge was unlawful. Whether the Board complies or forces me to litigate the matter, I have little doubt I will eventually be ordered reinstated. That will be quite a victory, and the back pay we can put to good use. The money will not, however, make whole my wounded self-esteem or my damaged professional reputation. Actually the likelihood of my being reinstated soon causes mixed reactions in all of us. Jules and Ira would both prefer that I stay at home, doing volunteer work of some sort to keep myself busy and interested. And even I must admit that there are many advantages to my staying at home, running the household myself, being relatively independent of domestic help, and having more time and energy to devote to Ira's interests.

I like working, however, associating with adults, concerning myself with professional problems, and collecting regular and substantial paychecks.

The other shock that this year - and the Republican Administration - have brought us was Lou Roland's suspension. I hope, and expect, that the outcome will be reinstatement with back pay for him. The exoneration, however, can hardly make up to him for all the humiliation and suffering his suspension has caused him and his family. Furthermore, he will in any event wind up substantially out of pocket because of his legal expenses.

We are grateful that Jules is out of Government service during this trying time, and that his practice seems to be making excellent progress. Although he had only $3000 in take-home pay, the firm has wound up the year with a substantial bank account, and the prospects for next year are very bright indeed.

If we could somehow persuade Ira to try a little harder and to do better in his schoolwork, things generally would wind up in very satisfactory style at the close of 1954.

1955

Anne won reinstatement in her job and returned to work in 1955. This was one of three occasions that she sued the Federal government for her rights and won each time. Her sister Clara's husband Lou was also reinstated in his position.

Jules' private practice is beginning to grow significantly and holds promise for the future. The problem that most concerns her is Ira's performance at school.

For their family vacation in August they went to Cape Cod, enjoying the beach, visiting Hyannisport and her family in Lawrence, Massachusetts.   -- RDH

Monday, January 31
Jules took Ira to school and took the car downtown to have something checked. He was to pick me up at noon and go to Baltimore to pick up the dishes. Meanwhile the school nurse called. Ira hurt his back in gym. We took him to the Takoma Park hospital for x-rays – nothing serious. Lunched at the Hot Shoppe, left Ira at school, and drove to Baltimore. After much running around and red tape, got the dishes and drove home. Fixed some supper while Jules unpacked the dishes. They are plain white porcelain, very attractive, and enough of them to create a storage problem.

Jules was supposed to go to a B'nai B'rith meeting but was too tired, so we stayed home and had a drink by ourselves.

Tuesday, February 1
Jules birthday. Took Ira to school and Jules to the terminal. Got our new dishes washed and put away. They are very attractive. Ira brought home his report card – 2 C's and 2 D's – the same as last time. It was a disappointment as we had all expected better. Jules received a card for a free dinner at the Stone House Grill. As Ira had a great deal of homework and we wanted him to have dinner with us, we went to the Grill rather than to a fancier place that would have taken more time.

Wednesday, February 2
A heavy and completely unexpected snow during the night, and it continued to snow most of the day. The county schools were out, so Ira spent most of the day sledding and had a glorious time. Jules took the car to work.

When Jules got home we all had a drink and hors d'oeuvers in the living room – Ira had root beer. Then we had an especially good dinner. After dinner we all played Scrabble. It was a very cold night, which made it seem especially cozy and pleasant indoors. I should have gone to Civil Service to discuss my case, but the weather discouraged me.

Thursday, February 3
Jules took Ira to school and took the car downtown. The driving still looked a little treacherous for me, and Jules is always glad of a chance to take the car.

When Ira got home from school, he gulped some hot cocoa and dashed off with his sled. It was cold but sunny, and he had a wonderful time.

Gayle telephoned, as he does almost everyday, to see if I had heard anything further from Civil Service.

Had an unusually good dinner served in great style in the dining room on our new dishes.

After dinner – for Ira alone- we took him and a friend to school for a variety show, and we went on to the Levy's for a very nice dinner. The Gangs were also there. The party was in my honor. Ira got home late, just before we did at about midnight.

Friday, February 4
A cold but sunny day. Thought Emily would call but she did not. Jules went downtown with Sid Gross and Irv Jaffe while I took Ira to school and picked Emily up at the terminal. Later went marketing. Drove carefully and had no trouble.

Ira went sledding after school, probably the last time for this snowfall.

Evelyn Promisel asked us to come over tomorrow night to play bridge. The Gangs had asked us to go dinner-dancing tomorrow night, which made four invitations for the same evening. I must bestir myself and start issuing some invitations soon.

Saturday, February 5
Jules took Ira to MCJC[50] in the morning for children's services. Later we picked him up and drove down to Jules' office. Lunched at the Hot Shoppe on the way home.

In the evening Jules and I went to the Grosses'. They had a congenial group and we had a pleasant evening. Everyone there was interested in my "case" and asked a great many questions. The matter has dragged on so long that I plan to go to the Commission next week and, if I do not get some satisfactory answers, will file suit.

Sunday, February 6
Poured all day. Considerably warmer than it had been. Jules got the fire going first thing, and we breakfasted in front of it.

Later we all got dressed and rode out to look at a couple of houses. Saw one we rather liked in the Landon School area. Then went to the McArthur to see "The Little Kidnappers." We all thoroughly enjoyed the picture. Then to the Villa Rosa for dinner. We were all very hungry by then so everything tasted especially good. Then home to play some Scrabble, finish the papers, and finally to go to bed. Telephoned Columbus. Mother much better.

Monday, February 7
Much warmer. Ira celebrated the change in weather by riding his bicycle to school. I drove Jules to his office and then went on to see Meloy at the Commission. He told me the veterans' decision would be out this week, and that the Commission would then see about getting the Board to comply with the Commission's directives. He was quite encouraging.

Bought Ira a black hat to go with the black trousers we ordered for him last Saturday. He was thrilled about it. He is becoming a little more conscious about his appearance. He is painfully self-conscious about his relative shortness. Hope he has a growing spurt soon.

---

50   Montgomery County Jewish Center.

1955

Tuesday, February 8
Still warmer. Ira went to school on his bike again. I took Jules to the terminal. Later I went to Frank's for a haircut by a Mr. Rudolph, whom I liked. Did some marketing too. It was a pleasure to be outdoors.
Fixed us a luscious steak for dinner, and we dined in style in the dining room.
Appreciate the fact that the days are getting longer, especially when I go to the terminal to pick up Jules in the evening. That and the warmer weather make one feel that spring is on the way.

Wednesday, February 9
Ira went to school on his bike. I took Jules to the terminal. Went to Buster's in Silver Spring for luncheon with Evelyn Promisel, but did not go downtown with her. It was well that I did not as I found, when I got home, that Ira had caught his hand in a machine at school and the nurse had been calling me and Jules and Evelyn, etc. Finally Clara was going to go over but reached me, and I took charge. His hand was x-rayed. There was no fracture but a bad cut, which was sutured. Got him home and in bed, and then picked up Jules. Ira felt well enough to come down for dinner. This is the first year we have not had school insurance. Jules was in Europe and I was negligent.

Thursday, February 10
Another warm day.
Ira insisted his hand felt all right and he wanted to go to school. Probably liked the idea of being the center of attention. We could not start the car so he and a friend hitch-hiked and Jules took a cab. I had someone from the service station come over later to fix the starter.
Picked up Ira after school.
Called Emily's mother and told her Emily should not come in tomorrow as I had to take Ira to the hospital.
Fixed us a rather elaborate dinner. Figured we could all do with a little cheering up after yesterday's accident and excitement.

Friday, February 11
Took Ira to school and Jules to the terminal – and there was Emily. She did not get my message. The morning was warm but it began to rain and get colder, and by afternoon it was snowing hard. Ira had a light jacket on, so I had to pick him up, but the driving was too bad for me to go to the hospital. I got stuck in the snow a couple of blocks from home and we had to walk. Jules was hours getting out on the bus, then had to walk from the terminal. After dinner he went out and drove the car home. It had stopped snowing by then. Later we relaxed by playing Scrabble.
The veterans were ordered reinstated today.

Saturday, February 12
Very cold but clear.
We had chains put on the car. Then drove to the hospital. Ira's finger was healing all right. I was very relieved to hear that. Then home, for a big brunch. Later we went marketing and picked up Ira's black pants. While we were out, someone left the material I am to use in the Heart Fund collection, so I guess I am stuck with that chore.

The snow-covered world today looked beautiful, but yesterday it seemed cruel and menacing. Hope I don't have to drive in anything like that for a long time.

Sunday, February 13
Still quite cold, and our furnace had not been working too well. Jules started the fire early and the furnace man got out in the morning, so we finally got the house cozy and warm again.
Clara called and said they were coming over, but I told her we were just leaving for a movie. They were not interested in joining us. We saw "On the Waterfront"[51] at the Langley. It was a very effective movie, and the acting was unusually good. Afterwards we went to the Langley Hot Shoppe for supper. It was a pleasant way to spend a cold dreary afternoon and evening.

Monday, February 14
Took Ira to school and Jules to the terminal. Made a fancy cake with Valentine trimming. Picked Ira up after school. Someone had bumped his finger so hard the splint was bent, so I had to take him to the hospital to have a new bandage put on. Got home just in time to pick Jules up. But I managed a good dinner, and the cake was a big success. Ira gave each of us a fancy Valentine. After dinner I received another "Valentine" – a telegram offering my job back beginning next Monday.[52] We called some people to come over to celebrate, but the only ones who came were the Rolands. We had a drink, and then coffee and cake. Hope we soon celebrate good news for Lou.

Tuesday, February 15
A warm pleasant day. Got a number of telephone calls from people congratulating me on my victory.
Picked Evelyn P. up about noon, and met Bea Lindner at the Hot Shoppe for luncheon. Ran into Mildred Stein, who joined us. Later we drove over to see the Stein house, a beautiful, expensive, ultra-modern home.
Later I picked Ira up at school and I picked Jules up at the terminal.
Called some people and invited them for Saturday night. Must get into the entertainment swing again.

Wednesday, February 16
Another warm day.
Took Ira to school and Jules to the terminal. Went downtown later with Evelyn Promisel. She took me to luncheon at the Nanking, a farewell to me as a daytime neighbor.
Ira had gone to the barber shop after school, so I got home before he did. He got a becoming haircut, and evidently he enjoyed the long walk very much. Hope his hand will heal soon so he can begin to get some real exercise before he begins to get stout again. His figure is very well proportioned now, but we are all hoping he will grow taller soon.

Thursday, February 17
A rainy day but still rather warm. Took Ira to school and Jules to the terminal. Ira had only

---

51   Elia Kazan movie about a longshoreman (Marlon Brando) and the violent life of the docks.
52   Anne had been dismissed from the Board a few months earlier after an FBI loyalty investigation. She appealed and threatened litigation. On review her dismissal was overturned, and she was reinstated.

a half-day of school so I picked him up at noon and took him to Washington Sanitarium to have the stitches removed. We have to come back on Sunday. We lunched at Kushner's on the way home. Later drove downtown to have his glasses adjusted to fit better. Then picked up Jules and went home.

Emily's mother telephoned to let me know Emily would be in tomorrow. I had suggested she check in advance to avoid what happened last Friday. Nate Ginsberg in town for the day. We went to the Willard to have cocktails with him in the evening.

Friday, February 18
A lovely warm day.
I took Ira to school and Jules to the terminal, and picked Emily up at the terminal. Although I felt that I should stay and work with Emily, Sylvia Benenson persuaded me to go with her and her sister Millie to the Peking, where we had a delicious luncheon. Did some shopping. Emily was gone when I returned, but I was home before Ira as he had gone to a basketball game.

After dinner - for Ira alone - we took him and a friend to school for a variety show, and we went on to the Levys' for a very nice dinner. The Gangs were also there. The party was in my honor. Ira got home late, just before we did at about midnight.

Saturday, February 19
Another warm day. Jules took Ira to MCJC for services. Later Jules and I went marketing. After we picked Ira up, we drove down to Jules' office. On the way home, lunched at Victor's Broilerburger Shop and did some errands.

Had a light supper at home. Then got busy preparing for our party. The Bellmans, the Levys, the Jaffes, the Silbermans, and the Winklers came.[53] We had drinks and stuff to nibble on, and later a fairly substantial supper. Everyone seemed to have a good time and stayed quite late. We were up until about 3:00 washing dishes and cleaning the living room.

Sunday, February 20
A beautiful day.
We took Ira to the hospital for a check on his finger. Have to go at least once more.
In the afternoon I collected on St. Andrews Way for the Heart Fund.
The Rolands[54] came over in the afternoon. We all went for a ride in the country in our car.
Increased Ira's allowance from $2.50 to $3.00 to take care of the extra bus fares he will have to pay at times because of my being at work.
Had a number of chores to do to get ready to start working tomorrow. It is going to mean quite an adjustment for all of us. But I can always quit if it does not work out all right.

Monday, February 21
Jules took me down as I wanted to get in on

---

53   Earl and Helen Bellman (Earl was NLRB colleague and frequent lunch companion), Bill and Ruth Levy (neighbors and best friends), Earl and Alice Jaffe (neighbors and close friends), Herb Silberman and wife (neighbors, Herb was NLRB colleague and Anne rode to the office with him occasionally), and Ralph Winkler (NLRB colleague with whom Anne frequently lunched and rode to the office).
54   Sister Clara and her husband Lou.

time. Checked in at the Personnel Office, then saw Powell. Was given a private office but down on the first floor. Was also given a case right away.

Eleanor, Mira, Helen and Grace,[55] who had taken me to the Watergate on my last day, took me again today. Later they brought a cake down for afternoon coffee. There was a big crowd, but I saved a piece to bring home for Ira.

Came home with Sam [i.e. Ross], Herb [i.e. Silberman], and Ralph [i.e. Winkler].[56]

Managed quite a good dinner.

Jules thinks I am undertaking too much - working and getting meals - but I am going to give it a try. Don't want another Margaret around the house.

Tuesday, February 22

Ira had to go to school, but Jules and I had the day off. Emily came in so I did not have the housework to worry about. It was a rainy day so Jules and I stayed in much of the day. In the afternoon we did a couple of errands, had a sandwich at Hofberg's, stopped in to see the Rolands for just a minute, then went to pick Ira up at school.

One of Ira's teachers had been discouraging him from signing up for college preparatory courses in high school. It had made him feel badly. Although he has not been a good student, we feel that what she is doing is very wrong. It has disturbed all of us.

55   Eleonor Schwartzbach, Mira Stevenson, Helen Rosen, and Grace McEldowney. Mira and Helen were regular coffee and lunch companions; occasionally Anne rode home with Mira.

56   This was the regular carpool from their neighborhood of people who worked at the NLRB.

Wednesday, February 23

A rainy day. Herb and Sam were to pick me up but, I later learned, forgot. Fortunately Jules, who had taken Ira to school, picked up a package at the Post Office (dates from California sent by Locker's parents) and brought it home, so he took me to work. Herb and Sam were very contrite. I came home with them.

Letter from Mother. She was happy about my victory, and expects a handsome gift to celebrate the occasion.

In the evening Jules and I went to a meeting at Blair to discuss high school curricula and related problems. It is a beautiful school – should be a pleasure to attend.

Thursday, February 24

Sam and Herb remembered to pick me up this morning.

Had morning coffee with Mira and Helen and luncheon with Mira. Still being greeted and congratulated extensively on my "restoration."

Came home with Sam and Herb, in a heavy and completely unexpected snowstorm.

Jules had left his office early, picked up Ira, and taken him to the hospital. His finger had not yet healed so he will have to go again.

Jules had also picked up some things for supper. That was a big help as we were a bit low on things that could be prepared in a hurry.

Jules went to an alumni meeting after dinner.

Friday, February 25

Emily's husband called last night. I told him Emily should come in this morning by 8:30. She did not. Ira got a ride and I went with Herb and Sam. Jules waited a while for Emily, but she did not appear. There was no word from her, so I did know whether she just did not come for some reason or came after we had all left.

Came home with Herb, Sam, and Ralph.

Did some housecleaning after I got home. Did not feel up to getting dinner also, so we went out to the Silver Restaurant, where we had a very enjoyable meal. Did a few errands, and then went home.

Saturday, February 26
Letter from Gertrude mentioning that Sandy Polster was bar mitzvah and that Ellen May had had her third child. When Jules and I drove downtown in the afternoon, we sent a bar mitzvah gift, but still have the baby gift to get. When we got home, I just had time to do some laundry before I fixed supper.

Later in the evening Jules and I went to the Koplows'. They had two other couples, none of whom we had ever met before. But the group was congenial and the evening was pleasant enough. Ira woke up after we got home, as he often does. Evidently he does not sleep very soundly when he knows that we are out.

Sunday, February 27
A cloudy, hot warm morning. Later it cleared up and grew still warmer.

We had a very enjoyable brunch. In the afternoon we went for a pleasant drive in the country. On the way home stopped at the hospital. The bandage was finally removed, but Ira had to be very careful of the finger for some time yet. On top of all that, he seemed to be coming down with a cold.

Telephoned Columbus. Mother was better but still not well. Fixed a really scrumptious broiled chicken dinner. Did some housework after dinner.

Monday, February 28
Ira did not feel too well but finally decided to go to school. I went down with Sam and Herb.

Told Powell I was ready to discuss my case. Apparently I am to report directly to him, with McGuiness sitting in, and am not to be subjected to the indignity of working under a supervisor.

Spent much of the evening on the telephone making some long overdue calls. Talked with Carol Pollack, Evelyn Promisel, Lou Roland, and Stasi Dunan.

Lou has not yet heard the result of his security hearing. He had been optimistic all along, but is becoming disheartened. It is an outrage.

Tuesday, March 1, 1955
Ira still feels punk in the morning, although he seems all right during the day.

Went down with Ralph, Herb, and Sam.

Emily came in today after we left (I had arranged with her yesterday when she called about leaving a key) and departed long before any of us got home, and did much less work than if I had been around. Got my back pay check today. By the time all the deductions were made, it seemed pretty insignificant.

Ira received a birthday credit card from Stone House Grill good for $1 at any time. Like that better than a free dinner on the birthday evening.

Wednesday, March 2
Ira's birthday. Jules is giving him some shares of stock and I am giving him theater tickets. Went down with Herb, Sam, and Ralph.
Took Eleonor, Grace, Helen, and Mira to luncheon at Hogate's to celebrate receipt of my back pay.
Pulled away from my afternoon tea to report a case to Powell and McGuiness. They scheduled it for discussion with Farmer tomorrow morning. I had planned to go with Jules for a conference about Ira at Eastern tomorrow morning, but decided I had better be available at the office.
Jules brought a lovely cake and ice cream home and we had Ira's favorite foods for dinner. He got a card from Milton Levin.

Thursday, March 3
Ira went to school on his bicycle for the first time in a long time. I went down with Ralph, Herb, and Sam.
Jules went to Eastern for the conference about Ira. Ira is not doing at all well and will almost certainly have to go to summer school.
I did not get to see Farmer after all.
Several people who had been downgraded were restored – and can thank me for it.
Max Rosenberg treated me to my afternoon coffee in celebration of my return.
Emily telephoned but I stalled her. Not satisfied with her work, but do not want to break off with her yet.

Friday, March 4
Went down with Sam, Herb, and Ralph. Had morning coffee with Art Leff, Bob Piper, Charlie Schneider, Sid Lindner, and Dave London.
Dave had brought some hamentaschen[57] so it was quite a party. Lunched with Earl Bellman and Lou Libbin.[58]
Had afternoon tea with Herb Silberman, Bob Mullin, and Sid Ascher.
Got in to see Farmer in the afternoon. He was surprisingly cordial – almost friendly. Think I did very well and he remarked about the speed with which I had prepared the case.
Jules and I went marketing although it was a nasty, rainy night. When we were ready to come home found our battery was dead but Jules got a rental battery without too much delay.

Year End Summary 1955

A very good year, on the whole. We have been relatively healthy all year, Ira's finger being the only thing that gave us any real trouble.

Probably the outstanding event, for me, was getting reinstated to my job. I have been treated shabbily since my return, but have learned to live with it, and with the hope that that, too, will change in time.

It was a great satisfaction also when Lou was reinstated to his job. Although we were both fairly optimistic most of the time that we would be reinstated, it was a long wait, and seemed a great moral victory when we finally went back to work.

Jules still has the problem in his office of being the minority member on practically every issue on which there is a divergence

---

57   A fruit filled pastry eaten during Purim.
58   Bellman and Libbin were NLRB judges and frequently had lunch or coffee with Anne.

of opinion. The relationship seems to be improving, slightly, however, and I hope will continue to improve as it would be a shame to break up the firm when the business is progressing most satisfactorily. Jules may want to change after he has had more experience in private practice, but that is definitely not to be contemplated at this time. The firm is just beginning to make some real money, and he ought to stick around to collect on his substantial investment in it.

Ira's school work continues to be a great disappointment, but we have stopped banging our heads against a brick wall on that subject. We shall do the best we can for him, and the rest he must do for himself.

Meanwhile he is definitely gaining height, which will help greatly to give him confidence in himself, a quality he needs to have bolstered. He is rough, noisy, and destructive, but at the same time he can be remarkably sweet, considerate, and loveable. If only he would take his school work a bit more seriously!

Jules and Anne at the beach

1956

This was the middle of the Eisenhower administration a period of stability for Anne and her family. Both she and Jules are well established professionally, and Ira was entering his high school years. Their extended family was largely intact, and they had a good group of friends. The death of the husband of Anne's sister, Janet, was a disturbing event of this year. A major turning point in her life was learning to drive and getting her own car.

Anne, Jules, and Ira went to Cape Cod and Hyannisport for the family vacation in August, also visiting Anne's parents. They took her parents on a side trip to Maine. -- RDH

Saturday, September 1
Although I went to bed early last night, I slept quite late this morning. Mattie did not come in, as she was moving.
Ira went to MCJC. Attended the Findling bar mitzvah. Many Labor Board people there. We marketed. Ira went swimming in the afternoon with Ronnie Goor.
Jules and I went downtown and did a few errands. Then to the Ambassador to see "The Bad Seed," which we found interesting. Then to Avignone's for a very enjoyable dinner. Ira ate with Ronnie. We stopped by to pick him up – brought the Goors a luscious cake from Avignone's – but he had gone on a date with Ronnie. Charlie's niece and fiancé and the Shaftels were there. Ira got home, and we finally left, about 1:00.

Sunday, September 2

A little cooler, which was a relief. I was feeling a good deal better.

Ed and Roberta Temple and their three daughters came over in the afternoon on their way to New England. We had a very enjoyable visit with them.

Later we had a charcoal-broiled supper on the porch. Everything was delicious. After supper Ira went to Silver Spring with Tommy Grimes.

The Levys stopped by with Linda, who took a notion she wanted to sleep over, and had a fit when her parents demurred, so they gave in to her, Bill went home for her things, and I gave her a bath and put her to bed.

Monday, September 3

A lovely day.

After breakfast, Jules went to the terminal to pick up Mattie, accompanied by Linda and Ira. Then Levys picked Linda up later, along with some toys she wrangled from Ira. We lunched at the Hot Shoppe. In the afternoon Ira went on a double date with Ronnie Goor. Later the foursome stopped in for a little while.

Edward telephoned Jules from Columbus. The doctor gives Mother S. only about 3 more weeks to live. Although she has been sick so long, this came as rather a shock to Jules. Nate Promisel[59] gave Jules some liquor for making out his will. Jules refused to bill him. We went to see "The Man with the Golden Arm."[60]

Tuesday, September 4

Called Silberman about a ride but he had left so I went with Jules. Ira went to school with a boyfriend. Got a cordial reception at the office. Had coffee with [Bill] Lubbers, Gearhart, [Dave] Davidson, Cameron, and Silberman – who mentioned that there were now 5 in the carpool, and I was out. A low blow.[61]

Lunched at Watergate Inn with Eleonor Schwartzbach and Grace McEldowney. Had tea with Lubbers, Urman, Janus, and McKinley.

Ira had boyfriends over in the afternoon and evening. Not ready to buckle down yet.

Came home with Silberman. New Years cards from Louie and Lucille. Postcard from the Vanderpools. Jules and I went marketing after dinner.

Wednesday, September 5

I went down with Jules. Had coffee with [Bill] Lubbers, Gearhart, [Dave] Davidson, Platt, Krasnecki and McKnight. Went downtown at noon to pick up my watch at Garfinkel's. It looked beautiful.

Had tea with Lubbers, Gearhart, Gillis, James and Urmen.

Jules left the office early, picked me up, and we stopped at a bakery for holiday stuff. Had an excellent dinner, served in style. Then to services at MCJC. Very warm so we stopped at Gifford's on the way home. New Year cards from the Gangs, the Abe Hymans, and the Clifford Schlezingers. Postcard from Edie

---

59 Nate and Evelyn Promisel lived in the neighborhood, and Evelyn was a close friend of Anne's. Their son, Larry, was about the same age as Ira.

60 An Otto Preminger movie starring Frank Sinatra about a gambler and former heroin addict returning from prison and trying to create a life without slipping into his previous lifestyle.

61 Not being a part of the carpool was a factor that led Anne to learn to drive and buy a car. She had resisted learning to drive up to this point.

Cohen, from Amsterdam, where she joined Hank who was already in Europe.
Called Ed but he was out. He called back later. Poor Mother S.!

Thursday, September 6
A warm day. We went to services right after breakfast. Iz Gromfine, who was distributing the honors, gave one to Jules.
Whipped up an excellent chicken dinner when we got home. The Gangs stopped in with their three children for a pleasant little visit.
Later we dropped in at the Promisels'. The [Sid] Lindners[62] and several other couples were there. We enjoyed the get-together.
Jules called Nate to ask about his Mother late in the evening but he was working. Bobbie said he would call back if he had anything new to report. He did not call.

Friday, September 7
Cloudy and cool.
Jules and Ira stayed at home but I went back to the office. Jules took me to the terminal and I went down on the streetcar.
Had coffee with Mira Stevenson, Helen Rosen, Lubbers and Urman. Lunched at Hogate's with Eleonor Schwartzbach and Grace McEldowney – a farewell to Eleonor's car, which she was selling. Had tea with Lubbers and Krasnecki.
Took my cancer test at Public Health. Will be notified of the results in 2 or 3 weeks.
Got a ride to Silver Spring with Max Rosenberg, and Jules picked me up there. Have not told Jules yet about the cancer test.

---

62   NLRB colleagues.

Saturday, September 8
Mattie came in. Jules and I went marketing at the Wheaton Co-op.
Fixed Mattie's luncheon. Then Jules, Ira and I went to look at cars. The sport cars will not serve my purpose, so we shall probably settle for a small American car. We lunched at Hofberg's, and Jules stopped at the office for a few minutes.
After dinner, Jules, Ira and I went to Silver Spring to see "Trapeze." It was rather good, especially the pictures of circus life. Then home for a snack, to look over automobile literature, and to bed.

Sunday, September 9
A lovely autumn day. Jules got up early and went to the bakery and delicatessen, so we had a scrumptious brunch.
Maury Adkins came over in the afternoon with some Democratic literature for Ira to distribute. Tommy Grimes helped Ira. Jules and I went to look at some of the Post's 1956 model homes while Ira was thus occupied. After we all returned, we went out again, to O'Donnell's in Bethesda for a very enjoyable dinner.
Cool enough at night to make a blanket feel very cozy. Don't suppose the cool weather is here to stay, but it is very pleasant for a while.

Monday, September 10
So cool that Jules put the heat on for a while this morning. It was very pleasant later in the day.
Jules took me down. Had coffee with Silberman, who assured me I could have a ride any time he was driving if I called and asked him. Downtown at noon. Had tea with

Loeb, Kerner, Friedman, Lee, and Goldberg. Took a streetcar to the terminal, where Jules picked me up. Fixed and ate dinner in a hurry. Jules had a meeting of the Civic Assn., exec. committee in the living room, while Ira and some boyfiends were making a tape recording for school in the den, and I was fixing and serving refreshments to both groups.

Tuesday, September 11
Mattie came in. I went down with Jules. Had coffee with Krasnecki, Lee Ricci, Cameron and McKnight. Downtown at noon.
Had tea with Jennie Sarrica, Mira Stevenson, Lee, Kerner, and Christopher.
Jules picked me up about 5:30, early for him. The Maine election went largely Democratic. We and our friends were jubilant about the results. Hope it is true this time "As Maine goes, so goes the nation."
Jules went to a Democratic precinct workers' meeting in the evening. Got more material for Ira to distribute as well as some tasks for himself.

Wednesday, September 12
Went down with Jules. Had coffee with [Bill] Lubbers, Gearhart, Davidson, Platt, Krasnecki and McKnight.
Lunched with Mira Stevenson. Had tea with Lindner and London.
Jules picked me up at 5:30. I called Mattie to tell her not to come in on Saturday, Yom Kipper. Also bawled her out for putting some things in the disposal that should not have been put in there, and for spilling my perfume. She tried to lie her way out of it, adding insult to injury. Jules called Columbus. No change in Mother's condition. It must be a terrible strain for the folks in Columbus.

Thursday, September 13
A warm day. I went down with Jules. Had coffee with [Bill] Lubbers, Gearhart, Loeb, Orman and Davidson. Went downtown at noon. Keep looking at clothes but not buying any because I have grown so darned fat – about 148.
Had tea with Lubbers, Krasnecki and Parlier.
To Hecht's in Silver Spring after dinner to buy Ira some clothes. Stopped later at Gifford's – as fat as I am! Home in time to hear Stevenson, and to watch him deliver a speech on TV. Found both the content and his delivery of the speech quite disappointing. So did Jules.

Friday, September 14
I went down with Jules. Had coffee with Christopher, Lee and Kerner.
A very warm day, but Mira and I nevertheless walked up to the House Office Building cafeteria for luncheon.
Had afternoon tea with Sperandro and Youngblood.
Jules picked me up early, and we had an early dinner. Then to services, which were held at the high school, in time for the Kol Nidre.
A note from Phyllis thanking us for the baby gift. She must have been reminded by Louie, as Jules mentioned to him on the telephone the other day. I called May Wagshal, who was quite sure Darbin had received the gift. Now I can pay the bill.

1956

Saturday, September 15
Not as warm as yesterday. I was tempted to skip services but Jules urged me to go. I began to get sickish, so drove home alone about 1:00, had a cup of coffee and went to bed. Jules and Ira stayed through the service, and fasted. Jules later had a headache, and went to bed for awhile. We all felt better along toward evening and had something to eat. When we took Ira to the Levys', where he was sitting tonight, we all stopped at the Langley Hot Shoppe for sandwiches. First time we used the automatic devices for calling in the orders. Seemed strange to Jules not to call Columbus to ask how Mother was after the fasting.

Sunday, September 16
A lovely day. We had a big brunch, read the paper, and relaxed. Later I did some laundry. In the afternoon we went to the Hulses'. They have a large place out in the country. There were several other couples there, most of them with assorted children. We sat around and talked, and some of the men and boys indulged in basketball, baseball, etc. Later Rosanna served a superb picnic supper, with delicious fried chicken, freshly-picked corn, tomatoes, fruit, etc., from their own crops, and everything in staggering abundance. She had a couple to do the cooking and serving. It was quite a shindig – and everyone there was an ardent Democrat.

Monday, September 17
Mattie came in. Lied all over the lot about the perfume and some other matters. Her lies were so obviously lies that they were quite ludicrous, but she stuck to them. Went down with Jules.
Had coffee with [Bill] Lubbers, Gearhart, Krasnecki, Sperandro and Davidson. Lunched with Emily Otis, Grace McEldowney and Vivian Asplund. Had tea with Rosanna Hulse, Krasnecki, Bernard and Davidson. Came home with Dick Brownstone. Jules came home quite late. After dinner we went shopping in Silver Spring. I bought a dress in Martin's.
Ira is in charge of a large group of boys for distribution of Democratic literature. He loves this stuff. Nate sent us some very good pictures he had taken of Mother S.

Tuesday, September 18
Went down with Jules. Had coffee with Lindner, London, Winkler and Stepakoff. Downtown at noon. Bought two dresses in Jelleff's French Room. A big help as we have a terrific social period on the horizon. Had tea with Parlier, McKnight and Waks.
Came home with Jules.
After dinner Jules went to a Democratic precinct workers' meeting. He went with Browner so I had the car. Ira and I went to the grocery store, but had time to pick up only a few items before it closed. Jules got home about 11:00. Hope he does not knock himself out with all his extra-curricular activities.

Wednesday, September 19
Mort Kramer had been riding down with Jules and me this week as he is attending conferences at the Statler. He works at the Bethesda Institute of Mental Health. Had coffee with Mira and Helen. Downtown

at noon with Mira. We had luncheon at Howard Johnson's, then separated to do our own shopping.

Had tea with Lubbers, Davidson and McNamara. Jules picked me up. We stopped at Hofberg's to order some things for tomorrow night. Rushed through dinner to go to the Civic Assn. meeting. Took Evelyn Promisel. Fitzgerald, who handles the coffee, could not come, so we had that to take care of too. Jules presided very ably.

Thursday, September 20
Mattie came in.
Went down with Jules and Kramer. Had coffee with Jennie Sarrica, Christopher and Lee. Lunched downtown. Had tea with Mira [Stevenson], Grace, [Bill] Lubbers, Bernard [Freund] and Orman.
Got a ride to Silver Spring with Sperandro. Met Jules there. Did some errands. Ate in a rush and dashed off to hear Stevenson speak at Blair. Had to listen to a lot of windbags but he was well worth hearing and seeing.
Afterwards Bill Levy, the Hulses, the Stevensons, and the Promisels[63] came over, and we had a nice little party. Expected more people, but many were turned away from Blair so they probably did not wait.

Friday, September 21
Went down with Jules and Kramer. Got all dressed up as I thought a Federal Bar meeting I wanted to attend was on today, but it was next Friday.
Had coffee with [David] London, Frank, Baisinger, [Ralph] Winkler, [Samuel] Ross, [Benjamin] Lipton and [Arthur] Leff. Lunched with Mira [Stevenson]. Had tea with Ormen and Lee. Home with Jules.
Ira had a postcard from Pam Vanderpool. I had a letter from Mother. She had given Ira an ink-well as we were leaving, but it had belonged to Louie and she wanted it back.
Ira had a meeting of his precinct squad. Various fathers were around to provide transportation. And some men stopped to see Jules on election stuff. It was hectic.

Saturday, September 22
Received a report from the cancer test I took at Public Health – favorable – so I told Jules about it for the first time. Ira and his crew were out distributing a Democratic flyer all morning.
Later Ira went fishing with Atkin, the precinct captain, and some other precinct workers on Atkin's boat.
Jules and I went to a supper party at Leedom's.[64] Did several errands on the way, including buying a new hat for me. Leedom had the entire staff, their spouses, and a few other people. He does not drink nor serve liquor, but the party was easier to take than we expected. We were home before Ira – minus any fish, but he had a wonderful time.

Sunday, September 23
A lovely warm day. We had a substantial but leisurely brunch. Then read the paper on the porch.
After a late luncheon, we took Jules to the airport as he had to be in New York for a

---
63   Evelyn Promisel

64   Boyd S. Leedom was the Chairman of the governing Board of the NLRB, 1955-1961.

conference tomorrow. The drive through the park was very pleasant, and even the drive home was not too bad, although it seemed the entire way that everyone was out for a Sunday drive.

I shall have to drive to work tomorrow, to get myself to work, to get down in time for Powell's stupid Monday morning conference, and to have the car downtown so Jules and I can go to a reception tomorrow evening connected with a World Bank conference.

Monday, September 24
A rainy day. Dropped Ira at Stuart's, then downtown. Managed to find space in a parking lot near the office. Coffee with [Paul] Bisgyer, Orman and Taub. Lunched with Kessel[65] and Bernard. Had tea with Christopher, Benedict and Robinson.

No word by 5:00 from or about Jules. I took a chance and drove over to a parking garage near his office and waited. He arrived shortly, shaved and put on some fresh clothes he had left in the office, and then we took off for the World Bank reception at the Mexican Embassy. There was an enormous crowd, several bars were set up in different rooms, and the buffet table was heavily laden and constantly replenished – quite a party!

Ira and Tommy collected dollars for Democrats.

Tuesday, September 25
Mattie came in. Went down with Jules.
Had coffee with Silberman, who again

---

65 Anne's close friend Thomas Kessel, Judge from 1953 and Chief Judge from 1975-1979. He gave Anne her last diary book for 1978.

assured me I could have a ride any time he drove. To a luncheon at the Shoreham given by Mrs. Eugene Black in connection with the World Bank conference. Style show by Elizabeth Arden. All very elegant. Came back in a Lincoln Premier the Ford people put at the disposal of Mrs. Remualdez.

Came home with Jules. Asked Libby, Paula, and Mrs. R. to have cocktails Friday night before the formal dance at the Shoreham, which does not begin until 10:00. Mattie rearranged her work so she could come in to clean up on Friday.

Wednesday, September 26
I went down with Jules. Had coffee with Frank, Baisinger, Ricci and Krasnecki. Lunched with Helen Rosen. Had tea with Eleoner Schwartzbach, [Lou] Libbin and Davidson. Came home with Jules.

After dinner we went marketing, mainly for refreshments for Friday, when we are having a few people in for a drink before the dance at the Shoreham. Stopped at Hannes for my evening gown, which needed a new zipper, but it was not ready as promised.

Mrs. Black had a tea this afternoon, but it meant a transportation problem and I just had too much to do.

Thursday, September 27
A cold rainy day.
Ira forgot his sandwiches, but we caught him at the Burk's before they left for school.
I went down with Jules.
Had coffee with Gearhart, [Bill] Lubbers, Davidson, [Max] Rosenberg and [Benjamin] Lipton. Lunched alone. Had tea with

Jennie Sarrica, Kerner, Bernard [Freund], Krasnecki and [Thomas] Ricci. Jules picked me up, and we went to a reception at the Anderson House given by Treasury Secretary Humphreys[66] for the World Bank conference. Quantities of food and liquor and people. Afterwards to a Democratic rally at the Indian Springs clubhouse. Ira and his crew had helped decorate the place, and I was much complimented on what a fine boy he is.

Friday, September 28
Mattie came in. I went down with Jules.
Had coffee with Helen, Letter and Krasnecki. Lunched with Mira [Stevenson] and Emily Otis. To the Statler in the afternoon to hear Leedom[67] address a Federal Bar Assn. meeting. Home with Jules, doing a few errands en route.
Ira went to Silver Spring for the evening with Tommy Grimes.
Jules and I got into formal clothes, and met the Friedmans, Lockers and Remualdezes[68] at La Salle du Bois. They were to come to our house for drinks, then go to the Shoreham dance given by the World Bank, but the R's were not going to the dance, Joe wanted to take them to dinner, we ate very late, I made the mistake of 2 martinis on an empty stomach, got very sick, and had to come home.

Saturday, September 29
I was still rather sick in the morning, and disgusted with myself. Jeanette Goor called to ask why we were not at the dance, which was a fabulous affair. Jules had to go to the office for a while in the morning. Talked to Joe while he was there – the Friedmans and the Lockers[69] got to the dance.
I felt well enough to get up around noon, but ate very little and stayed in the house all day. Ira went to a party in the evening wearing an "Ivy League" shirt he bought this afternoon, and looking quite handsome. Came home late, and had a good time.
Jules calls Columbus every few days, but it is always the same story – no change, hardly any sign of life.

Sunday, September 30
A lovely warm day, which inspired Jules to do a little work in the garden, and later inspired me to take a walk in the park with him. Ira played football, although it was really too warm for that. Later we went for a ride, then to the MacArthur to see an amazing British movie, "The Private's Progress,"[70] and then to the Peking for a Chinese dinner, which we all enjoyed very much.
Libby telephoned to ask how I felt.
I left the stole that matches my gown at La Salle, but when we telephoned we were told it had not been turned in. Too bad.

---

66   George M. Humphrey, Treasury Secretary 1953-1957.
67   Boyd S. Leedom, Chair of the NLRB governing Board.
68   Remualdez, Philippine last name, also the maiden name of Imelda Marcos, wife of Ferdinand Marcos, long time President of that country.
69   Jules' two law partners.
70   Richard Attenborough in a movie about a university student called into the British Army near the end of WWII, only to prove that he is not completely apt as a soldier.

1956

Monday, October 1
A lovely autumn day.
I went down with Jules.
After the meeting with Powell, there was a meeting in Leedom's office. He conducted a lottery to see which 5 of the 10 applicants would go to New York for the longshore election. I lost. Had coffee with Mira, Gearhart and Wilson. Lunched with Charlie Schneider. Had tea with London, Leff and Krasnecki. Got a ride home with Jack Mantell.
Jules and I did some marketing after dinner. Later listened to Eisenhower deliver a TV political address. It was a good speech, and well delivered, and he even looked well physically. Afraid it might have won him some votes.

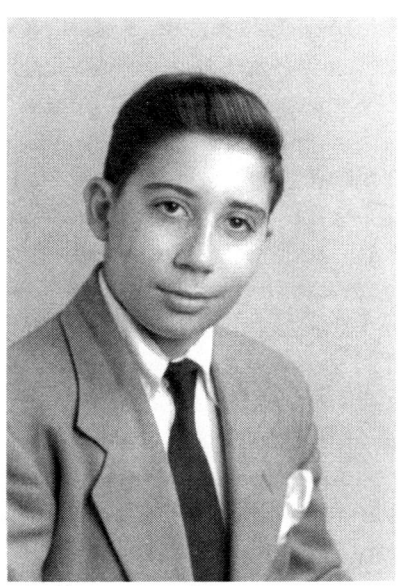

Ira

Year End Summary 1956

A very good year on the whole. Jules' practice seems to be thriving, although he is not happy about some of the peculiarities of his partners. Ira has grown taller, which is an important matter to him, and therefore, to us, but he is still doing schoolwork below the standard of which he seems to be capable.

My job is going along all right, although I do not relish the prospect of four more years of the present Republican leadership.

The big change in my life has been buying and driving my own car. I still prefer to ride with someone else driving, but being able to determine my own schedule has many advantages. The best part was the good health we have all enjoyed, and Ira's relative freedom from accidents.

We were all saddened, of course, by Jan's loss, and hope things will work out as well as possible for her and her children.[71]

About the folks, I don't know as they never write, and they have no telephone. The latest word any of us have heard from them was the letter they wrote Jan expressing their sympathy but explaining that they did not feel equal to going to the funeral.

---

71   This refers to the death of Joe Russcol, the husband of Janet, Anne's sister.

1957

The highlight of 1957 was the trip to a Bar Conference in London and the extended trip to the continent. This was Anne's first trip to Europe after dreaming about it for twenty years. She enjoyed traveling and discovering new places and people. She was still somewhat disturbed by the lack of professional recognition that she was receiving after being reinstated with the Board.   -- RDH

Friday, July 19
Breakfasted at home – we'll be eating out, after all, for 5 weeks. Closed up the house and left by cab about 9:00. A pleasant flight to New York, and then to a lavish but not too clean suite at the Plaza. Jules called his office – there was a letter from Ira – Joe read it – busy and happy.
Jules went to a conference. I lunched at Schrafft's and meandered along 5th Avenue without buying a thing. Then back to the suite to rest, read, and watch TV.
Jules and I had magnificent steaks at Gallagher's Steak House. Then saw "My Fair Lady" from the 3rd row of the orchestra, and loved it. Walked back, had a drink in the Oak Room, and up to bed.
Bon voyage telegrams from Ira and from the Levins.

Saturday, July 20
We had breakfast in the Oak Room with Arnsperger and Cohen. After they left, Jules and I went for a walk. Took Jan and her daughters to luncheon in the Oak Room. They all seemed to enjoy it. They were late getting down, so we had to rush. Jan had a cocktail so I had one to keep her company, and another at the airport with our charter group at Sabena's party in the Brass Rail. Bordered the plane about 5:00. We were in a small cabin with one other couple, to everyone's envy. There was so much liquor and champagne flowing, and so many people visiting our cabin, that it was a continuous party. The dinner was magnificent – shrimp cocktail, chateaubriand, French pastry, etc. There were perfume and other souvenirs.[72] The flight was quite smooth and it was a relief to get away from New York's hot and humid temperatures.

Sunday, July 21
Landed at Manchester about 9:00, a bit woozy from the champagne and lack of sleep. Breakfast in the dining room as Sabena guests. I had only tea. Picked up our rented Anglia, which Jules seemed to manage very well. Had a few showers, but the weather for the most part was delightful. Had sandwiches at the Grosvenor Café in Preston. Stopped early in the afternoon because I was so sleepy. Were fortunate in finding a room with bath at the Belsfield Hotel, a beautiful, enormous, corner room overlooking the gardens and Lake Windermere – but the bathroom was hopelessly antiquated. Walked around quite a bit. So cool and breezy that I wore a coat – a pleasant change from the hot, humid weather we left. Dined at the hotel. Visited after dinner with a very pleasant Scotch and English couple.

---

72 This was a time when air travel was still a special experience.

1957

Monday, July 22

Had a scrumptious breakfast at the hotel. Then visited with our new acquaintances, whom we enjoyed very much, for few minutes, and left. Another beautiful day with just a few momentary showers. We lunched at a trailer café near Brough. Stopped about 4:00 at the Royal Station Hotel in York. Got a lovely room with private bath overlooking the City Wall. Had tea in the lobby – quite a repast – and then walked for hours to the Minster, the Shambles, the Clifford tower, etc., etc. Back to the hotel for dinner, which was quite good. Then, as it was a pleasant evening, we went walking again. Enjoyed York very much, but hope we shall not regret stopping here as we should be in London to deliver the car and to get registered for the convention by about 6:00 pm tomorrow.

Tuesday, July 23

Had breakfast at the hotel. Because I overslept, and we had trouble starting the car, we did not get away until about 11:00. Were delayed at the New Holland Ferry, where we got our first terrible food at the Marine Café. Rained most of the afternoon, which delayed us more. We drove around for a quick tea at the Royal Restaurant in Stilton, skipped Cambridge reluctantly, and checked in at the Grosvenor after 8:00. Telephoned en route the time of our arrival.

Had a very good dinner in the Grill Room. Walked to Piccadilly Circus and took a cab back. Had a drink in the lounge. Received quite a bit of mail plus the suitcase Nate delivered. With all the delays, enjoyed our drive very much, the pleasant countryside, the interesting towns, and the courteous people.

Wednesday, July 24

We had breakfast in the hotel dining room. Then to the Savoy to register and pick up our material. Walked around and rode a double-decker bus. Lunched at the Regency Coffee Lounge – had cappuccino coffee for the first time. Later Jules had some appointments and I went walking myself. We met for tea in the hotel lounge. Then into formal clothes, and took a cab to Gray's Inn, where we had sherry, then dinner with three wines, including champagne, and much enjoyable conversation, particularly with the members of Gray's Inn, who answered the numerous questions patiently and interestingly. Jules and I, who were seated at different tables, enjoyed it tremendously.

Met Gene Leverson and Lee Anderson in the hotel lounge.

Thursday, July 25

Jules and I breakfasted together at the hotel, then took separate cabs to our section meetings. Mine was at Whitehall Court, and was followed by a luncheon. I enjoyed the whole affair. Back to the hotel to find letters from Ira and from Lucille, and was happy to get both of them. To a reception given by bankers at Fishmongers Hall, an impressive affair at an impressive place. Then stopped in at the International Law Section cocktail party at the Savoy. Back to the hotel to dress, and then to a reception and buffet given by Lord and Lady Makins at the English-Speaking union. Met a number of lords and ladies, and had quite a long chat with Sir Leslie and Lady Rowan. Back to the hotel for tea in the lounge with others attending the convention.

Friday, July 26
After breakfast at the hotel, I went to a section meeting and Jules took care of some business. We met later at Trafalgar Square and lunched at Chandos. Later to an assembly meeting at the Royal Festival Hall to hear the Prime Minister – a magnificent place and an interesting speech. Jules went to a Grotius Society[73] meeting. We had tea at the Coffee Inn.

Then to a magnificent reception by the P.M. at the Royal Gallery of the House of Lords. So many fascinating things to see there that we left, most reluctantly, because we were late for an appointment with the Bob Abrahams and some other people. We had supper and danced. It was after 2:00 a.m. before we got back to the hotel, but it was a grand day. Met more lords, ladies, ambassadors, etc., than I ever expected to meet.

Saturday, July 27
We had breakfast at the hotel. Then went shopping. Ordered some silverware at Jensen's for the Lockers. Lunched at Forte's. Then to Westminster Abbey. Later took a sightseeing bus to the Tower of London, etc. Unfortunately, rained almost ever time we got out of the bus.

To Simpson's for an excellent dinner. The Liftins called just before we left the hotel, and got tickets for the show we were seeing – "The Summer of the Seventeenth Doll," a very interesting play from Australia. Afterwards we all had a bite to eat at a Forte's, and walked around Piccadilly Square for a while. Cabs were scare, so we wound up walking back to the hotel. Doing more eating than walking though – I get bigger by the day.

Sunday, July 28
The Liftins came over in the Hillman they bought here. We all had breakfast at the hotel. Then drove to Hampton Court to walk in the beautiful gardens. Lunched at King's Arms there. Then to Windsor Castle, where we walked for quite a while. Had a delicious tea at an Ann Page. Stopped for a few minutes at Eton. Then back to the hotel for a little rest. Met the Liftins at Scott's for dinner. The food was good, but the place was a madhouse as it was one of the few good restaurants open on Sunday. So late when we finished dinner that there was time only to walk around a little bit, drive around a little bit, and then they dropped us at our hotel and went home. Enjoyed being with the Liftins, and it was helpful to have the use of their car.

Monday, July 29
Dave Reich joined us for breakfast. Tena was not up yet. Dave was going to visit an appellate court and suggested we join him, but we went shopping instead. Bought a sweater for Ira.

Jules went to a bankers' luncheon. I used the time to do some laundry.

Then to the garden party at Buckingham Palace. Saw, close up, the Queen, Prince Phillip, and the Queen Mother, all of whom seemed charming although I was not one of

---

73 Grotius Society was a British professional society to discuss the laws of war and peace and promote the study of international law. Since then it merged with another society to form the British Institute of International and Comparative Law.

the lucky ones chosen to be presented.

In the evening we attended a session of the House of Commons as guests of the Chancellor of the Exchequer, the tickets having been obtained for us by Sir Leslie Rowan.

Afterwards to an art show at one of the Royal Galleries. Back to the hotel to pack in readiness for leaving tomorrow.

Tuesday, July 30

Breakfasted in hotel, dispensed tips, took a cab to Waterloo Station, and a bus to the airport, and departed by Swiss Air. A lovely flight, a lovely luncheon, and lovely weather at both ends.

Checked in at the Baur Au Lac [Hotel in Zürich] in the most lavish suite I ever saw, enormous, beautifully appointed and furnished, with a balcony facing the lake and windows facing the canal. Someone from Knoll reserved it for us. I shudder to think of the cost. We walked into town, had tea at a café, and walked beside the lake.

We had flowers in the suite, but the Honecks sent more. Came later, to be our dinner guests, bearing a big box of chocolates. We had drinks served in our living room. Then to the dining room for a delicious dinner with wine. Danced under the stars. Later everyone went into Petit Palais for more dancing. We had champagne. I danced a great deal with Jules and Max. Elsa does not dance and does not speak English, but is beautiful.

Wednesday, July 31

A lovely day. We breakfasted at the hotel. Went shopping. Bought a recorder for Jane Friedman. Lentwyler, a business acquaintance, picked up the Honecks and us, took us to the Ermitage, a lovely place on the lake, for a lovely luncheon. Later, he picked us up and our baggage, took us to his summer home right on Lake Zug, where we had a drink. Then his wife, and their two children, drove us to the Grand National Hotel in Luzerne.

Bobbie and Nate arrived a little later. We had dinner in the hotel dining room, and then went walking around the town, telling one another about our travel experiences.

A wonderfully pleasant day, spoiled only by the fact that there was no mail from Ira awaiting us at Luzerne.

Thursday, August 1, 1957

Had breakfast in our room, at the windows facing the lake. Another beautiful day, and the Swiss National holiday, so everything was quite festive. We left at 8:00 for an all-day bus drive up to the Alps. Had a wonderful driver, an entertaining guide, and the front seats reserved for us. We stopped for coffee at a charming little village, stopped at the Rhone Glacier for the wonderful experience of walking through a tunnel in the glacier, stopped for luncheon at the Grimsel Pass, stopped for tea at a lovely inn, and stopped a few times for the camera fans to take pictures. It was a wonderful trip, and the clearest views they had had all summer.

Later had an excellent dinner at Harry's Dubeli. Walked around, enjoying the fireworks, the children with their lightened lanterns, etc., etc.

Anne Schlezinger

Friday, August 2

A beautiful day. We breakfasted in our room and then went for a walk. When we returned, Bobbie and Nate were breakfasting in our room, which is much nicer than theirs. We all went walking and shopping – we bought a clock for the den – grabbed a quick luncheon and then went for a very pleasant 2 ½ hour ride on the lake. Stopped at Weggies for a delightful tea on a terrace on the lake.

The Leutwylers came over in the evening, and, with Jules as the host, we had drinks at the hotel bar and then went to the Wilder Mann restaurant for a very interesting dinner, including, for some of us, beef fondue bourgignone and peach flambé, so there was much cooking at the table. A very enjoyable evening.

Saturday, August 3

We all had breakfast in our room, and then checked out. A Cook's car took us to the railroad station, where we took a train to Chiasso. Lunched on the train. My first ride on a European trip so it was interesting, as was the noticeable difference in the way of life between the Germans and Italian Swiss. From Chiasso we were taken by a hotel car to the Villa d' Este, a very elaborate, slightly decayed palace, beautifully located on Lake Como. This time Nate and Bobbie got the better of the two rooms in our suite.

Jules went for a dip in the lake as it was quite a warm day.

Later we dressed and had dinner on the open terrace – a good dinner and lovely surroundings. Afterwards we had drinks and danced on the part of the terrace reserved for drinking and dancing.

Sunday, August 4

We had breakfast on the balcony. Had box lunches prepared and walked down to the pier to take a boat ride, but the boats were too crowded.

Jules and I went swimming at the Villa. Later we ate our box lunches on the balcony.

In the afternoon we engaged a motor launch and a driver, and went for a delightful ride on the lake. Stopped at the Villa Carlotta to admire the gardens, the house, and the art works; and at Bellagio, a very interesting little town, to shop and have tea at a delightful outdoor café. The Dave Reichs arrived this afternoon and joined us for the evening. We had drinks on the terrace, then dinner on another terrace, then more drinks and dancing on the first terrace. I was not the only one who had to pinch herself occasionally to make sure it was not all a dream.

Monday, August 5

Two letters from Ira, in the same envelope, one written earlier than the other but which he had not found time to mail. Apparently he is, in his atrocious spelling and grammar, having a wonderful time. We breakfasted on the balcony. Then took a taxi to Como to shop, look around at the interesting town, have a thoroughly enjoyable luncheon at an outdoor café, and came back by boat. We bought Lucille a blouse and stole, and a number of scarves and ties for gifts. Went swimming with the Reichs when we returned. Later to Como by boat. Walked around and shopped some more. Then took a taxi to "Da Pizzi," an Italian restaurant on the other side of the lake, for a very enjoyable Italian meal, complete with souvenirs. Then a cab back to the Villa, where the Reichs joined us for drinks and dancing.

Tuesday, August 6
Breakfasted on the balcony and took a walk around the Villa grounds. About 11:30 a hotel car took us to the railroad station. We took a train to Venice, changing at Milan, and passing through familiar-sounding towns like Verona and Padua. We lunched on the train. At Venice took a motor launch to the Gran Danieli. Got lovely rooms with modern bathrooms facing the canal, but very noisy as they also face a loading dock constantly streaming with passengers and what appears to be one of the city's favorite promenades. Mail from Ira, Lucille and Gertrude. Jules and I went for a walk around St. Mark's Square while Nate and Bobbie napped. Later we all had dinner on the hotel roof terrace, an attractive spot and a good dinner. Then for a gondola ride, with the gondolier pointing out proud relics of the past.

Wednesday, August 7
We had breakfast on the roof terrace. Then went sightseeing. Very warm, so Bobbie and I bought gondolier hats to shade our heads. Went through St. Mark's Cathedral and the Doge's palace very thoroughly. Had a snack at an open-air café on the square. Back to the hotel to rest. Afterwards we took a boat to the Lido, a beautiful beach. Did not bring our swimsuits as B & N did not have any, but went wading at least. Bought a handsome gray bag at an exclusive shop at the Lido. Back to the hotel on the launch. We had dinner again on the roof terrace, and went for a walk afterwards. Then packed as we are leaving quite early in the morning for Florence. Would like to see more of Venice, but our rooms are terribly noisy.

Thursday, August 8
We were awakened at 6:00, had breakfast in our rooms, and then by motor launch to the station to get the train to Florence. An interesting trip through the Appenines, literally, as we were in tunnels much of the time.
Got very nice rooms at the Excelsior. Lunched in the dining room, except for Nate who was indisposed. Then the 3 of us took a sightseeing bus. Saw many beautiful and interesting works of art and places. Piazza Della Signoria, Palazzo Vecchio, Uffizi palace and Galleries, etc., winding up at Fiesole for the view.
Later all four of us had a very good dinner at Sabatini's. Then Nate took a cab back to the hotel while the three of us took a walk. The day had been hot and sunny, but the evening was pleasant.

Friday, August 9
Had breakfast in the dining room. Then all four of us took a bus tour – the Medici chapels, Pitti Palace and Galleries, etc., including the rooms that had been occupied by the royal family when in Florence. Rested a while. Then a light luncheon at a café called The Tabby Cat. Then shopping – bought several leather goods items for Jules, Ira, and gifts. Then Jules had to take me back to the hotel. The heat or the food or a bug got me down. I stayed in bed. The others had some tea sent up for me. I began to feel human again about 11:00, so got up and showered,

and joined the others in the lobby for a little while. There were a number of people around that we knew, some we had met on this trip, and it was all quite congenial. The evening again was pleasant after a hot, sunny day.

Saturday August 10
Managed to eat a little breakfast in the dining room and to accompany the others to the straw market just to see it. We went in a cab, and Jules and I returned shortly in cab. Had some tea in the bar. Later we had some luncheon in the dining room as we all wanted to avoid dining on the train. Left about 4:30 for Rome. A note from Ira when we arrived at the Excelsior Hotel. He is evidently having a grand time socially.
Later we took a cab to Pascal's for dinner. I was very hungry, but still not able to eat much. Took a cab back to the hotel, and then walked around a bit. It had been over a 100 [degrees] during the day, and it seemed that everyone in Rome was on the streets or in sidewalk cafes to get a breath of the cooler night air.

Sunday, August 11
Sunny and hot, as seems usual. We breakfasted in the hotel. Then went walking. Later took a carriage ride, with the driver pointing out some of the sights to see. Back to the hotel to rest. Lunched in the dining room. Then, with a sightseeing guide engaged by Nate, and a driver pointing out some of the sights to see. Back to the hotel to rest. Lunched in the dining room. Then, with a sightseeing guide engaged by Nate, and a driver and car engaged by the guide, we spent the afternoon touring old Roman remains. It was extremely interesting, but also extremely hot and wearing.
Showered and rested a bit after we returned. Then to Alfredo's – in two cabs – for a very good dinner with the Liftins and Nate's friends, the Kesslers. We took a motor bus back part way, and walked the rest.
Should be more enthused than I am about seeing the Coliseum, the Roman Forum, the monuments and relics I have read so much about it, but it is so terribly hot.

Monday, August 12
Breakfasted on the balcony, although it was already hot and sunny. Our guide picked us up about 9:30, and we went sightseeing – the Vatican and St. Peter's mainly – until about 1:30. Came back to the hotel, and lunched in the American Bar. Went sightseeing again in the afternoon – included the Capuchin Church, the synagogue, and the catacombs. Letters from Ira and Lucille, which were very welcome.
In the evening we had dinner with Bobbie, Nate and the Liftins at the Casino Delle Rose in the park. Sat on the balcony, with a good view of the floor show. The dinner was fairly good, and the floor show was relaxing. And we needed some relaxing after so much sightseeing.

Tuesday, August 13
Bobbie and Nate went sightseeing for another half day, but Jules and I had had enough. We had a late breakfast on the balcony, and then did some errands. Jules had a business luncheon date, so I lunched with Bobbie and

Nate at a sidewalk café. Later we all went shopping. I bought several pairs of gloves.

We had an excellent dinner at Giggi Fazi restaurant. Then to Baths of Caracalla to see the opera "Aida." Most of the voices were mediocre, but the setting and the production were superb. We drove out with the Liftins in their car while Bobbie and Nate and the Kesslers took a cab, but we all sat together. Afterwards we and the Liftins had gelatis at a sidewalk café, and sat and talked until all hours.

Wednesday, August 14
We had breakfast in the room. Went shopping - we all bought Borsalino hats or berets – then had a delicious luncheon at Alemagua. Rushed to get an earlier plane than originally planned. Left about 4:00. Had tea on the plane. A beautiful trip over the Mediterranean and the French Alps, but ran into heavy rain in Paris. Took an airport bus to the terminal, than a cab which dropped us at the Bristol and the others at the Ritz. Later we took a cab to the Ritz to pick up Bobbie and Nate to go to dinner, but many places were closed because of a religious holiday so we finally dismissed the cab and had a very good dinner at the Ritz Grill. Then took a cab back to the Bristol. Like our set-up there much better than theirs at the Ritz.

Thursday, August 15
Some showers, some sunshine, cool – quite a change from Italy.
We had breakfast in the hotel, then went for a walk. Bobbie and Nate came over later and we walked together until they had to leave, en route home, very reluctantly. We lunched at Round Point Café. Then took a boat trip along the Seine for a couple of hours.

At the recommendation of the concierge, we had dinner at Laparousse on the Left Bank. Had the specialties of the house – pressed duck, pommes soufle's, and a soufflé for dessert. It was an expensive meal, but everything was unusually delicious. Walked around a bit – the area was rather quiet because of the religious holiday – then took a cab to the hotel. Letter from Ira. Loving Columbus so much he is anxious to go to OSU.

Friday, August 16
Another showery day, but not enough so to keep us in. We breakfasted in the room. Then went walking and shopping – bought some perfume and scarves.

Had a very enjoyable luncheon in the Café de la Paix. Afterwards we took a bus tour of the city, stopping at the Louvre and Notre Dame. Later took a cab to Montmartre, and had a wonderful dinner, in a charming atmosphere, at Mire Catherine. Walked around afterwards, took the funicular down to Place Pigalle, and walked around there. Much too honky-tonk for my taste. Took a cab back.

Jules would like to walk far more than we do, and sometimes goes by himself, because I have had stomach trouble of one kind or another much of the time we have been in Europe.

Saturday, August 17
A little warmer and very pleasant. We had breakfast in the room. Then went walking and shopping – bought more gloves and

more ties. A couple in the tie shop engaged us in conversation – the Rosners of New York – and we shopped, lunched outdoors at the Café de la Paix, and took a cab to the Flea Market together. Found it an incredible place – such worthless junk on display for sale.

Later Jules and I had tea in the Bristol lobby. Still later we went to the Lido for dinner, champagne, and primarily, the show. It was most spectacular, and some of the acts were clever, and most of the girls seemed beautiful, but nudity is not my idea of entertainment. Did not get back to the hotel until about 3:00am.

Sunday, August 18
We slept quite late. Had breakfast in our room. Then went for a long walk. Later we took a sightseeing bus to Versailles. It was an interesting trip. I was having very painful cramps almost constantly, however, the palace was mobbed, it was hot inside because of the crowd, but then it was quite chilly outdoors when we went out to see the fountains turned on. I was very happy to get back to the Bristol. We had tea served in the room. Later we went down to the dining room, and I had some soup while Jules had a very enjoyable dinner. Later Jules went for a walk. He is tireless when it comes to walking while on vacation, especially in Paris.

Monday, August 19
A lovely day and I felt a bit better. We had breakfast in our room. Then went walking on the Champs Elysees. At a lovely Danish shop in the Champs, ordered a set of stainless steel in the same pattern we gave Lois for a wedding gift. Then walked some more, stopping at sidewalk cafes from time to time to have some refreshments and to rest. Later we went to the Auberge du Père Louis for a rather good dinner. Afterwards we again went walking on the Champs as it was our last evening in Paris. Were sitting at a sidewalk café when we saw Jack Levinson go by with a friend from New Jersey, Jean Moore. They joined us, and we sat and chatted until it was time to go home and to bed.

Tuesday, August 20
We had breakfast in our room. Took a cab to Sabena to buy our helicopter tickets as Jules had francs to use up. Tried to shop but had too little time so bought only a lipstick. Checked out, took a cab to the Invalides station, then a bus to Le Bourget, and then via KLM Airline to Amsterdam. Lunched on the plane.

Took a cab to the Amstel Hotel, where we were given a large attractive room overlooking the river, but with what seemed to me the most unimaginative possible furnishings. A long, charming letter from Lucille but none from Ira.

We went walking. Had cocktails in the very attractive lounge and dinner in the equally attractive dinning room, and then went walking some more. A cool, showery day, but a very pleasant one.

Wednesday, August 21
A lovely day. We had breakfast in the dining room. Then wandered about town for hours, stopping occasionally in a café for a snack and a rest. Even had herring at a herring stand.

In the late afternoon, we took a ride on the sightseeing boat along the canals and in the harbor. We both enjoyed it, although Jules had taken the same trip when he was here in May. We found our way back to the hotel on a trolley. Rested a bit. Then to the cocktail lounge for a drink. Later to the Five Flies for dinner – a very interesting, very old place, but the food was in my opinion only fair. Another couple from the hotel was there, the Smiths from Zurich. We had dinner with them, and found them an interesting couple.

Thursday, August 22
We had breakfast in our room. Then took an all-day bus tour. There was a small group on the bus, all friendly and congenial, and it was a lovely sunny day. We stopped at the flower auctions, lunched together at a café in Haarlem, went through the Peace Palace at the Hague, and stopped at some art galleries to look at some lovely Rembrandts as well as the works of other Dutch artists. The Liftins called in the evening, and came over to the hotel. We had a drink in the lounge and dinner in the dinning room. Then dashed down to the docks in a cab to get the last sightseeing boat of the evening so we could see the sights by night. There is much illumination and it was quite pretty. Said goodbye to the Liftins until Washington.

Friday, August 23
Another perfectly beautiful day. We had breakfast in the dining room. Then to the Rijks museum to see some magnificent Rembrandts. Checked out. Had the taxi driver take us through the Jewish quarter, where so many innocent people were killed and the physical destruction is still evident, on the way to the station. Went by train to Rotterdam, Lunched at a little café there. Took a helicopter to the Brussels heliport, stopping at Antwerp and the Brussells airport. Our first helicopter ride. The views of the cities and country side were wonderful, and the whole experience delightful. Checked in at the Metropole, and went walking. Had coffee at the hotel café. Later went to L'Epanle de Mouton for dinner – a small but famous place where many of the foods are cooked in front of you. Most of the guests were American, and everyone talked with everyone else. It was also a delightful (and expensive) experience.

Saturday, August 24
A sunny crisp day. We had breakfast in the dining room. Then walked around the city for about 3 hours, sightseeing and shopping. Lunched at a small cafe. Back to the hotel to rest and to pack. Had tea at the hotel sidewalk café. Then to the airport terminal. There was quite a reunion as the group who had started out together reassembled for the return trip. We took off about 11:00. Had a cold supper with champagne and followed by cognac, but nothing like the feast on the first trip. We were lucky enough to get seats again in the small cabin, but our companions were not as likeable as the Browns. And we had been told the plane would stop at Shannon, where we planned to do some shopping, but after the takeoff we were told it would be a nonstop flight.

Sunday, August 25
Got some sleep, and had a fairly good

breakfast. It was a very smooth flight, the first Jules made on a return trip without a stop. We landed in rain about 9:30. Went through customs with surprising speed. Got a cab to the La Guardia, and an American Airlines plane to Washington. When we got there, it was raining harder than ever, so we took a cab all the way home.

Telephoned Columbus. Talked to Lucille. Ira was out with the Lewins. He called back later, after Jules had left to pick up Pal at Ashton. He sounded happy and cheerful.

Had lunch on the plane. We went to the Langley Hot Shoppe for dinner. Then to the new Posin's to get some groceries. Must stock up, and find a maid, before Louie, Lucille, Howard, and Ira get here next Saturday.

Year End Summary 1957

1957 was a very good year. We seem to be hounded by the same two problems year after year – Ira's poor school work and my inability to find and retain competent household help. The first is the more serious, of course, the second more annoying than serious. Ira seems a little more serious about his studying, and works a little harder, as the problem of being admitted to college comes closer. He does not work nearly hard enough, however, particularly in view of all the work of previous years which he neglected and now lacks as a solid foundation for his present subjects.

I should appreciate, though, more than I do, that he seems to be a happy, healthy, well-adjusted teenage, very difficult to live with at times, but a great pleasure at other times. Jules is being very successful in his work. If he continues to do as well, my dream of retiring while we are still able to travel and have fun may come true.

My job goes along in what has now become a rut. I am still in an undesirable office, do no supervision and have not been restored in any measure to my standing before my discharge. The only difference to my ability and experience that the present administration pays is to assign very difficult cases to me, and to compliment my work from time to time.

1957 will always stand out as the year of my first trip to Europe – and what a wonderful, thrilling experience it was, from the Bar Conference in London to our travels on the continent.

It was good, too, to get to Lawrence for a few days, to see Mother and Dad getting along reasonably well, and to provide them with a trip to Boston, which they clearly enjoyed very much.

1958

This year brought deaths to the family. On the one hand, Clifford Schlezinger, Jules' nephew, died suddenly in Columbus, leaving a young family. He was the son of Jules' brother Lou. Within a matter of days Anne's father died in Lawrence, Massachusetts, her hometown. In both cases there were lingering questions that they might have been saved with proper medical attention. These cases lingered in Anne's mind. Ira was in his last year of high school.

Anne, Jules, and Ira went to Cape Cod for their August vacation, and they also helped wind up some of the business matters resulting from her father's death. They rented the family house. Anne's mother, Regina moved to an apartment in Washington to be nearer to Anne and her sister, Clara. Anne was concerned about how her mother would do in a new place, but it seemed to be the only choice.   -- RDH

Sunday, June 1
A quiet day. I read the paper, did laundry, cleaned house, etc. Ira studied much of the day, but took some time off to relax with Tommy.
About 7:00, a Rabbi Twersky called from Lawrence to announce that Father died this morning. I called Clara, who called Jan.[74] Then I called the Rabbi back to let him know we would come in tomorrow afternoon. Then Jules called, and, when he heard the news, said he would fly directly to Boston.[75] He called again later to say he would come home tonight and go with me. Louie called later to express sympathy and give me Jules' schedule. Poor Louie! Nate called about 12:30. Jules called later from the airport, got home by cab in a downpour about 1:45 am.

Monday, June 2
Left Ira with very little food in the house, and he had eaten out the last 2 nights, but he was very adult about it all. We and Clara had a pleasant nonstop trip to Boston leaving at 12:20.
Arrived in a downpour, which made Jan's plane late. When she arrived, with the three children, Jules rented a car and we drove to Lawrence. Mother was at home, alone, but in better shape than we had expected. Father died of a heart attack. She had not even called a doctor.
Jules made all the funeral arrangements, paid all the bills.
We checked in at the President Hotel, nearby, except Clara, who will sleep with Mother. Drove out to the Yankee Doddle, and had quite a good dinner there. Mother managed to eat a little. Her legal affairs are in a muddle but she does not want a local lawyer. A mess!

Tuesday, June 3
A beautiful cool sunny day, for which we were grateful.
Breakfasted at a grill near the hotel. Then to

---

74 Anne's two sisters Clara and Jan.

75 Jules was in Columbus for the funeral of his nephew Clifford Schlezinger who died unexpectedly on Thursday, May 29. Two deaths in the family within three days.

Mother's. Then to the funeral parlor for a last sad look. Then the funeral ceremony and burial. We were surprised and pleased that the synagogue and community did so well by him, and that Florence Webber and Bernie Gardner came from Boston. Afterwards we went out for a bite in shifts. Jules called the office and asked Joe to call Ira. We picked up schnapps and coke, and managed a minyan at the house that would have pleased Father but merely annoyed Mother. Later had Tom Collins, son of Henry C. who was Father's lawyer for many years, come up to discuss settling the estate. Mother decided we were trying to rob her when we were actually signing everything over to her. It was quite a mess.

Wednesday, June 4
Another beautiful day.
To Mother's after breakfast. She was in a slightly calmer mood, but refuses adamantly to budge from her determination to stay there alone at least for the time being. Collins came over with the forms for release of our interests, which we signed. Then we took Mother out for a bit of lunch. The candy Jules sent from Switzerland arrived today. We all left about 3:00, Mother still refusing to accompany any of us but in despair at the thought of being alone. We all felt sorry for her, although we all felt that her domination of and cruelty toward Father, and her refusal even at the very end to call a doctor, almost certainly hastened his death.
A pleasant trip back.
Ira had gone to MCJC yesterday before school to say kaddish for his grandfather. He took Clifford's and Father's deaths very hard.

Thursday, June 5
Back to the office. The few who knew of what had occurred over the weekend were sympathetic. I kept remembering plans I had for when Mother and Dad moved here, and wept each time I did so...
Cards of sympathy from Hilda Sommers and the Maybrooks, and a note from Helen Lee. The office sent a card to Lawrence.
We had chicken boxes sent in for dinner. The Rabbi came to call in the evening to express his sympathy. After he left, Jules and I went to the grocery store.

Friday, June 6
Downtown at noon. I was not really in the mood for shopping, and did not buy anything.
A sympathy note from Judge Leedom.
We had a very good dinner at home.
Afterwards Jules and I went to services at MCJC.[76] Ira was very tired so did not go. I had to get up three times for kaddish. It was an ordeal.
When we got home, Ira told us Gertrude had telephoned from Columbus to ask how I was and to express her sympathy although she had already done so by telephone. Jules has talked to Louie and Edward at the office. Apparently Lucille's house is crowded day and night with people shocked by Clifford's death.

Saturday, June 7
We are having beautiful weather, sunny but moderate. It is so sad that Father had to miss all this after surviving a rugged winter –and

---

76   Montgomery County Jewish Center.

to miss Father's Day and all our visits.

Jules went marketing with me. He also got the screens cleaned and put up. We lunched at Hofberg's. We had broiled chicken for dinner, which we ate in the dining room while watching television.

Ira went out on a date after dinner – a single date, for a change. Tommy is now "going steady." Glad Ira is not. That is what caused Joyce's trouble. Jules and I went for a ride so Jules could see the changes that were taking place on University Boulevard, etc.

Our Swiss candy arrived today.

Sunday, June 8

Nate telephoned to ask about Mother, to thank us for the Swiss chocolates, and to chat, just as we were leaving to take Jules to the airport for a quick business trip to Columbus. We are all getting tired of these frequent separations.

Ogden Fields telephoned to ask if I would chaperone the Blair dance on Friday, but I explained that I was hardly in the mood.

Sylvia Benenson called to suggest I drop in to see them, that they would come to see me, but Mollie was convalescing from an operation at their house.

Mary Wagshal telephoned to ask about Mother, etc. Had tried to call Clara but got no answer. I answered her questions. Gathered Sam[77] is offended because he heard thru her rather than directly.

Monday, June 9

There are a number of new recruits at the office, who are still in law school, working for the summer. I lunched with some of them. They seem so young, and make me feel so old. Ira and I went to dinner at The Silver.

A sympathy card from Ben and Lillian Wagshal, and a charming note from Florence and Arthur Gang.

Jules telephoned from the airport shortly after 11:00 to let me know that he had arrived, and took a cab home. He has had a hectic schedule lately, and I hope he will be able to stay at home and take it a bit easy for a while.

Tuesday, June 10

Staff meeting in the morning to announce that Kuskin[78] was replacing Compton as the Chairman's Chief Counsel. I ranked next to Kuskin for years, but that was years ago...Letter from Jan, still upset about Father, regretting that she had not visited and written more often. Jules called Sam Wagshal and explained why we had not called him directly. He said he would have gone to the funeral had he known in time. Jules and I dropped in on the Rolands for a while. They were quite elated. Then home. Still very warm, so we took Ira for a ride and stopped for ice cream.

Wednesday, June 11

Hope Piper had informed me that the staff would make a donation in Father's memory to any cause I designated. I asked her today to make it to his synagogue in Lawrence. A hot, humid day, but it was pouring when I left the office. I had an umbrella, but was

---

77 Sam Wagshal, Anne's cousin and close family connection in Washington.

78 Harry Kuskin. In 1965 he was named NLRB judge.

pretty wet by the time I walked to where I have to park these days.

An unusually charming note from Bobbie Schlezinger,[79] who so recently lost her own father.

It was so pleasant after the rain that Jules and I went for a long ride. We brought back some ice cream from Gifford's. Ira and Tommy and some other neighborhood youngsters were sitting enjoying the coolness and one another's company.

Thursday, June 12
Jules was taking the Chevy in for servicing, and I did not feel like trying to park the Buick where I park, so went down with Hazel.
Had a very enjoyable luncheon with Jules at the Occidental.
Got a ride to Silver Spring with Davidson. Ira picked me up at The Giant, where I got some marketing done.
Had put a rib roast on the automatic timer, the first one we had in a long time, and it was delicious. After dinner, Jules and Ira went to Silver Spring to buy some clothes for Ira. They came home to pick me up, and then we all went for frozen custards – how could I refuse when they had been so considerate that they would not go without me?
Sympathy notes from Madelyn and the Cantor.

Friday, June 13
The Board was having a cocktail party this evening as a farewell to Ray Compton. I did not go.
Got home to find a letter and a postcard from Mother, announcing that the downstairs tenants, on whom she had relied for various kinds of help, were moving, she was desperate; feared she was losing her mind; and wanted us, especially Jules, to come immediately. We called Jan in New York and the Rolands to alert them. Jan offered to go if Clara would keep her children, to which Clara very reluctantly agreed. We then called Mother, who sounded relatively well and cheerful, and the tenants were not moving, and she was managing affairs fairly well. Don't know what it all means.

Saturday, June 14
Had a maid in today, sent by the D.C. Employment Service, named Lena Croddock. She was a big woman, but seemed pleasant and a pretty good worker.
We took her to the terminal.
Later we all changed our clothes and went to O'Donnell's in Bethesda for dinner. Chose it mainly because Ira loves sea food and does not get it often. We all enjoyed our dinners. Later Jules and I went to visit the Levys. They were going to come to see us, but their children were being rambunctious. Their friends the Middlemans also dropped in. It was a pleasant evening.

Sunday, June 15
A pleasantly moderate day. Ira gave Jules *A Treasury of Jewish Folklore*, which seemed to please Jules very much.
Jules and I went to Wagshal's in the afternoon to deliver some perfume Selma asked Jules to get her in Paris; to visit Sam, who had written Mother, and maintains he would have gone

---

79   Jules' brother Nate's wife.

to the funeral if Selma, who knew about it Sunday night had not waited until Monday to tell him; and to buy some stuff for supper.

The Jeffes called after supper to ask us to go bowling with them, which we did, and to the Hot Shoppe afterwards, all of us. It was enjoyable, although the references to Father's Day kept reminding me of poor Pa.

Monday, June 16
A lovely day, sunny and cool. Started to go downtown at noon but it was so windy that I took a little walk and went back to the office. Lunched with Tom Sweeney and Ernie Dowd. Notes from Lucille and her sister Lillian Opperheimer. Poor Lucille, trying to be philosophical, and hide her heartbreak at losing her youngest child.

Jules telephoned Collins today to check on Mother's affairs, and to suggest that Collins urge her to install a telephone. She should have one – she and Pa should have had one all these years.

Ira finished school today, and went out in the evening to celebrate. Got in so late, I was asleep and did not know how late it was.

Tuesday, June 17
Jules took Ira to Blair to pick up the desk Ira made in shop. It was quite an ambitious undertaking for him, and there is much work yet to be done on it, but it should be a handsome piece when it is finished. Sam Wagshal telephoned in the evening. He had received a letter from Mother, complaining bitterly that her children were of no help, and appealing to him for help, although giving no indication of what she wanted him to do.

Jules and I went for a ride and had some ice cream. Ira was out with the boys for a while so he did not go with us.

A number of Philippine acquaintances are in town with President Garcia.[80]

Wednesday, June 18
Lena came in bright and early.

Jules took the Chevy back to Hicks. I rode with him that far and took a trolley the rest of the way.

Got a ride out to Giant with Max Rosenberg, and Ira picked me up there.

Managed to stay awake long enough to fix dinner, to eat, and to clean up afterwards, but that was about as much as I could manage as I was terribly sleepy. Tried to read but kept falling asleep over it, and the same with television. Did not want to go to bed too early for fear I would not be able to sleep through the night again. Finally stopped fighting, went to bed, and slept fairly well.

The Remualdezs gave us an attractive place mat set from the Philippines.

Thursday, June 19
Ira and Tommy went out early to try to get some caddying work, but it was a cloudy day and they earned no money.

I went down with Jules, but saw Hazel en route and switched to her car. Ira read a letter from Mother to me over the telephone – desperately unhappy but a little more rational. Jules received a letter from Collins, who had called on Mother and urged her, at Jules request, to get a telephone.

---

80   Remualdez contact that Anne mentions. See reference in next entry, June 18.

Downtown at noon but bought only some notepaper.

Jules picked me up after work and we went to the Pan-American building for a reception in honor of President and Mrs. Garcia. It was lavish, crowded and we saw very few people we knew. Ira had dinner out with Tommy. They are very excited about their weekend at the beach.

Friday, June 20
Pouring. Ira and Tommy were afraid for a while that their trip to Rehoboth would be called off, but they left about 10:00. I went down with Jules.

Kuskin told me to discuss a case with Loeb, a nice, bright guy but so much my junior I felt it was a slap in the face. Applied for a transfer to 3 other members' staffs and on the General Counsel's side, but was given no promises. Jules picked me up after work. We had a very enjoyable dinner at Blackie's "House of Beef."

Letter from Mother, worried about Collins. Sympathy note from Marvin and Lois. Ira's report car–fairly good–but he can do better.

Dickie Grimes told us Tommy called about 2:00 from Rehoboth - everything O.K. Wrote a letter to Mother, we took it to the S.S. post office, and stopped at Gifford's.

Saturday, June 21
Lena came in, a bit late.
Ira telephoned, collect.
Letter from Mother, still convinced that Collins is going to rob her. Clara called – she and Jan have received no mail at all from Mother since we were in Lawrence. She and Lou dropped in to read the letter I had received.

Jules and I went to a party at the Kaminstein's given as a farewell to Do Levy, who is moving to New York. Some of her old friends who were there included a social worker who played a part in Ira's adoption, and Sam Schwartz, his first pediatrician.

We stopped at a Hot Shoppe on the way home just for dessert and coffee, and then home.

Sunday, June 22
Jules and I slept fairly late. Had just finished brunch when Ira came home, much earlier than we expected him. Today was lovely but the weather was bad while they were at the beach.

The Gangs called and were going to come over, but we had an engagement with Nate. We picked up Nate at the Sheraton Park, and went to Jules' office for a drink. Then to Duke Zeibert's, where we had very good dinner. Took Nate to the station for a 6:00 train, and we went home, to digest the big dinners we ate. Ira ate as though he were making up for a number of inadequate meals while he was at Ocean City.

Year End Summary 1958

There have been many dark spots this past year. There was Clifford's sudden and untimely death, leaving a young wife, a small daughter, and an unborn baby. And poor Phyllis, living with the thought that another doctor might have performed a tracheotomy in time and saved Cliff's life.

And there was poor Father's death. He was much older, so his death was, to that extent, less tragic. But it was very sad nevertheless. If he could have lived only a little longer, he would have seen all of us. If Nate had not invited us to Philadelphia for his birthday party, we probably would have gone to Lawrence over the May 30 holiday. And if he had had any medical attention, maybe his life could have been saved.

So often, when I look at Mother's cozy apartment, her pleasant way of life, the medical attention she receives, the chauffeuring service, and the service and attention in general from the Rolands and us, I cannot help thinking how much Father would have enjoyed it. He wanted to move here for years, but she kept blocking the sale of the house. And with all Jules' and Collins' efforts, the damned house is not sold yet. How I wish I had insisted, while Father was alive, that they give it away if necessary to get rid of it, so he could have had some time to live here and to enjoy being near us all.

1959

In 1959 Ira graduated from high school and entered college. Jules' law practice was growing and doing very well. The same maid was with them the entire year, and she was reliable, making Anne's life easier in managing the household and working. Their family life was 1950ish.   -- RDH

Thursday, October 1

Had my immunization shots - updated at the District Building at noon. Shopped at the grocery store on the way home from work. New Year's card from the Lewins.
Had a delicious rib roast for dinner which Ira had put on for me.
Jules and I went to Silver Spring after dinner to do some shopping, but the stores were so crowded, and Jules was so agitated to get home to help Ira with a theme for school, that we accomplished virtually nothing. At this rate, I shall be doing my shopping for Mexico in Mexico.

Friday, October 2

Downtown at noon, but all I succeeded in buying was a girdle.
Got home before Rita left. Ira was at the library so she helped me a great deal in getting dinner started. We had a big, fancy chicken dinner, cleaned up, dressed, picked up Mother, and got to services in good time. The new auditorium looked quite impressive, and the service moved along well, but we missed Cantor Gewirtz. Mother enjoyed it all very much – the ride, the people, the service. New Year cards from Helen Lee, Lucille, the

Gangs, and the Levys. We should have sent some – go through this routine every year. Jules brought some lovely flowers home.

Saturday, October 3
A beautiful day, warm and sunny. We had breakfast, dressed, picked up Mother, and got to services at a reasonable hour. The Pearces (she knew Jules in Columbus, and they recently moved here) were coming out in the afternoon, so I called the Levys, Gangs, Elsons, and they all came too. The Pearces brought their Jr. High son and 16-year old daughter. Ira liked both very much and made a date with Phyllis.
We all enjoyed our little party very much. Jimmy Lindner and Larry Promisel dropped in later to visit Ira, so he had a very full day. New Year card from Phyllis, Clifford's widow, and the children. Poor things!

Sunday, October 4
A beautiful sunny day.
We all went to services again, I largely because of Mother, who enjoys going so much.
After dinner Ira went down to the Art Gallery to attend a lecture. Jules and I delivered Jonathan's bar mitzvah gift, and were asked to stay for dinner, but of course did not. Stopped in at Mother's to get some financial matters straightened out. She continued to insist on giving me $100 for the trip, which I finally accepted when she agreed to give Jan and Clara, both of whom she had given more than $50, another $50.
In the evening, Jules, Ira and I went to the Hot Shoppe for a curb-service snack. Hurried so Ira could do some studying.

Monday, October 5
Very hot – up to 90! I pulled out summer clothes again.
Downtown at noon. Bought a dress in Garfinckel's.
Rita came in. Ira was just leaving to take her to the terminal when I got home. It was too hot to cook, but I did so anyhow. We had a luscious sirloin steak, quite large, but every bit of it was eaten.
Ira went out after dinner, and was gone all evening, planning the school election campaign, on which he is, in my opinion, spending far too much time.
I should have gone shopping, but Jules had some work to do, and I did not feel like going alone.

Tuesday, October 6
Another hot day.
Downtown at noon, but did not buy anything. Went out early. Jules called just after I left to offer to go shopping or to lunch with me. He had argued a case in the Court of Claims in the morning, and felt it went well.
A gift handkerchief and a note from Bea Pearce for the party Saturday, which I felt, and Jules agreed, was making far too much of it.
Fixed supper at home for Ira. He was too busy with his electioneering to go out for dinner. Jules and I had dinner at Kushner's. Stopped in at Mother's to get her signature on a new lease form. Would have stayed to visit longer but had to go to the grocery store on the way home.

Wednesday, October 7
Downtown at noon. Bought some

underthings to take on the trip, and which I needed anyhow. Rita came in quite early. Had steak for dinner again, very good, this time with mushrooms.

After dinner Jules and I went to Hahn's in Silver Spring to try to get sport shoes for me to take on the trip, but did not find any I liked that were comfortable.

Directly home afterwards so Jules could check a theme Ira had written. Ira has put so much time and energy into his election campaign – I hope his studies do not suffer too much us a result.

Thursday, October 8
Got up with a headache, bad enough for me to stay at home. Too bad as I had some work at the office. I wanted to finish before leaving on vacation. But maybe I can do so tomorrow.

Felt well enough to fix dinner by the time Jules and Ira got home.

Jules and I went marketing after dinner although it was raining quite hard.

Jules went to see Judge Madden[81] this afternoon, at the hospital recuperating from an operation, and brought him a book. Madden sent me his regards. Thinking about him brings back many happy memories. Hope he recovers all right.

Thank-you note from Jonathan Levy.

Friday, October 9
Back to the office.

Shopped diligently at noon for walking shoes but did not find any. Might as well have lunched, instead, with Jules and Gene Levenson, who was visiting.

Completed my work, and left about a half-hour early. If Kuskin[82] wants to object, let him.

Long letter from Gertrude,[83] who will be on the Coast visiting Lois and her family when we are in Columbus for the Iowa game. Wrote primarily to tell us that Fred Reiter had died in New Zealand. Poor Anne Reiter.

Rita came in.

Don Mider is borrowing our folding cot while we are away.

Jules and I shopped for shoes – should have gone to services to hear Jonathan Levy.

Saturday, October 10
To the Jonathan Levy bar mitzvah at the Langley Temple in the morning. He did very well. To the house afterwards for luncheon and a reception in the back yard – worked out very nicely.

Ruth told me she bought some wonderful travel shoes in Slater's, so we went there and I bought a pair. Jules got a haircut and we did a couple of other errands.

Then home for dinner.

Ira went out afterwards on a date with Phyllis Pearce. Jules and I went back to visit the Levys, as they had urged us to do. There were only a few close relatives other than us. We

---

81   J. Warren Madden, the first Chairman (1935-1940) of the governing Board of the NLRB. The Board was known for being strongly pro-labor under his leadership. He was involved in the Potsdam Conference and the Nuremberg Trials, helping sustain the conviction of Alfred Krupp for crimes against humanity. He later served on the U.S. Court of Claims.

82   Harry Kuskin, Chief Counsel to Board member Leedom.

83   Gertrude Lewin, Jules' sister in Columbus.

took Bill's sister back to the motel later, so were there quite late waiting for her. But did not mind as we both liked her very much.

Sunday, October 11
We had brunch relatively early, as Joe and Mel were coming over about 1:00 for a discussion with Jules of some mail Jules received yesterday from Bob Wirth which may involve important new business for the office.
We had a very early dinner. Afterwards Ira picked up Mother, brought her to the house, and then all of us went to Kol Nidre services together. Mother has never been at all religious, but she seems to enjoy the services a great deal.
Clara telephoned to ask if I would bring her several things she wanted from Mexico.

Monday, October 12
A beautiful day – bright and sunny.
Ira picked up Mother and took her to MCJC. We left a little later, in a second car. Ira left after the sermon to pick up Phyllis Pearce and bring her back for a while. We left about 3:30, took Mother home, and went home.
Rita came in. Supposed to come in Saturdays while we are away. Broke our fast at home with a light snack. Later to Stone House grill for a heartier meal. Jules and I went marketing to stock the house for Ira and Pal. Then to Hechts, where I finally found a pair of red shoes I liked. Anne Reiter called. Too bad we shall not be here for Fred's funeral on Wednesday.

Tuesday, October 13
I got up early and watched the TV Spanish class with Ira. He left for school in the Chevy before we left for the airport in a cab. A beautiful day. Our plane was a little late but we had a very smooth trip. Bought a drink, then had steak dinner and champagne free. Stopped for a little while at Atlanta and New Orleans, drinks were free. There was no supper, but almost constant snacks and champagne.
Took a cab to the Reforma. Got a nice outside room on the 8th floor, but learned later it was extremely noisy as they were riveting right across the street.
Jules and I took a long walk, but neither of us wanted anything to eat or drink.

Wednesday, October 14
Poor Louie's[84] birthday. Spent much of the night in the bathroom, and awoke feeling very squeamish. Jules would not leave me, so I finally got up and we went for a walk. After a bite of breakfast in the hotel and some milk of magnesia, felt much better. We then went on a long walking tour. Had a light luncheon at the Sanborn's in the Del Prado hotel. Then on a Cook's tour, by limousine, of many interesting places, including the Cathedral, National Palace, Zocalo, Chapultepec Park and Castle, and the University.
Back to the hotel to rest. Then dressed, with raincoats as it was pouring, and took a cab the few blocks to the Jena restaurant. It was very good, but not so wonderful as I had been led to expect. Still pouring so we took a cab back. Missed our walk. Spent a little time in the lobby. Them to the inside room

---

84   Anne's brother Louie, who died in World War II.

to which we had moved for a good, quiet night's sleep.

Thursday, October 15
No longer raining, but quite overcast. We had breakfast at the hotel. Were picked up at 9:00 by a Cook's tour to the pyramids, this time only we two and a driver and a guide. Yesterday there were three and a driver, the guide in another car. The drive was interesting – people making so many things from cactus, women doing laundry in streams by flat rocks, the primitive types of housing. Stopped at the Guadalupe shrine, which was mobbed. A number of people making the long approach on their knees. Then to the pyramids, which we walked and climbed around, and found extremely interesting. Lunched at Sanford's Dept. Store. Jules made his business calls and later met me at the Anthropology Museum. More rain. We had a drink at the Del Prado. Had more drinks and dinner at the Villa Fontana, very nice, recommended by Mary Aarke in a note she left for us at the Reforma.

Friday, October 16
Walked over to the Hilton to arrange a Cook's tour to Toluca. Breakfasted there – in a big rush to make our tour – unfortunately as it was the best coffee I have had in Mexico.
The driver to Toluca was very interesting – again the sharp contrasts of wealth and poverty, modernity and primitivism. The market also was interesting but, at the same time, quite revolting because of the dirt and disease. We bought some cheap jewelry – not at fixed prices but too cheap to worry about it.
Had an excellent luncheon in the hotel. No rain for a change, so we did a good deal of walking.
Had dinner at the Focalare – fairly good food and music.
Wire from Mary Clarke in Acapulco. We called her. It seems improbable that we shall get together in Mexico.

Saturday, October 17
Walked over to the Hilton for a leisurely breakfast. It was good, but the coffee, like all the coffee hereabouts, tasted too strongly of chicory for me.
Did a great deal of walking and getting acquainted with the City. Did some shopping also. Bought a skirt for Clara and one for myself at one of the Maya shops.
Had an enjoyable luncheon at the Chalet Suizo, but the most enjoyable meal either of us has had in Mexico was dinner at the Quid. We liked the décor, the atmosphere, the music, and most of all the food – charcoal broiled steaks, sans continental sauces.
Hope Rita showed up to clean and launder for Ira.

Sunday, October 18
Had breakfast in the hotel. Picked up afterwards in a big Cadillac limousine with only a driver and one other passenger. Went to see the Tiffany glass curtain, then to Xochimilco, where we had a boat ride, and bought a lovely orchid and gardenias corsage.
Later lunched at a Pam Pam near the Hotel. Then to the bullfights by cab. Neither Jules nor I cared for the bullfights, which we

found gory and unsporting, so left at about the halfway point. Had drinks at the hotel. In the evening to the Belvedere Room on the Hilton Roof. We had a good dinner, a window-table, and enjoyed the dancing. The cool rainy weather we have been having, particularly on the boat ride this morning, finally gave me a case of the sniffles. I had expected much warmer weather than we have been having.

Monday, October 19
Had breakfast in the hotel. Then walked around and shopped some more – bought Rita a shirt – until it began to drizzle.
Jules had a business luncheon date. I would have gone shopping, but for my cold and the rain. Lunched in the hotel. Later Jules and I went shopping, in the rain, again, for the kind of bongo drums Ira requested, but again without success. Had cocktails in the hotel.
Did not go to the fiesta welcoming Pres. Mateos back from the U.S. because of the rain. Went to the Zocolo later. It was an impressive sight with all the illumination, and there were still large crowds there, but we did not stay to see what was coming on as it began to pour (most unusual weather, due to hurricanes in nearby areas). Had dinner at the hotel. Fortunate that we like the Reforma as we spend so much time there.

Tuesday, October 20
Had breakfast at the hotel. The Hertz man brought the car over about 11:00, and we took off, for one of the most beautiful, interesting, scenic drives ever. Shopped at Cuernevaca and did some sightseeing with a guide. Then on to the Victoria Hotel at Taxco, a hotel and a town unique in our experience. Had dinner there.
A message from Mary Clarke, whom we met later with a new friend, Allen McLean from Toronto, both staying at St. Prisca Hotel. We went with them for a walk, for a bus ride around the most incredible town, and for drinks in the beautiful patio of their hotel. We had supper at our respective hotels as we are all staying on the American plan. Then they came up here for the music, the dancing, the native dancers, and a few drinks. A lovely day in every way.

Wednesday, October 21
After breakfast we went walking and shopping. Met Mary and Allen, who went with us. Bought quite a bit of jewelry, including a bracelet and ring for me, at a Felipe Amore shop. Afterwards, had tequila cocktails on the Victorian terrace. A beautiful day, and Taxco is so unusual, we decided to stay another day.
After luncheon at our respective hotels, the four of us did more walking, and took another bus ride. Started for a drive in the Hertz Chevy, but it would not make the hill near the Victoria.
After so much walking and climbing, we had drinks again at the Santa Prisca.
Mary and Allen came up after dinner. We watched the native dancers, watched some Mexicans who were wonderful dancers dance, and did a little dancing and drinking ourselves. Very enjoyable.

Thursday, October 22

A beautiful day. We checked out after breakfast, picked up Mary and Allen, and set out for Acapulco. Stopped at the Spratling silver place and bought a couple of pins. A beautiful drive. We dropped off Allen at the Mozimba Hotel (he could not afford ours) and went to the Elcano. Got settled in our very attractive rooms, had drinks on Mary's terrace, and Jules and I went for a dip in the hotel pool.

Had lunch and dinner at the hotel, where we have to stay on the American plan, unfortunately, as the food is not very good. Had drinks in our room. Then to the El Mirador for a drink and to watch the diver. Expected to meet Allen there but he did not show up or call. Went for a lovely ride. Then sat on our balcony till bedtime.

Two wires from Hank about Arnsperger. No other mail.

Friday, October 23

A beautiful morning. After breakfast Jules and I went for a swim, both in the ocean and in the pool. Then for a ride. Mary delivered some camera equipment to Allen, who had a story about hearing a friend here had drowned, etc. Maybe. We rode around the town, which is, for the most part lovely.

It was cloudy and windy after luncheon. Jules went swimming anyhow. Mary and I just watched.

Saw a gorgeous sunset.

We all had cocktails and the Barroods, a young New Jersey couple with whom we had become acquainted, went to El Presidente's cocktail lounge, where there was music and dancing. We had a couple of drinks, listened to the music, watched some excellent dancers, and had a lot of fun.

Saturday, October 24

Pouring. All three of us had taken considerable trouble yesterday to make reservations for Oaxaca but the flight was cancelled. Mary left at noon for Mexico City by bus.

Jules went swimming during a brief lull in the rainstorms.

After luncheon we rested and read until time for cocktails and dinner. The rain had stopped so we took a cab to the Zocolo and walked around for awhile. As we were getting out of the cab on our return, ran into the Barroods, and all four of us turned around and took another cab to the Club de Pesca for a drink. Watched the dancing and the flirting, danced a little ourselves, and took a cab back to the Elcano, where there is absolutely nothing doing at night.

Sunday, October 25

A beautiful day. We went to the beach and pool first thing after breakfast, and stayed until we had to get ready to leave by cab for the airport and a 1:00 plane to Mexico City. Had a very pleasant flight. Back to the Reforma, where we were greeted warmly by the staff. Had luncheon there. Then picked up Mary Clarke at the Premier, and we all went for a long walk. When we returned, we had a drink at the Premier.

Later we all went to the Jacaranda, an impressively beautiful night club, with a terrific band and good food. We all enjoyed it tremendously. Jules told me he would have enjoyed it more without an extra woman, but Mary was so grateful that we included her.

Monday, October 26
Another lovely day. After breakfast at the hotel, we spent most of the day walking and shopping. Bought more shirts and jewelry, and bongo drums and maracas for Ira.
Lunched at a Hungarian restaurant. Later we had cocktails at the hotel. When Mary came over, we had some more. Then to the Quid (Mary's treat) for more cocktails and an excellent dinner. The maitre d' remembered us and was so pleased at the nice things we said about the place that he gave us a drink on the house.
Mary asked me to stay and go to Oaxaca with her, but I am leaving tomorrow with Jules. Have left Ira alone long enough, and Jules will have to leave so soon for New York.

Tuesday, October 27
Had breakfast at the hotel. Then took a cab to the airport, and a bit sadly, took off for home. Quite a rough trip to New Orleans, where we went through customs, but the rest of the trip was very pleasant. Ira met us with the Chevy. He had had a number of invitations to dinner, more than he could accept, and had had a dinner party himself, a foursome, for which he did all the cooking. He had been elected treasurer but we gathered, was running into some difficulties scholastically. His winter jacket had been stolen out of the Chevy parked near the school. But, in general, he maintained that he had greatly enjoyed our absence. We looked at the mail, unpacked, and went to bed in our own bed.

Wednesday, October 28
I was awake early so decided to go back to work. Took Jules downtown. He left about noon for meeting in New York with Hank Cohen and Arnsperger. Clara called me at the office – Ira had dinner one night at her house. I called Ruth Levy at the hospital, where she was recuperating from a hysterectomy.
Stopped at the grocery store on the way home to get some things for dinner. Learned when I got home that Ira was going to a banquet, which he had forgotten to mention earlier. It was being given by the Kiwanis to students selected for various reasons – Ira for his election campaign – to be members of the Key Club. I ate a rather helter-skelter supper by myself, did some household chores, and went to bed at a reasonable hour.

Thursday, October 29
Went downtown at noon to buy some trick-or-treat supplies. Cool, brisk weather, but pleasant.
Called Mort Friedman to let him know I was back in case the parking place was available. It was and had been all week.
Stopped at the grocery store on the way home. Expected Jules late tonight, but he got home by cab shortly after I did – just missed me at the office, and left N.Y. in too big a rush to call. I managed to stretch supper for the three of us. Helped Ira with a theme.
The romance between Helga and Bill Raffanti is evidently still going strong. A postcard from the Pearces asking us over Saturday evening.

Rita came in. Had come in the two Saturdays we were away.

Friday, October 30
What a pleasure to use the parking place this morning! Went downtown at noon. Jules went to services at MCJC after dinner.
Ira went shopping after dinner – bought a winter jacket in a hurry – came home and changed his clothes in a hurry – and went to MCJC as he felt Jules should not be there alone.
I was staying home because it was trick-or-treat night. We had a few children come before Jules left, but not one come afterwards, so I might as well have gone to services with Jules. He came home much earlier than Ira, who met a number of friends there.

Saturday, October 31
Rita came in. A rainy morning. Jules went to services. Ira went to Hecht' and exchanged his jacket for a larger size. I went marketing. In the afternoon Ira went to the MJC[85] homecoming football game. Jules and I had some luncheon at the Hot Shoppe and did a number of errands.
Later went to see Ruth Levy, home from the hospital. Gave her a book, and a pin we bought from Mexico. Gave Rita a shirt, some earrings, and some of our Halloween candy. In the evening Jules and I went to the Pearces'. There were two other couples. A pleasant evening.
Harlon spent the evening with Ira – and the trick-or-treaters. Invitation from the Millers to a cocktails party.

---

85   Montgomery College. Montgomery County Maryland.

Year End Summary 1959

It has been a very good year. It started off with Mother in the hospital, but she has been relatively well since then.

Ira has had a few months of college, and seems to have buckled down to studying a little more seriously than he ever did before, although, in my judgment, not nearly seriously enough. But he is enjoying school, and generally seems of a happier and easier–to–live–with disposition. Maybe it is because he has achieved his dream of owning his own car, in which he has great joy and pride despite the many problems and expenses which it causes him.

Jules seems to be getting along much better with his partners and his office setup than he did for a while, which makes him a generally happier person. That seems at least as important to him as the fact that the firm so far has been prosperous financially. Of course it is all part of the same picture. His partners defer to him more than they did originally because he is clearly the one who brings in most of the new business, and the one with whom most of the clients prefer to do business in person.

My job setup is still quite unsatisfactory, but I can live with it for the time being.

And Rita had been a loyal and reliable housekeeper for well over a year now, a situation that contributes greatly to the happiness of all of us–to Jules and Ira not only because of the work she does, but because it avoids the foul moods I fall into when I have the problem of finding and training a household manager.

1960

This was a quiet year, no major concerns. Anne did worry about Ira's grades and his transferring to a college of his choice. Their professional and social lives continue to be active. This was the last year of the Eisenhower era, basically quiet, and economically productive.

This was the twenty-fifth anniversary of the National Labor Relations Board. On August 25 Anne wrote, "I am so angry at the Board that I planned not to attend the 25th anniversary party, but Jules wanted to go, so I reserved 2 tickets." She was angry because of the slowness of her advancement within the organization. The anniversary party was celebrated in conjunction with the American Bar Association meeting in Washington that year. Anne also mentioned on August 28, "Then to the B'nai B'rith Building for the dedication of a museum dealing largely with Jewish contributions to the law. Justice Tom Clark was the principal speaker. There was a large crowd - this was on the ABA convention program - some of whom we knew."

In late November and December they went on vacation to Puerto Rico and Jamaica, but it was cut short because of a health crisis with Anne's mother, who later recuperated well. On the flight to Puerto Rico, Anne mentioned that it was the first flight on a jetliner that she made. -- RDH

Tuesday, November 1
A rainy morning.
Lunched in the cafeteria with Emily Otis, Mira Stevenson, and Helen Rosen – although it had cleared up and became a lovely day.
We had delicious steaks for dinner – all three of us. Jules and I went to the grocery store after dinner. Ira sometimes carries his lunches these days, and it is difficult to keep up with the things he wants.
A thank-you note from Edie Cohen for the flowers we sent her when she was in the hospital recently for an operation. It was apparently a minor one and she is all right again.

Wednesday, November 2
Rita came in.
A very pleasant day so I scooted downtown for a little while at noon just to get out of the building.
Had very good veal chops for dinner, and plenty of other food to go with them. But Ira had a yen anyhow to go to Gifford's – think he wanted to see how their political poll was progressing – and we finally let him talk us into going – Kennedy was comfortably ahead. Hope that is a true prognostication.
A lovely evening so Jules and I walked from Gifford's to the doughnut shop, and Ira picked us up there. The walk was pleasant.

Thursday, November 3
Bright but windy and cool. I started to go out, without a hat, but turned back because of the windiness. Lunched in the cafeteria with Henry Urman and Milt Janus.
A charming letter from Lucille.[86] She is such a darling.
Jules was working late this evening, and Ira was at school. I came home from the office.

---
86 The wife of Jules' brother Lou in Columbus.

Afterwards, went out to do some marketing. Then had supper at home by myself. Do not mind it occasionally. Ira came home after his class, and Jules did not come too late. He is struggling with a brief he had to prepare in a very limited time, poor dear.

Friday, November 4
A beautiful day so I was pleased to accept an invitation to drive out to Andrews' Air Force Officers Club for luncheon with Dennie Gooch, Bob Muldonian, and Paul Berry, in Dennie's Cadillac.
Rita came in. She had started a leg-of-lamb roast for me. It was delicious. We were all home for dinner, and we all enjoyed it very much.
After dinner Ira went out on a date to attend a school play, etc.
Jules and I went marketing.
Later telephoned some people about coming over Tuesday to listen to the election returns with us. So long since I have had a party, I hardly know how to go about preparing for one.

Saturday, November 5
We all had a very large brunch. Then Ira got busy with his studying, and Jules worked on a brief at home. In the afternoon he went to the office to work. I went down with him, planning to shop and have my hair done. But Clara called just before we left to tell me Mother had been to see Dr. Gusack, who seemed concerned about her, wanted her to go to the hospital for tests, but she refused so I did not feel like shopping. And it began to rain – so I did not get my hair done, I drove home. Jules came later on the bus, and Ira picked him up at the terminal. We had a very good dinner. Spent a quiet evening at home – as we were going out tomorrow.

Sunday, November 6
A pleasant day. We had a large and very delicious brunch.
Afterwards picked up Mother, took her for a ride, and to the Hot Shoppe, at her request, although neither Jules nor I really wanted anything. She seemed in better condition than she did last Sunday.
In the evening Jules and I picked up the Levys and drove out to the Bethesda Naval Officers Club, where we met the Gangs. Had a drink, buffet supper, and then another drink in the bar. There was a super abundance of good food, and everyone in our group seemed relaxed, talkative, and cheerful. Jules and I both enjoyed the evening, and got home at a reasonable hour.

Monday, November 7
A cold wintry day. Dashed downtown at noon anyhow to pick up some Merzetti slaw dressing which I needed for tomorrow night.
Rita did not come in today – is scheduled to come in tomorrow instead.
Jules was quite late getting home from the office. When he got home, we went to the Hot Shoppe for supper. Then to Hofberg's to order food for our election party tomorrow evening. Not sure how many were coming but ordered plenty of everything. Ira was at school this evening, but plans to stay up quite late tomorrow night even though he is taking midterms exams this week.

Tuesday, November 8

Jules and I voted in the morning, and then went on to work in separate cars. A lovely crisp sunny day. I went downtown at noon. Rita came in.

Jules picked up the Hofberg stuff on his way home.

The Naidens, who had declined, called to say they would come before going to another party, and were the first to arrive. Dottie Minshoff was coming alone, but Duke came with her, on his way out of town, and left when the Naidens did. The Grosses were both expected but Sid came alone. Paul and Rene Brand both made it. Then Duke called, had forgotten his suitcase, and Ira drove it and Dottie downtown to him. The Levys came late as David was not well. But we had a nice party. And our party won – almost certainly – in a nip-and-tuck race.

Wednesday, November 9

It looks like Kennedy is in – Nixon had conceded – but ballots are still being counted. I was at the office on time, gloating with my fellow Democrats. Rita came in today to clean up the party dishes.

Jules went to New York to see Arnsperger again.

I went downtown at noon. Ira and I had supper at home. He wanted to go out, but we had a good deal of food left over from last night's party – too much for him to use up in his lunch sandwiches – so we made an excellent supper of that. Bill Levy called to chat and to mention how much they had enjoyed the party last night.

Thursday, November 10

Spent much of the day packing and getting things ready to be moved to the new office over the weekend. Shall miss my free parking place. But being downtown will have advantages, and having a bright new office with a window, and alone, will be a big improvement.

Dorothy Edes called to tell me Jules was leaving New York about 9:35. He had the Buick at the airport so I did not have to pick him up.

He brought me, from Arnsperger, a handsome box of chocolates bought at Rumpelmayer's. It was good to have him back, particularly as Ira had class on Thursday evening, leaving me to have dinner by myself.

Friday, November 11

A holiday for Federal employees, but Ira had school. Left it up to Rita to work or not – she decided to work. Jules and I went downtown about noon, Jules to the office and I shopping. Had my hair done and bought some underpinnings. Then did some marketing and went home. Had planned rather an elaborate dinner only to be told by Ira that he was going on a hayride and had to leave before dinner could be prepared, so Jules and I had a feast by ourselves.

An out of town friend of the Lockers whom Jules also knew called him from the Lockers'. He went over to see him but I preferred to stay at home. Gusack was there – told him Mother is extremely anemic.

Saturday, November 12

A lovely day. But Pal had not been well; Jules

1960

and Ira took him to the vet's, and left him there for a prostate operation.

When they returned, Ira took off for the day. Jules and I took Mother for a long ride. Then we dropped Jules at home, so he would not miss any of the telecast of the OSU-Iowa game, and I took Mother to the Hot Shoppe. She ate, for her, quite a large meal, and seemed to be feeling better. OSU was trounced by Iowa, which means we take the Naidens to the Colony for luncheon.

Ira had to dash off early again for a date, so he ate out on the way, and Jules and I went to the Hot Shoppe's new Sirloin Room at the Wheaton Plaza for dinner – only so-so, we thought.

Sunday, November 13
A lovely mild day.
Took Mother for a ride in the afternoon again.
Bill Levy stopped by for a while, en route to meet Ruth, who had gone to New York for a family bar mitzvah.
Jules put up the storm-door glass inserts and did a few other household chores.
We had a very large rib roast for dinner – really should have had guests to share it. Jules and I have our vacation plans fairly well mapped out, finally. We will leave on the Friday after Thanksgiving Day for the West Indies, and be away for the following two weeks. We both need a real vacation.

Monday, November 14
A mild, pleasant day.
Parked my car at the Carter Barron fringe parking lot and took a bus down. The new office is bright and will, when organized, be very pleasant – a vast improvement over my last one. Jules took me to luncheon at Jack Hunt's. We were joined by Krasnecki and Max Rosenberg.
Tried two different places for coffee, neither of them very satisfactory. Found the trip home by bus not too bad.
Ira had class this evening. He did fairly well, for him, on his midterm exams, mostly B's but with a C – in Political Science.
Rita came in. Clara called. Gusack wants Mother to go to the hospital for tests.

Tuesday, November 15
Very warm. I went to work in a suit. Used the Carter Barron route again.
Lunched at Linda's with Mira Stevenson.
Had so many leftovers in the refrigerator – both chicken and beef – that we made a meal of them, and a very satisfactory meal. Ira went out later and picked up some Gifford ice cream.
A note from Phyllis Schlezinger, who wanted some information from Natalie Findling about the Parents Without Partners organization.
Jules went to Mother's before dinner to get some cards signed for a new bank account he had opened for her.

Wednesday, November 16
Another mild day. Parked at Carter Barron and rode the bus.
To Garfinckel's private sale at noon, but did not find anything I wanted to buy.
Had delicious steak dinners, all three of us together for a change. Rita came in. She

agreed to take Pal out on a leash. Had let him out before she was told not to, but Jules was still at home and managed to get him to return shortly.

Had to go to Mother's again to get her signature. Rushed through dinner so I could go with Jules, waked her when I called at 6:00, and then she fell getting to the phone, and was in such a nasty mood I walked out and waited in the car for Jules.

Thursday, November 17
Usually have company on my bus rides as more Board people use the Carter Barron route.

Lunched in the Embassy Room at the Statler with Jules, Ambassador from Haiti Bonhomme, and Mrs. B. A very pleasant luncheon, got some information for our vacation trip, and I rode back to the office with them in their chauffeur-driven limousine-with no one outside to see me, darn it!

Nate telephoned from Philadelphia. Will be in town, while we are away, to attend a convention, but will stay at a downtown hotel.

Jules was quite late getting home from the office. Neither of us was hungry, but we had to go out to do some errands, so had a bit to eat at the Hot Shoppe.

Friday, November 18
Was tied up all morning at a Board agenda with Leo Weiss. A pretty day so I took a little walk at noon – have to go out of the building to get anything to eat.

Ira wanted to eat out, so we went to the Silver. He went on from there to a school affair, and Jules and I did some marketing.

Rita came in. One of her jobs these days is to take Pal for a walk on a leash as he is not permitted to run loose. She loves it. The weather is delightful, and she would evidently rather do that than clean house.

She had agreed to come in twice a week to look after Ira while we are away – more than is necessary, but I did not want to cut her down too much.

Saturday, November 19
A lovely day. Jules took Pal to the vet's to have the stitches removed. Pal is still to be walked on a leash for a week. Glad we got this over with before going on vacation to save Ira the trouble. Jules and I spent much of the afternoon shopping for vacation clothes for me – no luck.

The Jaffes invited us to Thanksgiving dinner. I accepted with real pleasure.

Jules had a yen to eat out, so we called the Levys, who agreed to join us. I gave Ira dinner, and he went out. We went to Billy Martin's Carriage House in Georgetown. Had a good dinner. Took the Levys home, and then home ourselves.

Sunday, November 20
Gertrude telephoned to ask us to get some China in Jamaica for her to give Helen Lee. Jules went to see Mother on business. The Rolands stopped by, principally to ask us to buy some things for Clara. When they left, we called Coleman and Stanley to say we could not come over, and Lee asked us to bring back a dress for her granddaughter. We had a delicious rib roast for dinner.

Afterwards the Levys picked us up and we went to a meeting of the book club at the Zanoffs'. Neither of us had read the book, Snow's *The Affair*, but the Zanoffs have a lovely home, and we enjoyed the company and the evening. Must have the group meet at our house soon.

Monday, November 21
Another beautiful day. This has been a glorious autumn.
Downtown at noon, but did not find any clothes – too early for any selection of resort clothes. Ira had a class this evening. Jules and I had supper at home. Then went out to do some marketing.
Ira's friend Mike McKain just lost his mother. Ira was quite upset about it. Mike had been away at school studying for the priesthood. Ballots are still being counted and recounted in the remarkably close Presidential election, but I cannot believe that the recounts will affect the ultimate result – a Kennedy victory.

Tuesday, November 22
A lovely warm day. Chased downtown at noon, but shopped very lackadaisically, for lack of time and minus hope of finding anything I wanted to buy. Very busy cleaning my desk for my vacation.
We all had dinner together at home.
Later Ira went to the funeral parlor to keep Mike McKain company for a while. He is going to the funeral tomorrow morning. He is so upset about the death that he is even affectionate toward me occasionally, a real change in his attitude.
Jules went out to get some breakfast pastries, later for a walk with Pal – just very difficult for him to sit around for long.

Wednesday, November 23
A cloudy, drizzly day. I had my hair done, nevertheless, at Jelleff's. Walked there and back.
Rita came in. Will come in as usual on Friday, then on Tuesdays and Fridays while we are away.
Many "happy vacation" wishes from people in the office.
We all had dinner together at home.
Ira went to a party in the evening. Jules and I went to the store to get some frozen dinners, etc., for Ira. Spent the rest of the evening at home, reading, talking about the trip, making plans, etc.

Thursday, November 24
Jules went to Shupp's in the morning to pick up a pumpkin and a mince pie to take to the Jaffes' . We both did most of our packing in the afternoon. Then to Mother's. Jan[87] and Jeri were there. We took them to Clara's, where Cindy and Ricky were. Mother was going to the hospital tonight for tests. Hope all is well with her. Later to the Coleman – Stanley house, but no was at home except the dog. Then to the Jaffes'. Matt was home from school, but the other guests they had invited could not come, so there were just the seven of us, very cozy, and a very good dinner. The Levys called us there to wish us a happy journey. We went home relatively early to finish packing. Went to bed fairly early too.

[87] Anne's sister Jan and her daughter Jeri. They went to visit Clara, the other sister, and her children Cindy and Ricky.

Friday, November 25

A beautiful warm day. Rita came in.

Ira drove us to Friendship Airport, where we took a jet to San Juan, my first jet flight. Very pleasant trip. Lunched on the plane.

Cab to San Juan International – not our first choice, but our reservations got fouled up at the last minute – but more than adequate.

Rather late and a bit cloudy to go for a dip, and too far from town to go sightseeing. We had a drink in one of the hotel bars. Later took a cab to the Swiss Chalet, where we had an excellent dinner. Walked around a bit. Then took a cab back to the hotel. Sat in the lobby for a while, watched the gambling in the casino, had a drink, and went to bed.

Saturday, November 26

Had a very good breakfast at the hotel. Took a cab to the Old City, and then went sightseeing on foot. Warm, but there was a breeze. Enjoyed very much our luncheon at La Mallorquina, advertised as the oldest restaurant in Puerto Rico. Then to El Morro for a sightseeing guide. Caught the jitney back to the hotel.

Jules went for a dip, first in the ocean and then in the hotel pool. Then we had a drink on the verandah. Later we dressed and went to the Hilton (which had been our second choice, with a B'nai B'rith convention), a beautiful hotel, and we had a wonderful dinner in the Rotisserie Room. Back to the hotel. Joined by some acquaintances we made there. Had a drink together. And to bed.

Sunday, November 27

Warm and sunny, and we did not want to give up sunning and swimming altogether after breakfast, and spent the morning on the beach.

Later had a milkshake at the hotel. Then rented a Hertz Volkswagen, and drove to El Yunque, the rain forest. Got lost several times, but found our way. Enjoyed the trip, the fantastic foliage, the beautiful scenery, the squalid villages, with their TV sets and well-dressed families, and luncheon at a restaurant on top of the mountain. After we returned, dressed, and had some supper at the hotel, we relaxed in the lobby. Were joined by our frequent companions, the Hochalies, with whom we had our usual nightcap in the El Chico bar.

Monday, November 28

We had breakfast on the hotel verandah. Then went swimming, in between intermittent showers.

Drove to the Eldorado Beach Hotel, a beautiful place. Had luncheon on the terrace, and enjoyed it very much.

Back to the hotel. Jules went swimming again. I sat at the pool side.

In the evening drove and looked at hotels. Walked into the La Concha Lobby, and ran into Al and Laura Somers, he here for a Board hearing. We had a drink with them at the rooftop bar, admired the view and the hotel, and then, as they did not recommend the food there, we all drove to the Swiss Chalet for more drinks and a very good dinner. Took them back to their hotel, and then returned to ours, to pack for our trip to the Virgin Islands tomorrow.

Tuesday, November 29

Had breakfast at the hotel. Then checked out, and drove to the airport, leaving one suitcase at the hotel. Took Caribbean Airways to St. Thomas. By cab to Bluebeard's Castle, interesting but a bit musty in the damp weather, and it rained most of the day and all evening. During a dry moment, we walked into town. Jules got in touch with Jerry Freedman, a New York lawyer here for the winter. He and his wife Carrie took us to luncheon in town, and then drove us around the island sightseeing. That was a break for us, particularly as it was raining quite hard, which would have made it a bit difficult to get around by ourselves. Later they came up to Bluebeard's Castle to have dinner as our guests. Then for another ride – in the rain – and a drink and floor-show at the Hilton Virgin Isles Hotel.

Wednesday, November 30

Had an excellent breakfast at the hotel. Then walked into town. Ran into Jerry as we passed his "law office" but would not permit him to be imposed upon 'tho' he offered to take us around again – in the rain. Cab back to Bluebeard, checked out, cab to airport to check our bags, have a sandwich, and then another cab to a dock, where we took a very interesting and pleasant trip in a glass-bottomed boat over coal reefs, etc. Then to Smith's Fonay, an interesting spot on Synagogue Hill, for a drink. Cab to airport. Our plane was late, but we had a pleasant flight back to San Juan and the International Hotel. Had dinner at the Pavillon Room – a lot of fuss and feathers, but not very good food – a drink later at El Chico bar, and then to bed.

Year End Summary 1960

The actual year's end, at the Jaffe party, was very enjoyable. But other aspects of the end of 1960 are not so pleasant. Mother is probably going to be more of a care now than before the operation, and refuses to have a nurse or a maid in the apartment. Ira is concerned that his poor grades at school will not give him much choice of a college to which to transfer next year, and is inclined to blame all his troubles on me rather than on his neglect of his studies. He threatens occasionally to move out and work his way through college for the next couple of years, but, in his calmer moments, realizes he could not possibly manage such a program, financially or academically.

Rita leaving the way she did, without a word, was a disappointment. Although Alvin does not meet our needs, I find myself most reluctant to go through the process of training a new maid.

The job is working out fairly well, at long last. I finally got my 14 and supervisory status. Glad the Republicans lost out. Wish I knew how to go about it politically, or knew someone sufficiently influential, to try to get an appointment as a Board Member.

1961

This year marked a major change with Ira going away to college at Ohio State University. Jules had gone to college there, and his extended family still lived in Columbus. This year was also difficult for Anne in some ways. Ira had been an integral part of her life for almost twenty years, and he was an only child. His moving away to college must have left a significant vacuum in her life. She begins to focus more on her career to fill her life. From this point forward she begins to write in more detail about the office and her cases.

Anne and Jules took a driving vacation with Alice and Irving Jaffe[88] to Quebec and Nova Scotia. Anne said that they came back better friends than when they had left.

In her year end summary for this year she questions the meaning of why she is writing the diary, but her questioning goes deeper. She is really questioning the meaning of her life and what it will mean to those who come after her. -- RDH

Thursday, June 1

Pouring in the morning. Jules slept a bit later than usual, but hurried, and was ready in time for us to go down together. Clear and pleasant again by noon so I walked downtown.

Jules worked late. By the time I picked him up it was such a pretty afternoon that we drove home with the top down.

---

[88] Alice and Irving lived in Silver Spring and were members of the Sunday Night Book Club. Irving was an attorney and in the 1970's served as Assistant Attorney General of the United States.

Letter from Ira. He is getting all set for the summer quarter, registering for classes and arranging for housing, but is evidently very worried about getting passing grades for this quarter. Hope he does. This is one time I believe he has really tried.

Friday, June 2

Jules and I went down together. Warm and pleasant. Lunched at the Aviation Club with Mary Clark.

Jules and I came home with the top down on the Chevy. After dinner, before the top was put up again, we went for a ride. Stopped at Mother's to see if she wanted to go along, but it was late for her. Probably just as well as there was a short but violent thunderstorm before we got home.

No mail from Ira, but he will probably call on Sunday, and, as he will be home on Thursday, there may not be any more letters from him for a while.

Saturday, June 3

A cloudy, showery, humid day. Jules was very busy – getting the basement window fixed, the TV set adjusted, etc. I did the marketing, washed blankets, etc. Went shopping in the afternoon for slacks for Jules.

In the early evening we went to the Ontario to see "Saturday Night and Sunday Morning," a very good British movie, well acted. Then to Avignone's for a dinner we both enjoyed very much. Then to Hofberg's to pick up some things for brunch tomorrow. And then home – and it was still fairly early after all that. Even watched a little TV now that the set is working so much better.

Sunday, June 4
Ira telephoned. Looking forward to coming home. Still quite disheartened about his grades. Hope he does well enough to qualify for another quarter.
A lovely day. Jules mowed the lawn—once more before Ira's return.
We brought a big bunch of flowers when we picked up Mother. Stopped by to see if Mrs. Levy Sr. wanted to go along for a ride, but she was taking a nap. According to Jonathan, who answered the door, they are getting along fine.
Spent the evening reading, watching TV, and getting the house picked up and ready for Alvin tomorrow. Should do something about a new maid, but inertia keeps me stuck with the status quo.

Monday, June 5
Jules and I went down together. A lovely day so I walked downtown at noon. My work is piling up so that I don't know how I shall ever become current again. Yet, though I supervise about a fourth of the staff and issue about half of its case production, Kuskin[89] does nothing but complain about our not producing enough.
After dinner Jules suggested going for a ride before he put the top up. On the way, suggested we stop at the Jaffes'. Then suggested to them we all go for a ride and to Gifford's, which we did.
Letter from Ira, probably the last one, he pointed out, for this quarter. I said the same in my letter to him today.

---

89   Harry Kuskin supervised Anne at this point and later was Chief Counsel for Board member Boyd Leedom.

Tuesday, June 6
Awoke with a terrible headache and upset stomach. Spent the entire day in bed or in the bathroom, or dashing to one and tottering back to the other. I managed to drag myself out of bed in the evening, and to eat a little cereal for supper. Jules fixed supper for himself, as I could hardly bear even to look at food. Could not guess at what had made me so ill. Went to bed last night tired but otherwise feeling fine after our ride, visit with the Jaffes, and treat at Gifford's. Think it is the tension at the office, probably which lately has been greater than ever.
Postcard from the Levys from Miami.

Wednesday, June 7
Felt better, but very weak, and not well enough to go to the office. Jules called the office in the morning before he left. Hope evidently did not give Kuskin the message, and darned if he did not call me. As little sick leave as I take, and having been out sick yesterday, he might have surmised why I was not in today even if he did not get the message.
Jules persuaded me, when he got home, to go out to an air-conditioned restaurant and eat an adequate meal. We went to the Hot Shoppe. I was evidently hungrier that I had realized because everything tasted unusually good. Did some marketing, and then home.

Thursday, June 8
Back to work, rather unenthusiastically. It was really piled up for me!
Thought I might go shopping after work

before meeting Ira's plane, but it was pouring. Jules had parked the car so, when the rain stopped, I walked over to his office.

We went to Hogate's for dinner. Then to the airport, only to learn the plane had been much delayed leaving Columbus. We went for a long ride in the Virginia suburbs. Then back to the airport, picked up Ira and his bags, and home.

He does not have his grades yet, has signed up for a summer quarter in the hope that he made his 2.0 average, but rather dubious that he did make it. Have to wait and see.

Friday, June 9
We went down together in the Chevy, leaving the Buick for Ira, who ran around most of the day visiting friends, MJC, etc.

In the late afternoon Jules and I went to the Court of Claims for a ceremony farewell to Judge Madden,[90] retiring from the bench, and a reception afterwards.

Then home, for a bite to eat with Ira, and then we all went to the MacArthur to see "The French Mistress," a British film we all found very amusing. On the way home, stopped at Hofberg's for sandwiches and to pick up stuff for brunch, a meal to which Jules looks forward, particularly with Ira at home.

Saturday, June 10
Warm. Jules and Ira went to the bakery before lunch. Jules and I drove down to his office, and then did marketing and errands. Ira washed the Chevy, then took off in it and was gone all day.

---

90 See entry October 8, 1959

The Levys stopped by to show us their new Buick. We were obviously about to have dinner, so they left. Came back later and took us for a ride in the new car. Had sent some boxes of candy home from Florida, one meant for us, but the children thought they were all for them and opened all of them. They gave us what was left of one of the boxes. Came back to the house to visit and have a snack. Ira was out on a date. Got home very late.

Sunday, June 11
Ira, who got to bed so late last night, was nevertheless up very early and off to play tennis. He got back while we were eating brunch so joined us.

Later Jules and I took Mother for a ride and to Howard Johnson's. Tommy Grimes visited Ira for a while, and, later, Mattie Jaffes, who stayed and had dinner with us – cold chicken, etc.

Ira had an engagement in the evening at MJC Dean Thurston's house, so Mattie left when he did. We meet the Jaffes at the Wheaton bowling alley, bowled two strings, had a cold drink a the Hot Shoppe, all of us in the Chevy with the top down, then home.

Monday, June 12
Left Ira at home, waiting impatiently for the plumber, who came with a wrong part. Ira arranged to leave a door unlocked for him, and took off for the beach with a couple of boyfriends. Fed them first, apparently, and between him and the plumber and no Alvin, the place was a mess.

Bought some white shoes at noon. After

dinner Jules and I went to Hecht's to pick up his slacks, which had been altered. I looked at cotton dresses, but no luck. In this warm weather, I could use a good many of them, but am harder than ever to fit at my about 140 weight.

Several telephone conversations – Arlene Ulman, Evelyn Promisel, Ruth Levy.

Tuesday, June 13
Jules had to go to the airport on business, so dropped me at the office and kept the car. After work I walked over to his office. He worked a bit late, and it was quite warm, so we went to Junior's for supper – only-so-so. Then home.

Ira, who had been at the beach, got home about 11:00, very suntanned, healthy, and relaxed-looking. Apparently had a very gay time. Thought he might stay at home now for a bit, but he had promised some friends he would go sail boating with them, leaving early tomorrow morning.

Wednesday, June 14
Ira took off at about 6:00 am. Raided the refrigerator to take stuff along for luncheon. Alvin came in.

Surprised to find Ira at home already when we got home – more suntanned than ever. Apparently the water had been very rough, and he was somewhat less than enthusiastic about the whole outing.

The three of us had dinner together for a change.

It had been quite warm all day, but it rained and became a little cooler.

Ira is evidently very nervous – as we are also – waiting for his grades to arrive in the mail.

Thursday, June 15
Got up feeling rather woozy, but went to work anyhow. Felt much worse during the morning – even turned down a luncheon invitation from Jules – and had a late, light luncheon alone at the Hot Shoppe. Felt better later in the day.

Ira got his grades – is still in school – but just barely. He went out to a barbecue party before we got home. Jules and I went to the Sirloin Inn for dinner – broiled chicken and baked potato for me, and very good. Very cool evening. I was wearing a wool suit but was uncomfortably cool nevertheless. Made a wonderful night for sleeping, and I went to bed a bit early to take advantage of it.

Friday, June 16
A delightful day, sunny and brisk. I took a walk down Conn. Avenue at noon. Should have made a luncheon date but hesitate to take the time as Kuskin had piled so much work on me.

Set the oven controls in the morning, so we had a leg of lamb roasted by the time we got home. Fixed the rest of the meal, including orange muffins from a mix, and we had a really terrific meal. Deliberately skipped dessert, and went to Gifford's after dinner, as one of the rituals to observe while Ira was at home. He had eaten an enormous meal, but was still able to put away a banana split. Then we went home, and he went to Linda Saks' graduation party.

Saturday, June 17
We had a lovely big brunch. Then Ira took off to do some errands. Jules and I drove down to his office, and then did the marketing and some errands. By the time we got home from the last of the errands, Ira had left to go to a wedding of some friends, to be followed by a reception at the Shoreham Hotel.

Jules and I went to the Apex to see "The Big Deal on Madonna Street," an Italian movie, rather amusing, but more so, I am sure, if one knew the language. Ira had called a number of times while we were out. Had so much champagne he wanted to be driven home, but made it on his own. Was fine after some supper.

Sunday, June 18
Father's Day. Ira gave Jules a badminton set, installed it in the back yard, and they promptly gave it a workout.

In the afternoon Ira went to the MJC[91] graduation–got a yearbook which had several pictures of him in it. We took Mother for a ride and to Gifford's.

Telephoned the Lewins [Gertrude, Jules' sister], who will meet Ira's plane [in Columbus].[92]

We went to the Occidental for dinner – Ira really stoked up, from shrimp cocktail to banana cream pie – and then to the airport to see Ira off for the summer quarter at OSU – with our hopeful prayers that his grades will show some improvement as he becomes accustomed to the OSU requirements.

Monday, June 19
Alvin came in.

Jules and I went down together. Have to readjust our thinking again to Ira being away.

Louis telephoned in the evening from Columbus to tell us of Marvin's marriage – only the immediate family present – and the other local news, and to inquire about Ira. Had not heard that Ira was back in Columbus. The Levys stopped by in the evening with Linda, and visited for a while. Ruth is in the midst of getting all three children ready to go to camp, but she seems to take such chores in stride. Ira and Jules have installed our exhaust fan, but we have not needed it yet.

Tuesday, June 20
We went down together. Warm, but not unpleasantly so. We rode down and back with the top down on the Chevy.

After dinner we picked up Mother and took her to the Hot Shoppe for dessert. Went marketing afterwards. Clara is out of town this week, but she left Mother pretty well stocked with food.

No mail from Ira yet, but a good deal of mail for him, including one letter which had been forwarded here from OSU.

Jules did some pruning in the garden. No one to play badminton with as I don't care to. Glad the Levys stopped by yesterday as Linda played badminton with Jules for a while, and she and Ruth also played.[93]

---

91 Montgomery College.
92 Ira transferred to Ohio State University.
93 Ruth Levy (Anne's best friend) and her daughter Linda.

Wednesday, June 21
Poured all day. And very cool, lunched at the Roger Smith with Peg Pierce. Gave her a great many names of people who should be asked to attend the Madden[94] farewell dinner. We have already been invited, and accepted.
No mail yet from Ira. Thought there might be some today. Mother telephoned in the evening. Had received a postcard from Clara, in New Orleans, and having a wonderful time with other wives whose husbands are attending the same conference Lou is.
Notice from Henrique's in Jamaica that the platter we ordered had been sent to Helen Lee — what a long delay!

Thursday, June 22
Jules and I went down together. Cloudy and cool in the morning, but turned into a very pleasant day later.
Lunched at the Diplomat with Jonah Silver, recently rehired at the Board on McCulloch's staff.
Jules worked late and we did a couple of errands on the way home. Just got in when Ira telephoned — apparently homesick. There was a letter from him — such atrocious spelling! — and a letter for him from OSU, with a notice also to Jules, that Ira was on probation this quarter because of his poor grades last quarter. Ira is finding his present courses very difficult already. Not at all confident that he will get through college but glad he had some experience with it.

---

[94] See October 8, 1959 entry.

Friday, June 23
We went down together. A pleasant day. I walked down to Garfinckel's at noon. Ran into Paula Locker there, so we lunched together at the Aviation Club.
No mail from Ira. But there was a charming long letter from Lucille in Los Angeles where Marvin and Ruby are now living.
The Dr. Patrick we met in Jamaica stopped in to see Jules for a few minutes with his two children — brought a picture of us he had taken in Jamaica.
Did our marketing on the way home from the office.

Saturday, June 24
Got a permanent in the morning. Jules meanwhile went to the office, and was gone when I came home. I went shopping, and he came home while I was out. But we finally got together, and did some errands, including getting the Chevy car radio repaired, which took quite a while. A letter from Gertrude enclosing a picture of Lois's two little girls.
Jules and I went to the Silver Fox for dinner. Ran into Paula Locker there with a young man and woman and all four boys. She asked us to join them, but it was too large a party. Enjoyed the dinner but enjoyed the ride back through the park even more. Stopped at Hofberg's on the way home.

Sunday, June 25
Ira did not call today as he had called on Thursday. Hope he does all right this quarter, enough to get past his probationary status. At least now he knows better what is expected of him.

Took Mother for a ride and for dessert. A beautiful day, but she was sitting in her apartment watching TV. Does not even take herself for a walk around the block, or stir out of the apartment unless someone calls for her in a car. And the only reason is laziness and inertia. Clara even brings her groceries, so she does not have to go marketing.

Monday, June 26
Ann Elson came down to have luncheon with me at the Aviation Club. I had asked Alice Jaffe to join us, but, now that she is counseling instead of teaching, she is at school most of the summer. Mattie had not been able to find a job. Just as well probably that Ira is taking a summer quarter at OSU. No mail from him today. Postcard from Clara, from New Orleans, from which trip she had returned last Saturday. But she evidently had a wonderful time – her first trip without the children probably since she had children. They stayed with their respective friends. Shopping at Wheaton Plaza after dinner. Alvin came in.

Tuesday, June 27
A rainy cool morning and we both overslept a little. Instead of hurrying through breakfast, we went ahead, and Jules breakfasted at the Mayflower and I did later at the Drug Fair in the building with Vivian Asplund.
Went shopping at noon.
No mail from Ira. Hope he is not too discouraged about his studies to write.
Jules and I had dinner at the Sakura, a small Japanese restaurant in the Silver Spring Hotel – only fair. Afterwards we picked up Mother and took her for a ride and some ice cream – she had not been out of her apartment since we took her for a ride on Sunday.

Wednesday, June 28
Jules and I went down together. A pleasant day. There was a staff luncheon for Ray Molloy, who was leaving, but I skipped it and went downtown instead.
In the evening to the Madden[95] reception and dinner at the Bolling Officers Club. Neta Barghousen and Arnold Ordman[96] rode out with us. Saw many old friends. It was quite a sentimental occasion, Judge Fahy's[97] speech particularly making the old timers feel emotional. Helen Humphreys and Fannie Boyls, who had asked in advance to do so, were at our table, as were Jim Shaw, Abe Kaminstein,[98] Stan Metzner, and Ordman. After many fond farewells to the Maddens, we took both Neta and Arnold home, considerably out of the way, so we got home pretty late ourselves.

Thursday, June 29
Jules and I went down together. A pleasant day so walked downtown at noon.
<u>Jules was busy</u> as we were rather late getting

---

95 Judge J. Warren Madden, first Chairman of the NLRB governing board. See entry Oct. 8, 1959.
96 Judge and later General Counsel of the NLRB.
97 Charles Fahy, former General Counsel of the NLRB, who participated in Anne's hiring at the Board. At this time he was Judge of the U.S. Court of Appeals, DC Circuit.
98 Fannie Boyls and Kaminstein (Kami) were two of Anne's oldest friends at the NLRB from the 1930's.

home, but I managed broiled chicken and other goodies for dinner.

We went for a ride later, by ourselves, but had trouble, shortly after we started, with the radiator boiling over. Got it fixed, bought a new radiator cap, and went on our way.

Still no mail from Ira. It is rather worrisome, particularly as he was writing so frequently last quarter. But hesitate to call and give him the impression we are alarmists if it is just that he is busy.

Friday, June 30
I went to the dentist on the way to the office. Have to go back for a filling.

Felt a bit "icky" and having my teeth cleaned did not make me feel any better. But not sick enough even to go down to see the nurse.

Walked to Jules' office after work as he had the car. Ran into Bill Lubbers[99] on the way, who came along to see the office. Joe and Dorothy joined Jules and us for a drink, so it was quite a little party. Bill was duly impressed with the office.

Did some marketing after supper. Letter finally from Ira. Not very communicative, but mentioned that he broke his glasses. Don't know when we can get his prescription from Cox.

---

99   William A. Lubbers, later would be General Counsel for the NLRB.

Year End Summary 1961

Often wonder why, after all these years, I continue to write these fool things. I almost never look back in them for any purpose, and do not suppose, in view of the great number of these books that I am accumulating, that I ever shall go back over them. By the time I have the time, I shall probably not have the eyesight.

But I suppose, if it serves no other purpose, it is a form of self-discipline as I write my little page even when I find it a considerable bore and a great nuisance. Nor do I suppose that all this blithering will be of the slightest interest to Ira or to those who come after him. There is, after all, no vivid description of events of general interest, no profound thoughts, no clever writing, nothing of any interest to anyone who does not care about my routine, humdrum, day-to-day doings. Cannot imagine anyone caring. For one thing, anyone who liked reading could find so many things to read so much more interesting and worthwhile.

It might have been vanity and conceit when I began, and when some of the people I met and worked with seemed to my uncritical eyes among the world's greatest, and I a noteworthy person because I had met or worked with them. I am now, however, a little more realistic in my evaluation of people, including myself. I suppose, then, that I continue with this blithering nonsense year after year to be a habit which I am reluctant to bring to an end.[100]

---

100   Anne questioned herself at major turning

In any event, there were some very good things that happened this year. Ira did manage, with help, to get into Ohio State, and, what is more, he managed, on his own, to stay in. He might have stayed only by the skin of his teeth, but the point is that he did stay.

Jules and I had a very enjoyable vacation trip – our first with another couple who were not relatives – and we wound up, if anything, better friends than ever despite all the dour warnings.

And Mother seems to be getting along reasonably well, both with regard to her physical condition and the living-alone way-of-life she had chosen.

And I have had the experience of being on crutches, of being left alone in the house to manage the best I could, and of managing and surviving and getting rid of the crutches. Yes, all in all, a relatively good year.

Anne and Jules, 1961

---

points in her life, such as her marriage to Jules, and now with Ira leaving home for college. This is the most serious questioning of herself as to why she is writing the diary. Will any children or grandchildren be interested in it later? She is questioning her diary writing, but in a larger sense she seems to be thinking about her life. The so called "empty nest syndrome" must have been disturbing for her.

The Diaries

Part VI

1962 to 1967
Empty Nest and More NLRB Cases

Anne Schlezinger was 52 years old and entering the prime of her professional life. She and Julius were active in the judicial world of Washington. Both had been admitted as lawyers to the Supreme Court. They were in the same social circles with Supreme Court Justices, Federal Judges, and Attorney Generals. Anne had the reputation among her colleagues of being one of the best writers of case briefs in the NLRB, and she was proud of that recognition.

Ira graduated from college during this period and was married to Sandy, a turning point in his life. His transformation from student to a responsible adult with a successful professional career made Anne happy. The Sunday telephone calls from Ira and his family became a highlight of her week. Although she was originally hesitant about the marriage (as she was with her own marriage to Julius), her writing reflects how she relished her role as mother-in-law and grandmother.

After Ira left home for college Anne's attention turned more to her own professional life. This was a happy period for her, but there were issues. She had been with the National Labor Relations Board for twenty-five years, and men who had entered after her had already been promoted to positions as judges. She was frustrated with her lack of progress.

Anne began to push more actively for promotion as judge. Jules was not totally in favor of her making that change because it would mean that she would be away frequently. Since Ira was no longer living at home, it seems that Anne felt more freedom to pursue this appointment. She also aspired to being named to the Board, and in the March 5, 1965 entry she approached the Secretary of Labor, Willard Wirtz, to talk with him about the possibility of such an appointment. On March 8, 1965 Jules talked with Mark Feldman, another Kennedy-Johnson, official also inquiring about the possibility of an appointment to the Board, but again to no avail.

When Anne had asked about an appointment as judge in the 1950's, her supervisor had commented that her husband could support her, suggesting that such a promotion was not appropriate for a woman. In 1949 Burnita Shelton Matthews had been named by President Truman as the first woman judge of a United States District Court (District of Columbia), so Anne was aware that a woman could be named as a federal judge. However, in the NLRB no women were named judges until the 1960's, and the first was Anne's close friend, Fannie Boyls.

This period also began an active time of international travel for Anne and Jules. She had always been fascinated by the travels of her friends, and her entries frequently recount their trips to China, Latin America, Japan, and Europe among others. During these years she and Jules made repeated trips to Europe, and others to Mexico and Israel.

-- Ron Duncan Hart

Diaries. 1962 Through 1967.

1962

In late August and September Anne and Jules made a month long trip to Norway, Sweden, and later Amsterdam, and Geneva, where Jules had business appointments. Anne enjoyed the various countries with side trips and theater performances. On September 4 she wrote, "Another lovely sunny day - the best weather, I gathered, Amsterdam has had in a long time. Breakfast in the hotel dining room. Then to Mrs. V-N's [Van Nieuwkunle] by cab. With her to the flower auction at Aalsmeer, a lovely and interesting sight. Then to a diamond cutting plant. Had to restrain Jules from buying me a diamond wedding band…"

Anne was supervising six other attorneys at this point, which increased her workload. She felt that it was too many to supervise properly. Her mother was living in Washington and was ill frequently, which required Anne's attention. Ira was at college but communicated regularly. His forgetting her birthday that year was upsetting for her because it had never happened previously. Their social group continued actively. Anne visited frequently with Ruth Levy and Alice Jaffe. -- RDH

Sunday, July 1
A pleasant day. Jules went to Holberg's and we had a lovely big brunch. Ira washed the cars. Would have cut the grass but the mower would not work, so he went swimming at the Hardys'.

We had a magnificent steak dinner. I relented and let him drive the Chevy back to have over the holiday. He loaded it up with stuff from his room and took off very gaily with the top down.

We had called Mother for both brunch and dinner but she declined both. We went over there after Ira left and took her for a ride– which she almost never declines –and to Howard Johnson's for ice cream –which she practically insists upon.

Monday, July 2
We went down together – have only one car. A lovely day so I took a walk at noon.

A new legal assistant – Marty Fingerhut – had been assigned to me. After work I walked over to Jules' office, but he went for the car and picked me up.

After dinner we went to Hecht's in Silver Spring to do some errands. Ira called when we returned – had tried to call several times last night, apparently while we were out with Mother – had a great deal of trouble with the Chevy all the way back, taking hours longer than he should have, stopping at every gas station – and wanted to know what to do. We told him to have the darned thing fixed at any cost within reason. Poor kid.

Postcard from the Gangs on Cape Cod.

Tuesday, July 3
A rainy day. Brussell came in early and sprayed the house again. Hope it works this time. Lunched at the Roger Smith with Vivian Asplund.

After dinner we went to the Levys' to see a

portrait Ruth recently had painted and to say goodbye before they left on their western trip. The Jaffes came over also. We left at the same time, so suggested they stop by our house for a drink, but they counter-suggested the Hot Shoppe instead, and we wound up there. Sat around and chatted for quite a while as none of us had to worry about getting up early, particularly as rain was predicted, so they would not be playing golf.

Wednesday, July 4
Although rain had been predicted, it turned out to be a very pleasant day. We went for a ride in the afternoon. Stopped for Mother but she had taken a bath and did not want to get out. We went to the Wheaton Regional Park and hiked for a while. Very pleasant, when I was not turning my silly ankle.
The Harlows invited us to the cookout they have every 4th. Have always asked almost everyone in the neighborhood but us, so we declined. Went to O'Donnell's in Bethesda. Enjoyed the dinner very much. Thought we might stop at the Harlows' after dinner, but by them the party seemed very gay, and we were feeling very sober, so, although Marguerite had urged us to come, we stayed at home.

Thursday, July 5
We went down together. I went to the beauty parlor at noon.
Learned during the day that Max Goldman died of a heart attack Tuesday night. A number of us went to the Danzansky funeral parlor from the office for the funeral service, but the family decided not to hold a service. Ira called Jules a few times at the office, and finally reached him, to discuss the repairs on the Chevy, which will come to over $150. Walked to Jules' office after work, but he was good enough to walk to the parking lot for the car and come back and pick me up as I was tired by then, or possibly just lazy.

Friday, July 6
We went down together. Alvin came in. Lee Stanley called me for luncheon. I took her to the Lawyers Club. She had never been there, and enjoyed it very much. After work Jules and I met at the Plaza to see "The Sky Above and the Mud Below," a movie based on an exploration trip in New Guinea. Afterwards to Alex Stuart's for dinner. Had Alvin feed Pal so we did not have to rush home on his account. A thank-you for the wedding present note from Myron's daughter. Were glad to get it as it was so long since we had the gift sent from Lord & Taylor's that I was almost ready to ask the store to check and make sure that it was actually sent to the bride.

Saturday, July 7
A letter from Ira. Mentioned that he would call tomorrow. He usually does on Sunday.
Picked up Mother early in the afternoon. Jules dropped us at Garfinckel's while he went to the office, and picked us up later. I bought only a blue cashmere sweater, blouse style, with cool Norway in mind.
On the way home stopped at the Hot Shoppe. Jules and I had a snack while Mother ate, and thoroughly enjoyed, a fairly substantial meal. Then stopped at Hofberg's to buy stuff

for our supper, and Mother bought some items to tempt her appetite at home. Then took her home, tired but happy.

Sunday, July 8
A hot day. In the late afternoon, we took Mother for a long air-conditioned ride. Then to the house for a while. Then to O'Donnell's for dinner. Bill Levy called just as we were leaving – just back from a weekend in New York, his family having left for their trip out west, and wanted to have dinner with us, so we suggested he join us at O'Donnell's. He did not join us, but came over later to visit. We had cool drinks and fruit on the porch.
Not having heard from Ira, we called Nate, who said Ira had been out there, had been at the club with them, and had tried a few times to reach us – apparently when we were out with Mother for a ride and later for dinner. Were much reassured anyhow by our conversation with Nate.

Monday, July 9
We went down together. Jules left about noon for New York. Judge Leedom[1] back from a 3-weeks vacation.
Took Mary Clark and Dottie Minshoff to luncheon at the Aviation Club.
We had parked the Buick at the garage on H Street. I drove it home, the first time I have driven it that far and the first time I have driven it alone at all. I managed all right; although the brakes are so much faster than I am accustomed to that I almost went through the windshield a few times.
Ira telephoned – did not know we had talked to Nate last night – has picked up the car – enjoying his volunteer work at the hospital – will be home this weekend.

Tuesday, July 10
A lovely day, moderately warm and relatively low humidity.
I parked at Carter Barron and took the bus. Phyllis Schottenstein called – was coming into town – so we lunched together at the Hofbrau.
Jules called in the afternoon – was getting in earlier than he had expected. I left the office early to pick up the car, and met Jules at the airport when he arrived by Braniff at 5:35. It was too early to have dinner, so we went on home and ate at home. Jules always likes to eat at home – whatever we eat – when he has been away from home – even for just an overnight trip.
And now I am an experienced driver of the new Buick.

Wednesday, July 11
Jules and I went down together. A pleasant day so Mira and I bought sandwiches and took them to the park to eat.
Jules left early to pick up the lawn mower at the repair shop – then it was not ready – and I got a ride home with Dick Brownstone. Card from Ruth Levy and the kids in Chicago, and a long letter from Lucille.
Took the Buick to "Call Carl's" for lubrication. Had supper at the Charcoal House while it was being done.
Clara called to discuss vacation plans, Mother's

---

[1] Boyd S. Leedom, nominated by President Eisenhower as Chairman of the Board in 1955, replaced as Chairman by President Kennedy in 1961.

condition, etc. Phyllis Schottenstein called – will try to get her date to take her to Melody Tent Saturday night as we will be there.

Thursday, July 12
We went down together. I went first to the dentist's. Had my teeth cleaned, x-rayed, and one small filling replaced.
And then so busy for the rest of the day that I hardly found time to eat a sandwich and take a little walk at noon. And with it all, had a nagging headache on which aspirin seemed to make no impression.
We picked up some things at the grocery store on the way home, and had dinner at home. I was feeling better by then. Were sitting on the porch reading the paper in the evening when we heard loud crying from the Parkhill's house – Joe died this evening – had been in the hospital for a few days after a severe heart attack. And was so lively and happy at the Harlowe wedding party.

Friday, July 13
We went down together. I stopped at the dentist to have my filing polished. Saw Justin Douglas in the building.
Lunched with Vivian Asplund at the Willard Coffee Shop. Alvin came in.
Jules suggested staying downtown for a movie and dinner but I preferred to go home in case Ira came early. We had dinner at home. Later Jules went for a walk with Pal, and Ira called while he was out. Ira had just returned at 9:30 from a field trip, so decided to go to bed and come in real early tomorrow. I was disappointed that it would be so short a weekend, but it made good sense.

Long letter from Ellen thanking us for entertaining them while they were here.

Saturday, July 14
Ira got in early this morning – had left before daybreak – got both of us out of bed.
After breakfast Jules and I did the marketing etc. Ira went to visit friends. Rained, so he could not do his usual mowing and car-washing chores.
Jules stopped in at the Collins funeral parlor, where Joe Parkhill's body was, and had a long chat with Frances. Bill Levy came to dinner. We asked Mother also, but she declined. Too bad, it was an excellent roast beef dinner. After dinner we all went out to Shady Grove, the area theater in a tent, to see "Fiorelló." The place was gay, the production was a good one, we met a number of people we knew, and it was an enjoyable evening for all of us, including Ira.

Sunday, July 15
We all slept late, and were still eating brunch when Bill Levy called to let us know he just got out of a meeting. I told him to come ahead, and fixed brunch for him. Later Ira picked up Mother – she gave a gift of $10 – and we all sat on the porch and relaxed. Bill left in the afternoon.
We had dinner at home, then took Ira to RR station to get a 7:00 train back to Philly. Then took Mother home. Then home ourselves. The house seemed big and empty with just the two of us there, but it had been a very pleasant weekend, with Ira around, the show at Shady Grove, Bill Levy here for the

afternoon, dinner, and the ride to RR station to see Ira off.

Monday, July 16
I went down alone via Carter Barron. Jules stayed behind to go to the funeral service for Joe Parkhill at the funeral parlor.
Pouring at noon. I nevertheless went to lunch with Dick Brownstone at the Nichols Café. Would have been dryer eating in the drugstore, but the food was better at the Café.
Rode out to Carter Barron with Jules as we had arranged by phone. Was sorry we had as it did stop raining about 5:00. I would have got home earlier by hours, and Jules could have stayed later at his office as he would have preferred to do.
We had dinner at home.
Afterwards went to the grocery store, principally to pick up a few items for Alvin's luncheon tomorrow. She had a big appetite —and is a big woman.

Tuesday, July 17
We went down together. Alvin came in. Mary Clark took me to luncheon at the Aviation Club, and lent me some booklets about Oslo and Stockholm points of interest.
Had dinner at home.
Mother called to tell Jules about some mail she had received regarding hospital bills.
Alice Jaffe called and asked us to join them at the Apex to see a Russian movie, "A Summer to Remember." We did, and found the picture charming, particularly the children in it. Afterwards to a Howard Johnson for ice cream. Then home, and to bed, and at a reasonable hour as, by rushing, we made the earlier show.

Wednesday, July 18
We went down together. Lunched with Eleonor Schwartzbach and Vivian Asplund at Jack Hunt's.
Had a case on the subpanel agenda with Marty Fingerhut, my newest LA.[2] Am favorably impressed by him so far.
Had my passport photos taken at a little "joint" across the street from the office.
Bill Levy came to dinner. Would have stopped on the way home to pick up some stuff, but it was pouring so we "made do" with what we had.
Ira telephoned to say he was going to the Poconos Saturday with a boyfriend but would join us Sunday if we went to Atlantic City, as Jules wants to do. As Ira will not be spending the weekend with us though, we shall probably go to Rehoboth instead.

Thursday, July 19
We came down together. Had my hair done at the Roger Smith Hotel at noon. Mira was having hers done at the same time – today, after all, was payday. Picked up my passport photos. I always take poor pictures, and these were no exception. And so ridiculously expensive! Should have had Ira take them.
After supper we went over to see Mother as we shall not be seeing her over the weekend. Took her for a ride, stopped for ice cream, and gave her her biweekly allowance, due

---
2   Legal Assistant.

this Sunday. She seemed to be feeling well, and to enjoy her little outing very much, she mentioned how much she depended on TV for companionship. With her refusal to make friends, what would she do without it?

Friday, July 20
We came down together. Alvin came in.
I filed my passport application at the State Dept. Jules did so yesterday.
Jules picked me up after work. We went home first, fed Pal, and then went to Kushner's for dinner. Called Mother and Bill Levy to see if they wanted to join us, but both declined. After dinner we did some marketing, but not much as we are planning to go to Rehoboth for the weekend. Do not have a reservation so want to get there early. Cannot leave too early, however, as we have to leave Pal at the kennel, and cannot do so before 7:30 in the morning.
We got our book club, *Guns of August*, from the Library. It looks like slow, heavy going, and we must return the book in 2 weeks.

Saturday, July 21
A hot sunny day. We had breakfast at home. Then took Pal to the kennel and drive to Rehoboth. A pleasant trip except for a long delay at the Bay Bridge because of an accident. Then had trouble finding a place to stay. Wound up at the Holiday Motel. Changed to our swimming suits, and drove to the beach. Had a dip, lunched at boardwalk stands, and back to the beach. I had a slight headache, which grew worse. Dressed for dinner and drove into town, but had to give up and go back and to bed. Jules finally went to dinner alone, and went to the boardwalk for a while alone. By the time he got back I was feeling much better, except that I felt badly about messing up this evening.

Sunday, July 22
Got up feeling fine. We had breakfast at the Delaware restaurant, where Jules dined alone last night. Then to the beach, where we both had a lovely time. Later lunched at the Tip-Top restaurant. Had had to check out of our motel, so changed at the rest room – a nice, clean, new one and left about 3:30, slightly burned and feeling wonderful. Had a pleasant drive, beat the bridge tie-up, and stopped at a roadside farm stand for some fruits and vegetables. Because of it had dinner at home – and everything we bought there was delicious.
Ira called. Apparently he had a wonderful weekend. Stayed overnight at a boyfriend's house, and they went to the beach on both Saturday and Sunday. Could have seen him both days probably if we had gone to Atlantic City.

Monday, July 23
Went down together. Having learned that all staffs except Leedom's have an added grade 15, I asked Harry[3] about the vacancy on our staff. He said he would speak to the Judge. Did not commit himself, but gathered he would recommend me.
Had several compliments on my suntan acquired over the weekend. Jules and I did

---
3   Harry Kuskin, Chief Counsel to Board member Leedom.

some errands on the way home, so got home late. Had dinner at home anyhow. Still had some fruits and vegetables we got yesterday – still delicious.

Long mimeographed letter from the Bob Mathews – the second half of their extremely interesting account of their year in India on a Ford Foundation project.

Called Mother. Alice Jaffe and Bill Levy called us.

Tuesday, July 24
I went down alone via Carter Barron. Jules took the Chevy in to have the torn seat upholstery mended.

Harry told me he spoke to the Judge[4] about the 15 – made a big pitch in my favor, I gathered – but the Judge maintained that he was not ready to make a decision yet. What a rat!

I went to Carter Barron by bus, picked up the Buick, picked up Jules, and to Rayco in Silver Spring to pick up the Chevy.

Had dinner at home – a very good steak just right for two.

Long letter from Ira – apparently enjoying life in Philly to the hilt, for which we are grateful to the many who contribute to that enjoyment. Do wish he would learn a few of the rudiments of spelling – he mangles even simple words.

Received my passport – quick service!

Wednesday, July 25
We went down together. A rainy day. Attended a meeting of the Embryonic Professional Assn. being organized at the Board, held at noon, and then, in view of the time and the weather, lunched downstairs in the drugstore.

4   Boyd S. Leedom, member of the Board.

The office nurse and I have decided that what she has been treating as mosquito bites are hives – probably from eating so much fresh fruit. A letter from Lily Levine, in response to a note Jules sent about our being in London, sounding delighted at the prospect of seeing us again, and cordially inviting us to stay with them. We shall not take advantage of that invitation, but were very pleased at the warm note of pleasure in the letter.

Thursday, July 26
We went down together. Lunched with Mira at Laffel's. A lovely breezy day so we took a walk after luncheon. After work walked to Jules' office, and then we walked to where the car was parked at a lot on O Street.

Were in the middle of supper when the Middlemans stopped by looking for Bill Levy. They were very dressed up, and we were dining very informally.

Letter from Ira – not coming this weekend after all as some friends are planning a big party at the shore which he wants to attend. Postcard from the Leon Ulmans on vacation.

Called Alice Jaffe to say farewell. Irv left today for California, and Alice is leaving tomorrow to join him for a vacation.

Friday, July 27
I went down alone via Carter Barron. Alvin came in.

Had a case on the Board agenda with Leo Weiss.

Jules called me – Ira had called him – was coming home after all with a friend, Chuck Klein. Had Alvin make up the extra beds.

We went home separately, had supper, then went marketing. Bought enough for Ira and Chuck to have supper tonight, but they did not get in until about 11:00, and had just a snack. We all got to bed rather late.

Postcard from Ruth Levy from Lake Louise, enjoying most of the places she decided to go only because of Jules' strong recommendations.

Saturday, July 28
A beautiful day. Chuck slept quite late. After brunch, Ira took him to do some sightseeing, but, tho this was Chuck's first visit to Washington, he had little interest in sightseeing.

We did some errands. Drove to Jules' office to check the mail in the afternoon. Chuck and Ira were back in plenty of time for dinner. Bill Levy came over, and Ira and Chuck picked up Mother. We had roast brisket etc. – guess everything was good from the quantities eaten. Afterwards the boys took off, and we sat on the porch and talked and enjoyed the beautiful evening. The Promisels stopped by and asked us to go to a movie with them, but we preferred to stay at home and they declined to join us. After Bill left, we took Mother home – she had a wonderful time.

Sunday, July 29
A cloudy, drippy sort of day. We were all up long before Chuck. Jules and I finally went ahead and had brunch. Ira waited for Chuck. They took off afterwards.
Bill [i.e. Levy] came over for a while.
Ira "projected" a series of lovely colored pictures he had taken here, in Columbus, and other places, with a very entertaining commentary. Sorry we had not invited Mother. She would have enjoyed it. The Gangs came over later with Sharon. I gave the boys some supper, and they took off for Philly. Then Bill took off for a dinner engagement at the Zanoffs'. Then we changed our clothes and took off with the Gangs to the Bethesda Naval Officers Club for supper. Then to the Gangs' for a little while. Then home, very tired, but with much straightening out to do.

Monday, July 30
We went down separately, I via Carter Barron and the bus. Walked down to Garfinckel's at noon but did not buy anything. Am going to have to get busy shopping soon as there are a number of things I need before our trip to Europe.

Kuskin indicated again – in the course of a conversation – that he was unreservedly recommending me for the 15, but, I gathered, Leedom cannot bring himself to do it.

We had a delicious supper made up chiefly of leftovers from our weekend meals. Jules especially enjoyed it as cold roast brisket is one of Jules' favorite foods. And from her reaction Saturday, it seems that hot roast brisket is Mother's favorite food.

Tuesday, July 31
We went down together. Jules took the Chevy in to have some work done on it, getting it in as good shape as possible for Ira's use while we are away. Alvin came in.
A warm, sticky day, and – what with picking up the Chevy at Barry Pate's, where I met

Jules – we were a bit late getting home, so decided to eat out. Called Bill, who joined us. We had dinner at Cap'n Jerry's – quite good. Then back to the house. Bill and Jules chatted while I finished Tuchman's *Guns of August*, a magnificent book, but one that should be studied, not read as quickly as I did, and as all the Book club members will do who read it at all.

Year End Summary 1962

In 1962 and 1963 Anne did not write a year end summary. She did write summaries for 1964 and 1965, but they were the last, leaving the reader bereft of some of her most revealing thoughts about her life.

From 1931 to 1940 she had written monthly summaries, and from 1941 to 1961 she had written year end summaries. In these annual and monthly summaries she frequently evaluated her experiences. She talked about her fear of marriage because of her parent's problems, but at the same time she wanted to be married. She questioned herself as a wife and mother. She was always confident in her work, but she berated the fact that her promotions came so slowly. These summaries give the highlights of her feelings that are not revealed in the chronicling of facts of her daily life.

-- RDH

Jules, Anne, and Ira

1963

Most of the year was tranquil. Anne and Jules made a prolonged trip to London, Brussels, Amsterdam, Paris, Lausanne, and Frankfurt in July. Jules had business in some of those stops, and in others they met friends and were entertained by local families. In the middle of the Vietnam war Ira dropped out of Ohio State and joined the Maryland National Guard for a six month tour of duty. Afterwards he returned to OSU.

The major shock was the assassination of President John Kennedy in Dallas. The death and funeral of the President was a sad event, and the succession of Vice-President Lyndon Johnson to the presidency created changes in Washington circles. Anne's daily routine continued with the office, lunches, visiting her mother, and their social life with Levys and other Silver Spring neighbors and friends. -- RDH

Monday, August 26
We went down together. I walked downtown at noon, just for the walk.
Walked again after work, as I generally do while waiting for Jules to leave, and stopped at Magruder's to buy a few groceries, as I frequently do when I walk by in the afternoon. After supper we went to the library to get some books, and to get some information about a book that Nancy van Nieuwkuyk had asked us to send her. There was no information there. Having made a reasonable effort, I would forget about it - Jules bought her liquor when he went from Bremen to Amsterdam, as she requested - but he will continue to look for it.

Tuesday, August 27
A very pleasant day. We went down together.
I took Sonny Pressman, Irv Jaffe and Jules to luncheon at the Lawyer's Club - Sonny leaves tomorrow for the L.A. office. She knew Irv from Alien Property days. It was a very pleasant luncheon.
Afterwards a panel and a subpanel agenda. Anita was in today. Called me in the afternoon to tell me the ironing board - a very old one - had collapsed. After dinner, we bought one at Hecht's in Silver Spring, assembled it, and had it ready for Anita's next visit.
Letter from Lily and Mordecai Levine from their vacation spot in Yugoslavia. No letter from Ira. Would like to hear from him a little more often.

Wednesday, August 28
We went down together. Many did not go to work because of the big civil rights march, so there was very little traffic on our route. I had my hair done at Jelfeff's at noon. The downtown area was almost deserted. We were dismissed at 3:30 so we could get home before the march - a great success - broke up. We stopped at Lord & Taylor's and bought some bed linens, curtains, towels, etc., in preparation for Lucille and Louie's visit. Letter from Ira. He had been to Friday night services, and liked the Rabbi, a Captain, and liked his wife even more. Mentioned that he could hardly wait to get back to school. Hope he will be able to do so.

Sunday, September 1
A lovely day. Lucille's birthday and our 24th anniversary.
Ira telephoned. Would like to come home for Yom Kippur on a 3-day pass, but it seems so impractical. Talked quite a while. Ellen and Leonard also called from Columbus.
We had an enormous brunch – everyone just ate and ate. Picked up Mother and took her for a ride. Later to Olney Inn for dinner. Enjoyed the food, the atmosphere, and the ride there and back. The Levys telephoned, just back from their vacation, to let us know they were back and to wish us a happy anniversary. Nice to have a few people remember it.

Monday, September 2
Another beautiful bright day. Lucille and Louie had been undecided about leaving this afternoon and going half way or tomorrow morning and going all the way. Decided on the former. We were sorry as we had the makings of dinner, had planned to have the Levys and some other people over. But could not argue with their desire to break up the trip.
We had a big brunch. Drove over to Hofberg's later so they could pick up some pastries they wanted to take home. Gave Lucille my artificial flowers as she admired them and I was tired of them. We drove ahead of them to get them started on the right road.
The Levys asked us to go to a movie in the evening but we both preferred to stay at home by ourselves.

Tuesday, September 3
Back to work schedule! We went down together – in the Chevy to give it a little workout. The weather looked threatening at noon so I lunched in the drugstore. Was sorry afterwards as the rain never did amount to more than a few scattered drops. Anniversary card from Ira, with a note about how sorry he was not to be able to celebrate it with us.
I had fixed chicken for dinner last night – had bought enough to feed Lucille and Louie also – so we had plenty for tonight and some left for Anita tomorrow. Did laundry, etc., in preparation for her coming in tomorrow to clean and to iron.

Wednesday, September 4
We went down together in the Buick. Anita came in.
Walked downtown at noon. Lunched at the Hot Shoppe on the way back, Jules came in while I was eating, but no seat was available at the time and he decided not to wait.
Jules left the office late so we were late getting home. Had a simple, light supper.
Postcard from Jan[5] vacationing in Canada. Read Pat Frank's *Alas, Bablyon*. Found it interesting and depressing. Some of the people turned out finer and stronger than ever when faced with such awful problems, but others were so horrible.
Letter from Ira written before his call.

Thursday, September 5
We went down together, although Jules sometimes gets very fed up with getting up so early and hurrying downtown every morning to meet my early schedule.
Raining so I lunched in the drugstore with

---

[5] Anne's sister Jan, also known as Jean.

Arthur Leff.[6] Talked about a transfer to the Chairman's staff, but he had no "15" available and no prospect of one. Ought to shift at my present grade, but am reluctant to do so. Ought to file for a trial examiner's appointment application, but it means a very detailed application, and Jules does not like the idea. The jobs have been classified as "16" but it would require quite a bit of traveling.[7]

Friday, September 6
We went down together. Attended the Board's award ceremony at the new Interior auditorium at which a number of people received 25 years pin. I missed my own presentation last year. Got a chance to say hello to Fahy[8] and Herzog after the ceremony.

After dinner we did several errands. Bought a "snake" so Jules could try to fix a stopped-up toilet, the book for our Book Club meeting, some groceries, ice cream cones, etc. Ira's suitcase, which he sent back, was delivered today when no one was at home. Tried to call the express office but there was no answer. This is going to get more involved and expensive than the suitcase is worth.

Saturday, September 7
Worked on the stuck toilet with the snake, a hose, etc., but it remained stuck.
Ira's suitcase was delivered again while we were at home.
Down to Jules' office in the afternoon. While he went out for a haircut, I typed some notes to use when and if I apply for a trial examiner's job. It means writing practically a life history. And Jules is very unhappy at the mere suggestion that I might get a job that will involve traveling.
We had dinner at home. Then went to Silver Spring to see "The Great Escape,"[9] quite an interesting movie, well acted.

Sunday, September 8
Expected Ira to telephone but, although we were at home most of the day, he did not call.
I picked up Mother in the afternoon and brought her back to the house. Jules mowed the back yard. Jules and I – about the time we were ready to give up and call a plumber – got the stopped-up toilet unstopped. Had a very good rib roast for dinner.
Later in the evening, wrote letters to Ira and to Gesela Arnsperger. Then went over to see the Levys – a short visit. Got home in time to finish Gide's *The Immoralist*,[10] an odd

---

6 Leff was Chief Counsel to Board Chairman Frank McCulloch. Anne was inquiring about a transfer to McCulloch's staff.
7 This reflects Anne's continuing and growing interest in being appointed judge.
8 Charles Fahy, the former General Counsel for the NLRB, who originally interviewed Anne for the position with the Board. At the time of this meeting he was Judge on the U.S. Court of Appeal, D.C. Circuit where he served the rest of his life.
9 Steve McQueen and the famous motorcycle ride escaping the Nazis.
10 Novel by André Gide, one of the most important French writers of the twentieth century, about a classical scholar, Michel, who after marriage, gradually turns more toward hedonism than intellectual life. Traveling to Algeria he becomes more interested in young boys than women.

little story about a man I would have found it very easy to dislike thoroughly.

Monday, September 9
We went down together. Jules had planned to take back the new tire, which was defective, but I forgot until it was too late for me to go by myself. We put air in the tire on the way down and again on the way home. Long letter from Lucille. Hope she enjoyed herself as much as she indicated in her letter. Nate[11] telephoned from Philadelphia. Very enthusiastic about his latest European trip. Wanted to check on when we were going to Columbus. Will plan to go also for the Nov. 2 weekend. Otherwise would come here for that weekend as he has a convention here – has one wherever and whenever he wants to make a trip.

Tuesday, September 10
Jules took the tire back to Montgomery Ward's. I went down in the Chevy via Carter Barron. The Chevy is in rather bad shape. We probably ought to get rid of it rather than spend the money to fix it up again. But, once in a while, it is very convenient to have two cars available – at other times, just means two headaches.
Ira telephoned this evening. He chatted quite a while, about nothing in particular. We both gathered that he was quite homesick, and just wanted to hear our voices for a while. He seems to be more homesick now than at any other time that he has been away from home, probably because he dislikes very much what he is doing.

Wednesday, September 11
We went down together. Anita came in. Is trying to switch her Friday job so she can give us Tuesday and Friday, but her Friday employer is reluctant to change. To the beauty parlor at noon. Had two cases on the subpanel agenda, one with Chuck Thompson and one with Schneur Genach. Drive over to Tops to pick up some fried chicken, but then decided to eat it there. Later went to Gifford's for dessert.
Later watched some TV. Especially enjoyed an hour's program about the Greek Theater, with Alfred Lunt and Lynn Fontaine. Long letter from Ira. Disturbed that some of his friends are not writing to him. Has to learn people grow away from one another.

Thursday, September 12
We went down together. Rather warm and I was extremely busy at the office, so walked only to the bank at noon and ate a quick luncheon even though it was payday. Even if I wanted to apply for a trial examiner appointment, I would be unable to find the time to make out the detailed application.
So warm and humid when I was taking my walk while waiting for Jules that I spent part of the waiting time sitting in the Mayflower lobby enjoying the coolness.[12]
Postcard from Helen Lee, taking a vacation tour of the West Coast with the family. Must write – I have owed her a letter for far too long.

---

11   Jules' brother, the M.D. from Philadelphia.

12   Jules' office was across the street from the Mayflower Hotel.

Friday, September 13
We went down together. The weather had changed over night and it was very cool. And I had so much work on my desk that I hardly knew what to do next. Then got tied up all afternoon on the subpanel which I foolishly agreed to take over while Loeb is away.
Letter form Ira, much cheered by a big batch of letters from friends, and one package of goodies from a girl friend. Jules was not feeling too well so we ate a very light supper. The house was rather cold so, instead of starting the furnace, we read and watched some TV in bed. A safe ending to a Friday the 13th.

Saturday, September 14
Awoke with quite a bad headache – how I resent messing up so many weekends this way! Jules fixed his own breakfast. I got up later and dressed, but did not feel up to going with Jules when he went to the office and to do some marketing. Too bad as I would have liked to do some shopping downtown.
Mother telephoned. Had received a letter from Ira and was pleased at the attention.
Felt better by evening so we ate an early dinner and then went to the early show at the Apex with the Levys to see the Italian picture "8 1/2."[13]
Enjoyed it – sort of. Afterwards we went to the Hot Shoppe for refreshments. A pleasant evening and home at a reasonable hour.

Sunday, September 15
A cool, rainy day – but I was feeling much better in spite of the discouraging weather. It was the kind of day I could cheerfully spend at home, but we went over to Mother's in the afternoon. Visited with her for a while and took her for a long drive. Ira telephoned just after we got home. Had arranged to go to Columbus for Rosh Hashanah. May get a 5-day pass. He would have liked to come home, and we would have liked to have him, but it all got too complicated to arrange on the long-distance telephone. Besides, we are hoping he will get a 15-day pass when he finishes his basic training.

Monday, September 16
Another rainy day. We went down together. Started this afternoon on my office physical checkup. Nothing wrong, apparently, as far as the doctor could tell at this point. Raining quite hard in the afternoon so I let Jules pick me up although I hated to see him get in that traffic mess on Penn Avenue.
There were New Year's cards from the Levys (who also sent one to Ira) and the Lewins, and a letter from Ira, written, of course, before we talked to him yesterday. I have never known him to be as homesick as he seems to be these days, in his letters and in his telephone conversations.

Tuesday, September 17
We went down together in the Buick, the radio of which was broken by vandals, and the fan blows even when turned off, although it is doubtful that that is due to vandalism. Had to go to the HEW South Building for the rest of my physical exam at 1:00, so lunched in the dining room there for auld lang syne. Anita called to say she could not come in

---
13   Fellini's movie 8 1/2.

tomorrow. Had a good reason, but it was too bad it had to come up just before the holiday. She will try to come in on Saturday. A New Year's card from the Leon Brooks.

Alice Jaffee called to wish us a happy new year, and to chat. Matt is enjoying law school. I am frankly jealous. Called Evelyn Promisel to wish them a happy birthday. She has to work.

Wednesday, September 18
We went down together. Spoke to Kuskin again about the 15[14] – about a year and a half since he recommended me, is still recommending me, and Leedom[15] is still doing nothing about it. To the beauty parlor at noon. New Year's card and note from Sonny Pressman, who seems to be enjoying LA very much. Card form Lucille and Louie.

Jules picked me up about 5:00. We stopped to get a challah. Then home for a big chicken dinner – broiled chicken which I can prepare in a hurry and which we both prefer and then to MCJC[16] for Rosh Hashanah services. We have very good seats, next to the Bernie Cushmans,[17] and enjoyed the service. Too bad Mother refused to go.

Thursday, September 19
A lovely warm sunny day. We left for MCJC right after breakfast. The services ended about 1:00. Then home for dinner – cold broiled chicken, which we like at least as well as when it is hot.

Then to Saul Jaffe's open house party. A great many people we know. Enjoyed it very much, but felt badly because I lost the lovely gold pin Wyzanski gave me years ago, and which I have enjoyed so much. Evidently dropped it getting out of the car. By the time I realized it, it was gone. Sorry about that, and about not having taken leave for tomorrow also as Jules is going to services in the morning.

Friday, September 20
I came down alone in the Buick via Carter Barron. Jules went to services in the morning, and came down to the office in the afternoon. A warm day but I took a walk downtown at noon anyhow as the weather prediction is for much cooler weather moving into the area this evening.

New Year's cards from the Zeidmans and the Marvin Schlezingers. I have now heard from Helen Lee three times since I have written anything to her.

Anita called to say she could not come in tomorrow – was taking care of four small children whose parents had been called out of town – but she called again after to say they had returned and she would come in tomorrow.

Saturday, September 21
Cloudy and a good deal cooler. Anita came in. Glad to see her, to get the house cleaned and the laundry ironed. And she found the pin I was sure I had lost. Gave her an extra day's pay as she had been working for us for a year.

---

14 Her promotion to Civil Service 15 grade,
15 Board member who does not seem to have helped Anne's promotion.
16 Montgomery County Jewish Center.
17 Bernard Cushman was an attorney in Washington who worked with labor law and wrote about social legislation and labor law among other topics. He was involved with labor cases and the NLRB before the U.S. Court of Appeals, D.C. Circuit and the U.S. Supreme Court among others.

We did the marketing, and took a TV set and a radio to the repair shop in Kensington. Later Jules took Anita to the terminal and picked up the TV set which was ready.

Ann Elson called and invited us over next Saturday to break the fast with them.

Ira called. Back at camp. Got only a 3-day pass after all, but enjoyed Columbus very much, we gathered, especially the food. To the Flower to see a couple of British films.

Sunday, September 22
Jules went to the bakery before brunch. Felt free to do so as Ira had telephoned last night.
In the afternoon we picked up Mother, took her for a long ride, and stopped at Howard Johnson's for refreshments.
Later we went to Kushner's for supper.
Later yet we went to the Levys' for the first Book Club meeting of the season. Discussed Romain Gary's *Promise at Dawn* – and a very lively discussion it was. David Levy, unknown to most of us, was tape recording the discussion, and played it back while we were having refreshments. Enjoyed the evening, although we were rather late getting home for a Sunday night.

Monday, September 23
We went down together. Jules wanted to take the Buick in for servicing but was afraid I would be too cold driving the Chevy as the rear curtain does not work.
Extremely busy at the office, and got out quite late for luncheon, but walked over to the Hot Shoppe, which is far better than the Drug Fair and gets me out of the building for a little while.

Received a tray from Lucille with two figures on it labeled "Jules" and "Anne" and an inscription "Have a Drink with the Schlezingers." It was very cute. But had been badly wrapped and was dented. Hate even to mention it, she felt so badly about her gift from Israel having arrived badly dented.

Tuesday, September 24
We came down together in the Chevy, with the rear curtain down as it is unusable. It was cool but not too uncomfortable.
Had a case on the Board agenda with Robinson – my first since new member Jenkins came – but he did not participate.
Dashed to Garfinckel's at noon and bought a girdle in a hurry as I had a great deal of work but needed a girdle badly.
Picked up Mother in the evening and took her to the store. Offered to take her somewhere for dessert but she was not interested. But she enjoyed the extra weekday visit. Mentioned that the Rolands[18] were taking Joyce to OSU this weekend. Joyce has done very well. Poor Ira!

Wednesday, September 25
Anita came in. We came down together.
To the beauty parlor at noon. Had a case on the subpanel agenda with Marty Fingerhut. Scheduled for an agenda of some kind every day this week. Had Anita feed Pal. We went from work to the Stanley–Coleman house for dinner. The other guests were Bob and Nancy Asman, he of the NBC news bureau, she the

---

18   Anne's sister Clara, husband Lou, and daughter Joyce.

mother of two and a student at American U., and both charming. A pleasant evening and it broke up quite early. A letter from Ira. Thanked us for the money we sent him as a New Year's gift. From Lucille a newspaper clipping that Mildred Roth had died.

Thursday, September 26
We drove down together, but I dropped Jules at his building and parked in my garage as he was leaving later for New York.
We had a luncheon in the Board room for Mike Wolpert who is leaving – kosher delicatessen as we have three boys on the staff who would not be able to participate otherwise.
Did some errands on the way home. Did not notice until I stopped at the grocery store that the blankty-blank garage had left my lights on.
Fed Pal, and then fed myself. Read and watched TV and felt lonesome, but could not feel too sorry for myself as it was just the one night that I was to be alone.

Friday, September 27
I drove down alone and parked in my garage. Jules got back from New York about noon.
I had the subpanel 5 agenda today - had an agenda of some sort every day this week – and, when it finally ended, met Jules and we went home. It was early but we had a big dinner anyhow – delicious filet mignons – and then to Kol Nidre services, which we enjoyed. It had been a warm sticky day, and I had done a good deal of rushing around, so was in bed and asleep shortly after 11:00.

Awakened by a call from Ira, the guest of local Jewish families during the day but staying at the "Y." Almost made a surprise trip home but could not squeeze enough time out of his sergeant.

Saturday, September 28
To services about 10:00. Quite warm but the sanctuary was comfortably air-conditioned. We went home at the afternoon break and stayed at home. I went to bed, in fact, as I felt ill. When Jules broke his fast, I fixed some oatmeal for him, and ate a little myself. Felt much better afterwards. Had decided not to go to the Elson's, but then changed our minds. Glad we did. She had several couples stop by to break their fast. Put food out and let people help themselves very informally. It was pleasant, and we were home by about 9:30.
Letter from Ira, written before we talked to him yesterday. Confirmed in writing what we had gathered in a prior conversation – OSU was not encouraging about his coming back when he went there during the Rosh Hashanah weekend.

Sunday, September 29
A lovely day. Since Ira was unlikely to call, Jules went to the bakery before brunch. Later to Mother's. Brought her the Sunday paper and some rye bread. Took her for a long drive in the country and stopped at a produce stand to buy tomatoes, apples, etc. She gave us a note to Ira and $10 for a gift to him. The Levys telephoned to thank us for the anniversary card we sent them, and to tell us we had not missed much when we

decided not to go with them last night to see "A Thousand Clowns" at the National.

Jules thought the clocks were to be moved back today. Resulted in a crazy, mixed-up day time-wise.

Monday, September 30
We went down together. When it developed later that Jules was going to be quite late going home, I called a couple of people for a ride, without luck, then decided to try the bus rather than call any other. Found it quite satisfactory. It cost only a token plus 8 cents and a walk up the hill, but it was a lovely day and I was in no hurry.

It was close to 8:00 when Jules got home. Gave me plenty of time to fix a lamb stew from yesterday's left-over roast, and we both enjoyed the dinner very much.

When Paul Herzog was here for the NLRB awards ceremony, he suggested sending birthday cards to John Houston, which I did. Received a thank-you note, very cordial and quite touching.

Tuesday, October 1
Jules had to take the Chevy in for some repairs to the latest repairs. I took the Buick, parked at Carter Barron, and took the bus. A lovely day. At noon saw the "parade" honoring Haile Selassie. Got a good view of him and the President in an open convertible and of Jackie in the bubble-top car. And the bands and the banners and the crowds made it all very gay. But all the uniforms made me think of, and miss, Ira.

His OSU year book was delivered today. Did not find any photos in it we could identify as him.

Jules brought some delicatessen home for supper – unusually good corned beef which we both enjoyed very much.

1963 continued

Wednesday, November 20
We went down separately. Jules got a haircut yesterday and wanted to take his time this morning shampooing his hair. I parked at Carter Barron and took the bus.

Had various cases with various legal assistants on various agendas, so it was quite a hectic day. But did walk over to the Hot Shoppe for luncheon. Bad enough to have to eat in the drug store when the weather is bad without doing so just because I am busy – not when I have a boss like Leedom. Wonder what satisfaction he derives from giving the 15 to no one for all this time.

Thursday, November 21
We went down together. Some light rain in the morning, but by noon the sun was shinning brightly. I was very busy though, so did not take advantage of the weather. Walked only to the bank as it was payday, and to the Hot Shoppe for a quick luncheon.

Got my walk in after work before meeting Jules. We stopped at Kroger's to pick up some groceries. By then it was late and I was tired, so we got Chicken Delight boxes for dinner.

Letter from Ira, evidently feeling quite well but not altogether recovered from whatever ailed him. We had returned to Lucille the cute tray she sent us, which was dented. A new un-dented one arrived today.

Friday, November 22
A lovely day. Started leisurely as I was going first to Dr. Cox for a check of my glasses. Walked to the office from there. Anita came in. I had my hair done at noon. The brightness went out of the day just after I got back, when word got around that President Kennedy had been shot by an assassin. Government employees, in a state of shock, were dismissed early. I went to Jules' office and home from there. A letter from Ira. He called later. All weekend passes had been cancelled. He was attending services.
We called the Jaffes and asked them to come over, but they had asked some others, and asked us to join them, which we did. Charles and Ann Gordon and Harold and Mildred Inger were there. The talk was about the shocking events of the day.

Saturday, November 23
A rainy day. A day of mourning for the murdered John F. Kennedy. All radio and television programs were devoted to this subject.
We went out for a while in the afternoon to do some errands. Invited Mother to come along, but she declined because of the rain. We stopped for a few minutes at Jules' office. Tried to drive pass the White House, but only pedestrians were being permitted there.
In the evening Jules went to see "Lawrence of Arabia,"[19] which was playing at several of the local movie houses. I did not feel like going. Both the places where he stopped had such long lines that he decided not to wait and came back home. Letter from Ira explaining how Nate could get his army medical record.

Sunday, November 24
Cool but bright and sunny. We slept late, I particularly. Spent much of the day watching TV, the Washington programs in memory of President Kennedy, and the Dallas programs about Lee Oswald, charged with the assassination. Was watching when Rubinstein shot Oswald before Oswald, surrounded by police, could be moved from the city to county jail. An astonishing example of live TV news coverage. Another ineradicable blemish in the city of Dallas. Took time off in the afternoon to take Mother for a ride.
They Levys came over in the evening to talk and watch TV with us. Probably should have gone to the Capitol to view the casket but there were already such mobs waiting to do so.

Monday, November 25
No work today as President Johnson had declared it a day of national mourning.
Jules went to services at MCJC in honor of Kennedy in the morning. He picked up Bill and David Levy, who went with him.
Other than that we both spent most of the day watching the funeral services on TV. Very impressive. So many personages from all over the world. And Jackie was magnificent

---

19   Peter O'Toole's characterizaation of the life of T.E. Lawrence, British agent who encouraged the revolt of Arab tribes against the Ottoman Empire.

in everything she did. The children were adorable. The crowds watching behaved with great dignity and fitting solemnity. Showed the world watching TV we are not all maniacs.

In the evening with the Levys to a memorial service at Washington Hebrew Congregation. Enormous crowd. To a Hot Shoppe. Home.

Year End Summary 1963

This was the second year in a row that Anne did not write a yearly summary. Although it was a quiet year, she was more and more involved in professional activities and meetings. -- RDH

1964

In 1964 Ira graduated from Ohio State University, which made Anne very happy. He came home for a visit but took a job in Ohio and continued living there. She found the house "large and empty" after he left.

In July Anne and Jules traveled to Mexico for a convention, and she described visiting Mexico City and the pyramids of Teotihuacan, San Miguel de Allende, and Oaxaca. She was pleased with the people they met there and enjoyed parties and dinners.

On September 1 the important event of the year was their twenty-fifth wedding anniversary and a party with eighty guests. It was a huge success, and she was delighted with it. Anne was frustrated with the lack of professional advancement that she felt that she deserved. -- RDH

Saturday, August 29
Stopped at the Sheraton to see Nate, et.al., then to the beauty parlor while Jules picked up the Lewins[20] and the L. Schlezingers. Spotted Nate[21] near the White House so the Lewins went sightseeing with them We had a bite at a Hot Shoppe, picked up my corsage, and went home. We went to the party about 6:30 to check the table, etc. Everything looked fine. Guests began arriving about 7:00. It was a huge success. I have never been so complimented on a party or on my

20 Jules' sister Gertrude and her husband and brother Lou and wife from Columbus, Ohio.
21 Jules' brother Nate from Philadelphia.

appearance. Did not get much of the food that everyone raved so about, but managed to have a wonderful time at my own party. A number of the guests brought gifts, but we made no attempt to unwrap them tonight. The party broke up about midnight, the last guests leaving only when they saw us picking up the floral centerpiece to take home.

Sunday, August 30
We gave a brunch at the Sheraton for Louie, Lucille, Al, Gertrude, Nate, Bobbie, Mrs. Stern, Nan, Jo Ann and Dick, and the three of us. It was very good. Then they all came back to the house but Jo Ann and Dick left soon. The rest of us had champagne and/or lemon ice and things to nibble. Nate and his party left about 4:00 - after presenting us with a large hotray, something we have been wanting to get ourselves. Too hot and humid to cook the large rib roast I had, so later seven of us piled into the Buick and drove to Hogate's for a quick seafood supper.. Then to the airport to see the Lewins off for Columbus. Home again to glance at the paper before going to bed.
Telephone calls during the time we were home from Ruth Timmony and Judy Brachman thanking us for the lovely party.

Monday, August 31
Ira received his grades - a B, two C's, and a D. At least they were passing grades, and it seems he is pretty sure to graduate, which once seemed quite unlikely. We had brunch at home. Then took Louie and Lucille to the airport over the new beltway. Then Ira dropped us at our offices, took the car home, and picked us up after work. We picked up delicatessen for supper.
Ruth Levy wants us to come to dinner tomorrow. I hate to be difficult, but it depends on how I feel after having a tooth pulled. Clara and Lou called and came over. Brought an electric carving knife and a bottle of liqueur from Jan. Stayed for a drink and a visit, and to rave about the party. Glad it turned out so well as we give so few parties.

Tuesday, September 1
To Dr. Kaplan's to have a tooth pulled. Asked him why a cavity got so large that a tooth had to be pulled when I was seeing a dentist 5 or 6 times a year. He said he did not have the answer. Just pulled the tooth. Anniversary card from the Harlowes, New Year cards from the Levys and the Brooks, a beautiful flower arrangement from the Zanoffs, a set of lovely serving pieces from the Goors, a cloisonné picture from the Pachels, and a beautiful crystal and silver 3 – piece flower holder dish - container from the Saxes and Sam Wagshals.
To the Levy's for a magnificent roast beef dinner, several kinds of wine, an anniversary cake, a beautiful Steuben glass bourbon dish from Ruth and Bill and a stainless steel serving dish from the three children. Jules took Ira to the bus station later. Ira took the bus to Columbia [Maryland] and will drive the Chevy back.

Wednesday, September 2
A lovely day.

Jules felt like taking it easy and going down later, so I drove down and parked in my garage and he took the bus.

Lunched at the Washington Hotel coffee shop with Mary Clark, still commenting about the lovely party, as does everyone I run into who was there.

Evelyn Promisel called in the evening. She and Nate cut their trip short so they could get back in time for the party, then encountered so many delays en route from South America that they were 24 hours late getting home.

No packages or personal mail, for the first time in quite a while. Fixed dinner, did some washing and ironing, and wrote a few thank – you notes.

Thursday, September 3
Alvin called early this morning – I was up but she awaked Jules – to say she could come in today. That meant some scurrying around to get things organized for her, but I was glad to have her come. Found later she got a great deal of both washing and ironing done. Found also as we arrived home that Ira had arrived from Columbus in the Chevy a little earlier – all in good shape. We also had a New Year's card from the Schottensteins, a note from Evelyn Polster that the Kosak would be in New York later this month and she and Martin might join them there, and a beautiful silver and glass casserole from the Matlins. Jules and I went to Lord and Taylor's after dinner. Returned the linens we got from the Friedmans, and sent a purse as a bar mitzvah gift to Lenore Gross.

Friday, September 4
Hot and humid. I went downtown at noon anyhow but did not buy anything.

Had put a roast on the automatic timer. Ira came down in the afternoon to have Marie type some Form 57's, and was so long that we finally went home and he came later on the bus. Meanwhile I got the rest of the dinner prepared. Ira took off after dinner to give his friends, the Jacobys, some of the Form 57's to file for him. New Year cards from the Zanoffs and Martin Polsters. Telephone call from Phyllis Schottenstein, and one from Lil to tell us what a wonderful party we gave, how beautiful I looked, etc. etc.

I wrote some more thank-you notes but have a good many more to do. Will have to return some of the gifts just for lack of space to keep them all.

Saturday, September 5
Ira took off in the morning to spend the day at Reboboth Beach.

A thank-you note and two little glass and silver dishes from Jane Stern, Bobbie's mother, a lovely silver and glass trivet from the Fahy's and New Year cards-notes from Gertrude and Lucille.

To Lenore Gross's bar mitzvah. She did beautifully. Home afterwards to change and do errands, including returning McConnell's and Wagshals' gifts, which were lovely, but we had so many lovely things. Bought a hat at Garfinckel's in Spring Valley.

Ira came home about 8:00, quite sunburned but had a wonderful time.

We went to the bar mitzvah reception at the

Gross home, a lovely affair as theirs usually are. Many there who had been at our party, complementing us highly on the party and my appearance. And the Bisgyers gave us a gift – a chip and dip server.

Sunday, September 6
A beautiful moderate day.
Telephone calls from May Wagshal and Charlotte Middleman to thank us for the party, wish us a happy New Year, and, as to Charlotte, to postpone the book club meeting.
Ira went swimming at the Hardy pool. We went to see Mother. Her only comment about the party was to complain about a fancied insult by Alice Jaffe. She told Jules at the party she wanted to give us a check for an anniversary gift, but apparently forgot about it since the party.
We had a very good dinner – challah, broiled chicken, etc. Then dressed and went to Rosh Hashanah services at MCJC. The Levys had suggested we stop by afterwards, but we went home instead and had a snack and watched TV.

Monday, September 7
Ira went to services in a separate car. Left before us but arrived afterwards. Learned he got to MCJC, missed his watch, drove home again, and found it in front of the house where it fell off his wrist. How lucky!
Home for dinner after services- good cold chicken. Then in separate cars to Saul Jaffes. Saw a great many people we knew and met a few we did not. Left in about an hour, Ira to visit friends and we to go home and stay at home. Ira came back from his visits but went out again to make one more call. We had scrambled eggs for supper. I fixed some sandwiches for Ira when he came home, and then went to bed fairly early, feeling fine, but woke during the night with a miserable sick headache.

Tuesday, September 8
Much to woozy to go to work or to services. Stayed in bed almost all day. Jules and Ira had breakfast and went to services together. Then Jules went to the office and Ira came home – for a while.
I felt better in the afternoon and, by evening, was able to cook supper and even to eat some. We skipped dessert as a farewell to Jonathan, who is leaving tomorrow to enter the University of Miami, Ohio. We went over in both cars so the youngsters could ride with Ira with the top down. Drove out to the new Howard Johnson in Wheaton Plaza. Jules had stopped on the way home at Mother's on some business, reminded her of her remarks at the party, and she said she wanted to give us the check she promised for $100.

Wednesday, September 9
Jules and I drove down together. I parked in my garage as he was leaving in the afternoon for Orange to see Hank Cohen.
Did enough work today to make up for the holiday on Monday and the sick leave yesterday.
Gave Tom Ricci a ride out to Silver Spring

where he had left his car. Ira and I had supper together at home, read, watched TV, etc. He went out for a little while but spent most of the evening at home.

Edward Schlezinger telephoned to let us know that a Sandra Berlin was coming in tomorrow with her mother to look for a job. Old friend of the family, etc. He did not seem to know much about Sandra except that she was a lovely girl. We'll do what we can, of course.

Thursday, September 10
I drove down alone and parked in my garage.
Jules called from Orange – expected to be back about 5:30.
To the beauty parlor at noon.
Ira came down to the office in the late afternoon. Jules called me from his office at about 5:30. He went from there to an F.B.A. cocktail party at the Lawyers Club for a few minutes, and then picked up Ira and me at the office, and we went to the Golden Ox for dinner. Ira ate a fantastic amount of food – the large portion of roast beef plus part of Jules' regular sized portion. We drove directly home from there, glad to be all together again.

Friday, September 11
Have called some maids who were advertising for jobs, but no luck so far. Lunched at the Chez Francis with Vivian Asplund.
Met Jules at the Slather after work, and we stopped in for a while at an F.B.A. cocktail party there. Were joined by Lee Anderson and Neil Naiden. Jules and Neil each bought a round of drinks, and then we left. Picked up delicatessen at Hofberg's – unusually good – for supper for the three of us.
A note from Gertrude Levin thanking us for the weekend and the gift of linens from Ireland. A New Year's card from the Dr. Michaels. A reference to be filled in for Krusnechi for a TX job. And an invitation to a Tydings – for Senator affair.

Saturday, September 12
Cloudy and very cool. Ira took off after brunch for the President's Cup regatta and was gone most of the day.
A New Year's card from the Lewens from London, and a postcard from them on a vacation trip in Greece, and a New Year's card from the Zeidmans.
Called Linda and David Levy [i.e. Bill and Ruth Levys' children]. They expect their parents tomorrow night. Asked them to brunch but Linda had to go to Sunday School, so I said I would call them tomorrow.
In the evening to the Hay-Adams to pick up a Mr. Telst from Knoll.[22] Took him to Costin's for a very elaborate and expensive dinner, then drove him around to see the city by night. Stopped at the bagel bakery, and got home after midnight.

Sunday, September 13
A cool rainy day. I got up early anyhow to call Linda and David to arrange to have them over, but Ruth and Bill [i.e. Levy] answered – pushed through from Oxford last night.
Called Mother and invited her to dinner

---
22 Knoll was Jules' major German client.

but she did not feel like going out. Ira went out in the morning to pick up a *Post* – our service gets worse and worse – and in the evening on a date, but Jules and I stayed at home all day.

Had an especially good brisket for dinner. Mother would have enjoyed it very much as it was unusually tender as well as tasty. Got started reading *The Agony and the Ecstasy*, our book-club book, very long but easy to read as far as I have gone.

Monday, September 14
We all went downtown together, Ira for several job interviews he had arranged by himself or through friends. He was downtown all day and went home with us. We had excellent steaks for dinner.
Received some lovely red roses from Herr Telst, the German Jules and I took to dinner on Saturday.
A thank-you note from Lenore Gross for her bas [bat] mitzvah gift.
Ruth Levy telephoned just to chat for a while.
I called Alvin to find out if I should give up on her entirely. She has a beautician job so won't be doing housework any longer.

Tuesday, September 15
Ira came downtown with us, principally to keep an appointment with Dr. Eanet to have his teeth cleaned and x-rayed.
We left our offices about 4:00 so I could prepare a large dinner, eat and clean up afterwards, and get dressed in time for the Kol Nidre services. Managed to do so and get to MCJC in plenty of time. The place was jam-packed. I find it very uncomfortable to sit so long in such crowded conditions, but Jules finds pleasure at the thought of so many Jews turning out for religious observances at least once a year. I suppose his is the proper attitude.

Wednesday, September 16
A very pretty day.
We all went to services about 10:00, but in separate cars. I went home with Ira about 2:00. Jules stayed until the break at about 3:00. Jules and Ira both fasted, but I did not, although I ate very little. We all had dinner at 5:30, a tremendous meal.
I did some housecleaning, washing, and ironing, as well as the cooking and cleaning up afterwards. But I do not get the house cleaned properly – just too lazy and reluctant. And no sign of a maid although I have been fairly diligent in answering ads, checking references, registering at an employment office, etc.

Thursday, September 17
Another lovely day.
We all went down together, Ira for more interviews, which he is enjoying tremendously. He had an appointment at 11:30 in my vicinity, so stopped in afterwards, and we met Jules for luncheon at the Black Steer.
Pearl Berlin finally called at the Madison with her daughter, Sandra. The Solver Spring Employment Office called me about an applicant. With some misgivings about her

qualifications, I arranged for her to come out on trial Saturday.

Ira went out for dinner at the John Hardys'. Jules and I stayed at home. Ira came home fairly early, and went to bed rather early, more tired apparently than he will admit to us.

Friday, September 18
Ira stayed at home today. Did a great deal of work in the yard.
The Berlins, Mother and daughter, stopped at the office in the afternoon. Sandra had a job, had to find a place to live. I was not much help.
Ruth Levy called after dinner to ask if we wanted to go to a movie with them. I thought we had seen the picture they wanted to see, and I had a number of chores to do preparatory to a new – and, I am afraid, inexperienced, maid coming tomorrow. Have to remind myself about what needs to be done, and what is needed to do it with. And I know nothing about her character or reliability.

Saturday, September 19
Susie Lee Wingfield, sent by the Silver Spring Employment Office, telephoned about an hour earlier than scheduled, and Ira picked her up at the terminal. She did a fairly good job, but smoked heavily and worked in her bare feet – a little too casual for my taste. Ira took her to the terminal when she left.
Later Ira picked up Pearl and Sandra Berlin at the Madison and brought them out to the house. We had a couple of drinks, then – in a downpour – to Mrs. K's for a very good dinner. Then Ira took off with Sandra. Bill and Ruth came over to visit. They left so late that, by the time we drove Pearl back to the Madison and stopped at Hofberg's, it was about 2:00 when we went to bed. Ira got home about 2:30 – and he had done a lot of hard work in the yard today.

Sunday, September 20
Jules had a miserable night and did not feel well all day – we suspected the combination of liquor and his medications for allergies. Ira took off shortly after brunch to spend the day at the Hardy's, who were having some other friends Ira had not seem for a long time. He was staying there for supper. I had a leg of lamb for today's dinner but did not bother to cook it for just the two of us – and Jules not feeling well. We went to see Mother in the afternoon. She seemed well and chipper, but it was a cloudy rather cool day so she did not want to go out.
Ira came home relatively early - and went to bed.

Monday, September 21
We all went downtown together. Ira had one last interview – for this period – and then went home by bus. Called the Silver Spring Employment Office to report that Susie was not the answer to my problem.
Lunched at the Black Steer with Vivian Asplund.
Ira put on a roast while he was at home. We invited Mother to dinner but she declined. Ira went out after dinner with Sandra Berlin. He seems to have become quite fond of her. Don't know whether she is of him also, or is

making, the best of the fact then she does not know any other boys in this area yet. Jules is not yet back to normal but feels much better than he did yesterday, thank heavens!

Tuesday, September 22
Had a case on the Board agenda with Howard Abrahams.
Finally saw Dr. Eanet, who examined my teeth, and recommended that I see a periodontist to whom he would refer me. Indicated that he did not think Kaplan was the man for me.
Pearl Berlin called in the late afternoon to ask us all to dinner. Did not call earlier; she was waiting to see how Sandra felt after an all day CIA exam. We had cocktails in the bar and dinner in the dining room of the Madison, where they are staying. The dinner and service were excellent – that seems to be the Madison standard. Ira and Sandra took off after dinner for gayer places. We visited with Pearl for a while, and then went home.

Wednesday, September 23
Did not feel particularly well, and, as it was Ira's last day at home, I decided to stay at home. Spent very little time with Ira, however, as he was in and out all morning, and took off to play basketball all afternoon. A pretty day so that was understandable.
An anniversary gift from Lillian and Ben Wagshal – a lovely silver dinner bell – not much use for us, but very pretty.
We had dinner at home. Then took Ira to the airport. His plane left about 8:30. He had called his apartment – roommate last night from the Madison, and he agreed to pick Ira up at the airport in his brand new car. Ira will get his long promised new car for graduation.

Thursday, September 24
Went back to work, feeling fairly well, but later in the morning became very ill, and the medication which the nurse gave me merely nauseated me more. Finally felt well enough about 1:00 to take a little walk, and then felt well enough – it being a lovely day – to eat a little luncheon at the Hot Shoppe.
Skipped the Service Awards program in the morning at which Leedom[23] was the principal speaker.
Pearl Berlin called, had planned to leave tomorrow, but moved it up to this evening.
We had a very simple supper. Read for a while. Went to bed a bit early. The house seems large and empty again with Ira back in Columbus.

Friday, September 25
An Olivia Corgile telephoned before we left home – referred by the Silver Spring Employment Office. She is coming out tomorrow. I called Susie and told her not to come, a little regretfully, as she is a pleasant person, but her heavy smoking and padding about in bare feet not my "cup of tea."
A lovely day so I walked downtown at noon. Got tied up fairly late with Kuskin and Genach. When the discussion broke up, Genach and I walked over to the Cafritz garage to meet Jules, and we gave him a ride home. Spent much of the evening "picking up" the house and doing laundry in preparation or Olivia tomorrow.

---
23   Chairman of the NLRB governing Board.

Saturday, September 26
Olivia Corgile called right on time. Jules picked her up at the terminal. She made a much better impression on me than Susie did last week. She is engaged Tuesdays and Fridays, my preferred days, but I might settle for Thursday. Meanwhile, she is to come in next Saturday. Her reference had been in Europe but is due back on Tuesday. I stayed around the house all day although it was a lovely day. I got out a little while when I took her to the terminal so Jules could watch a televised football game. He had done the marketing and errands during the day.

At least, as a result of staying home all day, I have almost finished reading *The Agony and the Ecstasy*,[24] very good but too long.

Sunday, September 27
A lovely warm day.

Jules spent a good deal of time planting bulbs of various kinds that he bought yesterday and the chrysanthemums the Schofers had sent us for our anniversary. Ira had planted a number of things while he was home, so we should have a lovely showing this spring.

Talked to Mother on the phone but did not go over to see her.

In the evening, met the Levys at the Flower. We saw "The Chalk Garden,"[25] which we all thought was excellent. Afterwards to Howard Johnson's.

Evelyn Promisel called to chat about various things, including the fact that she is still looking for an anniversary gift for us. Wish she would forget about it.

Monday, September 28
Jules was going to do some more planting this morning and went to the office late, but it was raining quite hard so we went down together.

The rain stopped for a little while around noon so I walked over to the Hot Shoppe for luncheon. It let up also about 5:00, so I walked over to the Cafritz garage to meet Jules. He did his planting when we got home. Gave me time to prepare baked potatoes to go with the luscious porterhouse steaks he bought Saturday.

No mail from Ira. Surprising. Telephoned Sandra Berlin. She is getting along fine except that her work, principally filing, is extremely boring.

Tuesday, September 29
Jules got up with a bad headache. I had particularly wanted to drive down with him today as I was going to a party of female lawyers at Helen Rosen's house after work and could get a ride there. And it was pouring! But I drove- picked up Jack Brosnan and Gene Thomas – and later drove to Helen's, taking Roseanne Hulse, Nancy Sherman, and Marion Griffin. Helen had a beautiful home, her adopted son is adorable, and the party was very pleasant. But it was raining harder then ever, I was going home alone, she lives in an area I am not familiar with, and some of the roads thereabouts

---

24   Irving Stone's biographical novel (1961) about the life of Michelangelo. Over 700 pages.

25   A 1955 play by Enid Bagnold that tells the story of Mrs. St Maugham and her granddaughter Laurel, who was a special needs child.

were just about washed out. But I followed Mira part of the way, and managed to find my way home after she cut off, but I had some disturbing moments.

Wednesday, September 30
Another rainy day. We went down together. At 10:00 I went to see Dr. Baldinger, the periodontist to whom Dr. Eanet referred me. He will treat me – feels my teeth can be saved – but so did Kaplan and Birthright. A very busy afternoon, with cases on the subpanel agenda with Mira Stevenson, Bob Pfeffer, and Howie Abrahams.
Alice Jaffe called to comment on the picture of Jules shaking hands with the President of Mexico, which was reprinted in the Federal Bar News.
Nate sent us some newspaper clippings about a new hospital wing that was dedicated to him.[26] Still no word from Ira.

Year End Summary 1964

This had been a very good year in many respects. The brightest event, of course, was Ira's graduation, finally, from college. Just as gratifying was the way he went about finding a job, and his selection of a job on the basis of the kind of work and the kind of people he would be working with rather than the one that would pay him the largest starting salary.

He wound up his OSU career with many warm, close friendships, male and female. No serious girl-friend apparently, he has time for that now that he is embarked on his working career.

Things seem to be going well for Jules as well. His office relationships seem to be on reasonably good terms. And he has enough law practice and income to maintain his prestige and self-respect, although he would like to have a broader base to his practice with regard both to the number of his clients and the nature of their legal problems. But he finds such happiness and satisfaction in his family relationships that these feeling make up for many things he may lack.

And things have gone relatively well for me. I never did get the "15" but I did get rid of Leedom[27] as my boss, and that was almost as gratifying.

And, while I am a long way from being appointed a Board member, my activity as an applicant for the appointment seems to have raised me in the esteem I value, and

---

26 Nathan S. Schlezinger, M.D., Jules' brother who was a Professor of Neurology at the Jefferson Medical College in Philadelphia.

27 Boyd S. Leedom of North Dakota who served two terms on the Board but was not renewed by President Kennedy. He then took a position as an NLRB judge.

has, as far as I can see, done me no harm. And while my chances are slim, I can go on hoping until someone else is named to fill the Leedom vacancy.

Last – but by no means least – we have maintained good health throughout the family.

The only regard in which things have worked out quite badly for us is the business of not having a satisfactory maid. It makes a big difference on my feelings of relaxation at home, of my being able to entertain occasionally, and chiefly on my being able adequately to look after Jules and after Ira when he visits. But we manage to muddle though even that problem.

Julius and Anne
with grandsons David and Eric

1965

Anne continued to be frustrated by the lack of promotion. The high point of the year was Ira and Sandy's marriage. They decided to have the wedding in Columbus with the extended family where both had graduated from college. Anne would have liked the ceremony to be in Washington with more parties, announcements, and gifts surrounding the event.

Anne's mother needed regular attention, and they passed by her apartment frequently to help her.

They also bought a new Ford Mustang that year, which was a jazzy car of the moment. She was sad when Adlai Stevenson died and paid homage to him as a great man in American life.

Anne occasionally commented on President Lyndon Johnson's activities and military situation caused by the involvement in Vietnam. On July 28 she wrote, "The President, in a speech today, announced that the draft call would be increased, but that reservists would not be called up yet. Ira is in the active reserves." She was concerned about her son.

Their vacation that year was a trip through the lake country in New York, into Canada and then to Dayton, Ohio where Ira and Sandy lived, and Columbus to visit the extended family.

In March 1965 the United States made the first of ten manned space launches in the Gemini program with an average of one launch every two months. The first space walks were made, and the first dockings in space between two spaceships were executed, all this in preparation for the Apollo Moon program to come. Anne actively followed the space program and commented on it. -- RDH

Monday, March 1
We went down together. Wished we could be with Ira to celebrate his birthday tomorrow, but did the next best thing and called him this evening. He seemed pleasantly surprised. May have to work tomorrow, but had plans to step out with "the boys" Wednesday evening. Jules is upset about Wachtel having apparently raised his rent without a word of discussion. And moving would be such a complication!

Alice Jaffe telephoned to suggest we have dinner out together Sunday evening prior to book club meeting. Told us her father had fallen in his room, broke his hip, and is in the hospital. Sorry to hear it.

Tuesday, March 2
Ira's birthday. We went down separately, I in the Chevy via Carter Barron and the bus, Jules in the Buick via Covington's and the bus.

A pleasant day so I walked downtown at noon.

By bus to Carter Barron, then downtown to pick up Jules, and together to Covington's. I also stopped at the grocery store so supper was a bit late. Jules found his supposed rent increase was a stenographic error. We both felt much better.

Ruth Levy called to ask if we wanted to go with them to the Flower, but we saw the picture Saturday evening.

Louie Schlezinger called to discuss with Jules the draft of the will Jules had prepared for him.

Wednesday, March 3
We went together in the Buick. The turn signals and lights, that were damaged when Jules ran into another car on the way to Columbus, are now finally repaired. Took our vacuum to be repaired but needed only a new bag. Ate supper at the Charcoal Hut. Letter from Ira – making more friends, and is as busy and happy as he has been ever since he went to Dayton. Enclosed a clipping from a municipal paper mentioning him – his third press notice so far. Irv Jaffe called in the evening. Alice[28] is in the hospital again. This time it is an obstruction in the intestinal tract. What a shame! Just when she was beginning to feel better after the previous operation. And the only room she could get was in the Prince Georges County hospital, which is hard on Irv.

Thursday, March 4
We went down together. Had my hair done at noon. To Jules' office after work. It was pouring when we left there. He dropped me at O'Donnell's and, fortunately, found a place to park near both the restaurant and the theater. We met the Goors, Sheftels, and Schreibers at O'Donnell's, had a drink and dinner together, and enjoyed their company.

---

28   Irv and Alice Jaffe were close neighbors and friends with Anne and Jules. They were also members of the Sunday Book Club.

Then we all took off for the National and separated as we were the only ones sitting in the orchestra. Saw "The Odd Couple,"[29] which we found amusing. Saw a number of people we knew, including Paula and Kenny Locker. It was pouring again when we left the theater –so lucky to be parked nearby.

Friday, March 5
Went down together. Had some rain, some snow, some clear weather. The weather was bad around noon, so I lunched in the drugstore.
To Jules' office after work. Later we walked over to Dacos House for the Mathews' party – turned out to be their fifth anniversary. It was a very enjoyable party. Got a chance to tell Willard Wirtz[30] I was the same AFS seeking a Board Member appointment, and would be glad of a chance to talk to him about it. He was polite but completely noncommittal.[31]
After we left the party, we walked around to the Black Steer for dinner. Quite late by the time we finished so went directly home.

Saturday, March 6
Juanita came in late – but she came in. She has now tied the record for recent maids – 3 times. Left her alone while we went marketing. She seemed to get along all right, even delivered a message that Ira had called – Alice is getting along quite well but wants no visitors yet. We invited Irv and Mattie to dinner, but they spent the evening at the hospital and ate there. Offered to take Juanita home but she wanted to go to Silver Spring, so gave her a ride there.
We had a wonderful dinner – thick loin lamb chops, baked potatoes, fresh strawberries, etc. And I enjoyed an evening staying at home.

Sunday, March 7[32]
Ira did not call – probably because we talked to him on Monday evening. Had a very enjoyable brunch. Enjoy Sunday brunches all the more now that new maids have disrupted Saturday brunches.
In the afternoon we visited Mother. She seems well, and insists she is contented never going anywhere and never seeing anyone but Clara and us. In the evening to the book club meeting at the Levys'. Everyone came but Alice. We had a lively discussion of *Felix Frankfurter Reminisces*. Ruth had gone all out on the baking. We hardly made a dent in the four concoctions she served.

Monday, March 8
We went down together. Telephone call <u>from the Redevelopment Land Agency</u>,

---

29   A 1965 comedy by Neil Simon about two mismatched roommates, one organized and uptight, the other more disorganized and relaxed about life.
30   Secretary of Labor in the Kennedy and Johnson administrations. Wirtz could have been influential in helping Anne get the appointment as judge, but he seems to not have helped.
31   Anne was not promoted to full Board (i.e. NLRB) member judge status at the same rate that men were. Even Fannie Boyls, another woman serving since the 1930's had been appointed to judge in 1960. Anne tried on a number of occasions to receive the promotion until she finally did receive it in 1968.
32   This was "Bloody Sunday" when Civil Rights marchers were beaten at the Edmund Pettus bridge in Selma, Alabama. Anne seemed to be unaware of it.

which wanted Ira's address in order to offer him a job.

Jules had luncheon with Mike Feldman,[33] who is convinced my application will fail for lack of adequate political support and for that reason alone.

After work drove out to the Prince Georges County hospital to see Alice,[34] who seemed to be feeling fairly chipper. Irv and Mattie arrived to pick up a book for her but could not, in the limited time I had, find one suitable.

Then home for a late supper. Long letter from Ira, and we relished every mature, happy expression in it. Called the Levys to report on Ira's reference to Jonathan and our visit to Alice.

Tuesday, March 9
We went down separately, I via Carter Barron, as Jules was staying downtown for a meeting of the D.C. Bar. Assn. He "assumed" I would not want to go as the subject to be discussed dealt with the anti-trust laws — and I figured he was entitled to that much of an evening with "the boys."

A pleasant day with occasional sprinkle of rain, one as I was coming back from luncheon, and one as I was coming out of the grocery store on the way home. Jules noticed a favorable review in the *Wall Street Journal* of the book *The Ski Bum*, so he called Brentano's and ordered it sent out to Alice at the hospital.

Wednesday, March 10[35]
We went down together. After work I walked over to Jules' office. Later we went to the farewell party for Mike Feldman at the State Department. Our invitation was evidently an afterthought because Jules took Mike to luncheon on Monday, but we went anyhow. It was a brilliant gathering, including Supreme Court Justices Goldberg and Douglas, Bobby Kennedy, Sergeant Shriver, various Kennedy women, Senators, Representatives, Attorney General Katzenbach, Art Buchwald, etc., etc. Among those we knew and talked to were Charlie Horshy; Secretary of Labor Wirtz, who remembered me from the Mathews' party; and Harold Leventhal, just named to the Court of Appeals.

Home for supper. A long letter from Ira.

Thursday, March 11
We went down together. Jules called me at the office to let me know that Helga would be down tomorrow afternoon to spend a few days with us, that Alice's father died last night, and that Fred Naiden[36] was seriously ill. We did some marketing and errands on the way home. Had supper at home. Made up the bed for Helga in Ira's room as the den and downstairs bathroom, which we usually use for guests, is a very cold set-up in this weather, which had been rather cold and is expected to continue to be for awhile.

33   Mike Feldman served on the transition team in 1960 with Theodore Sorenson and Pierre Salinger among others as the Kennedy administration took over from the Eisenhower one. He was associated with foreign policy issues and later served in the Department of State before leaving in 1965. This discussion with Jules was evaluating the possibility of Anne being named to the Board of the NLRB.

34   Alice Jaffe, friend and neighbor.

35   Anne and Jules were frequently invited to events at the White House, Supreme Court, and Departments of State, Justice, and Labor, especially in Democratic administrations.

36   Family of Neal Naiden, Jules' law partner.

Ira telephoned – everything continues to be wonderful for him.

Alice called to thank us for the book. Accepted her father's death at 88 philosophically.

Friday, March 12

We came down together. I had my hair done at noon. Jules picked Helga up at Union Station in a cab and dropped her at my office about 3:30. I took her to coffee, introduced her to a number of people, then returned to do some work while she sat in the office and waited until it was time for me to leave. Jules left early, for him, gave Helga time to unpack, had martinis – her favorite drink, and then went to the Silver Spring Sheraton for dinner.

We have put Helga in Ira's room, which pleases her very much. She admitted that she was nervous when she was here before about sleeping on the first floor, and would be now again.

Saturday, March 13

A pleasant day. Juanita came in – on time- and four consecutive Saturdays is something of a recent record.

After brunch Helga and I went marketing. Then home to fix Juanita's lunch. Jules then took off for the office, and Helga and I went shopping at Wheaton plaza. She bought an evening dress.

Jules got back in time to take Juanita home. Had arranged a date for Helga with Gene Provost, the young lawyer who works for Wachtel, while Jules was at the office. Helga had dinner at home – rib roast of beef, etc. – but spent most of the afternoon and evening, until Gene picked her up about 9:30, getting ready for her date.

Sunday, March 14

Helga did not get in very late last night so was up in time to have brunch with us. She did not have much to say about the date – evidently not a great success.

Talked to Mother on the phone but did not visit her.

In the afternoon, the three of us drove out to see Alice at the hospital. Then for a long sightseeing ride. Stopped at Dumbarton Oaks to walk around the gardens a little and to go through the museum, which is a beautiful building worth seeing for itself, and which houses an interesting and beautifully displayed pre-Columbian art collection. Home for afternoon tea.

Later to O'Donnell's in Bethesda for cocktails – even on Sunday – and dinner.

Monday, March 15

Helga got up early – for her- and went down with us. She went to tour the White House, but it was closed, so she went to the Mellon Art Gallery[37] for a while. She came to the office about noon, and I took her to the Black Steer for luncheon. Then she went shopping. Came back to the office shortly with flowers she bought for me. She read the paper, etc., until I left, and we went to the Mayflower to meet Jules. Home for dinner. The flowers she brought were very pretty pink carnations.

We listened to the President's[38] civil rights

---

37   National Gallery of Art.
38   President Lyndon Johnson.

message to Congress – very good – and then to Gifford's at Helga's request. Long letter from Ira. Invitation to a black-tie dinner-dance from the Zanoffs. An old friend of Jules called to ask us to cocktails tomorrow. And Sandy Berlin called to chat.

Tuesday, March 16
Helga got up early and went down with us for the early White House tour which Jules arranged for through Ruth Timoney. I took her to Cleavers' for a second breakfast. We were joined by several people. Then she took off for Jules' office, and he took her by cab to Union Station.
After work Jules and I went to the Shoreham Hotel for cocktails with Angus Holmes, a law school classmate of Jules' whom he had not seen for many years. Afterwards to Avignone Freres for dinner. Then home.
The Levys called shortly after we got in to say they were going to drop in to see us. As we supposed, they brought some of Ruth's delicious home-made hamentaschen. Very sweet to remember us year after year.

Wednesday, March 17
We came down together. Rained and/or snowed most of the day so I lunched in the drugstore and, after work, waited at the office until Jules picked me up.
Long letter from Ira. Mentioned that he had driven to Miami University and visited Jonathan Levy.[39] We read that part of his letter on the telephone to the Levys, who seldom hear from Jonny.

39   Son of Anne and Jules' best friends, Bill and Ruth Levy.

I had plenty of household chores to do. Nevertheless enjoyed an evening at home with no guests to be entertained.
Long letter from the Edes to Jules at the office explaining and apologizing for the delay in taking care of his fee.

Thursday, March 18
We started down together in the Buick, but it began acting so strangely that we took it to Covington's. I went the rest of the way on an "express" bus which cost 60 cents. Jules took a cab home and drove down in the Chevy, and got to the office about the same time I did.
I met him after work and drove the Chevy home from Covington while he picked up the Buick.
Ira telephoned – talked at considerable length, which bothers us as he insists on not calling collect.
Apparently everything is going very well at work and otherwise. He is planning a big open-house party, to which he has invited people from Columbus as well as the many friends he has made in Dayton. What a guy!

Friday, March 19
We came down together. Very busy at the office but managed to slip out long enough to have my hair done at noon. Jules was tied up late at the office so I walked over there after work. It got so late we decided to eat downtown. The last time we were at the Golden Ox I had felt badly and did not enjoy my dinner at all, so we went there again, and I made up for the last time.
Then home to do some chores and get ready

for – I hope – Juanita coming tomorrow. Read *Candy*, which Stella Zanoff lent us. Thought it putrid. Felt we should apologize to Wachtel, to whom Jules sent the book when Wachtel was ill.

Saturday, March 20
Surprised when I awoke to find it snowing. Juanita made it in despite the weather. Jules took me marketing, and then went to the office. He got back in time take Juanita home. Before he left, we watched the President's press conference on civil rights. He also announced some appointments, including Sam Zagoria as Board Member – a former newspaperman, non-lawyer, administrative assistant to Senator Case. That's that![40]
Evelyn Promisel called to ask if I wanted to go along to see their new home-site, but, in view of the weather and Jules not being available, I declined.
Accepted the Levys' suggestion, however, to go to a movie in the evening. They picked us up, and we went to the Silver to see "36 Hours." Then to the Potter Coffee House for some very enjoyable refreshments.

Sunday, March 21
We had a large and very enjoyable brunch. Afterwards Jules went to the office again. He is working on a reply brief in his indigent-defendant case. I went over to see Mother, never going anywhere, never seeing anyone but the Rolands and us and, occasionally, Jan and her children.[41] Jules came home in the late afternoon, very tired. He is much of the time not really busy, with the result that it is quite a strain on him when he does have to work under pressure. And he is determined to do a good job on this criminal appeal even though it involves no fee, not even expenses.

Monday, March 22
We went down together. There was, of course, a good deal of comment and gossip around the office about the new Board member and the staff changes he is likely to make.
I was very busy, primarily because of getting ready for some rather difficult cases scheduled for tomorrow's Board agenda, so settled for a quick sandwich at the Hot Shoppe for luncheon.
After work walked over to the Cafritz garage to meet Jules. Then home. I had made a big batch of broiled chicken on Saturday, and we had enough left over for dinner this evening. Called the Jaffes. Alice is at home and evidently getting along very well.

Tuesday, March 23
We drove separately as Jules had to go to the Rockville courthouse in the morning. I had a couple of cases on the Board agenda with Mira,[42] and then one by myself. She waited for me, and then we went to luncheon together. It was quite late by then, so we went to Chez Francois and had a big luncheon together plus a martini.

---

40   That was the opening on the Board to which Anne had been hoping to be named. Mike Feldman's prediction on March 8th about what was required receive the appointment seems to have been fulfilled.
41   This refers to Anne and her two sisters Clara (Rolands) and Jan.
42   Almira Stevenson, Anne's colleague at the NLRB.

Jules called me after I got home to say he would be working late but would be home for supper. Just as well that I had a large late luncheon. No mail from Ira for a few days now. It is not an unreasonable period, certainly, but he has spoiled us by being such a frequent letter writer.

Wednesday, March 24
We came down together. After work I walked over to Jules' office. Later we picked up the car, and then Bill Levy at his office, and went to Hogate's, where we met Florence and Arthur Gang, and had a very enjoyable dinner. Then to the Arena Theater. Ruth [i.e. Levy] joined us there during the first intermission as she had classes this evening. The entire Book Club was there except the Jaffes – who had turned their tickets over to the Hillers. The play was "He Who Gets Slapped." It was not very good but we did see it through. The Middlemans and the Zanoffs left before it was completed. Long lovely cheerful letter from Ira.

Thursday, March 25[43]
I overslept – apparently forgot to set the alarm. Jules slept later, so I went ahead, without breakfast, via Carter Barron. Had breakfast later in the drugstore. Joined by various individuals, including Art Leff[44], who asked me in front of the others if I was a disappointed candidate.[45] These people have a different idea than I do about keeping a confidence. He did tell me, though, that some very complimentary things were said about me at a recent administrative agenda, so maybe I will at least get a "15"[46] at last. Another letter from Ira, enclosing a copy of letter recommending him to a Dept. of Commerce official for appointment to an interurban committee, and saying some highly complimentary things about him. We are so proud of him!

Friday, March 26
Jules was leaving the Buick at Covington's to have some work done on it. I followed him in the Chevy, and we went down together.
A cool cloudy day. Looked constantly like it was going to rain, as predicted, but it did not. Meanwhile, discouraged by the weather, I cancelled my beauty parlor appointment, and did not stand around on the curb to greet the astronauts, Grissom and Young, in their Presidential honors parade, much as I admire these men.
Ira called in the evening. As seems to be customary these days, he was bursting with good news about his appointments to intercity committees, speeches he was making, and the chance that the office might send him to an M.I.T. seminar for two weeks this summer.

Saturday, March 27
Juanita came in. I am more than ready to

---

43   The Selma to Montgomery march (March 22 to 25) led by Dr. Martin Luther King, Jr arrived to the state capitol in Montgomery with a large rally, but there is no mention of it in the diaries.
44   Chief Counsel to the Chairman of the Board at the time, Frank McCulloch.
45   Reference to Anne not being named to the Board of the NLRB.
46   Civil Service grade 15, the highest before moving into the executive ranking system.

have her coming in on a weekday but she has none available. Jules got up with a very bad headache but went to the office anyhow. I did the marketing.

Ruth Levy called about —among other things — a joint gift from the book club for the Zanoffs' 25th anniversary. I declined to participate. The group did not send me a gift as a group, and some not as individuals, although all came to the party. In the afternoon I developed an annoying headache, but was able to keep going. Fixed an especially good rib roast dinner, and was able to eat some myself. Did not feel up to going out; however, even to visit Alice Jaffe as we had tentatively planned to do.

Sunday, March 28
Still had a slight headache today. Was able to get up and have brunch with Jules. We called Lucille and Louie because Jules had not heard from them since he sent them a draft of Lucille's new will. All was well with them. They had in fact written to us yesterday. Jules went to the office in the afternoon. I slept much of the afternoon – my best treatment for this headachy condition.[47]

Felt much better in the evening, but was too lazy to get dressed and go to see Alice Jaffe, as Jules suggested.

Jules talked to Mother on the telephone, but neither of us visited her. I would have if I had felt better during the day.

Monday, March 29
Jules expected to be working quite late so, although it was a rainy morning, I went down myself via Carter Barron. It stopped raining later and was fairly warm, so I thought I would scoot downtown, but the White House area was roped off because of the President's reception of the Upper Volta president, and I did not feel like walking around it.

Got tied up late in the conference with the Chairman. Got a ride to Carter Barron with Jack Mantel and Harry Kushin. Began to pour again as we got there, and I had both my umbrellas at the office.

Finally got home. Finished my supper about the time Jules called and said he was coming home for supper. What a day – after a sick weekend!

Note from Lucille and the itinerary for their planned trip. Sounds wonderful.

Tuesday, March 30
Jules had to take the Buick back to Covington for a small adjustment, but was afraid waiting for it might make me late, so I went ahead via Carter Barron. I had a case on the Board agenda with Howard Abrahams.

Got tied up a bit late on a rush job so rode out to Carter Barron with Jules instead of taking the bus. A note from Alice Jaffe thanking us for visiting her in the hospital and for the book. Called her to offer to drop by this evening, but Mattie said she had gone to a meeting at school. That's a good sign.

Announcement of Jane Friedman's marriage, and her home address in Rhode Island. Understand that even her parents were not at the wedding.

---
47   The migraine headaches which she suffered.

Wednesday, March 31
We came down together. Have several rush matters at the office, and am really being run ragged – knowing, of course, that no one really appreciates it.

Met Jules after work at the Avis parking garage. We did some marketing on the way home.

Long letter from Ira telling us, in writing, some of the honors and responsibilities that have been given him, that he had mentioned on the telephone last Friday. We did not often have occasion to brag about him when other parents bragged about the scholastic achievements of their children, but he is making up for it now at the beginning of what we trust will be an illustrious career.

Year End Summary 1965

An eventful year indeed, as far as Ira is concerned. Not all of it was joyful to me... but it has seemingly all worked out happily for everyone.[48] Ira and Sandy seem to be completely in love with each other, and the baby is adorable. I would have preferred a known courtship period, plans, parties, announcements, gifts, etc...But all's well that ends well. As for Sandy's conversion, she seems to be more observant of Jewish customs than Ira is, and, as far as I can tell, sincerely so. And Ira is even more ambitious since he married, works hard at his job and at school, and seems determined to be able to provide his family with a good life even if it requires some sacrifice for a while.

Jules seems to have settled down in a fairly comfortable, interesting, challenging, remunerative, pleasant practice. Having Marie stay so long has been a great help to him.

Mother has seemed to stay well, as has the rest of the family as far as we know.

The situation in my job seems considerably improved. I have not been given the promotion that I feel has been unfairly withheld for so long, but Zagoria is a big improvement over Leedom in any event.

---

48   Ira and Sandy were married by the family rabbi in Columbus. Just as Julius and Anne had done twenty-six years earlier, they had a small family wedding although Anne would have preferred a big one.

1966

Anne was focused on cases at the Board, and Jules was traveling frequently for his work.

In July they went to Geneva for the meeting of the International Bar Association. From there they went to Warsaw and a visit to Chopin's birthplace, then on to Moscow and Leningrad. They met with Russian lawyers at the "Friendship House," visited the Kremlin, and went to "the most magnificent theater we had ever seen, for a beautiful production of 'La Boheme.'" They also attended services at the principal synagogue of Moscow. About that experience Anne wrote, "What a pitiful sight! We and some other American tourists were the only ones in decent clothing. The local people were all elderly, all very shabby as was the temple." (July 22, 1966) From Leningrad they flew to Helsinki and a short visit of Finland, then to Paris and back to the United States.

In August Ira, Sandy, and David came for a vacation visit, which Anne enjoyed. Anne and Jules drove to Columbus for Thanksgiving to meet Ira, Sandy, and David. Anne commented, "David looked adorable, walks remarkably well and seems very bright and happy." Ira and Sandy had a second son, Eric, in December 1966.   -- RDH

Sunday, May 1

Jules got the front lawn mowed after brunch. Just as well because it was raining again later. We went to visit Mother, who seemed to be feeling fine.

Jules wanted to go to a movie after dinner, but I preferred to stay at home and watch TV on a rainy evening. We had an early supper and he went by himself to an early movie. I felt badly about letting him go alone. On the other hand, he likes movies generally far better than I do, and it would be quite all right with me if he went occasionally without me. Probably should not start such a practice, however, when he is already upset about the prospect of my traveling as a TX.[49]

Monday, May 2

We went down together. Another rainy day. In getting out of the car with my umbrella, purse, briefcase, etc., I apparently dropped my gloves. That was the end of them. My best black gloves, of course. And the diamond I lost is not covered by insurance – but that I could not help – I think.

Jules and I got our passports renewed by mail. That was a big help. We both need new smallpox shots before our trip.

Jules did not pick me up until about 6:00. By the time we got home, fixed dinner, etc., the evening was pretty well shot and so was I. Some of these frozen foods – what with preheating the oven, etc. – take longer than they are worth.

Tuesday, May 3

We went downtown together. The nurse at the office gave me a smallpox inoculation. Not raining for the first time in a long while so I celebrated and walked downtown at noon.

---

49   Trial Examiner for the NLRB, a position as a judge that requires extensive traveling to trial venues.

Mary Clark called – is taking the TX exam also on Saturday and was delighted to hear I would be there too. By coincidence, I saw her when I was waiting for Jules and she was on her way to the Lawyers Club. Asked us to join her for a drink but it was already about 6:00 and we decided to go on home. Decided on the way that, as it was so late, we would have supper at Irv's Corner. The food, strictly kosher, was only fair, but it made a nice change from cooking anyhow.
No mail from Dayton.[50]

Wednesday, May 4
We came down together. A pleasant day as I walked downtown at noon. Sent Sandy from Garfinckel's a lovely embroidered handkerchief "from David"[51] for Mother's Day.
Had put a rib roast on the automatic timer this morning, so we had an especially good dinner. Letter from Ira – all well, all busy, and David progressing beautifully.
Bill Levy called. Would like us to take Guild subscriptions with them for the coming year, but I don't want to be committed until I see what develops on the TX matter.
A beautiful evening. Jules went out to get some doughnuts for a TV snack – and to get out for a little ride.

Thursday, May 5
We went down together.
Pay Day. My check has been reduced by increased withholdings. Very busy, but took a little walk to the bank at noon.

50 Reference to Ira and Sandy who were living in Dayton.
51 Ira and Sandy's first son, David.

Jules picked me up about 5:30. We did some marketing on the way home as I shall be tied up all day Saturday and he does not want to have to do it himself. Juanita will be in, so he will not have the house to himself. I shall have to leave about 8:00 to get to the Commission building by 9:00, so will not even be fixing breakfast for him. Poor Jules – he is so unhappy about the whole matter. I am not altogether happy myself about the prospect, but feel that I have to do it. It will be most embarrassing not to be qualified. On the other hand, if I am appointed, Jules and I both will hate the traveling required in a TX job.

Friday, May 6
We went down together. Had a beauty parlor appointment but cancelled it – I just was not in the mood. Went downtown at noon but did not buy anything other than my luncheon.
The nurse at the office gave me a tetanus shot, and she and the doctor agreed that my smallpox inoculation was a "take."
Jules picked me up about 6:00. Suggested we drive around the Civil Service Commission area to see what the parking situation was. Looked pretty hopeless to me. Suggested also that we dine out to relax me. I would have preferred that he offer to drive me down. We had a drink and dinner at the Embers. He apparently enjoyed the food more than I did. Then home.

Saturday, May 7
Left very early. Finally parked by a 20 minute

meter near a special no-parking sign for today. The exam began at 9:00. We had an hour for luncheon, which I ate in the cafeteria with Mary Clark. Time was up at 3:30 but I turned my papers in shortly before that.

No ticket on the car, and a beautiful day. Juanita had the house nice and clean – even worked a little after time. A cute Mother's Day card with a reference to something yet to come.

Jules and I had a drink. Later with the Levys to O'Donnell's for supper with them, the Jaffes, and the Hillers. They had all been at a City College affair. Jules and I had had a bite to eat with our drink so were not very hungry, but it was a lot of fun anyhow. Ran into Vivian Asplund there, just back from a vacation trip in South America.

Sunday, May 8
Jules offered to fix breakfast in honor of Mother's Day, but it seemed to me we would both be happier if I did so. He helped, as he always does, Mother's Day or not.

Ira and Sandy called. Their gift, not yet ready is, as we had guessed, a photo. Hoped it would be of all of them, but it is of David alone. A beautiful day. We picked up Mother in the early afternoon, took her for a ride, and then back to the house for the rest of the day. Our area is a beautiful sight these days, with masses of cherry blossoms, dogwood, azaleas, tulips, etc., in bright profusion.

We had delicious broiled chicken for dinner. And I made enough so we can have it cold a couple of times.

Monday, May 9
We went down together. It had rained last night and this morning, and was a good deal cooler. It was not raining at noon but looked threatening so I was cowardly and lunched in the drugstore.

A number of people have asked me about the written exam. I avoid stating the problem too explicitly, and have not looked up the case on which it was based, lest I learn I was completely off base. Will be glad when this whole ordeal is over, one way or the other.

Jules picked me up about 5:30. We had cold chicken – very good – and dinner was a cinch to prepare. Watched a TV program with LBJ on his home area in Texas. It was very good although I fell asleep before it ended at 11:00. Must have been more tired than I realized.

Tuesday, May 10
We went down together. Mary Clark called me, very elated because she found the case on which the exam question was based, and she had the right answer. So I learned did the other two from the Board. I did not. We are supposed to be graded on our reasoning, not on getting the right answer, but I was terribly disheartened. Went to Garfinckel's at noon and bought two outfits, but that did not cheer me up as I hoped it would. If I did flunk, it would be terribly embarrassing. And I won't find out until after our trip to Europe. The strain is going to be very hard on me. Sorry Mary called as, in my ignorance, I felt fairly confident of having done a passing job. Slept very badly brooding about how I

got off track. Afraid it won't help that I am a "whiz" at writing Board decisions.

Wednesday, May 11
We went down together. Wore my new suit and my fur piece. Received many compliments on my appearance.
Ogden Fields asked if I wanted a ticket for the $100 Democratic dinner tomorrow evening. I did not. Jules picked me up about 6:00, and we picked up Bill Levy. Had drinks and a very enjoyable dinner at Gusti's with the whole book club except for the Middlemans. Then to the Coliseum to see the Bolshoi Ballet. The Middlemans joined us there with their three daughters. The performance was exciting and beautiful, we had first-row seats, and many notables were present, including Humphreys,[52] Gen. Taylor, and the Bob Kennedys.
Letter from Ira. David is wearing a brace on one foot, and Sandy has not been feeling well. They have their troubles.

Thursday, May 12
Jules thought he might be quite late this evening but I decided to go with him anyhow, and to try to get a ride home if need be. He got so busy at the office, however, that he did not go the meeting he had planned to attend, and was able to pick me up about 5:30. In the meantime, I am reading *The Rabbi*, which we got from the duplicate pay collection at the library, during the periods I spend waiting for Jules, and have almost finished it. Just as well, as Jules and the Levys are counting on reading the same copy before the book club meeting on the 22nd.
I keep hearing details about the TX appointment procedures, some that perk me up, some that let me down. Will be glad when the matter is finally settled.

Friday, May 13
We went down together. To the beauty parlor at noon. The NLRB golf tournament was held this afternoon so the office is very quiet and I was able to get a good deal of work done.
Walked over to Jules' office after work. He was ready to leave shortly after I got there. Offered to take me to a cocktail lounge downtown because he thought I looked so pretty, but I did not feel that getting my hair done called for that much of a celebration.
We went home, doing some marketing on the way.
Had been trying to reach Phillip Kan to have him over again. He finally called back this evening, and is coming to brunch on Sunday. Means we shall have to do a little more marketing tomorrow. And this is Friday the 13th.

Saturday, May 14
Bill called fairly early – he was picking up his brother-in-law Sidney at the Sheraton to take him to the new Pancake House for brunch and wondered if Jules wanted to go along. Jules did.
Juanita came in, very late. Had a toothache. I made it clear she should feel free to leave early, but she worked the whole day. She

---

52   Vice-President Hubert Humphrey and wife.

took a message for us that Lee Stanley had called. When I called back, Lee asked us to dinner tonight, some people had cancelled at the last moment because of illness. We had nothing planned, and I did not feel I had to stand on ceremony with her, so we went. There were two other couples there, all very interesting people, and we had a very enjoyable evening.

Sunday, May 15
Phillip Kan came to brunch. He had been asked to come about 11:00, and showed up almost an hour late, having decided to go to church. In any event, we had a pleasant brunch. Later took him for a ride around the Maryland campus. He had a car. Left in the middle of the afternoon. Talked to Mother on the telephone but did not go over to see her. It was a lovely day but I did not want to go for anther ride. Jules had some work to do in the yard. We had the paper to read. And, before we knew it, it was time to start preparing for dinner.
I have finished Gordon's *The Rabbi*, the book club choice. Enjoyed it very much, and Jules is enjoying it. Should have bought it and later turned it over to Sandy and Ira.

Monday, May 16
We went down together.
All morning at a conference in Zagoria's office. At one point he commented about "when" I became a TX, which I amended to "when and if."[53] This is being talked about so much around the Board that it will be terribly embarrassing if I do not get a passing grade. We stopped at Mother's on the way home to give her her money and to visit for awhile.
Note from Sandy, which we were glad to get it as it indicated that she was all right. But apparently the brace is bothering David[54] a great deal, and is making them all unhappy. Hope it does the trick in short order.
Jules finished *The Rabbi* and was very enthusiastic about it.

Tuesday, May 17
Jules woke during the night with a terrible headache, took a couple of tablets, and was able to fall asleep again. He slept late, but got up in time for us to go down together, at his insistence. He skipped breakfast and ate later at the Mayflower. He spent a good deal of time there as the ALI[55] meeting began today. We rushed home and had a snack as the painter, Mitchum, was due to come over at 6:30. He called to say he would be delayed until about 7:30 so we had the rest of our supper. He recommended, and we agreed, a combination of light and dark brown. The Harlowes wandered over while we were discussing it, and agreed that it should look well, and would be somewhat different from the trim on other houses in the neighborhood.

Wednesday, May 18
ALI discussion. Then lunched with Pachel, Mike Feldman, Bill Wise, and Jules. Pachel

---

53 Anne did receive Trial Examiner (Judge) status two years later in 1968.
54 Grandson David.
55 American Law Institute

was not staying with us as he had to go back this evening.

Back to the Mayflower at 5:00 for the ALI reception. In addition to the bars, there were lavish buffet tables this year, so people stayed longer than usual. The best feature, from my point of view, was seeing people I see only on this occasion. Roger Traynor mentioned that he had sent the Commission a very good reference. Paul Herzog never received the form. Charles Fahy and Charles Wyzanski were not there, which was a disappointment. The painters got started at the house.

Thursday, May 19
We went down together.
Payday so I walked over to the bank at noon. Walked over to the Mayflower after work to meet Jules. Many of the ALI people had already left, so we did not linger. Drove by a house an agent had told Jules about – the size we wanted and well located but older than I like. By then it was a bit late and Jules was hungry and we were in the neighborhood of the Peking, so we went there for dinner. The place was not at all busy, and the food and the service both were excellent. And, when we got home, there was a long letter from Ira. David is growing accustomed to the brace, and, in general, all seems well with them. We were surprised to find out that the painters did no work at the house today.

Friday, May 20
We went down together. The painting crew had arrived and started working before we left.
I had a beauty parlor appointment at noon, but my operator was running so late that I finally got irked and left.
After dinner we picked up the Levys and went to the Silver to see "The Flight of the Phoenix," a fairly interesting movie. Then to the Hot Shoppe for a cold drink, which we had in the car. As we had gone to a late showing of the movie, by the time we took them home and got home ourselves, it was quite late for us.
Leaving the windows slightly open because of the painting, and getting a lot of bugs in the house as a result.

Saturday, May 21
The painters arrived bright and early.
Jules left for the office – to interview the client in his current indigent appeal case – before Juanita got in. Jules gives up his Saturdays so the non-paying client won't have to take any time off from his job.
I went shopping in Silver Spring – not very successfully.
We both enjoyed our dinner – broiled loin lamb chops – very much, but we both were sort of headachy – probably from the paint – so we went for a ride. Stopped at Gifford's for sundaes. They were no good for us, I suppose, but they certainly did taste good, and I was feeling much better.

Sunday, May 22
I woke up feeling very icky. Was still in bed when Ira called. Sandy also was not feeling well, but Ira and Jules had a nice chat. I got up later, but ate very little brunch.
Ira mentioned that Louie had been ill so we

called him. Later Ellen called to give us Susie's schedule. The Levys picked us up about 6:30 and we went to the Zanoffs' for dinner. She had the whole book club plus the Middleman girls, the two Zanoff boys and the girl-friend of one of them. The dinner was delicious, and the discussion of the book – *The Rabbi* – was lively and stimulating. Altogether a lovely evening after the miserable way I began the day.

Monday, May 23
Feeling much better. Went down alone via Carter Barron as Jules expected to be late. Downtown at noon but did not find anything to buy in the little time I had. Most of the morning in Zagoria's office and most of the afternoon at the sub-panel agenda with Hoffman and Randazzo. Claire Edes called in the evening from Chicago to ask if Nikki could stay with us for several days while he looks for a place to stay as he will be working at Labor again this summer. It was highly inconvenient and he can well afford to stay downtown, but I could not refuse. He will arrive Thursday, and Susie on Friday.
Phyllis Schottenstein called. Susie will spend some time with her also. I hope to make it separate visits, not a joint affair. Tried to call Juanita. I now have three telephone numbers for her – but did not succeed.

Tuesday, May 24
We went down together. Had a case on the Board agenda with Eleanor Schwartzbach. We lunched afterwards at the Roger Smith. Mitchum has completed his paint job – delayed by frequent bad weather. The colors were suggested by him – tan and dark brown –and we were very pleased with the result. Finally with much difficulty reached Juanita by telephone. She will come in tomorrow. This is an added expense for Nikki's uninvited visit as I was not going to bother to have Juanita in for an extra day for Susie. I wonder if it occurs to any of the Edes that Ira never calls on them when he is in Chicago because they are practically total strangers and he would not do it just to save a hotel bill.

Wednesday, May 25
Mitchum was at the house in the morning – still had some touching-up to do.
Juanita came in, cleaned, did some ironing, and made up Ira's bed for Susie and a bed in the den for Nikki. A rainy day so I lunched in the drugstore.
Letter from Ira.
Home for supper. Then out to Hugh Jascount's house in Greenbelt, where the staff was having a party in honor of Sterling Lee's marriage. Most of the staff was there, plus a number of spouses. It was crowded but everyone was cheerful and the evening was fairly enjoyable. As it was a work-night, we had a good excuse not to stay too late.

Thursday, May 26
Did a lot of chores in the morning in preparation for our house guests. Went down together.
Should have taken advantage of the golf tournament awards luncheon to take some extra time at noon, but had too much work.

Nikki got to Jules' office about 4:00. They picked me up about 5:30. Stopped at the grocery store on the way home. Then home to fix dinner. By the time I finished clearing up, it was fairly late and I was fairly tired, so spent the rest of the evening reading. Jules did also. Afraid Nikki was a little bored with it all, but he is a big boy, with plenty of spending money, and self-invited, so I did not feel I had to make a special effort to entertain him.

Friday, May 27
Jules, Nikki and I had breakfast and went down together. Nikki took off for a day of apartment hunting, etc. Jules picked up Susie Schottenstein at the airport about 4:30, and then picked me up at about 5:00, and we went on home. Nikki had left word at Jules' office that he would not be home for dinner. We decided to give Susie a treat and take her to the Japanese restaurant for dinner, but she would have enjoyed a Hot Shoppe hamburger more. Then to MCJC[56] as I have jahrzeit[57] for my father. There was a bar mitzvah, so I think Susie enjoyed it. We stayed for the refreshments as there were a good many children. Home late and got Susie right to bed. Nikki was there – had got himself something to eat – but had not found a place to live. Letters from Ellen and Lucille about how excited Susie was about the trip.

Saturday, May 28
Juanita came in.
<u>We took off af</u>ter brunch. Dropped Nikki

56 Montgomery County Jewish Center.
57 The anniversary remembrance of the death of a family member or other person.

in Georgetown to look for a place to live. Then we took Susie to the zoo and to the new Smithsonian building, where we saw many interesting exhibits and a chalk-talk by the "Dick Tracy" cartoonist. Had some luncheon at the cafeteria there. Home in the late afternoon. I had left a leg of lamb and some baked potatoes with instructions for Juanita to start them. Had more than enough for Nikki but he did not show up or call. Susie enjoyed the meal very much and ate a great deal for such a little girl. After dinner we drove out to Wheaton to do some shopping. I bought Susie a pair of white gloves. She had an attractive white purse, and seemed delighted with the gloves.

Sunday, May 29
A beautiful sunny breezy day. We all had brunch together. Nikki stayed behind to make some telephone calls when we took off with Susie for the Capitol, the art gallery, and another Smithsonian building. Then back to the house. Jules took Susie out to Wheaton Regional Park for a while but I stayed at home and read the paper. After they got back, we had a light repast, and went to the McArthur to see "Born Free,"[58] which we all enjoyed. Then to the Hot Shoppe where Susie had a hamburger, which she enjoyed far more than the dinner at Sakura. Then home to get Susie to bed. She seems to be enjoying herself – does not want to go to Phyllis's tomorrow, and is not homesick at all.
<u>Nikki found an </u>apartment. Good!

58 A 1966 movie set in Kenya about a British couple rescuing and raising an orphaned lion cub. Beautiful scenery, strong identification with nature.

1966

Monday, May 30
Another beautiful day.
Phyllis Schottenstein came over while we were still at brunch. Later took Susie to her place in Arlington, and will put her on the plane tomorrow. I suggested to Nikki it might be a good time for him to move today to his new place. It was not yet available but he moved to his aunt's house in Silver Spring. Jules did a lot of work around the house, washing windows on the outside, putting in screens, and mowing the lawn.
Ellen called after Susie left–too bad. The Edes called Nikki at the aunt's while he was not there or here. Visited Mother for a while. Very relaxing this evening having the house to ourselves. I was glad to stay at home and enjoy it.

Tuesday, May 31
Went down together.
Meant to call Susie to say goodbye, but got tied up as soon as I arrived at the office, and by the time I had a free moment, she had left.
Herman Levy, whom I had called about an apartment for Nikki or his fiancée and her girl-friend, called back to say he had not found an apartment but would be glad to show them all around town, and his mother would put up the girls for a few days if necessary. Very generous of them.
Juanita was supposed to call about coming in one day this week, but no word. Probably would not occur to her to let me know if she can not come.
Rene Brand called and asked us over for an informal supper on Friday and to see their new home.
<u>Lighted a memorial candle for my father.</u>[59]

Wednesday, June 1
We came down together.
Had a beauty parlor appointment but, for the second consecutive time I walked out because my operator was running so far behind time. And I had the Brown subpanel agenda this afternoon, with 5 cases on it. Jules did not feel well, so went to bed after we got home. Got up about an hour later feeling much better. And, after a dinner of a luscious porterhouse steak, baked potato, etc., he felt even better.
We called Nate[60] to wish him a happy birthday. He was not at home but Bobbie was. Learned at least that Jo Ann had received our gift but was way behind on writing thank-you notes, and that Nate and Bobbie would be here for a convention next week for several days.

Thursday, June 2
We have made a "soft landing" on the moon. Hooray for us![61]
To the beauty parlor at noon – a different one. Did not have to wait, but did not care too much for the way my hair was done.
A long letter from Ira with some small photos of David, looking very chubby and adorable.
Philip Kan telephoned to tell us he was leaving for Hong Kong for the summer. Asked if there was anything he could bring

---

59 Yahrzeit candle lighted on the anniversary of the death.
60 Jules' brother Nathan, his wife Bobbie, and their daughter Jo Ann.
61 This was an unmanned landing on the moon, part of the preparatory explorations on the moon before the first human mission that was in July, 1969.

me from Hong Kong when he returned in the fall. I was tempted to take advantage of his offer but did not.

Learned today that Tom Ricci, one of my TX references never received a form. Wonder why, when he is a former chief to a chairman and for many years an outstanding TX.

Friday, June 3
We went down together. Had a case on the Board agenda with Eleanor Schwartzbach, and was in conference most of the rest of the day – the big-end-of-the-fiscal-year rush.

Jules picked me up about 5:30, and we went home, freshened up, relaxed a while, and then to the Paul Brands' for dinner. They are in a very attractive small house in Somerset. We liked both the house and the location very much. There were no other guests so it was a quiet evening but very pleasant and restful. And we went home at a reasonable hour.

The U.S. has two astronauts in orbit again.

Year End Summary 1966

The 1965 year end summary was the last one that Anne wrote. So, there are no concluding observations for 1966, nor for subsequent years. -- RDH

Jules and Anne in Moscow

1967

The big event was Anne and Julius' first trip to Israel. The 1967 war was June 5-10 during which Israel occupied the West Bank, the Sinai, and Jerusalem. Anne and Jules went three months later. As late as March, she was contemplating that they might travel to Hawaii for the American Bar Association meeting and go to Japan from there. At the end of May and early June, they made a short road trip to Montreal and enjoyed sightseeing and shopping. They followed the United Nations Security Council meetings about the war in Israel, and she mentions (June 11) of watching Moshe Dayan on "Face the Nation". She called him, "My idea of a real hero." By July 12 she mentioned that they were planning to go to Israel.

Bill and Ruth Levy bought an apartment, leaving their Silver Spring house. Anne mentioned that they, too, were considering buying an apartment, rather than air-conditioning their house. Ira was completing his master's degree, which pleased Anne, and Jules had a very successful year in the law practice.

Most of her entries describe the minutae of daily life from invitations, lunches, letters, gifts, and visits with friends. She repeatedly refers to her mother who needed regular attention from Anne to solve everyday issues from loneliness to groceries and medicine.   -- RDH

Friday, September 1
Down together. A beautiful day. Really shopped at noon but did not find anything. Eleonor "took me" to afternoon tea as a farewell and anniversary gift.
Letter from Ira, and an unsigned card we decided was from the Levys.
David Levy brought some snow tires over to store in place of the ones Jonnie took. Apparently we have become the regular storage place.
Went shopping at Wheaton plaza in the evening. Bought a number of small items.
No word form the Martin Polsters. Glad I did not turn Ruth [i.e. Levy] down flat for Saturday evening. The Polsters might have dropped us a note – after all, they raised the whole subject.[62]

Saturday, September 2
Juanita came in for a little while. Gave her some clothes and items from the refrigerator.
Anniversary card from the Zanoffs. Jules went downtown. I went to the beauty parlor in Silver Spring. A beautiful day.
Talked to Mother on the phone. Will get over to see her tomorrow. In the evening to the Levy's.[63] The Jaffes and Gangs were also there. Linda was at home but both boys have returned to school. We had drinks, including some champagne which the Gangs brought as a new-home gift. Later there was coffee and cake. An enjoyable evening but ran very

---

62   This was their 28th wedding anniversary.
63   The Levys, Jaffes, and Gangs were at the heart of the Sunday Night Book Club, and close friends for Anne and Jules for decades.

late. We were the first to leave – well after midnight.

Sunday, September 3
Ira called in the morning – had tried to reach us Friday and Saturday – to wish us a happy anniversary and bon voyage. They are fine, excited about a new home. A beautiful day. Took Mother for a ride and stopped at the Hot Shoppe. The Levys picked us up about 3:00 and took us to National Airport in their new Volvo. We took a National flight to Kennedy, a bus to El AL, where we found an orchid corsage sent by the travel agent.[64] Walked, had a drink, etc., and took off almost an hour late. About an hour later were served a pretty good dinner. The flight was smooth but we were unable to get very little sleep because of a baby who cried during much of the night. Stopped an hour in Paris. Discovered my wallet, with about $200 and my suitcase key were missing. It was Jules' idea that I carry that much cash against my preference.

Monday, September 4
Had a bagels, cream cheese, and box breakfast. Later quite a mediocre luncheon. Told the steward and stewardess about my lost or stolen wallet but they were amazingly indifferent. Told the airport El Al people when we landed in Tel Aviv about 3:30. Expect it was stolen in the very crowded El Al terminal. Have a very faint hope I might have left it at home. Took a terminal bus and then a cab to the Dan Hotel. The bellboy managed to get my suitcase opened by breaking the lock and to fix it so I can use it unlocked. We went walking, had a pretty good supper in the hotel Grill Room, and did some more walking and talking to people on a bench at the walk along the beach. To bed about 10:00, very tired, but off schedule and slept very fitfully.

Tuesday, September 5
We had breakfast in the coffee shop. Went walking and shopping – I bought a knit suit at Franchette's.
Had a pleasant luncheon at Zuckerman's. Later went swimming at the beach in front of the hotel. Found the water too warm. Made some tour arrangements. Did a good deal of walking. Had fruit juice at a sidewalk café. Inquired again at El Al if my wallet was found, although I am sure it was stolen, not lost, or – a 1 in a million chance – left at home.
Much to-do around the hotel for a big wedding. Watched some of it.
In the evening we went to the Casbah for a very good dinner beautifully served. Took a cab there and back, but walked along the beach after we returned – sat in the lobby a while – and, after reading a newspaper, to bed.

Wednesday, September 6
Our guide, Montag, picked us up about 8:30. Had a very interesting trip; although we did not care for him and the air conditioning in the car was a joke. We walked about quite a while in Jaffa, saw Roman ruins, a flea market, new settlements, the Silver

---
64   What a gesture.

agricultural school, and, in the Gaza strip, much evidence of the recent war, many strangely garbed Bedouins, women with large loads carried on their heads. Stopped at the kibbutz Yad Mordechai and at the Weizman Institute. Had luncheon at a very pleasant café in Ashkelon. Back to the Dan about 5:30. Paid off the guide – an expensive way for two people to go sightseeing.

Had dinner at the Ron – very good, an attractive place, and we were the only diners. Then went walking, had dessert at a café, talked to some people in the hotel lounge, and to bed.

Thursday, September 7

Had breakfast in the hotel. Left on a bus tour about 8:30. Found it all very interesting. Spent some time in Beersheba, had a drink at the Ein Gold Hotel, stopped in Dimona for gas, went through the fascinating Dead Sea Valley, and for a swim in the Dead Sea – most unpleasant, and left a garter belt behind when I decided to skip the hose. On the way back our excellent guide pointed out the formations called Lot's wife and King Solomon's Temples. Lunched at Shefech Zobar guest house in Sedom. Stopped on the way back at a Bedouin settlement, one of the first indication they may be getting weaned away from their nomadic way of life, and for refreshments at the very pleasant Desert Inn in Beersheba.

Dined at a chicken grill on Dizengoff Street, had dessert at a sidewalk café. Watched movies about Israel at the Hotel. Saw Abba Eban[65] there.

Friday, September 8

We had breakfast in the hotel. Then to the travel agent's to make some arrangements; to Franchette's to pick up my knit, but they decided it needed more adjustment; and by cab to Hertz. The driver gave Jules a receipt as Hertz was to reimburse us, but "forgot" to return Jules' pen. We are making a good many involuntary contributions on this trip – I particularly.

Picked up a Cortina, then our bags, then the knit, and hitchhiking soldiers all along the way. Stopped at Ceasarea to see the very interesting Roman ruins, where we had refreshments, mainly cold drinks. Met some interesting young kibbutzim [i.e. *kibbutz nikim*] from London. Stopped at Ein Hod, the artist colony, but it was closed, for siesta or Shabbos. Got to Haifa, a beautiful city, and a beautiful room in the beautiful Dan Carmel Hotel. Attended services and visited a nearby Yeshiva. Drove down to the port at night for a very good dinner at the Bilu Cellar. Then back up the hill to visit in the lounge until bedtime.

Saturday, September 9

Went sightseeing after breakfast in our rented car. Stopped to see the Bahai Temple and gardens. Then drove to the Druse villages. Had coffee and cake at the Beit Oren Kibbutz[66] – very pleasant. Walked around

---

65 Foreign Minister of Israel (1966-1974), pri- or to that long time ambassador to the United States and the United Nations. From the 1940's to 1970's he had a major role in shaping Israel's ties to the United States and Western Europe.

66 Kibbutz Beit Oren is located near the Oren Valley and the Carmel Nature Reserve national park,

in the old city of Acre, which we found especially interesting after *The Source*.[67] Stopped for a bite to eat on the verandah at Fredi's Inn, outside Acre, which we enjoyed. Then to Rosh Hanikra, the Lebanese border. All told a very interesting and enjoyable tour. Then back to the hotel, picking up hitchhiking soldiers returning from Shabbos leave.

Had dinner at Balfour Cellar, kosher, not very good. The bread, for one thing, was stale, as it had been at breakfast. No baking since Friday afternoon.

Walked in the town, which was very crowded. Then back to the hotel lounge for a while.

Sunday, September 10
After breakfast we turned in the car at the Hertz place in the hotel. It went right out again. We regretted several times during the day that we had not kept it. By the time we finished the red tape, the city tour bus had left. We took a private car and guide for a couple of hours to go to the Carmel monastery, Elijah's Cave, and the very impressive Technion Institute.

Went swimming in the afternoon. Had snacks at the pool side and later in the lounge. Spent a very lazy afternoon as we shall be making a strenuous 2-day tour starting tomorrow to the Galilee.

Had an excellent dinner, beautifully served, in the magnificent La Ronde Room at the an area referred to as "little Switzerland". The Kibbutz was founded in 1939 by immigrants from Poland and Russia, who had socialist goals.

67   A 1965 novel by James Michener recreating the long history of the land of Israel from Biblical times to the present.

hotel. Then to the lounge to visit with the few acquaintances we have made. Think we have found a couple to share a car and guide to Jerusalem.

Monday, September 11
Left our suitcases at the hotel and took overnight bags. Picked up a cab to the bus station, then the bus about 11:00. We stopped at Acre, in a copper working shop, the Arab market, the Jezzar-Pasha mosque where a few men were washing and praying, and then on to a very nice luncheon at the Dolphin. Then on to Safed. Shopped in the late afternoon at the Kibbutz Ayelet Hashahar. Had a very good dinner, heard an illustrated lecture about the kibbutz, watched a TV program from Lebanon, bought a Passover platter for Sandy and Ira, and enjoyed talking to some of the other passengers but especially to the bus driver and guide. The driver had been a tank commander and the guide a frogman in the last war – the driver's fifth, and their stories were fascinating. Our room and bath were far better then we had expected. A fine day.

Tuesday, September 12
Went for a walk in the beautiful gardens. We lost our camera last night but it was picked up and left at the lodge. Had breakfast and left about 8:30. Drove through much magnificent scenic country – the Hula Valley, free after 19 years of Syrian sniping. Rode along the Lebanese border and into ex-Syrian territory, with many signs of the war still there. Stopped at the Tel Hai cemetery, Banias, Capernaum to see the synagogue and Byzantine church, along the Jordan [River] and the Sea of Galilee.

Lunched at the Ginton Hotel in Tiberias. Drove by Cana and stopped in Nazareth to go through the Church of the Annunciation.. Welcomed back to the hotel with lovely room and basket of fruit. Dined at La Ronde with the Silvermans. Saw a folk dance program. Finally to bed, but not to sleep – probably too tired.

Wednesday, September 13
Left about 9:00 with the Silvermans of Montreal and "Doovid." Passed Meggido. The Jordanians in Jeneen noticeably unfriendly. Went through some beautiful and some very desolate looking country, at times side by side. Had an interesting stop at the Samaria synagogue, and a very good luncheon in an Arabic restaurant, Matam O'Gama, in Nablus. Went through villages of mud huts, refugee camps and Arab communities, deserted since the war. Were stopped from going to Damiya because of recent shooting. Did see the city and oasis of Jordan, the oldest city in the world. Saw the ruins of the Omyad Hisham Palace. Walked over the Tel Sultan, already showing several layers of Jordan civilization. And stopped at the Dead Sea. To King David Hotel in Jerusalem about 6:00. Walked. Ate in the Grill Room at table next to Moshe Dayan.

Thursday, September 14
We went on a bus tour in the morning, which took us to the Jaffe Gate in the wall of the Old City and then left us to walk. Saw the Dome of the Rock – magnificent. Walked into the bazaar and bought a gift for Timmy; up the Via Dolorosa; through the Church of the Holy Sepulcher; and to the Wailing (now West) Wall, where we each said a prayer, separately, as the sexes are fenced off. Lunched in the hotel coffee shop with an attractive Canadian couple named Siegel who were on the tour. Then went with them by cab to the Rockefeller Museum in former Jordan. Found it quite interesting. We took a cab back to our hotel. Later to dinner at the Moriah – very good and quite inexpensive. Our hotel room has tremendous space, a wonderful view of the gardens and the old wall, but half the time no hot water.

Friday, September 15
Took another morning bus tour. Drove through some of the better residential areas. Stopped at the Kennedy Memorial, which I found impressive. Stopped at the Hadassah Hospital. Saw the Chagall windows[68] there – had seen them on display in New York before they were sent to Israel. Stopped at the Memorial to the Martyrs – deeply touching – and at the Herzl Memorial and others. Involved much walking.
Lunched in the hotel coffee shop.
 Then to the Youth Center for an entertaining talk on synagogues, and the on a tour of four different types of synagogues – all rather poor and depressing in my opinion. Had dinner again at the Moriah, with dessert and tea at our coffee shop. Complimentary individual bottles of musatel from the hotel.

68   Twelve stained glass windows with Judaic symbols and designed by painter Marc Chagall located in the Abbell Synagogue at the Hadassah Ein Kerem Hospital, Jerusalem.

Saturday, September 16
In the morning a guide took a group of us, walking (no cars allowed there), to services at an ultra orthodox Hasidic synagogue. It was quite a sight and sound!

Afterwards some of us dropped out of the rest of the tour and went to the Israel Museum. Saw the Billy Rose sculpture garden, the Dead Sea Scrolls in the Dome of the Book, and as many of the museum exhibits as we could, and were deeply impressed by it all. Later lunched in the hotel coffee shop with the Segals, an attractive couple from Montreal.

In the late afternoon to a lecture at the Ezry Gallery about the synagogue tour. Then took a cab to the Gondola, where we had a pretty good dinner. Walked around in the very crowded downtown area, then took a cab back. Visited with acquaintances in the lounge. A beautiful evening, the moon almost full.

Sunday, September 17
On a bus tour in the morning. Saw many Jewish graves shockingly desecrated by the Jordanians. Stopped at the Spring of Shiloah, where several children were drawing water; Gethsemane, the Tomb of Mary, Tomb of the Kings, Mount of Olives and Mount Scopes. Lunched in the hotel bar with Segals of Montreal.

On another tour to Bethlehem. Stopped at the Tomb of Rachel. To Hebron to see the Tombs of the Patriarchs, a relatively large clean Aral bazaar, a glass factory, and, back in Bethlehem, the Church of the Nativity. Bus to downtown. At a very interesting little shop called Baruch's bought yarmulkes, taluses [*tallitim*],[69] a mezuzah, and a pair of slippers. Then to Fink's for a rather good dinner and conversation with people at the next table. Back to the hotel to have dessert, read the paper, and rest my poor abused feet.

Monday, September 18
Checked out after breakfast. Took a cab downtown, then a cheroot [*sherut* or shared taxi] to Tel Aviv. Only three other passengers, one a lawyer named Ayon, who had gone to school in the U.S., and who appointed himself sightseeing guide, which made the trip very pleasant. Cab to Dan Hotel. Went out to do some errands, but it was siesta time. Later to Fanchette's to have an adjustment made-almost bought another outfit. Then to the travel agent, but found the flights to Eilat, which Jules was very anxious to make, were completely booked for the days we were free. Back to the hotel. My ankle is bothering me considerably so we had supper in the Grill Room. The Segals came over and joined us – they are at the Sheraton now. Saw Moshe Dayan at the hotel. Jules and I took a walk on Dizengoff Street later – I hobbling along by then but still trying to get ahead.

Tuesday, September 19
After breakfast at the hotel, we went shopping. Bought a number of gift souvenirs. Checked out about noon. Barbara Segal stopped by just before we took off by bus for Sharon, the resort hotel where we are to rest up from all the sightseeing. We went for a swim in the

---

69 A *tallit*, or prayer shawl worn by men.

sea. Very refreshing, but it was difficult for me with my bum ankle to walk in the sand and to stand in the surf. This is a place to rest all right. We had tea in the lounge, sat around the lobby, read, did some laundry, sat on our verandah, had dinner, sat around the lounge some more, and went to bed early, largely for lack of anything else to do. Cannot even walk back and forth to our room as Jules insisted on the more expensive, which happens to be farther from everything.

Wednesday, September 20
Went to the beach after breakfast. Back about noon. Made the mistake of going to the dairy bar for luncheon – so many choices on the buffet, and so good, that we both ate far more than we had intended. Back to the beach in the afternoon. Cannot tell whether my ankle is better or worse as a result. Later we took a bus to Tel Aviv. Ran into the Segals, who presented me with a charming pottery bell and Jules with a booklet about the 6-day war. We had a delicious and delightful dinner with them in the Maccabean Room at the Sheraton. They had an engagement later and so did we – with Danny Jacobson, whom we knew from IBA meetings. He took us to visit some relatives. Very pleasant. Later back to the Sharon by bus.

Thursday, September 21
We went to the beach shortly after breakfast, and stayed a few hours. I spent little time in the water, which was delightful, because, with my bum ankle, I fall easily and have difficulty getting up. Jules spent a good deal of time in the water, in the sun when I was in the shade, and stayed at the beach after I left. By evening he realized he had a painful sunburn.

After dinner – which was pretty bad – there was an Israeli song and dance program. It was pretty amateurish, but watching it was something to do. Jules went back to the room about halfway through the program – too uncomfortable with his sunburn to sit through it. He bought a paperback of Malamud's *The Fixer* to read.

Friday, September 22
After breakfast we took the bus to the Accadia, the nearby resort hotel which is in the Dan chain. It had lovely shops, and we bought a number of things there. Jules coaxed me to buy some jewelry for myself, but I was still too conscious of having lost almost $200. Ran into the Engels, whom we had met in Jerusalem and who visited us at the Sharon. Smeared Jules with the sunburn cream we bought. Went down to the beach, Jules to sit in the shade and I to go wading only. Meanwhile our stuff was moved to a first-floor room, which I had wanted to take in the first place because of my ankle. Jules attended services at the hotel. Back to the Accadia by bus for dinner with the Engels – Dutch treat. They are pleasant people. Back to the Sharon by bus. A good night bar of chocolate for each of us in the room.

Saturday, September 23
We went to the beach after breakfast. Jules kept a jersey on and went wading only.

Too bad, but it seemed best in view of his sunburn, which is better. The beach was extremely crowded – everyone spending his Shabbos holiday there. The Segals called to say goodbye – and to remind us of an Israeli girl who will be visiting us shortly.

Jules and I both feel regretful at leaving Israel and the Sharon. Spend a good deal of time just looking at our favorite views there.

Got most of our packing done this evening, and settled our accounts with the Sharon so we could get an early start tomorrow morning. Left a call for 5:00, went to bed early, but could not fall asleep on this schedule.

Sunday, September 24
Left by cab at 6:00. Bought some chocolates at the airport. Left at 8:00. Again had seats by ourselves. A beautiful day – fine views of Greek islands, Florence, Genoa, the Alps, and Paris, where we stopped. Bought more souvenirs. A lovely trip. Ate much of the time. Through customs without difficulty. Had to wait about an hour for the Washington plane. Bill and Ruth were at the airport and took us home. My wallet was not at home. Pretty sure I know when it was "lifted" in New York, but that is small comfort for a loss of almost $200, some keys, but, fortunately, no credit cards as far as I can tell. Unpacked, did some laundry, and looked through the mail. Should have done some grocery shopping – the Levys offered to stop – but I was too tired and had too much to do in the house.

Monday, September 25
We were both up very early. Stopped at the Hot Shoppe in Silver Spring for breakfast. Cordially greeted at the office, and had to answer many questions about the trip. Found the check I left for Zagoria for the parking place had been returned to me. Lunched with Marion Ladwig – in a hurry - and then to the bank and to the beauty parlor. Called Ira and Sandy. All was well. They are flying in on Saturday for a week. Tried to reach Juanita but did not succeed. Could not reach Mother, or the Rolands, for quite a while, and was growing concerned, but they had all gone to the airport to see Joyce, who had been visiting, off for New York. We were both tired and went to bed rather early. Seem to be having more trouble than usual adjusting to the time changes of our return trip.

Tuesday, September 26
We had breakfast at home – for a rather pleasant change. Felt fine – and in fact, had been congratulating myself on not having been ill on the entire trip – when I was hit with a sudden and intense headache. Went to luncheon at Laffal's with Eleanor, but could barely talk or eat. She did enough talking for both of us, and ate much of my luncheon as well as her own.

Postcard from Bobbie and Nate, on a vacation trip in Canada.

Reached Juanita. Her niece is ill. She will call tomorrow about when she can come. Our high-holiday tickets from MCJC.[70] Pretty bad. Jules was so upset he went tearing off to MCJC. No one was there so he came home, and later went over again, and again nobody was there. Too bad, with Ira and Sandy going with us.

---

70   Rosh Hashanah and Yom Kippur services at Montgomery County Jewish Center.

Wednesday, September 27

Went down together. Jules called MCJC on the phone. We had misunderstood the marking on the tickets, which are all right. A pleasant day. Took a pleasant walk by myself at noon. Went marketing on the way home. No word from Juanita. New Year's card from the Michaels. We still seem to be having trouble getting adjusted to the time change. Get very sleepy early at night, go to bed early, and then are wakeful very early in the morning.

The 30th anniversary of my coming to work at the Board –and of my meeting Jules. I stayed too long at the Board. Don't appreciate as I should how well my marriage has lasted.

Thursday, September 28

Went down together. A rainy day so I lunched in the drug store. Leet offered me his parking ticket for next week, but I shall be out part of the time so turned it down.

Letter from Ira enclosing a newspaper clipping about the park plan he originally prepared, referring to him several time by name; a leaflet about the Dayton U. graduation exercises with a picture of him and a chap from Nigeria, the only ones getting a master's degree in public administration; and a list of other things they would need next week. We went shopping for some of the things on the list. Wachtel is moving to larger quarters in a new deluxe building on Connecticut Avenue. Jules is moving with him. It will mean considerably higher overhead expenses. No word from Juanita. Trust she will be in on Saturday.

Friday, September 29

Went down together. A pleasant autumn day so I took a walk at noon. My ankle and feet seem to have recovered from whatever ailed them on the trip.

Letter from Marvin Harmatz at the office. New Year's card from the Edes with a note commenting very favorably on Ira, who visited them on a recent trip to Chicago. Called Mildred Michael to tell her we would not be at the book club this Sunday. Called Ruth to chat with her – Bill is out of town. Jules and I had supper at Crisfield's. Then did a number of errands. Picked up a toaster-oven with TV stands, which I think will be very handy for us.

Saturday, September 30

Juanita called to say her sister was still ill so she could not come in. I pleaded with her to come in for a while at least. She arranged to have a neighbor look after the children and came in for a half day, which was a big help. I gave her some candy and perfume from Paris. Ira called to confirm his time of arrival. We borrowed a high chair and crib from the Grimes. Picked up the kids at the airport about 5:00. They had a lovely trip and looked and felt great. We had a big rib roast dinner after the children were fed. Then, after the children were put to bed, we spent the evening having a pleasant visit. Gave Sandy the bracelet, and both of them the various other things we brought them from Israel. They seemed very pleased. They brought us strudel and homemade preserves – delicious.

Ulaine Naiden, Julius, Anne, Neil Naiden

Anne, Jules, and an unidentified companion at a reception

Part VII

1968 to 1978
Grandmother and Judge

Anne Schlezinger was named judge of the National Labor Relations Board, based on more than thirty years of experience as a lawyer in the same institution. References to the cases that she was hearing become more detailed after 1968, and she traveled extensively to preside over cases. Anne was 58 years old when she was named Trial Examiner, then in 1972 (age 62) her title was changed to Administrative Law Judge. NLRB Administrative Law Judges work with the same guidelines as the United States District Court judges.

During these years Anne led a hectic professional life, and she was a proud mother grandmother. She delighted in Ira's success as a planner and administrator in the health field, making frequent references to his achievements both locally and on the national scene. She waited for the Sunday telephone calls from Tulsa, where Ira and his family lived. She asked for cases when possible in Tulsa to spend time with them. Anne was an interesting mix between strict trial judge and caring grandmother.

When she was in the office in Washington, her frequent lunch companions were Mira (Almira) Stevenson, Jenny Sarrica, and Fannie Boyls, the latter her oldest friend in the NLRB. In the early years at the NLRB her lunch companions were normally men, largely because there were few professional women. By the 1970's more women were named to professional positions in the NLRB. As a result she worked on cases more often with women, and they frequently lunched together. She still had lunch on occasion with men colleagues, but her network of professional colleagues include more women.

In 1973 Anne and Jules bought an apartment closer to downtown, which made their lives easier. They no longer had to care for the larger house and distance was less of a problem. They were nostalgic about selling the house that had been their home for twenty-four years, the home where Ira had grown up, and where they had established a good set of friends. Anne rarely had the assistance of a maid at this time, so she normally prepared dinner unless they ate out. She frequently made hamburgers that Jules called "Anneburgers", a term that appears more and more frequently in her entries.

Jules' office was across the street from the Mayflower Hotel in Washington, which became an occasional meeting place for them. During this period Jules' law firm merged with the Morgan, Lewis, and Backius, a large Philadelphia mainline law firm.

Anne enjoyed dressing well and being admired for the way she looked. On January 31 she wrote, "Warm enough that I wore my red antelope coat - still more admired than my mink."

-- Ron Duncan Hart

Diaries. 1968 Through 1978.

1968

Anne and Jules started the year with a trip to Dayton, Ohio to visit Ira and Sandy and their children, David and Eric. Their days were busy with the children, and at night the four adults would go out for dinner or on one occasion to the movies to see "The Graduate".

Martin Luther King, Jr. was assassinated on April 4 in Memphis, and they heard about it in the evening. Jules' brother Nate and wife Bobbie arrived that same night for a visit, and they stayed listening and discussing the news of the assassination. Dr. King's funeral was on Tuesday, April 9th, Anne's fifty-eighth birthday.

Bobby Kennedy was assassinated in June, bringing another shock.

In April Anne and Jules installed central airconditioning in the house in preparation for the summer. In April she also read Oscar Lewis' book *The Children of Sanchez* about poverty in Mexico City. His theory of the "culture of poverty" had been widely discussed during the 1960's. President Johnson's "War on Poverty" program had generated interest in understanding poverty with the thought it could be solved. Lewis' writings made important contributions to this discussion.

On Friday, June 7 Anne was sworn in as a Trial Examiner with the Board; it was the same day as her father's *yahrzeit* (the anniversary of his death). They went to services that night to say kaddish for her father. Later that month she attended a conference in Williamsburg on legal issues as a representative of the Board.

That summer they saw stage productions of "Fiddler on the Roof" and "Man of La Mancha," which Anne wrote about enjoying very much.

That August Anne and Jules traveled to Rio de Janeiro where they stayed in the Copacabana Palace. They also visited Sao Paulo before going to Buenos Aires and on to Peru. They traveled with Neil and Ulaine Naiden. Neil was the newest partner in their law firm, and part of the trip was for business purposes. While they were on the trip, the Soviet Union invaded and occupied Czechoslovakia.

Sam Zagoria was Anne's supervisor at the Board during this time, and she worked well with him. -- RDH

Thursday, May 16
We went down together. I parked the car after dropping Jules at the office. He went to Philadelphia later by train with Naiden. When they got back in the evening, Naiden had a car downtown and brought Jules home about 7:30. I had eaten but fixed some supper for Jules. He had talked to Nate and Bobbie on the phone. The birthday celebration for Nate is still evidently a secret from Nate. Quite late in the evening I got a telephone call from Ogden Fields, who said the Board had met late in the afternoon to make its TX selections, that Zagoria had given me a big boost, and that I had been selected and would be told officially tomorrow.

Friday, May 17
Lock told me I had been selected as a TX. Zagoria was not coming in today so called Welles last night, and Welles was not coming in today so asked Lock to deliver the message. Later I got word from the personnel office that the appointment would be effective June 17.[1] Had my hair done at noon I had Leet's parking ticket, so dropped Jules this morning. Picked him up about 5:00 and we did some marketing on the way home. Took Ruth, Bill and Johnnie Levy[2] to Giffords to celebrate my TX appointment. Ira called to see if my Mother's Day gift had arrived. Eric has had another bad fall and cut face and both boys were exposed to infectious hepatitis.

Saturday, May 18
My Mother's Day gift arrived, a week late – 6 handsome coffee mugs. And Juanita came in, a week late – and gave the house a good cleaning. Discovered we have termites in the house. Called a few exterminators but all were too busy even to talk about the problem. At Mildred Michael's suggestion, we picked up the Dubits couple, friends of the Michaels, and Mildred and Mike, and drove to Chez Francois, where we met the Levys, Jaffes, and Zanoffs. We had dinner, and then walked to Constitution Hall to see the Bolshoi Ballet. Had seats – expensive ones – so far front that we could not see the dancers' feet. Afterwards took our riders home, and then ourselves.

Sunday, May 19
We called Ira – told him his gift had arrived and we were delighted with it – he seemed pleased, and is still thrilled about my appointment. We went to see mother in the afternoon. It began to pour after we left the house, and continued until after we got home. Jules was pleased – he had put down some fertilizer before we went. Jo Ann telephoned – she and Dick were here visiting some friends. They had planned to stop by, but had to hurry back to Philadelphia. We are scheduled to stay with them, when we come for Nate's birthday celebration. Jules told mother about my appointment. Mother called Clara, who called and congratulated me, and chatted about a number of things.

Monday, May 20
We went down together; I dropped Jules and parked in my garage. A number of people called or came by to congratulate me on the TX selection. Picked up Jules about 6:00. Directly home as he had an exterminator coming at 6:30. Said what we had were carpenter ants, not termites, but quite destructive also. Letter form Lucille. They are coming for the May 30 weekend, but are worried about the reports of riots, violence, and poor people's marches here. Joe Randazzo called me today on the tie-

---

1   At the age of 58 and after 31 years with the NLRB, Anne was promoted to Trial Examiner, a position as a judge to hear cases within the NLRB. In 1972 she would be named a full trial judge.

2   The Levy family, Jules' and Anne's closest friends for decades.

line.³ He was delighted to hear about my TX appointment. I frequently receive "regards" from him via TXes [i.e Trial Examiners] before whom he tries cases in the Buffalo region.

Tuesday, May 21
Went down together. Jules dropped me – I returned Leet's parking ticket. Mira Stevenson celebrated my appointment by taking me to the Roger Smith dining room for a cocktail and luncheon. Zagoria, Jenkins and Welles were there. Some came over to congratulate me. Later Welles told me I would be welcome to stay until I went on vacation, Zagoria having already cleared it with the Board. I would still be sworn in on June 17 as a TX. Jules has another exterminator out tonight. He confirmed the carpenter ants diagnosis. Went to see Dr. Roggenhamp this afternoon and had some annoying corns removed.

Wednesday, May 22
We went down together. Told Welles I would be glad to stay on until vacation time if it did not prejudice the TX decision against me. He is to discuss the matter with Bokat.⁴ Lunched at Marty Laffal's with Al Sommers and Bill Avrutis. Jules picked me up about 5:45 and we went to the Law Institute⁵ reception at the State Department. It was a lovely evening so we were able to enjoy the balcony. Saw a number of people we enjoy seeing at these affairs. There was an abundance of good liquor and good food. Enjoyed it all. Long letter from Ira. Still very enthusiastic about the trip to San Francisco and the things they bought there which are not available in Dayton.

Thursday, May 23
We went down together. More cool rainy weather. Almost 6:00 when Jules picked me up. Ogden Fields had asked for a ride home. I was glad to oblige. By the time we dropped him it was a bit late to get fresh fish at Giant as I had planned for dinner. Instead we went to Fred and Harry's for dinner. Letter from the Board confirming my appointment subject to security clearance and a medical checkup. Guess it is really official now. No word as yet about my being detailed back to Zagoria's staff temporarily, but I do not care too much whether or not that is arranged.

Friday, May 24
Went down together. A cool, rainy day. Jules asked me to go to a luncheon of the Law Institute today, but it was an international law section, I thought I would not know anyone, and declined. He told me later there were many there I would have known, including Wyzanski.⁶ I did not see Pachel after work. He came in just for the day. Letter from Barbara Segal of Montreal – whom we met in Israel. She is bringing her two boys to Washington and wondered about getting Senate passes. We can arrange it for her –

---

3   A special direct line to the NLRB.
4   George Bokat, Chief Judge, 1961-1972
5   American Law Institute.
6   Charles Wyzanski. Anne worked with his father's law firm in Boston originally, then she came to Washington as his legal secretary when he was Solicitor General in the Department of Labor.

through Timmy – and will be pleased to do so. We found Barbara and her husband Ralph – who is not coming – an unusually charming couple.

Saturday, May 25
Juanita came in. Would like to have her come during the week – before Louie and Lucille get here – but her son has broken his arm! We did some errands and marketing. Stopped at Hofberg's for a sandwich. Ran into Evelyn Braverman Herrup[7] there with her mother. They came back to the house with us for a visit. Naiden called to say Ulaine was feeling on the up side and would like to go out for dinner. We went to their house, had a drink, and then to the City Tavern Club in Georgetown for dinner. Talked about the trip to South America we may take together. Had a pleasant walk around Georgetown. Took them home and then ourselves.

Sunday, May 26
Ira called early. All were well and sounded very cheerful. They hope to come here for a visit over the 4th. A lovely day. Jules wanted to do some work in the yard, and then some work he brought home form the office, so I went alone to visit mother. She seemed well but tired. Fixed a rib roast for dinner – the first time in quite a while – and we both enjoyed it very much. We had a tentative engagement to go to a movie with the Levys, but I was just as well pleased when Ruth called and said they were too tired to go. They had gone to a late show last night with Jonathan, and are expecting David home on vacation tomorrow.

Monday, May 27
We went down together. A cold, rainy day. I was tied up all morning at a case conference in Zagoria's office. Lunched in the drugstore – first time in a long time. I may be selected for a federal TX [i.e. Trial Examiner] conference in Williamsburg the week beginning June 9. Sounds tempting, but that is going to be a somewhat hectic time for us. Bobbie telephoned to check on when we would be coming up for Nate's birthday. He knows nothing about it as yet. Juanita promised to let me know this evening if she could come in on Wednesday to get set for Louie and Lucille, but not a word. She is so good about coming or calling on Saturday but not during the week.

Tuesday, May 28
Went down together. Another cool, rainy day. Those poor people in Resurrection City![8] Lunched again in the drugstore. Decided to accept the invitation to the Williamsburg conference. Jules may be away much of that week also. And I should get back while Bobbie and Nate are still here and before the

---

7   A friend who Anne met in Baltimore at the Harvard/Navy footbal game on October 16, 1937 with a group of young professionals from Washington. By December of that year Anne was calling her the best new friend.

8   Dr. Martin Luther King, Jr. was working on the Poor People's Campaign when he was assassinated. One month later Resurrection City was built as a shantytown on the Washington Mall to continue his work for economic reform. It was built in the area where the "I Have a Dream" speech had been given.

Segals get here. Jules is very busy. Picked me up yesterday and today about 6:00. Stopped at the grocery store. And after dinner had to do some housecleaning, make up the den beds, etc. No word from Juanita. And no word from Louie and Lucille, who were supposed to telephone tonight to let us know how far they had come and when they expected to arrive in Washington.

Wednesday, May 29
Awoke during the night with a miserable sick headache, and was still very ill in the morning. Jules called the office to tell them I would not be in, called the beauty parlor to cancel my appointment, and told the air conditioning men who were doing some work to lock up when they left and not disturb me. Louie and Lucille arrived about 4:00 on a beautiful sunny afternoon. Yesterday in a downpour they had a blowout, and by the time they got organized they felt it was too late to call. Jules came home early – his office is in the throes of moving – and I was feeling much better by then, so we went to Mrs. K's for a very enjoyable dinner. Gave Louie and Lucille the gifts we had brought them from Israel.

Thursday, May 30
Some periods of sunshine but a good deal of rain. We had a big brunch, which everyone seemed to enjoy. Bobbie telephoned to let us know that we as well as Louie and Lucille would be staying at the Elkins Park House. Did some sightseeing in the afternoon- the riot damage, Resurrection City in a sea of mud, etc. Talked to mother on the 'phone but did not invite her along in view of the rain. Had a delicious rib roast for dinner. Called the Levys to see if they wanted to join us in having dinner out tomorrow. They were having some relatives to dinner, and urged that we stop by after dinner. I would like to show off their apartment but doubt that we will have the time.

Friday, May 31
Jules took me to the bus stop and I went down on the bus. Downtown at noon. Bought a dress at Garfinckel's. Met Lucille there and shopped with here a bit. After work to the beauty parlor. Then to Jules's new office in the Ring Bldg., still very cluttered, but it will be handsome when completed. To the Knife and Fork for a very good dinner. Then home. Letter from Ira. Invitation to a Metzger cocktail party on the 14th. Just finished reading the mail when Ira and Sandy called. All fine. Wanted to get in touch before we took off, and to greet Louie and Lucille. Spent the rest of the evening packing and getting ready to take off in the morning.

Saturday, June 1
We had brunch at home. Jules went out to pick up 3 dozen cheese Danish we were bringing Nate, and some stuff for us. We took off about 9:30. Stopped at mother's for a minute. Then on to Elkins Park House, after a very pleasant drive in Louie's Chrysler Imperial, and checked into our very pleasant rooms. Lunched at Stauffer's in Benson East. Then to the house. Gertrude and Ed were

already there, and Lynn and little Bobbie arrived a little later – all a complete surprise to Nate. Later a number of their close friends joined the family for cocktails, delicious and varied hors d'oeuvres, and a magnificent dinner. Afterwards some of the folks played cards and the rest of us had an entertaining conversation. A lovely day and evening.

Sunday, June 2
We had a bite at a Toddle House on the way to Nate's. Later to Jo Ann and Dicks' apartment for a very elaborate and delicious brunch. Joan and her boyfriend Nick Kass joined us for the day. Afterwards back to E.P.H.[9] to rest. Had thought of going back tonight but were persuaded to stay over. Later to the Locust Club for an excellent dinner. Back to the house to see movies of Bobbie and Nate's South American trip, which we found very interesting. Nate seemed pleased with the shirt Jules gave him and with his other gifts, particularly the cheese Danish. We made our farewells and went back to E.P.H., where we made our farewells to Louie and Lucille. Found Bobbie had paid in advance for our rooms there.

Monday, June 3
We had some coffee and a bagel in the commissary before Nate picked us up and took us to the RR station. Got a train due to leave at 9:20, but it was late and lost time at each stop. Had a second breakfast in the diner. Cab to the office. Walked to Jules' office after work. Naiden gave us a ride home. Had a very good dinner – cold roast beef, etc. Letter from Barbara Segal about her plans for her visit here. Invitation to the wedding of Sol Lindenbaum's daughter. Jules is going to be away much of the next week and I may be away all week. It is going to complicate things, with Bobbie and Nate and the Segals coming to Washington around that time.

Tuesday, June 4
Went down together. A pleasant day. Walked downtown at noon. After some on-again off-again talks, I have definitely been invited to attend the Federal Bar Examiners' conference in Williamsburg next week. Jules picked me up about 5:30. Had another very good dinner of left-overs. Accumulated a lot of goodies while we had guests, and are enjoying using them up. Florence Gong called asking more questions about travel in Mexico. Max Rosenberg called to ask some questions about travel in Europe. Meanwhile we should get busy and make our plans for a South American trip a little more definite.

Wednesday, June 5
Robert Kennedy was shot at a celebration of his victories in the primaries. Developed later it was by a Jordanian angered by Kennedy's pro-Israel stand. We went down together. Walked to Garfinckel's at noon. Bought some underthings. Had a case on the Panel agenda with Don Samuelson which ran a little after 5:00. Walked to Jules' office and he and Naiden were at the travel agent's mapping out our South American trips. They are beginning to sound a little

---
9   Elkins Park House.

more definite, and to sound very interesting. Mother called. Even she had heard the news about Kennedy, and even she, in all her self-centeredness, was deeply shocked to hear of his being shot so senselessly.

Thursday, June 6
The newspaper headlines had Kennedy battling for his life, but the later news on the radio was that he died. A great tragedy for his family and his country. Very busy trying to finish up work at the office but took time to walk downtown at noon. Very warm. Walked to Jules' office later. We took Timmy to Georgetown, went to Lord & Taylor's and bought a graduation gift for Jonnie Levy and I bought two pairs of shoes. Then home to do some household chores. Had hoped Juanita would come in midweek last week and this week, but she did not make it – or call – either week. Probably ought to change to someone who could give me more time.

Friday, June 7
Went down together. To the beauty parlor for a permanent. Was sworn in as a TX so I can go to the conference as a TX although the appointment does not actually go into effect yet. Jules picked me up about 5:30. We did some marketing on the way home. After dinner to MCJC for services as it was my father's jahrzeit. It was also Hebrew School graduation. And there was a special prayer for Robert Kennedy and his family. Made it quite a long service. We stayed for the Oneg Shabbat[10] afterwards – quite elaborate, because of the graduation I suppose. Received late this afternoon a large supply of reading material for the conference.

Saturday, June 8
Juanita came in – a welcome sight. Ruth called and we made a date for a movie this evening. Clara Rosen called. She and Duffy were in town for a niece's wedding. Had some down time in the late afternoon, but we could not work out a mutually convenient time to get together. Jules delivered Jonnie Levy's graduation gift while I did some shopping. Long letter from Ira – upset about the latest assassination – but otherwise all was well. The Levys picked us up and we went to the movie at the Silver. Then to Giffords. They invited Jules to supper tomorrow night. Very nice. Watched on TV some of the Kennedy funeral rites. Very sad.

Sunday, June 9
Happened to waken early and got up. Read the *Post*, had brunch, did some laundry, and packed. Called mother – talked to Jan, Cindy, and the latter's fiancé, who were visiting. Jules drove me to Jim Fitzpatrick's house. Henry Jolette joined us, and we drove together to Williamsburg. Had a drink with the group, supper at the cafeteria with some of them, and then to a lecture/discussion which ran to about 10:30. Mark Massell, the speaker I used to know him in early New Deal days. Called Jules. He had supper at the Levy's. Ira had called this evening after returning from a weekend in Toledo to celebrate his brother-in-law's birthday.

---
10   Food and conversation after a service.

1968

Monday, June 10
Breakfast in the cafeteria with some of the men. Then to the meeting. Complained to the conference arranger about paying $21 for my room. The men were all sharing $21 rooms. I got moved to a smaller room in a different building for $14 a day. Drove over with some of the fellows to the Coach House for luncheon then back to the conferences. Later drove with some of the fellows to Rick's in Yorktown for an excellent seafood dinner. Might have done some sightseeing afterwards but it was pouring so we called it a day. Called Jules. He had just come in. The Germans arrived this evening and he took them to dinner. Hope he misses me as much as I miss him.

Tuesday, June 11
Walked over to the cafeteria for breakfast. Met some of the conferencees there. Walked over to the Cascades conference room. Had a very dull session with a William & Mary professor. Showers at noon, so some of us took the bus through the restored area and back to the Cascades dining room for luncheon. Back to the meeting. Judge Grimes of N.H., who had dinner yesterday and luncheon today with the same group I did, was the moderator, and the discussion was interesting and informative. Later a number of us went back to Tom Garcia's room (he is the civil service chap in charge of the conference) for a drink. Then about 10 of us went to the lodge for a very good dinner. They dropped me later at my room. Jules called just after I got in. He had just got in from dinner with the Germans. Going to Orange tomorrow.

Wednesday, June 12
We had a free morning. It poured early in the morning, but, fortunately, stopped before I started on my morning of sightseeing. Did much of it by myself, helped greatly by the free historic area buses. Met a couple of HEW conferencees, and had a pleasant drive with them to Jamestown. Pouring again when the conference broke up about 4:30. I took the bus to the information center, saw the movie "The Making of a Patriot," and during a lull in the rain took the bus into the downtown shopping area. Did not find anything I cared to buy, but had a satisfactory supper, and, when it began raining hard again, took the bus back to my room, and, when I got bored with the TV, went to bed early.

Thursday, June 13
A lovely day, weather and otherwise. Walked to the cafeteria for breakfast. One of the morning speakers – a last minute substitute – was Sam Zagoria, who said some very complimentary things about me. He lunched with a group of us at the Cascades and then took off. After the sessions were over, Bill Ellis gave me a ride back to my room. I had several choices of people and places for dinner, but wanted to dine at the inn, so went there with Wabs, Jalette, Simon, and Meyer. Had a delicious dinner, with wine, deliciously served, and we all enjoyed it very much. Back to the room after dinner to get packed and ready to check out tomorrow.

Have to make an 8:30 session and take off right after the session.

Friday, June 14
A beautiful day. Breakfasted at the cafeteria with Blackburn and Garcia. Our session began at 8:30 and concluded about 1:30. Checked out, lunched at the lodge with Fitzpatrick and Jalett, and then had a pleasant drive with them to Jules' office. He was just back from New York. We cleaned up and went to the Stanley Metzgers' cocktail party in their charming Georgetown home. Did not stay long, but took off for the Washington Hilton. Then with Bobbie, Nate, Lynn, and Bobette, we went to the Tokio for dinner, which was good but the service was atrocious. Home about 11:00. Letter from Ira written on Wednesday and a thank you note from Lucille written last Monday. Got partly unpacked before I tumbled into bed.

Saturday, June 15
Juanita came in. Did some marketing. Later picked up mother, and took her to the Charcoal Hearth in Langley Park for luncheon, which she enjoyed very much. The Segals called – are at the Congressional Hotel – and we shall see them tomorrow. In the evening we picked up Nate, Bobbie, Lynn, and Bobette and took them to Hal's for dinner. Had delicious lobsters – for which little Bobette already had a grand passion. Afterwards to a little walk around the waterfront, did some sightseeing from the car, and took them all back to the Hilton. Visited a little while. Lynn went out on a date so Nate and Bobbie had to babysit or we might have stepped out with them.

Year End Summary 1968

The year 1968 saw political turmoil with the assassinations of Martin Luther King, Jr. and Bobby Kennedy, civil disorder in African American neighborhoods in many cities, anti-war protests and student activism in universities, and the student protests in Europe, especially Paris that led to the downfall of the government of Charles DeGaulle.   -- RDH

Jules and Anne at Macchu Picchu

1969

Anne and Jules started the year with a driving trip to Miami where Jules' brother Lou and his wife Lucille had an apartment. They shopped, had dinners, and visited the Everglades. The first day back at the office was Monday, January 13; Anne wrote," Back to work. My suntan was much admired. The best news at the office, however, was a copy of an order adopting my decision in D.M.A. Knitwear, my first case, no exceptions having been filed. I needed some reassurance about my work as I worry a good deal about it. Have been accustomed too long to operating as one of a team and anonymously. Now I must work alone and in my own name." This was the first case she had ruled on as a Trial Examiner, and her decision was completely upheld. The year was busy with cases from Texaco to Dyna Technology and others. Among the places she traveled to hear were Beaumont, Texas, Chicago, Detroit, and Albuquerque.

Her friend Alice Jaffe was in and out of the hospital this year. Her family news ranges from her mother to Ira and Sandy with scattered references to others.

Their August vacation was to Seattle, Victoria (Canada), Portland, and San Francisco, where they celebrated their thirtieth wedding anniversary.

While in San Francisco, Anne visited the NLRB regional office on September 3 and met people she knew there. Then, she wrote, "To the State Supreme Court to listen to some arguments." They went to Yosemite for a couple of days and then on to Los Angeles.

On the trip back they flew into Tulsa, where Ira and Sandy had moved some months earlier. They stayed for Rosh Hashanah[11] services on September 12. Anne was delighted to see Ira and Sandy's house and to see how active they were in the Jewish community.

-- RDH

Thursday, May 1
I dropped Jules who was leaving later for New York. Lunched at Giggi's in Georgetown with Jo Klein.
My picture appeared in the Federal Bar "Forum," taken at the Judicial reception with Judge Brown and Bessie Marglin. I was surprised, after all my fussing yesterday, to be rewarded with a Dayton assignment.
Just got home when Jules called from his office. Tried to call from New York to tell me he would be back early but all the circuits were busy. I picked him up, and we stopped for dinner at the Three Aces. He decided to go to Dayton also if I would go in for the weekend. We called Ira, and it was all right with them – even with Eric if we promised to bring some "play dough."

Friday, May 2
We went down together. I went down at noon to do some errands. Got a ride down with Hugh Jascourt. Could not get a beauty parlor appointment. Walked back. Checked out the matters involved in the Dayton case when I was told it had been called off. Told Jules. We decided not to go.

11   Jewish New Year.

When we got home, called Ira and explained. Spoke to Sandy and the boys also. Called Juanita, who was not in, and cancelled the message we would be away for the weekend.

A letter from Sandy. And an announcement of the birth of Jo Ann's baby together with a thanks for the hospitality note from Bobbie.

Saturday, May 3
About 10:30 I called to see if Juanita was coming in. She had not received my message last night but said she would come. We took off to shop for a toilet for the upstairs bathroom, and spent most of the day doing so. Selected one at Sears to be installed Tuesday morning.

Ruth suggested a cookout dinner tomorrow at our house as it would be Bill's birthday and he misses the cookouts they used to have at the house. Glad Juanita was in to clean up the porch. Ruth also suggested we stop over for dessert and a visit this evening. By that time, however, we were both quite tired, and would be seeing the Levys tomorrow, so called it for this evening.

Sunday, May 4
A beautiful day. We had brunch. Read the paper. Picked up Mother and took her along to Katy's and Gifford's. She also bought some things at each place. Bill, Ruth and Linda came over about 5:30. Johnny, home for guard duty, came over a little later. We had a drink. Charcoal – broiled steaks on the porch and ate out there – Bill preferred it to the air-conditioned dining room. Ruth had brought a number of items, including a birthday cake. We furnished the ice cream. Sat on the porch afterwards and talked until Linda became obviously bored, and they all left. Took us the rest of the evening to clean up, but it was all very enjoyable.

Monday, May 5
We went down together. I parked the car. Was told later that I had an assignment of a case in Akron for tomorrow. Went home and packed a bag and had some luncheon. Back to the office. Later picked up Jules and went to the airport. Took off on the 6:40 plane to Cleveland. Johnny Levy was on the plane and we shared seats. Had dinner on the plane. By the time I got my bag, it was after 8:00. I got an 8:30 coach to the Akron Tower Motor Inn. It turned out to be more of a hotel, with porters to be tipped, and a $14.56 rate. But I was given a very attractive and quiet room. By the time I unpacked, washed up, read some papers for the hearing tomorrow, and watched some TV, it was time for me to go to bed.

Tuesday, May 6
I had breakfast in the coffee shop. Walked to the City-County Building. The hearing was in a courtroom, handsome but rather warm, and no one was able to get it cooled. It was a warm day, and the hearing was quite heated at times. I lunched in the tea room at the nearby Polsky's department store. Ate very little as I was headachy. The hearing closed about 5:10, too late I felt to go back tonight. Walked back to the Akron Tower,

left my attaché case and took a walk, and then, having seen no place I liked in the area that was open, dined in lonely elegance in the Tower's dining room.

Called Jules. He had tried to reach me. He has been working hard and long hours. My absence is a help in leaving him free to work late.

Wednesday, May 7

Had a quick breakfast in the coffee shop. Then checked out and got the 8:00 coach to Cleveland. Had a long wait there as the earliest plane I could get was at about 11:15. A sandwich was served on the plane. I got a cab at the airport and was in the office about 12:40.

Jules picked me up about 6:00. We picked up chicken boxes on the way home for supper. The new toilet which was to be installed first thing yesterday morning did not get installed. Jules "raised the roof" so the plumber agreed to do it Saturday morning, a big concession apparently. Hoped to get a number of things done before the kids' visit but I shall have little chance to do any of them.

Thursday, May 8

We went down together. I parked. As I got out of the car, the seat jammed and could not be moved. I just left it. Later recalled I had been doing some laundry in the upstairs wash basin, and could not recall finishing it or turning off the water. Was worried, but could not bring myself to call the Harlowes again. Had a pleasant luncheon at Blackie's with some of the TXes. Picked up Jules about 5:45, the parking lot attendant having moved the seat with no difficulty. Went directly home – I had finished the laundry and turned off the water. Letter from Helen Lee.

Clara called – asked us to stop by for a visit tomorrow evening – to discuss their trip to Europe.

Friday, May 9

We went down together. The travel agent could not get the reservations I wanted. Should have called earlier in the week myself. And should not have agreed to the reopening on a Monday morning requiring that I leave on Sunday.

Pouring at noon. Would have liked to get my hair done, but did not. Lunched downstairs with several TXes. Attended a staff meeting in the afternoon – [Chief Judge] Bokat's usual pitch for more work, longer hours, and quicker decisions.

Picked up Jules about 5:45. Did some marketing on the way home – things he can use while I am away.

After dinner we went to Clara's. Had a drink and, later, cake and tea, and talked about travel in Europe. Lou spent a good deal of time in Europe during the war but this will be Claire's first trip.[12]

Saturday, May 10

The plumber installed a new toilet in the upstairs bathroom – that will save much running up and down stairs. Juanita came in – very late but she came. Did a number of errands.

Later Jules mowed the lawn for the first time

---

12   Anne's sister Clara and husband Lou.

this summer. The boy who was supposed to do it showed up when Jules was about halfway through. Ruth was out of town for the weekend. We invited Bill to dinner but he was tied up with chaperoning Linda and her date. He missed a wonderful steak.

We talked about going to a movie but wound up staying at home and watching TV. Later I fixed banana splits. They were yummy. A pleasant relaxing evening. I will get enough of traveling tomorrow.

Sunday, May 11
Ira called. We spoke to all four. The boys were excited about having gone to a movie and eaten popcorn.

We stopped to visit Mother on the way to the airport. I got the 4:30 plane to Chicago, a dinner flight. A long wait at O'Hare. Then back on a United flight at 7:05 EST, and, after a stop at Muskegon, to Flint at 8:55. Took a group cab to the Voyager. Pleasant enough room. But I was sorry to leave Jules, who was not feeling too well. And I was angry at myself for granting a recess until a Monday instead of a Tuesday, and for not making a reservation myself when I could have gotten a quicker trip through Detroit, rather than wait for the travel agent when the Detroit Flint flight was all booked.

Monday, May 12
After a cold night, a cool but sunny morning. Breakfasted in the coffee shop. Then to the hearing which ended before noon. The Company representative offered me a ride to Owasso. I accepted – it would balance my ride to Detroit with the GC [i.e. General Counsel]. But hated to leave Flint with its shops, etc., for Owosso with the rest of today and all of tomorrow stuck in a motel. Got a very attractive room in the Pines. Called the office to leave word where I was. Asked them to notify Jules. In the evening called Jules. Agreed I was nutty to let myself get stuck this way in Owosso. So I watched a lot of TV, did some reading, did some work, and felt very bored and lonely. Jules mentioned there was a letter and a package for me from Ira. Wonder what it is.

Tuesday, May 13
Still cool but warmer than it had been. But I was stuck in a motel room. Wonder if Kessel[13] thought he was doing me a favor by giving me this free day. Gave me plenty of chance to rest – and not much else. Glad at least I was at the Pines, where there is a fairly good dining room, rather than at the Mel Manor, where there are no eating facilities at all. And another interesting thing about this place is watching small planes land in back and wheel up into the parking lot alongside the cars. But it all palled very soon. There are aspects of the job I like very much, but I am getting fed up with so many absences from Jules, and doubt that I shall continue for the prolonged period that I might otherwise find this job attractive.

Wednesday, May 14
A lovely sunny mild day. Optimistically checked out, but cautiously reserved a room

---

13   Anne's friend, Thomas Kessel, who coordinated case assignments and was later Chief Judge.

for tonight. One of the motel operators gave me a ride to town. The attorneys discussed settlement and seemed hopeful of reaching agreement, but did not, and we began the hearing – I very disappointed – about 3:00. Recessed about 6:00. Maguire, the reporter gave me a ride to the Pines. Had dinner there. Later called Jules. He was a bit fed up with my absence. Juanita had called and said she would be in tomorrow. I much prefer to have her come when I am there, but did not voice any objection. And there is plenty of work at the house if only she will use a little imagination as to what should be done.

Thursday, May 15
Big breakfast party at the motel so no ride. Took a cab. Was first one there and the building was locked. But it was a bright sunny day. Pushed through with virtually no recesses and only a 30 minute break for luncheon, and got a good deal of testimony on the record. Then granted the Respondent's motion for an adjournment over the GC's objection. Accepted a ride with the GC – with the Respondent's sanction – to Detroit as I could get no satisfactory flight out of Flint. Left Detroit about 6:30 and arrived in Friendship about 7:30. Called Jules who had just got home. I took the coach to the Sheraton and he picked me up there. Letter from Ira with some newspaper clippings about him, and a pretty yellow slip for my Mother's Day gift. Ruth called to ask if I got back.

Friday, May 16
We went down together in the Olds which Jules parked. Found another assignment on my desk – just a 1-day case in Baltimore – but complained and got rid of it. Had my hair done at noon. Walked to Jules' office after work. Hank Cohen was there. Later we walked to the Madison to pick up Doris, and drove to the Four Georges. Had drinks and a fabulous dinner – Hank trying to outdo Arnsperger, with Jules picking up the tab. Then walked around in Georgetown. Liked Doris far more than I had ever liked Edie. They are taking off tomorrow for the Greenbier. Dropped us at the garage. The Olds would not start. Had to wait for a AAA truck. Got home very late.

Saturday, May 17
Juanita came in. We did a good deal of marketing. Had to call AAA again – the Olds apparently needs a new battery. The kids arrived about 3:30, earlier than I had expected them. David got sick on the way so there were things to be laundered right away. And I got busy preparing dinner – a rib roast, etc. By the time it was ready, they had all recovered a little from the trip, visited with some neighbors in the yard, and seemed to enjoy the dinner very much.
Mother called to see if they had arrived all right. She sounded well. Ira spoke to her and promised to go see her – which he would do in any event.

Sunday, May 18
Jules went to Katz's to get stuff for brunch. Ira and the boys went along. They also went out to the Wheaton Regional Park where the boys rode a train and horses. Later they

went downtown to take the barge trip on the canal.

Sandy has been having terrible headaches so stayed at home and in bed. I decided to stay at home with her and read the paper. The boys came back bubbling over with the fun they had.

We cooked steaks on the hibachi for dinner – they were delicious. Talked to Mother on the phone. Ruth called just back from a weekend in New York.

Ira went out to make some calls in the evening. Sandy went back to bed.

Monday, May 19
I went down in the Mustang. Jules took the Olds to Paul's. Ira got on the phone, had Sandy's doctor in Dayton call Dr. Porter on St. Andrew's Way, brought Sandy in to see Porter, and got a different prescription for her. I went home a little early and stopped at the grocery store on the way. Jules had won his first Government Contracts case. While waiting for him to get home, we chilled some champagne, fixed *hors d'oeuvres*, and got dinner started. It was a pleasant surprise for him and enjoyable for all of us. Between the new prescription and the champagne, even Sandy was feeling better. They boys are in great shape, eating well, sleeping well, and seeming to enjoy very much visiting with us and being in this area.

Tuesday, May 20
The boys got up and had breakfast with us while Ira read the paper and Sandy slept. They stayed home while the air conditioning people checked the operation. Then they came downtown, picked up Jules and then me, and we all went to Hall's at the waterfront for luncheon.

Got word that Jerry Williams had died. Poor guy. He had more than his share of woe. Bill Levy called to say Ruth would stop by on the way home from a Maryland U course about 5:00. I went home early, the kids all left for dinner at the Jacoby's, and I picked up Jules in Silver Spring, before Ruth arrived – Bill had been mixed up on her schedule. Sandy and Ira brought the boys home and went out again. Sandy is evidently feeling much better.

Wednesday, May 21
Had breakfast with the boys. Jules dropped me at the office on his way to a meeting in Virginia. Mira Stevenson called and offered me a ride to Jerry Williams' funeral this afternoon. Very thoughtful. But I declined as I expected the kids to come down in the afternoon. They did not get down until about 5:00, picked me up, parked in Jules' garage, and took a tour of Jules' offices. Then we all went in Ira's station wagon to Hogate's for cocktails and dinner. Sandy is apparently feeling much better. David went to the doctor yesterday with an ear infection but he seemed much better. Later the two boys rode home with us. Long letter from Lucille and Louie, preparing to go to Columbus for a couple of months.

Thursday, May 22
The boys had breakfast with us. After we left, they all took off to spend a little time

at Rehoboth. The Law Institute is in session. I met Jules, Mike Feldman, and Pachel[14] for Pach's annual luncheon party.

After work I picked up Jules and Pach and we went to the ALI[15] reception in an old Smithsonian building. Saw the Trainers and a number of others, and there was an abundant spread of food and liquor, so we would have been glad to spend some time there, but left early, dropped Jules at the office and I drove home. Ira and Sandy left as soon as I got home with John and Pat Hardy. I put the boys to bed – no trouble at all. Jules came home much later by cab.

Friday, May 23
The kids announced they were leaving Saturday rather than Sunday. Made various excuses but were firm. They came down to the office in the forenoon, I introduced them around a bit, and then we went to Blackie's for luncheon. Jules joined us there. Ira et. al. picked me up about 4:00. I had put on a rib roast, and we had an excellent dinner.

Later to the Levys' to see Linda and her date dressed for the prom. Then we all went to Gifford's. Ruth and Bill came back to the house for a while. Then Jules and I drove them home. Stopped in Wheaton on the way home for bagels, enough for the kids to take some home with them.

Gertrude Lewin called – had been in Dayton and wanted to know where Ira was.

Saturday, May 24
Juanita called – had a tooth pulled and could not come in because it was damp. She really let me down this week. The kids took off after brunch. We gave them some stuff to take along, including two bottles of very expensive liquor. Jules left a little later for the office, while I got busy with housework. Resent Juanita never letting me know she won't come in advance so I can do a little at a time instead of letting it accumulate for her. She knew I hoped she could come in a few extra times this week. Had I known they would leave today rather than tomorrow, as originally scheduled, we would have attended the Trial Examiners Conference banquet. Ira called about 9:00 – had a pleasant trip back – the boys were happy to be home again, Ira and Sandy no doubt.

Sunday, May 25
A lovely day but I awoke feeling headachy. Felt better after a while, and managed to prepare and eat a good brunch.

Jules went to the office in the early afternoon. I did some household chores. Then went to see Mother. She was in one of her moods – everyone was taking advantage of her, and Ira and his family came to see her just because she gave him some money, and their whole attitude changed because she gave him $10, and when Jan called that evening she would hang up on her, etc., etc. The book club meeting at the Middlemans' was on *I Never Promised You a Rose Garden*.[16] Surprised that Dana, who is living through such an experience, was present and participated,

---

14 A long time colleague who was later named Attorney General for the state of Pennsylvania.
15 American Law Institute.
16 A 1964 novel by Joanne Greenberg that is a semi-autobiographical account of a teenage girl's battle with schizophrenia.

and that the author of the book and the characters in it are all relatives of Ruth's.

Monday, May 26
Jules took me down, and then went to his allergy doctor for a shot. A beautiful day. Had my hair done. Sorry to do it when I was leaving rather when Jules could enjoy it, but was unable to get an appointment last Friday, and was tied up with the kids anyhow.
In the late afternoon took a cab to the airport – Jules would have taken me but was waiting for some important papers coming by messenger.
Got a Northwest plane leaving at 5:30, a dinner flight. Changed to North Central – what a hike! – and arrived at Flint at 7:50, 6:50 CST. Took a cab to the Voyager. Got a room like the previous one I had there but two stories higher. Unpacked, watched some TV, read and finally fell asleep.

Tuesday, May 27
A lovely day - sunny and cool. I had breakfast in the coffee shop. Walked to the Federal Building – turned out to be farther than I was told. After some question we were permitted to use a handsome District Court room, but were told it was only for today. Arranged for use of the bankruptcy court room for tomorrow. The hearing went along fairly well. I lunched at a nearby cafeteria. The GC rested and we adjourned about 5:30. I walked back – needed the fresh air. Had supper late in the coffee shop.
Called Jules but got no answer. He called me before I could call again. Had been at Mother's. Jan had called him, alarmed because Mother's phone was not answered. He found out her phone was out of order. The Rolands have left for Europe. We shall have to take care of her shopping, etc.

Wednesday, May 28
I had breakfast in the coffee shop. Then checked out. The desk could not get a cab for 30 minutes so I went out on the street and got one. Began at 9:00, recessed an hour at noon, and finished about 3:00. Trouble again getting a cab so the GC, with permission of others, took me to the Flint airport, where I had a long hot wait – in the 80's and no air conditioning – for my 6:05 plane. It stopped at Detroit. Served dinner between Detroit and National, which we reached about 9:15 D.C. time. Jules was waiting. By the time we picked up my bag and drove home, we got home after 10:00. I caught up on the *Washington Post*, unpacked my bag, talked to Jules and went to bed.

Thursday, May 29
Jules was having the plumber in this morning as the new toilet does not work right. As I got in so late last night, I waited too and talked to the plumber. He fixed it. Then we had trouble with the Mustang. With all that I was in at 9:30. A very hot day – up to 97 – so I ate in the building. Ethel Denny was in the area so dropped in to see me – brought some of the news from the other building.
Jules had parked the car. Too hot for me to walk to his office so he picked me up. We picked up some groceries as the stores will be closed tomorrow. Then home for dinner and a

relaxing evening of reading, watching TV, and nibbling – which I cannot do in a motel room.

Friday, May 30
Lighted a yahrzeit candle for my father last night but decided not to go to services tonight as his name was read at the services last Friday. A hot day. We did not do much of anything during the day. Talked on the phone to Mother and to the Levys. Will do Mother's marketing tomorrow as the Rolands have left for Europe.
In the evening we went downtown. Had supper at Gusti's. Then to the Fine Arts Theater to see "Goodbye Columbus." I did not care much for the parade of sexual activity nor the vulgarization of Jewish middle-class life. Stopped on the way home at Gifford's for dessert.

Anne

Saturday, May 31
Juanita came in. We did the marketing for Mother. Visited her for a while when we delivered her groceries. Did our own marketing and some errands, including sending a baby gift to Jo Ann's son. Fixed a delicious lamb stew, tossed salad, etc., but it was pretty well spoiled for me when the garbage disposal went on the blink. Left the mess and the dinner dishes, and we went to Roth's in Silver Spring. Met the Levys there. Also ran into the Middlemans with some friends of theirs. Saw "The Prime of Miss Jean Brodie," a more intelligent and less sex-filled picture than I had seen in some time. Did not go anywhere afterwards – too late and I wanted to get home and see about the disposal.

Anne, Sandy and Jules with David and Eric

1970

Anne had her sixtieth birthday. Her headaches continued to bother her, and her mother was becoming more difficult. For their thirty-first wedding anniversary they were in New York City for a dinner party given by a couple of Jules' clients, and a few days later they left for vacation to Denver, the Rocky Mountains, Mesa Verde National Park, and Aspen. Then they flew to Tulsa to visit Ira, Sandy, and the boys.

They were back in Washington in time for the champagne reception at Ohr Kodesh Synagogue for the unveiling of stained glass windows and ark for which they had made a "significant donation".

Anne was back into the office routine of hearing cases. She had lunch occasionally with Fannie Boyls, one of her oldest friends at the NLRB.

At the end of December they drove to Miami with Bill Levy and his son David. While Anne and Jules visited with his brother Lou and wife Lucille, the Levys rented a car and drove to Key West.   -- RDH

Sunday, November 1
Ira and Eric called in the morning. Sandy and David were arguing about what David would wear to Sunday School, and were too busy with that matter to come to the phone. But all was well otherwise.
We visited Mother. Then to Beth El in Bethesda for the Aviva Gang[17] – Ed Hord wedding, a lovely ceremony. Then to the Gangs' home for the reception. There was a large crowd, many of whom we knew, and we both enjoyed it very much. Bill wanted us to go to something at the Community Council this evening, and Paul Brand wanted us to stop at his house to visit, but Jules and I were both agreed that we preferred to go home and to stay at home.
As far as we could see there were no Halloween tricks. It was a pretty lackadaisical affair which was ok with us.

Monday, November 2
We went down together. Should hand in my Brooklyn decision for stenciling, but have nothing else on which to work.
Picked up Jules about 5:40.
Letter from Ira, which he told us yesterday he had written, enclosing a $500 check. Still owes about $2400. Thank-you note from Aviva for the wedding gift. And a note from a Walter Kaufman, who worked at the Board about 18 years ago, and used my name as a reference for a California bar admission. I have no recollection of him at all. Won't worry about it until I get the reference form. May not get one. But certainly will not recommend anyone I do not know just because he has stated that I have known him for 18 years.

Tuesday, November 3
Raining hard when we went to Parkside School to vote. Then to the office. I dropped Jules and parked.
Would have had a hearing in Tulsa this week but the case cancelled. Hope I get an

---

17   Aviva, the daughter of Florence and Arthur Gang, close friends of Jules and Anne for more that two decades.

assignment on Thursday. Really finished with my Brooklyn decision but have not turned it in because I have no other case on my desk.

Picked up Jules about 5:50.

We had lamb chops for dinner, one of Jules' favorite foods.

Called Ruth who is feeling much better. Spent the evening listening to election results and forecasts. Looks generally favorable to the Democrats, but they have lost a few major races to the Republicans, including some right here in Maryland.

Wednesday, November 4
We went down together. I dropped Jules and parked. Pleasant enough at the time, but began to rain late in the morning, and poured most of the day. A particularly heavy downpour at the time I left the office, with thunder and lightning although the temperature was quite cool. And I had parked at the far end of the lot. At least I was able to pick up Jules at his door although he got wet just coming across the sidewalk. I lost a pair of almost – new gloves in the process of dashing into the house with umbrella, briefcase, etc.

An appointment card from the dentist for a week from tomorrow. The day after the holiday. And I am due for an assignment. Life does get complicated for a TX.

Thursday, November 5
Went down together. Got long overdue vouchers on several trips, but the clerk who did them credited me with too much money and I sent them back. That means much more delay. Turned in half the Brooklyn decision yesterday for stenciling, and the other half today. Got an assignment of a 2-day case in Atlanta. Starts Monday at 10. Hate to leave on Sunday or get stuck on Wednesday, a holiday. Could have had a 1-day case in Pittsburgh on Thursday but had a dental appointment. Probably should have postponed it and taken the 1-day case. Jules offered to take me shopping this evening but I decided against it. Instead picked up some fresh salmon steaks at Giant, and we had a very enjoyable dinner at home. Jules will have plenty of eating out next week.

Friday, November 6
Went down together. A beautiful day. Went with Ivan Peterson to the Summer Lawrence funeral at a church in Bethesda. Later to the Democratic Club at the Watergate for luncheon. Back to learn [Chief Judge] Bokat and others had been looking for me because my Brooklyn decision is urgent, but it is being stenciled. Not so urgent that I was taken off the Atlanta case. And the Employment Office and a maid they referred were also calling – Vera Wright. Got a Board decision in my Baton Rouge case – affirmed with a footnote modification. Stopped at the grocery store on the way home, and then home for dinner. Had some picking – up and other chores to do around the house preparatory to having a new maid come in. Wish I could find someone for more than one time but doubt that it is Vera.

Saturday, November 7
Had about given up on Vera when she called, an hour late, bus trouble. Jules picked her up. She seemed to do a pretty good job, but was suffering from a head cold, and this made her seem sullen. Jules did some work in the yard. I helped Vera in view of her late start. About 4:30 we drove her into town – she will call if she can come again, had no phone, and is trying to get a full-time job – and then went to Georgetown to pick up the print we had left to be framed. Stopped later for a drink and dinner at the Charcoal Hearth. Then home. Tried the print in various places. Decided to put it in the dining room. It is quite large and had bright strong colors so cannot go just anywhere. Jules likes it much more than I do, although I like it better now that it has been framed.

Sunday, November 8
Ira called. We talked to all four. All well and happy.
Stopped to visit with Mother. Then down to Fran O'Brien's. After we got there Jules realized he did not have the tickets. Went home and back in record time. We ate a very quick brunch and got on the bus. Neil and Fred Naiden were present. It was a lovely day and an exciting game, but the Redskins lost. Back on the bus to Fran O'Brien's. Then home to finish reading today's *Post*. Did some laundry and other chores. Then packed to go to Atlanta for a case with a 2-day estimate. Jules may have to go out of town on Wednesday or Thursday. What a crazy setup.

Monday, November 9
Jules insisted on taking me to the airport; got there in plenty of time for the Delta 8:10 flight which left about 8:30. Served a lavish breakfast. Took a bus to the hearing room. About a half-hour later the case was settled. Changed my plane reservation, cancelled the hotel, went for a ride and a lovely luncheon on the top floor of the Regency Hyatt Hotel, a spectacular place. Then back to the office where I picked up my bags and went to the airport in plenty of time for the 3:50 plane, particularly as it did not take off until 4:50. Had a pleasant flight. Was served a "snack." Called Jules from the airport. He picked me up. I did not want any dinner. He did but preferred to have it at home. So we went home, and I fixed dinner for him.

Tuesday, November 10
Went down together. I dropped Jules and parked. As I got out of the car, noticed something was leaking and smoking. Took it to a nearby station and I was told I needed a new hose. Turned out it needed a new water pump which, with labor, anti-freeze, etc., came to about $55. Had Jules come over. He agreed to do it. Lunched with Fannie Boyls [i.e. her old friend at the NLRB].
Got my Brooklyn case signed. Met Jules at the station. He wrote the check and we drove home.
Pleasant note from Sandy, just about the most pleasant event of the day.
I suppose I shall be sent out again next week. Have the transcript in my Detroit case but it is a very short one.

1970

Wednesday, November 11
A mild but rainy day. Jules could not work in the yard because of the weather so we went shopping. I bought a winter coat at Garfinckel's. We also bought some picture books, and hung the print of the stained-glass ark in the dining room. It looks very well there except that a living-room lamp throws reflections on the glass covering the picture. We had dinner about 5:30. Jules left shortly after dinner in the Oldsmobile for the airport and New Jersey – left early in view of the weather and bad driving conditions. I offered to take him to the airport but he preferred to leave a car at the airport in case he came home late in the evening. Expects to come home tomorrow.

Thursday, November 12
Awoke with a slight headache, and it was a rainy day, but I felt I had to go down as I had a dental appointment. Then could not start the Mustang. Stopped a neighbor who could not start it either but gave me a left to Silver Spring. Took a bus and walked a few blocks to the office. Got a ride in the Board car to and from the dentist. And got a ride to Bisgyer's house with Curly Sommers, and a ride home with Paul.

Jules called about 7:30 from Knoll to let me know he would be late. He got home about 11. He tried to start the Mustang but could not. Did not want to spend much time on it at that hour. Thought it was not anything serious, but probably caused by getting wet during a great deal of rain while we were driving the Olds yesterday.

Friday, November 13
We went down together in the Olds. I parked it. Warned the attendant to be careful in view of my costly experience the last time I parked the Olds there. He said he would be. Found the radio left on when I started the ignition, and I was pretty sure I had not left it on. Picked Jules up about 5:40. We stopped on the way home at the Sakura for a very enjoyable dinner. Al Berg telephoned in the evening. He and Bert were in town for the weekend and Monday, when Al had some business. Asked us to lunch with them tomorrow but Jules said we could not make it. Told me it was because I had a maid coming in but I suspect the real reason was he hated to miss the telecast of the OSU-Purdue football game.

Saturday, November 14
Vera came in, again about an hour later than she said she would. Jules picked her up at the terminal, and later took her back to the terminal. She shows no appreciation for that service, and seems disgruntled that she does not earn more in the short day she worked. Letter from Ira with a copy of a long article about his work complete with a picture of him. Very impressive. Watched Ohio State on TV beat Purdue, just barely. Vera "hates" football. After dinner we met the Levys at the Apex. Saw "Lovers and Other Strangers," which we found amusing. Raining hard when we got out so, to avoid Ruth getting in and out of the car, in the rain at a restaurant, we went to their apartment for dessert. Great help to park in the building in this weather.

Sunday, November 15
A cloudy day. We both slept rather late. Were just getting up when Ira called. Talked to him and the two boys. David sang "America the Beautiful," and did it very well.
Jules did some work in the yard but the leaves were very wet to handle.
Went to visit Mother. Watched football on TV. Had excellent steaks for dinner. A lovely relaxing day until Lillian Wagshal [i.e. Anne's cousin, daughter of Sam Wagshal] called to tell us Mark Winkler died. I had called Cathy when I heard Mark was ill, and understood he was getting better. I called Clara, who will let Mother know tomorrow. Lillian did not know what the funeral arrangements were but understand he would be buried on Tuesday. Jules has people coming in from out-of-town for a conference but will try to arrange to go to the funeral.[18]

Monday, November 16
I went downtown alone in the Mustang, which started with no trouble. Jules was driving to Baltimore for the day with George Edgar to see a client.
A chilly day so I wore my new coat. Seemed good and warm.
I went home alone. Seemed so early compared to the evening I wait for Jules. He called about 6 from the office and came on home. He had been in Baltimore most of the day. Had called Sue and asked her to try to postpone the meeting he had scheduled for tomorrow with a number of out-of-town people, but found a note on his desk that she had been unable to do so. He will not be able to go to the memorial service for Mark but will come to the house later.

Tuesday, November 17
We went down together in the Olds. Jules dropped me and parked.
I got a ride in the afternoon with Sid and Lila Asher to the memorial service, non-sectarian, for Mark at a funeral parlor in Virginia. There was a large crowd. Afterward I got a ride to the Winkler home with Clara and Lou. There was a large crowd there also, a bar and food. Cathy was being very brave. The three girls were there, two with fiancés. Gertrude and her husband came from Boston and their son from Atlanta. Florence's son came form Kansas, where he is a city planner with a private firm. And Harold – whom I had not seen for so many years – was there from California. Jules came later. Afterwards we went to the Flagship for dinner. Then home. Mark had asked about us a week before he died but was too sick for visitors. Sad.

Wednesday, November 18
We went down together in the Mustang. I parked. It seems to be working pretty well now.
Still somewhat depressed about Mark's untimely death.
Picked up Jules about 5:45.
Received some of the savings bank insurance checks. They trickle in throughout the month. It is a nuisance because I have to

---

18 Funerals for family and friends begin to be more frequent in this time period.

keep records of those that come in, in case by the end of the month I have not received all twelve. Too bad when I made the payments all those years through one bank that the insurance people cannot arrange to have all the checks sent to me from one point. And this is going to go on for the rest of me life.

Thursday, November 19
We went down together.
Got a haircut and permanent, both needed badly. Lost a scarf in my rush. Also got word that my Detroit case, in which I have a decision completely drafted awaiting the briefs due Monday, was about to be settled. I am going to have to do a good deal of traveling in the next few weeks before I have cases ready for drafting. Was given an assignment in Chicago, a short simple case. Would like to get a few such cases to be able to get out some production. Vera was to call today to let me know whether she would come in on Saturday. Did not hear from her. Assumed she got the full-time job she was desperately anxious to find so she could arrange a real Xmas for her 11-year old son.

Friday, November 20
We went down together. Made my travel arrangements. Lunched at Blackie's with Fannie Boyls.[19] On the way back to the office it rained, hard, and we had no umbrellas.
Got a form issued from Chairman Miller, noting I issued less than 9 cases last fiscal year (I issued 8), and warning that he would

---

19   Fannie Boyls and Annie joined the NLRB at about the same time and remained friends for decades.

be watching my production this fiscal year. Then I got word my Chicago case was off. Got a stipulated case to do, which I dislike, a hot cargo case at that, which I hate. By the time I picked up Jules at 5:30, I had acute indigestion. Vera called us as we got in – tried yesterday, she said, but the line was busy – so I told her to come.
Felt better later, ate a light supper, and spent the evening reading.

Saturday, November 21
Vera came in, quite late. Later left quite early, explaining that she was very tired. Wonder what she would do if she did not get picked up and taken to the terminal.
We watched the telecast of the OSU-Michigan game, a victory for OSU, which goes to the Rose Bowl. Jules enjoyed the game tremulously, and was delighted with the victory, particularly as Michigan beat OSU last year.
Had lamb chops for dinner – very good. Stayed home in the evening – as well as all day for me – in view of the hectic schedule we will have tomorrow with the visit to Mother, brunch, football game, dinner, trip home, and then out again shortly to the book club meeting at the Levys.

Sunday, November 22
David called to tell us he had sent a note, which he wrote, to Great Grandma, enclosing his school picture. We spoke also to Eric and Ira. Sandy was not feeling well.
Talked to Mother on the phone but did not stop by. As it was, just managed to get down to the Anthony House in time for brunch,

the bus to the game, and a trouncing of the Redskins 45-21 by Dallas. Back by bus. Had a very good steak dinner. Then home to rest a little while before changing and going to the book club meeting at the Levys'. The book was *The Selling of the President* by Joe McGinness.[20] It stirred up a very lively discussion so that we all stayed a good deal later than we generally do. Suspect the Levys were glad when we all left.

Monday, November 23
We went down together. Got to work on the hot cargo case, a type of problem with which I am quite unfamiliar.
The weather turned much cooler during the day. Glad it waited until today. I picked up Jules about 5:45. Stopped at the grocery store on the way home. When we got home, found inside the storm-door an 18-pound turkey. I did not care to cook one that big, nor to give it to the Levys as we did last year and never got a smell of it. I had asked Jules to find out if Knoll was sending us one so I could pre-arrange to get smaller turkeys or something else instead, but he had not done so. This one came from Katz's so he took it back there. They were very gracious about it – gave him a smaller turkey, some veal chops, and the reminder in cash.

Tuesday, November 24
We went down together – in the Olds as it has a much more efficient heater and it was a cold day.
Getting straightened out on what is involved in my hot cargo case, it is a novel question so the Board may or may not see it my way. Seemed to be getting the same rash on my right hand as I had last year and a few times previously. Switched to using only Ivory soap, and using the salve Dr. Stolar prescribed last time. If that does not do the trick I shall also start using rubber gloves to do dishes and laundry, as the doctor also prescribed.
Not getting a flu shot as the Health Unit discourages it again this year. Hope I do not get a repeat of the runny-nose problem I had so long last year.

Wednesday, November 25
Were going down in the Mustang but had trouble getting it to start so took the Olds. Jules had to get to the dentist for a 9 o'clock appointment.
Chilly but not so cold as it has been. Walked to Adam's Rib for luncheon with Mira Stevenson.
Was assigned two relatively short cases, both in Milwaukee. It will be a cold trip but, with my use-or-lose annual leave, should hold me for a while. I picked up Jules at 5:40. We went home for dinner. As we are eating out tomorrow, had no great preparations to make. Jules wanted to go out or, if we ate at home, to have a turkey and all the trimmings and guests. It was so long since I had cooked a turkey that I did not want to risk it with guests expecting a treat.

---

20   McGinniss examines the role of publicity and image-making in presidential campaigns, analyzing the 1968 campaign of Richard Nixon by Roger Ailes and Frank Shakespeare, who argued that image was more important to voters than substance.

Thursday, November 26
A pleasant relaxing day. We slept relatively late. Had a leisurely brunch. Read the paper. A mild day as Jules worked in the yard and I did a few chores in the house. No word from Vera so don't know if she will be in this Saturday. Later went to visit Mother. She had a printed note from David thanking her for the money she sent. She was going later to Clara's for dinner. From there we drove out to take a look at Columbia, an impressive "new town," and then to the King's Contrivance for dinner. The food was only fair and the service quite disorganized. Vera was supposed to call today to let me know about Saturday. Did not hear from her. Maybe she called while we were out – to give her the benefit of the doubt.

Friday, November 27
We went down together in the Mustang, which started with no difficulty. Made my travel and hotel reservations. A lovely mild day so I had my hair done at noon. Was pleasantly surprised to find my lost scarf waiting for me. Its value was sentimental – Ira gave the scarf to me. Vera called – said she tried to call yesterday but got no answer – and would come in tomorrow, by 9:30 or not at all. Have no idea why it is so difficult for her to get to the Silver Spring terminal before 10:00 or 10:30 but tolerated it since it meant Jules could eat his breakfast before he picked her up. The 9:30 deadline she imposed on herself so she could get away earlier. We are scheduled to have dinner tomorrow evening with the Naidens, Pehles, and Olsons in celebration of Ulaine's birthday. Could be an interesting evening.

Saturday, November 28
A pleasant mild day. Nevertheless Vera not only did not make it by 9:30, she did not make it at all.
Neil called to cancel the dinner as Ulaine had a sore throat – he said. My guess is she just did not want a big birthday celebration. Ira came through – with a cheerful letter and another favorable clipping. Went shopping at the mall. Bought a birthday gift for Eric and Chanukah gifts for both boys.
Jules felt that he was getting a cold so we stayed in this evening. Had terrific steaks for dinner. Jules' cold did not affect his appetite, and he ate a tremendous dinner. Spent a quite evening, doing household chores, reading, and watching some TV.

Sunday, November 29
Ira called in the morning. We talked to all four. Sandy was still hoarse but feeling better. Thanked David for his note to Mother, which pleased her very much.
A mild day for a football game, but we had to give up our tickets for the game to some company officials, prearranged when we got the tickets. Jules might not have gone anyhow because of his cold. We did go to Jandel's to look at fur coats on sale but did not see any I cared to buy. Stopped at Mother's on the way home – I visited while Jules waited in the car. Then home.
Clara called later – could not get an answer to Mother's phone – I called and got a

prompt answer – she must have been dozing when Clara called.

Called the Levys. They left Bill's mother in the hospital, brought the father back with them.

Monday, November 30

Went down together in the Olds – could not start the Mustang. Could not blame the weather as it was very warm. In the 60's today and scheduled to be in the 70's tomorrow – just when I am leaving for several days in Milwaukee for two cases. And got briefs in the Detroit case after all.

Jules insisted he would take me to the airport, but I did not see the point as he would then go back to work. Got a ride with Jack Dyer who was dropping Mel Welles at the airport also. Got a United 6 o'clock non-stop, with dinner, to Milwaukee. Took a limousine to the Sheraton Schroeder. Was given a satisfactory room on the 18th floor with a fine view.

Tuesday, December 1

Very warm – 58 when I got up – but very windy. I had breakfast in the coffee shop. Walked around a while but the wind was discouraging. Then to the hearing in the Capital Court case. Lunched at the Clock nearby. Was told in the afternoon that my second case had been postponed. Recessed at 5. Should be able to get home tomorrow night.

Walked back to the hotel. Much colder. Had dinner in the Hunt Room at the hotel. Called Jules after dinner. He had just got home. Thought Kessel[21] might have told him when he sent the message to me about the second case postponement, but he had not. So I had the pleasure of telling Jules I would not be away all week, but would probably return tomorrow evening. He seemed glad to hear it.

Wednesday, December 2

Had breakfast in the coffee shop. Then walked over to the Regional office. The weather was much cooler, but sunny and very pleasant. Resumed the hearing at 9:30. Finished in a couple of hours. Back to the hotel. After had luncheon at a nearby Pancake House. Checked out and took the limousine to the airport. Got the 3:25 United plane. Got to National about 6:15, and found Jules waiting for me. We stopped at the Cantina for a delicious dinner. Then home.

Invitation to Neil Naiden's annual party on the 16th, this one to be a buffet as well as cocktail party, and to be held at the City Tavern Club. Jules may be out-of-town, and I may be also. I had expected Jules before this to have arranged our own Club cocktail party, but he had not.

---

21   Kessel case coordinator

1971

Anne and Jules began the year in Miami where they enjoyed the sun and beaches. Jules was always a fan of Ohio State football, and they watched on television as OSU played in the Rose Bowl, but his team lost.

As soon as they were back in Washington from the trip, Anne flew to Buffalo for a case. On NLRB trips as a judge, she was most of the time either in a local courtroom or in the hotel, reading, reviewing case work, or watching television. She and Jules usually talked by telephone at night. He was also traveling extensively, and their conversations were usually about the day's events for each one.

In April she had a kidney stone attack which hospitalized her for a short time. As soon as she was out of the hospital, they left for Tulsa where she had her sixty-first birthday and they had the Passover Seder with Ira and family. Jules gave Anne a "lovely gold bracelet" for her birthday.

On their wedding anniversary they traveled to Yugoslavia, arriving to Belgrade then continuing later to Sarajevo, Split, and Dubrovnik. On their return they stopped in Rome and London for short visits in each.

At this stage in their lives the children of their friends are getting married, and this year the son of her long-time colleague, Ralph Winkler, got married, as did the son of their close friends, the Jaffes.   -- RDH

Monday, March 1
We went down together, after managing not only to get ready and to have breakfast but also to do some more putting away from last night. A pleasant mild day so Sid Ascher and I walked into Georgetown and had luncheon at Chez Odette. Enjoyed the walk and the luncheon very much.
We picked up some fresh rockfish on the way home. I broiled it, with crushed pineapple – read a recipe once for mixing maui – maui that way. It was delicious.
A bomb exploded this morning in the Capitol. A shocking and frightening event.
Finished putting away the dishes and whatnot we had not taken care of last night.

Tuesday, March 2
We went down together. A cloudy and considerably cooler.
Received copies of my Tonarranda decision which was issued yesterday.
Had planned to call Ira to wish him a happy birthday, but by the time we got home and got ourselves organized and thought of it, we decided it was too late. The boys would have gone to bed, and Ira and Sandy would not doubt be celebrating, and we would probably have talked only to a baby sitter. Sorry we did not think of it a little earlier.
And sorry I did not get my hair done today. Rain was threatened all day but did not come. It no doubt will tomorrow, and I shall arrive in Tulsa unkempt – as usual.

Wednesday, March 3
Awoke to a snow covered scene. It was soon

washed away by rain which fell all day. The weather reports indicate we shall have some bad weather on our trip. Ivan Peterson offered me a ride to the Guy Peterson party this evening but I had decided not to go.

Picked Jules up about 5:40. Did a couple of errands on the way home.

Got pretty well packed and organized to go in the evening, but did not haul anything out to the car as it was raining quite hard. Have a large quantity of fish and other Passover foods, which we understand are hard to get and experience in Tulsa, and some toys we had at the house. Did not get a chance to shop for other gifts we would have liked to bring with us.

Thursday, March 4

Woke again to a snowy world, this time icy and cold as well. And no *Post*. Jules dropped me at the office. Picked me up about 12:30. We stopped for a sandwich at a Howard Johnson. Then took off. Ran into all kinds of weather, all bad. Slowed us down a good deal but Jules pushed on through all the way to Columbus. Stopped at the Marriot Inn where we stayed on our last trip. Had a very good dinner in the Showboat Landing dining room. Called Gertrude to see if she would join us for dinner but it was too late. She did agree to come to breakfast. Called Edward and Madelyn after dinner. That was all the calling and visiting we could do as it was after 10 by the time we got back to the room after dinner. Watched some TV. Should have better driving weather tomorrow.

Friday, March 5

Gertrude came over in the morning, and we had a very pleasant breakfast and visit together. Then took off. The weather was chilly and windy, but bright and sunny. We stopped for a light luncheon at a Stuckey's outside Indianapolis. Then drove past cities like St. Louis – not seeing anything of them – until we stopped for the night at the Arrowhead Motel in Springfield, Missouri, and had a pretty good dinner in the dining room. The motel was rated excellent by AAA, and their dining room was recommended. We found it second-rate, would have preferred to be at one of the newer places in the vicinity. But for one night it was certainly adequate. And tomorrow we will have a relatively short trip.

Saturday, March 6

We had breakfast at the motel. It was raining and/or snowing, at the time and continued until we got close to Tulsa. We stopped at a delicatessen in Tulsa for a sandwich. Picked up some goodies there to bring with us. Then to the house. Visited with the baby sitter until the boys got up from their naps, then with the boys. Sandy and Ira got back a little later from their weekend. Both looked fine, in clothes made by Sandy. Ira with a $100 check for his speech. A couple from Pittsburgh, whom they knew when they all lived in Dayton, stopped, on their way to visit parents, for dinner. Sandy managed drinks, *hors d'oeuvres*, and a lovely dinner. She is quite a girl. And the boys looked wonderful and behave wonderfully. Ira seems tired but very happy in his work.

Sunday, March 7

Managed to get a reasonable amount of sleep on a terrible mattress there. Had a very nice breakfast. Ira went to play basketball. We took the boys to Sunday School and picked them up later. We all went to the Book and Art Fair at David's school – Jules bought the boys some books. Afterwards we all had luncheon at a Big Boy. Home to rest for a while. To the Synagogue – the boys in costume – for the Purim party, including dinner. It was enjoyable except that the very amateurish entertainment lasted much too long. Each of the boys got a gift toy, which they liked. But they like much better the things we brought . Ira seems delighted with the Mustang. And Sandy was pleased with the various foods we brought.

Monday, March 8

After breakfast we went with Ira and the boys to AAA to get title to the Mustang transferred. Later took David to school, and, at his request, I went in to meet his teacher. We had some luncheon at the house with Eric – Sandy had to drive a neighbor somewhere. Ira came home early and we all went to the airport. Bought "cowboy" hats there for the boys. We left about 5:10. A pleasant flight and a fairly good dinner. Took a cab home from National.
Looked at the mail, did a few household chores, unpacked, and I went to bed fairly early as I did not feel too well. Did not sleep well on the terrible guest bed we get in Tulsa, and must have eaten something during the day that I could not digest.

Tuesday, March 9

Went down together in the Olds. Found an assignment on my desk, left there Thursday afternoon after I took off, calling me to be in New York at 11 this morning for 4 days. Got it reassigned as, among other reasons, I had a dental appointment on Friday. And I thought the assignment was unreasonable. But now I am in the "doghouse" with both Kessel[22] and [Chief Judge] Bokat.
Jules and I stopped at the grocery store on the way home.
Clara called us to let us know she and Lou were going to Italy later this month. We must make some decisions soon ourselves about our tip to Europe this summer – where to go after the London Bar conference, etc.

Wednesday, March 10

Went down in the Olds. Jules is anxious to start shopping for a second car.
Lunched at Blackie's with Fannie Boyls.
Jules was not feeling well so I picked him up about 5:15 and we went directly home. He went to bed for a little while, then ate a light supper, and seemed to be feeling better in the evening. No word from Uyzella, who was supposed to call yesterday or today to let me know whether or not she was coming in on Saturday. Don't know whether to call the agency for someone else, and don't want to leave a dirty house when I go out of town as I am certain to do next week. Maybe she will yet call.

Thursday, March 11

Went down together in the Olds.

---

22   Anne's friend Thomas Kessel who was coordinating case assignments.

The Board adopted my decision administratively in Capitol Court (Milwaukee), no exceptions having been filed.

Lunched at Blackie's with Al Somers.

Got an assignment of a case in Memphis, Tennessee, beginning Tuesday and estimated to run 3 to 4 days. This will be my first hearing anywhere in Tennessee.

Picked up Jules about 5:40. Picked up laundry and some groceries on the way home.

No word from Uyzella. I have not called the agency for someone else. Jules wants to shop for a car on Saturday, which I cannot do with a new person. Will have to try to do some cleaning myself.

Friday, March 12
Went down together. To the dentist later in the morning. Then to the beauty parlor. Back to the office to make my plane and motel reservations.

Picked up Jules about 5:30. He has not been busy this week, which makes him despondent. But things should pick up for him next week.

We went home, cleaned up, then to the Shanghai in Silver Spring for dinner. From there to Ohr Kodesh for a talk by Leo Rosten, whom everyone – and there was an enormous crowd – found very entertaining. Stayed for the Oneg Shabbat and to talk to a few people we knew. Then home. Uyzella called after 11 – said she tried a number of times but the phone was always busy, and she would be in tomorrow.

Saturday, March 13
A lovely warm day. Uyzella, even with getting picked up, did not get in until about 10:30. She managed to clean the two bathrooms, but did not touch the basement or the bathroom there. Suspect it was not lack of time but a matter of principle with her. We spent much of the day shopping for a replacement for the Mustang. Lunched at Hofberg's. After Jules had taken Uyzella to the terminal, we did some errands, and then went to the Sakura for a very enjoyable Japanese dinner. Picked up some things for brunch on the way home. Will be eating at home for a change. But I get so annoyed with these maids these days that I cannot settle down to cooking after they leave. Gertrude called – David Daniels' brother died.

Sunday, March 14
Cloudy and a good deal cooler. And I seem to have a head cold, mild but annoying.

Ira called, we talked to all four. It was very warm there, and they all seemed to be bubbling over with cheer. We went to see Mother in the afternoon. She seemed well. Jules did some yard work after we got home, I did some work in the house and got ready for my trip tomorrow to Memphis.

We have a lot of decisions to make about the kind of new car we are going to get, where we will go in Europe if we go on the Bar Association charter trip, when we should schedule the cocktail party we should give after not entertaining for so long etc., etc. Will plan when I get back from Memphis.

1971

Monday, March 15
Jules dropped me at the office. Lunched at Blackie's with Sid Ascher and Ben Lipton. A mild day with some hard showers, but fortunately I did not get caught in any of them. My sniffles are bad enough without that. In the afternoon took a cab to National and an American flight to Memphis at 4:50, nonstop, and a pretty good dinner was served. Then by limousine to the Pilot House Motor Inn. Was given a large room on the 14th floor. Got the impression, however, there were no dining facilities. Should have checked that on the phone in advance but did not suppose a downtown city motel would not have at least a coffee shop. But for tonight at least it did not matter one way or the other.

Tuesday, March 16
I was right about the eating facilities in the motel – there are none. A pleasant day so I walked to a nearby restaurant for a pretty bad breakfast. Then a very short walk to the Federal Building and the hearing, which it appears, will run for a few days. Lunched at the snack shop in the building. After we adjourned for the day, I walked back to the motel, and a little later walked to the 100 Building for dinner in the Top of the 100 on the 38th floor. Got a window table with a magnificent view, and had an excellent dinner beautifully served – but so lonely. Then back to the room. Called Jules, who sounded as lonely as I felt.

The cold was very bothersome during the hearing today, but seemed a little better by evening.

Wednesday, March 17
Walked to the cafeteria in the 100 Main Building for breakfast, back to the hotel, and to the hearing, all short distances, and it was a lovely day. Took another little walk during the luncheon recess, and had a quick but very satisfactory luncheon in a coffee shop in a department store. Adjourned when the General Counsel rested at 4:30. Walked to the motel and left my attaché case. Out again, and had a late tea, or early dinner, in the tea room at Lowenstein's Department Store.

The Respondent's counsel, an able and attractive young Mr. Nichols, indicated that he would finish early tomorrow. Did not change my Friday reservation, but should be able to get home tomorrow evening if all goes well at the hearing tomorrow.

Thursday, March 18
Walked over to 100 Main Street for breakfast. The hearing concluded about 11:30. I called the office. Checked out, got a limousine to the airport, and just made a plane ready to depart. Called Jules from National and he picked me up. Stopped at Montgomery Mall to leave off a Garfinckel dress in which the material had come apart. It was not a new dress but, for over $160, that should not have happened. Went to Hecht's also and sent a tablecloth and napkins to Sandy as she was unable to get the right size in Tulsa. Had a very good fish dinner at Crisfield's. Picked up a few things at the grocery store. And finally home. Bill Levy called to chat and suggest we get together on Saturday. Alice Jaffe called to suggest we get together on travel in Britain if we go to the London Bar conference, and

also that we join a theater group on April 2, which we agreed to do.

Friday, March 19
We went down together. Poured most of the day. There was a TX conference luncheon at Blackie's. I was offered a ride if I would go but decided to skip it and stay in the building. Picked up Jules about 5:30. Did a couple of errands on the way home, but went home for dinner. We had both had enough of eating out for a while.
Uyzella called later in the evening. Said she had tried earlier but got no answer. It is a nuisance that she does not have a phone or one where I can leave a message for her. Suggested calling her at one of her places of work but she did not like the idea for some vague reason. Wonder if she has other regular jobs.

Saturday, March 20
A cold windy day. Uyzella came in, just as late as last week. And left early, and in between, although she does a good deal of hard work, could not wash out a few nylon things for me – no hand laundry – and evidently never uses the basement bathroom.
Bill called to say Ruth was not feeling well so we would not see them tonight. Spent much of the day shopping for a car. Bought a green 2-door "Duster" by Plymouth.
Also watched a TV basketball game which OSU lost in the overtime period. The set worked fine for the game but went on the blink almost right after that. And the set upstairs had not had a picture for a long time. So we stayed home and read "Up the Organization," which we both find quite dull.

Sunday, March 21
Read part of the paper. Then had a big very enjoyable brunch. In the afternoon went to see Mother. Clara and Lou left yesterday for their European vacation.
A lovely crisp sunny day so we stopped at Katz's and did a few other errands, including buying the paperback *Up the Organization*, our next book club book.
Had broiled veil chops for dinner. They were delicious – should have been, as they cost over a dollar a piece.
No call from Tulsa. They were looking forward to a warm weekend when they could go to the lake. This was probably that weekend as Tulsa was fairly warm. Our one TV set is "on the blink."

Monday, March 22
We went down together. Lunched at Blackie's with Sid Ascher.
Picked up Jules about 5:20. He has not been busy lately, and it bothers him a great deal, and worries me as it bothers him. It is not at all the money involved but the prestige among his partners.
Picked up our downstairs TV set and took it out to the store in Rockville where we bought it. Pouring at that time. Stopped at a Steak-a-rama in the area for supper, which we both enjoyed very much.
Invitation to the wedding of Cathy Winkler's second daughter. Jules has cancelled our Bar Assn. trip to London. Afraid Europe would be just too crowded with tourists in July.

1971

Tuesday, March 23

We went down together. Decided I could not prolong any longer my "revisions" on the Hooker Chemical decision waiting for the Tulsa assignment. Asked Kessel if I could get a short case next week without prejudicing my getting the Tulsa case. He agreed.

Picked up Jules about 5:20. We took the upstairs TV – which for a long time has had sound but no picture – to a repair shop.

Ira and Sandy called fairly late. They had four college students as house guests – two of their Dayton neighbors plus two of their friends – and Eric had another accident requiring stitches on his face. They had been at the lake, with their guests, for the weekend. If I get the Tulsa case, Ira will be here during part of the time.

Wednesday, March 24

We went down together. Turned in Hooker Chemical to be stenciled.

Called Mother to make sure she was all right and still had enough food on hand. She was and she did. Jules tried to get tickets for "Hair" at the National – which he saw in New York – but nothing available until May. Jules got word that the old TV set was fixed. Stopped on the way home to pick it up. It seemed to be working fine. Ridiculous that we had it all these months with sound only, no picture. Watched a 2-hour presentation of "Jane Eyre" which I enjoyed. And we were able to watch the news, to which we have become accustomed so long, we prefer it to listening to the radio.

Thursday, March 25

We went down together. Signed Hooker Chemical and sent it to the other building for issuance.

Uyzella called – will be in on Saturday. Lunched at Blackie's with Sid Ascher.

Was assigned a 1-day case in Atlanta which was fine with me. Picked up Jules about 5:15.

Note from Ira, written in haste so illegible in spots, but we are glad to hear from him in any event. Got Mother's shopping list as it may be easier for us to stop on the way home tomorrow then to do it on Saturday.

Jules watched a championship basketball game on TV probably the reason he got this old set fixed in a hurry.

Friday, March 26

Snowing fairly hard in the morning although not much was sticking to the ground. Too bad as I would have gone to the beauty parlor otherwise.

Called Garfinckel's about my dress, but the promised call-back never came.

My Atlanta 1-day case postponed. I was given instead a case in Grand Rapids with a 2-3 day estimate. Spent most of the day making and unmaking travel and hotel reservations. Would have much preferred the Atlanta assignment for a number of reasons.

Picked up Jules about 5:15 and Nelson Baines at his office whom we gave a ride home.

Picked up some groceries on the way home for ourselves. Will do Mother's marketing tomorrow. Her list is not a very long one.

Saturday, March 27
Awoke with a headache but made myself get up, shower, dress, and have some breakfast. Away so much, I did not want to spend a Saturday sick in bed. Uyzella came in, a little earlier than usual. We did the marketing for Mother, and a few errands for ourselves. Lunched at Hofberg's.

We both took Uyzella to the bus terminal, and then went on to a movie in Bethesda to see an Italian movie, "A Case of Jealousy," which we found entertaining. Then to the Yenching Palace for dinner. Since Jules had reduced his beef eating because of the cholesterol problems, he has become fond of chicken cooked in various Oriental styles. His favorite is Chicken Teriyaki at the Sakura.

Sunday, March 28
A lovely warm sunny day. Even warmer no doubt in Tulsa. No call. We figured the kids were at the lake.

Jules did some work in the yard. I stayed in all day – talked to Mother on the phone but did not go to see her – and read the paper, did some chores, and got my bag packed to leave tomorrow for Grand Rapids. Had broiled veil chops for dinner, which we enjoyed, Jules particularly. But about the time I was going to dress to go to the book club, Jules got sick to his stomach and had an excruciating pain in his back. After he threw up his stomach felt better. And after I persuaded him to get into a hot tub, his backache disappeared. But I called the Zanoffs and said we would not come. And we bought the book and both of us read it.

Monday, March 29
Jules was feeling much better. We went down together. He dropped me. Later after calls to Mother and Jules – took a cab to National and left at 11:55 on Allegheny. Stopped at Baltimore and South Bend, with luncheon served between the two, and then Grand Rapids. Took a cab – there was no limousine service – to the Pantlind. It is a very old hotel but I was given an adequate corner room, with not much of a view although I could see a bit of a river from one of the windows. Later had supper at one of the several dining rooms in the hotel. Back to the room to study the file in tomorrow's case, read a detective story, watched some TV, and went to bed. The hotel was full of conventions but my room was quiet.

Tuesday, March 30
Had breakfast in the hotel. Later walked the couple of blocks to the Federal Building for the Rospatch Corporation hearing. Lunched in a nearby café. The hearing closed about 4:00. I called the office. Should have checked out of the hotel at noon, and headed for the airport after the hearing. But had not, and did not. Not that many flights available from Grand Rapids.

Walked back to the hotel. A crisp day but sunny and pleasant.

Had a very good dinner in the Pub Room at the hotel. Afterwards called Jules. He is still not busy at the office and wants to go to New York tomorrow to "promote." Will meet me and turn over the car. Was feeling much better. There is a note from Sandy and a postcard from the Rolands from Venice. And the Jaffes called to remind us we had a date for Friday night.

Wednesday, March 31
A lovely warm day. I had breakfast in the hotel. Then took a cab to the airport and the 10 o'clock United flight to Washington. Jules was not at the airport, so I called him at the office. He postponed his trip to New York a day.
Had a sandwich on the plane so took a cab directly to the office. Received exceptions in my Chicago backpay case so now have three cases before the Board. Kessel asked if I still wanted the Tulsa case – up to a 5-day estimate. Said I did. Jules picked me up about 5:30. We stopped at Kushner's for supper, and at the grocery store, and had dessert at home. Garfinckel's called to report that they were reweaving the tear in my blue dress. Hope I get it back soon as it is one I use a great deal.

1972

Once again, they began thinking about moving to an apartment closer to downtown and their offices. Bill and Ruth Levy, who had moved to an apartment some years earlier, encouraged them. In recent years Anne had been running the household without a regular maid. Occasionally someone would come in to help her on Saturdays. The situation with Anne's mother continued unchanged.

She worked closely with Tom Kessel during these years, and he made the assignments for the hearings over which she would preside. On August 9 she wrote, "My Commercial Letter decision was featured in the *Daily Labor Letter.*"

A major event this year was the change in her title from "Trial Examiner to Administrative Law Judge." Trial Examiner were in fact judges, but this name change recognized that status. After decades of having lunch outside with friends, she began to take her lunch from home occasionally and work through the lunch period. Her old friends Fannie Boyls and Mira Stevenson were frequent lunch companions when she did go out. She had cases for which she had to travel at least two weeks out of the month, which meant that she was on planes and in hotels regularly.

In August Anne and Jules took a vacation trip to Portugal, stopping in Lisbon to visit with Hank Cohen and his wife, who were now retired. From there they went to Seville, visiting the Cathedral and the Alcazar. Then, they went on to Algeciras and a trip across to Tangier. Back in Spain they stayed a few days in Marbella, then went to Granada to visit the Alhambra, about which Anne wrote, "I thought very overrated, and the magnificent gardens of the summer palace." From Granada they traveled to Madrid where they visited the Prado Museum and the city of Toledo before returning home. They arrived home on their anniversary. 　　　　　　　-- RDH

Thursday, August 31
We got up early, had a quick breakfast in the dining room, were picked up by bus to a terminal, and then by another bus on a Cook's tour to Toledo. Found Toledo interesting; though hours were spent on the glories of the cathedral, moments on the old synagogue converted to a church and then to a museum, reminders again of the virtual extinction of Jews in Spain. Back to the hotel about 2. Did some walking. Lunched at the little café nearby, El Borro.[23] Interesting. Bought gloves for me and a wallet for Jules at a Loewe's in the Palace Hotel.

Later walked to Horcher's for an excellent dinner. Many staying at the Ritz, who have come to recognize one another, were also there. We walked back after dinner, only a few blocks, but rather dark deserted streets. Feel safer walking in Europe than at home.

Friday, September 1
We had a leisurely breakfast in the dining room. Then checked out and took a cab to the airport. Bought 2 pairs of earrings. Our plane was jam-packed. We were put in first class. Ate and drank and chatted our way across. Would have had a long wait for an American Airlines plane out of Kennedy so took a cab to La Guardia and just made the 5 o'clock shuttle. Took a cab home. All in order, except *Posts* had been piled up even though I had cancelled it.

Anniversary card from Lucille and Louie. Document about hospital labor relations from Ira asking for my comments on it. Another publication showing my title has been changed from Trial Examiner to Administrative Law Judge.

Went to bed early by local time but late by Madrid time. Glad to have the weekend to get readjusted.

Saturday, September 2
We both awoke and got up very early by local time.

No word from Dorothy Covington, who had promised to call and come in today. We went downtown, Jules to the office and I to the beauty parlor. Later I picked up Jules and saw his elegant new offices. We did some marketing on the way home. Jules had picked up a few essentials before breakfast. Jules offered to take me out to dinner in honor of my hairdo, but it was a rainy day so we ate at home.

Postcard from Gertrude in Hawaii with Lois and some of Lois's children. Thank-you note from Ohr Kodesh for a donation Jules made to repair the damage done by hurricane Agnes.

23　　A *borro* is a young male lamb.

1972

Sunday, September 3
Got up early. Still not readjusted to local time. We both went to Katz's to do some marketing. Had brunch after we got back. Later we went to see Mother. Took her for a ride. Stopped at some country stands where we bought some fresh produce. She did also.

Afterwards drove out to Sumner. Met the Levys there. The office was closed for the weekend but we walked around to see what progress had been made.

Met the Levys at Wu's in Rockville for supper. They have problems with Linda – after seeing her in Naples, they got word that Greg has been discharged from the service and he and Linda are coming home. And David's wife is starting medical school, but David does not know what he will be doing.

Monday, September 4
Got up at a reasonable hour. Seem to be back on D.C. time.

After brunch we did some shopping. Many of the suburban stores were open today. All I bought was another pair of gloves at Garfinckel's in Montgomery Mall. We looked at appliances with a view to our choices for the apartment.

Called Alice. She had had a second operation on her throat.

We had a yummy dinner at home, lamb chops, fresh corn, etc. No call from Tulsa.

Watched some of the Olympic contests. Proud of the young Jewish American, Spitz, who won 7 gold medals in swimming, a real record time.

Tuesday, September 5
Back to work. Much comment on my tan and trip. Found the Board had affirmed me in Forbes Pavilion.[24] Lunched at the Red Coach with Mira Stevenson.

Picked up Jules about 5:45. Went to Garfinckel's with a suit he bought there on which threads kept pulling. He had worn it a good deal but got a full credit for it. We had some supper there at a Hot Shoppe while waiting for his salesman, and the rest of the supper at home.

Letter from Ira and large sketches of the boys made in Taos for our anniversary gift. The glass on them was broken, we had shreds of glass to clean up, and we did not think the sketches were good of the boys.

Shocked by the murder of Israeli Olympic athletes by Palestinian guerillas in Munich.

Wednesday, September 6
Went down together. Dropped Jules at the doctor's for an allergy shot. Gave my secretary, Gloria Reid, one of the wallets I bought in Tangier. She seemed very pleased with it.

Picked up Jules about 5:45. Picked up some groceries on the way.

Copies of some Tulsa paper clippings - one about Ira's appointment to a national hospital board, and one about Sandy's defeat in a doubles tennis match. The Ruchels called and asked us over on the 17th. We declined as it was Yom Kipper. They called the people who had already accepted and changed it to the Friday before so we accepted. The Biekerts

---

24 Referring to the Board having sustained her decision after having reviewed it.

may be in that Friday, which will complicate things. Paul Brand, who had retired, called and asked us over, we to say when. We called Irv Jaffe - Alice better but cannot talk much.

Thursday, September 7
Went down together. Lunched at the Red Coach with Sid Ascher.
Did not get an assignment. [Thomas] Kessel apparently is not sending out any of the Jewish judges during the holiday period even though the holidays come on the weekends. We picked up some holiday food items on our way home. Ira called. We talked to all 4. He had lost our itinerary so did not write while we were away or know exactly when we were scheduled to return. The two boys are in school, and all sounded well and happy. Ira expects to be at National airport for 2 hours next Wednesday on his way to Charleston. Is doing a great deal of traveling.

Friday, September 8
Went down together. Jules had a date to lunch with Irv Jaffe so I gave Jules the earrings I had bought in Spain, to send via Irv, with the message that Alice did not have to call about it in view of her throat trouble.
Lunched at Blackie's with Maller, Ascher, and Hinkes.
Jules left about 5. We went directly home. I fixed broiled chicken, etc., for a holiday meal. Then we went to services at Ohr Kodesh.
New Year's card from the Sam Meltons in Columbus. Get very few cards now, probably because we have neglected over the years to send them. Have also cut down considerably on the number of postcards I send from vacation trips.

Saturday, September 9
We had breakfast – not brunch – and then went to services. After we came home in the early afternoon, had luncheon which was more like a dinner. Then to the annual open house on Rosh Hashanah at the Saul Jaffes'. It was pleasant as we see people there we do not see the rest of the year. We did not stay long. Went home and read the paper. I also did some washing, ironing, and housecleaning. A long time since the house has had a thorough cleaning. Will try to get someone in next Saturday as the holiday next week starts on Sunday.
Removed with great difficulty the broken glass that remained on the pictures of the boys.

Sunday, September 10
I woke up with a bad headache. Managed to get up, and to fix breakfast for both of us, and to eat some. Felt better afterwards but not well enough to get dressed and go to services again. Jules went by himself. We had some luncheon when he got home. Then went to see Mother. She seemed well. Nate called from Philadelphia to arrange for a football outing to Columbus on a weekend we could all make it. Agreed on a weekend in early November. Naiden had not indicated anything about Redskin tickets this year. He and Ulaine[25] are getting divorced, and he no doubt has tougher things to worry about than tickets to football games. I was shocked to hear of their divorce plans. She will move to Denver.

---

25   Neil and Ulaine Naiden, close friends to Jules and Anne. Neil was Jules' law partner.

Monday, September 11

I went down alone. Jules took in the Olds, which was making peculiar noises, and it turned out needed a new water pump. Turned in my Harrawood decision for stenciling. Gloria was out sick but expected back next day. Glad to wait a day to have her do it.

Peterson offered me the use of his garage space for the next two weeks when he would be on vacation. Too bad it was not this week as I shall have to use the car at noon one or two days this week. But very nice of him in any event.

Jules got a ride out to the Olds place in Bethesda with Pehle so I got home relatively early, and had dinner well on the way by the time Jules got home.

Tuesday, September 12

Went down together. Lunched at the Black Ulysses with Abe Muller and Harry Kuskin. Got caught in a light shower on the way, but hardly enough to get wet.

Got exceptions in the Commercial Letter case. Asked the parking lot guy if I could use the car tomorrow and repark it. His predecessors permitted on the rare occasions I requested it, but the guy me a brusque "no." Picked up Jules about 5:50. Had a very good supper on the way home at Crisfield's. Went home for dessert.

Holiday greeting card from the Zanoffs. By coincidence it was just like the card we received from the Meltons.

Mildred Michaels called to set the date for the book club meeting. Mike had been very ill but is feeling better.

Wednesday, September 13

I went down separately as Jules was going to New York for the day and leaving a car at the airport. I parked on the street at a 2-hour meter place, and at noon drove to the airport to meet Ira's plane. It came in on time at 1, but no Ira. Drove back to the office. Lost my parking place, and too stubborn to go on the lot, but finally managed to park parallel, between 2 cars, for the first time – and no meter. Called Tulsa. Sandy told me Ira's meeting had been changed and he had so written me. But I received no such note, not even when I got home. Had just finished my supper when Jules got home, ready for his supper. He ran into Biekert – they are not coming here this weekend. Just as well, with the holiday. A holiday greeting from someone in New York, whose signature we could not read.

Thursday, September 14

We went down together. I parked on the street. At noon I picked up Jules and we drove out to Sumner Village. Met with agents of the builders about some changes we wanted made. Had a quick luncheon in the shopping center there and went back to work. I parked on the street again, in a non-meter place.

Got an assignment in Evansville, Indiana – again – a 2-day case beginning Thursday.

Picked up Jules about 5:45. Did some marketing on the way home. Had dinner at home, late, and I did some laundry after dinner – later. Grateful for all the non-iron fabrics. Would be in a bind if most of our laundered items had to be ironed.

Friday, September 15
We went down together. I parked in the lot for the first time in days and the last time for a couple of weeks. Lunched at Blackie's with Mira Stevenson and Abe Muller.
Got a short-form affirmance – not even a footnote in my Huntington Piping decision. A maid, Catherine Smith, called me at the office and will come in tomorrow. Jules was tied up late at the office and I got caught in a massive traffic jam on the way to pick him up so we got home late. Did some quick picking up in the house, changed clothes, and went to the Ruchels'. Did not eat as we thought from the early hour it was for dinner, but only snacks were served with the drinks. But they had a large group, most of them from the office, and we enjoyed the evening.

Saturday, September 16
Jules picked up Catherine Smith at the terminal. She seemed as old as the hills and did only a second-rate cleaning job.
Jules went to the office right after brunch. I had brought some work home and spent much of the afternoon on it. When Jules came home we both took Catherine – insisting she wanted the job and it was not too hard for her – to the bus terminal. Then we did some errands.
Had dinner at home. Then spent a quiet evening reading and watching a little TV. Later just to get out a bit – we drove into Silver Spring for frozen custard cones. Then home again.

Sunday, September 17
Ira called. Apologized about the note advising me of his change in schedule, which he wrote but forgot to mail. Sandy was removing splinters from David's foot and Eric was in bed.
Had a very good brunch, visited Mother, picked up a few things at the grocery store, and had a big dinner. Then changed and went to Ohr Kodesh. Walking from the parking lot, and talking to Saul Jaffes in back of me, I stumbled and fell. Seemed uninjured except for my dignity and my ankle, which was extremely painful. Sat – literally – through the services, which seemed interminable. A couple of men helped me out of the building while Jules got the car, and Jules got me into the house and upstairs with considerable difficulty.

Monday, September 18
Jules got up and dressed for services. Offered to come home early and take me to a hospital for x-rays. I was in considerable pain, knew from experience Dr. Porter would send me to a hospital, so Jules took me to Holy Cross. Took a long time but I was finally told there were no broken bones, and given instructions and a prescription for a pain killer. Jules took me home then and went to services. Got my prescription filled on the way home. I called the office in the morning to be put on sick rather than annual leave. Called later to tell them I could not possibly travel on Wednesday so my case in Evansville will have to be reassigned. Jules managed dinner with my directions. Clare Jaffe called to inquire about me. Ruth Levy called and learned of my silly accident.

1972

Tuesday, September 19
I came downstairs in the morning and Jules gave me some breakfast. Then he took off for the office. I called him a couple of times during the day to avoid having him call when I was not near a phone. Got calls that I was able to answer from someone urging the reelection of Nixon, from Mrs. Graham of the Employment Agency whom I told Katherine Smith was nice but too old for this job, and from Gertrude[26] to let us know the good tidings that Elaine and Milton had a son.

Jules picked up a barbecued chicken on the way home, and with it managed a very good dinner. The experience is valuable for him as he hardly knows how to turn on the correct burner on the stove. Meanwhile, thanks to the codeine and time, pain is much eased, but I cannot step down on the injured foot. Probably mental more than physical.

Wednesday, September 20
I got downstairs, and Jules gave me some breakfast. After he left I tried to walk without holding on to furniture, and did manage a few steps. Felt I succeeded in getting over the psychological bar, if that is what it was. Could not do much as there was still a good deal of pain.

In order for Jules not to have to stop again at the store, we had cold chicken and other things on hand for a very adequate dinner. Jules called Gertrude to congratulate her on the birth of her new grandson, Adam Harold Lewin.

---

26   Jules' sister, Gertrude Lewin, in Columbus.

Instead of my last ankle soaking, soaked all of me in bubble bath, and laid out my clothes in case I felt up to going to the office tomorrow.

Thursday, September 21
With some misgivings I got dressed and went down with Jules. He parked in Peterson's garage space, and then walked to the doctor's for his shot. I managed to get a good deal of work done on my current draft decision. Gloria brought me coffee from time to time. Fannie brought me a sandwich from downstairs, and we lunched at my desk. The sandwich was terrible, and I had indigestion all afternoon. My ankle bothered me a good deal also. Not a good idea to go in but at least I will not have to chase around the hospital to get a leave slip signed by a doctor.

Sprinkling on the way home. Stopped at the Sheraton for dinner as we could park in the garage. Then home, and glad I was to get there. Did not even get out of my chair to talk to Florence Gang when she called.

Friday, September 22
Marguerite Schwartz, the Mordecai Levine daughter in New York, called to ask for a recommendation of a New York divorce lawyer.

I called Katherine Smith. Got no answer. Before I could call again a Margaret Parker, referred by the agency, called me. The Rabbi called to ask how I was getting along. Jules called and put on Nate Ginsberg, whom neither of us had seen in many years.

Good thing I stayed at home today. There

were some calls I did not answer as I was soaking my ankle or too far from the phone. And did not go to the phone in the evening when Dorothy Covington called – lost our number – got it from the agency weeks after she was supposed to call. Too bad as she was a good cleaner.

Saturday, September 23
Margaret Parker came in. She appeared not much younger than Catherine and much heavier, a better cleaner but not much, and left a wrong telephone number when she left. Jules went to the office for a while. He got back in time to take Margaret to the terminal even though she left early.
Later we went to the Sakura for dinner. Gave me a chance to get out of the house. Also picked up some things at the grocery store. I found I could get around pretty well holding on to the grocery cart that I was ostensibly pushing. Home to rest my ankle, watch some TV, and take a bath as the easiest way to soak my ankle, as I am supposed to do more often than I do.

Sunday, September 24
A lovely mild day to watch a football game, and the Redskins were playing at home. We were supposed to get tickets from Naiden, but he had been away a good deal, and either gave them to someone else or neglected to give them to anyone, which would be worse. Maybe just as well we did not get them or I might have tried to go.
Took Mother for a ride. Had supper at home. Then changed clothes and went to the Michaels' for the book club meeting. It was a small group – Ruth and Charlotte were ill and the Zanoffs were not back from vacation. Neither of us had read the book, one by Barbara Tuchman. Alice took the occasion to thank me for the earrings I brought her from Spain. I managed pretty well despite me ankle.

Monday, September 25
I decided to go back to work. Went down together. Jules was carrying a heavy attaché case so suggested I drop him. First time I drove since I hurt my ankle but managed all right. Parked in Peterson's garage space. Had to put up with a lot of jokes about skiing and football accidents, but got along fairly well. Lunched at my desk. Picked up Jules about 5:45. Managed to prepare a fairly simple dinner. The ankle is still very painful. Hope I am not doing too much walking. Letter from Ira apologizing for not having written for so long. Mentioned that Sandy was still playing in tennis tournaments and was starting her fall sewing – so of course she cannot be expected to write us a note for months at a time.

Tuesday, September 26
Went down together. Dropped Jules and parked in Pete's place – that is a big help at this time.
Cancelled my dental appointment for tomorrow. Don't feel up to that much getting around yet.
The painters started today on the exterior trim of the house. Glad the threatened showers held off.

Picked up Jules about 6. We stopped at the Shanghai in Silver Spring for a very good supper. Had dessert at home. Hope to be able soon to do more marketing, cooking, laundry, etc., as my ankle is getting stronger, but it is still very painful at times, and my walking is still very unsteady much of the time. Everyone assures me the effects linger for months.

Wednesday, September 27
Went down together. The painters arrived as we were leaving but had to quit shortly afterwards as it rained most of the day.
The stationery I ordered, imprinted with my title of Judge,[27] arrived today. I was pleased with its appearance. Now have to find some occasion to use it.
Picked up Jules about 5:40. Although it was pouring at the time we stopped at Snider's for a few groceries. Then I fixed dinner, did the dishes, and did some vacuuming where the painters had walked in wet shoes. Pleased that my ankle permitted me to do all that. It is beginning to show noticeable improvement each day but has room for much more improvement.

Thursday, September 28
We went down together. The painters did not come today. They had called and said they would not in order to give the wood a chance to dry.
My "assignment" was the Celanese case reopening at the Court of Claims on Tuesday.

We went home after work. Later to the Trojan Horse dining room in Silver Spring for dinner in honor of the Levys' wedding anniversary. The dinner was only fair, it was very expensive, and Bill as usual paid a good deal less than his fair share and Jules floating the difference. But I managed fairly well on the hobbling around, and it was a reasonably enjoyable evening.

Friday, September 29
I drove down alone as Jules had to go to Rockville to argue a motion. First time since I sprained my ankle that I drove all the way. Managed all right.
Lunched at my desk and read part of the *Post*. Beginning to like this routine. Got home relatively early. Jules got home about 6:45 even though he stopped to pick up a few items at the grocery store.
No maid called. Just as well, we both looked forward to a Saturday without one. It will mean more work for me, as some cleaning has to be done, but I am beginning to hobble around much more efficiently, even on stairs. Mother called to ask about my ankle.

Saturday, September 30
Did not sleep late but enjoyed the idea that we did not have to get up early because of a maid. We read the paper, had a leisurely brunch, and then went to a Bath and Kitchen shop in Bethesda for ideas for the apartment. Then out to Sumner[28] to transmit some of these ideas. Everything still very inchoate

---

27 Anne was very pleased with the title Judge Anne F. Schlezinger.

28 Sumner Village where Anne and Jules were buying a condominium apartment.

as to what changes it will be feasible for us to make. Stopped at the Woodmoor delicatessen on the way home to pick up some goodies to have for the weekend. Ran into Wachtel there and visited with him for a while. Then home. Did some housework and laundry – the disadvantages of not having a maid – and spent the evening at home.

Jules and Anne

1973

Anne and Jules bought an apartment and moved from their Silver Spring house. Since she and Jules were traveling frequently, Anne felt lonely at times. On April 4 she wrote, "Had dinner at home alone. Read the paper, watched some TV, did a few chores, and by then it was time for bed. Cannot complain about Jules leaving me at home alone as he has not done so for quite a long time. It is lonely, though, and I am conscious of all the outside doors to this house." On November 7 she wrote, "Will be glad when Jules gets home tomorrow. Have had enough of being alone." There are many other similar references to loneliness.

The Watergate scandal had broken, so Anne refers to it occasionally in her entries. On April 30 she wrote, "Watched Nixon performance on TV as he tried to explain the innocence of himself and his closest advisers, including those whose resignations he had reluctantly accepted, in the Watergate bugging and cover-up mess."

In late May she had a case in Tulsa and was able to spend some time with Ira, Sandy and the boys. Jules joined them for the Memorial Day week-end. In early August Ira had a professional conference in Rockville, Maryland and stayed a few days with them. Anne wrote on August 2, "We all had breakfast together. Seems like old times…"

In September they went to in Mexico for vacation. They were in Puerta Vallarta for a few days resting, and then went to Guadaljara and Morelia to see indigenous crafts before going to Mexico City. Jules had some business meetings, but they had time to visit Puebla, San Angeline, Chapultepec Castle and other places of interest.

This was the time of the 1973 war in Israel, and on October 9, Anne wrote that they went to a Rally for Israel at the Ohr Kodesh Synagogue, and then said, "The reports of what is occurring are rather discouraging. This is already a costly war for Israel."

The October meeting of the Sunday Night Book Club discussed *Bury my Heart at Wounded Knee* at Anne and Jules' house.

On December 14 Anne and Jules moved from the Silver Spring house to the Sumner Village apartment. At the end of December they met Ira and his family in Miami for several days. They saw Jules' brother Lou and wife Lucille, visited Disney World with their grandsons, David and Eric, and spent time on the beach.   -- RDH

Monday, July 30
We went down together. Jules called in the morning to let me know the closing might be off as 2 serious purchasers were discussing a contract. I had a cocktail at luncheon with Mira Stevenson at the Chesapeake, to celebrate. Jules called later to tell me we would be stopping at Sumner to sign a sales contract. When we got there, however, one potential purchaser had been unable to get the financing, and the other had evaporated without signing anything and had gone through a similar process several times before about the same apartment. We all felt pretty let down. We had dinner at Hamburger Hamlet. Then home. Note from Ira with a newspaper clipping about my Riverside Industries decision.

Tuesday, July 31
Went down together. Jules cancelled an appointment to have a new gas meter installed. Made it when he expected to be "closing" at 10:15. I was going to the office to meet him there. But the closing was postponed, and we thought it might be better to have one car with Ira coming.
Lunched with Fannie Boyls at the Georgetown Plaza. Not very good. Ira called later from Jules' office. I picked them up about 5:45. We had a great dinner – filets, corn, string beans, salad, etc. – and we were eating and watching the TV news in considerably less than an hour after we got home. Took a ride later to orient Ira to where he is going to be attending conferences tomorrow in Rockville. Then home. He went to bed early.

Wednesday, August 1
The three of us had breakfast together. Then Ira took off for Rockville and we downtown. No further word about a purchaser or a closer for the apartment.
Thought, if I could get the 2 Columbus cases next Thursday and Friday, Jules might join me for the weekend, and it would be a good schedule for both of us. One went off, however, so I would have to go to Moraine and Columbus, and miss one of the ABA receptions.
Picked up Jules about 5:45. Ira got home later than we did. Watched the TV news.

Then took off - in a downpour - for dinner at The Phase, very nice but the place was almost empty. Then home again. Invitation to a reception the Levys are giving to present David's wife to their family and friends.

Thursday, August 2
We all had breakfast together. Seems like old times, except that I would have had a maid around and more food on hand. But we managed well enough. Ira then took off for HEW in Rockville and we for our offices. I did not get an assignment. Jules had some clients in from Germany. They brought him a very nice bottle of Scotch.
Jules also was advised that Flynn was still waiting to hear from Brown, but I don't expect any reasonable offer from him. I picked up Jules about 5:20. Stopped at the Sheraton Park for him to register for the ABA convention. Then home. Had a large and very good dinner. Offered to invite the Levys and some others over but Ira decided he preferred to go out and visit John Hardy. He had had a long phone conversation with Mother, and we all talked to Sandy.

Friday, August 3
We had breakfast together one more time. Then Ira went to Rockville to see some people, down to Jules' office where he called me, then left the car in the garage and took a limo to National for a 12:30 plane.
Lunched with Jennie Sarrica and Mira Stevenson at the Black Horse Tavern.[29] Was advised by Jules that Brown will not make an offer. Not surprised. We had two cars downtown so I drove home alone, a little earlier than I usually do when I wait for Jules. Dinner seemed a cinch to prepare when there were just two of us. And I should start eating less than when I was preparing rather large and elaborate dinners for Ira.

Saturday, August 4
Read the paper early. After brunch pitched in on the laundry and cleaning. Don't know when I shall have a maid again. The phone repairman came. Later we went shopping. I bought a dress at Saks 5th Avenue, and Jules bought a number of small items. Did some marketing on the way home.
The Levys have an ad in the *Post* this weekend to rent their Sumner Village apartment, so were staying in with the hope of answering calls.
We were both tired and glad to have dinner and spend the evening at home. We are also pretty well reconciled to moving into our apartment in Building 2.

Sunday, August 5
We had a lovely big brunch. Read the paper for a while. Telephoned Mother to explain why we would be unable to see her today. Then dressed and took off for some ABA[30] meetings at the Sheraton Park. From there to a reception at the Washington Club in honor of Jules' partner Bracken. It was a beautiful place for a reception, and a very beautiful

---

29 Black Horse Tavern was a favorite lunch place during this time. Anne occasionally refers to Blackie's [House of Beef] was another favorite restaurant for lunch. Mira Stevenson and Fannie Boyls are her most frequent lunch partners during this time.
30 American Bar Association.

buffet table and bar. From there to another ABA reception at the Decatur House, also a lovely place for a reception, as well as very bountiful food and liquor supplies. And saw many people we knew at both receptions, some of whom we had not seem for a very long time. With all the party food, had just a snack when we got home.

Monday, August 6
Debated on the way down who should park the car. Finally Jules took it as he might need it to go to Rockville, but he did not go.
Went to the beauty parlor at noon. Jules arranged the "closing" for Thursday although it could have been next Tuesday! I recommended changing to Tuesday. After work met Jules at the Mayflower for an OSU – alumni – ABA party. Then to the Washington Hilton for a BNA-ABA party. A terrible mob scene but saw a good many "Labor Law Section" people we knew. Jules was very hungry by then – these were not parties with lavish buffet tables – so we went to the Yenching Palace for supper. Took part of it home as there was more than we could eat.

Tuesday, August 7
Went down together. Lunched at the Chesapeake with Mira Stevenson and Jennie Sarrica. Told Leff,[31] who is making the assignments, I would like one the latter part of next week in view of the Tuesday afternoon closing.
Picked up Jules about 5:45. There were a couple of ABA affairs we considered attending, but wound up going home, cooking a couple of our precious steaks – completely unavailable now – and watching the rebroadcast of the Watergate hearings. Will miss the hearings when they are in recess. Best program by far on TV this summer. And they may resume in sections before subcommittees with less TV coverage.

Wednesday, August 8
Went down together. Jules was taking Gene and Jack Levinson, here for the ABA convention, to luncheon, and urged me to join them. I did, at Paul Young's. They are by now a couple of dull old bachelors. Made Jules and me feel very lucky by comparison. Returned to find the Board decision affirming me in Carbide Tools, a case involving a good many issues, so was very pleased by that.
One of the secretaries at the office is going to take over my parking place for September. That will save me having to cancel it for the month with the question whether I would be able to resume in October as the lot is so very crowded these days.

Thursday, August 9
Went down together. A hot sultry day. Lunched at Blackie's with Sid Ascher.
Tried to convince Leff, who was making the assignments, that I should get one, but was unsuccessful.
Picked up Jules about 5:45 and drove out to Sumner Village. Went through the apartment with a finisher to point out what needed yet to be done. One of the first

---
31   Arthur Leff, who in 1973 was back in the Division of Judges and responsible for case assignments.

potential purchasers is interested again and coming in this weekend. If not sold, we settle on Tuesday, and get busy selling the house, moving, buying furnishing, etc.

Had some supper at Hamburger Hamlet. Then home. Should do something soon about selling the house. Jules procrastinates, I suspect, because he hates the idea of selling it.

Friday, August 10
Went down together. I was feeling rather "icky" most of the day, but not sick enough to stay home or to go home. The pollution alert was still in effect – the most protracted one yet.

Was advised that the parties will probably reach a stipulation in the Memphis case that will make a resumption of that hearing unnecessary. Have about finished the decision in the Saginar case but waiting for the Union's brief due next Friday. Picked up Jules about 5:45. Stopped at the grocery store on the way home. Went home for dinner.

Jules is worried about how to proceed in selling our house in the present tight-money market as it appears certain we shall settle for the apartment.

Saturday, August 11
After brunch Jules got busy and cleared out some of the accumulation of "junk" in the storage closet. Plenty more to do.

Later we went shopping for gifts for David Levy and his wife and for Irv Jaffe's birthday. Later met the Levys at the Apex and saw "Day of the Jackel,"[32] – not so exciting as the book but a pretty interesting movie as movies these days go. From there to the North China restaurant. About 9:45 when we got there but, fortunately, Bill had a made a reservation as it was still crowded at that hour. Had a very good dinner and pretty good service as the crowd began finally to thin out. They will move into Sumner Village if they don't rent their apartment.

Sunday, August 12
We read the paper for awhile. Then had a lovely brunch. A very hot day but the pollution alert was finally ended. We drove out to the produce stands and bought some fresh vegetables. Later visited Mother and took her to the Hot Shoppe. She told us the Rolands had gone to a beach for a long weekend. Had a terrific supper of steaks, fresh corn, string beans, tomatoes, etc.

Jules was tempted to call Sumner Village as this was the last weekend before we settle. Did not call as we were sure Karras would have called us if there was a possible purchaser.

Monday, August 13
Went down together. Lunched with Jennie Sarrica at Chez Odette. She and Mira Stevenson have assignments later this week in Detroit. They can travel together and have company at meals, a nice setup compared to usual aloneness.

Picked up Jules about 5:45. Stopped at the grocery store on the way home. Letter from Nate enclosing his itinerary for a trip he and Bobbie are making, again, to the Iberian

---

32   A 1973 movie about a foiled assasination plot against Charles DeGaulle. Mystery/thriller.

Peninsula. We sat down this evening and made a few decisions on our trip to Mexico. Planned to go about September 1 but Jules has a court argument on September 6. And have been so busy with house - apartment problems have done virtually no vacation planning.

Tuesday, August 14
Went down together. Lunched with Mira Stevenson at Blackie's.
Picked up Jules about 3 and drove out to the law office where we were "closing" on the apartment. Jules had checks with him totaling over $26,000. Glad he was handling it. Most of it was beyond my comprehension. He even got a change made in the form language over strong opposition. Drove out then to Sumner to pick up the keys. Agreed to come out on Saturday to be shown the storage setup and some other details of living at Sumner Village. Home for dinner.
Called Bill and gave him the benefit of Jules' experience at the closing so Bill can demand the same change, etc.

Wednesday, August 15
Went down together. Lunched at Blackie's with Asher, Lipton, and Ohlbaum.
Got word that the parties will probably enter a stipulation in the Memphis case making it unnecessary for me to go there to resume the hearing. Asked to go somewhere else, preferably where I could pick up 2 or 3 short cases. Letter from Ira, first word since he left here, sent Air Mail, apparently because Phil Howell is in town for a few days and refused to call us because he felt it might seem an imposition. We shall try to reach him. We like him very much for himself and because he is a very good friend of Ira's.
Called Alice Jaffe. She will post a notice at school about our house for sale.

Thursday, August 16
Went down together. Jules called to tell me he had been advised that an Israeli couple with 3 small children wanted to rent the apartment but at considerably less than the asking price and with a 3-year lease. He turned it down.
Had asked Leff and Goslee for 2 or 3 short cases. Got a 1-day case in Fort Worth.
Picked up Jules about 5:45. Went to the Shade Shop with one of the new shades that does not work properly. Did a couple of other errands. Had dinner at Kushner's. Then home.
Jules had reached Phil Howell today. He will come to Jules' office tomorrow afternoon, and we will take him to dinner. The question remains where we shall take him.

Friday, August 17
Went down together. Lunched at the Chesapeake with Jennie Sarrica.
Got word about 4 that the Fort Worth case was off. Got an assignment instead in Brooklyn starting Monday morning. Could not get a plane ticket, or a reservation on American, and the case had a 3-day estimate. Picked up Jules and Phil Howell at 5:45. We went for a ride, a walk in the Georgetown area, and then to La Pauvre Immigrant for a drink in the cocktail lounge and dinner in

the dining room. Most of the conversation was Phil raving about Ira, partly because he thinks very highly of Ira, and partly no doubt because he knew we would never tire of the subject. Then took him back to the Burlington Hotel, and went home to read the morning *Post*.

Saturday, August 18
Did a little more closet cleaning. Then over to Sumner Village. Went through the apartment with Ferreter – still things to be done, and got our keys – but someone was using our storage bin and put on his own padlock. Ran into some of the Levys. Went to see their apartment. It had some features much nicer than ours. Then went to look at washer-dryers. Home for supper.
Later dressed and went to the Levy party in the party room at the Irene. They had a lot of family, a lot of friends, and very lavish buffet and bar. They tried to reach us last night to come over for a little celebration with Irv and Alice of Irv's birthday but we were out with Phil Howell. It was a lovely party and we both had a very good time. Home quite late.

Sunday, August 19
Ira called. We talked to all four of them. They all sounded fine. Then to a brunch party at the Jaffes' in honor of Irv's birthday. Alice had told Irv she was having just relatives and a few close friends but it was a mob scene and a great reunion for a lot of us old-timers.
Stopped to visit Mother on the way home. Did some cleaning, laundry, fixed a big dinner, and packed. Too bad the way this trip worked out, as the real estate agent Jules picked had been ill but may come back to look over the house tomorrow evening. But the Grimes have been advertising, posting the house for sale, etc., and their house is in far better condition than ours, but theirs has not been sold. Don't know what their condominium deadline is.

Monday, August 20
Jules and I got up earlier than usual, and he took me to National. I missed the 8:00 shuttle, could not get on the 8:30 American, but got on the 9:00 shuttle. Took a cab from La Guardia and got to the hearing in good time. Spent a good deal of the time discussing settlement but finally went to hearing. Recessed at 5 with an indication we would go all day tomorrow. Checked in at The Gotham. Then walked over to Stouffer's for dinner. The dinner was pretty good, and I enjoyed taking a little walk on Fifth Avenue. But it had been a long and tiring day so I went back to the room, watched some TV, and went to bed relatively early. Decided to check out tomorrow but make a reservation in case I had to stay over.

Tuesday, August 21
Checked out, made a reservation, had some breakfast, and got to Brooklyn for the 9:30 resumption. Took about a 20-minute lunch break-over the reporter's opposition as he was trying to get in another hearing – and finished about 2:30. Took a cab to La Guardia, and took the 4:30 American flight.

Called Jules office. He had been in conference all day in Chantilly but left word he would pick me up – I had sent him a message when I expected to get in – at the shuttle gate. I walked over there. He got there about 6. We stopped at the Empress in Silver Spring for supper. Then home. He took Howell to dinner last night. Announcement of marriage of Ricky Ruscoll.[33] No announcement bearing on the sale of either house or the apartment.

Wednesday, August 22
Went down together.
Lunched at Blackie's with Jennie Sarrica.
Got exceptions to my decision in the Tulsa case. Issued an order closing the hearing in the Memphis case. And signed my decision in the Saginaw case. The real estate agent Jules called is still sick but will try to come this weekend. We have lost out on two good weekends for sale of houses before school opens. But as mortgage money is so hard to get it might not have made any real difference. Ruth Kline called and invited us to a party on September 22. Had to decline as we shall be returning late that evening from Mexico according to our present plans.

Thursday, August 23
Went down together. Lunched at Blackie's with Ben Lipton and Sid Ascher. Kessel gave me a choice between 2 cases in different cities in Texas and one in Chicago. Chose the one in Chicago.
Picked up Jules at 5:45. Started to go home but he suggested we look at washers and dryers. Drove out to Landover Mall. Got a good salesman at the Dalmo Store and believe we have narrowed down our choices. Had a very enjoyable dinner at the House of the Liu there. Then picked up a few groceries and went home to have dessert and read this morning's *Post*.

Friday, August 24
Wenn down together. Made my travel arrangements.
Lunched at Jason's with Maller and Ascher. Invited Gloria to come as my guest in honor of her birthday but she asked for a rain check.
Bought a $25,000 Treasury note. Ran into several other ALJ's [i.e. Administrative Law Judges] at the Treasury. Picked up Jules about 5:40. Went home. Fixed lamb chops for dinner. Very good. Are going to have to eat our meals at home pretty much until we leave for Mexico as I would like to use up all the meat we have in the freezer. The Levys are running an ad in the *Post* all weekend to rent their Sumner Village apartment. Would like to rent it for a year or so and then move into it.

Saturday, August 25
Had breakfast and read the paper for a while. Then dressed and went to Sumner Village. Put some stuff in our storage area as we found someone else using it last week. But much remains to be done in the apartment. Did some bawling out with no satisfaction. Then went shopping. I need some things for our trip to Mexico but did not find anything I wanted.

---

33 The son of Anne's sister Jan.

Then home. Fixed a big brisket for dinner. It was delicious. And Jules has enough food he likes and does not have to cook to last him much longer than I shall be in Chicago.

Did some laundry and house-cleaning. Should get a maid in soon to give the house a good cleaning before we show it to potential buyers.

Sunday, August 26
The real estate saleswoman Jules had called was supposed to call by noon about coming to see the house, but did not. I decided we had wasted too much time on her, called an agency, got a Mrs. Miller, who came out on schedule and got a 60-day contract for multi-listing the house.

Took Mother for a ride and milkshake, which she enjoyed very much.

Had lamb chops for dinner. Had to use them up as they were not in the freezer.

Evelyn Kaplan, Jules' real estate choice, called this evening. Told her we had switched and why. It is in the same agency so she may yet be the one to sell it, but not the one to get the contract.

Monday, August 27
Jules arranged to have the painter in early tomorrow to see about re-doing a ceiling at Mrs. Miller's suggestion. And the whole swarm of agents will go through the house during the day. Wish the house were cleaner than it is. What a time for me to be away!

Jules dropped me in the morning. I left the office about 3 for National. Took a TWA flight at 4. Dinner was served on the plane.

Got to Chicago about 5 CST. It was hot and humid in Washington, with a pollution alert again for several days. It was also hot and humid in Chicago.

Took the bus to the Palmer House. Was given a pleasant large room on the 21st floor. Spent a long evening reading and watching TV. Probably should have come in tomorrow for an 11 o'clock hearing.

Tuesday, August 28
Had a leisurely breakfast in the coffee shop. Took a walk, although it was a hot and humid day. Then to the Federal Building for an 11 o'clock hearing in a case with union respondents. It was bitterly fought on every question, answer, objection, and ruling.

Lunched at Bergdoff's.

Recessed about 5:15. Had not finished the first witness.

Had dinner later in the Steak House, one of the several dining rooms in the hotel. Jules called later. Letter from Ira indicating we overlooked Sandy's birthday. Jules will send her a check and an apology. A thank-you note from the David Levys. Jules had been out to the apartment. Much of the cleaning, etc., had finally been done. And several real estate salespeople have been through the house.

Wednesday, August 29
Had breakfast in the coffee shop – a good deal earlier than yesterday as the hearing resumed at 9. Counsel was more argumentative and wordy than ever. Recessed for luncheon about 1:30. I had a sandwich at a nearby café. Then back for a long afternoon. No chance

of finishing tomorrow. Think I will adjourn tomorrow instead of a holiday weekend. Counsel cannot make it next week as it may have to be continued until I get back form Mexico – which is suffering a series of devastating floods and earthquakes.

Had called and left a message this afternoon for Claire Edes. Had an early supper at Berghoff's. The Edes[34] called and urged me to come to dinner or for the evening, but I "took a rain check" until I return next month.

Thursday, August 30

Had breakfast in the coffee shop. The hearing resumed at 9:30. Ran until about 2:30 with no luncheon break. Then adjourned until October 2. Called Kessel[35] to let him know, asked him to let Jules know I would be home this evening.

Checked out, took the bus to the airport, and got an American flight at 4:30. Had dinner on the plane. Got in at 7:10 and called Jules at the office. He picked me up. He was completely broken out in a rash, which had affected one eye, looked terrible and apparently felt miserable. He saw an eye doctor today, is seeing a dermatologist tomorrow, and suspects it may be an allergy. Hope he clears it up so he can make the trip to Mexico. A real estate agent with a couple leaving the house when we arrived.

Friday, August 31

We went down together. Lunched with Jennie Sarrica at Adam's Ark. Drove there in her Lincoln Continental.

Jules called in the afternoon. Had been getting massive injections at Dr. Soolar's, falling asleep, and getting more injections. The doctor did not want him to drive home. I picked him up about 6:30 and drove directly home. An agent had been in the house and left his card.

Jules napped, ate some supper, and napped some more. He had shingles, and the doctor does not know yet whether Jules will be able to take off for Mexico on Friday. We may go later just for the Knoll[36] meetings in Mexico City.

Postcard form Bobbie and Nate[37] in Portugal.

Jules with Anne

---

34   Sam and Claire Edes, old friends.
35   Coordinator of case assignments.
36   Jules' important German client.
37   Jules' brother Nate and his wife.

1974

Anne and Jules started 1974 meeting new people in the apartment complex. Anne's mother was in the hospital. The doctors reported that she was doing well, but she could no longer live by herself. Ira recommended Randolph Hills Nursing Home, which Jules, Anne, Clara, and the mother accepted. The family moved her there on April 17.

Anne was busy traveling much of the year, hearing cases in various places. On April 23 she wrote, "My Carbide Tools decision, short-formed by the Board, has been ordered enforced in a default judgment by the Court of Appeals. Goslee indicated he was going to give me 2 cases in Detroit next week. Unfortunately they are spaced so I would be away all week, and the second one is a secondary boycott case." Both she and Jules were traveling almost weekly.

Anne's entry for Sunday May 5 tells about her life at this time. She wrote, "Ira called early, somewhat to my surprise, as I told Sandy on Friday I was coming in or would let her know. We talked to all four. They all seemed fine and glad I was coming. Too bad Jules could not join us.

"Had a brunch. Read the *Post*. Finished the cleaning. Packed.[38] Picked up our bakery items, etc., etc.[39]

"Jennie[40] called - had unexpected guests and could not come. Clara called to chat about mother's condition and insurance.

"The Levys, Jaffes, Michaels, and Middlemans came - the last with a bottle of wine for a new-home gift. All admired the apartment. We had a pleasant and interesting discussion of "The Partners" and other subjects, all enjoyed the Gourmet Shop desserts, it was a pleasant evening, and we were up very late cleaning up."

In August they took the first driving vacation in many years and returned to Quebec, which was especially important to Anne, and Nova Scotia. For their thirty-fifth anniversary on September 1 they were in Halifax.

Back at the office Anne had lunch with Fannie Boyls, her oldest friend at the NLRB, on September 10, and she wrote, "Lunched with Fannie Boyls at Blackie's. She is one of the large group planning to retire in December. I should probably add my name." The thought occurred to her, but she never retired. On September 16 she wrote, "New Year's card from the Levys, addressed to "Mr. and Judge." She mentioned on other occasions receiving mail addressed the same way. She enjoyed being addressed as Judge. -- RDH

Monday, September 30

Took my bags down but kept the car – just in case. Ran into Kessel and mentioned my problem. He insisted it was no problem, called Atlanta, which called back after a check with the parties and okayed the changes. I went home at noon and changed

---

[38] She was traveling the next day to Tulsa for a case she was hearing there.
[39] The bakery items were for the Book Club that was meeting at their apartment that night.
[40] NLRB colleague Jennie Sarrica and Anne's sister Clara.

my clothes. Brought a coat down for Jules as the forecast was for much cooler weather this evening.

Picked up Jules about 6, we parked near Fran O'Brien's, met Neil and Eva Naiden there for drinks – on Jules – and dinner, included in the football tickets. Then by bus, also included in the tickets, to the stadium to see a very enjoyable football game as the Redskins beat the Detroit Broncos 30 – 3. By the time we got back downtown on the bus and drove home, we got home about 1, and to bed about 2, and set the alarm for 6 o'clock.

Tuesday, October 1
We got up about 6 and left about 7. Jules ate breakfast downtown. I was served breakfast on my Delta flight to Atlanta. Got a limo to the hearing. Arrived well before 11. Got counsel talking settlement. To their surprise and mine, the discussion went on at length and culminated in a settlement. I called the office, sent word to Jules, cancelled the hotel reservation, and took a United flight at about 6. Dinner was served and tasted very good after a light luncheon with the reporter, Betty Batson, at Morrison Cafeteria. Arrived late. Jules was waiting. We went home. The trouble with the settlement is that I am certain to have to go out again next week.

Wednesday, October 2
Up early again. I took Jules downtown. He got a cab to National for the 9 o'clock shuttle to New York.

My Gilbert Intl. decision, excepted to both GC [General Counsel] and Respondent, was short-formed by the Board.

Lunched at Blackie's with Mira Stevenson. It was a chilly day. I was cold in the office and when I went out for luncheon.

Jules called about 4:30. Expected to take the 6 o'clock shuttle. We agreed I might as well go home, and he would take a cab. He called again from National about 7:20. Then came running in for some money as the cabbie could not change a $20 bill. Then he had some supper.

Nate called to make plans for a football weekend in Columbus.

Thursday, October 3
We went down together. Lunched with Fannie Boyls at Blackie's.

Was assigned a 3-day case in Rockford, Illinois. Found I would have to drive from O'Hare as connecting flights were too early or too late. Kessel was adamant about changing, but finally, when I said I would retire first, gave me a 4-5 days case in Baton Rouge, starting Monday morning. I would have to leave early Sunday afternoon to make connections, but at least I would not have to drive. And have to leave there early Friday morning as the afternoon connections are all booked.

Picked up Jules about 5:45. Picked up a few groceries on the way home. Had "Annie burgers" for dinner – very good.

Friday, October 4
Went down together. Decided I could probably get to the hearing on Monday

morning instead of Sunday afternoon if it was changed from 10 to 11. It was, and I changed my reservation accordingly.

A pleasant day, warmer than it was been lately. Lunched at Circle One with Mira Stevenson and Jennie Sarrica.[41]

Picked up Jules about 5:45. Did a couple of errands on the way home – mainly looking for a laundry – cleaner where we can stop on the way to and from work. We both had eaten big lunches so stopped at Hamburger Hamlet for a light supper, which wound up costing as much as complete dinners. Then home. My "New Yorker" did not come today – first time it has missed since April.

Saturday, October 5

A beautiful sunny day. Jules called AAA first thing. When the Olds got started, we took it to a gas station for a battery charge, in 2 cars, came home in the Duster, had our brunch, did the cleaning, and read *The Post*. In the afternoon went to pick up the Olds. Jules drove it and did some errands, and I did some using the Duster. Later we walked to the shopping center to pick up a few things but mainly to take a walk as it was a lovely afternoon.

We had broiled veal chops for dinner, and baked potatoes, among Jules' favorite food. Bought the potatoes at the health store in our shopping center. Spent the evening reading, watching TV, and talking.

---

41 Almira Stevenson and Jennie Sarrica (Goicoechea) were friends, NLRB judges, and frequent lunch companions.

Sunday, October 6

We read *The Post* – I even did the crossword and double-crostic puzzles, ate brunch, and did our house-cleaning. Were glad to find the Olds started all right. Jules admits the battery was run down by his garage people playing the radio. But he won't park in my garage when I am away. Went to see Mother. A beautiful warm day but did not take her for a ride. She has a notion that all her troubles are caused by a cold, and now has 3 electric heaters in the apartment, and worries if they are enough. On the way home stopped at the Rock Creek delicatessen and picked up some things for supper. Ate in the living room watching the news, etc., on TV. Jules took a walk. I packed. Hard to know what to take or what the weather will be.

Monday, October 7

Jules and I got up at 6 and left about 7. I had breakfast on the Delta flight to Baton Rouge. Got to the hearing just a minute or two late. The hearing room was terrible. Managed to get it changed to a magistrate's courtroom across the street. Looks like this is going to be a long hearing. I lunched at a cafeteria with the reporter, Mary Bagby. Recessed at 5:30. Although staying elsewhere, the reporter gave me a ride to the Prince Murat Inn. Got quite a nice room across a large courtyard from the main building. Had dinner in the dining room, very much alone, as I was the first guest and very few came in later. And the food was only so-so. But this is it for the next few days as this looks like a long hearing.

Tuesday, October 8
Had breakfast in the coffee shop. Liked it better than dinner in the dining room. The reporter picked me up about 8:15. The hearing resumed at 9. I lunched at a sandwich shop with the reporter. A lovely sunny day, the temperature about 85. Glad I brought a couple of light-weight dresses. Recessed about 5:30. The reporter, who uses the face-mask system, was exhausted after her stint of almost non-stop talking. The reporter gave me a ride to the motel. I have invited her to dinner as my guest. She usually types in the evening but will try to make it tomorrow. I was reaching for the phone to call Jules when he called me, just back from a day in Chicago. There was a letter from Ira. All was well. Went to the dining room alone. A young man named Ogden, also alone, joined me. An art director in Mississippi.

Wednesday, October 9
Mary Bagby did not say anything yesterday about picking me up this morning. Surprised when she called from the lobby. Came over for breakfast. We ate together. Then to the hearing at 9. We lunched together at the cafeteria. Although we shall be in session tomorrow, one company counsel will be absent so asked for the adjournment date to be set. Set it for Nov. 5. Called to Kessel to let him know. Recessed at 5:30. Bagby gave me a ride back to the motel.
Later I had dinner alone in the dining room. Getting pretty fed up with the place, the solitude, the very limited menu. The coffee shop is not open for dinner and there is not a dining place in the vicinity of the motel. Would certainly like to get home tomorrow evening.

Thursday, October 10
I met the reporter in the coffee shop and we had breakfast together. Then to the hearing. Recessed for lunch shortly after 12. Appeared then that I could get away in time for the afternoon flight, but could not get a reservation through to Washington. Drove to the State Capitol with the reporter. Friend of hers who works there gave us the grand tour. Took so long we had to skip luncheon. During a recess I bought some candy bars for both of us. Adjourned about 4. I had received no call –back from Delta. The reporter took me back to the motel. Then she took off for her home in Fort Worth.
Called the office. Asked that Jules be told I could not get back tonight. Was told I had an assignment for Tuesday. Should not have called yesterday about the adjournment. Had dinner once more in the dining room.

Friday, October 11
Got up and packed early. Had been told at the desk that the courtesy car would take me to the airport whenever I wished but there was some delay this morning. I had breakfast in the coffee shop, left about 8, and took a 9 am flight, with a change in Atlanta, to National. Luncheon was served on the second half of the trip. Took a cab to the office. Called Jules. Saw my hearing Tuesday was in Columbus and started at 1:00, so did not complain. Made my arrangements for travel but not for a motel. Called the Lewin shop. Milt insisted

I stay with Gertrude.[42] Would rather stay at downtown motel. We shall see.

Jules had parked in my garage. Picked him up about 5:45. Went home, then to the Woodmont deli for a shabbos[43] dinner, and then to services as Jules had yahrzeit for his mother.

Saturday, October 12
We both got up early, and had a relatively early brunch. I did all of Jules' cleaning. Walked to the shopping center where Jules bought some toilet articles. Then Jules packed. I did not want to drive back from Dulles alone so took him downtown to get the bus to Dulles. Realized as I drove home, with a stop at the grocery store, that Jules had forgotten his raincoat unless it was packed. Just got in the door when he called from Dulles. He did forget the coat. Thought of it after he got on the airport bus. We agreed he should buy a new one although he likes this present one, which he bought in London, very much.

I had dinner alone. Spent most of the evening reading. Watched some TV. Glad Jules was asked to come to Germany, but sorry it had to be over a holiday weekend.

Sunday, October 13
Got up rather early and rather headachy. Had some oatmeal, read a little of the *Post*, and went to bed again. Felt much better when I got up the second time.

Ira called. I talked to all four. Sorry Jules missed the call. I called Mother but did not go over to see her. Did not want to do all that driving alone.

In fact did not go out at all although it was a lovely autumn day. I cannot complain about Jules being away as I am away so much myself. But I am never away over a weekend, and try hard to avoid being away even part of a weekend. It is much easier to be alone when one is most of the day at the office.

Monday, October 14
Had a leisurely breakfast and read the *Post*. Then went to the beauty shop in our shopping center for a shampoo and set. It cost almost 3 times what I pay downtown, but the work was a little better, and my hair was very dirty. Did a couple of other errands, but did not go to any of the holiday sales.

Gertrude called in the early evening to confirm my arrival tomorrow as reported to her by Milton.

A little later Jules called to let me know he would not be home until Saturday afternoon and to ask for Gertrude's telephone number in case he had to get in touch with me while I am in Columbus.

Later I packed so I could get an early start.

Tuesday, October 15
I drove down to the office, parked in the garage, took care of some office matters, and took a cab to National for the 10 am United flight to Columbus. Gertrude picked me up at the airport. We drove downtown and lunched at the Lazarus Tea Room. Then Gertrude sat in on the hearing for a while, but had to leave after a while. The Graham

---

42   Jules' sister Gertrude Lewin in Columbus.
43   Shabbat.

Ford hearing recessed about 5. I called Gertrude, who picked me up. We went to her apartment. Invited her and some others to let me take them to dinner. Only Gertrude and Madalyn were able to accept. We went to the Longhorn. The dinner was good, an inexpensive affair as none of us had a cocktail or dessert. Madalyn came back to Gertrude's and we visited a while longer. Then she left and we went to bed.

Wednesday, October 16
Gertrude and I had breakfast. Then she drove me to the hearing and went on to her office. The hearing resumed at 9:30. When we recessed for lunch, I ate at Lazarus with the young girl reporter. Finished the hearing about 3. If Jules were at home or if I were at a motel, I would have tried to get the late afternoon flight. Instead called Gertrude, went home with her and relaxed for a while. Then to Elaine's. Brought her kids some candy. Then the three of us drove to a new and very beautiful Garden restaurant where Gertrude was having a dinner party. We were joined by Madalyn (Ed could not make it), Milton, and Ellen and Leonard. Enjoyed it very much. Elaine and Milt came back to the apartment for a while. When they left, we watched the 11 o'clock news and went to bed.

Thursday, October 17
Gertrude and I had breakfast. Then she took me to the airport, and I got the 9:25 TWA flight to National. A lovely day and a pleasant flight, with a snack. Took a cab to the office. After going through some of the stuff on my desk, postponed the Baton Rouge resumption from November 5, Election Day, to November 6, changed my travel reservations, well in advance, as I will probably be coming back on Friday evening. Left the office a bit early and went home. Called the *Post* Tuesday when our paper did not come. It still did not, nor yesterday's, but today's was there. Also a letter from Ira and a note from Ellen about coming to Florida in February. She told me in Columbus about the plans.

Friday, October 18
Overslept badly. Changed the alarm time but apparently omitted some step in setting it. But got to the office in good time by dressing in a hurry and skipping breakfast.
A chilly day but sunny. Lunched with Mira Stevenson at Blackie's.
Picked up a few things at the grocery store on the way home.
Another letter from Ira. Our package for David's birthday had arrived, but the birthday party had not been held when this letter was written.
A very quiet evening. The phone did not ring once. I fixed and ate dinner. Read this morning's *Post*. Did some household chores. And read a little in one of the *New Yorkers*. I am months behind in reading them.

Saturday, October 19
I had breakfast and read the *Post*. Should have gone marketing but I was not sure when Jules would get in. Figured I would go to the store on the way back from picking him up at the

limo terminal downtown. When he called, however, he had already arranged to take the bus from Dulles to Bethesda. Not sure which motel was the bus stop, I stayed at home and he took a cab from the motel. He was very enthusiastic about what he accomplished on the trip. He was also suffering from time-lag, and was totally uninterested in a meal. I had a light supper, and he joined me just for a bite. He unpacked, looked at the *Post*, and went to bed early, and, apparently fell asleep right away.

Sunday, October 20
We read the paper for a while, had brunch, and Jules took a nap. I did some housecleaning. He did not, but I did not make an issue of it. Ira called. We talked to all four. David thanked us for his birthday gift but indicated he needed money for paints for some models. He is broke because he has to pay for a bike tire he wrecked. Would like to send him the money but don't want to disrupt Ira's discipline.
In the late afternoon – after watching the Redskins trounce the Giants – we went to visit Mother. From there went to Kushner's. It was very crowded and we had a long wait, but at least the dinner was excellent when we got it. We went home from there. By the time we finished the *Post*, it was time for bed.

Monday, October 21
We went down together – first time in quite a while – in the Duster. The Olds battery is dead again as Jules found yesterday. Will probably get a new one next Saturday.

Went to the library and lunched at Blackie's with Mira Stevenson. Picked up Jules about 6. Stopped at the grocery store on the way home. He wanted to go to a political-candidates presentation at Ohr Kodesh after dinner, but I was not inclined to get dressed and go out again at that time. He did not mind too much as there was a football game broadcast he wanted to watch.
Looks like our apartment is going to be cold again this winter in spite of the assurances that the heat has been "adjusted."

Tuesday, October 22
We went down together. Made the mistake of telling Kessel I had given Wanda a decision to stencil and had no other case on my desk. Got 4 volumes a few minutes later of the Baton Rouge transcript, but Kessel said he would give me a case nevertheless. Picked up Jules about 6. Went out of our way to stop at a particular gas station and got caught in slow-moving traffic, so went to Hamburger Hamlet, nearby at that point, for dinner. Had rotisserie chicken which this evening was unusually good. Then home.
Some chap called Jules. Has lived in the area for years but just got Jules' number from Edward, one of the several Schlezingers he has known for years.

Wednesday, October 23
Went down together. Jules called me in the morning to let me know we had both been invited to a reception at the British Embassy which I would have to miss as I would be back in Baton Rouge. Too bad.

Picked up Jules about 5:25. He is apparently still suffering from jet lag as he said he had felt groggy much of the day. We had a big steak dinner. Soon after we finished clearing up, he was snoozing on the sofa, which is quite unlike him. Hope he is not coming down with something. There is a good deal of flu around my office and elsewhere.

Thursday, October 24
Went down together. Was assigned a 2-day case in Indianapolis. Made my arrangements, and then was told the case settled. Persuaded Kessel to hold off another case.
Went to the NLRB service awards ceremony as it was a chance to chat with Fahy[44] and other old-timers.
Picked up Jules about 5:40, feeling much better. We went home for dinner. Clara called. They are going to New York for the long holiday weekend.
Thank-you letter from David for his birthday present. I have sent him and Eric money for trick-or-treat.[45] David said Sunday he had forfeited his allowance for a long period for carelessness with his bike, and needed some. Wrote that this was not to undermine his discipline.

Friday, October 25
Went down together. Decided not to go to FALJ[46] luncheon although I was offered a ride and several escorts.
Eva Naiden called in the late afternoon to report that Neil was not feeling well and they would not be able to use their theater tickets this evening. We offered them to a few people at Jules' office and mine, but many had already left, or had other plans, and the rest had seen the play, and it was too late to call people in the suburbs. The tickets were wasted. We went to the Kennedy Center, had some supper in the cafeteria there, saw "Sherlock Holmes" which we both enjoyed very much, and which was playing to standing room audiences, and went home after the show.

Saturday, October 26
Bill Levy called in the morning, said he tried yesterday evening, to ask if we wanted to dine out with them tonight. I suggested instead having dinner tomorrow before the book club meeting. They agreed. Had AAA out right after breakfast to charge the Olds battery again. Then drove to Montgomery Mall, Jules to get a new battery at Sears and I to do some shopping at Garfinckel's. Did some errands and picked up some delicatessen for supper. Had some luncheon at the Mall. Were out most of the day, but it was a pleasant warm day, which helped.
Spent the evening resting, reading, and watching TV. Decided to let the weekly cleaning go until tomorrow and Monday as I prefer doing that in the early part of the day.

Sunday, October 27
Ira called early. We talked to all four. David thanked us for the Halloween check. Eric had too many other things to talk about.
Telephoned Mother but did not go over.

---
44   Charles Fahy, old colleague, and Judge U.S. District Court, D.C. Circuit
45   Grandsons David and Eric
46   Federal Administrative Law Judges.

Jules wanted to watch a football game and we were having dinner early with the Levys – then they called, had been at a reception, did not want to eat. After brunch we did some cleaning and laundry. Walked to the shopping center twice to do errands and to get out on a lovely day.

Had dinner at home. Then to the book club meeting at the Michaels'. Lasted later than usual in view of the holiday.

Set our clocks back an hour, the beginning of dark evenings.

Monday, October 28
Another lovely warm day. Read the paper. Had brunch. Did some housecleaning. Then went to see Mother. As it was so warm, took her for a long ride which she enjoyed very much. On the way home did some errands. Called the Naidens about the second series of plays, just as a gesture as they have seen only one of the three shows so far, but Eva called back after talking to Neil and asked us to get tickets for them also. Their tickets for "Sherlock Holmes" were wasted, which was a shame.

Jules would like to drive to Columbus next weekend. If the weather stays like it is now, I shall be sorry I asked that we fly instead.

Tuesday, October 29
We went down together. George Powell, who is retiring in December, took a group of us in two cars to Fellowship House for a very pleasant and interesting luncheon. The awards committee chairman called. Apparently my records are fouled up again – or still – but I have over 40 years of government service. Jules had to go back to the Watergate apartments for a conference so left the office about 5:15 – dark already nevertheless. We went home, had dinner, he changed his shirt, and went back downtown. Got home again about 10:30.

We are ready for trick-or-treaters but wonder if any will come.

Wednesday, October 30
Went down together. Later went to the other building to get a flu shot. Also made an appointment for a cancer test.

Lunched at Blackie's with Mira Stevenson. Picked up Jules about 5:45. He had tried to call Gertrude at the shop to let her know our schedule, but she and Milton were both out. Called her at home later this evening. She insisted she would pick us up and have a borrowed car for Jules. He had wanted to drive in the first place, or to rent a car after we got there.

We had broiled loin lamb chops for dinner for the first time in quite a while. Outrageously expensive but very good.

Thursday, October 31
Went down together. A lovely warm day. Went up to about 80. I went to the beauty parlor. Walked there and back.

Picked up Jules about 6. In honor of my hairdo, and in view of the scarcity of food at home before our departure for the weekend, we stopped at Old Europe for dinner, which turned out to be quite enjoyable. Then home. Invitation to the bar mitzvah of Frank Itkin's son. Surprised me as I know Frank slightly and his family not at all. And it is the Saturday of the Thanksgiving weekend. Jules would like to go away that weekend even if not to Tulsa.

1975

Anne's mother continued to be a concern for her. On January 5 she wrote, "In the afternoon we went to visit mother. Her mind plays more and more tricks on her. It is probably due to a combination of old age and being so much alone."

On January 8 her entry has two comments that reflect her concerns, she wrote, "Stopped for milk on the way home. Spotted a good-looking whole strip of beef and splurged. The butcher cut it up into beautiful-looking steaks. Should come in handy when Ira and the family are here.

"Betty Murphy was named to the Board. Wonder if my speech at the meeting of 'executive women', about never having had a woman Board member, did her any good. Could not have hurt her."

Betty Southard Murphy was the first woman Chairman of the NLRB, but Anne mentions it only casually after the visit to the butcher. She had aspired to be a Board member, but at this point she knew that it would not happen. Mira Stevenson continued as an important lunch companion, but Fannie Boyls had retired in December, 1974 and was no longer there. On February 28 she wrote, "Received a desk pen set engraved for my 35 years of service, 2 years late. My records are apparently still fouled up."

In February Anne and Jules made a vacation trip to Palm Beach, but as an indication of her frequent travel, Anne had a hearing in Texas immediately before the trip and one in Brooklyn immediately afterward. She was regularly in and out of airports.

On May 29 Anne wrote, "A number of messages on my desk including one that the doctor wants to see me about the Georgetown report on my cancer test. I consider that a bad omen. Jules asked me to meet him for luncheon but I was in too blue a mood. Will see the doctor Tuesday morning."

On June 3, she wrote, "Got a ride to the other building to see Dr. Anderson. He told me, as I had feared, that the Georgetown clinic report was rather ominous. I walked back to the office to collect my wits." Another meeting the next day suggested that she should have more tests. Anne was 65 years old. She continued working and traveling a full schedule even with her concerns about health.

Their social life was filled with dinners with the friends and comings and goings as people went on vacations. As an experienced person in Washington, Anne repeatedly received requests to assist a son, daughter, niece or nephew with an internship or recommendations about jobs.

In August they went to Cape Cod for vacation, repeating a trip they had made many times years earlier.   -- RDH

Sunday, June 1

Read part of the *Post*. Then had a large brunch. Did our Sunday cleaning chores. Then read more of the *Post* and rested.
Showered, dressed, and went to see Mother. She seemed well. Stopped at the Rock Creek delicatessen on the way home to pick up a few things. The kids called after we got home. Both boys got very good final reports from school, David did splendidly in a swimming

meet, and Eric is on a winning baseball team and did well in his first piano recital. And they all sounded well and happy. Had supper at home. Then I caught up on the ironing I had permitted to accumulate.

Monday, June 2
We went down together. To the other building in the morning for a meeting of the committee on an ALJ[47] conference with some of the Board people.
Got a report that my cholesterol test was ok. Too bad I could not do as well on the cancer test. Picked up Jules about 5:30.
Had "Annie Burgers," fresh asparagus, fresh peaches, etc., for dinner. We both enjoyed it very much. Read the first story in *The Pagan Rabbi*, our book club selection, and waded through a second story. Disliked them very much and do not intend to read any more of the book. Curious to see if anyone else in the book club will have enjoyed the stories.

Tuesday, June 3
Got a ride over to the other building to see Dr. Anderson. He told me, as I had feared, that the Georgetown clinic report was rather ominous. I walked back to the office to collect my wits. Called Dr. Ney and made an appointment to see him tomorrow afternoon, with the Georgetown report which the nurse sent to me.
Jules invited me to luncheon but I was in the mood for anything gala. Picked him up about 6. Went home for dinner as there were some steaks in the refrigerator I did not want to keep there any longer. They were delicious and the meal was, Jules told me, a banquet. Then watched some TV and went to bed, worried about my appointment with Dr. Ney.

Wednesday, June 4
We went down together. Told Goslee about my problem as I should ordinarily be going out. He was sympathetic as his wife had had these problems. Said he would give me a short Philadelphia case if it fitted my schedule.
My appointment with Ney was 3:30. I checked and was told he was running late so went about 4. He took me about 5. But it was worth the wait as he was very reassuring. His clinical test, like that of the office doctor and of the clinic, showed nothing, and he said the other tests were of value only if properly interpreted. He suggested a double-check with another doctor. I agreed.
We met at the garage, had supper at Hamburger Hamlet, and then home.

Thursday, June 5
We went down together. I got an appointment to see Dr. Klopp a week from tomorrow. Goslee gave me the Philadelphia case, a nice short one, but it means missing the first meeting of the ALJ conference committee.
Jules called to tell me Liz Coleman died. Lunched with Jo Klein and Milt Janus at the Embers Restaurant, complete with cocktails. Our $36,000 salaries are still frozen but our checks have gone from $897.90 to $915.40 because of a recent change in tax laws.

---

47   Administrative Law Judge.

Picked up Jules about 5:45. Went home. He had a big luncheon also, so we both settled for a very simple light supper. Then finished reading the Post, watched some TV, and went to bed.

Friday, June 6
We went down together. Made my Philadelphia trip arrangements. Had a ceremony in the afternoon for some retirees.
Picked up Jules about 5:45. Made a sudden decision as we were driving through Georgetown to go see "The Passenger," a bit weird for my taste. Turned away from a few restaurants because we did not have a reservation, but got a table and a very pleasant dimmer with wine at Chez Odette. Then home.
Letter from Ira enclosing a bulletin about a swimming organization particularly mentioning David's accomplishments, and a cassette of Eric's piano recital. Will have to bring a machine home from the office on which to play it.

Saturday, June 7
Read the *Post*. Had brunch. Did our cleaning chores. Then went shopping at Montgomery Mall. Did not buy anything of interest. Did some marketing on the way home.
Postcard from Bobbie and Nate, in Malaysia, having a wonderful trip. Too bad I shall be in Philadelphia while they are away. And Jules would like to discuss this cancer report with Nate. As it is, we shall wait to see what Dr. Klopp comes up with on Friday the 13th.

A lovely day, but breezy and rather cool, so neither of us went to the swimming pool. Signed up, however, for a pool party a week from tomorrow including food at $3 per person. Unexciting but a way to get to know some neighbors.

Sunday, June 8
The kids called fairly early as they were going on a float trip down the Illinois River.
Jules went to see Mother. Picked up Clara and Lou on the way. Got a new power of attorney signed with them as witnesses. Another sunny but cool and breezy day. We went for a walk in the late afternoon just to get me out of the apartment for a while. We had supper at home. Went to Farrell's for dessert – had a coupon for one free hot fudge sundae when one other was purchased.
Packed the few things I shall need for what I expect to be a very short trip. Accepted the invitation to Howard's wedding in New York on a Sunday morning, with the book club meeting that evening, but Jules thinks we can get back in plenty of time.

Monday, June 9
Jules drove me to National in plenty of time for a 8:55 flight in which I was ticketed. But the travel agent made a mistake. The plane left at 9:20. Had to take a cab – very expensive – to get to the hearing at 11. During the luncheon recess, checked in at the Holiday Inn, lunched there, and back to the hearing. When we adjourned about 5, the GC counsel rested, but the Respondent thought his case might take all day tomorrow. Leaves me not

knowing whether or not I shall check out. Walked back to the motel. Later had dinner in the motel dining room, not very good, but very crowded, as the whole area is with tour groups. Probably should have called Jules to tell him I would not be in as early tomorrow as I expected, but it was all so indefinite.

Tuesday, June 10
A lovely day. I had breakfast at the motel. Got an extension of the check-out time from 12 to 2. Then to the hearing which resumed at 9. During the lunch break checked out of the motel. The hearing concluded at about 2:45. I telephoned the office, asked that Jules be informed of my schedule, and got to the airport in plenty of time for my flight, scheduled for 4:40, but late, on a commuter Allegheny flight. Pleasantly surprised to find Jules waiting at Page airport. He had parked in my garage expecting me back early, had to leave his office in the middle of his day to pick up the car but was there. We stopped at a Roy Rogers for sandwiches and milk shakes. Then home to read the *Post* and relax and feel glad to be at home.

Wednesday, June 11
We went together. Got a Board decision in my long Baton Rouge case, affirming me with a couple of minor additions requested by the General Counsel. The Board still has several of my decisions under consideration. There is a long Tulsa case on the docket. I was tempted to ask for it and Jules and urged me to do so. I did not, however, as at this point I felt I should wait and see what develops at my appointment on Friday with Dr. Klopp. Picked up Jules about 5:45 and went home for supper.
Bill Levy called. Has been offered yet another job, and thinks he will take it.

Thursday, June 12
We went down together. The Tulsa case was given to Bud Friedman. I suggested he call Ira to say hello. They have met at a Saul Jaffe Rosh Hashanah party.
As I am not going out, should get one more case out this fiscal year. Gave my secretary the first few pages to start stenciling.
Was on the way to pick up Jules when a tire went flat. Was able to call from an apartment lobby, and reached Jules just before he left the office. He walked over to where I was sitting. Could not get any of the nearby stations to send someone to change the tire so drove it a block to a station. The tire was no good anyhow. Had dinner afterwards at the Old Europe. Then home.

Friday, June 13
Went down together in the Olds. Find it a big nuisance in the garage but managed. Saw Dr. Klopp at 10. He also told me a clinical examination showed no problem, but he had not yet received the x-rays, so I shall have to come again when he does. He would not, without them, do a biopsy, as the Georgetown report recommended. Picked up Jules about 5:40. Went to Hamburger Hamlet. Then to the Avalon to see a new Peter Sellers movie. I found it too wacky to be really funny. Then home.

Letter from Ira enclosing a tentative itinerary for the upcoming western trip. It sounds wonderful. They are enjoying the planning very much. Hope they enjoy the trip as much as they anticipate.

Saturday, June 14
Gertrude called in the morning. Will come back with us from Howard's wedding for a short visit. Had to tell her there was some question of our going because of the cancer report.
We had brunch. Then to Montgomery Mall. Jules bought two tires for the Plymouth. I shopped and did not buy a thing. Then to Saks 5th Avenue to buy a wedding gift for Howard. Stopped at Wagshal's to get a box, etc.
When we got home, did some cleaning and laundry. Did not want to let it ride as we may come back from New York next weekend with Gertrude, if ---. It is annoying after all this time not to know if Georgetown alarmed me unnecessarily, or discovered something the doctors cannot find in clinical tests.

Sunday, June 15
Ira and the two boys wished Jules a happy Father's Day and Grandfather's Day. Sandy had disappeared at the moment. David is still doing great on the swimming. Eric's baseball team lost the first two playoff games.
Jules went to the pool in the afternoon. I stayed home and read the *Post*. We had spent much of the morning over brunch and household chores.
In the late afternoon we both went to the "pool party." Ate a grilled hamburger and a hot dog, chatted with a few people, realized again how many people at Sumner Village we did not know, and went home for the rest of our supper.

Monday, June 16
Went down together. Meeting in our library of conference committee with Board representatives. Then I went to Social Security to inquire about benefits I can claim under Medicare, but not sure it would be to my advantage. Took a bus back. It was crowded. I suddenly noticed my bag was open and a black hand was lifting my wallet. Caught it in time. Unabashed, he merely said "excuse me." Jules had asked me to lunch with him but I did not want to take the time. Almost an expensive bus ride. Jules and I stopped at the library. Then home for dinner and the evening. Glad just to relax after the bus incident.

Tuesday, June 17
We went down together. Later I picked up Jules, we parked at Hecht's and went to the courthouse nearby where I attested to my signature on the Coleman will. Had a sandwich in Hecht's restaurant.
Goslee accompanied by Kessel checked on availability for assignment. Kessel later asked about the reference to my medical appointments. I told him. Picked up Jules about 6. We stopped on the way home for supper at Argentine Steak House. Did not care for the food. Went home for dessert. The maintenance people were supposed to

glue a loose rubber molding in our freezer but had not done so. Will have to get G.E. out now that our warranty is ended [i.e. call G.E. repairmen again to their house].

Wednesday, June 18
Went down together. Klopp's secretary refused to call Georgetown again about the x-rays, so I got on the phone and finally was referred to someone who checked and said they were sent out yesterday so should be received tomorrow. Notified Klopp's office. Picked up Jules about 5:45. Went home for dinner. The freezer had been repaired, but the repairman's note indicated he was doubtful that it would hold. And Jules' Father's Day package finally arrived, a jacket, very nice, but too small.
We had delicious porterhouse steaks for dinner. Made the beef we got last night look ridiculous. Did some chores, getting ready for a house guest.

Thursday, June 19
Went down together. Called Klopp's office – no x-rays yet. Was assigned a case in Boston for next Thursday and Friday. Jules said he might join me for the weekend. Hot and humid, but Mira and I braved the weather, walked to Georgetown, and had a pleasant luncheon at Mr. Smith's.
Picked up Jules about 5:45 and went home. He went for a dip in the pool while I did some chores. We had supper at home when he got back.
Letter from Ira, and, separately, notes from the two boys thanking us for the $10 checks I sent each of them recently. Glad to get their notes, but sorry to see they are getting Sandy's habit of writing only in order to express thanks for a gift.

Friday, June 20
Went down together. Klopp received the x-rays about noon, leaves his office about noon, I am to see him Monday morning. Dudley Brown called – had arranged for me to go by myself to look at fabrics at Knoll's. Signed Akron Convalescent. Got exception and a supporting brief in Stone & Webster, and a brief in support in Wickham. The exceptions were filed by Ropes & Gray. Lunched at Blackie's with Mira.
Eve Miller called – to try to get together – but they are away far more than we are. Clara called. Told her my medical shenanigans. Picked up Jules about 5. Stopped at the grocery store to buy things to have when we get back with Gertrude. Had supper at home. Did some laundry. Packed for the weekend. And finished reading this morning's *Post*.

Saturday, June 21
A cool night and a beautiful day. We had breakfast, drove to National, and took the 9 o'clock shuttle. Then a cab to the Plaza. Got a very pleasant room, but the hotel is going through a big renovation. We went walking. Wound up at Wolf's for luncheon. Back to the room to rest a bit. Then more walking. Back to the hotel for tea in the Palm Court. When we got to the room had a message to call Ed. He and Gertrude had called several times but their earlier messages were not

delivered. Took a cab to the Barclay where they were staying, and to a dinner party at the hotel. Met the bride and her family. Joan's in-laws were there also, and a couple of old friends of Howard's. Broke up about 11. Howard gave us a ride back nearly to the Plaza as we asked to get out and walk back. A beautiful evening.

Sunday, June 22
Another beautiful day. As the wedding "brunch" would be late, we took a walk and had some breakfast at Rumpelmayer's. The wedding took place at noon, in a small room at the Plaza, followed by a very nice brunch. I assumed Gertrude would bring her bag so we would go from here but she did not. We took a cab to her hotel, had to wait for her to leave, with the taxi running, but she finally came down with her enormous bag, and we went to La Guardia. Got the 5 pm shuttle. Drove home. Cleaned up. Had very light supper. Then went to the book club meeting at the Michael's. Plenty of room for Gertrude as the Middlemans did not come. We all enjoyed the evening. But found when we got home that Gertrude left her sweater at the Michaels' so we will have to stop there sometime to pick it up before Gertrude leaves.

Monday, June 23
We all had breakfast and went down together, I to see Dr. Klopp, Gertrude to go to the Hirshhorn Gallery.
Klopp said he could see what Georgetown was talking about and recommended a biopsy at the hospital. I understood him to say "in and out" but his appointment clerk said I would go in Monday, the 30th, and leave probably Wednesday morning.
Gertrude did not show up by 1 so I got myself a sandwich. She went to Jules' office later. They picked me up about 5:30. We stopped at the Michaels' to pick up Gertrude's sweater. And stopped briefly at the grocery store. Then home. I fixed steaks for dinner. Everything turned out very good. Spent the rest of the evening reading and watching TV. Gertrude is planning to leave Wednesday about the same time I go to Boston if my case does not settle, as seems likely.

Tuesday, June 24
We all had breakfast and went down together. Dropped Gertrude at Kennedy Center where she got a tour bus. Klopp's office confirmed my going to the hospital Monday between 1 and 2. Jules and I decided to scrap our plan to spend the weekend in Boston.
Gertrude called about 1. Could not make if for luncheon. I lunched with Jules at Blackie's. Got a Board decision in Oak Apparel, affirming me and finding one more violation. And got the record in my Philadelphia case so have work again. Gertrude came about 3, read the *Post*, we picked up Jules and Charlie Smith, stopped at Charlie's apartment for him to deliver 4 frozen trout he caught, then home to put the fish in our freezer. After went to dinner at Le Caprice. It was very good. Then home, I to pack. Gertrude announced she would stay home in the morning so we shall have to pick her up later.

Wednesday, June 25
Gertrude was up when we left, but stayed at home to rest, take a walk, and pack. I picked up Jules later and we went home. Had a sandwich. The travel clerk called me at home – found I was due $4 more on a voucher. Then we all went to the airport. I took an American flight to Boston at 3, got in about 4, with the temperature about 20 degrees cooler than at home. Took a limo to the Holiday Inn. The room was fair, certainly not worth what it cost, and the dinner I had later at the Inn was pretty bad. Will check out in the morning and, if I stay another night, go to the Parker House for about $10 a night less. It was not available tonight but I have a reservation there tomorrow night.

Thursday, June 26
Had breakfast. Then checked out. The room came to $31.71, much more than the current allowance. Then to the hearing. The parties had been talking settlement, as I had been advised previously, but I suggested one more attempt. They reached agreement about noon.
Called the office, which called Jules, and told me he was going to Philadelphia on the train and would be back later. Also told me a call from the hospital for insurance data had been referred to Jules. I lunched at the Parker House. Got the limo there. Took a Delta flight at 2:48, then a limo to Bethesda, and the Sumner Village shuttle home. Jules called form [i.e. from] the R.R. [i.e. railroad] station. Had to go to the office garage to get the car, got a sandwich, then home about 9. I should have left a car in my garage.

Friday, June 27
We went down together. A showery day, but Mira Stevenson and I walked to Blackie's nevertheless. Told her of my hospital plans. Have told very few at the office. But she will be away next week on a hearing, and she has become pretty much my regular luncheon companion. Picked up Jules about 6. We stopped on the way home at O'Donnell's for supper. Stopped afterwards at the grocery store. Then home. Jules would have liked to make it a movie-and-dinner evening, but there was no picture I was interested in seeing, and I was not in a mood to celebrate anything.

Saturday, June 28
Slept relatively late. Then read part of the *Post* had brunch, did some housecleaning, and then dressed and went to Montgomery Mall. I bought a purse, but that was all I found to buy. Did a few other errands. By then it was raining so we went home.
Immediately took out of the freezer the fish Charlie Smith gave us. Hours later had to run some cold water over them to complete the thawing. Then broiled them. They were delicious. There were four, enough for two others, but I did not feel much like having a dinner party, and had to cook them all, so we ate them all with no difficulty. Not sure I knew how to fix them, but my method worked very well.

Sunday, June 29

Another cloudy showery day. Expected Ira not to call last Sunday as he said he would be away, but thought he would before leaving on his trip in a couple of days. He did not and we did not call him. If he was not at home, Sandy is just too uncommunicative. Jules went to see Mother to check on the mail. There was none, but he could not check on the phone as she does not hear or understand us well on the telephone. I did not go. Had a good deal of work to do after being away last weekend and having a house guest and getting ready to go to the hospital.

Later we went to the Sir Walter Raleigh for dinner and to Gifford's for dessert, in large part to get me out of the apartment at least as far as Bethesda.

Monday, June 30

We went down together, I with a small overnight bag. I parked the car.

Was going to attend a meeting of the ALJ conference committee at 10, but when it was postponed to 11, I skipped it.

Walked to Circle One at noon with my bag. Met Jules there for luncheon. Then we walked to G.W. Hospital.[48] He left shortly. I went through a number of tests, etc., before being shown to a semi-private room, which I shared with an older woman named France. More tests in the room. Klopp stopped by. Said all this was necessary now but not for the biopsy he did years ago because it was very superficial one. Jules came by in the evening. I had had supper, much as it was.

---

48   George Washington Hospital.

When he left to go to dinner, I read for a while and then to bed.

Tuesday, July 1

I was awakened early to be given a couple of shots. That and the ride on the stretcher made me a little nauseous. I was given some oxygen, which helped. I was then put to sleep. Was taken to the recovery room, and later back to my room. When I came fully awake, my chief problem was a sore throat caused by a tube inserted in the operating room. Caused me to spit up a cup of tea so got only a liquid diet supper. Jules came over at noon and again in the evening. Brought the *Post* and a letter from Ira, who had accepted a job with a Tulsa hospital, enclosing a clipping from a newspaper about it.

Klopp came by and said I could go home this afternoon or evening, but with my sore throat and squeamish stomach, decided to leave in the morning.

Wednesday, July 2

Up early. Had breakfast. A woman doctor with 3 men doctors accompanying her, told me if I went home I could change the dressing myself, but, when I said I could not, none of them offered to do so. Jules picked me up about 9:30, paid the bill the cashier said was not covered by insurance, and took me home. It looked great. He had even made the bed. He then went to the office. Clara and Lee Stanley called to ask how I was. Poor Lee is terribly lonely. In the evening Ira called – had tried a number of times – told him about my hospital stay – glad he reached us as they leave tomorrow on their big trip – talked to all four. Gertrude called from Columbus. Bill Levy called to chat with Jules – suggested getting together so Jules told him about me. Fixed lamb chops for dinner – tasted great to both of us.

Thursday, July 3
Jules had a leisurely breakfast, read part of the *Post*, and left at the time he would generally to go to the office.
After the several calls yesterday, no one called today except Jules. I spent the day reading, napping, watching TV, and feeling lazy and bored.
Jules came home about 6:30. He picked up a few things at the grocery store on the way home. We had Annie Burgers for dinner. Even I found them delicious, and I had not worked up much of an appetite. Made a cake from a mix. It turned out very well. I have really become lazy about cooking.

Friday, July 4
Got up very early, read for awhile, and then went back to bed. When I got up again, found my toilet would not flush. Murray and a handyman came over but could not fix it. I tried it later, and it was ok, so cancelled Murray's call for a plumber. Heard the building was having water pressure trouble. Went shopping. Ran into Kessel, who seemed glad I had no serious problem so far. Did some marketing. Got some watermelon and strawberries. When we got home, did some apartment cleaning. Then Jules went to the pool for a quick dip. Does not like to linger there when he is alone.

We had a yummy dinner, thanks to stuff we bought at Wagshal's, our fresh fruits, etc. Ate on the balcony, a nice change, but involved a lot of to-and-fro.

Saturday, July 5
We went out early to the Bethesda farmers' market, but did not beat the crowd, and did not get home-grown tomatoes, our main purpose in going. Then home for a big brunch. Did some cleaning and read the *Post*. Jules went for a quick dip in the pool when he finished his cleaning chores.
Bill Levy called in the morning. We arranged to meet them to see the movie "Jaws." The movie was pretty good, but I found the book far more absorbing. Afterwards we walked to a nearby Howard Johnson for dessert and to chat for a while. But it is not the old relationship – for whatever reason – and probably never again will be.

Sunday, July 6
I woke up early and got up. The dressing is not conducive to lying in bed. Fortunately the *Post* was delivered early, and I got started on it. Later we had a very enjoyable big brunch.
Did our cleaning chores, Jules later went to the pool. Was there a while. We had delicious loin lamb chops for dinner. After cleaning up, we went for a, for me, fairly long walk as I had not been out all day. Met some neighbors on the way and stopped to chat a few minutes. Then home to rest, read, and watch TV. Not visiting Mother during this period not only because of the operation, but also because of her enviably nasty remarks each time I go.

1976

Jules was an intense Ohio State University football fan all of his life, so on New Year's day they watched on television as OSU lost to UCLA in the Orange Bowl. Anne frequently reported the results of OSU games and Washington Redskins games, and they occasionally attended them. She does not seem to have been particularly interested, but she knew the results because of Jules' interest in the game. She frequently read while he watched games.

Anne and Jules went to Sanibel Island near Tampa for a few days vacation in late February. Like recent years the travel schedules for both were hectic. They had a complicated choreography of who was meeting whom at the airport or dropping the other one off, or taking the car, or a taxi. Anne seemed to thrive on the busy pace.

Between on-site hearings, anywhere from Brooklyn to Detroit, Chicago, or Houston and writing up her opinions of the individual cases in the office, Anne was busy. More and more references appear in her entries about the status of her cases. On April 19 she wrote, "Got exceptions in a Cleveland case. A close question. I might be reversed. Makes 5 of my cases before the Board." The final comment refers to the review of cases by the members of the Board itself. On April 20 she wrote, "Was notified that my Youngstown case had been settled. Too bad it could not have waited until I got there. I have not had a 'disposition' for about a year. And I do not want to travel next week although I am the logical candidate to do so."

She did not want to travel the next week because she had medical appointments in her continuing concern about her health. They flew to Tulsa for Passover.

The year included receptions at the Carter White House, seeing the Texas trilogy at the Kennedy Center as well as other plays, concerts, books, and movies. Cultural events were a frequent highlight of their lives.

In August Jules and Anne made a vacation trip to Hawaii with a stopover in San Francisco. They celebrated their thirty-seventh anniversary in Hawaii. On the return trip they stopped in Columbus for a wedding and a visit with family members.

Back at the office, Anne left the next day to hear a case in Tulsa and a visit with Ira and the family. On her arrival back in Washington Clara called. Anne wrote, "Clara telephoned. Mother's fantasies are becoming worse and more varied, and are a real problem. We shall see for ourselves on Sunday." Since Clara was in town all of the time, she was the constant contact with the mother. Anne notes many calls from Clara about issues with the mother.

In September Anne's old friend Ruth Weyand was arguing a class action suit in the U.S. Court of Appeals, Fourth Circuit against General Electric for sex discrimination under Title VII of the Civil Rights Act. In an interesting connection between generatons, Ruth Bader Ginsberg prepared a brief in support of that case on behalf of the Women's Law Project. -- RDH

Monday, March 1
We went down together. A lovely warm day – got up to a record 80 – and the forsythia and other shrubs and trees are in bloom. Glad we came back early from Florida.
Lunched with Mira Stevenson at Blackie's.
Got out an Order denying motion to reopen record in the Chicago case. My two Detroit case transcripts are still missing.
Picked up Jules about 5:45. Did some errands on the way home. Had porterhouse steaks for dinner. Tasted especially good as we ate fish almost every evening at Sanibel [i.e. Island off the coast of Florida]. Finished reading the *Post*, watched some TV, and got more laundry done.
Talked to Mother. She seemed better but said she was not. Thanked me for the postcard.

Tuesday, March 2
We went down together. A cool cloudy showery day, but still warm for this time of year, and more flowers and leaves coming out everyday.
To Blackie's for luncheon again with Mira Stevenson. Picked up Jules about 5:45. Went home for dinner. Had delicious veal chops – from our last trip to Katz's. How did we ever manage without freezing compartments?
Jules called Bill to let the Levys know we were back, and to ask about Bill's trip to Brussels for an international conference on the problems of Russian Jews. Apparently it was a very exciting experience for Bill.

Wednesday, March 3
Went down together. Kessel mentioned that he did not want to send me out next week but might have to as there is such a large docket.
Jules, who had been very busy since he got back from Florida, could not get away from his desk until about 6. We stopped at the Hamburger Hamlet for supper. Then home.
Gertrude telephoned from Columbus to let us know Helen Lee's two boys were engaged to be married, and Pam already married, had a baby, as Helen Lee is now a grandmother. Hard to believe as she was so long the problem child herself. Nice of Gertrude to let us know.

Thursday, March 4
I went down alone as Jules was staying down this evening to have dinner with some clients.
Lunched with Pat Kirkwood and Mira Stevenson at one of the French cafes in Georgetown. Made a pleasant change.
As I did not have to wait for Jules, I left a little early, beat the traffic rush hour, and stopped at the grocery store for a few things we needed. Will not be able to get them tomorrow as Jules wants me to stay downtown for dinner with Horst Hasskarl, here from Germany for his first trip to the States. Jules got home about 10.

Friday, March 5
Switched to the Olds so we would have more room for a visitor. In the process forgot some shoes in the Duster I planned to wear.
To the dentist at 11:30. Warm and lovely so I walked there and back. Dr. Kelser's office called – wants the x-rays they took.

Picked up Jules about 6:30 and Hasskarl at the Madison, and went to the Canard for a very good dinner. It was a showery evening, but we walked around Georgetown a bit between showers. Then we drove him around to see something of the city at night. Then to his hotel and home. People had been working in the windows in the apartment. We could tell by the dirt left behind.

Saturday, March 6
We read the *Post*, had brunch, and did some cleaning. Hasskarl took a morning bus tour. Then called us. We picked him up, with his bags, took him to Hogate's for luncheon, then to the Capitol for a quick look-see before it closed, and to the Congressional Library. We then drove him out to Dulles. He bought us a farewell drink, and we parted. He seemed a very pleasant and intelligent young man.
We then drove home. Had just a snack at home as neither of us was hungry enough for a meal. Then read, watched some TV, and relaxed until bedtime, and enjoyed just being by ourselves.

Sunday, March 7
Read part of the *Post*. Did some cleaning and laundry. The kids called. Still trying to trace the Valentine candy they sent us. And still full of news and excitement about David's swimming accomplishments. In the late afternoon we went to visit Mother. She was better but still had some pain. Absolutely refuses any medical help. Did some marketing on the way home. Had supper. Then to the Michaels' for the book club meeting. A lively discussion of Mee's "Meeting at Potsdam."[49] The Middlemans were not there. We will take their turn which is next, and they will then presumably take ours. Irv told us Mary Clark died of cancer.

Monday, March 8
Went down together. Dropped Jules at the doctor's for an allergy shot. He now gets them twice a week. Dr. Kelser's office asked me last Friday to bring in the x-rays they took, but I forgot to bring them from home. Picked up Jules about 5:35, sleepy from the effects of the shot, and went home.
Letter from Ira enclosing an article from a medical journal that he co-authored with a doctor. Also an inquiry from a candy company as to whether we received the candy Ira sent us as a Valentine gift.
Did some chores getting ready to be away Wednesday through Friday.

Tuesday, March 9
Awoke to a white fairyland of snow-covered trees. As it was reported the snow would turn to rain, and I hate to park the Olds, we went down in the Duster. There was more snow than was predicted but we managed all right.
Got a belated notice that no exceptions were filed to the second, as well as the first, of 2 cases I heard in Newark. But exceptions have been filed by Surface Industries in my McAlester case.

49   Charles L. Mee, *Meeting at Potsdam*. 1975. Analysis of the meeting between Truman, Churchill, and Stalin at the end of World War II to make agreements on post-war Europe.

Bought my x-rays from home but did not deliver them in view of the weather. Picked up Jules about 5:40. Stopped at the grocery store. Had some fresh asparagus with our dinner, our first of the season. It was delicious.

Wednesday, March 10
Jules left early to get a train to Philadelphia. I went down a little later in the Duster. There was still some frozen snow on the streets but I had no trouble. All set to go to Cincinnati when the case was cancelled. Given a choice for next week. Will probably wind up with Syracuse as it is the only place with one short case. I went home a little early. Jules got an early train back, went to the office, and got home about 6:45. He had called me from the office so I waited to fix dinner until he came home. He had talked to Bobbie and Nate while in Cincinnati. He heard later when he talked to his secretary that I would be at home.

Thursday, March 11
We went down together. The snow had just about disappeared. It was mild and pleasant at noon as Mira Stevenson and I walked into Georgetown and lunched at the Charing Cross. Ran into Lou Roland there. His office recently moved into the Georgetown area. Did get the Syracuse assignment. Made the hotel and travel reservations. Would have gotten a Tulsa 3-day case, but Kessel thought the Kothe firm was involved, and the firm had demanded, under the Freedom of Information Act, a list of all my decisions, in connection with the exceptions in the McAlester case. Picked up Jules about 5:45. Went home for dinner and the evening. He has a Britisher coming in tomorrow. We may be taking him to dinner and to Dulles, or we may not.

Friday, March 12
We went down together in the Olds in case we took Milne of England to dinner and to Dulles. Rained much of the day and on-and-off all evening as well. I was parked in Jules' garage after work and went up to the office to meet Milne. Then we walked to the Cantina. Had a very good but hurried supper as Milne does not like to eat on the plane. Then drove him out to Dulles. Then home. Found a package waiting for us. Turned out to be some hamentaschen from Sandy. They were delicious. We were glad to have them as we had not bought any.

Saturday, March 13
We late slept relatively late. Looked at the *Post*, had brunch, then went downtown. Jules had to go to the office a while. I got my hair cut. Did some errands on the way home.
Eastern Airlines called to notify me my first class seat was changed to Y class for the Syracuse trip.
Into evening clothes and to the Kennedy Center for the M-L-B[50] night. There were cocktails in a private room, then a show – we saw "Rex," only all right – then to another private room for an omelet supper. Bought tickets while we were there to a show for next Saturday night. Home very late, for

---
50   Jules' law firm Morgan, Backies, and Lewis.

us. Left most of the young associates still at Kennedy Center.

Sunday, March 14
Jules slept late but I slept a good deal later. We read part of the *Post*. Then had brunch – no eggs in view of last night's omelets.
Bill Levy called to chat. Ruth is getting over an allergy attack. Did a good deal of cleaning and laundry as we did not do any yesterday. A pleasant afternoon so we went marketing. Needed some things and wanted to get out. Fixed a rib roast for dinner, with roast potatoes, fresh asparagus, etc. – and hamentaschen with our Jell-O for dessert. We both ate a great deal and enjoyed it very much.

Monday, March 15
We went down together. A relatively mild day, but the prediction is for heavy snow starting this evening. It never came. Lunched at Blackie's with Mira Stevenson. Picked up Jules about 5:45. Went home for dinner. Did some laundry and other chores preparatory to being away the latter part of the week.
Ira called. We talked to all four. They had been in Dallas over the weekend for a swim meet in which David performed commendably. Ira is coming here for a week, but not at Passover, and asked us to come there for Seder so he won't have to take the boys out of school to come here for Seder. We did not decide.

Tuesday, March 16
We went down together. The attorney in the Abrahamson case had filed with the Board a request for special permission to appeal. ALJ's order. Picked up Jules close to 6. We had cold roast beef at home, but he decided en route he felt like having chicken. Stopped at Hamburger Hamlet. For the first time in a long time they had rotisserie chicken, and it was delicious. A cold, windy, rainy night so we were glad to get home. Of course our living room is uninhabitable in this weather but at least the den is fairly comfortable. I packed boots for the trip to Syracuse tomorrow.

Wednesday, March 17
We went down together. Jules dropped me and my suitcase, and parked in his garage. I was promptly notified my case had been settled. It was lucky as the weather in Syracuse was very bad, but if I had been told yesterday I would have had the car.
Jules picked me up about 5:40. Went home for supper. And unpacked. Second week in a row I have been cancelled out of a trip on the day I was to leave. If I went and the case settled, I would get credit for a "disposition," but this way all my preparations are just a total waste of time. And I shall run through my backlog soon at this rate.

Thursday, March 18
We went down together. Thought, as the Cincinnati and Syracuse cases were short ones I would get another short one, but I got a 5-day case in Philadelphia. Lunched at Blackie's with Mira Stevenson.
Signed a decision in one of my Detroit cases. Never got the transcript in the other.

Made travel arrangements. Then case was postponed. Three in a row. Picked up Jules about 6. Stopped for supper at a new crêperie, The Magic Pan. We both enjoyed the place, the food, and the service. Then home. Wore my mink coat today, maybe for the last time this season.

Friday, March 19
We went down together. A pleasant day, but I agreed to lunch with a group that eats sandwiches in one of the group's office. I got my sandwich downstairs. Some brought them from home. Did not care much for the arrangement. If I am going to eat in, would just as soon do so at my own desk and read the *Post*. Picked up Jules about 5:40. We did a couple of errands on the way home but went home for supper nevertheless.
Bill Levy called. David and Margie have a son. Ruth went out to Chicago. Clara called. She and Lou are taking a trip to Hong Kong in May. Also she needed more money to cover her expenditures for Mother.

Saturday, March 20
A beautiful warm sunny day. We did more than our usual cleaning stint today as we shall have little time for it tomorrow. Then went marketing and shopping. Enjoyed being out in the warm sunshine and seeing the beautiful spring foliage.
Later dress and drove to the Kennedy Center. Had supper in the cafeteria. Then saw "The Heiress." We both enjoyed it. Thought Jane Alexander was particularly fine in the leading role. And saw a number of people we knew at the theater. But went home after the show, and had an after-theater snack at home. To bed at a reasonable hour as Bill is coming to brunch tomorrow.

Sunday, March 21
The kids called early as they had a busy day ahead. Ira again urged that we come for Seder. We probably shall. Bill arrived about 11, and we had brunch. He stayed and visited for a while. After he left, went to visit Mother. She seemed and looked better.
The day started out very warm, but got cloudy, we had showers, and then it grew cooler. But most of the day was very pleasant. Jules went for a walk after we got home. I got started on the *Post*.
Florence Gang invited us to a birthday party for Arthur on the 10th of April, the day after my birthday.
We had delicious porterhouse steaks for dinner, with all the trimmings.

Monday, March 22
We went down together. There is a short Columbus case on the docket which will probably be combined with another Ohio case. I asked Kessel for it. Jules is anxious that I get to Columbus to see Louie and Lucille.
Picked up Jules about 5:45. Went home for dinner. The candy Ira sent – originally in plenty of time for St. Valentine's Day – arrived today. We opened it after dinner. A fresh box was sent when the fist one did not arrive, and the candy was delicious.

Jules got a letter from Milne enthusing about our taking him to dinner and to Dulles, and about having kissed a judge.

Tuesday, March 23
We went down together. Jules had made the Tulsa plane reservation for Passover. I called Tulsa in the afternoon. Only Eric was at home. Left a message with him that the candy arrived and that we were coming on the 13th.
Joe Randozzo called. In town from Buffalo for a Supreme Court case argument for which he will be sitting at counsel table.
Picked up Jules about 5:45. Went to O'Donnell's for dinner. It was good, but the place was very busy and the service very slow. Then home. Seemed pleasant and quiet in the apartment after the hustle and bustle of the restaurant even when we turned on the TV.

Wednesday, March 24
We went down together. Received a Respondent memorandum in lieu of a brief in the Abrahamson case, urging delay of a decision until the Board rules on its appeal from my ruling denying a reopening. That is going to be a long decision as the procedural issues will take pages to discuss. Picked up Jules about 5:30. He was able to get away that early today but expects to work all day Saturday, and has to go to New York Sunday for an early meeting with Bickert Monday morning. He then has to rush back to the office to file papers in a Knoll case in court on Monday. We went for dinner and a relaxing evening.

Thursday, March 25
We went together. Kessel told me the Columbus case was off, and the Cincinnati case was being combined with me in some Kentucky town. I wound up with a 2-3 case in Orlando. Would have been glad to go Sunday as Jules is going to New York on Sunday, but the case starts at 1:00 so I shall go Monday morning. Picked up Jules about 5:45 and drove out to Lord & Taylor's. Bought an adorable dress for Nan's new baby, and sent it c/o Bobbie, as Jules got, then lost, Nan's present address. Walked to the nearby Magic Pan for supper. It has become popular and was very crowded, but we did not have to wait too long, and enjoyed the food, Jules especially.

Friday, March 26
We went down together. Completed my travel arrangements for the Orlando trip. The Board denied the Abrahamson appeal on the ground there was ample notice to appear. I was pleased to be affirmed. A lovely day so Mira Stevenson and I walked into Georgetown and lunched at Café de Paris.
Picked up Jules about 6. Went home for dinner. Had "Annie Burgers," which Jules and I both thought tasted especially good.
Ira told us on the phone he sent my birthday gift very early as the mail was so slow these days. It came today, the package in excellent shape. As was told by Ira, I will not open it before April 9.

Saturday, March 27
Jules was up early and read part of the *Post*.

I slept later. After I got up we had breakfast. Jules left for the office right after breakfast. I had thought I might go shopping, but the weather turned cool and showery, and I stayed at home. Worked on a draft decision I had brought home to the point where it was ready to be stenciled. Plan to drive to the office, park in the garage, give Judy the decision, and take a cab to the airport.

Jules came home about 6. We had delicious steaks for dinner. Jules was shocked to learn I had not been out all day, and offered to go out for dinner and/or a movie, but I was just as content to stay at home, finish the *Post*, and watch some TV.

Sunday, March 28
We were both up fairly early. Read part of the *Post*. Then had a big brunch. Letting Jules skip the cleaning chores this weekend in view of his schedule. We took a couple of walks as it was a lovely day. He left about 4 to catch the shuttle at 5. Ira called after Jules left. Glad we are coming, but Wednesday would be better for them. Our reservations are for Tuesday evening. David did not do well in his last swim meet. He was very disappointed. Sandy did not get on the phone.

Eva Naiden returned a call I made when she was out of town – about possibly getting subscriptions to a Wolf Trap opera series. She will talk to Neil, he will talk to Jules, etc.

Monday, March 29
Drove down to the office, parked in the garage, left the draft I finished over the weekend with Judy, and then got a cab to National and a National flight, with breakfast, to Orlando. Took a long time to get my bag. Then no limo. Took a cab to the Kahler Inn, checked in, dropped my bag in the room, and walked to the courthouse. Got there with 5 minutes to spare. A very disputatious group of lawyers. Ran until 5:30. Walked back to the Kahler, unpacked, and had supper in the dining room. Only fair. But the hotel is comfortable. And it is only about a half block from the County Courthouse. Tried to call Jules but did not reach him. And fell asleep early while watching TV.

Tuesday, March 30
Had breakfast in the dining room. Then took a little walk before resuming the hearing at 9:15. During the luncheon recess got a sandwich at a nearby café – pretty bad. Recessed about 5:30. Looks like we shall be going all day tomorrow. Then took a walk, and went back to the Kahler. Had dinner in the dining room.

After several tries reached Jules. He worked late and stopped for supper on the way home. He had called Lucille. She is fine but Louie is completely senile. I have been trying for a long time to get a Columbus assignment so I could, at Jules' urging, visit Louie, but it appears Louie would not know if I was there.[51]

Wednesday, March 31
The hearing resumes at 9:30 so I had time for breakfast and a walk before hand. Counsel,

---
51 Jules' brother Louie and his wife Lucille.

who said yesterday he would need all day, finished about noon. Recessed for lunch. Tried to get on a plane this evening but it was filled. Back for closing arguments. Then to the hotel. Called the airline again, got a seat, packed, checked out, took a cab to the airport, and, after a long wait, got a 6:55 flight, with dinner. I had made a collect call to the office, asked that Jules would be notified, and he was waiting for me at National. It was raining hard but the Olds was parked nearby. He had eaten dinner so we went home. I had lugged a bag of oranges from the airport. Found they were not very good.

Thursday, April 1
We went down together in the Olds. Jules dropped me. The Duster was still parked in my garage. Was surprised not to get an assignment. Kessel told me he had declined to give me a rest from traveling, but I had not done that much recently. Suspect he had another reason.

Because I did not have an assignment and did not have to pick up Jules, I left early, went home, read the old *Posts* and then today's, and fixed steaks for dinner when Jules got home close to 7. Then did some chores, did some reading, watched some TV, and went to bed.

Friday, April 2
We went down together. Received from clerical personnel a pin, scotch-taped to a pink slip "honoring" my 40 years of service. Signed the decision in the case I heard in Brooklyn.

Picked up Jules about 5:45. Stopped at the Yenching for dinner, which was very good. Then to the Avalon to see "Greenwich Village," a fairly entertaining movie. Then home for dessert, to finish this morning's *Post*, to do some other reading, and to watch the news on TV. I have almost finished the book club book but Jules, who will have to report on it, has not started it yet.

Ira and Sandy

1977

This year started like many others, but it would be irrevocably different. Anne continued her hectic pace of official travel until she was stricken ill while traveling in December.

They started the year watching the televised OSU game in the Orange Bowl, a game OSU won.

Her work continued to be a focal point of her life, but new issues were beginning to appear. On January 4 she wrote, "There was a meeting at noon at the other building on women's rights. Several of the female ALJ's[52] went and asked me to join them, but I decided to skip it. Ate at my desk."

In February they took a winter vacation trip to the French speaking island of Guadaloupe. They spent time relaxing. On February 6 Anne wrote, "Then into our bathing suits and down to the beach, which was lovely, and crowded, almost all French-speaking, the little ones naked, the women and girls topless. Spent a very relaxed day, at the pool, on the beach, reading in our room."

In April they flew to Tulsa for Passover, having the seder with Ira and his family. On the second night seder, April 3, Anne wrote, "Had another fine seder and dinner. They gave me my birthday gift to avoid having to entrust it to the mails. It was a beautiful gold Cross pen and pencil set, each engraved 'Her Honor'. I thought it was a lovely gift. Expected, and would have been glad to settle for, one of Sandy's pottery pieces." On this trip they drove out to see a farm property that Ira and Sandy were considering buying.

Back in Washington Anne wrote on April 14, "Jules picked me up about 4:30. We went home. Relaxed a little while. Then dressed and drove to the Shoreham for the ABA[53] Anti-Trust reception and dinner. The law firm had 3 tables. We happened to sit at a table with some GE [i.e. General Electric] lawyers, and had some interesting conversation, not too serious. Griffin Bell, the AG,[54] was the speaker. Not as funny as his predecessor speakers, Art Buchwald and Mark Russell, but entertaining."

They traveled to Germany in June on a combined business/vacation trip. Jules' most important client for many years was the German company, Knoll. They were in Heidelberg, then in Salzburg they saw a presentation of "Don Giovanni". They visited Vienna where they saw a production of Verdi's "La Forza del Destino" before returning to the United States.

In July Ira, Sandy, and the boys came to visit them. On July 14 Anne wrote, "In the afternoon Sandy and the boys went to Jules' office, they picked me up, we picked up Ira, and drove home. Later dressed and went to La Nicoise for a delicious but very expensive dinner. It was Ira-and-Sandy's anniversary, and St. Bastille Day, so the restaurant was crowded and noisy. Ira gave Sandy a beautiful little dress watch. We gave them the Olds[55] and $200.00 to buy themselves gifts. And they enjoyed the dinner very much they each said."

---

52 Administrative Law Judges.
53 American Bar Association.
54 Attorney General of the United States.
55 Anne and Jules' Oldsmobile.

Anne continued to have concerns about her health, and on September 5 she wrote, "I went to bed about 11, feeling fine. Awoke during the night with dizzy spells. The bed and the room seemed to revolve, and it took great effort to walk to and from the bathroom." She went in for another check-up, but the doctors found nothing. Then, in November and December she had more problems, but she maintained her work schedule until she entered the hospital. -- RDH

Monday, November 14
We got up early and left early for the airport. Jules parked to help me in with the bags. Luckily as I was misinformed as to the airport. It was the commuter one. He took off then for breakfast and the office. I took the 7:55 flight, on a tiny cramped plane, to New London with a stop in Philadelphia. One of the attorneys got on there, was met, and gave me a ride to the motel. Had some breakfast there. Took a cab to the 1:00 hearing in the City Hall Council Chamber. This evidently will be a long hearing with constant argument among counsel. Recessed at 5:30. Got a ride back to the motel. Had a pretty good fish dinner. Joined the reporter, a young woman who was on the plane from D.C and is staying at the same motel. Used the steam bath setup in the room. My back still aches.

Tuesday, November 15
Had breakfast at the motel. Took a cab to the hearing with the reporter. More interminable arguments among counsel. Was told the hearing was covered in the press and on TV news but did not see any of it.
Lunched at the Captain's Inn with the reporter. Not good food or service. Back for a few more hours of wrangling. Someone attending the hearing gave the reporter and me a ride to the motel. I rested awhile. Then had dinner at the motel.
Called Jules. Ira and the kids called last night. Ira had misunderstood Jules the other day and thought I was not leaving until today.
Took a steam bath again. Do not know if it helps anything. Still coughing and still have headaches.

Wednesday, November 16
Had breakfast in the dining room. Becoming well known there.
Shared a cab with Ruth McLean, the reporter, who is going home this evening. Another cat-and-dog hearing. Lunched with the reporter at the Whaler. A lovely mild sunny day. We finally recessed about 5:40 so the reporter could make her plane at 7. She got a ride to the airport. I got a ride to the motel.
Had dinner in the dining room. Getting very tired of eating there twice a day.
Took a steam bath again tonight. Cannot see that they are doing any good, but might as well use it while it is available. Guess it cannot do any harm.

Thursday, November 17
Raining in the morning, but mild. I had breakfast in the dining room. Then took a cab to the hearing. Things went fairly smoothly. I lunched at again at the Whaler. Then in

the afternoon we got into a real hassle about the GC motion to amend the complaint. I finally recessed, to announce my decision tomorrow. Got a ride back to the motel. Later had dinner in the dining room. Jules called. Will meet me tomorrow at 6 at the commuter terminal. Am going to leave on the 3:30 flight on which I am booked. Have no idea when we will resume. Were going to adjourn for a week but the amendment, which I shall probably allow, may mean an adjournment until January.

Friday, November 18
Had breakfast in the dining room. Checked out. Took a cab to the hearing. Adjourned until after New Year's about 1:00. The reporter and I took a cab to the airport. Lunched there. We got the 3:30 commuter to National with a stop at Philadelphia. Got in about a half-hour late. Jules was waiting. We stopped at the Peking for dinner. Then home. I was coughing badly again. We both had newspapers to read.
Ed called Jules yesterday about some jointly-owned property. There was a note from Gertrude about that and other matters, and assuming we were going to Tulsa for Thanksgiving. Jules was tempted to call and say we were not so she could ask us and we would drive there, but I did not want to ask for an invitation.

Saturday, November 19
Jules went out in the morning to pick up some things we needed for brunch. Then had a lovely brunch and did some cleaning before getting tied up with TV for the historic arrival of Sadat from Egypt for a visit to Israel,[56] and the Ohio State-Michigan football game. OSU lost, and Jules lost some bets. He told me his M-L-B[57] allocation was cut $10,000 when other partners got substantial increases, a number of them now getting over $200,000. This was a blow to his ego in his last year as a partner.
We did some marketing and errands. Jules offered to take me out for a fancy dinner but, the way I was feeling; it seemed wiser to eat simpler food at home. Had broiled loin veal shops, boiled potatoes, apple sauce, etc. We enjoyed it and it was much better for me.

Sunday, November 20
We watched the Sadat-Begin ceremonies and listened to the speeches at the Knesset. Thrilling.
Ira called. First time in quite a while both of us talked to all four of them. Ira has sent the bill for the Knoll turkey. Glad they were able to use it.
We had brunch. Did a good deal of cleaning and laundry. Then, as it was a mild day, drove out to Katz's for some groceries, but mainly to get me out of the apartment. I was feeling better but not really well. Not as well, in fact, as I was feeling towards the end of the week in New London.

56   Anwar Sadat, President of Egypt, made this trip to Israel, starting a peace process that eventually ended in the first peace treaty between Israel and an Arab country. In 1978 Sadat and Menachim Begin, Prime Minister of Israel, jointly won the Nobel Peace Prize. In 1981 Sadat was assassinated by radicals opposed to his having negotiated with Israel.
57   Jules' law firm.

Had dinner at home. Feel it is better to eat simple foods when my stomach is queasy much of the time.

Monday, November 21
We went down together, A rainy day so Jules dropped me and parked in his garage. His office will be on holiday status next Friday so I will take the day on annual leave. Thought getting back to the office routine might make me feel better but I still cough, spit, urinate, and have vague pains in the stomach and other parts of the body. Eating lunch in the building did not help. Jules picked me up about 5:20. We went to the library, the grocery store, and home for dinner. I went to bed fairly early. Kept the TV set on for a while. Jules stayed up to watch the Redskins game, which they won by one point. I slept through the night, a change from getting up 2 or 3 times.

Tuesday, November 22
We went down together. Jules was getting a shot so I dropped him and parked. Another rainy day so glad to be able to park in the nearby lot. I felt much better this morning. Hoped I had licked whatever ailed me. But during the day was again coughing, spiting, etc. And although my backache is much better, I now have a very painful spot at the top of my right leg that Jules think is related to my back weakness. If it persists over the long holiday weekend, I will break down and try to see a doctor next week. I picked up Jules at about 5:20. We went home, read the *Post*, watched the news, and later had supper.

Wednesday, November 23
We went down together. Another rainy day, so Jules dropped me off.
Not raining at noon. Was persuaded to go out for luncheon with Mira Stevenson. We walked to La Chaumiere, had a very good luncheon, and walked back, before the rains resumed. Sending my 40-year award back to have the middle initial corrected. Wonder what part will get damaged in the process. Jules picked me up shortly after 5. We went home. Had dinner at home. He has conceded that we will have a non-turkey Thanksgiving dinner rather then go to a restaurant as I did not want to prepare a turkey. Did not get other things I might have needed to make it a more festive meal as he did not make this concession until tonight.

Thursday, November 24
I went to bed early last night, fell asleep early, and slept around the clock. Still coughing and still have a good deal of pain in my right leg. The weather cleared up for a while in the afternoon. Jules went out a couple of times for walks and to get out. I stayed in.
Nate called from Philadelphia while Jules was out. They are going to be in New York a couple of weekends next month and suggested we join them one of these weekends.
Fixed a brisket, etc., for dinner. It was not a turkey, but the brisket and all the go-withs turned out just delicious. Jules admitted, a little reluctantly, that he enjoyed the dinner very much.

Friday, November 25
We had a simple brunch. Had run out of a number of things. Later we went out to do some marketing and errands. Picked up my mink coat. Not in the mood to go shopping for 4 Chanukah gifts so will send the kids a $1000 check and let them buy their own.

My leg was much more painful this afternoon and evening. I went on a regimen of a couple of analgesic pills every 4 hours. And agreed with Jules I would try to get a doctor's appointment Monday morning.

We had half a cold chicken in the refrigerator so dinner was a cinch to prepare and very good. Later Jules went to the Ohr Kodesh for the special services marking Porath's anniversary as our rabbi. I decided to stay home.

Saturday, November 26
A cold very windy but clear day. We read part of the *Post*. Then had a sumptuous brunch. Jules suggested he would do the cleaning without help from me, but my leg was a little less painful so I did my share. Later dressed and went out to do some errands, mainly to get out. Someone was in my garage space. Took a little time to get the car moved. Then Jules went to the gym for his exercises and to the barber shop for a haircut.

We had delicious strip steaks for dinner, and plenty of tasty trimmings. By evening, however, I was again in terrible pain. Could not sit, stand, walk, or even lie down without extreme discomfort. Agreed we would go to the Sibley emergency room tomorrow.

Sunday, November 27
Felt better in the morning. Decided to go to Sibley after brunch. Read part of the *Post*, had a delicious brunch, and felt well enough to do the cleaning chores. By then felt well enough to skip Sibley and hope to see a doctor tomorrow. Drove out to see Mother. She seemed in better physical and mental condition. Then home. Had a very good dinner at home. Was feeling fine, the apartment clean, I am clean and in clean clothes. Then, shortly after dinner, got an attack of so much pain in my leg that I could only moan and groan. Then were warnings of a sleet storm, which did not come. But that and the way I felt kept Jules from going to the Porath reception, which he had been looking forward to both of us attending. He had sent a $25 contribution for the festivities.

Monday, November 28
Felt better this morning so went down with Jules. Called Ney's office to try to learn what the trouble was, and got an appointment for 3:30. Nancy Sherman asked me to have lunch but I declined as I had better eat in the building.

Ney saw me – more than an hour late – preformed various tests, decided the leg trouble was related to my back problems, gave me some prescriptions, exercises, etc., but had the worst and most prolonged pain all evening and during much of the night. Spent hours groaning with the pain, making poor Jules unhappy and unable to sleep. Finally managed to fall asleep about 1 am.

Tuesday, November 29

A chilly rainy day, and I was in a good deal of pain in the morning, so decided to stay home. Did all the things Ney ordered but had recurring bouts of great pain.

Jules got a prescription from Ney for a stronger pain killer. He brought it home about 6:30. I was able to take it twice, 4 hours apart, and still had terrible pain. Jules called Nate to answer questions Nate asked on the phone. He talked to Bobbie, then to Nate who called when he got home later. Told each other about my woes. Nate said I should get in a hospital for tests. Ira called. They were out of town for a swim meet. Ira thought I should be in a hospital for tests. And Jules said that, when he talked to Ney, Ney recommended that I go to a hospital for a real check.

Wednesday, November 30

Jules had to leave fairly early for a court appearance. I had some breakfast with him. Tried not to go running for a codeine pill every 4 hours, but had to give in to the pain. Jules came home about 3 and drove me downtown to be x-rayed at the office of a Dr. Hagen as prescribed by Dr. Ney. We went home then. He had arranged things at the office so he could stay home. Later we had a light supper. Jules had eaten a big luncheon. And my appetite had been dulled by all the pills. Decided to try to skip the evening codeine pill unless the pain became unbearable. Did get through the evening and night without one.

Thursday, December 1

A relatively balmy day, I felt better, and was tempted to go to the office, but did not because it would be difficult for me to cope there with an attack of pain. Could take a pill, but could not go to bed and moan and groan in misery. Had to take a codeine pill at 2. Jules picked up some things at the grocery store and got home about 6:30. I was having considerable pain so took a codeine pill about 7. The pain continued acute nevertheless until about 9:30.

Jules talked to Clara this afternoon about a problem regarding her brother. He told her of my problems. Nate called to ask how I was before they leave for New York in the morning. He insists I be examined by a gynecologist. The gate house called to report there was a package for us, and then we forgot to pick it up because of my pain and suffering.

Friday, December 2

Jules went to the office.

Mira Stevenson asked Kessel where I was; he learned I was on sick leave, and both of them called me.

Talked to Nay on the phone. He told me to go ahead with the other pills, and it they do not work I would be placed in traction in a hospital. But I was suffering more today from nausea than from my leg. Finally in the evening and again during the night threw up – it seemed all the medication – and felt a little better. Jules stopped at Schupp's on the way home but I could not eat any of the goodies. He also picked up the package, an assortment of foods from Hickory Farms in Tulsa. Ira called in the evening. Will use some of the $1000 gift to buy a guest bed. Clara called to inquire about me.

Saturday, December 3
We had breakfast, not brunch, and a very light one for me. I took the first one of the new pills. Had been feeling very nauseated, and that set off a series of throwing up – medicine, food, blood – some before I made it to the bathroom, creating a mess to be cleaned up. Bill Levy called. Jules mentioned that I would not be at the book club tonight and he might not be. By then I was taking only water and feeling a little better, and he had been out today only to do a couple of errands, so I insisted he go. He did for a little while. Arrived late, by which by then Bill had informed everyone about my problems and left early, before refreshments were served. Jules has been so attentive. Hope I can get well soon and make it up to him.

Sunday, December 4
I tried to eat some breakfast but it was difficult to choke anything down without immediately feeling all choked up. But no more throwing up. And no more pills.
A pleasant sunny day so Jules got out to go to the gym, to do errands, and to take walks. Clara and Alice called. This was the first night of Chanukah. Jules lighted the candles, said the blessing, and gave me a beautiful full-length terry-cloth robe in a golden brown from Neiman-Marcus. We had some cold chicken and other things in the refrigerator, so he was able to prepare a very good dinner. I managed to choke down a little bit of applesauce and a small glass of milk. Will be glad to call Ney tomorrow and find out what's next.

Monday, December 5
A rainy day. Jules took off for the office. I called Ney's office about my weekend problems. He arranged for me to go to GW [i.e. George Washington Hospital] between 2 and 3. Got a hold of Jules, who came home, had some luncheon, and drove me to the hospital. Got a private room. The only private facilities were a bed washbasin, but they will try to move me tomorrow. Jules left them. Ney is out of town. Meyers is to be in charge. Meanwhile various young interns did a lot of checks on me.
I was able to eat some of the supper. Jules came by about 7, while some tests were going on. I urged him to leave shortly after that so his own supper would not be too late. He called me when he got home as I requested. Just feel better knowing he is at home and is ok.

Tuesday, December 6
Was able to eat some of the breakfast. Jules called from the office. Ira called last night. Wanted to come or call me. Jules persuaded him to wait until called in case my room was changed. It was not.
Ney came to see me. And a gastrointestinal, man, Dr. O'Keefe. Survived more distressing tests. Developed a bad case of diarrhea. Jules came to see me at noon and in the evening.

Clara called during the day but at a very bad time for me so our talk was very brief.

Ate part of my lunch and part of my dinner. Get no more food or liquids, except the IV to which I am still hooked up, until after the barium tests and enema tomorrow.

Wednesday, December 7
I went down early for the upper GI x-rays. An ordeal. Later got rid of the IV – one less ordeal. Was visited by groups of doctors several times, by Dr. O'Keefe and Dr. Ney, who is having a gynecologist look at me also. He and O'Keefe think the bleeding was due to the reaction to the pills, but will keep checking. There were also some orthopedists. Meanwhile my leg continues to hurt. Jules called a few times. Tied up in an important client matter but came over in the evening. Ira had called and suggested coming this weekend but I told him to wait until I knew what was going on better. Nate called Jules last night. Also wants me to see a gynecologist etc., etc. Poor Jules happened to visit when I was having a lot of leg pain. I was not good company, but I could not help it.

Thursday, December 8
Jules went to the Alien Property Xmas luncheon so did not come over at noon.

Had two more tests – one by a sonar machine and a liver scan. Had a long talk with Ney. Looks like I will be in the hospital much longer then I had expected.

Alice called twice when I could not talk to her. Did talk a few minutes to Clara. When Jules came in the evening, he brought the Hagen x-rays at Ney's request. I was in a good deal of pain and had been given a liquid diet all day and a lot of laxatives in the evening. Urged him to go home but he insisted on visiting. Said Bill Levy called from New York to ask how I was.

Friday, December 9
Although pretty empty then, the nurse gave me an enema in preparation for the barium enema, a horrible experience but done by a considerate Dr. Got cleaned up. Lunch, when it came, tasted great. Jules came for a very nice visit during the lunch period. Clever get-well card from Nate and Bobbie.[58] Tom and Mira[59] called – heard from Jules where I was after trying constantly to reach me at home. Jules tells me Ira calls every night and argues that he should come this weekend. He called me this afternoon, right after I had taken a shower, and was pleased to hear me sounding so well.

Jules came over in the evening. Poor guy does not like so much eating out alone, so much cooking for himself, so many household chores to do, and all in a very cold apartment.

Saturday, December 10
Dr. Meyers came to see me. Said he had been in yesterday but I was not available. He agrees with Ney there is something in the stomach that must be biopsied. Does not care if I use the traction device or not, so used it very little.

58 Jules' brother Nate and wife Bobbie.
59 Tom Kessel, Chief Judge and Almira Stevenson, Judge and close friend.

Clara called in the afternoon when I was able to chat with her. Jules came about noon. Went home later to do some chores and watch the Redskins win a game. He came back later in the evening to visit. Brought me a note from Gertrude sent to the house. He had called her about my illness. She apparently assumed I would be home by now.

Jules left to have dinner at home. He called me when he got home. Nate called. Coming for Xmas.

Sunday, December 11
The orthopedic people came down to see how the traction was working. Last time I tried to use it , no one available knew how to hook it up. They agreed to remove it as bed rest apparently did the trick for me.

Jules came about noon. Surprised both of us when Ney stopped in so we could both ask questions. He approved my getting rid of the traction. There will be a full body scan, then exploratory surgery. Clara and Lou stopped by to visit. Brought some pretty flowers.

Ira, Sandy and the boys called. It was nice to talk to all of them. Ira called Jules last night. Wants to have Steve call Ney for a report.

Jules left relatively early to go to Duke's for dinner and then home. Called me when he got home.

Monday, December 12
Had an uncomfortable night. Jules told me Lucille[60] called thinking I was at home, and Bill called from New York. Alice Jaffe called me.[61]

The orthopedists stopped in. Did not question my discarding of traction. Ney also stopped in. The body scan will be tomorrow morning. O'Keefe also stopped in. Glad Jules was there at the time so they could meet. He was to come back later to draw fluid out of the stomach. Did not think any was there but, later, found there was. Also changed some of my medications so I would not be a constant diarrhea sufferer, and discussed diet with me, mainly to drink much less milk. Jules went home for dinner. Called me when he got home.

Tuesday, December 13
I was taken down shortly after 7 for a body scan. Jules called a couple of times from the FDA conference at the Hilton – we got Xmas cards from Lee Stanley and the Edes. I got a note from Florence Gang.[62] The Naidens[63] called just before taking off for New York. McKelway stopped in twice, Ney once, and O'Keefe is urging major exploratory surgery as long as I am undergoing surgery. Will know tomorrow. Jules left fairly early for the FDA banquet and reception. Planned for a long time to have me go, and arranged tickets for Knoll and office wives on that basis. Another wife got my tickets. Too bad. Jules had looked forward for a long time to our being there together.

Wednesday, December 14
Ira called – had called Jules late last night. Gertrude[64] called – had called Jules late last

---

60 Wife of Jules' brother Lou in Columbus.
61 Bill Levy and Alice Jaffe, both close friends.
62 All close friends for decades.
63 Closest friends from Jules' law firm.
64 Jules' sister Gertrude Lewin of Columbus.

night also. Clara[65] called. Some beautiful flowers from the Pehles. Jules called a few times and came at noon. I had conferred with various Drs., including Ioline, a surgeon. It was agreed the surgery today would be replaced by more radical surgery tomorrow, after a kidney x-ray today. Jules discussed it with Ney on the phone. I had the x-ray. Was visited by a new crew, anesthesiologists, etc. Jules came over again in the early evening. We read the paper together.

I had trouble falling asleep from shortness of breath. Used the oxygen mask almost all night.

Thursday, December 15
Jules called early. Then Ira, who talks to Jules every day. I suggested he cut down on the calls since they are coming here, but would not hear of it. Florence Gang telephoned. Alice Jaffe came to visit and brought a plant. Meanwhile, very handsome plant from M-L-B,[66] a big surprise to both of us. Visits also from Drs. Ioline, Cohen and Ney. And various very unpleasant procedures like a spinal tap.

Meanwhile I am having great difficulty eating the hospital food, and get weaker and weaker.

Friday, December 16
No entry

Saturday, December 17
No entry

---

65   Anne's sister.
66   Jules' law firm.

Sunday, December 18
A rainy day. Jules arrived fairly early. I got rid of the IV again; and was given some food at last.

Gertrude called. Debbie has a baby girl.

Ira called to confirm they would be here on Friday of Xmas weekend. Clara and Lou stopped to visit on their way to the Arena Theater. Seemed like beings from another world.

Peg Pierce called. Also in the hospital for some surgery.

Jules had supper in the hospital cafeteria. Went home shortly afterwards. Not much fun visiting me. I am either asleep or too groggy to talk.

Monday, December 19
A rainy day and Jules had a 9:30 appointment so did not come by in the morning. Some of the doctors stopped in including Ney who was encouraging about licking this situation by treatments. Jules came over for a while at noon.

A plant from the Michaels. They also came to visit in the evening. Everyone who comes in from the cold looks so healthy and energetic. Wonder if I shall ever be one of them again.

No more entries in December.

1978

Anne was in and out of the hospital in the early part of the year. The inside cover of her diary for 1978 was inscribed, "To Annie, With my best wishes. Tom Kessel." Her long time supervisor and now Chief Judge Kessel of the NLRB had given it to her as a get well gesture. The pages for January 1 through 15 were empty, as were the last pages of December, 1977. These were the only gaps in her diary in 47 years.

She tried to do work when she felt better but was not always successful. Anne began writing entries again on January 16, 1978 while she was still in the hospital. Her handwriting was uncommonly shaky. She pushed for going home that day, and they let her. She was so happy to be home. She wrote steadily through the remainder of January, February, and March. In February Anne was back in the hospital for a few days, and she continually had day trips to one of the doctors or to the hospital for tests or treatments. In March they made a trip to Columbus for a wedding. She tried to do NLRB work completing her cases, and the Chief Judge Kessel told her that she could work at home. She took materials home with her. We pick up her narrative on April 3.   -- RDH

Monday, April 3
We went down together. Jules dropped me at the office. I packed my briefcase with a big load of work, left word that I would be working at home tomorrow, and was picked up by Jules at about 12:30. We stopped at a Roy Rogers for luncheon, not because we cared for their food, but because it was quick and had plenty of parking area. Might have gone home for luncheon but I will be eating at home tomorrow alone while Jules is out of town for the day. Jules went back to the office. Came home about 6:30. We had a delicious dinner – broiled veal chops – but got a call from Tulsa while we were eating. Spoke to all four. They sounded so happy for various reasons that the pleasure of talking to them more than made up for having our dinner interrupted.

Tuesday, April 4
Jules had to go to New Jersey for the day. He could have taken me to the office, but expected to get back too late to take me home. I could get myself home, but rain – which did not come – had been predicted. So took work home yesterday and left word I would work at home today. Jules in fact got in early, and came directly home from National at about 3:30. Elaine Naiden called – to my great surprise. Neil told her some time ago of my illness. She had an extra ticket for a concert tomorrow night and asked me to join her. I accepted. Hope it does not turn out to be too much for me. Birthday card form Madelyn and Ed. They certainly have been maintaining close relations with us.

Wednesday, April 5
A beautiful day. Jules dropped me at the office. Had a stream of visitors, who heard I was back and came in to wish me well and offer any assistance I might need.

Jules picked me up about 12:45. We went home. Lunched there. Jules then went back to the office.

Telephone calls from Clara, who asked about my visit with Mother, and from Jo Klein,[67] who is eager to get back to work.

We hurried through dinner. Elaine picked me up and drove to the Kennedy Center. We parked at the Center at my request and expense. Her seats are on the second balcony and she usually parks at the boat landing free of charge. But we enjoyed the concert and I enjoyed getting reacquainted.

Thursday, April 6
Jules dropped me at the office. Dr. Cohen was at a conference so I was scheduled for the clinic tomorrow.

Getting through the accumulated piles of reading material on my desk pretty well. Have found Board decisions in several of my cases, all short form affordances, which was gratifying.

Jules picked me up about 12:30 and took me home. It would be all right with me to work a little later but that is the best time for him to take off from the office. Still working very conscientiously.

Friday, April 7
Jules dropped me at the clinic. Understood I would get a treatment but, after some tests, was told my blood count was low and I would probably get the treatment next week. Meanwhile got permission to go to Tulsa, and to work full days when I preferred. Was

---
67   Josephine Klein, who was named Judge at the NLRB two years before Anne.

also told my present weight of 128 would be a good one to maintain.

Jules picked me up, too early to stop for luncheon. I did not feel like going to the office. Went home. Although it was a lovely sunny day, I did a good deal of napping, and was asleep when Jules came home. Woke up, however, in time to prepare and eat dinner. Although I am gradually feeling better and stronger, I still do a great deal of sleeping.

Saturday, April 8
A lovely spring day. We read part of the *Post*. Then had brunch. Went out to do our marketing. Made a few stops largely to be out in the sun. Then home to put away our groceries and to do the cleaning chores. When Jules said he was taking a car in for gas and washing, I went along. He dropped me at Neiman Marcus. Admitted when he joined me he did not have a birthday gift for me because of spending lunch hours taking me home, and was going to get one today. We shopped together. Got a pair of earrings and a necklace. Had sodas at Swanson's. Did some other errands. Then home. A lovely day. Had a late supper. Watched some TV and read. And by then, it was time for bed.

Sunday, April 9
Another lovely day for my birthday. We read part of the *Post*. Then had a delicious brunch. Later did our cleaning chores.

Mary Rains called – did not know I had been ill – and asked us to dinner on the 29th, but that was the book club date so I had to decline. I was inclined to accept and skip the book club but Jules insisted we had to go there as it was a prior engagement.

Many of the good restaurants are closed on Sunday, but Harvey's was open, and we went there for a delicious dinner. The service was excellent too. A very pleasant birthday and a very enjoyable weekend.

Monday, April 10
We went down together. Jules called and said he could take me home about 12:30. I would have liked to stay longer but agreed to go then. We stopped for luncheon at the Magic Pan.

Ira telephoned. Got confused by his calendar note and thought today was my birthday. The mail, which came late, included a very pretty blouse, size 12; Sandy picked it out for me.

Mildred Michael called to check on how I was getting along. And Medicare called to check on my Medicare number. Maybe it was just as well I came home as early as I did.

Jules went to the rec center to take his exercises when he got home. Then we had dinner, read, and watched some TV.

Tuesday, April 11
We went down together. Jules called later to say Gang asked him to have lunch and it was Gang's birthday. I told him to go ahead. He took Gang to the Federal City Club. Later picked me up about 2 and took me home. He is burned up at the firm's insistence on his retirement as a partner, confirmed today by Curtin. The firm makes exceptions but will not for Jules. And the modern trend is not to push people into retirement, in the government not even after age 70.

Charming note from Debbie thanking us for the gift we sent the baby and saying again how glad she was that we got to Columbus to visit. Postcard from Ruth, in Germany, and having a very enjoyable trip.

Wednesday, April 12
Was getting dressed to go the office when I became aware there was something wrong with my vision. Told Jules to go ahead without me. Later I called my office to tell them to put me on sick leave. Hoped the problem would clear up itself, but it got worse. I was seeing everything double, and could not read or watch TV. It was a long day.

Hope if it does not clear up by then, the clinic will be able to do something about it tomorrow.

Birthday card from Gertrude, a little late, but she never forgets.

Thursday, April 13
My eyesight was much worse. Jules dropped me at the clinic early. Did not get a treatment as my white cell count was lower than it was last week. Saw the ophthalmologists and neurologist, and Dr. Cohen did a bone marrow test. Gathered the eye problem might be a weakened muscle which will adjust itself or a symptom of the spread of the lymphoma. So busy with tests I got no lunch. Jules picked me up at 3:30, took me home, and stayed at home. I had some soup for a belated luncheon, and later was able to eat some supper, but felt miserable, and the patch on one eye did not help.

Friday, April 14
Jules went to the office early. Came home to take me to the hospital at 12:45 for a head scan. Was told I was to go to the clinic. Dr. Cohen gave me a spinal tap. Reported the bone marrow test was ok, the head scan was ok, the low blood count and eye problem might be from a virus. Then found lymphoma in the spinal tap. The world changed. I am to give up working, to get household help, to go to the clinic twice a week, and apparently to deteriorate pretty fast. No longer any hope for complete remission but only to control the spread. Got a treatment this evening. Left about 7:30. Ate a little supper but threw it all up. Went to bed. Cannot read or watch T.V.[68]

Saturday, April 15
A beautiful spring day. I had woozy moments but was able, with Jules' help to fix and eat a very good breakfast, do some laundry, over Jules' objection, do some cleaning. He went to the Farmers Market early. Later I went to the grocery store with Jules. He went alone to Wagshal's. Told them the bad news. Told Clara the bad news. He tried unsuccessfully to call Gertrude and Ira. He reached Ira late in the evening and told him the bad news. I went to bed early as the eye patch bothered me greatly. Listened a while to the TV set, which has no picture, but must have dozed off.
Thank-you note from Annie Safdi for the wedding gift.

---

[68] This was the day that Anne received the terrible news that she would not get well, and that her deterioration would be fast.

Sunday, April 16
A beautiful day, but I was feeling very weak. Did not know I would fall apart so fast. Had a pleasant brunch. Ira called. Insists I will surmount this latest blow also. Talked to all four. As we could not hope to go to Tulsa for Seder now, we drove out to Katz's to buy some Passover foods for ourselves. Walked in with Jules, but had to walk right out again and wait in the car, as I felt so disgustingly weak. Directly home after Jules picked up a few things.
Did manage to fix veal chops, etc., for dinner. We both enjoyed the meal. I managed to read the paper, not easy with a patch over one eye. Jules reached Nate with the news late this evening. I was in bed.

Monday, April 17
A beautiful day. And I felt a little better. Went to the office to arrange for reassignment of my cases, except Hechinger which I will try to complete. Jules picked me up about 11:30. We went home for luncheon.
My Tulsa case, Oertle's, affirmed by the Board, was affirmed by the 10th Circuit.
Did some work on Hechinger's at home. Apparently did too much with only one eye functioning. Got tired and rather groggy in the late afternoon.
Managed to eat some supper and even to help with preparing and cleaning up. But did not feel like reading or watching TV afterwards, so got into bed early and listened a while to the TV that had no picture.

Tuesday, April 18
Jules took me to the clinic. I had a spinal

treatment, a chest x-ray, something very unpleasant for my throat problem as I spit up my breakfast. Then to the hospital in a wheelchair for radiation treatment. Back to the clinic for chemotherapy.

Dr. Ney was at the clinic. Congratulated me on my great progress. Had not heard the news. Jules came over to take me home. I was able to eat and retain a little supper and my current medications. Card from the Zanoffs, who just heard of my illness, and a call from Claire Jaffe, who also just heard. Quality Care is sending Evelyn Clipper out tomorrow.

Wednesday, April 19
We went to GW [i.e. George Washington Hospital] for my radiology treatment. Got home shortly before Evelyn arrived. A mature women, very pleasant and a steady worker. I worked on my decision for a while and read the *Post*. Ralph Winkler called. Invitation to Michael Cantor's bar mitzvah in St. Louis. Fixed supper and was able to eat some with Jules. Evelyn left on the 3 o'clock shuttle. The shuttle is scheduled to end the 28th.

Ira had called Jules at the office when Jules was out. He called back but Ira was out. Ira called this evening. Wanted to tell Jules he had Steve, who was in Boston, call Dr. Cohen for a prognosis. It was not optimistic. The cancer cells in the spine were reduced, not eliminated, and the radiology may or may not cure my eye problem.

Thursday, April 20
Jules took me to GW for radiology. Then home. Evelyn came at 10. She pulled a few boomers yesterday but seems a good worker and a very nice person. But she is here only until someone else is available, and has other full time work. Very disappointing. And the other one could not work the hours I needed.

Note from Ira with a newspaper photo of Eric helping prepare the Temple for Passover. The nursing home invited us to Seder with Mother on Monday but Jules declined. Chester Cooke of the office called. Will start mailing my checks again. Kessel called, just back from out-of-town.

After supper Jules went out to get some things at the store for Passover. When he returned I made haroset,[69] hard boiled eggs, etc., for the Seder. Jules ordered a chicken stuffed with matzo meal dressing from Wagshal's.

Friday, April 21
Had a good night's sleep and felt better then I had in several days.

Got radiology and then to the clinic for a spinal treatment. Jules came over. We left about 1:15. Lunched at a Swenson's on the way. I rested but Jules ran around picking up two haggadahs[70] – all ours were left in Tulsa – the roast chicken, a bone, etc. Kessel called. Ricci will write decisions in some of my cases. I will discuss them with him, read and sign them. Much prefer it to notifying

---

69   Sweet fruit paste eaten during Passover.
70   Passover story book.

all the parties I am incapacitated. I will try to finish Hechinger's. Bill Levy called Jules from New York about me. Jules heard from Gang that Jaffe is ill. Pehle gave Jules a bottle of Passover wine. We had a lovely Seder service and a very enjoyable Seder dinner. We were both happy with what we managed although of course we would have preferred observing the occasion with the kids.

Saturday, April 22
Dr. Cohen called to check on my medications as he was not at the clinic when we left. Tina Reich called to check on how I was. Clara called to report she saw Mother who thought I might be dead. Charming note from Debbie with a photo of her baby.
Took my mink coat to storage and did some more grocery shopping. Had very good Passover foods for breakfast and luncheon, and a somewhat shortened but lovely Seder service and dinner.
Quality Care called to offer us one of the best nurse's aids – Ruby. Jules and I turned her down. The agency may not have anyone else available on my terms but will not consider Ruby again. Did not like her character or work. Wish it was Evelyn who was available.

Sunday, April 23
Ira called early – for Tulsa – before the rest of the family was out of bed. Was pleased to hear how well I did for the Seders. They had discussed bringing their Seder here but decided it would not feasible.
Went to see Mother. She thought at first Jules was there with a second wife, and wished him happiness after his long devotion to a sick wife. She realized later who I was. Then home. Katz's etc. were closed. He called Clara to tell her about the visit, and Irv whose lump was found to be benign, and who got home from the hospital in time for Seders with Matt and Dan and their families.
Had a very good and enjoyable Passover dinner. Jules went for a walk in the afternoon and after dinner.
The rabbi called to check on how I was doing and if I could come to services.

Monday, April 24
We had breakfast. Then Jules took me to GU for radiation therapy. Then home. Jules went to the office.
Called my office to report I would try to work at home today, Wednesday, and Thursday, and be on sick leave Tuesday and Friday, the clinic days. Lunched alone at home. Worked before and after it. Calls from Alice Jaffe and Claire Jaffe, not related, and later in the mail a notice of a donation made by Claire and Saul in my name. Call for Jules from Ohr Kodesh urging not only contributions but attendance at affairs. He agreed only to the former.
Had a good dinner although mainly finishing up leftovers. We read and watched some TV. Then to bed, I about 11, Jules a little later.

Tuesday, April 25
Jules took me to Radiology, and then walked me over to the clinic. Got a spinal treatment. It is to be once a week. Some encouraging signs but Dr. Cohen doubts there will be any improvement in my eye problem. Ran into

Bob Cohn from the office. Looked great. His cancer was caught in good time. Mine was not. Jules picked me up, and we lunched at home together. Delia O'Hara called to chat for a while.

Jules got home a bit late. We had a very good veal chop dinner, a bit hurriedly as Nancy Sherman was coming with her husband to deliver some material from the office. We had Passover wine and macaroons. Chatted with Nancy, and watched her husband – not a conversationalist – make clever little objects with pipe cleaners. Tina Reich called about going to luncheon, but will call again in the morning.

Wednesday, April 26
A cool showery day. Jules went to the office after breakfast. I worked at home. Tina Reich called – we are to lunch Friday at Florence Gang's house. John Irving called – just heard about my illness. Evelyn Clipper called – can come tomorrow.

Fixed a small rib roast for dinner. It was good but rarer than I prefer. Ate a large dinner. Ira called from his office while we were eating – they plan to come to visit, while Jules is in New York, and over Mother's Day.

Later in the evening got a severe headache. Felt a little better after a long session in the bathroom. Nate and Bobbie,[71] leaving soon for Japan, called and chatted with Jules while I was in the bathroom as he did not know I had been indisposed until I felt better, which I was pleased to accomplish.

Thursday, April 27
A cool showery day. Jules took me to GU[72] Radiation. Saw Dr. Rogers, who seemed just a little more hopeful about the eye problem. Then to Dr. Cohen. Evelyn came in shortly after Jules took me home. She drove me nuts. I had a headache, at times tried to work and at times to rest, but she insisted on discussing every few minutes possible different arrangements involving her and various family members, involving detailed descriptions of people, numerous phone calls, giving me telephone numbers for everyone she mentioned etc., etc. I was delighted to have her leave.

Kessel called about cases. Helen Rosen called to offer her services in any way I wished. Jules stopped at the grocery store. Eric Zeidman called from Woodbridge, Va. – will be assigned at Walter Reed – Jules called back when he got home. Lucille called to ask about me and Leonard to discuss business with Jules.

Friday, April 28
A pleasant sunny day. Jules took me to the Radiology Clinic. Then home. Would have stopped at the office but had the luncheon date. Jules went to the office and to the dentist. Alice Jaffe called – lunch to be at Tina Reich's; Florence Gang to pick me up. The Reich home is nearby and very attractive. We had an enjoyable luncheon and interesting conversation. I did not stay long. Florence took me home. Glad I went, and Jules was pleased that I did.

---

71 Jules' brother and his wife.

72 Georgetown University.

Ruth Levy, back in town for a few days, telephoned. Invitation to a party by her offspring in honor of Stella Zanoff's birthday, enclosing an old photo of a very good looking young woman. Gertrude called from California where she is still visiting Lois and family for Passover.

Saturday, April 29
A beautiful warm sunny day. Charlotte Middleman called early to urge us to come tonight to the book club. We planned to do so. After brunch drove to Montgomery Mall. Bought a new wig and did some other shopping. To the Gourmet Shop and home for luncheon, our last Passover meal. Later to Safeway to market. Later yet we had a light supper. Then to the Middlemans' apartment at The Irene. Everyone was most cordial and welcoming. I was treated as a guest of honor. Neither Jules nor I read the book, but enjoyed the discussion. Stayed awhile for the refreshments, but we left while others were still at the table. I changed the clocks. Had a full but pleasant day, did not do too much or get too tired, and was delighted to be able to get out and give Jules a chance to be with friends.

Sunday, April 30
A beautiful warm sunny day. We read part of the *Post*. Had a very pleasant brunch. And did not feel I had to nag Jules to do the vacuuming. In the afternoon Jules and I went out to do some marketing. I enjoyed getting out for a while with him.
Later dressed and drove to Ohr Kodesh for the annual Night-of-the-Corp party celebrating Hitler's death. Saw many old friends for the first time in a long while, and was touched by the warmth and cordiality of their greetings. Enjoyed the evening very much, and the early schedule, good food, etc. Ira called in the evening. We talked to all four. They will arrive on the Tuesday Jules leaves for N.Y. Jules has urged Ira to come when he is here, not take the kids out of school, and let me manage with friends, but Ira insists on subbing for Jules.

Monday, May 1
To Radiology with Jules. Then he left me at the office and went on to his office. I found the roof over my office was leaking again. Went down for coffee with a group of ALJ's.[73] Did not get much done but enjoyed the bull session. Jules took me home about noon. We lunched at home.
Helen Rosen called. Later picked me up. We went to the grocery store – I mainly for the ride – and then she drove me around some very pretty-homes-and landscapes in our vicinity. A lovely sunny day. It was a pleasant outing for me.
Helga and Fritz are in N.Y and coming to Washington. Jules hopes we can take them to dinner Friday evening.

Tuesday, May 2
Jules took me to Radiology for my 8:30 treatment. Then he walked me to the clinic and left for the office. Cohen wanted me to

---

73   Administrative Law Judges, the NLRB term for judge.

have a chemotherapy treatment as well as the spinal one, which was prolonged and difficult. Had scheduling problems so we decided to try to do it today. Jules came over at noon and took me to the Le Gaulor's for luncheon. The clinic gave me the treatment in the late afternoon, but Jules could use the time at the office. He picked me up about 6. We stopped at the Round Table for some supper. Then home, for dessert later. The pharmacist was unable to fill a prescription of the strength prescribed. Will have to get it changed tomorrow. The nausea, backache, severe headache, etc., which I was told to expect did not come.

Wednesday, May 3
Jules left for Whippany, New Jersey, in the morning. I called the clinic and People's pharmacist about problems in furnishing Decadon pills of the prescribed dosage. Jules called in the afternoon from Whippany, and later from National to let me know he landed about 6:30. He stopped for the Decadon, but there was a mix-up and they were unavailable. I had a few to tide me over until I got a new supply. Jules and I had some supper. Then read the *Post* and relaxed.

I had set my schedule, and done a lot of housework today, only the basis that Evelyn would be in tomorrow to help get the place ready for Ira et al. She called about 10:30 to report she had to go to the dentist tomorrow. Got into other notions but I told her merely to call when she found she could come in one day. Very annoying.

Thursday, May 4
Jules took me to Radiology. He picked up the pills at GU that People's had so delayed. Gave Bob O'Malley a ride downtown. With Evelyn not coming in, would have gone to the office, but it was a cool, rainy, nasty day, so I decided to go home instead. Did a good deal of office work at home, and some housework. Does not appear that Evelyn will get in before the kids do, if she ever comes again. Jules got tied up at the office. Did not get home until after 7. I had dinner ready, so we ate shortly after he arrived. Plan to stop at the office tomorrow. Have a draft ready for final typing and, hopefully, then for stenciling and issuance.

Friday, May 5
Jules took me to GU. Then to the office and went to his office. He picked me up about noon. Stopped for luncheon at a French café-patisserie on the way, and brought some things home.

Kessel called – pressured me to get out the cases - I told him what I thought of the idea with my present difficulties. Alice Jaffe called to chat a while. Helga was having dinner with us although Fritz was tied up at a business dinner which she cancelled for herself. We picked her up at The Madison, then drove to La Bagatelle, where we had a very good dinner and a delightful visit. Took her back early, and made no engagement for tomorrow, regretfully, in all the circumstances. Nate called – leaving on their trip tomorrow early – hoped to come here before leaving but could not work it out.

1978

Saturday, May 6
I got up early, as I generally do these days, and Jules followed shortly. We read part of the paper. Had a very pleasant brunch. Then each of us did a good deal of cleaning. Jules hoped to go to the office but decided to put it off until tomorrow. We went to Giant and did, for us, a big marketing. For dinner fixed a beef stew which we both found delicious. Sorry there was not more of it for another time but we ate it all up.

Clara called to report her latest visit to Mother. Helen called - tried to reach me yesterday and in the evening – we had a tentative engagement yesterday which I assumed was off because of the bad weather – but I should, of course, have called. She will take me home from the clinic on Tuesday.

Sunday, May 7
Awoke with a persistent annoying cough. Had an excellent brunch except that our coffee maker did not work correctly. Ira called. We talked to all four. The weather there is cool and rainy, as it is here. Ruth Levy called a little later. Asked if we wanted to go out to dinner with her and Bill. Did not. In the conversation, she offered to pick up the kids at Dulles unless dashing to Philadelphia for the birth of Linda's baby. Very nice of her. I accepted. Helen Rosen is going to take me home from the clinic.

Jules and I did some more marketing. Then he took off for the office. I did some chores at home. The weather turned pretty in the afternoon but Jules is quite harassed getting ready for the Knoll meetings. We had a very good supper at home, read more of the *Post*, and tried to relax.

Monday, May 8
No entry

Tuesday, May 9
A cool rainy day. Jules took me to Radiology. Dropped me there. I went from there to the Clinic for, much later, a spinal treatment. Jules stopped at the clinic before leaving for the airport. Dropped, I hope, worrying about me. Helen [Rosen] came to the clinic, brought me some goodies which, after we got home, the kids and I had for luncheon. Ruth [Levy] picked up the kids at Dulles and brought them home. During supper Charlie Smith from Jules' office brought us some fresh-caught frozen trout. Jules called from N.Y. to check on whether Charlie, who had trouble calling us about the fish, had made connections.

Anne Schlezinger

Julius, Anne, Ira

Anne Freeling Schlezinger

April 9, 1910 to August 15, 1978

Tuesday, May 9, 1978 was the last entry Judge Anne Freeling Schlezinger wrote in her incredible career as a journal writer. Her good friend of thirty years, Ruth Levy, was picking up Ira, Sandy, David, and Eric at the airport. Since Julius stayed with her every day, he made a postponed business trip to New York. Ira and his family came to be with Anne while Julius was gone. Anne was looking forward to Ira's visit, but her strength of will could not stop the deterioration of her condition. Eventually she fell into a coma, and in spite of her resistance, her active mind came to rest.

The references in this last entry reflect her basic concerns with daily life for forty-five years: her husband Jules, family (Ira and his family), food (goodies that Helen brought and trout that Charlie Smith brought), friends and colleagues. She did not mention work that day because she had to go to the hospital for a radiation treatment. She had been at the office only a few days before, and she was still trying to work even with the disease in an advanced state.

Her son, Ira, was visiting regularly from Tulsa during those first months of 1978, as the disease worsened. First, they found lymphoma, then as she was weakened from radiation treatments, she had a stroke and organ failure. She knew that she was dying, and she told Ira and Julius that she wanted to die at home in dignity with a proper gown. She did not want to wear a hospital gown again, nor suffer the indignity of a doctor entering her room with interns talking about her condition as if she were not there. They honored her request, and she went home.

Anne Schlezinger's diary covers the heart of twentieth century America. From the 1930's as a growing nation with a struggling economy in the Depression years, she experienced misogyny and anti-Semitism as a young lawyer, through the fear and loneliness as a wife and young mother left during World War II to the Communist scares and McCarthyism of the 1950's and the Civil Rights challenges of the 1960's, space travel to the moon, and the political turmoil of the 1970's.

Anne Schlezinger's story is the story of twentieth century America and more specifically of Jewish America. It is the story of a woman who stubbornly embraced her dream of recognition as a professional although she did not visualize herself as a person who was transforming life for American women. She enjoyed being a professional woman and working in law. She thrived on intellectual challenge, and she was at her best when she was being grilled by a Congressional committee or overseeing a difficult case with a major corporation.

Anne Schlezinger and women like her opened paths toward equal rights for women in homes, workplaces, and the larger public sphere of life. Anne had aspired to be appointed to the Board of the NLRB in the 1960's, but she never mentioned it in terms of being the first woman, rather she seems to have considered as realization of professional achievement. Although she was not successful, she lobbied for a woman to be named to the Board, and her efforts were rewarded in 1975 when the first woman was named, Betty Southard Murphy, who served as Chairman from February, 1975 to April, 1977.

Twenty years later in 1997 Wilma B. Liebman was named to the NLRB Board, and in 2009 she became the second woman to chair the Board. Anne Schlezinger's aspirations were too early historically for her dream to be realized, but she contributed to opening paths for women who followed her.

-- Ron Duncan Hart

Epilogue

Orit Rabkin

The Art of Women's Diary Writing: Anne Schlezinger

One day in late 1930 twenty-year-old Anne Freeling (later Schlezinger) walked into a bank and received her first, small, black, bound journal. At the bottom of each page, clichéd messages appeared in tiny print about the security of the bank's bonds and the honesty of its employees. In this promise of the American dream young Schlezinger began her diary writing with an entry every day without fail for almost forty-eight years. Selections from Anne Schlezinger's diary see publication here for the first time and against the expectations of its author.

Reading the diary reveals a strong woman who cared deeply for her family, did not give in to mediocrity, and worked hard to get ahead in her career despite setbacks. The tension created between work and family life--her husband, Jules--and especially when it took her away from her only child, Ira, remained throughout the most powerful theme. The diary reflects a strength as it moves forward in time from the young Schlezinger, law student, to that of a working mother in the 30's and 40's and into a seasoned professional. As the reader knows, she in fact became one of the first women – and a Jewish woman -- Federal labor judges in the United States.

She wrote her diary clearly for herself as sole audience. In other words, she never imagined its publication. In her summary of 1961 she wrote:

> *Often wonder why, after all these years, I continue to write these fool things...do not suppose, in view of the great number of these books that I am accumulating, that I ever shall go back over them...But I suppose if it serves no other purpose, it is a form of self-discipline...Nor do I suppose that all this blithering will be of the slightest interest to Ira or to those who come after him.*[1]

As this passage illustrates, she almost never read through the diaries herself nor could she fully understand the habit she had developed over the span of so many years. Still, she would continue daily entries almost to her death in 1978. When she did contemplate a readership, she thought of her son, Ira, and his progeny yet never a broader audience that publication affords. Ultimately, she viewed her diary as a personal exercise, one involving only herself without imagining it might interest anyone else. Reading her diary proves she had much to say that would interest a larger audience. Her private diary is filled with her life experiences, with which many readers can and will strongly identify.

---

1   Year End Summary 1961.

Why would a reader not be interested in the everyday routine of a woman who lived through the Second World War, a woman who achieved so much professionally, and a woman who shared her innermost anxieties about her family and work at a time when the "professional woman" was relatively a new concept? "There is, after all," she writes, "no vivid description of events of general interest, no profound thoughts, no clever writing, nothing of any interest to anyone who does not care about my routine, humdrum, day to day doing".[2] She implies that philosophical musings about the "condition of man" are the stuff of literature; she excludes the mundane from proving interesting. Worse still, she assumes her writing lacks sophistication or profundity, which simply is not the case. Instead, her diary proves to be a relevant, contemporary feminist text, one that will prove interesting to a variety of different readers. Furthermore, as feminist scholarship has pointed out for the last forty years or more, Schlezinger's assumptions appear to espouse a patriarchal definition of literary worth, one that deserves a thorough reworking to allow many works written by women the literary respect they deserve. Like many women of her generation, Schlezinger internalized those patriarchal values. In addition, like many women of her generation, she found sophisticated ways of resisting and negotiating these values in her writing.

Women needed to negotiate family responsibilities against the desire to write. Francesca Sawaya, in *Modern Women, Modern Work* (2004), outlines that for most white, middle and upper-class women in the United States (and elsewhere, as in England), everyday life consisted of running one's home and overseeing the education of one's children. In general, then, male writers could more easily perceive of themselves primarily as professional writers, artists working at their craft while women writers could do so much less. Male writers perceived themselves as creating great masterpieces since they existed in the sophisticated culture of professionalism, while women thought they had "nothing" to write about.

One of the most famous feminist writings, one taught repeatedly and quoted constantly, comes from Virginia Woolf, whose work emerged at the same time that Schlezinger began her own writing. In 1928, Woolf wrote the seminal *A Room of One's Own*. She imagines there "what would have happened had Shakespeare a wonderfully gifted sister".[3] Basically, his sister would receive no education while William would be sent to school. While William left to work in London theaters, she would be forced into an early marriage. Even by the nineteenth century, where Woolf "found several shelves given up entirely to the works of women" finding the time and opportunity to write was not simple.[4] To this day, the argument repeated most often from *Room of One's Own*, echoes its title: "In the first place, to have a room of her own, let alone a quiet room or a sound proof room, was out of the

---

2 *Ibid.*
3 Woolf, 1999:48.
4 *Ibid.*, 56.

question…"⁵ The difficulty in finding a "room of her own" had a long history and did not improve enough by the time Woolf engaged in her professional writing career.

In addition to the fact that mere physical conditions often made it more difficult for women to write, feminist scholarship has argued that the literary establishment privileged masculine themes over feminine "domestic" themes seen as focused on child rearing or the running of one's household. These have been left out of the literary canon more often than not. Merle Feld includes in her *A Spiritual Life, A Jewish Feminist Journey* (1999) a poem by Rachel Adler, one specifically relevant here: *My brother and I were at Sinai* Adler opens,

>He kept a journal
>of what he saw
>of what he heard
>of what it all meant to him".⁶

The speaker in the poem explains that she, too, wished she could record what she saw and heard on that monumental day:

>It seems like every time I want to write
>I can't
>I'm always holding a baby
>and then
>time passes…"⁷

Since the stand at Sinai, the speaker argues, men had been the ones blessed with the leisure to observe and record. Men have been the ones able to travel, to experience, have had the leisure to write about the monumental events they witnessed. They are the ones with the chance to develop their writing craft. Women, on the other hand, tended to find themselves left behind in this regard. Then, the same men decided that writing about monumental struggles against nature, monumental descriptions of travels, that those types of experiences constitute literature. A woman writing about domestic experience, of having held the child in her arms, of worrying about her family, those experiences became devalued as almost antithetical to "great literature."

Adler's poem concludes by stressing that the brother's version of the events can only tell part of the overall story: "If we remembered it [the event] together," the speaker in Adler's poem concludes, "we could recreate holy time / sparks flying".⁸ A woman writing about her private life shares with her readers a different kind of experience. It offers a literary complement to masculine writing, proving no less interesting and no less able to deliver insights into the "human condition." There are two monumental stories at play, then: the masculine and one different but no less monumental, the feminine-domestic. Anne Schlezinger's diary

---

5   *Ibid.*, 54.
6   Feld, 1999: 205.
7   *Ibid.*
8   *Ibid.*

adds a voice that complements that of so many stories already out there; the monumentally of her voice offers forty-eight years of a woman's story. An early twentieth century example illustrates the point well. Schlezinger's apprehensions about the worth of her writing echoes eerily Virginia Woolf's semi-autobiographical story "The Legacy." In it, Gilbert Clandon's response to Angela's, his wife's, private diary is that she left "nothing in particular" behind.[9] While Schlezinger did not show her diary to her family, Angela outright forbade her husband from reading it; "After I'm dead," she would tell him when he caught her writing, "perhaps".[10] In both these cases the women did not wish their diary read.

Women writers have been painfully aware of a larger patriarchal dismissal of their work. They reacted by deprecating their written creations. As part of the reaction to the denigration of women's writing, feminist scholars have long argued that women's private journals are significant, and show the worth of women's experiences. Amy Wink explains, that diaries are as "significant as forms of women's autobiography and records of women's experiential history".[11] These should be privileged no less than men's. Like Adler's poem argues, the experiences of women as well as the experiences of men can greatly enrich literary tradition, both working together to complete the picture, as it were. Woolf has Clandon learn a crucial truth about his life with his wife, a truth he could never have accessed without her diary. He learns that Angela killed herself basically to get away from him. Schlezinger enjoyed a much happier marriage, yet similarly it is her diary that allows us to access her experiences.

Indeed, the post-World War I scholarly establishment's aesthetic standards for literature erected a bifurcation where the domestic and feminine were devalued in the face of the masculine point of view. For example, F. R. Leavis' influential *The Great Tradition* (1948) aimed at "finally" setting the rules in the face of the plethora of publications by minorities, women, and others during the first half of the twentieth century. He declared it high time that someone established specific measures of quality. Too many writers by then had written what too readily, in his eyes, was accepted by the literary establishment as literary. It was time to "try and establish the essential discrimination" between literature and non-literature.[12]

Specifically focusing on novelists, he pronounced Jane Austen, George Eliot, Henry James, and Joseph Conrad as the only worthy novelists in the English language, concluding firmly that "there are no novelists in English worth reading" apart from these.[13] His kindness toward the two women novelists here needs more careful consideration. Literary history is filled with examples of women publishing yet only these two entered his consideration. Furthermore, literary history is inundated with women publishing anonymously in an at-

9   Woolf, 1989: 281.
10 *Ibid*.
11 Wink, 2001, xi.
12 Leavis, 1948:1.
13 *Ibid*.

tempt to avoid the possible damage to one's good name, an issue male writers rarely faced. This was true of Austen, George Eliot, or (to quote an American example) Catherine Maria Sedgwick (often referred to as the American Maria Edgeworth) who was regarded as one of the first original American women writers. She initially published anonymously dedicating her first novel, *A New England Tale* (1822) to Edgeworth. Second, Leavis fails to mention what Woolf also describes, the fact that Austen wrote exactly between social visits and her family's demands on her time. She had no room of her own and wrote in the family room, constantly interrupted. There existed no situation under which she would be considered a professional writer, who would possess her own space and time to write.

Furthermore, and for some of the reasons already enumerated, his demands for quality easily excluded many other women writers and minorities. Leavis demands "significant" awareness "of the possibilities of life" in order to label a novel great.[14] He means that the writing must have historical significance, without descending to "simple" concerns focused merely on human nature. Such concerns produce an effect of "monotony".[15] Two ways to achieve this literary transcendence included attention to content and to literary technical abilities (think back to Schlezinger's complaint that her own writing offers "no vivid description…no profound thoughts, no clever writing…"). The content, as already discussed, needed to include the monumental stories rather than the small moments. The possibilities of life, concerns transcending "simplicity" translated into the masculine experience.

Second, the technical qualities of the writing needed to be able to reflect the same. The writing must be concerned with form or style as means as an end unto itself. Literary grandeur must show originality of technique, "having turned their genius to the working of their own appropriate methods and procedures".[16] At the same time, then, according to Leavis a great literary work both needs to discuss matters of historical magnitude rather than sink to mundane human moments and needs a particular style of writing so that its concern with aesthetic value would occupy center stage. Any discussion too invested in the primitive domestic cannot hold historical significance. Next, Leavis presented himself as qualified to judge so called appropriate methods involved in the creation of great literature. Consequent literary theory, specifically theory written during and since the 1960's, questioned the cultural biases of such a declaration. The main criticism focuses on his white, protestant, male, point of view.

The feminist reply to the ingrained patriarchal assumptions we find in Leavis extends beyond Woolf's early angry retaliation against the disadvantaged situation in which women found themselves. The seminal work by Sandra Gilbert and Susan Gubar, *The Madwoman in the Attic: The Woman Writer and the Nineteenth-Century Literary Imagination* (1979), changed the literary-theoretical landscape. They began with the premise that there exists a

14   *Ibid.*, 2.
15   *Ibid.*, 4.
16   *Ibid.*, 7.

"common, female impulse to struggle free from social and literary confinement through strategic redefinitions".[17] Women found a way to evade and conceal their anger and their criticism by burying it deeply inside of their work, disguising it, as it were, to avoid direct criticism. Crazy women in nineteenth century novels – the madwoman in the attic of Jane Eyre, for instance – safely express the author's anger against patriarchy. These melodramatic characters, as they call them, "act out the subversive impulses every woman inevitably feels when she contemplates the 'deep rooted' evils of patriarchy".[18] As I will demonstrate further on, Schlezinger does exactly that. She does not directly attack patriarchy, as Woolf did in her writings, but articulates subdued anger to express her clear criticism of patriarchy. When she tries to study, when she tries to date, or when faced with women who completely "buy" into, as it were, the patriarchal role of the woman searching for a husband rather than for an education or a career, her submerged anger becomes clear. In this way, her diary reveals itself as an example of a feminist text, one that resists the general culture's patriarchal assumptions and conventions.

In a more current argument for understanding the strength of *Pulling It All Together*, Steven Knapp takes on Leavis' "formalist" measure of literary value. Knapp's fascinating treatment of the literary world entitled, *Literary Interest: The Limits of Anti-Formalism* (1993) asks the question on its very first page, "what, if anything, makes literary discourse special?"[19] He argues that "the meaning of the work goes beyond what its author intended". A larger meaning can be identified, a meaning beyond the author's intended plan, a meaning possibly extending beyond what he or she could ever foresee.[20] Knapp argues that one of the characteristics of a literary text remains the fact that it allows the reader to feel as if the singular example expands outwards from the text into her own life. It is the difference, again in Knapp's words, between what a "text means and what it exemplifies".[21] A work needs to be able to allow readers to feel as if they have gained a kind of "knowledge" from the encounter with the text. Knapp calls this a kind of "imaginative experience" because the writing allows readers to feel as if they had learned from the particular experience shared by the author even though the lesson is personal and sometimes unintended by the author.[22]

In this respect, a work does not need to, as Leavis and others would have it, transcend "small human moments" in order to impact a reader deeply. For example, reading Schlezinger ask herself in a most private moment, "Have given up almost all frivolities – for a career? I wonder if it will ever be, and if it does come to pass, will it be worth while,"[23] might

---

17   Gilbert and Gubar, 1979: xii.
18   *Ibid.*, 76-77.
19   Knapp, 1993: 1.
20   *Ibid.*, 6.
21   *Ibid.*, 7.
22   *Ibid.*
23   January 16, 1931.

encourage the reader to expand the question outwardly and into her own life. Schlezinger answers the question during a lifetime of diary writing about her career and her family.

Current literary theory finds itself increasingly dealing with questions of the cultural meaning of the literary in place of attempting to catalogue characteristics of the same. In other words, instead of conversations regarding what a work of literature needs to demonstrate in order to be counted as great – a certain style judged as aesthetically superior, content transcending the mundane, etc. – critics ask about the relationship between the culture and the produced literary piece. Basically, as Jonathan Culler puts it, "To ask 'what is literature?' is in effect a way of arguing about how literature should be studied" and, just as importantly how *Pulling It All Together* can be experienced.[24] Frank Kermode clearly makes the same point in his book *Pleasure and Change: The Aesthetics of the Canon* (2006). He contemplates the relationship between aesthetic value and a world in which the literary canon changes. He writes, "Changes in the canon obviously reflect changes in ourselves and our culture".[25] Reading Schlezinger's diary now, decades after it was written, makes the kinds of cultural changes Kermode describes palpable: her entries reveal nothing less than both the social values with which she daily wrestled—the tension between traditional gender roles and modern ones.

Next, a reader should take into account that reading the published version of such a private diary requires a different kind of approach than reading a novel. Schlezinger favored the genre that allowed her maximum freedom, maximum privacy, and the ability to describe life's smallest moments--what she made for dinner and who called or wrote that day. Like Angela Clandon in Woolf's short story, she chose to privately describe the minutest details in her life as a woman. In place of large gestures toward the meaning of life, large philosophical musings, Schlezinger chose what Lynn Bloom describes in *Inscribing the Daily* as the "truly private diary," one that tends toward a "bare-bones" type of work, "written primarily to keep records" of visits from neighbors, public occurrences, etc.[26] Such a diary seems "coded for personal use," making it a challenge for an outside reader to fully understand the context of each entry. There are almost no gestures toward the reader. Instead, the reader needs to trust Schlezinger and allow her to tell her day at her pace, allowing her to reveal what she wants to reveal. A reader needs to understand that the diary references itself and its writer and not an outside audience.

The result is tremendously intimate. A narrative voice almost whispers its short, private, coded messages like a secret on which the reader intrudes. There are no long descriptions of characters' or long monologues built to expose the characters inner life. The reading experience resembles much more closely reading a modernist text like Woolf's Mrs. Dalloway or James Joyce's *Portrait of the Author as a Young Man*. An internal logic drives the narrator

---

24 Culler, 2007:275.
25 Kermode, 2004:36.
26 Bloom, 1996:25.

who is occupied primarily with their own process leaving the reader to feel a guest out of place at best and an intruder, at worse. Yet, like to Joyce's or to Woolf's writing, the reader is drawn, curious about these intimate moments offered suddenly to her.

Throughout her decades of entries, Schlezinger adheres overall to a style that keeps a strict internal uniformity. The entries are always very short, usually prescribed by the physical measurements of the small page on which she writes. Early in the 1930's, for example, her entries would typically read, "Very warm, Breakfasted with Peggy. She wants me and Jean to move with her".[27] The sentences are kept to a minimal length and a reader would not understand who Peggy might be, who Jean might be, and where exactly they are to move from, and other details. Over time, the reader begins to learn about the characters and their stories. Another entry from November 23, 1938 reads:

> *To the beauty parlor in the morning. Was in the office a very short time before Jack took Condon, Swope, Jules and me out for cocktails to celebrate his raise…Then to do an errand with Jules. I got some lovely black satin mules…Then to a Jewish restaurant for dinner with Mr. and Mrs. Schlezinger* [Julius' parents], *who seem to be good, plain, simple folk. We got along fairly well.*

Here the reader receives two different pieces of information. First, that Schlezinger spent the morning both getting her hair done before spending some time in her office. Later, she went on an errand before meeting her future in-laws at a restaurant. If she were writing in a more expanded narrative style, she may have shared with her readers her apprehension about the upcoming dinner. She might have shared what she imagined Jules' parents might be like based on what he had described to her. Perhaps she would include her conversation with her hair-stylist, telling her nervously about how that night she must look perfect for Jules' parents. The reader, however, receives none of these pieces of information, none of these narrative elaborations. Instead, the reader remains to wonder about the hair appointment. Was it set up for that morning to look her best for meeting the Schlezingers? Part of the pleasure of reading becomes these small moments of realization, that she most probably did have her hair done before meeting her future in-laws.

To the patient reader a sophisticated depth reveals itself. Early in her diary writing-career, she shares her struggles against the expectations for her gender. Her barely subdued anger in the early entries reveals a woman who expected much from herself and from others around her. She accepted notions of domesticity and her own inferiority as a diary writer, one writing in a decidedly feminine fashion. At the same time she angrily records her disgust with women who behave in stereotypically feminine ways. Basically, under the short entries about women whom she perceives as silly and men whom she perceives as useless, she reveals herself as a

27 January 5, 1931.

woman who demands to be respected for her intellect. At the same time, she struggles with wishing to fit into a feminine world of hairdos, dances, and dates. She simply refuses to accept a world where the latter takes precedence over the former. The barely subdued anger acts as her private resistance to these expectations, her private space to air her frustrations. Only careful reading of the entries reveals to the reader the intricate depths of her criticism.

Her entries from January 1931, while in law school, almost daily include reactions of disappointment and anger aimed both toward the young men and the women around her. Thus, when she does go out it often results in short angry entries like: "Lloyd and Mim drank more than they could manage…—mostly drunken fools—".[28] She reacts against men who feel superior intellectually. She does not outwardly write that her intellect surpasses theirs. Rather, she tends to stress how they bored her or tended to drink too much as she does in the example above. Their conversations she describes as "inane," or "unentertaining".[29] Meanwhile, the girls around her mostly annoy her. These are the girls whose lives are dedicated to pleasing these same men she finds so unimpressive. For example, the following entry represents Schlezinger's general attitude. She writes:

> *Peggy in the room after school. Wants me and Jean to go out to the dance tomorrow night with some law students. Pleaded much studying, but she and Jean teased until I finally consented to go. Very much dissatisfied with my refusal powers. Must strengthen them…I would not have surrendered if they had not been law students. May mean future business.*[30]

There is a great satisfaction in the story. A reader, after all, enjoys special hindsight. We know that she will have a successful life and will rise to historical importance. Peggy drags her out of the house to socialize too much, as far as Schlezinger was concerned. Again, the reader must wonder what Peggy teases Schlezinger about. Considering Schlezinger wishes to study and Peggy wishes to go out, the reader could infer the teasing has to do with that. Schlezinger regrets and even betrays anger at her self for not being strong enough to withstand the teasing. She excuses herself when she thinks about her future profession. While other young women study subjects which bore them, hoping to marry as quickly as possible (see entry from January 11, 1931), Schlezinger resists on the one hand but still finds herself going out. Her excuse for not studying in the particular case is not one of finding a husband. She could just as easily have written that at least that way she might find a husband more quickly.

Clearly, however, young Schlezinger focuses on a career more than on her social life. She consoles herself that by going out, she builds her future career. The second entry, from Tuesday, January 6, 1931, stresses young Schlezinger's impatience with women whom she

---

28   January 1, 1931.
29   January 2 and January 4, 1931.
30   January 5, 1931.

views as undependable. Interestingly, here she couples that undependable quality with attractiveness. Schlezinger reacts in this entry to the woman who dresses in order to hunt for a husband, an attractive woman who feels no need for education because for her success means only finding a husband:

> *Sally Penn in the office. As attractive and as dependable as a bubble. Wants to go on a 'real big date' with her some night. Her idea of a good time—plenty of liquor, laughter, and loving. Not mine except for one ingredient.*

Laughter is probably the only ingredient that would be included in her idea of a good time. Again, the reader can be satisfied that while the others seem to disappear from the story (both Peggy and Sally are left behind), Schlezinger, the hard working, diligent, serious one, will enjoy success.

Her plight, then, as personally specific to herself as she presents it, will resonate easily with readers. She quickly judges others in her earlier age but arguably does so because she expects so much of herself as well as from others. She balances complaints about the stupidity or dullness of others with demands of herself for more studying. Then, when she does well at work, she feels pride. After a rush job for her boss, she hears him say that "not many people rated 100% in their work" under which she beams.[31] She wishes desperately to both belong with the young men and women her own age yet is painfully aware that her dedication to her studies and to bettering her mind with hopes of a future career sets her apart.

On one occasion she admits that she "wore white chiffon and looked unlike the rest of the crowd".[32] She cannot completely do away with her wish to fit in with the rest of her contemporaries. The instinct to fit in along with the determination to break the conventions of her time echoes into the lives of present-day readers. Many will feel the familiar dilemma of conforming to peer-pressure versus resisting it. Stephen Knapp would step in here to remind us that as specific as her story appears, it also leaves room for others to read and to feel that they, too, can relate. The story unfolding over the years will exemplify the lives of so many contemporary readers.

Meanwhile, Schlezinger's style of writing undergoes an interesting change over the years. The writing grows more inclusive. The reader moves from complete outsider to being allowed more space inside of the text. For years our diarist consistently wrote in this bare manner. The change arrives later, as Ira grows up and while the Second World War has been raging for a few years. Interestingly, especially at the hardest junctures of her life, her writing becomes more detail-oriented. Schlezinger begins a new habit—she summarizes what she calls the "civilian" calendar year (rather than the Jewish Year whose ending is celebrated around September or October depending on the changes in the moon-based Jewish calendar).

---

31 September 16, 1937.
32 January 1, 1931.

Epilogue

Compare, then, entries such as above (which again dominate most of the writing) with these comments from her Year End Summary 1943: "...now that Jules is in the Army, I am filled with doubts as to whether I should continue to work or stay at home with Ira." Schlezinger explains that Jules is in the army and continues describing her dilemma in detail: "It has been bad enough to leave Ira as much as I have, but to continue leaving him..." The reader receives in this entry the whole context for concern over continuing to work. More than anywhere else in her diary she departs from her usually self-contained style and ventures into her own narrative voice. An interesting tension is then created between the pleasure of peeking into a private diary almost like a voyeur and between the sudden realization that one is being included. The change does not take away but adds to the sophistication of the text, and the particular interest that it can produce for a reader.

The satisfaction of a life unfolding slowly over the years does belong first and foremost to Schlezinger. The expanded style allows her, it seems, to talk more fully to herself, first and foremost, about the events around her. In the Year End Summary 1944, she writes: "And so 1944 had dragged to a close. I do not suppose I have ever been so well satisfied to have any other year of my life come to a close". With her husband in the army, feeling forced to leave her job and worrying that she thus effectively ended her career, and her problems with her aging mother, the year had been particularly difficult. In published form, the additional details are transformed into an appeal for understanding at the same time that for her, the external audience remains unknown. Part of the tension is created, therefore, between two types of writing. The one can be defined as a private awareness, a private reflection, as the quote from the beginning of this paper suggests. If nothing else the diary serves Schlezinger as a way of thinking about her life as a form of self-discipline.

The second awareness arrives later, during the year-end summaries. Those are moments where Schlezinger suddenly takes on the voice of a narrator aware both of the importance of her small recordings as crucial for her but also seeming to communicate to a larger audience. These moments of expansion are evidence of an awareness, despite herself, of the importance of the small moments she collected all year. They accumulate in knowledge, a meaning larger than her, even when she does not directly explain it in these terms. She transforms herself into the well-wisher, the mother spreading her good wishes over the world. For example, as 1944 ebbs, she writes "I hope and pray that 1945 will not only reunite our family but will also bring joy to the world".[33] Suddenly, for a few long sentences, Schlezinger sounds as if she is fashioning her New Year speech to an audience rather than summarizing for herself a few relevant events of the day. Again, those moments heighten the monumental importance the collection of private smaller moments had become over the years. What she had to say as a writer in those moments of well-wishing, those moments of year-end summation, adds another layer to the voice of the private diary writer.

33   Year End Summary 1944.

Schlezinger joins another tradition in addition to the women-diary writers described above. She also joins a Jewish American literary tradition. In addition to writing her private diary in a particular feminist mode—the mostly submerged criticism of patriarchy—she is also writing while living the life of a Jewish American woman. In terms of Jewish American writing, Schlezinger's diary occupies a specific literary juncture. Her parents immigrated to this country along with countless others arriving during the great immigration that began around 1881 following the pogroms that began in Russia.

That immigration ended in the 1920's with the change in immigration laws with over a million Jews having entered the country from Ellis Island. That early immigrant generation began a rich literary tradition in Yiddish and also in English (see Irving Howe, *The World of Our Fathers*). One of the most important values or one of the most central dreams for many of the immigrants was transforming into an American. Writing in English allowed the immigrants to either stress the dissonance with their new country and language or to argue for their assimilation. Schlezinger's diary represents a bridge between those Jewish American immigrant voices that felt they had to fight to be counted as American and those who would later take increasingly for granted that they were both American and Jewish.

Mary Antin famously opened her *The Promised Land* (1912) with the following words: "I was born, I have lived, and I have been made over… I am as much out of the way as if I were dead, for I am absolutely other than the person whose story I have to tell".[34] She described the hardships of emigrating from Russia to America coupled with the struggle to "become" American. Her book turned her into a symbol for some of the transformative powers of the United States. The whole point of her narrative, however, is her absolute success at becoming completely American, or as she says, having been reborn American as if the Russian Jew in her completely died.

One of her greatest triumphs was learning to speak English without an accent. For her, the question of assimilation meant everything. Only a few years later, another young immigrant woman by the name of Anzia Yerzierska began her publishing career. She found her niche by writing in the voice of the immigrant who never quite caught on to the intricacies of "proper" Standard English or Americaness. Her short stories and several novels were written in a heavily Yiddishized English. Her semi-autobiographical novel, which currently enjoys renewed critical attention, *Bread Givers* (1925), describes the life of a young immigrant, Sara Smolinsky, who grew up in the United States to became an English teacher to other immigrant children. Smolinsky tells her mother in her immigrant English, "But won't you be proud of me when I work myself up for a school teacher, in America?"[35] Her mother promises her she would be happier to see her married but Smolinsky, like Schlezinger only a few years later, opts for an education.

Similarly, Abraham Cahan published in English after beginning his career exclusively in Yiddish as the first editor of New York's *Forvertz* (Yiddish Daily Forward). Supported by one

---

34   Antin, 1912:3.
35   Yerzierska 1925:172.

of America's leading intellectuals at the end of the nineteenth century, William Dean Howells, Cahan began publishing stories like "Yekle" (1896) about a man who wanted nothing more than to achieve what Antin had been able to brag about, and what Sara Smolinsky fought so hard to achieve, unaccented English and the title of having successfully Americanized.

Twice in the opening pages of the story, Cahan describes Jake motioning what he believes to be "a Yankee jerk of his head" or giving what he thinks is "a Yankee wink".[36] He explains to a fellow factory worker that he likes America because "Here a Jew is as good as a Gentile".[37] For that reason, one must not be a "greenhorn" (someone obviously fresh-off-the-boat). At the same time that he lectures over the importance of assimilation, his heavily accented English weighs heavily on the readers' ability to comprehend him. Cahan transcribes the accent in order to stress the extent of Jake's failure to internalize American English despite his confidence in his own Americanization. For example, in the same speech about America as above he explains, "I want to know that I live in America. Dot'sh a' kin' a man I am! One must not be a greenhorn…"[38] The Yiddish and English compilation, again, further exposes the failure at assimilation which by the way will not stop him from branding his wife, once she arrives with their son from Russia, as a greenhorn. The same themes return later in his only full-length novel in English, *The Rise of David Levinsky* (1917).

Anne Schlezinger writes at a time, then, when ethnic Jewish writing is very popular, like the works of Cahan or Yerzierska who in fact enjoyed most of her success during the 1920's and into the 1940's. Schlezinger's relationship to her own Americaness stands in complete opposition to Yerzierska's, Cahan's, or even to Antin's. She does not make an argument for assimilation into an American lifestyle. Instead, she lives such a life. There is no need for lengthy discussion on the subject. Exactly this lack of discussion argues most strongly for the fact that she has assimilated successfully and therefore represents the new Jewish American voice of which she is one of the earliest examples.

In place of hugely dramatic, epic tales of transformation or failures at transforming from Jewish European to American, the themes become, in a strange sense, less Jewish per se or perhaps less "ethnic." Saul Bellow or Phillip Roth described (Phillip Roth still does) every day life, getting married, getting along with siblings or lovers without feeling they needed to highlight specifically the Jewish aspects of their lives. The Jewishness, the feeling of Otherness still haunts the works but only as very general backgrounds. That one was born American and that one is American becomes a kind of quotidian given. Phillip Roth, who began his writing career in 1959 (with the publication of *Goodbye Columbus*) famously argued that he was not a Jewish American writer but an American writer who happens to be a Jew. Mary Antin could never have dreamt of such a statement. Nothing else defined her relationship to America more than her Jewishness.

36 Cahan 1896: 3, 5.
37 *Ibid.*
38 *Ibid.*

Still, a reader might ask why Schlezinger does not reflect more on her life as Jew in America when stories of European Jewry would certainly begin to drift back to the United States. She almost refuses to include in her diary the fate of European Jewry during the Second World War. One almost wants to ask her if she heard or knew what was happening. Again, all a reader can do is read her entries and see what is reflected there. Does she refuse to discuss such things? She did occasionally talk about wanting the war to be over.

She does signal here and there that she realizes the situation is dire but she seems to keep her diary as a kind of refuge for herself, a place where she can talk about her husband, her son, her mother, what she cooked for dinner rather than worry about reflecting much on the larger historical context. Her diary offers the reader a different story. It offers a complementary narrative to the larger historical one. It is enough to keep the larger historical context in mind to add another layer of meaning. Meanwhile, the diary remains an intimate, powerful look into the everyday life of a Jewish American woman.

The diary expands from the private diary into a type of knowledge communicated to other readers. The diary transforms itself into an exemplar for a modern woman who negotiates work and family life. Schlezinger writes in a 1943 entry:

> *There is, of course, some satisfaction to being a professional career woman at a fairly substantial salary, but the satisfaction is much diminished by the amount of thought I have to devote to maids, marketing* [grocery shopping or general shopping for the house], *housework, and first and foremost Ira's care and welfare.*[39]

Clearly, her smart, demanding, hardworking nature helped her not only through law-school but also do well as a career woman. Different women will easily sympathize with Schlezinger's extraordinarily contemporary dilemmas. In this, another simple, mundane moment, Schlezinger spells it out clearly the dilemma: "The Board conference today took only a few minutes since everyone was in agreement. Two cards from Mother… Ira was, as usual, delighted when I got home."[40] In her plain way, the entry stresses the important part of the day, coming home to Ira.

Prof. Orit Rabkin specializes on the relationship between Jewish and American identities found in early twentieth century English-language authors in the United States. Her research has focused on writers from Emma Lazarus to Anzia Yerzierska and Abraham Cahan, including Anne Schlezinger. She holds a B.A in English from the University of Haifa, Israel (1999) an M.A in American Literature from the University of Oklahoma (2004) where she teaches while completing a Ph.D. dissertation.

---

39   Year End Summary 1943.
40   May 4, 1942.

Bibliography

Antin, Mary. 2001. *The Promised Land*. New York: Random House.
Atwood, Barbara and Mary Ann Richey. 1998. *A Courtroom of Her Own: The Life & Work of Judge Mary Anne Richey*. Durham, N.C.: Carolina Academic Press.
Bayer, Linda N. 2000. *Ruth Bader Ginsburg*. New York: Chelsea House Publications.
Bloom, Lynn. 1996. "I Write for Myself and Strangers: Private Diaries as Public Documents" in *Inscribing the Daily Critical Essays on Women's Diaries*. Cynthia Anne Huff and Suzanne L. Bunkers, editors. Amherst: University of Massachusetts Press.
Brokaw, Tom. 1998. *The Greatest Generation*. New York: Random House.
Bronte, Charlotte. 2006. *Jane Eyre*. London: Penguin Books.
Cahan, Abraham. 1970. "YEKL." *Yekle and The Imported Bridegroom and Other Stories of the New York Ghetto*. New York: Dover Publications.
Culler, Jonathan. 2007. *The Literary in Theory*. Stanford: Stanford University Press.
Edwards, Willard. 1940. "Juvenile Jurists: The NLRB's Curious Personnel," in *Saturday Evening Post*. Vol 213, Number 8. Pages 29 ff.
Feld, Merle. 1999. *A Spiritual Life, A Jewish Feminist Journey*. Albany: State University of New York Press.
Friedman, Jane M. 1993. *America's First Woman Lawyer: The Biography of Myra Bradwell*. Amherst, New York: Prometheus Books.
Gilbert, Sandra and Susan Guber. 1979. *The Madwoman in the Attic: The Woman Writer and the Nineteenth-Century Literary Imagination*. New Haven and London: Yale University Press.
Ginsberg, Ruth Bader. 1978. "Women At The Bar - A Generation of Change," in *University of Puget Sound Law Review*. 1 (1978-1979). Pages 1 ff.
Goor, Ronald S. 2010. Personal Interview. Bethesda, MD.
Gross, James A.
    1974. *The Making of the National Labor Relations Board: A Study in Economics, Politics, and the Law*. Albany: State University of New York.
    1981. *The Reshaping of the National Labor Relations Board*. Albany: State University of New York Press.
    1995. *Broken Promises: The Subversion of U.S. Labor Relations Policy, 1947-1994*. Philadelphia: Temple University Press.
Hartmann, Susan M. 1998. *The Other Feminists: Activists in the Liberal Establishment*. New Haven: Yale University Press.
Hochschild, Arlie. 1989. *The Second Shift*. New York: Viking.
Howe, Irving. 1976. *The World of Our Fathers*. New York: Harcourt Brace Janovich.

Joyce, James. 1991. *Portrait of the Artist as a Young Man*. New York: Knopf.

Kermode, Frank. 2004. *Pleasure and Change: The Aesthetics of Canon*. New York: Oxford University Press.

Knapp, Steven. 1993. *Literary Interest, the Limits of Anti-Formalism*. Cambridge and London: Harvard University Press.

Labor Relations Reporter. Washington: Bureau of National Affairs.

Leary, Margaret. 2009. "Michigan's First Woman Lawyer," in Law Quadrangle: Notes from Michigan Law. Fall. http://www.law.umich.edu/newsandinfo/lqn/lqnstories/kilgore/Pages/default.aspx

Leavis, F.R. 1948. *The Great Tradition*. New York: G.W. Stewart.

Leonhardt, David. "A Market Punishing to Mothers," *New York Times*, Wednesday, August 4, 2010, B1, B6.

Linton, Richard J. 2004. *A History of the NLRB Judges Division: With Special Emphasis on the Early Years*. Washington: National Labor Relations Board.

Mossman, Mary Jane.
    2005. "Defining Moments for Women as Lawyers: Reflections on Numerical Gender Equality." *Canadian Journal of Women and the Law*. Vol. 17. Pages 15 to 25.
    2006. *The First Women Lawyers: A Comparative Study of Gender, Law and the Legal Professions*. Oxford: Hart Publishing.

Nadell, P. 2003. *American Jewish Women's History*. New York: New York University Press.

Nadell, Pamela S. and Jonathan D. Sarna. 2001. *Women and American Judaism: Historical Perspectives* (Brandeis Series in American Jewish History, Culture, and Life). Waltham: Brandeis University Press.

Perry, Leslie S. 1947. "Facts about Jim Crow," in *Fourth International*. November-December. Vol. 8, No. 9.

Reinharz, Shulamit.
    2010. *Observing the Observer: Understanding Our Selves in Field Research*. New York: Oxford University Press.
    2001. *A Chronological Chart of Women's Sociological Work*, Working Papers Series, #1, Women's Studies Program, Brandeis University. 3rd edition.

Rosenberg, Rosalind. 1982. *Beyond Separate Spheres: Intellectual Roots of Modern Feminism*. New Haven: Yale University Press.

Rosner, Jennifer. 2010. *If a Tree Falls: A Family's Quest to Hear and Be Heard*. New York: Hadassah-Brandeis Institute and the Feminist Press.

Salkin, Patricia E. 2009. *Pioneering Women Lawyers: From Kate Stoneman to the Present*. Chicago: American Bar Association.

Sawaya, Francesca. 2004. *Modern Women, Modern Work: Domesticity, Professionalism, and American Writing, 1890-1950*. Philadelphia: University of Pennsylvania Press.

Schlezinger, Ira. 2009. Personal Interviews. Oklahoma City, OK.

Sedgwick, Maria C. 1995. *A New England Tale: or, Sketches of New-England Character and Manners*. New York: Oxford University Press.

Smith, J. Clay, Jr. (Foreword by Thurgood Marshall). 1999 . *Emancipation: The Making of the Black Lawyer, 1844-1944.* Philadelphia: University of Pennsylvania Press.
Stern, Nancy. 2009. Personal Interview. Boston, MA.
Strebeigh, Fred. 2009. *Equal: Women Reshape American Law.* New York: W.W. Norton & Company.
Wagshal, Sam. 1950. "The Most Unforgettable Character I've Met," in *Reader's Digest.* January. Pages 12 to 14.
Wink, Amy. 2001. *She Left Nothing Behind in Particular, The Autobiographical Legacy of Nineteenth-Century Women's Diaries.* Knoxville: University of Tennessee Press.
Wisse, Ruth. 2000. *The Modern Jewish Canon, A Journey Through Language and Culture.* New York: Free Press.
Women Lawyer's Journal. Vol.2, No. 4. Women Lawyers' Club. Jamaica, New York City. February, 1913.
Woolf, Virginia.
    1989. "The Legacy." *The Complete Shorter Fiction of Virginia Woolf.* Ed. Susan Dick. London: The Hogarth Press.
    1999. *A Room of One's Own.* New York and Burlingame: Harcourt, Brace & World.
Yezierska, Anzia. 1963. *Bread Givers.* New York: Persea Books.

Index

A

Abba Eban 453
Adlai Stevenson 310, 431
Administrative Law Judge 461, 497, 498, 526
Alger Hiss 147, 164, 320
ALI 445, 446, 477. *See also* American Law Institute
Alice Jaffe 319, 335, 66, 402, 406, 408, 424, 430, 432, 434, 439, 440, 471, 493, 511, 552, 553, 559, 561, 562
Allen Rosenberg 124, 311, 313
Almira Stevenson 311, 313, 438, 518, 551
Al Sommers 300, 464
American Bar Association 66, 124, 152, 179, 384, 451, 508, 544
American Law Institute 445, 464, 477. *See also* ALI
American Radiator 68, 165, 169, 172, 173, 190, 193
Apollo Moon program 432
Army 66, 110, 170, 202, 207, 208, 215, 219, 228, 229, 231, 233, 237, 247, 275, 356, 576
Arnold Raum 154-160, 162, 163, 166, 169, 172-175, 187, 188, 198, 263, 264, 315, 320, 332, 333, 338, 348, 398
Art Buchwald 434, 544
Arthur Leff 312, 333, 413, 509
Ascher 315, 338, 348, 489, 493, 494, 495, 500, 509, 513. *See* Sid Ascher
Atomic bomb 250
Attorney General 68, 296, 315, 320, 325, 392, 434, 477, 544. *See also* Griffin Bell, Herb Brownell, Nicholas Katzenbach

B

Baba 100, 108, 111, 123, 126, 127, 128, 130, 149, 177, 179, 185, 224, 226, 227, 267, 268, 269, 271, 274, 276, 277
Bar 65, 66, 67, 97, 98, 105, 110, 113, 114, 124, 147, 152, 179, 354, 356, 358, 364, 368, 384, 430, 434, 441, 451, 467, 471, 491, 492, 493, 494, 508, 544
Bar mitzvah 263, 316, 325, 329, 330, 331, 332, 333, 334, 336, 337, 338, 339, 347, 349, 376, 377, 387, 423, 424, 448, 525, 558
Beeson [Albert C.] 331, 334, 335, 337, 338, 339
Bellman [Earl] 320, 322, 331, 332, 334, 335, 338, 345, 348
Bernie Balicer 299, 308, 321
Bill Levy 314, 354, 386, 387, 404, 405, 406, 407, 408, 409, 438, 442, 444, 476, 480, 493, 523, 528, 534, 539, 540, 550-552, 559. *See also* Ruth Levy
Bill Lubbers 399
Bisgyer [Paul] 265, 7, 66, 67, 105, 123, 330, 331, 355, 483. *See also* Paul Bisgyer
B'nai B'rith 341, 384, 390

Board [National Labor Relations Board] 260, 262, 264, 269, 275, 276, 278, 280, 281, 285, 287, 295, 300, 308, 311, 313, 315, 293, 319, 320, 321, 324, 325, 326, 327, 331, 333, 337, 340, 342, 344, 349, 354, 356, 358, 372, 377, 384, 388, 390, 391, 393, 397, 398, 401, 404, 407, 408, 413, 416, 417, 418, 428, 430, 431, 433, 434, 437, 438, 439, 441, 443-445, 447, 450, 459, 461, 462, 464, 480, 481, 483, 486, 492, 497, 499, 509, 516, 517, 525, 526, 528, 529, 531, 535, 539, 541, 555, 557, 580. *See also* NLRB
Bobby Kennedy 434, 462, 470
Bob Freehling 292, 293, 312, 315 328
Bokat [George] 464, 473, 481, 491
Boyd S. Leedom 354, 356, 404, 408, 430. *See also* Leedom
Bradford Machine 354
Buckingham Apartments 178, 220, 257, 266, 275

C

Cape Cod 259, 283, 320, 341, 349, 369, 402, 525
Carbide Tools 509, 516
Carol Pollack 299, 338, 347
Carpool 267, 298, 299, 310, 311, 312, 314, 316, 327, 332, 346, 350
C.C.F. 75, 78. *See* Mrs. Fuller
C.E.W. 113, 123, 149, 150, 162. *See* Charles Wyzanski
Chanukah 227, 487, 548, 550
Charles Fahy. *See* Fahy
Charles Wyzanski 68, 89, 104, 115, 116, 126, 148, 159, 162, 163, 173, 186, 446, 464. *See also* Wyzanski
Churchill [Prime Minister Winston] 205, 222
Claire Edes 235, 278
Claire Jaffe 558, 559
Claire Rosen 186, 201, 203, 204, 211, 238. See Claire Edes. See also Edes
Clara [Freeling Roland] 23, 24, 30-33, 38, 65, 66, 69, 87-89, 91, 93, 97-100, 102-112, 114, 118, 123, 126-134, 138, 139, 141-145, 149-152, 154-160, 163-165, 167, 169, 171, 172, 177, 179, 183, 185-189, 192-204, 206-210, 214, 217, 219, 220, 224-226, 228, 229, 232, 236, 241, 244, 246, 247, 250, 251, 256, 259, 260, 262-266, 268, 271-273, 276-278, 283, 286, 289, 291, 293, 294, 303, 306, 308, 315, 319, 323, 335, 341, 343-345, 369, 371, 372, 374, 376, 378, 379, 382, 385, 387-389, 396-398, 404, 422, 433, 437, 463, 468, 473, 484, 487, 488, 491, 494, 516, 523, 527, 530, 534, 535, 540, 549, 550-553, 555, 557, 559, 563. See Freeling/Frihling Family. See also Rolands

D

Dave Rein 164, 168, 169, 194, 195
David and Eric [Schlezinger] 462, 479, 507, 523, 470. *See also* Grandsons
Department of Labor 67, 68, 96, 113, 123, 126, 137, 161, 240, 464
Dick Brownstone 292, 299, 307, 311, 314, 315, 321, 326, 328, 330, 331, 353, 404, 406
Dixie Mercerizing case 292
Dorothy [Surrey] 74, 126, 127, 129-133, 138-141, 144, 152, 164, 165, 167, 168, 171, 179, 186, 187, 193, 203, 206, 214, 255, 286, 386, 399, 498, 504. *See also* Surreys
Duffy Edes 204, 223, 279, 303, 304, 308, 330

Index

E

Edes 200, 201, 203, 204, 205, 206, 207, 223, 234, 235, 238, 263, 264, 278, 279, 303, 304, 308, 330, 386, 436, 447, 449, 459, 515, 552. *See* Claire Edes, Claire Rosen, Duffy Edes
Edith Bisgyer 307. *See also* Paul Bisgyer
Ed Rains 273, 334
Eleanor Schwartzbach 86, 271, 447, 450
Emma Fall Schofield 86
Eric [Schlezinger] 323, 441, 470, 462, 463, 471, 479, 480, 485, 487, 491, 495, 502, 507, 523, 524, 526, 527, 529, 541, 558, 560, 565
Evelyn Promisel 323, 330, 335, 342, 343, 344, 347, 350, 354, 395, 416, 423, 429, 437. *See also* Promisels

F

Fahy, [Judge Charles] 52, 55, 150, 151, 186, 193, 195, 211, 251, 398, 413, 423, 446, 523
Family Friends. *See* Levys, Jaffes, Gangs, Pachels, Promisels, Purcells, Naidens
Fannie Boyls 31, 398, 433, 461, 480, 482, 485, 491, 497, 507, 508, 516, 517, 525
Father 73, 78, 82, 93, 97, 99, 100, 110, 136, 147, 200, 203, 230, 239, 266, 273, 276-278, 281, 283, 291, 309, 317, 319, 333, 334, 354, 369, 370, 371, 373, 375, 396, 529, 530. *See also* Freeling/Frihling Family
Federal Judges. *See* Madden, Fahy, Wyzanski, Harold Leventhal
Frances Perkins 137, 270, 271
Freeling/Frihling Family. *See* Mother, Father, Baba, Clara, Jean, Jan, Louie, Wagshals

G

Gangs [Florence and Arthur] 276, 290, 292, 294, 311, 313, 330, 342, 345, 350, 351, 374, 376, 385, 402, 409, 451, 452, 480
Garfinckels 105, 278
Gates Rubber 202
Gear Mfg. 261
General Motors 160, 192, 199
George Bokat. *See* Bokat
Geraldine Novelty 270, 271
Gertrude Lewin 295, 298, 319, 377, 477, 503, 520, 553. *See also* Schlezinger Family
Gladys Burch 132, 139, 141
Goors 240, 247, 248, 249, 251, 255, 256, 263, 264, 266, 275, 284, 290, 349, 422, 433. *See also* Jeanette, Ronnie
Grace McEldowney 285-287, 297, 314, 346, 350, 351, 353
Grandsons 445. *See* David and Eric
Griffin Bell [Attorney General] 544
Gromfine [Iz or Israel] 275, 276, 280, 289, 297, 299, 351

H

Haile Selassie 419
Hank Wenzel 299, 308

Harold Leventhal 157, 434
Harry Kuskin 325, 371, 377, 393, 407, 501. *See also* Kuskin
Headache 86, 90, 144, 149, 169, 203, 249, 269, 310, 313, 316, 324, 338, 353, 377, 393, 405, 407, 415, 424, 429, 439, 445, 458, 466, 483, 496, 500, 560, 562
Hebrew School 311, 312, 315, 325, 331, 338, 468
Hecht's 278, 286, 289, 294, 296, 304, 326, 338, 352, 395, 402, 411, 493, 529
Helen Rosen 311, 313, 314, 324, 326, 330, 333, 334, 337, 346, 351, 355, 384, 429, 560, 561, 563
Henry Lehman 160, 164, 198, 206, 213, 261, 264
Herb Brownell 315
Herb Lipsitz 315, 331
Hitler [Adolf] 161, 561
Hooker Chemical 495
Horshy [Charles] 161, 168, 169, 173, 186, 193, 434
Housekeeper 282, 306, 309, 317, 328, 383
House Un-American Activities Committee 124. *See also* Allen Rosenberg, Martin Kurasch, Joseph Robinson, David Rein, Nathan Witt, Ruth Weyand
Hyannisport 259, 320, 341, 349

I

Irene Shriber 264, 268, 277, 278, 279, 282, 284, 285, 287, 303, 306, 308
Irv Jaffe 311, 342, 411, 432, 500, 510
Irv Levy 306
Iz Gromfine 288, 289, 297, 299, 351

J

Jaffes 333, 336, 345, 388, 389, 393, 394, 403, 420, 424, 437, 438, 443, 451, 463, 489, 497, 500, 502, 512, 516. *See also* Alice and Irv. Children Saul and Claire.
Jan [Freeling/Ruscoll) 319, 338, 357, 358, 369, 371, 372, 374, 376, 389, 412, 422, 437, 468, 477, 478, 513
Jean [Freeling/Ruscoll] 65, 68-78, 80, 81, 85-89, 91-93, 95, 98-100, 104-109, 114, 119, 120, 136, 145, 148, 153, 157, 173, 219, 249, 250, 271, 281, 289, 319, 338, 336, 412, 479, 573, 574
Jeanette [Goor] 178, 220, 228, 241, 243-246, 249, 250, 252, 265, 266, 280, 356. *See also* Goors
Jennie Sarrica 352, 354, 356, 508, 509, 510, 511, 513, 515, 516, 518
Jewish 65-68, 95, 106, 109, 111, 115, 118, 123, 124, 170, 175, 179, 259, 278, 282, 285, 286, 299, 322, 331, 338, 339, 342, 367, 370, 372, 384, 416, 418, 440, 448, 456, 459, 471, 479, 499, 500, 567, 569, 572, 573, 576, 577, 579, 581, 583, 585, 586. *See also* Seder, Passover, Kol Nidre, Bar Mitzvah, Chanukah, Synagogue
Joe Friedman 156, 165, 212, 241, 243, 253, 259, 296, 302, 315, 319, 323, 327, 328, 330
Joe Robinson 124, 152, 154-156, 207
Joe Ruscoll 153
Jo Klein 471, 527, 555
Judge Emma Fall Schofield 86
Judge [Warren] Madden 271, 377, 394
Justice 123, 126, 132, 133, 135, 137, 154, 158, 161, 169, 228, 239, 291, 313, 315, 320, 323, 327, 384, 434
Justices Black, Goldberg and Douglas 154, 434

Index

K

Kaminstein [Joe] 123, 210, 259
Kessel [Thomas] 355, 562, 474, 488, 491, 495, 497, 500, 513, 515, 517, 519, 522, 523, 529, 530, 534, 536, 538, 541, 543, 549, 551, 554, 558, 559, 560
Knoll 486
Kol Nidre 149, 185, 352, 378, 418, 426
Kommy 120, 171, 123, 126, 127, 128, 130, 131, 132, 133, 134, 138, 139, 140, 141, 142, 141, 143, 144, 147, 149, 150, 151, 152, 154, 164, 165, 166, 167, 171. *See also* Kaminstein
Krasnecki 320, 350, 351, 352, 353, 355, 356, 357, 387
Kurasch [Martin] 124
Kuskin [Harry] 325, 371, 374, 377, 393, 395, 325, 371, 374, 377, 393, 395, 407, 409, 416, 428, 407, 409, 416, 428, 501

L

Labor Dept 99, 138, 139
Laura Sommers 300
Lawrence [City of] 81, 84, 91, 92, 100, 101, 105, 108, 110, 114, 117, 127, 128, 130, 136, 147, 151, 169, 184, 185, 189, 193, 194, 238, 253, 265, 306, 320, 341, 368, 369, 370, 371, 374, 375, 420, 481
Lawyers Club 425
Lawyer's Guild 152
Leedom [Boyd] 354, 356, 357, 370, 377, 393, 404, 407, 408, 409, 416, 419, 428, 430, 431, 440. *See also* Boyd S. Leedom
Leff [Arthur] 312, 327, 330, 333, 338, 348, 354, 357, 413, 438, 509, 511
Leo Weiss 388, 408
Levys 259, 322, 337, 345, 350, 353, 372, 376, 377, 385, 386, 388, 389, 393, 394, 396, 402, 411-413, 415, 417, 418, 420-422, 424, 425, 429, 433, 434, 436, 437, 443, 444, 446, 447, 451, 452, 458, 536, 463, 465, 466, 468, 472, 477, 479, 480, 483, 485, 486, 488, 499, 505, 508, 510, 512-514, 516, 524. *See also* Ruth Levy, Bill Levy
Lindner [Sid] 376, 324, 325, 328, 330, 331, 333, 335, 337, 338, 344, 348, 352, 353
Louie 120, 140, 147, 149, 183, 226, 227, 302, 322, 332, 335, 336, 350, 352, 354, 368, 369, 370, 378, 411, 412, 416, 422, 432, 439, 447, 465, 466, 467, 476, 498, 541, 543. *See* Freeling/Frihling family
Lou Roland 177, 199, 204, 207, 214, 251, 259, 275, 319, 323, 340, 347, 538
Lucille [Schlezinger] 183, 226, 227, 302, 319, 322, 335, 336, 350, 359, 362, 363, 364, 366, 368, 370, 373, 375, 384, 397, 404, 411, 412, 414, 416-419, 422, 423, 439, 448, 463, 465, 466, 467, 470, 471, 476, 480, 498, 507, 541, 543, 552, 560. *See also* Schlezinger family

M

Madden [Judge Warren] 153, 158, 186, 193, 271, 377, 394, 397, 398
Mae [Wagshal] 81, 82, 100-111, 140, 142
Mass Knitting Mills 124
Max Rosenberg 285, 299, 310, 311, 313, 314, 323, 325, 331, 332, 333, 335, 336, 342, 467

McCarthy [Senator Joseph] 124, 175, 299, 323
MCJC 285, 299, 310, 311, 313, 323, 325, 331-333, 335, 336, 342, 345, 349, 350, 370, 378, 383, 416, 420, 424, 426, 448, 459, 468
Mentors. *See* Mrs. Fuller, Mrs. Mann, Charles Wyzanski
Migraine 67, 145, 157, 317, 439
Mira [Almira Stevenson] 314, 329, 330-334, 337-339, 346, 348, 351-354, 356, 357, 404, 408, 430, 438, 461, 464, 476, 486, 497, 499, 502, 507, 508, 509, 510, 511, 517, 518, 521, 522, 524, 525, 530, 532, 536, 538, 539, 540, 541, 547, 549, 551
Moshe Dayan 451
Mother 65, 78, 85, 91, 93, 97-100, 105, 110, 136, 145, 147, 148, 163, 167, 172, 184, 186, 190, 196, 197, 200, 202-206, 208-219, 223-230, 232-235, 237-239, 241-253, 256, 261, 263, 265-273, 276-278, 281, 283, 288, 289, 291-293, 298, 300, 302, 303, 306, 309, 313, 317, 319, 322, 325, 330, 333, 334-336, 339, 342, 346, 347, 350-354, 360, 368-376, 378, 383, 385-398, 400, 402-409, 412, 413, 415-418, 420, 424, 426, 427, 429, 433, 435, 437, 439-443, 445, 449, 451, 452, 458, 463, 468, 472, 474, 475, 476, 477, 478, 479, 480, 482, 484, 485, 487, 492, 494, 495, 496, 499, 500, 502, 504, 505, 508, 510, 512, 514, 518, 520, 522, 524, 526, 527, 533, 535, 536, 537, 540, 548, 555, 558, 559, 560, 563, 580. *See also* Freeling/Frihling Family
Movie 128, 140, 151, 167, 181-183, 186, 192, 195, 201, 202, 204, 206, 207, 211, 221, 223, 227, 231, 234, 242, 243, 250, 253, 256, 260, 261, 268, 269, 270, 272, 273, 276, 278, 279, 281, 282, 285, 289, 292-294, 298, 302, 303, 307, 312, 316, 320, 321, 336, 338, 344, 350, 356, 392, 396, 403, 405, 409, 412, 413, 415, 420, 427, 437, 441, 446, 448, 465, 468, 469, 474, 496, 510, 529, 532, 534, 542, 543
Mrs. Fuller 69-74, 76, 79, 80, 82, 83, 88, 92, 94, 96, 97, 105, 108, 110, 112, 113, 130
Mrs. Mann 85, 86, 89-91, 95, 98, 99

N

Naiden [Neil] 387, 319, 322, 425, 434, 460, 462, 465, 467, 482, 488, 500, 504, 517, 523, 542, 554
Naidens 386, 387, 487, 524, 552
Nate [Nathan Schlezinger] 40, 8, 69, 71, 170, 123, 124, 125, 148, 172, 175, 191, 192, 319, 328, 330, 332, 334, 335, 336, 338, 345, 350, 351, 353, 359, 361, 362, 363, 364, 365, 369, 371, 372, 374, 375, 388, 404, 414, 420, 421, 422, 423, 430, 449, 458, 462, 463, 465, 466, 467, 470, 500, 503, 511, 515, 517, 527, 538, 548, 549, 551, 552, 557, 560, 563. *See also* Nate and Bobbie, Schlezinger family
Nate and Bobbie [Schlezinger] 313, 362, 363, 67, 462, 470, 551, 560
National Labor Relations Board 123, 124, 125, 148, 172, 175, 191, 192, 319, 384, 401, 461
Nat Witt 150-153, 158, 192
Nicholas Katzenbach (Attorney General) 434
NLRB 123-125, 128, 149, 150, 152-155, 158, 164, 175, 177-179, 183, 190-194, 198, 202-204, 210-212, 219, 221, 234, 250, 260, 271, 275, 281, 295, 309, 319-333, 337, 338, 345, 346, 348, 351, 354, 356, 371, 377, 398, 401, 413, 416, 419, 428, 430, 433, 434, 438, 441, 444, 461, 463, 464, 471, 480, 482, 485, 489, 516, 518, 523, 554, 555, 561, 583. *See* National Labor Relations Board

O

Oak Apparel 531

Index

Ohio State University 392, 396, 421, 535
Ohr Kodesh 6, 480, 492, 498, 500, 502, 507, 522, 548, 559, 561
OSU 365, 387, 396, 397, 398, 411, 417, 418, 419, 430, 483, 485, 489, 494, 509, 535, 544, 546. *See* Ohio State University

P

Pachels [Iz and Reba] 170, 212, 216, 223, 270, 317, 334, 336, 422
Passover 276, 278, 292, 454, 561, 489, 490, 535, 539, 541, 544, 557, 558, 559, 560, 561. *See also* Seder
Paul Bisgyer 265, 269, 289, 295, 303, 307, 308, 312, 330, 331. *See also* Edith Bisgyer
Phil [Wagshal] 100-111, 119, 128, 131, 140, 145, 149, 179, 200, 205, 224, 233-235, 238, 239, 283, 313, 332, 511, 512. *See also* Wagshal
President Dwight Eisenhower 60, 267, 259, 310, 311, 314, 315, 319, 320, 329, 349, 357, 384, 404, 434
President Lyndon Johnson 411, 431, 436
President John F. Kennedy 420
President Roosevelt 84, 86, 87, 100, 115, 127, 138, 140, 142, 175, 177, 191, 222, 240, 241, 242
Promisels [Nate and Evelyn] 259, 336, 337, 351, 354, 409. *See also* Evelyn Promisel
Purcells [Morris and Pearl] 262, 263, 264, 270

R

Ralph Winkler 24, 50, 52, 205, 261, 311, 312, 314-316, 324-326, 328-335, 345-348, 354, 465, 489, 558. *See also* Ralph
Read/reading 6, 7, 9, 12, 13, 14, 17, 19, 20, 26, 27, 28, 38, 39, 45, 53, 62, 65, 76, 77, 80, 81, 84, 85, 99, 100, 107, 110, 114, 126-129, 130-132, 137, 140-144, 151-153, 155, 156, 159, 166, 167, 168, 180, 181, 192, 194, 195-198, 200, 201, 204-206, 209, 212-215, 221, 222, 224, 224, 226, 228, 239, 245, 249, 250, 254, 263, 264, 272, 273, 278, 279, 282, 289, 295, 296, 299, 301, 307, 353, 354, 358, 364, 369, 373, 374, 381, 389, 393, 399, 405, 410, 415, 425, 426, 429, 436, 444, 445, 448, 452, 456, 457, 462, 466, 468, 472, 474, 476, 478, 479, 482, 485, 487, 489, 494, 496, 500-502, 504, 505, 510, 512-514, 518, 520, 522, 523, 526, 527-529, 530-537, 539, 540, 542-544, 546-548, 553, 555-563, 567, 569, 570-574, 576, 579
Remualdez 355, 356, 373
Republican 85, 86, 311, 319, 320, 338, 340, 357
Resurrection City 465
Reynolds Pen 265
Rolands [Lou and Clara] 8, 177, 204, 208, 210, 251, 276, 277, 284, 290, 291, 296, 298, 303, 304, 306, 308, 310, 313, 323, 324, 327, 335, 336, 339, 344, 345, 346, 371, 372, 375, 388, 417, 437, 458, 478, 479, 497, 510. *See also* Clara. *See* Lou Roland
Ronnie [Goor] 87, 178, 220, 221, 222, 240, 241, 242, 243, 244, 246, 248, 253, 254, 255, 256, 263, 264, 265, 266, 267, 268, 275, 320, 321, 349, 350. *See also* Goors
Rosh Hashanah 183, 322, 415, 416, 418, 424, 459, 471, 500, 528
Ruscolls [Joe and Jan] 338. *See also* Jan
Ruth Bader Ginsberg 67, 536
Ruth Jewell 133, 142

Ruth Levy 319, 330, 335, 336, 345, 382, 383, 395, 396, 402, 404, 409, 422, 426, 427, 432, 436, 439, 451, 476, 497, 502, 561, 563, 565. *See also* Levys

Ruth Weyand 124, 125, 128, 149, 212, 281, 535

S

Sam Efron 296, 330

Sam Wagshal 65, 100, 263, 267, 291, 336, 371, 373, 484. *See also* Mollie, Phil, Mae

Sam Zagoria. *See* Zagoria

Sandy [Schlezinger] 347, 401, 431, 436, 440, 441, 442, 443, 444, 445, 447, 454, 458, 459, 460, 564, 462, 466, 471, 472, 476, 477, 479, 480, 482, 485, 487, 489, 490, 491, 493, 495, 496, 499, 501, 502, 504, 506, 508, 514, 516, 529, 530, 533, 538, 542, 544, 545, 552, 556, 565

Saul Jaffe 416, 528. *See also* Jaffes

Schlezinger Family. *See* Mother S., Nate and Bobbie, Gertrude Lewin, Lucille (wife of brother Lou Schlezinger)

Schneider [Charles] 193, 316, 327, 328, 330, 331, 333-335, 348, 357

Schulson [Hyman] 150, 153, 154, 158

Secretary of Labor Wirtz 97

Seder 276, 278, 290, 292, 489, 539, 540, 447, 558, 559

Shell Chemical case 155, 156

Shopping 67, 75, 76, 80, 87, 98, 103, 109, 119, 128, 129, 131, 132, 138, 139, 142, 144, 149, 154-157, 159, 164, 165, 170, 172, 180, 184, 186, 194, 196, 197, 205, 206, 209, 248, 268, 271, 272, 276, 284, 289, 290, 292, 294, 300, 306, 307, 314, 321, 326, 331, 332, 345, 353, 354, 360-363, 365, 367, 370, 375, 376, 379, 380, 382, 383, 385, 386, 388, 392, 393, 397, 398, 401, 409, 415, 435, 446, 448, 451, 452, 457-459, 468, 469, 478, 481, 483, 487, 491, 492, 494, 495, 499, 501, 508, 510, 514, 518, 520, 523, 524, 527, 534, 540, 542, 548, 559, 561, 580

Sid Ascher 315, 338, 348, 489, 493, 494, 495, 500, 509, 513

Sid Lindner 324, 325, 328, 330, 331, 333, 337, 338, 348

Silver Spring 184, 259, 266, 275-277, 281, 288, 289, 291-293, 320, 343, 351-356, 372, 375, 377, 392, 398, 402, 408, 411, 413, 425, 427, 428, 433, 435, 446, 449, 451, 458, 476, 479, 483, 487, 492, 502, 505-507, 513

Smith Committee 124, 177, 185, 189, 191-193, 195, 199, 203

Solicitor 68, 96, 101, 114, 117, 119, 123, 126-137, 139, 150, 161, 211, 464

Stanley Surrey 166, 167, 214

Stasi [Dunan] 281, 286, 303, 305, 306, 308, 311, 313-316, 321, 325-328, 347

Sumner Village 441, 455, 456

Supreme Court. 117, 125, 134, 138, 143-147, 154, 156, 158, 177, 179, 187, 211, 277, 290, 291, 298, 308. *See also* Justices Black, Goldberg and Douglas

Surreys 165, 168, 171, 184, 185, 189, 193, 198, 203, 206, 214. *See also* Dorothy and Stanley

Synagogue 111, 123, 364, 370, 371, 441, 455, 456, 498. *See also* Ohr Kodesh

T

Taft-Hartley Act 125, 177

Television 66, 259, 287, 299, 304, 305, 307, 310, 311, 312, 315, 323, 325, 371, 373, 420, 489, 535

Theater 40, 45, 87, 92, 133, 149, 151, 155, 158, 171, 181, 186, 197, 208, 234, 305, 314, 348, 402, 405, 433, 441, 494, 523, 540

Index

The Secretary 132, 137. *See* Frances Perkins, Willard Wirtz
The Solicitor 117, 126, 127, 128, 129, 134, 135
Toland [Edmund] 192, 193, 194. *See also* Smith Committee
Tonarranda 489
Trial Examiner 190, 192, 198, 211, 221, 262, 441, 445, 461, 462, 463, 465, 471, 497, 498. *See also* TX
TX 425, 441, 442, 444, 445, 450, 462, 463, 464, 465, 468, 481, 494

V

Vivian Asplund 24, 353, 398, 402, 405, 406, 425, 427, 443

W

Wagner Act 125, 177, 183
Wagshal 8, 65, 100, 109, 123, 126, 131, 186, 195, 200, 225, 234, 238, 263, 267, 270, 272, 287, 289, 291, 319, 332, 336, 337, 338, 352, 371, 372, 373, 424, 428, 484, 529, 534, 557, 558, 584. *See also* Mae; *See also* Mollie; *See also* Phil; *See also* Sam
Wenzel. *See* Hank Wenzel
White House 101, 132, 146, 188, 205, 278, 280, 314, 420, 421, 434, 435, 436, 439, 535
Willard Wirtz 401, 433. *See also* Secretary of Labor
Williamsburg 462, 465, 467, 468
World Bank 355, 356
Wyzanski [Charles] 89, 96-98, 100-106, 108-110, 114-116, 118, 120, 123, 126, 132, 133, 137, 141, 146-149, 154, 158, 159, 161-163, 166, 169, 171, 173, 186. *See also* C.E.W., Solicitor

Y

Yom Kippur 123, 149, 325, 412, 459

Z

Zagoria [Sam] 437, 440, 445, 447, 458, 462, 463, 464, 465, 469
Zanoffs [Stella] 389, 409, 422, 423, 436, 438, 439, 447, 451, 463, 496, 501, 504, 558

Kol Bat Series
Gaon Books

Voices of Jewish Women
Vanessa Paloma, Editor

Kol Bat (voice of the daughter) is the mirror image of the Biblical phrase Bat Kol, which refers to the echo of a feminine voice responding to unanswerable questions from the heavens. Through this collection, contemporary women speak with insightful voices in the worlds of academia, religion, activism, arts and beyond.

Titles

Volume 1. Vanessa Paloma.
Mystic Siren: Woman's Voice in the Balance of Creation. 2007.

Volume 2. Nina S. de Friedemann.
African Saga: Cultural Heritage and Resistance in the Diaspora. 2007.

Volume 3. Silvia Hamui Sutton.
Cantos judeo-españoles: simbología poética y visión del mundo. 2008.

Volume 4. Susan Vorhand.
The Mosaic Within: An Alchemy of Healing Self and Soul. 2009.

Volume 5. Angelina Muñiz-Huberman.
The Confidantes. 2009.

Volume 6. Isabelle Medina-Sandoval.
Guardians of Hidden Traditions. 2009.

Volume 7. Carol Rachlin.
Seasons of Rita: the Biography of a Sauk Indian Woman. 2010.

Volume 8. Rabbi Min Kantrowitz.
Counting the Omer: A Kabbalistic Meditation Guide. 2010.

Volume 9. Sandra K. Toro
By Fire Possessed: Doña Gracia Nasi. (2010).

Volume 10. Anne Freeling Schlezinger.
Pulling It All Together: Diaries by One of America's First Jewish Women Judges. (2010).

Volume 11. Patricia Gottlieb Shapiro.
Coming Home to Yourself: Eighteen Wise Women Reflect on their Journeys. (2010).

Volume 12. Vanessa Paloma.
The Mountain, the Desert, and the Pomegranate: Stories from Morocco and Beyond. (2010)

Forthcoming:

Volume 13. Sandra K. Toro.
Princes, Popes and Pirates. (2011).

Volume 14. Angelina Muñiz-Huberman.
A Mystical Journey. (2011)

Volume 15. Isabelle Medina Sandoval.
Crypto-Jewish Secrets. (2011).

Volume 16. Estrella Jalfón de Bentolila.
Haketía: Language and Culture. (2011)

Volume 17. Susana Weich-Shahak.
The Sephardic Romancero from Morocco. (2011).

Volume 18. Gloria Abella Ballen.
The Power of the Hebrew Alphabet. (2011).

Published in collaboration with

Gaon Institute

A 501 c 3 organization that supports
tolerance and diversity.
www.gaoninstitute.org